KT-420-020

GCSE
WORLD HISTORY
1870 to the Present Day

Peter Lane

Letts

EDUCATIONAL

Every effort has been made to trace all copyright holders but, if any have been inadvertently
overlooked, the publishers will gladly receive information enabling them to rectify any error
or omission in subsequent editions.

First published 1984
Revised 1987, 1989, 1992, 1994
Reprinted 1992

Letts Educational
Aldine House
Aldine Place
London W12 8AW

Text: © P. Lane 1984, 1987, 1992, 1994
Design and illustrations: © BPP (Letts Educational) Ltd 1984, 1987, 1992, 1994

All our Rights Reserved. No part of this
publication may be reproduced, stored in
a retrieval system, or transmitted, in any
form or by any means, electronic, mechanical,
photocopying, recording or otherwise without
the prior permission of BPP (Letts Educational) Ltd.

British Library Cataloguing in Publication Data

A CIP record for this book is available from the British Library.

ISBN 1 85758 312 4

ACKNOWLEDGEMENTS

Thanks go to the following Examination Groups for their permission to use GCSE examination
material:

    Midland Examining Group
    Northern Examinations and Assessment Board (formerly the Northern Examining Association)
    Northern Ireland Schools Examinations and Assessment Council
    Scottish Examination Board
    Southern Examining Group
    University of London Examinations and Assessment Council (formerly the London East Anglian
    Group)
    Welsh Joint Education Committee

The author would also like to thank his colleagues Richard Maples (teaching for the Midland and
London based Groups), Joan Kennedy (teaching for the Southern Group and, previously, an
assistant examiner for the London Association) and Richie Greig (an assistant examiner for the
Scottish Examination, for which he also prepares pupils).

Photographs and prints by permission of BBC Hulton
Picture Library; *Daily Mirror*; Mansell
Collection pp. 14, 25; Popperfoto.

Printed and bound in Great Britain by
WM Print Limited, Walsall, West Midlands WS2 9NE

Letts Educational is the trading name of BPP (Letts Educational) Ltd

CONTENTS

INTRODUCTION

A Guide to Using this Book

This book has been written to help candidates for GCSE and similar examinations to gain the knowledge and to develop the skills which will enable them to give their best performance in the history examination. It has been written with the help of several examiner-teachers and under the guidance of experienced teachers. The author and the team of examiners and teachers have taken into account the material published by the various Examining Boards. Opposite you will find an outline of the *Aims* which these Boards have set for our subject. More importantly, you will also find the *Assessment Objectives* (1–4) which candidates have to bear in mind when studying and when answering examination papers. On pp. viii–xi you will see that various papers in your examination have been designed to test one or more of these Objectives: it is obviously important that you should understand what these are and how you may achieve them.

In Units 1–45 of this book you will find all the necessary topics you need for this examination: such factual material is the basis for our subject. In Unit 47 you will find a selection of the types of questions set by the various Examining Boards. You should use these as part of your revision. The long experience of examiners has shown that many candidates become nervous and lack confidence in the examination room because of inexperience and poor preparation for the examination. As a result they do less well than they, and their schools, expect. This books aims to provide the preparation which will allow candidates to approach the examination with more understanding and greater confidence.

The Examination Syllabuses

It is important that you study the table on pp. xii–xiv. Find the columns that refer to the examination for which you are preparing and read the relevant notes on pp. viii–xi. If you are in any doubt, please check with your teacher or, if you are a private student, write to the Board (p. xv) for a copy of the syllabus. In the relevant column of the analysis table you will find: (a) the number of examination papers to be taken; (b) the topics which make up the syllabus for your particular examination and, for many Boards, the papers in which these will be examined. Not all Boards require all 40 topics into which the Units have been divided. Various symbols in the column indicate that the topic is included in your syllabus. *Note:* Units 40–45 deal with developments in various countries after 1988. Cross-references in earlier Units will tell you if you need to study these Units.

Studying material in Units 1–45

Work your way through as many of the necessary Units as possible. Your teacher will advise you on which Units have been particularly chosen for study by your school.

Preparing for the Examination

Study the examination hints provided by experienced examiner-teachers (pp. vii–viii) and, in particular, note the advice given about last-minute preparation.

Understanding the questions

In Unit 47 you will find examples of the various kinds of questions set by your Board. Broadly these are divided into:
(a) structured questions based on one or more pieces of evidence;
(b) structured questions (as above) which require some source evaluation;
(c) questions based on a number of sources requiring evaluation and interpretation.

Coursework

See pp. vi–vii.

GCSE

THE AIMS OF THE EXAMINATION

Each history course has to aim to achieve:
▶ the stimulation of interest in and enthusiasm for the study of the past;
▶ the development of a feeling for the past;
▶ the acquisition of knowledge and understanding of human activity in the past, linking it, as appropriate, with the present;
▶ an understanding of the nature and use of historical evidence;
▶ an understanding of the development over time of social and cultural values, particularly in those courses or parts of courses on British History;
▶ an understanding of the nature of cause and consequence, continuity and change, similarity and difference;
▶ the development of essential study skills such as the ability to locate and extract information from primary and secondary sources; to detect bias; to analyse this information and to construct a logical argument;
▶ the furthering of methods for the discovery, interpretation and communication of knowledge about the past;
▶ the provision of a sound basis for further study and the pursuit of personal interests.

Assessment Objectives

It is essential that you study these Objectives. You will see from the table of analysis of syllabuses that different papers are set to test a candidate's level of achievement of these Objectives.

The examination will assess a candidate's ability to:

1 recall, evaluate and select knowledge relevant to the context, to analyse and synthesize such knowledge, and to deploy it in a clear and coherent form;
2 make use of and understand the concepts of cause and consequence, continuity and change, similarity and difference;
3 show an ability to look at events and issues from the perspective of people in the past ('empathy');
4 show the skills necessary to study a wide variety of historical evidence such as primary and secondary written sources, statistical and visual material, artefacts, textbooks and orally transmitted information:
● by comprehending and extracting information from it;

● by interpreting and evaluating it–distinguishing between fact, opinion and judgement; pointing to deficiencies in the material as evidence, such as gaps and inconsistencies; detecting bias;

● by comparing various types of historical evidence and reaching conclusions based on this comparison.

What Grade will I get?

The grade awarded to each candidate will depend upon the extent to which the candidate has met the Assessment Objectives. It might conceal weakness in one aspect of the examination which is balanced by above average performance in some other. If you study carefully the material below, you will see that to obtain a high grade (Grade C) you will have to have done very different quality work compared to the work required for the award of a low grade (Grade F). You will see this almost immediately if you compare the requirements for each Grade under the requirement numbered '7' in each case.

Grade Descriptions

Grade descriptions are provided to give a general indication of the standards of achievement likely to have been shown by candidates awarded particular grades. The grade awarded will depend upon the extent to which the candidate has met the Assessment Objectives overall and it might conceal weakness in one aspect of the examination which is balanced by above average performance in some other.

Grade C

Candidates will be expected:

1 to recall and use historical knowledge, accurately and relevantly, in support of a logical and evaluative argument; to distinguish between cause and occasion of an event; to show some capacity both to analyse and to synthesise historical problems; to show that change in history is not necessarily linear or 'progressive'; to compare and contrast people, events, issues and institutions;
2 to be able to look at events and issues from the perspective of other people in the past; to understand the importance of looking for motives; to display sufficient imagination in seeing the past through the eyes of those living at the time;
3 to demonstrate comprehension of a range of evidence either by translating from one form to another (e.g. explaining accurately the information contained in a bar graph) or by summarizing information given in a document; to answer accurately questions demanding specific information to be extracted from the evidence;
4 to demonstrate adequately the limitations of a particular piece of evidence, e.g., point to the use of emotive language and to generalizations based on little or no evidence; to identify deficiencies in sources and to indicate other types of evidence that the historian would need to consult in relation to the topic and period in question;
5 to compare and contrast two or more different types of evidence, showing where they contradict or support each other, and write a coherent conclusion based on them, even though all aspects may not be taken into account;
6 to communicate clearly and coherently in a substantially accurate manner.

Grade F

Candidates will be expected:

1 to recall and display a limited amount of accurate and relevant historical knowledge; to show a basic understanding of the historical concepts of causes and consequence, continuity and change, sufficiently supported by obvious examples; to identify difference and similarity;
2 to show occasional insights into why and how people acted as they did in the past;
3 to show ability to comprehend straightforward evidence; to extract partial and/or generalized information;

4 to demonstrate obvious limitations of a particular piece of evidence; to list some of the evidence needed to reconstruct a given historical event;
5 to make simple comparisons between pieces of evidence; to list the major features of two or more pieces of evidence, without drawing conclusions from them;
6 to communicate in an understandable form.

Coursework

Each of the Examining Groups requires candidates for GCSE to submit coursework. In the table of analysis on pp. xii-xiv you will see the marks assigned to this work by your Board, as well as the Assessment Objectives which this work is meant to examine. Each Board has its own requirements concerning this work and it is important that you understand what your particular Board demands. However, there is some practical advice which will help you, no matter which examination you are taking. I am grateful to examiner-teachers for these important suggestions.

ORGANIZATION OF COURSEWORK

▶ Jotter—if using a jotter, use a separate one for each unit of work.
▶ 'Science-type' note books will prove useful as permanent holders of all notes and pupil tasks. However, you may find that it is difficult, if not impossible, to insert new material into such a book.
▶ Loose-leaf A4 ring-binders have the benefit that you will be able to add new material to previous work, which may also be improved on or discarded at a later date. This updating or improving on your work during the year may well be an important feature of your coursework. Diagrams and/or slides can be inserted into the ring-binder in see-through folders. However, note that you are NOT allowed to submit your final work in a ring-binder.

THE LAYOUT OF THE WORK

▶ Headings should be used to differentiate aspects of each topic: you might illustrate these or pick them out in red capital letters.
▶ Use paragraphs (each separated by a space) for each item of information, detailed at some length.
▶ Sentences and not a series of notes must be used. Make sure that each sentence is complete and full and that it is factually accurate.
▶ Highlighting of important points by underlining of certain words or phrases will improve the appearance of your work.
▶ Summarize your conclusions with a single page at the end of your work.
▶ Contents: use a series of headings at the start of your work to show the examiner the logical way in which you have laid out the work which follows.
▶ Illustrations should be used to enhance your written work. If you are drawing a diagram, make sure you use a ruler when drawing straight lines. If you are using coloured pens or shading, make sure that this work is done neatly. Do not forget to add explanatory notes to photographs or slides and other illustrative material.

SKILLS TO BE DEVELOPED

▶ You have to develop your ability to write a sustained answer. Examples of such writing should be a part of your coursework.
▶ As well as such written work, examples of slides, videos and computer programmes may be attempted. You may submit tapes of oral reports or photographs of artefacts, with accompanying descriptions and commentary.

▶ Interviewing skills can be shown by, for example, a taped interview of a person being asked pre-arranged questions intended to provide you with specific information.

▶ Historical diaries and records of visits should be encouraged. Each item used in such work should be detailed and follow a logical sequence: for example, an account of a visit to a museum should show:

● what you hoped to gain from the visit;

● what you saw;

● how far the experience of the visit was relevant to the topic being pursued.

▶ Handling of sources: your coursework should show your ability to interpret various types of source material, and to use these as bases for arguments you wish to make. In developing your argument, you will be expected to show an ability to arrange work logically, to explain it fully and to arrive at correct conclusions.

CONSULT YOUR TEACHER

Before you decide what work you wish to do consult your teacher and be guided by his or her advice. Teachers will know whether the examiners will accept some work or not (e.g. they will not necessarily accept the 'story' of your local football team, although you may find it interesting). Teachers will know what sources are easily available that will be useful for you. Your teacher will help you to improve your work during the two years. Make sure that you follow any suggestions which may be made.

DOING THE WORK—ON TIME

Make sure that you keep up to date with your coursework by doing the work regularly. Try not to get behind with it. You cannot do good work if you leave most of it until the last few months or weeks. Start it at the beginning of the (one or) two-year period of study for the examination, and make sure that you have each piece completed in good time to be accepted by your teacher. There is a dead line—a date by which the whole of the completed coursework has to be submitted to your examiners. Find out from your teacher what this date is, and aim to have your coursework ready well before that date.

MAKE YOUR WORK AS GOOD AS POSSIBLE

Do take a great deal of care with your coursework and make it as good as you can. Unlike the examination—where you have a limited time in which to show the examiners what you understand and can do—you can normally take as much time as you like with your coursework. Because the mark for this work is added to the marks you gain in the written examination, your final grade can often be better than it would otherwise have been if you obtain a high mark for your coursework.

EXAMINING GROUPS DIFFER

Make sure that you understand what your Group demands —as to length and number of assignments, the Assessment Objectives being examined in each piece and the total value of coursework. Your teacher will provide this information; if you are a private candidate you can get the information from the syllabus, which is available from the appropriate Group's address shown on p. xv.

▨ A revision programme ▨

Why Revise?

You may know people who do not seem to do much preparation before examinations, yet who still obtain high marks. You may also know people who spend a great deal of time at revision, some even studying up to the day of the examination. It is impossible to define 'the best method' for all candidates, because people are different and what suits one may not do for another. But long experience has shown teachers and examiners that most people learn more, gain in confidence and perform better in examinations after they have made suitable preparations by a sensible programme of revision.

Planning Your Revision

Some people prefer to read a Unit several times before testing themselves to see whether they can remember the work they have studied. Others prefer to make notes as they read and to use these notes for revision purposes. Almost everyone learns best by tackling small portions of work. Study one Unit, test yourself on it and then decide whether you have understood the Unit. By the time you have gone through all the necessary Units you should have a list of topics which need further revision to help you overcome your weaknesses.

A Revision Timetable

A complete revision requires a good deal of time and needs sensible planning. The following timetable is based on the assumptions that the examination will take place in mid-June. If your examination takes place in May, November or January, obviously you will need to change the suggested dates.

▶ **End of March**
● Check how well you did in the mock examination so that you can see which topics you need to study carefully.
● Make up a timetable using the units in this book and any other topics which you need to study.
● The timetable should cover April and May and you should plan to do extra work during the Easter holidays.
● The timetable should be drawn up to allow you to finish your revision by the end of May. This will give you two weeks for further revision of your weaker points and a final revision of the main points in the days before the examination.

▶ **April and May**
● Allow yourself about one hour every day for history revision.

▶ **June**
● Revise the main points, using the examination questions in Unit 47. Make a list of the main points needed to answer any of the questions in that section.

▶ **Examination day**
● Make sure that you arrive at the examination in time and that you have with you all the things you think you might need – pens, pencils, ruler, crayons and eraser.

Taking the Examination

▶ **Read the paper carefully**
Almost every Report made by examiners complains that candidates did not understand the questions asked or failed to use the information supplied in the examination paper. If the examiners ask you to 'Give an account of Gladstone's domestic policies', they expect less analysis than they expect from answers to 'Account for Gladstone's defeat in the Election of 1874'. If you are asked to 'Give an account of Disraeli's domestic policy in his ministry of 1874-80', do not waste time by offering accounts of his foreign and imperial policies.

▶ **Tick off the questions you intend to do**
As you read through the paper tick off the questions which you think you could answer. Then check the instructions at the head of your examination paper to see how many questions you have to do, and from which sections, if the paper is sub-divided into sections.

Having ticked off a number of questions, go back through the paper and choose those which you intend to do. As you do this, number the questions—1, 2 and so on—to remind yourself which question you intend to tackle first, which next and so on to the end. Always do first the question which you think you can answer best; this will give you confidence to go on with the rest of the paper.

▶ **Plan each answer before you start**

This refers to those questions which require you to write either an essay or a brief note on some item. It does not refer to the fixed-response questions.

▶ **Time yourself**

If you only answer half the questions asked for, you cannot expect to get more than 50 per cent even if you get full marks for each answer. It is important to attempt to answer the required number of questions. To help you do this:

● **Before the examination**, practise doing questions in the time allocated. This is important because you have to find out how much you can write in the 25 or 30 minutes which you can spend on a question in the examination.

● **In the examination room**, make a note of the time which you will allow for each question. If, for example, you have to do four questions in two hours you will have 100 minutes in which to write your answers (if you have spent 20 minutes on planning). This means that each answer should take 25 minutes. So if you start writing at 2.00 pm you should finish your answer to your first question at 2.25 pm, your second answer should be finished at 2.50 pm and so on.

● **When answering the paper**, keep an eye on your proposed timing and on the clock. When you get to the end of the time allocated to an answer, stop writing, even if you have not completed the answer. Leave a space and, if you have time, complete the answer later. It is better to have answered all five questions (if that is the number required), even if the answers are incomplete, than to answer only three – which you might do if you take five minutes more for this answer and a further five minutes for another.

▶ **Answering the questions**

You should remember that examiners have to mark a large number of papers. They will appreciate it if your work is neat, although they will not object if you have crossed out such things as plans for answers. They will object to a sort of shorthand which some candidates use, such as 'Pam' for Palmerston or 'Dizzie' for Disraeli. They will not give you any credit for the use of 'etc' since they will think that this means you do not know any more. If you really do know more, then you should write it down so that the examiners can award the marks you deserve.

Notes on the Table of Analysis

It is important that you read the section which refers to the Board whose examination you intend to take. These notes will help you to understand the table of analysis on pp xii–xiv.

UNIVERSITY OF LONDON EXAMINATIONS AND ASSESSMENT COUNCIL

Assessment

The scheme of assessment is common to both the syllabuses outlined.

Paper 1 (40 per cent of the total mark) comprises questions based on a piece of source material. Each question will be divided into two parts. The first part comprises FIVE write-a-sentence/paragraph questions intended to test Objective 1. The second part comprises short essay questions intended to test Objective 2.

Paper 2 (30 per cent of the total mark) comprises questions that require the analysis of pieces of evidence, and is intended to test Objective 3. A variety of forms of evidence will be used. Usually, each question will comprise a series of sub-questions based on one or more pieces of evidence.

Coursework (30 per cent of the total mark). Candidates will be required to submit THREE assignments aimed at testing Objectives 1, 2 and 3. These assignments may be related to ANY of the topics on the syllabus. No assignment should be longer than 1500 words, and the total for the three assignments should be about 4000 words.

Syllabus A: Modern World History

Candidates are advised to study SIX topics. At least ONE topic must be chosen from each Group (i.e. one out of six). In the examination candidates will be required to answer questions on FIVE of these topics.

Paper 1 will consist of TWENTY questions, TWO of each of the topics listed as A1-I1 in the table of analysis on p. xii. Candidates must answer ONE question on each of THREE topics.

Paper 2 will consist of TEN questions, one on each of the topics listed as A2–J2 in the table of analysis. Candidates must answer TWO questions.

Coursework. Assignments may be related to any of the topics on the syllabus.

Syllabus B: British and European History from the mid-18th century

In spite of the title of this syllabus, candidates do not have to study both British and European History. They have to answer questions on TWO sections of the TEN listed in the syllabus. This book contains material on THREE of those listed in the syllabus. You should note that, if you concentrate on European History, you have to choose chronologically adjacent topics; i.e. you have to take EITHER Topics H and I OR Topics I and J. You cannot take Topics H and J. Notice that in Paper 2, the Nominated Topics are relevant to the Topics chosen in Paper 1.

If you choose to study both British and European History, you should notice that you have to take TWO sections (one from British and one from European History) which cover, roughly, the same period of time, e.g. if you take Topic H from this book; you would have to study Britain, 1867–1918 from the British section. Material on FIVE of the British History Topics may be found in the companion book, *Revise GCSE History, 1750 to the Present Day.*

Paper 1 consists of TEN sections each with THREE questions. Candidates have to answer THREE questions taken from TWO sections.

Paper 2 consists of TEN sections, each of ONE question, on a nominated topic. Candidates have to answer TWO questions. Note that the nominated topics will be changed every two years.

Coursework. Assignments may be related to any of the topics the syllabus.

MIDLAND EXAMINING GROUP

Assessment

The scheme of assessment is common to all the syllabuses offered by the Group.

Paper 1 (40 per cent of the total mark) will test the Core Content (listed as C1-C3 in the table of analysis on p. xii). It will consist of SIX structured questions, of which candidates must answer ANY THREE. Questions may make use of source material, but no evaluation of sources will be required. TWO questions will be set on EACH of the THREE Core Units.

Paper 2 (30 per cent of the total mark) will consist of ONE question set on each of the Optional Topics (listed in the table of analysis), and candidates must answer TWO questions. All questions will make use of source material. All questions will be structured and will include sub-questions requiring the evaluation and analysis of the source material provided.

Coursework (30 per cent of the total mark). Candidates will be required to submit either ONE piece of work or TWO shorter pieces of work on a subject related to Modern World History. Each piece may consist of several shorter pieces of work related to a common theme, provided that the finished assignment has between 2000 and 4500 words.

Syllabus 1607: The Modern World, 1914 to the Present Day

Paper 1 will examine the three sections of the Core Content:
1 The Search for International Order between 1919 and 1929 (C1 in the table of analysis)
2 The Collapse of International Order in the 1930s (C2)
3 Tension and Cooperation since 1945 (C3)

Paper 2 will examine the NINE Optional Topics listed as TA–TI in the table of analysis. Candidates have to answer questions on TWO of these Topics.

Coursework. See assessment above.

Syllabus 1612 (E): British and European History, 1789–1914

Paper 1 will examine the Core Content, THREE sections dealing with British History. The material for this Paper can found in the companion book, *Revise GCSE History, 1750 to the Present Day.*

Paper 2. Material for TWO of the Optional Topics can be found in this book (listed as OE/F and OE/G in the table of analysis); material for other Optional Topics may be found in the companion book.

Coursework. See assessment above.

Syllabus 1613 (F): British and European History,1867 to the Present Day

Paper 1 will examine the Core Content, THREE sections along with British History. The material for this Paper can be found in the companion book, *Revise GCSE History, 1750 to the Present Day.*

Paper 2. Material for FIVE of the Optional Topics can be found in this book (listed as OF/A–D and F in the table of analysis on p. xii). Material for TWO of the Optional Topics can be found in the companion book.

Coursework. See assessment above.

NORTHERN EXAMINATIONS AND ASSESSMENT BOARD–Syllabus B

Assessment

The scheme of assessment will consist of THREE components.

Paper 1 (30 per cent of the total mark) in which all questions will be compulsory and based on a variety of sources related to *Conflict in the Modern World* (Th. 1 on the table of analysis on those p. xiii).
   A variety of structured questions will be set including requiring a short or a more extended written response.

Paper 2 (40 per cent of the total mark) will contain questions based on Themes 2 and 3.
   In Theme 2, candidates will be expected to have studied (a) ONE of the following (Themes 2A(1-3) in the table of analysis):

   1 The Russian Revolution: Lenin and Stalin
   2 Germany 1918–39
   3 Communist China
and
(b) EITHER *The USA in the 1920s and 1930s* (Th. 2B in the table of analysis) OR *Britain 1905–51*, the material for which may be found in a companion book, *Revise GCSE History, 1750 to the Present Day.*

In Theme 3, candidates will be expected to have studied ONE of the three sections listed as Th. 3(a)-3(c) in the table of analysis.

This paper will be divided into four sections:
   1 Based on the candidate's choice from Th. 2A
   2 Based on the candidate's choice from Th. 2B
   3 Based on the candidate's choice from Th. 3
   4 Based on the syllabus content as a whole

For sections 1, 2 and 3 structured questions requiring a short and more extended written response will be set. The fourth section will be an essay/extended writing section. Candidates will be required to answer FOUR questions – ONE from each of the four sections.
   Notice that in both written examination papers a wide variety of historical evidence will be used to test candidates' skills.

Coursework (30 per cent of the total mark) will be based on *Colonialism* (Th. 4 in the table of analysis) and *Human Rights* (Th. 5). For Theme 4 a candidate's work should be based on a study of any ONE area of the world to illustrate all given aspects of colonialism:

   (a) The pre-Colonial Experience
   (b) The Origins of Colonialism
   (c) The Colonial Experience
   (d) The Growth of Nationalism
   (e) The Achievement of Independence
   (f) Post-independence

   For Theme 5 only ONE of the following has to be studied:

   (a) Divisions in Ireland from the mid-19th century to the present day
   (b) The Jews 1880 to the present day
   (c) The changing position of women in Britain
   (d) Civil Rights in the USA
   (e) Apartheid in South Africa

Material on (a) and (c) may be found in the companion book, *Revise GCSE History, 1750 to the Present Day.* Each candidate will be expected to submit a minimum of THREE and a maximum of SIX assignments, a maximum of TWO of which should be based on each of Themes 4 and 5. Candidates will be expected to submit a total minimum of 3000 words and not more than 6000 words.

NORTHERN IRELAND SCHOOLS EXAMINATIONS AND ASSESSMENT COUNCIL

Assessment

Paper 1 (50 per cent of the total mark) consists of two sections A and B).

▶ Section A (25 per cent). Candidates have to answer ONE compulsory source-based question: a number of sub-questions will be set on a selection of source materials. Candidates also have to answer ONE essay-type question from THREE set questions.

▶ Section B (25 per cent). The requirements will be the same as for Section A.

Paper 2 (30 per cent of the total mark) in which candidates will have to answer TWO compulsory source-based questions and ONE structured essay question (from two questions).

Coursework (20 per cent of the total mark). Candidates have to submit THREE assignments based on a Local Study. One (750-1000 words) has to satisfy Assessment Objectives 1 and 3, one (500-700 words) has to satisfy Assessment Objectives 2 and 3, and one (500-700 words) has to satisfy Assessment Objectives 2 and 3.

Syllabus

All candidates have to take TWO papers and submit course-work.

Paper 1 consists of TWO sections (A and B).

▶ Section A *A Modern World Study*. Candidates have to answer questions on ONE of:

   (i) Israel and the Arab World (A1 in the table of analysis);

   (ii) The USA in the Modern World (A2).

There are also TWO other options, the material for which may be found in the companion book, *Revise GCSE History, 1750 to the Present Day*.

▶ Section B *A Study in Depth*. Candidates have to answer questions on ONE of:

   (i) Germany 1919–39 (B1 in the table of analysis)

   (ii) Russia 1917–29 (B2)

   (iii) China 1934–53 (B3)

Paper 2 in which candidates have to answer questions on a study in development on ONE of:

   (i) Medicine through time

   (ii) Energy through time

Note that the material for this paper is not available in either of the *Revise GCSE History* books.

Coursework. A local study – see previous page.

SCOTTISH EXAMINATION BOARD

Standard Grade

Assessment

The Board offers THREE papers – Foundation, General and Credit. Candidates have to know the level for which they have been entered: Foundation (F), General (G) or Credit (C). The level for which you have been entered determines the number and nature of the papers which you have to take in the examination. School assessments will be used as a guide for deciding which level and how many papers you have to take in the examination.

Syllabus

The course is based on FOUR units of study.

Unit 1 Changing Life in Scotland and Britain. Candidates have to study ONE of the periods:

   A 1750s–1850s

   B 1830s–1930s

   C 1880s to the present day

Material for this Unit will be found in the companion book, *Revise GCSE History, 1750 to the Present Day*.

Unit 2 International Cooperation and Conflict. Candidates have to study ONE of the periods:

   A 1790s–1820s   (NOT covered in this book)

   B 1890s–1920s   (B in the table of analysis)

   C 1930s–60s   (C)

Additional material on this Unit will be found in the Companion volume, *Revise GCSE History, 1750 to the Present Day*.

Unit 3 People and Power. Candidates have to study ONE of the following:

   A USA 1850–80   (A in the table of analysis)

   B India 1917–47   (B)

   C Russia 1914–41   (C)

   D Germany 1918–39   (D)

Unit 4 The Historical Investigation. This is to be undertaken on the advice of your teacher.

WELSH JOINT EDUCATION COMMITTEE

Syllabus A: Modular

Candidates will be examined on FOUR Modules:

▶ 1   Crime and Punishment in England and Wales

▶ 2   A Study in Depth: In this book you will find material on TWO of the Options offered by the Board:

   F   Lenin and the Russian Revolution (marked F in the table of analysis on p. xiv).

   G   Hitler's Germany, 1933–1939 (marked G in the table of analysis on p. xiv).

   Material on other Options will be found in the companion volume, *Revise GCSE History, 1750 to the Present Day*.

▶ 3   A study in Welsh History

▶ 4   ONE of the following twentieth century world history Options:

   A   The Arab-Israeli Conflict

   B   The Rise of Communist China

   C   Japan – the Silent Super-Power

   D   Super-Power Relations since 1945

   E   The UN and the Third World, An African Perspective

   Material on each of these Options is marked A – E in the table of analysis on p. xiv.

Assessment

Paper 1 (25% of the total mark) will examine Module 1.

Paper 2 (25% of the total mark) has TWO sections:

▶ Section A Evidence questions of graded difficulty on a variety of source material on your chosen Option.

▶ Section B Essay-type questions with candidates having to answer ONE from the THREE on their chosen Option.

Paper 3 (25% of the total mark) will examine Welsh History.

Module 4 will be examined by coursework assignments on their chosen Option. This coursework will consist of:

   1   An extended essay (including an oral)

   2   TWO written exercises.

Syllabus B: Aspects of 20th century World History

The TWO examination papers (see below) are based on SEVEN Topics, listed as T1-T7 in the table of analysis on page xiv.

Paper 1 (40 per cent of the total mark) will test, mainly, Assessment Objective 1 (see p. v) and consists of three sections (A, B and C).

▶ Section A (16 per cent). Candidates have to answer THREE of the FOUR stimulus questions requiring responses in continuous writing.

▶ Section B (12 per cent). Candidates have to answer ONE of TWO questions in which they will be offered a series of stimulus material on a general theme, each of which should stimulate a piece of continuous writing.

▶ Section C (12 per cent). Candidates have to answer ONE of THREE questions of the open essay variety. The questions may be structured.

Paper 2 (40 per cent of the total mark) consists of two sections (A and B).

▶ Section A (20 per cent) consists of THREE compulsory questions, each dealing with ONE of the three key concepts: cause and consequence; change and continuity; and similarity and difference. This Section deals with Assessment Objective 2 (see p. v).

▶ Section B (20 per cent) consists of ONE compulsory question and will consist of a variety of sources dealing with ONE of the seven Topics listed in the table of analysis. Candidates will be expected to respond freely to the various sub-questions that will be set.

Coursework (20 per cent of the total mark) on *An aspect of 20th century Welsh history*. Candidates have to write TWO coursework assignments; they should consult their teachers as to the topics which may be offered, the method of examination and the nature of the investigation which they have to follow.

Table of Analysis of Examination Syllabuses

Boards: **University of London Examinations and Assessment Council** (syllabuses A, B, 1607) and **Midland Examining Group** (syllabuses 1612 (E), 1613 (F)).

For each syllabus the three columns are Paper **1**, Paper **2**, and **C/W** (coursework).

#	Syllabus	A 1	A 2	A C/W	B 1	B 2	B C/W	1607 1	1607 2	1607 C/W	1612 1	1612 2	1612 C/W	1613 1	1613 2	1613 C/W
	Fixed-response	•			•			•			•				•	
	Structured essays		•			•			•			•			•	
	Evidence-based		•			•			•			•			•	
	Source evaluation			•			•			•			•			•
	Assessment objectives (see page v)	1+2	4	2–4	1+2	4	2–4	1+2	1,2+4	1–4	1+2	1,2+4	1–4	1+2	1,2+4	1–4
	British component	Opt	Opt	Opt	Opt	Opt	Opt	Opt	Opt	Opt	Comp	Opt	Opt	Comp	Opt	Opt
1	Germany 1870–1914				H											
2	France 1870–1914				H		•									
3	Russia 1855–1914				H		•		TB							
4	The Eastern Question 1870–1914				H		•					OE/G			OF/B	
5	Africa 1870–1914				H		•					OE/F			OF/A	
6	The Far East 1870–1918															
7	The United States of America 1870–1917															
8	International Relations 1870–1914				H		•					OE/G			OF/B	
9	The First World War 1914–1918				H	H	•		TA							
10	Russia 1914–1928	G1		•	H/I		•		TB						OF/C	
11	Russia 1928–1941	G1		•	I		•		TB						OF/C	
12	Peacemaking – Germany and Austria				I			C1	TC							
13	Peacemaking – Turkey				I			C1								
14	The League of Nations	E1		•	I		•	C1	TC						OF/D	
15	Germany 1919–1933	F1														
16	The United States of America 1917–1932		H2	•				C2	TD							
17	China and Japan 1914–1949		A2	•				C2	TE							
18	International Affairs 1919–1929	E1		•	I			C1								
19	The United States of America 1932–1941	H1	H2	•	I		•	C2	TD						OF/D	
20	Hitler's Germany 1933–1939	F1		•		I	•	C2	TC							
21	Italy 1919–1939	F1		•	I											
22	The British Empire 1918–1939	A1		•	I											
23	International Relations, 1930–1939	E1		•	I		•	C2								
24	Spain 1919–1939				I		•									
25	The Second World War from 1939 to 1942	I1		•	I		•	C3								
26	The Second World War from 1942 to 1945	I1		•	I		•	C3								
27	The United Nations Organization	E1	I2	•	J		•	C3								
28	International Relations 1945–1953			•	J		•	C3								
29	Russia 1945–1988				J		•	C3								
30	Eastern Europe 1945–1986		G2	•	J	J	•									
31	Western European Integration				J		•									
32	The United States of America 1945–1988	H1	A2	•	J			C3	TF						OF/F	
33	China 1949–1986			•					TE							
34	The Indian Sub-continent 1939–1986	A1	J2	•					TH							
35	The Far East 1945–1986		B2	•					TH							
36	Africa, South of the Sahara 1945–1986	B1	C2	•					TF/I							
37	North Africa and the Middle East 1945–1986	C1	C2	•					TG/I							
38	The Third World and some of its problems		E2	•												
39	The road to détente		I2	•	J		•	C3								

Annotations in the right-hand (C/W) columns of syllabuses 1607, 1612 (E) and 1613 (F): **See assessment on page ix**

Syllabuses 1612 (E) and 1613 (F), Paper 1 (British component, Comp): **Core content: British History — See *Revise GCSE History, 1750 to the Present Day***

Syllabus 1612 (E): **Other options: British History — See *Revise GCSE History, 1750 to the Present Day***

Table of Analysis of Examination Syllabuses

Syllabus	Southern Examining Group										Northern Examinations and Assessment Board		
	2 (1169)					5 (1173)					B		
Paper	1A	1B	2A	2B	C/W	1A	1B	2A	2B	C/W	1	2	C/W
Fixed-response	•					•					•	•	
Structured essays		•	•	•			•	•	•			•	
Evidence-based	•	•				•	•				•	•	
Source evaluation	•	•		•	•	•	•		•	•	•	•	•
Assessment objectives (see page v)	4	1, 2+4	1+2	1, 2+4	3+4	4	1, 3+4	1+2	1+2	3+4	2+4	1+2	4
British component					Opt			Opt	Opt	Opt	Opt	Opt	Opt
1 Germany 1870–1914							2						
2 France 1870–1914													
3 Russia 1855–1914						1	1				Th1	Th2A(1)	
4 The Eastern Question 1870–1914								11			Th1		
5 Africa 1870–1914								11					• Th4
6 The Far East 1870–1918													• Th4
7 The United States of America 1870–1917											Th1		
8 International Relations 1870–1914								11			Th1		
9 The First World War 1914–1918			1	1		1			13				
10 Russia 1914–1928			2	2		1	1+5					Th2A(1)	
11 Russia 1928–1941			2	2			5					Th2A(1)	
12 Peacemaking – Germany and Austria		2						12			Th1	Th2A(2) + Th3(a)	
13 Peacemaking – Turkey		2						12				Th3(a)	
14 The League of Nations		2						12				Th3(a)	
15 Germany 1919–1933			4	4			6					Th2A(2)	
16 The United States of America 1917–1932			3	3			8					Th2B	
17 China and Japan 1914–1949		2	5	5								Th2A(3)	
18 International Affairs 1919–1929		2						12			Th1	Th3(a)	
19 The United States of America 1932–1941			3	3			8					Th2B	
20 Hitler's Germany 1933–1939			4	4			6				Th1	Th2A(2)	
21 Italy 1919–1939		2											
22 The British Empire 1918–1939		3									Th1	Th3(a)	• Th4
23 International Relations, 1930–1939		2	2					12			Th1	Th3(a)	
24 Spain 1919–1939		2											
25 The Second World War from 1939 to 1942			6	6					14		Th1		
26 The Second World War from 1942 to 1945			6	6					14		Th1		
27 The United Nations Organization												Th3(b)	
28 International Relations 1945–1953	1	1										Th3(b)	
29 Russia 1945–1988	1	1					5					Th2A(1)	
30 Eastern Europe, 1945–1986	1	1											
31 Western European Integration												Th3(c)	
32 The United States of America 1945–1988	1	1					10				Th1		• Th5
33 China 1949–1986			5						5				
34 The Indian Sub-continent 1939–1986		3									Th1		• Th4
35 The Far East 1945–1986	1	1											• Th4/5
36 Africa, South of the Sahara 1945–1986		3											• Th4/5
37 North Africa and the Middle East 1945–1986				7								Th3(b)	• Th4/5
38 The Third World and some of its problems				7									• Th4
39 The road to détente	1	1									Th1	Th3(c)	

Material on Topic 7 (Britain, 1919–45) is in
Revise GCSE History, 1750 to the Present Day

Table of Analysis of Examination Syllabuses

No.	Syllabus	NSEAC 1A	NSEAC 1B	NSEAC 2	NSEAC C/W	SEB 1	SEB 2	SEB 3	SEB 4	WJEC A 2	WJEC A 4 C/W	WJEC B 1	WJEC B 2	WJEC B C/W
	Paper (headings)	1A	1B	2	C/W	1	2	3		2	4 C/W	1	2	C/W
	Fixed-response	•	•				•	•	•		•	•	•	
	Structured essays	•	•				•	•	•		•	•	•	
	Evidence-based	•	•				•	•	•		•	•	•	
	Source evaluation	•						•						•
	Assessment objectives (see page v)	1–4	1–4	1–4	1–4					3+4	1–4	1	2, 4	3
	British component	Opt				Comp	Opt	Opt	Opt			Comp		
1	Germany 1870–1914													
2	France 1870–1914													
3	Russia 1855–1914									F				
4	The Eastern Question 1870–1914						B							
5	Africa 1870–1914													
6	The Far East 1870–1918								A					
7	The United States of America 1870–1917						B							
8	International Relations 1870–1914						B	C						
9	The First World War 1914–1918									F		T2	T2	
10	Russia 1914–1928		B2				B	C				T2	T2	
11	Russia 1928–1941		B2					C				T1	T1	
12	Peacemaking – Germany and Austria		B1				B		D	G	A	T1	T1	
13	Peacemaking – Turkey	A1					B					T1	T1	
14	The League of Nations		B1				B		D	G		T1	T1	
15	Germany 1919–1933		B1				B					T1/3	T1/3	
16	The United States of America 1917–1932	A2									B, C	T4	T4	
17	China and Japan 1914–1949				B3			C						
18	International Affairs 1919–1929		B1	B2						G		T4	T4	
19	The United States of America 1932–1941	A2						C				T3	T3	
20	Hitler's Germany 1933–1939		B1					C	D					
21	Italy 1919–1939													
22	The British Empire 1918–1939	A1						C	B	G	A			
23	International Relations, 1930–1939		B1	B2										
24	Spain 1919–1939													
25	The Second World War from 1939 to 1942		B1	B2				C				T5	T5	
26	The Second World War from 1942 to 1945		B1	B2				C				T5	T5	
27	The United Nations Organization							C			E	T6	T6	
28	International Relations 1945–1953			B2				C			D			
29	Russia 1945–1988										D			
30	Eastern Europe 1945–1986										D			
31	Western European Integration											T7	T7	
32	The United States of America 1945–1988	A2						C			B			
33	China 1949–1986				B3			B			B			
34	The Indian Sub-continent 1939–1986							B				T6	T6	
35	The Far East 1945–1986	A1			B3						C			
36	Africa, South of the Sahara 1945–1986											T7	T7	
37	North Africa and the Middle East 1945–1986										A			
38	The Third World and some of its problems										E	T6	T6	
39	The road to détente										D	T7	T7	

Column groups: **NSEAC** = Northern Ireland Schools Examinations and Assessment Council (MODULAR); **SEB** = Scottish Examination Board (STANDARD); **WJEC** = Welsh Joint Education Committee.

Notes appearing across the table:

See assessment on page ix (Northern Ireland Schools Examinations and Assessment Council)

Material for this section is NOT covered by the *Revise GCSE History* books (Northern Ireland Schools Examinations and Assessment Council)

See *Revise GCSE History, 1750 to the Present Day* (Scottish Examination Board)

See assessment on page x (Welsh Joint Education Committee)

■ Examination Boards: Addresses ■

To obtain syllabuses, past examination papers and further details, write to your Examination Board.

MEG   **Midland Examining Group**

1 Hills Road
Cambridge
CB1 2EU

Tel: 0223 61111

NEAB   **Northern Examinations and Assessment Board**

12 Harter Street
Manchester
M1 6HL

Tel: 061 953 1180

NISEAC   **Northern Ireland Schools Examinations and Assessment Council**

Beechill House
42 Beechill Road
Belfast
BT8 4RS

Tel: 0232 704666

SEB   **Scottish Examination Board**

Ironmills Road
Dalkeith
Midlothian
EH22 1LE

Tel: 031 663 6601

SEG   **Southern Examining Group**

Stag Hill House
Guildford
GU2 5XJ

Tel: 0483 506506

ULEAC   **University of London Examinations and Assessment Council**

Stewart House
32 Russell Square
London
WC1B 5DN

Tel: 071 331 4000

WJEC   **Welsh Joint Education Committee**

245 Western Avenue
Cardiff
CF5 2YX

Tel: 0222 561231

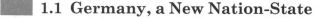

1 GERMANY, 1870–1914

1.1 Germany, a New Nation-State

After 1871 Germany was one of the most important states in Europe. However, in 1870 Germany did not exist as a unified state. To understand her importance after 1871, we have to see how Germany came into being.

THE GERMAN CONFEDERATION, 1815
(see Fig. 1.2)

In 1815 when Napoleon was defeated, there were 39 separate states in the German Confederation. Each had its own ruler, government and foreign policy. Some states were powerful.

▶ **Austria**, largely Catholic, was the most powerful. Under the Hapsburg monarchs Austria had gained an Empire in Europe, containing Poles, Hungarians, Italians, Croats, Slovenes—as well as Germans.

▶ **Prussia**, in the north, largely Protestant, had become increasingly powerful. But in 1815 she was unable to stand up to Austria.

▶ **Bavaria, Hesse-Cassel, Hanover, Westphalia, Saxony and Wurttemberg** were other large states. These, and the many smaller states, usually followed Austria in domestic and foreign policies.

THE PRUSSIAN ZOLLVEREIN

Prussia had grown from its eastern origins in Brandenburg. By 1815 it included agricultural regions in East Pomerania and East Prussia and industrial regions in Silesia and the Rhine Provinces.

In 1816 the Prussian government abolished customs duties on goods passing from one region of the state to another. This led to lower prices, a growth in trade and a rise in living standards.

In 1819 several smaller states joined this customs union, which remained under Prussian control. The larger states refused to join on those terms—they wanted a share in running the customs union.

In 1826 the Catholic states of Bavaria and Wurttemberg formed their own customs union. They could see the benefits of such a union, but were too jealous of Protestant Prussia to join the older Prussian-dominated union.

In 1833 Prussia enlarged its customs union—and called it the Zollverein. New states were admitted on a basis of equality—tariff policies had to be agreed by all the states and not imposed by Prussia. Hamburg and Hanover still refused to join.

In 1849 Austria applied to join the Zollverein. The application was rejected by Prussia's friends; they wanted to end Austrian control.

In 1853, the Zollverein signed a commercial treaty with Austria—a sign of its independence of Austrian influence.

In 1867, after the Austrian War (see below) the Zollverein was reorganized to include all German states, except Austria, Hamburg and Bremen.

The importance of the Zollverein

The removal of internal tariff barriers was one of the reasons for the industrial expansion of Germany. The customs union gave Germany an economic and industrial unity long before it had any political unity. It gave Prussia the leadership, in economic and industrial affairs. Later this gave her the chance to take the political lead.

ATTEMPTS TO FORM A UNITED GERMANY, 1848–50

You do not have to know in detail the attempts made in 1848–9 to create a united Germany. You should note the following:

▶ In 1848 there were many revolutions throughout Europe, when 'liberal' revolutionaries tried to force their rulers to become constitutional rulers.

▶ In Prussia and other German states, the liberal revolutionaries forced rulers to produce democratic constitutions. In 1849–50 most of the rulers withdrew those constitutions. Only in Prussia did the King maintain the constitution.

▶ In 1848–9 representatives from all the German states met in the Frankfurt Parliament. These liberals offered the crown of a united Germany to Frederick William IV, King of Prussia.

He refused it because:

● he did not think a monarch should accept a crown from 'the gutter' of a democratic Parliament;

● he was afraid that Austria might declare war on Prussia if he accepted the crown;

● the liberal constitution gave the monarch only a limited power.

THE DEVELOPMENT OF PRUSSIA, 1850–62

The population continued to increase. Many factories were built; steam power was introduced. A railway system provided the basis for:

▶ industrial growth, in iron, steel, coal and engineering;

▶ increased trade, as goods travelled more quickly and cheaply;

▶ a modern postal system.

A modern education system was developed.

This industrial revolution made the Prussian people prosperous and the ruler richer. Other German states admired Prussia's achievement. This helps explain why many joined the Zollverein.

THE CHALLENGE TO AUSTRIA, 1857–62

In 1857 Frederick William IV became too ill to rule. His brother, William, became Regent in 1858. In 1861 William became King of Prussia.

A former soldier, the new king appointed Roon as Minister of War and Moltke as Chief of the General Staff. He decided to increase the size of the army.

The Prussian Parliament, (the Landtag) did not like the new taxes needed to pay for the doubling of the size of the army. In 1861 Parliament approved the new taxes—by only one vote. In 1862 Parliament refused new tax increases. This threatened William's plans for the army. What would he do? He appointed Otto von Bismarck as Minister-President.

OTTO VON BISMARCK

He was born in 1815, son of a Prussian landowner ('Junker'). In 1847 he was Prussian representative at the Diet (of the Confederation) at Frankfurt. He was opposed to

1

the liberal revolutionaries in 1848, and approved the King's refusal to accept the German Crown.

In 1851 he was again Prussian representative at the Diet. In 1859 he was sent as Ambassador to Russia. In 1862 he was transferred to Paris.

King William I had to find someone to overcome the opposition of the Prussian Liberals to his army plans (see above). Roon suggested that he send for Bismarck. As Minister-President, Bismarck also failed to get Parliament to vote for the increased taxes in 1862. He simply announced that the new taxes would be imposed and collected in spite of Parliament's opposition and anger.

The King realized that the people would accept such behaviour only if Prussia benefited from it. This helps to explain Prussian policy after 1862.

1.2 German Unification and the Three Wars, 1864–71 (see Fig. 1.2)

In 1864 Bismarck persuaded Austria to join Prussia in a war against Denmark to get back the duchies of Schleswig and Holstein from the Danes. After defeating Denmark, the two German states ruled the duchies jointly.

Bismarck laid his plans for a future war with Austria:

▶ He won Russian friendship by refusing to let foreign troops cross Prussia to go to the help of the Poles who were in revolt against their Russian rulers in 1863 (see Unit 3).
▶ Italy became an ally when Bismarck promised her Venetia (part of the Austrian Empire) on Austria's defeat.
▶ France, under Napoleon III, agreed to remain neutral after Bismarck hinted that France could have Belgium or some Rhineland states once Austria had been beaten.

In 1866 Austria and Prussia quarrelled over the way in which the duchies were being governed. A war broke out. Within six weeks the Prussian army was everywhere victorious. The main reasons for Prussia's unexpected victory were:

▶ the superiority of the Prussian army, organized by Roon and Moltke, and supplied with better weapons by the Prussian industry;
▶ Austrian difficulties with her subject peoples;
▶ Bismarck's success in isolating Austria from possible allies.

Austria and Prussia signed the Treaty of Prague, 1866.

Under this treaty:

▶ the old (1815) German Confederation was abolished;
▶ a North German Confederation was set up, under Prussian leadership (Fig. 1.2);
▶ the Catholic states of the south were left alone;
▶ Prussia took no territory from Austria, except Venetia, which was given to Italy;
▶ Prussia annexed Holstein and retained Schleswig.

This was a lenient treaty. Austria would be less likely to seek 'revenge' on Prussia. It brought the war to a speedy end, before France and other countries had time to interfere as they might have done.

The Franco-Prussian War, 1870–1, was almost inevitable because:

▶ Bismarck wanted such a war. He built up a new army, on the Prussian model, from the North German Confederation;
▶ Russia agreed to stay neutral in the event of such a war when Bismarck supported her breach of the Treaty of Paris (1856) and her building of naval bases on the Black Sea;
▶ Italy agreed to remain neutral, when France refused to withdraw a French garrison from Rome, which prevented the Italians from capturing that city for their new unified state;
▶ France was made to appear an aggressive country. When Napoleon III asked Bismarck for his 'promised reward' (see above), he was outwitted by Bismarck.
● When Napoleon III suggested that he should occupy Belgium, the British were angered, and remained neutral when Bismarck went to war with France.
● When he suggested that he should take some Rhineland territory, the Catholic states of southern Germany were alarmed, and less opposed to Prussia than before.
● When he suggested that he might buy (and take) Luxemburg, he only succeeded in driving all the German states more firmly into Bismarck's 'camp'.

We are not concerned about the details of the war. You have to note that:

▶ the much-fancied French army was defeated;
▶ the North German army surrounded Paris (autumn 1870);
▶ Napoleon III abdicated;
▶ a republican government was set up to continue the war;
▶ Paris was forced to surrender (January 1871) after a long siege.

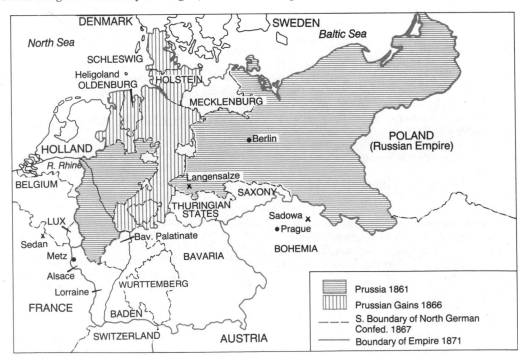

Fig. 1.2 The Prussianization of Germany, 1861–70

THE CREATION OF THE GERMAN EMPIRE, 1871

At Versailles, once the home of the Kings of France, France and Prussia signed a preliminary peace to end the War.

Here, too, Bismarck announced the creation of a new German Empire, made up of the old North German Confederation plus the Catholic states of southern Germany. Only Austria was excluded.

THE TREATY OF FRANKFURT (MAY 1871)

This was signed after negotiations which followed the Treaty of Versailles. In this harsh treaty:

▶ Alsace and Lorraine were ceded by France to Germany. These lands had many valuable coal and iron deposits;
▶ France had to pay an indemnity (or compensation) of £200 million to Germany;
▶ France had to allow a German army to remain in occupation of France until this compensation had been paid.

1.3 Bismarck's Domestic Policies

THE CONSTITUTION OF THE GERMAN EMPIRE, JANUARY 1871

The Empire consisted of a confederation of 25 states. The rulers of the states (kings, dukes, etc.), had great power in the internal affairs of their own states.

The King of Prussia became the Emperor of Germany (the Kaiser). He had a great deal of power:

▶ he had full control of the army, and, later, the navy;
▶ he alone could declare war and make peace treaties;
▶ he appointed all the Ministers in the Empire, including the Chief Minister (or Chancellor). The Cabinet was responsible to him and not, as in Britain, to Parliament.

The German Parliament consisted of two Houses or Chambers:

▶ **The Bundesrat** consisted of 58 delegates appointed by the state rulers. The number of delegates from each state varied; Prussia, the largest state, sent 17 delegates. Since only 14 votes were needed to get any measure rejected, Prussia in fact controlled the Bundesrat, the more important of the two Houses.
▶ **The Reichstag** was elected by universal manhood suffrage in a secret ballot. This was a much more democratic system than Britain had in 1871. There were 382 members in the Reichstag; half of these came from Prussia which had 60 per cent of the Empire's population—in the industrial Ruhr, the Saar and Upper Silesia.

The powers of the Reichstag were very limited:

▶ its consent was needed for the levying of new taxes, but not for the continuation of old taxes;
▶ it could debate proposals for new laws sent to it by the Bundesrat and it could suggest amendments. The consent of both Houses was needed for any new laws. Because Prussia controlled the Bundesrat, the Reichstag had little chance of pushing through anything which Prussia might not like;
▶ it could be dissolved by the Emperor with the approval of the Bundesrat. The Emperor could then call fresh elections.

The Prussian Parliament (or Landtag) was not elected by universal manhood suffrage but by a system of three-class voting. This gave control of the Landtag to the wealthier, landowning class. Since Prussia controlled the Bundesrat and dominated the Reichstag, it was, in fact, these wealthy landowners who had a great deal of influence throughout the Empire. After the fall of Bismarck their influence was to become even stronger.

The Chancellor, or Chief Minister, was appointed by the Emperor. He was responsible only to the Emperor. Bismarck was the first Chancellor of the German Empire. As long as he could control the Emperor, he could do almost what he wanted. It was only when a new Kaiser decided to exercise his full powers that Bismarck lost control. Between 1871 and 1890 the German Empire and the whole of Europe were dominated by Bismarck.

POLITICAL PARTIES IN THE REICHSTAG, 1871

The National Liberals were the largest party in the 1871 Reichstag. They represented the interests of German industrialists. These wanted the new Empire to succeed. They wanted a long period of peace during which industry and trade might grow.

The Conservatives, with about a hundred seats in 1871, represented the interests of the aristocrats and the rulers of the states. Many of these complained of the Prussianization of Germany (see below).

The Centre Party, with about sixty members, represented the interests of the Catholic Church. Most of them came from the northern Rhineland and Bavaria, which had once looked to Austria for leadership. Many of them resented control by Protestant Prussia.

The Socialists were not a large group in 1871. They were to become very important, as we shall see below.

There were approximately a hundred other members in the 1871 Reichstag. Few of them were fervent supporters of Bismarck and Prussia. But few of them could agree on how best to oppose the new power.

BISMARCK'S IMMEDIATE PROBLEMS, 1871

In Germany, as in most other countries in Europe, there were racial minorities. There were a few million non-Germans—French (in Alsace and Lorraine) Danes (in Schleswig) and Poles. In Austria such minorities provided major problems. This did not happen in Bismarck's Germany because:

▶ they were relatively few in number;
▶ they were scattered throughout the country;
▶ they had little in common; e.g. the French wanted to get back to being ruled by France and were not concerned about Poles or Danes.

Local 'nationalism' existed in large states such as Hanover. This might have made them less fervent German nationalists.

The Catholics were to become a major problem (see below).

Industrial towns created social problems—sanitation, water supply, refuse disposal and housing. It was from these towns that there emerged a strong working class political party.

THE PRUSSIANIZATION OF GERMANY

Criminal and commercial law

A common code of law imposed throughout the Empire ended the inconsistencies which existed when each state had its own legal system. A code of civil law and a central court of criminal appeal were also set up.

The Prussian mark became the basis for a single monetary system.

Education

This was organized on the Prussian model. New textbooks were issued; children from all the states had a common education.

BISMARCK AND THE CATHOLICS

Protestant Prussia had defeated Catholic Austria and France, as steps towards unification. Many Catholics resented this. The Centre Party seemed more concerned with Catholic affairs than with German affairs.

Bismarck thought that everyone ought to work in the interests of the Empire. This was a centripetal (or centralizing) policy. The Catholic Church looked to Rome and the Papacy and not to Berlin and the Empire. This was a centrifugal (or going away from the centre) policy. Bismarck decided to attack the Church in Germany.

Bismarck and Papal Infallibility, 1870

In 1870 the Vatican Council (a meeting of all the Catholic bishops and leaders) announced its decisions about Papal Infallibility. This said that when the Pope makes a statement *ex cathedra* (i.e. to the whole Catholic Church) on a question of faith or morals, he is guided by God, so that he can never be wrong.

Few people noticed that there were very few occasions when the Pope spoke in this way. Many, wrongly, thought the Council was claiming that the Pope could never be wrong on any issue. However, most Catholics accepted the new teaching.

Some Catholic professors and teachers in Germany refused to accept it. The Pope demanded that they be sacked from schools and universities. Bismarck supported these 'old' German Catholics, as they were called—the 'new' Catholics having accepted the new teaching. Bismarck argued that education was a state matter. He claimed that the Church had no right to sack the old Catholics from their teaching posts. The Church, on the other hand, insisted it was right. Catholic students were forbidden to go to lectures by opponents of Papal Infallibility or to services led by Old German Catholic priests.

The Kulturkampf

This was the campaign by the State against the Church. The Centre Party took up the struggle on behalf of the Church. The National Liberals supported Bismarck.

In 1872 the Jesuits, the leading Catholic teaching order, were expelled from Germany. The Pope refused to receive the German Ambassador to the Vatican, who was recalled to Germany.

In 1873 all German schools were placed under the control of government inspectors; in the past Catholic schools had been inspected only by churchmen.

Marriage had once been a Church-only ceremony. In 1874 the law was changed; all marriages had to take place before government-appointed officials.

Falk was the Minister of Church Affairs (Public Worship) in Prussia. In May of 1873, 1874 and 1875 he introduced a series of laws in Prussia (the May Laws):

▶ the Church was forbidden to publicly excommunicate 'old' priests;
▶ all candidates for the priesthood had to study at a state university for three years and pass a state examination before starting their priestly studies;
▶ the state had to approve the appointment of Catholic clergy to teaching posts, and could refuse that approval if it wished;
▶ all Catholic schools, colleges and universities had to be open for inspection by state officials;
▶ all religious orders were either dissolved or expelled.

The Church and the Kulturkampf

The Pope declared the May Laws to be invalid. The Catholic clergy defied the Laws; many were sent to prison; others were fined; more were expelled from Prussia and Germany. Ordinary Catholics supported their bishops and clergy. The Centre Party gained more support and seats.

Bismarck calls it off

The Socialist Party had grown in strength because of the continued industrialization of Germany. Bismarck wanted the support of the Catholic Centre Party in his struggle with the Socialists (see below).

The Liberals supported Bismarck against the Church. They might not do so if he fought the Socialists. He needed the Centre.

In 1878 a new Pope, Leo XIII, let it be known that he was ready to arrive at a compromise with Bismarck and Falk.

In 1879 the Falk Laws were suspended and later repealed. Religious orders, other than the Jesuits, returned to Germany. The state kept the power to inspect schools and to hold civil marriages. Otherwise the Church recovered all its old power.

The Catholic Centre Party now supported Bismarck's government.

BISMARCK AND THE SOCIALISTS

The Socialist Party

The German Social Democratic Party (SDP) was set up in 1869 by Bebel, a follower of Karl Marx.

Marx (1818–83) was a German who lived most of his life in exile in London. Together with a German industrialist (Engels) he produced the *Communist Manifesto* (1848) and *Das Kapital*, the first volume of which appeared in 1867.

Marx believed that the workers (or proletariat) should rise in a violent revolution against their capitalist bosses (landowners and employers). After the overthrow of the capitalist system, they would set up a communist system in which:

▶ all the means of production, distribution and exchange would be owned collectively (i.e. by all the people);
▶ there would be no private industry, investment or banking;
▶ everyone would be rewarded 'according to his needs' after he had worked 'according to his ability'.

Bismarck hoped that the democratic constitution (see above) would win the support of the masses for the new Empire.

The industrial revolution had created many social problems. It was these problems which led to the growth of the SDP. Few German socialists thought that a violent revolution would be needed to change things. They hoped that a strong Socialist Party would persuade the government to pass the needed reforms.

In 1871 the Party won only three seats in the Reichstag. In 1877 it won 12 seats and had 500,000 votes. Bismarck was alarmed at this growth.

In 1878 there were two attempts to assassinate the Kaiser. Bismarck claimed that these had been organized by the Socialists.

The campaign against the Socialists

The Enabling Law (1878) allowed the government to declare a state of emergency whenever it wanted to. This Law allowed the police to break up political meetings. Socialist publications were banned. Over 1500 leading socialists were arrested.

The Party continued to grow. In 1890 it got one and a half million votes; in 1914 over four and a quarter million.

Bismarck and a fresh approach

Bismarck realized that he could not crush socialism. He introduced a series of reforms, hoping to win popular support:

▶ national insurance against sickness (1883) for all workers;
▶ national insurance against accidents at work (1884);
▶ a system of old age pensions (1889).

This 'generous' policy failed to draw support away from the Socialists. In 1896 (after Bismarck's fall) the SDP was the second largest party in the Reichstag.

Bismarck's fall in 1890 was due, in part, to his quarrel with the new Kaiser over the way to deal with the Socialists.

BISMARCK AND THE TARIFF QUESTION

The National Liberals were Bismarck's main supporters. They had seen how Prussia gained from the Zollverein (see above). This led them to demand international free trade. They hoped that such a policy would benefit the whole world.

By 1879 other European countries had become industrialized. They sent their goods into free-trade Germany. This led German industrialists (Liberal supporters) to form the National Economic Union to demand a German tariff on foreign imports.

Bismarck's main supporters in Prussia had been the land-owning Conservatives. These Junkers became wealthier as industrial workers bought their agricultural output. But by 1879 American farmers were selling huge quantities of wheat in free-trade Germany. This harmed the interests of the Junker class. They joined the Liberals in their demand for a German tariff.

Bismarck might have rejected these demands from industrialists and farmers, but there was also a military need for a tariff.

Since 1866 and the time of the North German Confederation the central government had got its money from:

▶ postal and telegraph services;
▶ such low import duties as existed;
▶ contributions by each of the states to the central government.

By 1879 Bismarck realized that this revenue would have to be increased because his foreign policy needed a larger and better-equipped army, and a network of roads and railways to carry the army to the frontiers when war broke out. He also needed money to pay for the larger Civil Service needed to run the Empire, and for the social welfare system he planned.

He might have got this money from new taxes approved by the Reichstag. This would give greater power to that House. Bismarck did not want this to happen. Tariffs would provide the money needed. So, reluctantly, he brought in a system of protective tariffs (May–July, 1879). The Liberals opposed him, but they ceased to be a problem, because:

▶ many joined the SDP to campaign for more social reform;
▶ many more, fearing socialism, joined the Conservatives.

1.4 Bismarck's Foreign Policy, 1870–90

COLONIAL EXPANSION

In 1870 Bismarck thought that Germany ought to concentrate on her industrial development, and that attempts to gain colonies would annoy Britain which might become an ally for France and help her regain Alsace and Lorraine.

After the introduction of the tariff system he realized:

▶ colonies could provide raw materials for German industry;
▶ they would also be markets for German goods;
▶ they could be 'living space' for the growing population.

In 1882 a German Colonial Union was formed to campaign for the acquisition of German colonies.

In 1884 Bismarck called an international conference in Berlin. Here the major Powers agreed on the division of Africa. Germany gained the following:

▶ 1885: South West Africa, Togoland and the Cameroons;
▶ 1890: the naval base of Heligoland by agreement with Britain;
▶ 1890: Britain recognized German claims to German East Africa (later called Tanganyika) while Germany recognized Britain's claims to Kenya and Zanzibar.

Unit 8 also develops the important topic of Germany's foreign policy.

1.5 The Fall of Bismarck, 1890

In 1888 William I died. Bismarck had usually been able to rely on his support and had generally got his own way with this Kaiser. The new Kaiser, Frederick, was married to a daughter of Queen Victoria. She and Frederick disliked Bismarck; they wanted a more liberal and democratic system of government. But within three months of coming to the throne, the Kaiser died of cancer.

1888 was the year of the Three Emperors: Kaiser William II succeeded his father, Frederick. This Kaiser was only 28 years old. He had never got on with his parents, but had always admired his grandfather, William I. He was born with a paralysed left arm which prevented him from being as active as other members of the aristocracy and made him bitter.

By 1890 the young Kaiser had quarrelled with Bismarck about:

▶ the Socialists: William II opposed Bismarck's attempts to crush Socialism; he wanted to come to terms with the SDP;
▶ the colonies: the Kaiser thought Germany ought to have more;
▶ a navy: the Kaiser wanted to challenge British sea power;
▶ foreign policy: the Kaiser wanted to side openly with Austria-Hungary, even if this meant a quarrel with Russia (see Unit 8).

In 1890 Bismarck was forced to resign.

BISMARCK'S SUCCESSORS

Von Caprivi was Chancellor from 1890 to 1894. He allowed the anti-socialist laws to lapse (1890), hoping the welfare system would lead to a fall in support for the Socialists. In fact the party continued to grow.

Hohenlohe (1894–1900) tried to get the Reichstag to renew the attack on socialism (1895) but failed.

Admiral Tirpitz was appointed German Naval Secretary (or Minister) in June 1897. He drew up plans for a large German navy, and helped found the German Naval League to popularize the demand for a navy. His appointment and policies were steps along the road to war. Other steps were:

▶ 1890 the acquisition of Heligoland;
▶ 1895 the completion of the Kiel Canal between the North Sea and the Baltic.

Colonel-General von Moltke (son of Bismarck's Moltke) became chief of the German General Staff. He got the support of the Kaiser for a larger German army. This was welcomed in Germany because:

▶ it created a demand for iron, steel, coal and engineering products so that it helped German industry;
▶ the larger army was seen as a sign of German importance.

Bülow was Chancellor from 1900 to 1909. He had to face opposition in the Reichstag from parties opposed to the increasing power of the militarists such as Tirpitz and Moltke. But this opposition was unable to restrain the Kaiser and his ministers.

Bethmann-Hollweg became Chancellor in 1909. The chief interest of his government lay in foreign affairs (Unit 8).

Unit 1 Summary

▶ The unification of Germany and its federal constitution.
▶ Bismarck's three 'wars of unification', 1862–71.
▶ Bismarck's domestic policies, 1871–90.

2 FRANCE, 1870–1914

2.1 The Franco-Prussian War, 1870–1 (See also Unit 1.)

Napoleon III, nephew of Napoleon I, became Emperor of France in December 1852, after a *coup d'état*. By 1870 he was unpopular.

During the Austro-Prussian War of 1866 (see Unit 1) he remained neutral, hoping that Bismarck would reward him with (a) Belgium, (b) the land on the left bank of the Rhine and/or (c) some territory in Southern Germany.

Negotiations with Bismarck brought trouble for Napoleon. Russia and Italy supported Bismarck. (See Unit 1.)

The Spanish throne was vacant after a revolution. The Spanish asked Prince Leopold, a relative of the King of Prussia, to accept the throne. This request led to a war. The French told the Prussian king that they would not agree to his relative becoming King of Spain; Bismarck hoped France would declare war. The Prussian King let Bismarck down: he persuaded his relative to withdraw his acceptance of the Spanish throne. The French demanded that the King make an official renunciation of his relative's claim to the throne. However, the King refused, during an interview with the French Ambassador whom he met at the spa town of Ems. The King sent Bismarck a telegram about the interview, and Bismarck altered the Ems telegram to appear as if the King had been rough and abrupt with the French Ambassador. He then published the Ems Telegram. The angry French public marched to the Imperial Palace to demand war on Prussia.

THE FALL OF NAPOLEON III

The French thought that they would win the war, but their army was badly organized, and army supplies were lacking: there was not enough ammunition; weapons were not as modern as those used by the Prussians.

The Prussian army, on the other hand, was well organized: Roon and Moltke had made their preparations. The railways took armies to the front quickly, and Prussian industry produced the munitions.

MacMahon was defeated at Worth in August 1870. Bazaine was defeated by a second Germany army and forced to take refuge in the fortress town of Metz. Napoleon and MacMahon marched to relieve Metz. They were defeated at Sedan and Napoleon surrendered on 2 September 1870.

2.2 The Difficult Establishment of the Third Republic

The Germans continued to advance and besieged Paris. Gambetta, a leading opponent of Napoleon III, proclaimed a French Republic in Paris (September 1870).

A Provisional Government of National Defence was set up in Paris to lead France in the struggle against the invaders. Gambetta escaped, in a balloon, from Paris to raise fresh armies in the south and west. These untrained and badly armed men were unable to drive the Germans from Paris.

In January 1871 Paris surrendered and an armistice * was signed.

The Provisional Government had not been elected by the French people. It did not have the power to make a peace treaty. After the armistice a National Assembly was elected to decide whether to continue with the war or to make peace. This Assembly met at Bordeaux, January 1871. It agreed to the Treaty of Frankfurt (see Unit 1).

THE ASSEMBLY VERSUS THE PARISIAN REPUBLICANS

The Republic of 1870 was created by Parisians. Republicans wanted to continue the war. However, the majority of the French people were peasant farmers, and they wanted the war to end. In the elections for the National Assembly (January 1871) the peasants chose men who wanted to make peace. The majority of these supported some form of monarchy—although they did not agree who should be ruler. They did not try to bring back a monarch immediately. They realized that such a monarch would have been blamed for the harsh terms of the Treaty of Frankfurt. The Assembly therefore elected an old politician, Thiers, as Chief of the Executive Power. It did not call him President, nor did it proclaim a Republic.

THE PARIS COMMUNE

The people of Paris resented the fact that the Assembly on leaving Bordeaux met at Versailles, the old monarchical palace, and not, as they demanded, in the capital. They also resented the monarchist majority. Parisians wanted the Assembly to proclaim a Republic. They had been angered and humiliated when the German army marched, in triumph, through the streets of Paris—and more angered by Thiers' having allowed this 'march of the victors'. The German occupation of forts to the north of Paris was a constant reminder of the humiliating Treaty.

The Assembly passed two Acts which angered Parisians:
► during the war all property rents within Paris had been suspended. The Assembly decided that they should be repaid to landlords—with interest.
► the people of Paris had raised their own National Guard as part of their defence during the German siege. The Assembly decided to disarm the National Guard, to end payment to its members and to remove its cannons from the city.

Troops loyal to the Versailles government were sent to get the cannons (March 1871). The Parisians resisted and fighting broke out. There then took place the formation of the Commune:
► as in revolutionary cities in the south (Lyons and Marseilles), the red flag was flown over the Paris Town Hall;
► a General Council (or Commune) of ninety members was elected to govern Paris. Paris was to be self-governing and completely independent of the Assembly.

You should note that the members of the Commune were drawn from every social class. It was *not* a communist gathering.

Thiers and the Commune, March–May 1871

Thiers was determined to bring the Commune down. He

could not allow 'the tail (Paris) to wag the dog (France)'.

The Germans allowed the Assembly's forces to attack Paris, and even handed back prisoners of war to MacMahon to help. In May he forced his way into Paris. Fierce street fighting continued in the barricaded streets. The supporters of the Commune made a last-ditch stand in the Père Lachaise cemetery. Many buildings were destroyed, many hostages shot, including the Archbishop of Paris.

The Versailles forces finally won (May 1871). Many supporters of the Commune were executed and others exiled.

The effects of the Commune

Many Parisians remained hostile to the Thiers government—and, later, to the Republic which succeeded it. The uprising frightened many European leaders. Bismarck used this fear in his policy of isolating France (see Unit 8).

Thiers was popular with the rich French who had feared that the Commune might be the beginning of another revolution like that of 1789. They gave generously to the loans floated by the government to pay off the compensation demanded at Frankfurt. The £200 million was paid in less than three years and the German army withdrawn sooner than Bismarck had imagined.

THIERS, 1871–3

Thiers had already played an important part in recent events:

▶ he was head of the Bordeaux Assembly which made peace;
▶ as head of the Executive Power he put down the Commune;
▶ he had got the loans to pay the German compensation.

Once the German army of occupation was withdrawn, he reorganized the French army and brought in a strict law of conscription.

As a reward for his work, the Assembly declared him President of the Republic, although the majority of members were monarchists.

Thiers supported the claims of the Orléanist candidate for the throne. But by 1873 he realized that it would be impossible to bring back a monarch. He suggested in 1873 that the Assembly should write a republican constitution. The Assembly rejected the proposal, and in May 1873 forced Thiers to resign. MacMahon, a monarchist, was chosen to succeed Thiers.

THE MONARCHISTS' PLOT, 1873–5

There were three possible claimants to the throne:

▶ the Bourbons were the family overthrown in 1791, restored in 1815 and overthrown again in 1830. Their leader in 1873 was the Comte de (or Count of) Chambord, grandson of the king deposed in 1830;
▶ the Orléanists (who had had Louis Philippe as King from 1830 to 1848) were represented by the Comte de Paris, Louis Philippe's grandson;
▶ the Bonapartists put forward the claims of Napoleon III's son, the Prince Imperial, aged seventeen.

The Royalists agreed that the claims of the Prince Imperial could be dismissed. Napoleon III even more than his uncle, the great Napoleon, was not of the royal 'race'.

The Bourbon and Orléanist factions finally agreed that the old and childless Chambord would be King, and that the younger Paris would be named as his heir. Then they threw it all away. Chambord refused to accept the tricolour flag as the national emblem. The flag of his France would be the white flag of the Bourbons, with its lilies (or *fleurs de lis*). MacMahon said 'The guns would have gone off on their own' because there would have been widespread opposition to this rejection of the flag which had been the national emblem since 1791.

Royalists hoped to wait until Chambord died, when the Comte de Paris would become King. But MacMahon summed up the position when he admitted, 'It is the Republic which divides us least.'

THE REPUBLICAN CONSTITUTION, 1875

Gambetta rallied the anti-royalist forces in the Assembly which in January 1875 voted by a majority of one vote in favour of a republican constitution. A president was to be head of state. He would be elected every seven years by the members of the two Houses of Parliament.

The royalists only agreed to allow the constitution through on condition that the President was given very great powers:

▶ he chose the ministers to form the government;
▶ he could introduce laws himself;
▶ if the Parliament passed anything with which he disagreed, he could demand further debates in Parliament;
▶ on the advice of the Senate (below) he could dissolve the Chamber (below) and call for fresh elections.

There were two houses in the French Parliament:

The Senate or Upper House was to be elected every nine years by an electoral college chosen by each department throughout France. This is an example of indirect elections.

The Chamber of Deputies was the Lower House. Every four years all men over the age of twenty-one were entitled to vote for members of the Chamber. This is an example of direct elections.

Ministers, although chosen by the President, were responsible to the Senate and the Chamber, which had the right to reject government proposals. If the government were defeated on a major issue, there might be fresh elections. However, it was more usual for there just to be a change of government. There were many short-lived governments—fifty by the time war broke out in 1914.

The Republic was called the Third Republic. There had been a First Republic from 1793 to 1805 and a Second from 1848 to 1852.

MACMAHON'S FINAL YEARS, 1875–9

MacMahon was President in succession to Thiers. After 1875 he used his powers to try to prevent republicans from getting too much of their own way.

Fresh elections were called in 1876. These resulted in:

▶ a republican majority in the Chamber of Deputies;
▶ a monarchist majority in the Senate.

In 1877 MacMahon used his powers in union with the Senate to dismiss the Chamber and call for fresh elections. He hoped for a monarchist majority, but did not get it. He appointed a monarchist, the Duke de Broglie as Prime Minister.

But MacMahon's hopes were dashed by the French people. In 1878 the republicans gained a number of seats in the Senate so that they controlled that body as well as the Chamber. MacMahon acknowledged that he had lost. He resigned to make way for Jules Grévy, a republican. In 1879, the republicans had the Presidency and control of both Houses of Parliament. It seemed as if the republic was, at last, safe.

WHY DID THE MONARCHISTS FAIL AND THE REPUBLIC SURVIVE?

The legacy of Napoleon III. His reforming activity and his aggressive foreign policy made a 'liberal' republic appear as an attractive alternative.

The royalists failed to present a realistic alternative. The republic appeared to MacMahon and other members of the upper classes as the most logical alternative. It was already an attractive alternative as far as the middle classes were concerned.

The extreme left was not a threat, particularly after the defeat of the Commune. There was no danger that a liberal republic would pave the way for extreme socialism. This deprived the right-wing monarchists of a possible argument against the republic.

The economic depression, of the 1870s did not affect France as much as it did Germany and Britain. Thiers had laid a firm basis for economic recovery (see above) so that the royalists could not argue that republicanism led to depression.

The republic was in many ways a constitutional monarchy in disguise, although it was liberal and democratic in appearance. It was not likely that this republican government would pass any truly radical measures. Indeed, although there were to be many changes of government by 1914, almost all of them were very conservative and similar in outlook. There was too little for royalists to disagree with.

2.3 Domestic Policies, 1879–87

Jules Ferry was Prime Minister 1881–3 and 1883–5. His governments were responsible for:
► pardoning exiled and imprisoned supporters of the Commune;
► allowing trade unions freedom—although the government did not repeal the old Laws of Association under which unions and other organizations had been persecuted;
► removing press censorship;
► tackling the question of education (see below).

EDUCATION

The importance of education had been recognized by the republican, Gambetta, who declared that the French had not been beaten by the Prussian army but by the Prussian schoolmasters. Prussian education had turned out a more intelligent workforce, more intelligent soldiers and the technicians who produced the munitions.

The French educational system—primary, secondary and university—was controlled by the Catholic Church, which republicans blamed for the failure of the French system. They also accused the Church of being monarchist and anti-republican. Gambetta said '*Cléricisme, voilà l'ennemi*' ('Clericalism, there is the enemy').

A national, government-supported system of primary education was set up for children between the ages of six and thirteen. Priests, monks and nuns were forbidden to teach in these schools.

State secondary schools (or *lycées*) had been set up by Napoleon I for boys. Ferry established similar schools for girls. It was forbidden to provide religious instruction in these schools, which were staffed by laymen and laywomen. Priests and nuns were free to give that instruction outside school hours.

The Jesuits were expelled from France. Other religious orders were allowed to exist provided that they registered as required by the Laws of Association. These 'authorized orders' could run their own schools, which received no financial help from the government. These private schools (or *écoles*) were supported by richer Catholics.

2.4 Republican Problems

Grévy and Ferry were not always popular with the French Parliament. When Ferry tried to bring in Factory Acts to improve conditions for workers, the Senate rejected them.

As the fear of a monarchist revival died out, divisions appeared among the republicans. They split into rival groups. One result of this was frequent ministerial changes.

This 'in-and-out' series of governments made the republican form of government less popular. Monarchy, after all, provided a stable form of continual government.

In 1887 Grévy was succeeded by Carnot.

In 1886 President Grévy's son-in-law was involved in a financial scandal concerning the sale of honours.

In 1887 a French frontier official, Schnaebele, was arrested on French soil by a German policeman. This was a reminder of the power of Germany and the loss of Alsace and Lorraine. Grévy and, later, Carnot seemed unable to stand up to the Germans.

Many French people looked for someone who might take charge of the country. Such a one might:
► make France great again—and stand up to Germany;
► bring strong government—and fewer ministerial changes;
► get rid of corruption;
► end the quarrel with the Church (a wish of Catholics);
► ensure the continuation of the Republic (the wish of the anti-Catholics).

GENERAL BOULANGER

Many people thought that such a saviour existed in the shape of the Minister of War, General Boulanger. Handsome (unlike most of the politicians), frequently seen riding on his black horse (a reminder of military power) he became very popular as he demanded the reforms which many people wanted to see.

He demanded that the Presidency should be strengthened (which pleased the monarchists). He asked that the army be strengthened (and those who hoped to regain Alsace and Lorraine supported this).

In 1888 six constituencies chose him as their Deputy. He then demanded the abolition of the Senate (which pleased the radical republicans) and called for democracy in the army (which pleased the left-wing and the anti-clericals).

In 1889 it appeared that he might get elected for many more seats in the Chamber. Those who supported him (the Church and army, the anti-clericals and radicals, the fervent republicans and the anti-Germans) hoped that he might lead a march on the Parliament, dismiss the two Houses and seize power.

The government finally took courage. It accused him of treason—plotting the overthrow of the republic. Instead of standing up to the government, Boulanger ran away to Belgium. Three years later he committed suicide. The republic had come through one crisis. Another was waiting to threaten it.

THE PANAMA SCANDAL, 1889–92

In 1869 the French engineer, Ferdinand de Lesseps, completed the Suez Canal. In 1879 it was proposed to build a Panama Canal, and de Lesseps was asked to take charge of the project. A company was formed, money borrowed from the public, hoping that the new canal would be as successful as the Suez Canal. In 1889 the company went bankrupt, long before the canal was complete.

The reasons for de Lesseps' failure were many:
► he had underestimated the difficulties involved;
► he had made serious errors in engineering;
► the climate made working very difficult.

In 1892 an investigation showed that much of the money raised was used to bribe politicians to support the scheme. De Lesseps was sentenced to five years in prison, but this did not help investors in the bankrupt company.

This corruption led many French people to have less confidence than ever in the republican system. Others blamed the financiers for the bribery and for the company's collapse. Some of the financiers (bankers, stockbrokers and others) were Jewish. This led to an outburst of anti-semitism in France. It was this anti-semitism which provided the republic with yet another crisis in 1894.

THE DREYFUS AFFAIR, 1894–1906

In 1894 an army Captain, Alfred Dreyfus, was charged with having sold military secrets to the Germans. The main evidence against Dreyfus was an unsigned document called the *bordereau*, said to be in his handwriting.

An army court-martial found him guilty. He was degraded (stripped of his rank, all the buttons and decorations torn off his uniform in front of the soldiers of his regiment). The army court then sentenced him to imprisonment for life on Devil's Island.

However, the Dreyfus family argued that the trial had been unfair, the defence had not seen all the papers involved, and that Dreyfus had not written the *bordereau*.

A Colonel Picquart became convinced of Dreyfus's innocence. In 1896 he claimed that Major Esterhazy had forged the *bordereau*. This accusation divided French public opinion.

The anti-Dreyfusards supported the army court-martial and argued that Dreyfus was guilty. This was the 'party' of:
▶ the wealthier families which produced most army officers;
▶ the monarchists who saw a chance to weaken the republic;
▶ the clergy, opposed to attacks on the Catholic Church;
▶ the anti-semites. Dreyfus was a Jew—one of the few non-Catholics to become an army officer. Most officers had been trained at the Catholic military academy, St Cyr.

The Dreyfusards said Dreyfus was innocent and the Catholic officer-class was guilty of anti-semitism. This 'party' consisted of:
▶ those who wanted a more democratic army and were opposed to the Catholic domination of the forces;
▶ the anti-clericals who argued that the Dreyfus case showed how right they were to attack the Church;
▶ the republicans. The case damaged their form of government and showed that the army was outside government control;
▶ many literary men, who wrote pamphlets and books supporting Dreyfus's innocence.

In 1898 an army court found Esterhazy innocent. Emile Zola, a leading novelist, then wrote a famous letter headed '*J'accuse*'. This was published in the socialist newspaper *L'Aurore*. Zola accused the army of corruptly mishandling the affair. There was a good deal of public argument over this letter; France became bitterly divided between the Catholic right and the Republican left. Zola, arrested and found guilty of treason, fled to Britain.

The government brought three documents before the Chamber of Deputies to show Dreyfus's guilt. Picquart said that two of the documents had nothing to do with the case, while the third had been forged. A Colonel Henry confessed to having forged the document—and then committed suicide.

In 1899 Esterhazy (see above) fled to Britain, where he confessed to having forged the *bordereau*. This led to the calling of a Court of Cassation which laid aside the verdict at Dreyfus's first trial and ordered a fresh one.

In spite of the admissions of Henry and Esterhazy, the army court-martial again found Dreyfus guilty, but reduced his punishment to one of ten years' imprisonment. The government stepped in to give Dreyfus a pardon—but said nothing about his guilt.

In 1906 the case was re-opened. A Court of Cassation laid aside the result of the second trial, declared Dreyfus innocent and said Esterhazy was guilty of forging the *bordereau*. Dreyfus was restored to the army, where he was promoted and given the highest award in France, the Legion of Honour.

ANOTHER CLASH WITH THE CATHOLIC CHURCH, 1901–7

It is difficult for us to understand the hatred which the Dreyfus Affair aroused in France. Families were divided; old friends quarrelled; there was even street fighting.

It is also difficult to understand the important part played by religion in French affairs during this period (1870–1914).

We have seen how Ferry and Grévy limited the power of the Catholic Church. The bitter arguments over the Dreyfus affair led to a more violent attack on the Church.
▶ Waldeck-Rousseau became Prime Minister in 1899. It was his government which was responsible for three attacks.
▶ A new Law of Association (1901). Older Laws of Association said that any association or society with more than twenty members had to be approved by the government. These laws had not been rigorously enforced and many religious orders had been formed without government permission. The new Law of 1901 said that:
● non-religious societies were legalized;
● religious associations had to seek permission;
● they had to submit their rules for government approval;
● all unauthorized associations were banned from teaching.
▶ Religious orders which did not apply for or failed to get government sanctions were suppressed.
▶ Over 1500 religious houses were closed.

In 1904 Waldeck-Rousseau resigned. His successor, a former Jesuit priest, Combes, was violently anti-Catholic.

In 1905 the Law of Separation was passed. This ended the Concordat (or agreement) between the French government and the Vatican, reached in 1802. The government stopped the payment of salaries to Catholic priests, although it continued to pay pensions to retired priests. All churches and cathedrals became state property. Associations for public worship (*Associations culturelles*) were to be formed. The government would give permission to such associations to use churches and cathedrals.

Jews and Protestants formed their own associations. Pope Pius X forbade French Catholics to do so.

In 1907 the government relaxed the law. Priests could negotiate for the use of churches—without forming an association.

Many people had seen the Church as a menace to the republic. It had supported MacMahon, Chambord, Boulanger, the anti-Dreyfusards and seemed to be very powerful. It is worth noting that the attacks on the Church after 1875 were supported by the majority of French voters. No minister lost power because of a Catholic revolt at the ballot box. It is possible that the power of the Church had been more apparent than real. Certainly by 1905 it had ceased to be an important issue in French politics. Only a minority of French people remained loyal to the Church.

2.5 Socialism and Syndicalism

SOCIALISM

France was slow to become industrialized. The majority of the people were peasant farmers and lived in small villages.

Industrial workers were relatively few in number. Trade unions were small, and until the 1890s there were few socialist Deputies in the Chamber. France was very different from Germany where the Socialist Party was a very large one (see Unit 1).

In 1884 trade unions were legalized, although workers employed by the government were not allowed to form or join unions.

Trade unions set up their own Labour Exchanges in industrial towns where they organized unemployment benefit and other social services for their members.

Alexandre Millerand was the Socialist leader who helped the party to grow. Many radicals joined the party when the republican governments did little for the working class.

In 1893 Millerand led 45 Socialist Deputies in the Chamber and, in the unstable republican system, had a little influence.

In 1899–1902 he was a minister in Waldeck-Rousseau's government which:
▶ in 1900 reduced the working day to 11 hours;

▶ in 1904 further reduced it to 10 hours;
▶ failed to enforce these regulations properly.

Millerand was a moderate. In 1902 he was expelled from the Party, which had been re-organized on Marxist lines. The next significant leader of the Party was Jean Jaurès, who was assassinated in Paris on 30 July 1914 because of his opposition to French entry into the war.

SYNDICALISM

The failure of republican governments to do much for the working class led to demands by workers for more direct action.

French trade unions were known as *syndicats*, and have given their name to an extremist movement called syndicalism.

Syndicalists aimed at:
▶ destroying Parliamentary institutions by strikes and sabotage;
▶ giving the workers in every industry complete control of their industry.

It was the syndicalists who fixed on May Day as a day for working-class demonstrations and marches.

By 1900 about half a million men belonged to the organiza-tion which had nothing in common with the moderate trade unions of Great Britain or the moderate Socialist Party of Germany.

In 1909 the syndicalists organized a nation-wide railway strike. The minister concerned with the railways, Aristide Briand (a moderate Socialist) called all the striking workers up for military service. To have continued the strike would have allowed the government to put workers on trial for treason. The strike was broken.

In 1912 a European war appeared possible. A coalition government was formed to ensure national safety. Syndi-calism became less important.

Unit 2 Summary

▶ The Franco-Prussian War and the fall of Napoleon III.
▶ The difficult establishment of the Third Republic.
▶ The domestic policies of the Third Republic.
▶ Threats to the Republic: Boulanger, scandals, Drey-fus and the Catholic Church.
▶ Socialism and syndicalism.

---

3 RUSSIA, 1855–1914

3.1 Tsar Alexander II, 1855–81

The ruler of Russia was known as the Tsar, or Emperor. Alexander II became Tsar in 1855 during the Crimean War. That war had shown how inefficient Russia was. Her industry was unable to supply enough munitions, her agriculture was unable to supply enough food, and her Civil Service was unable to organize the war.

Once he had made peace with Britain and France (1856), the Tsar decided on a policy of reform.

THE RUSSIAN PEASANTS

Most of Russia's agricultural land was owned by the Tsar himself, the small number of nobles, and a larger number of lesser nobles or gentry. The majority of the Russian people living on the land were serfs, or semi-slaves.
▶ They had to work three days a week for their owner.
▶ They paid most of Russia's taxes in a poll tax.
▶ Their masters could sell them; punish them severely without trial (flogging was common).
▶ They could be conscripted for service in the forces.

Each serf family had about 6 hectares (15 acres) to farm for their own benefit—but they did not own the land.

The effects of serfdom

Agriculture was inefficient. There was no incentive for serfs to work hard: any profit would go to the owners.

Industry was developing, but there was a shortage of labour. Serf labour was not free to move to the factories.

Revolutionaries from Western Europe might be able to persuade the downtrodden serfs to revolt. Alexander II said, 'It is better to abolish serfdom from above rather than await the time when it will begin to abolish itself from below.'

The Edict of Emancipation, 3 March 1861

Few nobles agreed with the Tsar's ideas. Even these demanded payment for their loss of slaves and land. Forty-four million peasants were set free by the Edict. They could now own land, they were free to move from the estates—but they had to carry passports to show the police when asked, and they did not have to work on the nobles' land. However, the former serfs did not become owners of any land immediately—they had to pay for it.

Government surveyors divided the land between the former owners and the former serfs. On average a former serf family got about 3 hectares (8 acres)—less than when they lived on a master's estate. That land had to be paid for. It was valued by a government official. The government paid the owner, and the ex-serfs paid instal-ments for forty-nine years.

The mir (or village commune) became, as it were, the new owners. Each year the 'elders' of the mir divided up the 'freed' land according to the numbers in each family. The mir collected the debt instalments.

Discontented peasants

The population increased from 50 million in 1850 to approximately 82 million in 1900. The annual division of the land by the mir after 1861 led to every family getting a smaller and smaller plot. Most peasants remained inefficient. They produced enough to feed their families, but few produced enough to sell for profit. This led to food shortages in the growing towns.

Many peasants gave up farming because they could not pay the annual instalments. Some became workers for more successful ex-serfs (called *kulaks* in Russian). Some went to work in industrial towns. Here they lived in primitive conditions (see below).

LOCAL GOVERNMENT REFORM

The nobles and the gentry had run the countryside—seeing to the building of bridges, hospitals and schools. Then, after the Emancipation of 1861, it was necessary to find some other way to govern the countryside.

The mir or commune was the bottom rung of the ladder of government. There were elections in each mir to choose its leaders.

District councils (zemstvos) had been controlled by the nobles. After 1861 these councils were elected by nobles, townspeople, and peasants, the former serfs. These zemstvos looked after the building and maintenance of roads and bridges and ran the country's improved school system. The district zemstvos were a second rung on the ladder of government—above the mir.

A third rung on that ladder was the provincial zemstvos. Delegates went from various district zemstvos— a case of indirect election. They looked after the public health system and chose magistrates for the new law courts.

DISCONTENTED LIBERALS

Democratic elections to the mir and the district zemstvos pleased many liberals—nobles, gentry and townspeople. This partial democracy also made them discontented, because government-appointed Provincial Governors could ban any demand of a zemstvo, and while the Tsar had created three tiers or rungs of government (mir, district zemstvos and provincial zemstvos) he was unwilling to call a national council or Parliament. He went further. The members of the various zemstvos were forbidden to meet in national conferences to discuss common problems. Maybe the Tsar feared that such a gathering might have led to a demand for a constitutional government.

OTHER REFORMS BY ALEXANDER II

The press

Censorship was relaxed; writers could criticize the government. Alexander hoped to bring his critics into the open. Newspapers and journals flourished—the number of national newspapers increased from 6 to 16 by 1881.

The legal system

As in other countries, judges and magistrates were appointed for life and could not be dismissed by the government. Equality before the law of all Russians was proclaimed, trials had to be held in public. The system of trial by jury replaced the system by which a nobleman-judge or magistrate had tried cases.

However, there were limits to the legal reforms: political offenders were not tried by jury; peasants had their own special courts; so too did editors of critical newspapers. These could not even speak in their own defence during a trial.

The army

In 1874 all classes became liable for military service—and not only the peasantry. Length of service fell from twenty-five to fifteen years. Flogging of soldiers was forbidden.

Education

Primary education

District zemstvos built 10,000 schools as a means of tackling massive illiteracy.

Secondary schools

There were two kinds of schools:
▶ the old-fashioned schools taught mainly classics (Latin and Greek) and did not offer science;
▶ modern schools offered science.

Universities

These admitted only students from the old-fashioned schools. The government thought that science was 'dangerous'.

ALEXANDER AND POLAND, 1863

Russia had expanded its territory at various times so that it included many non-Russian peoples. The Poles were one such people—their country had been seized by Russia during the Napoleonic Wars.

In 1863 the Poles rose in revolt because:
▶ the reforms created a 'liberal' atmosphere;
▶ the defeat in the Crimean War (1853–6) suggested that Russia might be too weak to put down a revolt;
▶ the Italians had risen against Austria (1859–61).

The incident which sparked off the rising was the closing-down of the Polish Agricultural Society in Warsaw. Anti-Russian demonstrations took place, which led to troops firing on the crowd.

Napoleon III of France wanted to help his fellow-Catholics in Poland. Bismarck refused to allow French troops to go through Prussia—and so gained Russian friendship (see Unit 1). The rising was put down with great cruelty.

Alexander II and his ministers then encouraged Russian nationalism (they blamed the Poles for trying to break up the Russian Empire), pan-Slavism and the union of the Slavs of South-Eastern Europe under Russian leadership (see Unit 4).

3.2 Revolutionary Developments

The reforms of Alexander II led to the growth of revolutionary movements, because:
▶ each reform whetted the appetite for more;
▶ educational development created a more literate people able to read and understand the arguments of Radicals;
▶ the land reform left many people dissatisfied;
▶ industrial towns created their own problems.

NIHILISTS

Nihilists (from the Latin word *nihil* meaning 'nothing') were a group of revolutionaries who thought that everything from the past had to be destroyed, so that a new society could be built. Using the greater freedom of the press, the movement won a great deal of support; many thousands joined. However, the old system did not go away peacefully, so the nihilists began to use terrorist tactics. Bombs, guns and knives were used in attacks on government officials and in 1866 on the Tsar himself.

The government then turned to repressive methods:
▶ Thousands were arrested and exiled to Siberia.
▶ Since many leading nihilists were students, there was an attempt to restrict entry to universities to those who could be shown to be 'reliable'—i.e. loyal to the Tsar.
▶ Editors of newspapers could be dismissed if they did not reveal the names of writers of nihilist articles.

NARODNIKI

The *Narodniki* (the name given to the many thousands of students) went in the early 1870s to preach revolutionary ideas to the peasants. They were not very successful because:

▶ most peasants could not understand the ideas;
▶ peasants were shocked by the free-and-easy behaviour of the 'townies';
▶ the local priests had great influence and persuaded people to attack the students.

The movement fizzled out, but it led Alexander to tighten up university entrance.

SOCIALISTS

Socialism, as taught by Marx (see Unit 1), had some influence in the 1870s in Russia.

The village commune attracted some Russian revolutionaries. They saw it as the ideal socialist society, where land held by the commune was shared out according to the families' needs. Some socialists, imitating the Narodniki, tried to preach the need for a peaceful revolution by the peasants. Others, led by Michael Bakunin, once a nihilist, wanted a violent uprising to sweep the Tsarist system away.

THE DEATH OF ALEXANDER II, 1881

The Tsar had started out by being 'The Liberator' and had made many important reforms, but he had failed to satisfy all the people. Unable to get more changes by peaceful means, they turned to terrorism.

In 1866 there was an attempt to assassinate Alexander II. In 1879 he survived two further attempts on his life. In one, five shots missed him. In another, his Winter Palace was dynamited—but the Tsar was away.

In 1880 the dining room in the Winter Palace was mined when, again, the Tsar was away, and a mine on a track along which his train was travelling did not explode.

In 1881 the terrorists killed Alexander in a bomb attack.

3.3 Tsar Alexander III, 1881–94

The new Tsar declared that his father's reforming policies had been wrong and had failed. He promised to 'turn back the clock' and undo the reforms. In this he gave a free hand to his chief Minister, Pobedonostsev.

POBEDONOSTSEV

This man had been Alexander's tutor in 1865. Alexander III made him the Chief Procurator of the Holy Synod controlling the Russian Church, a powerful organization. Pobedonostsev was responsible for many harsh policies.

The secret police (the Okhrana) were given greater powers to hunt down revolutionaries and terrorists. More people were imprisoned, executed or exiled.

Education

Universities

Entry was restricted to classical students. Teachers were spied on and critics of government sacked.

Secondary schools

No child from the working class or from the peasant class was allowed to go to secondary school.

Primary schools

These were put under the control of the Church, and obedience to the government was taught to all children.

The press was more closely supervised. Fourteen newspapers critical of the government were shut down.

Land Captains—drawn from the old nobility—were appointed with powers over all other local officials. They also replaced magistrates appointed by Alexander II.

Minority races

The Baltic regions of Latvia, Estonia and Lithuania had been allowed to retain their own languages and customs. Now they had to teach the Russian language, which became the official language for use in courts, press and in dealings with government officials. In Poland Russian was made compulsory in all schools.

The Lutheran (Protestant) Church was persecuted.

The Jews

Attacks on Russian Jews had often taken place in the past. Under Pobedonostsev there were more serious attacks or pogroms. Jews were not allowed to live in the countryside but only in towns; fewer of them were allowed secondary education; and priests of the Orthodox Church encouraged people to attack Jews and their homes having labelled them 'Christ killers'.

This anti-semitism allowed people to take out their anger (at the Tsar and the government) on the Jews.

3.4 Russian Industrialization

The idealistic Narodniki (see above) thought the Russian peasants were the important section of Holy Russia. However, the Russian Church was opposed to most of the Narodniki's ideas—attacks on the Tsar, the need for a revolution and socialism. The Church believed that Holy Russia was a 'better' country than any of the 'pagan' countries of Western Europe. Pobedonostsev shared this belief and opposed Western ideas such as jury service, free press and science in schools.

But Holy Russia was poor, inefficient and militarily weak. If Russia were to be stronger, if her people were to have a better standard of living, then industrialization would have to take place. And with industrialization would come Western ideas on trade unions and demands for political development.

Some industrialization had already taken place. In 1855 there was only one railway in Russia. By 1860 over one thousand miles of line had been opened and by 1888 13,000 miles. This gave a boost to the development of the iron, steel and coal industries. A textile industry had also been started and was centred on two or three industrial areas.

Foreigners played an important part in Russian industrialization. British textile firms supplied the machinery for the Russian textile industry—and the skilled workpeople needed to run it. John Hughes from South Wales formed the New Russian Company to build factories in the Donetz Basin. Siemens of Prussia built the Russian telegraphic system and had factories in St Petersburg. The Nobel brothers of Sweden began the Russian oil industry and in the 1880s built the first Russian oil tankers. France, now Russia's ally, provided a good deal of the money needed to pay for the machinery and raw material which Russia had to import (see Unit 8).

PAYING FOR THE INDUSTRIALIZATION

The Russians had to pay interest on money borrowed from France and other foreign lenders. They also had to repay the money borrowed over a period of years. Russia earned the money for those payments by exporting wheat.

To get this wheat the government increased taxes paid by peasants—and got the money in the form of grain. Thus the peasants were left even poorer than before.

Industrial workers, too, suffered from this export of wheat. Prices were kept high because there was never enough grain available. Sometimes there were famines—

but exports had to be maintained if possible. The shortage of food and the high prices added to the burdens of industrial workers who already suffered because of poor housing, poor working conditions and low pay—and from not being allowed to have trade unions.

But there was another price to be paid: the number of town workers increased—and they were less under Church control than were the peasants.

Holy Russia became 'diluted' with westernization. Foreign industrialists taught people the benefit of working (selfishly) for a profit, showed that science was essential (and so attacked Pobedonostsev's ideas).

SERGEI DE WITTE

De Witte, Minister of Finance 1892–1903, was responsible for the attempt to industrialize Russia at that time. Foreigners played major roles in this industrialization. It was fitting that the Minister should be a foreigner, of Dutch ancestry.

Agriculture was Russia's main industry. De Witte thought that to be strong, Russia had to develop industrially. In 1892 he obtained foreign loans for the building of the Trans-Siberian railway, completed in 1902.

By 1900 coal production had reached 15 million tons (compared with over 200 million tons in Britain).

Cotton production in Central Asia allowed the textile industry to grow in Poland and the Moscow region.

Wool, iron and steel and other industries also grew. Between 1885 and 1900 the output of industry multiplied by three and the number of industrial workers reached three million.

Tariffs on imports of goods which Russian factories could produce helped the development of new industries.

Government income had to be increased to get the money to pay for the foreign loans (see above). De Witte managed this in various ways. One was to give the government the sole right (or monopoly) of selling alcoholic drink. This gave the government an interest in increasing sales of such drink (which provided one quarter of government revenue). This tended to increase the amount of drunkenness.

3.5 The Development of the Revolutionary Spirit

The **Social Revolutionary Party** (SRP) was founded in 1901 out of earlier attempts to rouse the peasants (see above).

The peasants' standard of living fell as a result of industrialization. They had to pay most of the taxes. One sign of their poverty was the high death rate, the result of poor living conditions and poor diet.

In 1882 a Peasants' Land Bank was set up to help peasants to buy land. But interest rates were very high, while payment of the instalments for land grants made after 1861 left little money for new purchases.

The SRP hoped to incite the peasants to a violent revolution. To encourage them the SRP carried out terrorist acts against Land Captains and other government officials.

Alexander III was often attacked. In 1887 a plan to assassinate the Tsar failed, and the plotters were arrested and tried. One was Alexander Ulyanov. His execution caused his younger brother, Vladimir, to become a revolutionary; he was better known as Lenin.

The Liberals (known from the Russian initials for their **Constitutional Democratic Party** as the Cadets), hoped to persuade the Tsar to give Russia a British-style parliamentary government. They drew most of their support from the zemstvos.

The Social Democratic Labour Party (SDLP) was formed in 1898. It had its main support among the industrial workers. Its policies were Marxist, and it did not believe that terrorism could succeed.

The SDLP was often attacked by the secret police.

THE CREATION OF THE BOLSHEVIK PARTY

Lenin's career is typical of most leaders of the SDLP;
▶ in 1895 he was arrested;
▶ in 1897 he was again imprisoned;
▶ he was exiled to Siberia from 1897 to 1900 and then forced to live abroad.

Lenin and his fellow-exiles published a newspaper, *Iskra* (*the Spark*), which they smuggled into Russia. In 1903 the committee producing *Iskra* had meetings in Brussels and, after being driven from Belgium, in London. During these meetings they argued over the question 'What should a revolutionary party be like?'

Some, led by Trotsky, wanted the SDLP to become a mass party like the SRP.

Others, led by Lenin, wanted the SDLP to be a small party. Every member ought to be a dedicated revolutionary who understood fully what the Marxist revolution would be about.

The argument ended with a vote:
▶ the majority (*Bolsheviks* in Russian) agreed with Lenin;
▶ the minority (*Mensheviks* in Russian) agreed with Trotsky.

3.6 Tsar Nicholas II, 1894–1917

In 1894 Alexander III died a natural death.

Nicholas II said that he would follow the 'principle of autocracy* as firmly and unswervingly as my late father.' There would be no Russian parliament.

Personally, Nicholas was a kind man and a good father—but had no idea of the problems facing Russia.

Alexandra, his wife, was a German princess, a reminder of the influence of foreigners on Russian history. She had no sympathy with reform. She had a great influence over Nicholas II.

V.K. PLEHVE

Plehve became Minister of the Interior in 1902, when his predecessor was assassinated. He was in charge of the domestic government.

Plehve's policies were like those of Pobedonostsev (see above):
▶ he organized anti-Jewish demonstrations and pogroms*;
▶ he pressed on with the Russianization of such regions as Finland, Armenia, Poland and the Baltic Provinces.

But his policies were different in some ways:
▶ he was frightened at the success of the SDLP in winning support among the industrial workers;
▶ government spies were sent to work in factories. They tried to persuade men to strike—so that possible leaders of industrial workers could be picked out and arrested.

He believed in the idea of a Holy Russia of peasant people loyal to the Tsar and the Church. This opposed de Witte's policies. In 1903 Plehve persuaded Nicholas to sack de Witte. But the discontent continued, with terrorist attacks, workers' strikes and peasant riots.

It was Plehve who persuaded the Tsar to have 'a short, victorious war' against Japan. This would win support for the Tsar and help to put an end to the unrest in Russia.

THE RUSSO-JAPANESE WAR, 1904–5

The course of the War will be examined in Unit 6. Here you have to note the following:
▶ it began on February 4 1904 and lasted until the signing of

the Treaty of Portsmouth (USA), September, 1905;
▶ poor leadership led to heavy defeats on land and at sea;
▶ heavy casualties affected many Russian families;
▶ the transport system was unable to cope with the demands to carry military supplies as well as peacetime goods. There was a shortage of food in industrial towns.

3.7 The 1905 Revolution and the Establishment of the Duma

UNREST IN RUSSIA, 1904–5

In 1904 Plehve was assassinated by Social Revolutionaries.

The Union of the zemstvos demanded constitutional reforms. They wanted free speech, fair trials, the abolition of the secret police, a Russian parliament.

The SDLP organized a series of strikes and demonstrations. They wanted an end to the war and to rule by the Tsar.

The peasants in various regions rioted. Land Captains and members of the nobility were killed.

BLOODY SUNDAY, 22 JANUARY 1905

Fig. 3.7 Bloody Sunday, 1905

Father Gapon, a Russian priest, was a government spy sent to work among industrial workers. The SDLP planned to hold a massive anti-Tsarist demonstration in the capital, St Petersburg in January 1905. To stop the SDLP getting the credit for a demonstration, Gapon and other government agents planned their own.

Industrial workers and their families gathered from all parts of the capital to march to the Tsar's Winter Palace, carrying their petitions:
▶ they complained about low wages, poor housing, high prices, long working hours;
▶ they asked for some sort of Parliament;
▶ they said they were loyal to the Tsar.

Nicholas, fearing the demonstration, had gone to another palace at Tsarsko Selo some miles away. The guards at the Winter Palace, frightened that the demonstrators might

turn violent, fired at the mob. A hundred and thirty people were killed and over three thousand injured. The rest fled.

DEEP UNREST

Strikes took place in industrial towns.

Sailors on the battleship *Potemkin* mutinied in June 1905. No other ship in the Black Sea fleet tried to stop the mutineers on the *Potemkin* as they bombarded the port of Odessa.

In October 1905 a railway strike started in Moscow and became a national railway strike. Food did not get to industrial towns.

Trotsky created a number of workers' councils (or soviets) in factories in St Petersburg and Moscow.

Non-industrial workers—teachers, lawyers and doctors—supported the soviets and the demand for the overthrow of the inefficient and cruel system of government.

THE OCTOBER MANIFESTO, 1905

De Witte, who had opposed the declaration of war, was recalled as Chief Minister (October 1905) after the signing of the Treaty of Portsmouth which ended the War.

The Tsar issued a Manifesto in which he promised reforms: a Russian Parliament (or Duma) would be called, and he would make no new laws without the Duma's approval. Many people were satisfied with this development.

The Liberals welcomed the constitutional development which they had been demanding for many years.

Many strikers went back to work hoping that an elected Duma would pass the reforms they wanted.

The soviets, led by the SDLP, did not think that the Tsar's promises were enough.

Peasants in the countryside did not see how a Duma would help them; they continued to riot.

The Tsar got his army back from the Far East (December 1905) and felt more secure. The leaders of the soviets were arrested.

In December 1905 Moscow workers began an armed rising. This was put down by the armed forces. The Tsar's advisers knew that the revolutionaries would not be satisfied by the promises of October 1905.

The French made fresh loans in April 1906.

The Russian People's League was a right-wing organization which carried out terrorist attacks on reformers of all kinds.

In May 1906, just before the first Duma was due to meet, Nicholas issued his Fundamental Law of the Empire:
▶ autocracy, God-given, could not be subject to a Duma;
▶ control of government spending and of taxation would not be left to the elected Duma;
▶ the Duma would have only a very limited power to introduce new laws.

Thus the Tsar had tricked those who had anticipated reform.

ELECTING A DUMA, 1906

There was a complicated system of voting:
▶ most men were allowed to vote in a secret ballot, but direct elections only took place in the large towns;
▶ most representatives were elected by an indirect system which had been designed to make sure that the landowners and the non-socialist peasants would get elected.

It was hoped that this would produce a conservative Duma loyal to the Tsar.

THE FIRST DUMA, MAY 1906

The Liberals (or Cadets) won the majority of seats. They demanded full control of government taxation. They reminded the Tsar of the October Manifesto and the promise of constitutional government.

The Tsar's answer was to dismiss the Duma and call fresh

elections. The leading Cadets fled to Viborg in Finland. They issued a Manifesto, inviting the voters not to pay taxes or serve in the army.

 ### 3.8 Stolypin's Policies

THE SECOND DUMA, FEBRUARY–JUNE 1907

Peter Stolypin became Prime Minister in succession to de Witte. A conservative, he wanted to 'carry through effective reforms but at the same time face revolution, resist it and stop it.'

For the elections to the Second Duma Stolypin:

► refused to allow some candidates to stand for election;
► imprisoned known anti-Tsarist candidates;
► took many voters' names off the voting lists;
► threatened Jews with death if they dared vote.

In spite of all this the second Duma proved to be more radical than the first. Moderate and constitutional Liberals lost seats, and the revolutionary-minded SDLP won 65 seats.

Stolypin asked the Duma to condemn terrorism. It refused. The Tsar demanded the arrest of the SDLP members on the grounds of treason. The Duma refused to agree.

This Duma, like the first, was dismissed.

LATER DUMAS, 1907–14

The electoral laws were further changed in 1907: Social Democrats could not stand as candidates, and possible trouble-makers were arrested and imprisoned.

The third and fourth Dumas (1907–14) were 'loyal' to the ideas of the Tsar and Stolypin.

STOLYPIN'S REFORMS

Revolutionaries remembered Stolypin's repression: after the failure of the 1905 'revolution' some 1500 people were executed. Stolypin's answer was that 4000 officers had been assassinated or injured by terrorists. Russianization was also pushed through in Finland and other regions. The Jews were again harshly treated, elections were 'fixed' and the Duma made 'harmless'.

Many peasants remembered only his reforms: the mir was abolished, peasants could now own or rent their own land without any interference from the commune, and Peasant Banks helped peasants to buy their own land. Many did so. These richer peasants (or kulaks) were the more go-ahead. They made their land profitable. One result of this was that there was enough food for the town workers and for the export trade; while another result was

that the kulaks became much more loyal to the Tsar—and opposed to the revolutionaries.

TOO LITTLE, TOO LATE?

In spite of his reforms, Stolypin was unpopular with many people. In 1911 he was assassinated in a Kiev theatre in the Tsar's presence.

By that time Rasputin had become a strong influence. He was a monk who had gained the reputation of being 'a holy man'—in spite of his wild style of life. The Tsar's wife, Alexandra, was a religious woman who, after 1905, came under Rasputin's influence. In 1907 the Tsar's son, Alexis, seemed to be dying from haemophilia. Rasputin prayed over him and the boy lived. This confirmed the monk's reputation with the Tsar and his wife.

By 1912 there were many sordid stories of the way Rasputin lived with many ladies of the Tsar's court. These stories lessened people's loyalty towards the Tsar. But in July 1914, when Russia went to war against Austria–Hungary, the Tsar seemed secure on his throne: industry was growing; the influence of the SDLP failing; the countryside was at peace. More kulaks enjoyed the ownership of their land, the influence of the SRP was failing.

It was the First World War which was to show how slender was the hold which the Tsar had over his people.

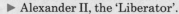 ### 3.9 Russian Foreign Policy, 1870–1914

► The Balkans 1875–8 (or the Eastern Question) (see Unit 4):
► The Russo-Japanese War, 1904–5 (see Unit 6).
► The Franco-Russian Alliance, 1892–5 (see Unit 8).
► The outbreak of the First World War (see Unit 8).

Unit 3 Summary

► Alexander II, the 'Liberator'.
► The growth of revolutionary movements.
► The reactionary government of Alexander III: Pobedonostsev.
► De Witte and the industrialization of Russia.
► The formation of the Bolshevik Party.
► The autocracy of Nicholas II: Plehve.
► The 1905 Revolution and the establishment of the Duma.
► Stolypin.

---

4 THE EASTERN QUESTION, 1870–1914

 ### 4.1 What Was the Question About?

Today we might think that the Eastern Question must have been concerned with Asia. However, Asia did not play a major role in world affairs until the end of the nineteenth

century (Unit 6). The Eastern Question was about the Turkish Empire.

There were three main parts to the Question.

► Turkey had, in past times, conquered large areas of South-Eastern Europe. By the early part of the nineteenth century it was clear that the Turks were no longer able to control that large Empire. There were many rebellions and, in Greece, a successful independence movement. So one part of the Question was, 'Can Turkey survive?'

▶ Greece was the first of the Christian states to break away from rule by the Muslim Turks. During the nineteenth century other Christian peoples tried to follow that example. The Turkish Empire was crumbling. The second part of the Eastern Question was: 'What will happen to that Empire?'

▶ The European Powers each had their own interests in the affairs of Turkey. So the third part of the Question was: 'What would the Powers do as Turkey crumbled?'

THE INTERESTS OF THE GREAT POWERS

Russia

Russia was the largest of the Slav nations. Many Slav peoples lived inside the Turkish Empire—Serbs and Slovaks in particular. These, and the Bulgars, Rumanians and Albanians, also had a religious link with Russia. They were all members of the Orthodox Church. So Russia made herself the champion of the Slavs (and developed the pan-Slav movement for that purpose). Thus if these nations rebelled against Turkey, Russia would help them gain their independence. The government hoped that they would be grateful and allow her to influence their trade and foreign policies.

Russia also wanted an outlet to the Mediterranean Sea. To achieve this she could do one of two things:

▶ she could help one of the Christian peoples to gain control of the Aegean Sea coast where Salonika could become the Russian-dominated outlet for Russia's trade;

▶ she could capture Constantinople (Fig. 4.1), gain control of the Dardenelles and develop her Black Sea ports.

Britain

Britain saw Russia as a threat to British India. Russian expansion in Central Asia brought Russia to the borders of Afghanistan—and India. Russia was also seen as a threat to British interests in Persia and the Middle East. Britain did a great deal of trade with the countries of the Middle East. If Russia expanded, she would threaten that trade. In addition, the Suez Canal had been opened in 1869. This 'life line of the Empire' allowed British ships to get quickly to Australia, New Zealand, India, Malaya and Hong Kong. If Russia got her outlet on to the Mediterranean, she might threaten this Canal and British trade.

So Britain's policy in the Eastern Question was:

▶ to maintain Turkey as a buffer against Russia;

▶ to oppose the creation of a number of small, independent states, which would become Russian satellites*;

▶ to oppose Russian policy all the time.

Austria–Hungary

Austria only became closely involved in the Eastern Question after 1870. By then she had lost her power in Italy and in the German Confederation (see Unit 1).

The Austro-Hungarian Empire included a number of Slavonic peoples—Serbs, Croats and Slovenes (the southern Slavs) as well as the Slovaks (or northern Slavs). The Emperor of Austria-Hungary, Francis Joseph, and his ministers, decided to try to extend Austria's power in a south-easterly direction. This would achieve two objects. It would:

▶ make up for the losses in Italy and Germany;

▶ stop the creation of a Russian-backed Slav nation in Serbia which would attract the support of Slavs living inside the Austro-Hungarian Empire. If they succeeded in freeing themselves, Austria would be even less powerful.

THE INTERESTS OF THE CHRISTIAN SUBJECTS OF TURKEY

In Fig. 4.1 you can see that part of modern Greece became independent of Turkish rule in 1830.

Turkish government in the nineteenth century was cor-

Fig. 4.1   The Balkans, 1878–1914

rupt. Its ministers thought only of making money for themselves. Higher taxes paid by the Christian peoples brought no benefit to those peoples. This government was also inefficient. The Turkish rulers became lazier and put Christians into positions of authority. In addition, they were cruel. This was shown by the frequent massacres of Christian peoples.

Backed by Russia, the peoples of the Turkish Empire began to develop ideas of self-government.

4.2 Crises, 1875–8

THE CRISIS OF 1875–7

In 1875, the peoples of Bosnia and Herzegovina rebelled because of ill-treatment of Christians and increasing taxation. In 1876, Serbs, Montenegrins and Bulgarians joined in. The Turks' answer to the rebellion was even greater cruelty. Men, women and children were driven into local churches where they were burned alive. The news of these Bulgarian atrocities attracted widespread attention:

▶ Gladstone, leader of the Liberal Opposition, wanted Britain to drive the Turks, 'bag and baggage', out of Europe;

▶ Austria saw a chance to take Bosnia and Herzegovina;

▶ Disraeli, the British Prime Minister, feared a break-up of Turkey and a Russian advance;

▶ Russia claimed that she had to go to the help of the Christians suffering under Turkish misrule;

▶ Bismarck said that he had no interest in Turkish affairs— he had enough to cope with in Germany (see Unit 1).

THE RUSSO-TURKISH WAR, 1877–8

Russia was the only power which helped the Christians. Austria-Hungary remained neutral. In May 1877 Russian troops crossed the River Danube. In July 1877 they reached Plevna, where the Turks held out until December 1877. The fall of Plevna allowed the Russians and Bulgarians to sweep on towards Constantinople. Britain sent a naval force to the Dardanelles and threatened to declare war on Russia if she continued her advance.

In January 1878, the Turks signed an armistice to end the war.

4.3 Peace Treaties, 1878, and Their Effects

THE TREATY OF SAN STEFANO, 1878

Turkey lost most of her European Empire. She kept only outlying areas of Bosnia, Herzegovina, Albania and the region of Thrace guarding the roads to Constantinople.

Bulgaria became independent. She was given territory which stretched from the Danube to the Aegean Sea. This gave her the long coastline and the port of Salonika.

Rumania, Serbia and Montenegro were given their independence. This pleased the Slav peoples. Serbia, who thought of herself as the leading Slav nation in the region, hoped that she might one day get Bosnia and Herzegovina.

Russia took Kars and Batum, as well as part of Bessarabia. Rumania, which lost part of Bessarabia to Russia, was given the Dobruja as compensation.

The other powers and the Treaty

Britain threatened to make war on Russia if this Treaty remained in force. She was alarmed at the break-up of Turkey—the buffer to Russian advance, and at the creation of Bulgaria with its long coastline. Britain believed that through this satellite Russia would threaten British interests in the Mediterranean.

Austria-Hungary was alarmed by Russia's advance and by the growth of Serb nationalism. She saw this as a threat to her ambitions in Bosnia and Herzegovina (see above) and to the safety of the Austro-Hungarian Empire. Serbia might encourage rebellion by Slavs inside that Empire.

Bismarck of **Germany** feared a war between Russia on one side and Austria-Hungary, Britain and Turkey on the other. He did not want to see his Dreikaiserbund break up (see Unit 8). So Russia gave way and agreed to hold an international conference to arrange the future of the Balkans.

THE CONGRESS OF BERLIN, 1878

Before the Congress met in June, the major Powers had made a number of secret agreements. Bulgaria was divided into three parts (Fig. 4.1):
▶ a northern part, independent under a Bulgarian prince;
▶ a central part, Eastern Rumelia, under a Christian Governor-General, but under the rule of the Sultan;
▶ the southern part, including Macedonia and the coastline was given back to the Sultan.
Britain gained Cyprus. This would be a naval base from which Britain would keep an eye on Russian progress.

Russia kept Kars, Batum and part of Bessarabia. Serbia, Montenegro, and Rumania retained their independence. Austria, which had played no active part against Turkey, was allowed to administer Bosnia and Herzegovina.

The diplomatic effects of the Congress of Berlin

Bismarck, chairman at the Congress, had supported Austria's demands to be allowed to occupy Bosnia and Herzegovina. Russia, a member of Bismarck's Dreikaiserbund, was angered by Bismarck's attitude. This was to play a part in the future of international relations (see Unit 8). Austria was grateful for Bismarck's support. She agreed in 1879 to a formal Alliance with Germany (see Unit 8).

THE FAILURE OF THE CONGRESS SETTLEMENT, 1878–1908

The Sultan of Turkey promised the Congress that he would never again ill-treat his Christian subjects. In fact, massacres took place at regular intervals, the worst being the Armenian Massacres of 1895–6 when 30,000 were killed in Armenia and another 6000 in Constantinople.

Bulgaria and Eastern Rumelia united in 1885. The new and larger state did not turn out to be a Russian satellite.

Serbia and Montenegro were angered by Austria's control of Bosnia and Herzegovina. This led to increasing friction between them.

4.4 The Revolt by the 'Young Turks', 1908

Patriotic Turks were angered by the break-up of the Empire. They wanted a democratic country run on Western lines.

Army officers led a successful revolt in 1908. They forced the Sultan, Abdul Hamid ('Abdul the Damned') to promise to bring in a system of parliamentary democracy. In 1909 he tried to go back on his promises. He was deposed by the revolutionaries.

The new government promised Christians equal rights with Muslims. This gained support for their revolution. In fact they, like the deposed Sultan, did not keep their promises. This was to be a cause of trouble in 1912 (see below).

THE EUROPEAN POWERS AND THE REVOLT OF 1908

Many liberals in Western Europe welcomed the news of the revolution and the coming of 'democracy' to Turkey.

Austria's foreign minister, Aehrenthal, persuaded the Russian foreign minister, Isvolsky, to agree that Austria could annex Bosnia and Herzegovina. This made these Slav provinces a part of the Austro-Hungarian Empire. Russia agreed to do this because Austria promised to agree to persuade the other powers to allow Russia to have the right to send her ships through the Dardanelles (see Fig. 4.1).

Austria cheated. Having annexed the two provinces, she did not keep her promise to Russia. Russia was angered by this. But, as we shall see in Unit 8, she was in no fit state to go to war about it.

Serbia was angry. The annexation seemed to mean the end of the Serbian dream of a large Slavonic kingdom. But without Russia's help, Serbia could do nothing.

4.5 The Balkan Wars, 1912–13

THE BALKAN LEAGUE, 1912

Turkey had a counter-revolution in 1912, the democratic system was overthrown and the old repressive system brought back.

Venizelos, a Greek statesman, realized that the Christians in Turkey would suffer even more harshly than ever. He persuaded Serbia, Montenegro and Bulgaria to join Greece in the Balkan League. He hoped that they would persuade the Turks to deal fairly with their Christian subjects.

THE FIRST BALKAN LEAGUE WAR, 1912–13

Italy took advantage of the unrest preceding the revolution to seize Tripoli, the last remaining part of the Turkish Empire in North Africa (Fig. 5.1). War was declared by the Italians in September 1911.

In 1912 the Balkan League declared war on Turkey. Austria and Germany thought that Turkey would win. In six weeks the forces of the League overran European Turkey, except for Eastern Thrace around Constantinople.

This success alarmed the major powers. Russia feared that Bulgaria would seize Constantinople. Austria feared that Serbia might gain an outlet on to the Adriatic by taking the region now known as Albania (Fig. 4.1). The major powers forced the League and Turkey to end the fighting and come to a Conference to settle affairs.

THE TREATY OF LONDON, 1913

Turkey was allowed to retain only Eastern Thrace. The League's members then tried to agree on a division of the rest of the region. They could not agree, particularly over the division of Macedonia—and went to war with each other.

THE SECOND BALKAN LEAGUE WAR, 1913

Bulgaria claimed that she had supplied most of the army in 1912. She wanted the largest share of Macedonia. Thus Bulgaria attacked Serbia when she occupied part of Macedonia.

Serbia was joined by Rumania (which had not fought in the first War of 1912–13), Montenegro, Greece, and Turkey, which saw a chance to get back some of her former territory.

Bulgaria was easily defeated and forced to agree to a treaty.

THE TREATY OF BUCHAREST, AUGUST 1913

Turkey made small gains, including the city of Adrianople.

Serbia and Greece kept those parts of Macedonia gained by the Treaty of London.

Austria insisted on Albania having the Adriatic coast between Greece and Montenegro. This kept Serbia land-locked.

Rumania gained territory on the Black Sea, from Bulgaria.

THE EFFECTS OF THE BALKAN LEAGUE WARS

Serbia became a larger country. This alarmed Austria, which was concerned about the effect of this expansion on the 7 million Serbs, Croats and Slovenes living in her Empire. She had prevented Serbia gaining the port she wanted on the Adriatic. This angered Serbia.

Like Serbia, Austria wanted ports. She had her eye on Salonika which, with other parts of Macedonia, went to Greece in 1913 (see Fig. 4.1). This ensured that Austria maintained her ambition to expand to the south—even if it meant war.

In 1913 the Kaiser told Austria that he would support her if she went to war with Serbia. So too, would Turkey—anxious to get revenge for earlier defeats, which left her much reduced in size.

The Serbs, on the other hand, allowed terrorist gangs, such as the Black Hand, to train on Serb soil before undertaking terrorist activities inside the Austro-Hungarian Empire.

Russia declared that, in the event of a war between Austria and Serbia she would support Serbia. So too, presumably, would Russia's ally, France (see Unit 8).

4.6 Sarajevo, 28 June 1914

The heir to the Austrian throne, the Archduke Francis (Franz) Ferdinand, supported Slav claims to greater control by Slavs of their own affairs—but inside the Empire. In June 1914 he and his wife made a tour of Bosnia and Herzegovina. On 28 June they were in the Bosnian capital, Sarajevo. They were assassinated by a Bosnian student—Gavrilo Princip. Princip, a member of the Black Hand, had links with Serbia.

Austria used this assassination as an excuse for declaring war on Serbia. We will study this in more detail in Unit 8.

Unit 4 Summary

▶ Defining the Question and the interests of the Powers.
▶ Rebellion, 1875, and the Russo-Turkish War, 1877–8.
▶ San Stefano and the Congress of Berlin, 1878.
▶ The Young Turks, 1908.
▶ The Balkan Wars, 1912–13.
▶ Sarajevo, 28 June 1914.

5 AFRICA, 187 –1914

5.1 The 'Dark' Continent

In the 15th and 16th centuries Portuguese and Spanish sailors had found a route around the Cape of Good Hope to the Far East. In the 18th century the British, Spanish and Portuguese had set up trading settlements along the African coast (Fig. 5.1).

For Britain in particular, Africa was a valuable trading area. Slaves were collected in ports in West Africa, taken to the Spanish colonies in South America and to the British colonies in southern North America, there to be sold at great profit.

When the slave trade was abolished (1807), European powers maintained trading links with the coastal regions. But until 1850 little was known about the African interior.

DIFFICULTIES FACING THE DEVELOPMENT OF THE INTERIOR

Even after European explorers had found out more about

Fig. 5.1 European possessions in Africa, 1875

Africa, they faced many problems. The climate was hostile. Diseases such as malaria and sleeping sickness killed many people and animals. Africa's physical features presented many obstacles:

▶ the north was mainly a desert, difficult to cross;
▶ south of the desert was an almost impenetrable forest;
▶ the coast provided few good harbours;
▶ the rivers were obstructed by rapids and waterfalls. Many of these were near the coast and blocked attempts to explore.

The native people were also hostile. This is hardly surprising, given the Europeans' record as slave-traders.

Transport was a major problem. Many rivers were not navigable—or only with difficulty. Camels were needed in the northern desert. Horses were killed by disease-carrying tsetse flies. The development of the railway and, later, the steamship were major aids in the work of opening up Africa.

5.2 Explorers, Missionaries and Traders

THE WORK OF THE EXPLORERS

From around 1790 to about 1870 a number of explorers, mainly British, undertook voyages of exploration into Africa. Many of the explorers were helped by the Royal Geographical Society of Great Britain. Its members wanted to know more about the geography of the vast land mass of Africa. Because of their work Africa became better known. They wrote books and pamphlets about their voyages, they lectured to large audiences, and they interested other people in the possibilities that existed in Africa. In particular they gained the attention of Christian missionaries and, later, of European traders.

But the explorers did not go out to Africa to help develop trade. They were interested only in gaining knowledge.

THE WORK OF THE MISSIONARIES

Christians in many European countries believed they had a duty to bring Christianity to the African people. Catholics founded religious orders for this work. Protestants in Britain founded the London Missionary Society.

In 1840 David Livingstone was sent by the London Missionary Society to Africa. His work turned out to be part exploration and part religious. In the Cape Province he quarrelled with the Dutch because of their ill-treatment of black people. But Livingstone, like other Europeans at

that time, thought that white civilization was superior to black. Europeans felt they had the duty to give the black people the blessings of Christianity, better social conditions and increased trade.

In 1841 Livingstone went to work in the interior—in Bechuanaland. In 1849 he crossed the vast Kalahari desert. On this journey, he was the first European to find Lake Ngami (which has since dried up). In 1851 he came across the River Zambesi, along which he explored to the west (1853–4) until he reached Luanda. This journey proved that the Zambesi's rapids and gorges would be major obstacles to its use as a trading route. In 1855 he followed the Zambesi to the east. He came to the falls which he named Victoria Falls. He reached the coast at Mozambique, the first recorded person to cross the continent.

In 1856–7 he lectured throughout Britain. This led to the formation of the Royal Niger Company (see below). In 1858 as British consul for the east coast of Africa he was instructed to explore east and central Africa. On his voyage he had the use of a steamboat, which made travel easier, but he still had to face the problems of rapids, waterfalls and gorges. In 1859 he located Lake Nyasa.

During these various journeys he was frequently attacked by Portuguese slave-traders. Only in 1873, the year of Livingstone's death, was the slave market on the island of Zanzibar finally closed.

In 1865 Livingstone journeyed to find the source of the Nile. Travelling from Portuguese East Africa, he went through the region we now call Zambia. For six years he lost contact with Europeans—a reminder of how inaccessible most of Africa then was. During that time he located more lakes, explored Lake Tanganyika and mapped thousands of square kilometres.

H.M. Stanley, a Welsh-born reporter, was sent to look for Livingstone. In 1871 he met up with him at a camp near Lake Tanganyika. Stanley left after four months, but Livingstone stayed behind and died in May 1873.

THE WORK OF THE TRADERS BEFORE 1870

European traders had long been active in the coastal regions. With the ending of the slave trade, some tried to develop trade with African peoples living further inland. The difficulties they faced are outlined above.

The world-wide fall in agricultural prices around 1870 led to a fall in the incomes of many traders and firms. This, too, led to an attempt to develop trade with the interior. It was hoped that this might lead to new sources of different raw materials, and to new untapped markets for the sale of European goods.

5.3 Governments and Africa, 1870–1914

European governments played little part in the development of African trade before 1870. Most statesmen agreed with Disraeli: 'Colonies are a millstone around our necks'. The reasons for this view were the expense involved in gaining colonies, as well as wars with local people and/or with some rival European country. This had happened in India, Canada and the West Indies.

The British also had the American experience to look back on. They helped to found 13 separate colonies on the eastern seaboard of America. They had spent money to defend those colonies from the American Indians and the French. Then in the 1770s the colonists had rebelled, won their War of Independence and left the British with nothing save a larger National Debt.

GOVERNMENTS AND CHARTERED COMPANIES

In the next section we will examine the so-called 'Scramble

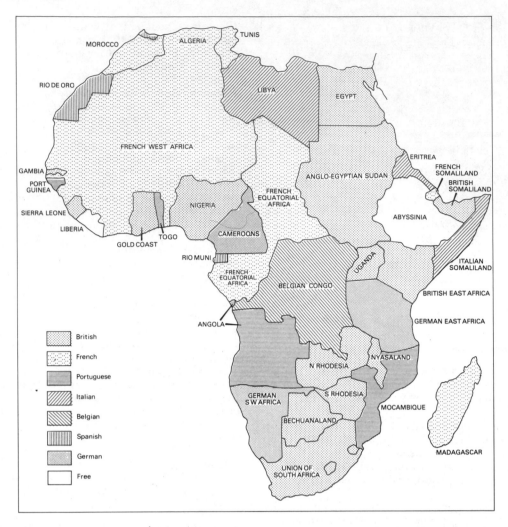

Fig. 5.3
Africa, 1914

for Africa' which took place in the 1880s and 1890s. In this 'Scramble' almost all Africa was divided out amongst the European powers (Fig. 5.3). This development was carried out by trading companies which governments encouraged to develop certain territories.

If a territory (e.g. Nigeria) was to be developed so that trade could increase, someone had to spend (or invest) a large amount of money. This was required for: building harbours and railways, establishing trading posts and clearing forests for agricultural development.

Firms were willing to do this only if they thought they had a good chance of making a profit. To help to guarantee a profit, governments gave companies the sole right (or monopoly) of trade in an area. Examples of such companies were:

▶ the Royal Niger Company (formed 1884) which advanced British trading interests in what is now called Nigeria;
▶ the British East Africa Company (formed 1887) which developed the area now known as Uganda;
▶ the British South Africa Company formed by Cecil Rhodes in 1889 for the development of the region north of the Cape—now known as Botswana and Zimbabwe.

Having got the government's approval (or charter), these companies sent out traders to develop the area named in their charter. These would make agreements with local chiefs. Often the chiefs gave the whole of an area (e.g. Nigeria) to the Company in return for a rent fixed by the Company. Companies got the sole right to mine wherever they wished. Chiefs also agreed not to allow anyone else to trade or mine in their territory.

The governments of the European countries helped by founding schools of tropical medicine to discover ways of preventing tropical diseases from spreading. They also funded agricultural development in the universities of home countries, where scientists developed new strains of seeds or new breeds of animals better fitted for the tropics.

Trading policies (including tariffs) were meant to help the country's own Companies.

There were frequent clashes between workers of one Company and Europeans working for a rival Company. French and British traders in Nigeria often clashed, as did German traders in German East Africa with British traders in Uganda. There were also clashes with native chiefs and peoples who resented the way in which the Europeans 'stole' their land. (See section 5.7 for the effects of Europeanization on the Africans.)

Companies provided private armies to guard their officials. They also called on governments to send armies to defend the territory granted to them in their charters. There were frequent wars with Ashanti, Matabele and Zulu peoples.

Sometimes it appeared likely that a particular Company was going to have to give up trading because its management was not able to make the region profitable. Then governments stepped in to declare the region a colony. The British government acquired colonies in this way in:

▶ Nigeria, 'bought' from the Company in 1899–1900;
▶ Uganda, handed over by the Company in 1893;
▶ Kenya which only became a separate colony in 1920.

It is important to note that the flag followed trade.

5.4 The 'Scramble for Africa' in the 1880s and 1890s

In 1875 European powers held small coastal strips (Fig. 5.1).

By 1914 the whole continent had been colonized. Only Abyssinia in the east and Liberia in the west were independent. This was achieved without a European war.

Colonial rivalry, the jealousy of one country for another, was one of the causes of war in 1914 (Unit 8).

REASONS FOR THE 'SCRAMBLE'

Colonization of Africa became possible, after 1875, because transport became easier with the development of the steamship (for river travel) and the railway, and because knowledge of the interior was increased by the work of explorers, missionaries and earlier traders.

The decline of Turkey (see Unit 4) made it easier for Europeans to seize colonies in North Africa. Naval strategy explained the seizure of certain coastal regions. Britain, for example, extended its control over southern Africa, Egypt and Aden to safeguard trade routes through the Suez Canal and the Indian Ocean.

The balance of power helps to explain why, if one country made a gain in Africa, others felt they had to do so.

National pride in France needed some boost after the defeat of 1870–1 (Unit 1). This helps to explain French interest in gaining African territory. New nationhood in Italy and Germany explained ambitions in these countries to gain colonies in Africa and elsewhere.

Economic forces were, however, the most important (see below).

The economic reasons for the 'Scramble'

Raw materials, obtained cheaply from an African colony, would boost profits and employment of a domestic industry.

Markets for some European goods could be created among the African peoples. This had been true before the abolition of the slave trade and of slavery. As the coastal regions became less profitable after these reforms, Europeans pushed further into the interior in search of new markets.

Tariffs by European countries and by the developing USA (see Unit 7) made it increasingly difficult for countries to sell goods abroad. This forced them to look for new markets, or face industrial decline and rising unemployment.

Many rich people in Europe had become used to lending money to firms in their countries. As each country achieved a certain level of industrialization, there were fewer chances of such lending. This caused the potential lender (or investor) to look for new places in which to invest. The French, for example, lent money to help Russian industrialization (see Unit 3).

Africa provided a good prospect to investors because:

▶ there were mines—for gold, diamonds, copper and other metals which could be profitably sold in the industrial world;

▶ there were other raw materials—palm oil, cocoa and coffee which could be grown at a profit;

▶ profits on an investment would be higher in Africa than in Europe because land and labour were cheap and plentiful.

Marxists, such as Lenin, and economists, such as the Englishman, Hobson, noted this drive for colonies as a desperate attempt by the capitalist system to keep going—it could no longer depend on the industrialization of the white man's world.

5.5 European Colonies

THE BELGIAN CONGO—THE SPUR TO JOINT ACTION

King Leopold of the Belgians set up an African International Association in 1876. This was the first example of government involvement on a large scale. He claimed the Congo region, explored and mapped by Stanley (see Section 5.2 above), who was financed by the Belgian king.

France then acted by claiming control of the Lower Congo, and Britain claimed Egypt.

Bismarck realized that there was a danger of war between rival claimants to the same regions. He called a Colonial Conference in Berlin, 1884–5. Representatives of all European powers drew boundary lines across the map of Africa and agreed on each other's claims. The boundaries made little sense. Villages were cut in half; tribes were divided between one country and another. But the division was done peacefully.

FRENCH AFRICA

North Africa

This area had already been colonized by France. The city of Algiers was occupied in 1830; Algeria was acquired in 1839, although it was not developed until after 1870. Tunisia was claimed and conquered in 1881. The French argued that Tunisians were causing trouble on the border with Algeria.

Bismarck encouraged this expansion because:

▶ it took French attention from Alsace and Lorraine (Unit 1);

▶ it brought France into conflict with Italy which also wanted to gain a North African Empire. This ensured that Italy would not side with France in the event of a Franco-German war.

Morocco was on Algeria's western border and France seized it to stop frontier incidents.

West Africa

The French had had trading posts on the mouths of the River Senegal and Congo. After 1880, explorers pushed inland. They pushed north to link up with Algeria—crossing the huge Sahara desert to do so. They also pushed east across the Sudanese grasslands south of the desert. This brought them into conflict with Britain.

East Africa

French missionaries and traders had developed Madagascar, which the French claimed officially in 1885. Somaliland was claimed in 1888.

GERMAN AFRICA

Bismarck had not been interested in colonial gains. However, a German African Society was set up in 1878 to interest people in African development. The Colonial League (1882) led the demand for a German overseas Empire. Economic reasons led Bismarck to agree with the imperialists who wanted a larger Empire.

South-west Africa

German traders settled north of the Orange River, northern frontier of the British Cape Province. When attacked by natives, they asked Bismarck for help.

In 1884, at the Colonial Conference, Bismarck obtained all the region between the Orange River and Portuguese Angola. Britain kept the naval base at Walvis Bay in this region.

The British did not easily accept this German expansion in South-west Africa. The British argued that this was the 'natural' region for expansion from the Cape. However, in 1884 Britain needed German support over the Egyptian question (see below). In return, she conceded South-west Africa.

Togoland and the Cameroons were claimed by a German explorer in 1884. British and German traders often clashed with each other, but their governments took no part in such incidents.

East Africa

In 1884 Germany claimed a large area of East Africa—today mainland Tanzania. To the north were the British colonies of Uganda and Kenya; to the south were British colonies in Northern Rhodesia (modern Zambia). Clashes between the British and German governments seemed likely because traders from the two countries fought for trade, and boundaries between the various territories were not clear.

An Anglo-German agreement, 1890

The danger of a colonial war was averted by an agreement, in which the boundaries of German and British East Africa were agreed. Germany granted Britain control of Zanzibar, and Britain returned the island of Heligoland, seized in the Napoleonic Wars. The Germans wanted it as a naval base.

ITALIAN AFRICA

Italy, like Germany, was a 'new' nation, united by a series of wars and agreements between 1859 and 1870.

The Italians claimed colonies for prestige reasons. Eritrea, a narrow strip of desert was occupied in 1882. Somaliland, another desert region, was seized in 1889. Abyssinia was attacked in 1896. The Italians suffered a major defeat at Adowa and the attempted seizure was called off. Tripoli was claimed in 1911 (see Unit 4 and Fig. 5.1).

BRITISH AFRICA

Zanzibar was acquired in 1890. The Zambesi was accepted as the boundary between British and Portuguese East Africa (Mozambique) in 1891. Uganda and Kenya were acquired when the East Africa Company faced bankruptcy in 1892. Nigeria was acquired from the Royal Niger Company in 1900.

Egypt, the Sudan and South Africa deserve longer treatment.

The British and Egypt

The Suez Canal had been opened in 1869 (see Unit 2). It was built and owned by a French Suez Canal Company. The Khedive, or ruler of Egypt, owned almost half the shares in the Company. The Canal ran through his territory. In 1875 the Khedive needed money to pay gambling debts. Disraeli, British Prime Minister in 1875, borrowed the £4 million needed to buy the shares, from the bankers, the Rothschilds. (Parliament was not in session at the time. To have waited for Parliament to meet might have lost Britain the chance to gain these shares.)

After 1875 Britain and France governed Egypt jointly. Both countries appointed commissioners and other officials to ensure that Egypt remained peaceful, that the Canal ran properly and that the shareholders got their annual interest.

In 1881 there was a nationalist revolt led by a young officer, Arabi Pasha, who wanted to drive the foreigners from Egypt. The French withdrew their officials. Gladstone, British Prime Minister in 1881, sent in a naval force and an army led by Sir Garnet Wolseley. The naval force bombarded Alexandria (1881). The army defeated the rebels at the battle of Tel-el-Kabir (1882).

The British then appointed Sir Evelyn Baring (later Lord Cromer) as Consul-General. It was Baring who transformed Egypt into a modern state by the time of his retirement in 1907.

Britain and the Sudan, 1881–5

The Sudan had been claimed by the Khedives of Egypt. It was administered by Egyptian officials from Khartoum. In 1882 Gladstone sent Baring and other officials to govern Egypt—but refused to send any to the Sudan.

In 1883 a religious fanatic, the Mahdi, led the Sudanese in a nationalist revolt against their Egyptian rulers. Gladstone claimed that this Egyptian affair had nothing to do with Britain. However, in 1884 public opinion forced him to send out a British force to bring Egyptian officials back from the Sudan. General Gordon was given command of this force.

When Gordon got to Khartoum, he disobeyed orders. He decided to stay in the Sudan and to defeat the Mahdi. The Sudanese rebels besieged Gordon in Khartoum. Gladstone refused to send a relief expedition to help Gordon until, in 1885, he again gave way to public opinion. The expedition arrived at Khartoum two days after Gordon was killed, when the Sudanese overran the capital.

Britain and the Sudan, 1896–8

In 1896 General Kitchener was sent to avenge Gordon and to reclaim the Sudan for British-controlled Egypt. He built a railway line up the Nile valley, along which his army approached Khartoum.

In 1898 at Omdurman, the Sudanese (or Dervishes) were mown down by the modern rifles and field guns. Sudan came under Anglo-Egyptian rule. Three days after the battle, Kitchener heard that the French, under Captain Marchand, had reached the Nile at Fashoda. This was part of the French drive across the Sahara Grassland.

The Nile was important to Egypt. The cotton crop depended on the waters from the Nile. Control of the river would lead to control of the Egyptian economy. For several weeks the rival armies faced each other across the Nile. Newspapers in Britain and France became warlike. In the end, the French agreed to withdraw. The Nile was recognized as a British interest. In return, the British recognized French claims in parts of West Africa. The fact was that the French had retreated. This led to ill-feeling in France against Britain.

◼ 5.6 Britain versus the Boers ◼

THE BRITISH AND SOUTH AFRICA UP TO 1879

Dutch settlers had colonized the Cape of Good Hope. The British had seized this during the Napoleonic Wars and had retained it by peace treaties signed in 1815. In 1820 British settlers and missionaries arrived. They disagreed with Dutch treatment of the black population.

After the abolition of slavery (1833) the Dutch (or Boer) settlers left the Cape. On their Great Trek they crossed the Orange River and founded two new and independent republics—the Orange Free State and the Transvaal.

The British extended their holding. In 1843 they occupied Natal and built a naval base at Durban. In 1867 diamonds were discovered at Kimberley in the Orange Free State. The British seized part of the Orange Free State, Griqualand. Another part of the Orange Free State was seized in 1868 and named Basutoland.

In 1877 the Zulus, led by Cetawayo, attacked the Boers in the Transvaal. Disraeli sent a British army to defend them and announced that Britain had 'temporarily' annexed the Republics. The British lost the battle of Isandhlwana but defeated the Zulus at Ulundi (1879). This saved the Boers, who demanded an end to British occupation.

THE BRITISH AND SOUTH AFRICA, 1879–99

Disraeli refused to withdraw from the two Boer Republics. In 1880 Transvaal announced its independence. Gladstone, British Prime Minister in 1880–5, called a conference to discuss the future of the Boer Republics. The Boers attacked the British army before this conference had finished its work. This was the start of the First Boer War. At Majuba Hill (1881) the Boers defeated the British.

Gladstone's announcements of British withdrawal and of British recognition of the independence of the Boer Republics was seen as a result of that defeat.

Because of the expansion of German South-west Africa, the British declared that Bechuanaland was a British protectorate (1885). The Boers were caught in a British pincer movement.

In 1885 gold was discovered on the Rand in the Transvaal. Cecil Rhodes founded the British South Africa Company. Rhodes made an agreement with the Matabele people. The Company gained control of the territory to the north of Bechuanaland and the Transvaal (now part of Zimbabwe).

As Prime Minister of the Cape Colony, Rhodes aimed at enlarging British interests in Africa, building a Cape-to-

Cairo railway through British-held territory, and enlarging British South Africa.

Paul Kruger was the Boer President of the Transvaal. He and his fellow-Boers did not play any part in the development of the gold and diamond holdings on the Rand. This development was the work of non-Boers, known by the Boers as 'Uitlanders' or 'Outsiders'. The Boers refused these 'foreigners' any civil rights:

► they could not vote in elections;
► they could not hold official positions;
► the tax system was organized to hurt the industrialists more than the Boer farmers.

Chamberlain, the British Colonial Secretary (1895–1903) encouraged Rhodes to plan for a British drive to the north. Rhodes had appointed a Dr Starr Jameson as administrator of Matabeleland (now part of Zimbabwe). Jameson and Rhodes plotted with the 'Uitlanders', who were to rise in rebellion against Kruger; Jameson and Rhodes would attack the Republics. At the last minute the 'Uitlanders' called off their rising. Jameson's raid did take place.

The Boers praised Kruger when the Jameson raid ended with the capture of its leader and the defeat of his small force. Rhodes was forced to resign as Prime Minister of the Cape. The German Kaiser sent a telegram to congratulate Kruger.

THE SECOND BOER WAR, 1899–1902

The Uitlanders sent a Petition to the British government. In this they outlined their complaints against the Kruger government and asked for British help.

Chamberlain sent an army to the Cape, which Kruger saw as a threat. When the British refused to withdraw this army, the Boers invaded the Cape.

The War (1899–1902) falls almost naturally into three periods:

1 October 1899–January 1900

The Boers had the larger forces and took the initiative. They besieged British forces in Ladysmith (Natal), Kimberley (the Cape) and Mafeking (Bechuanaland). In December 1899 there was a 'Black Week' when British attempts to relieve these towns failed.

2 February 1900–August 1900

Lord Roberts and Lord Kitchener led large armies which relieved the besieged towns and captured Johannesburg and Pretoria (the capital of the Transvaal).

3 The guerrilla war

Many people thought the Boers would now give in. However, they continued a guerrilla war. Kitchener then enclosed large areas behind lines of barbed wire guarded by fortified blockhouses. Behind the wire he destroyed farms where Boers might have helped the guerrillas. Women and children were herded into concentration camps, where poor hygiene and bad administration caused the deaths of thousands.

TREATY OF VEREENIGING, 1902

The Boers were forced to ask for peace. This led to the signing of a Treaty. This said that:

► the Transvaal and the Orange Free State were annexed by Britain;
► the Boers were to get self-rule inside a Federal Union;
► £3 million was to be paid to the Boers as compensation for the damage done to their farms.

The creation of the Union of South Africa, 1910, was welcomed by the Boer leaders, Smuts and Botha.

5.7 The Impact of European Intervention

THE BENEFICIAL IMPACT OF EUROPE ON AFRICANS

Africans gained some benefits from European involvement. Europeans waged war on slave traders. While some of these were European (mainly Portuguese), after 1833 the majority were Arabs. They took slaves from various parts of East Africa, using Zanzibar as a slave market until the Europeans closed it down in 1873. The Portuguese and Arabs could not have got the slaves without the co-operation of many African chiefs.

Education for African children, by Christian missionaries before colonial governments accepted this responsibility, opened up employment opportunities for many Africans.

Medical treatment was largely provided at mission hospitals.

Medical knowledge of tropical diseases was increased by European study. This led to the development of cures for various diseases and for campaigns to wipe out the causes of others.

Transport by road, rail and steamship made travelling easier.

Industrial development of mines, plantations, local industries as well as commercial development of harbours, railways and office centres increased job opportunities for Africans.

An African middle class of prosperous, educated and town-dwelling Africans was created. This class led campaigns for the end of colonial rule after 1945 (see Units 36 and 37).

THE UNFORTUNATE EFFECTS OF EUROPE ON AFRICA

Even Livingstone thought little of African civilization (see section 5.2). He and other Europeans helped to destroy it. African religions were condemned as 'pagan', and Africans were persuaded to become Christian, or 'Black Europeans'. Being a Christian brought some benefits (education, job prospects); many Africans became 'mealie Christians'—converted in appearance only.

Many religious customs were condemned without a full understanding of their importance to Africans. One of the main reasons for the later rebellion by the Kikuyu of Kenya was the tribal memory of the way in which Scottish missionaries had tried to wipe out female circumcision (see Unit 36).

Attacks on their religion and customs left many Africans with no firm roots—in African tradition or in their new-found Europeanized Christianity.

Many tribes were driven from tribal homelands to allow for European economic development. Settlers took the best land, ignoring the effect this had on the native people.

Until the second half of the twentieth century there was little African involvement in the government of the colonies. This helps to explain some of the problems faced by Africans since the end of colonial rule (Units 36 and 37).

AFRICA AND EUROPEAN CRISES

There were clashes of interest in various parts of Africa:
► British and French interests clashed in West Africa and at Fashoda;

► British and German interests clashed in East Africa and in South-west Africa.

However, only at Fashoda in 1898 did it seem that war might break out.

In Unit 8 we will study the development of international relations. We will see how the British and French became more friendly, settling their differences over Egypt. Britain recognized French interests in Morocco—but that led to a protest from Germany. In 1905 and 1911 there was fear that a major war might break out.

Unit 5 Summary

► Why Africa remained 'the unknown continent'.
► Explorers, missionaries and traders.
► Government aid to the development of Africa, 1870–1914.
► The 'Scramble for Africa'.
► Belgian, French, German and British colonies.
► Britain versus the Boers.
► Did Africans gain or lose from European intervention?

6 THE FAR EAST, 1870–1918

6.1 Europe and China, 1793–1870

Foreign traders and governments had forced Chinese governments to allow Europeans to trade in China. In 1793 the first attempt was made by the British to trade in China.

In 1839–42 the Anglo-Chinese War, or the Opium War, was fought. As a result of victory the British forced China to:

► hand over Hong Kong to the British (Fig. 17.1);
► open up five ports (Treaty Ports) to foreign trade.

In 1856, the Arrow War involved a British-registered ship caught smuggling into China. The British government waged another war. France became involved because of the murder of a French missionary. The Chinese were defeated and forced to sign the Treaty of Tientsin (1858).

In 1858–60 the Chinese government was faced with a revolution by a religious-led movement known as the Taiping Rebellion. This threatened the government. At first it was supported by foreign traders and governments who hoped to get increased privileges as a result of the divisions in China. In 1860, difficulties with the Taipings made it impossible for the government to carry out the 1858 Treaty. Anglo-French armies attacked the capital, Peking, burned the Summer Palace and forced the Emperor to sign the Treaty of Peking (1860). By this treaty:

► eleven more Treaty ports were named;
► the British and French won trading rights in the Yangtse Valley.

In 1860–4, the British and French armies now helped the Chinese government to put down the Taiping Rebellion.

At that time, the Emperor of China ruled as an autocrat*. The royal family were known as the Manchus. The Manchus (from Manchuria—Fig. 17.1) had invaded China in 1634, defeated the last Ming Emperor and imposed 'foreign' rule on China.

The success of foreigners in the nineteenth century showed the Chinese people that their Manchu government was inefficient. This was not entirely the fault of the government:

► Chinese industry was backward and could not produce modern weapons;
► Chinese pride was responsible for the contempt in which they held Westerners ('red-haired devils' or 'barbarians').

Few Chinese thought they could learn from the despised West.

The Manchus were still blamed for the way in which Western countries won concessions in China.

There were many large towns in China where some industry and commerce was carried on. But the majority of the people were peasant-farmers. They had a very poor standard of living because:

► their methods of production were inefficient;
► landlords took most of the crops they produced;
► government taxes took some of what was left.

This inefficient and corrupt system came under increasing pressure during the 19th century as the population grew. One result of that pressure was a number of famines which swept through China, killing millions.

6.2 Japan

THE OPENING OF JAPAN, 1853, AND ITS INDUSTRIALIZATION

Catholic missionaries had gone to Japan in the 16th and 17th centuries. By the middle of the 17th century the Japanese had driven most of these foreigners out. Japan remained 'closed' to foreigners for two centuries.

In 1853 an American naval force, led by Commodore Perry, went to the harbour of Yokohama. Perry had a letter from the President of the USA asking for permission to trade with Japan, and safe harbours for American ships in bad weather. In 1854 the Japanese opened their country to foreign trade.

The Meji leaders of Japan then set about making their country as Westernized as possible—so that they could stand up to the foreigners with their large ships, heavy guns and efficiency.

Industry

Japanese were sent to work in the industries of every country and to learn the reasons for Western success. Foreigners were also invited to help Japan. Industries, railways and shipyards were built with foreign help, but by 1900 Japan no longer needed foreign help. She had already become a major industrial power.

Fig. 6.3   The Russian octopus

Effects of Westernization

The Japanese army was trained by German officers; the Japanese navy was trained by British officers.

Western-type schools were set up, modelled on those of France and Germany.

Modern methods of banking and business were copied from the United States.

A new constitution was written (1868). Parliament, the Diet, was elected by the people. It only met for three months a year. Power remained with the Emperor and his advisers.

6.3 Russia and the Far East, 1856–90

A major factor in Russian foreign policy was the attempt to get an ice-free port, to allow importing and exporting of goods all the year round. Russia tried to get such a port in the Baltic and on the Aegean (see Unit 4).

This policy made Russia look like an aggressor. The cartoon (Fig. 6.3) illustrates Japanese fears—but it also illustrates the fears of Britain and other countries.

In 1853 Russia had tried to win control of the Dardanelles to allow her to use her Crimean ports freely. This led to the Crimean War and Russia's defeat. Russia then turned to the Far East and to Central Asia.

In 1858 she advanced from Siberia eastward into the Amur Province. Then in 1860 she set up the Maritime Province on the Pacific Coast (Fig. 17.1).

The port of Vladivostok ('Mistress of the Pacific') was built, and the Trans-Siberian Railway built to link it with Moscow. The railway was not completed until 1916. This railway had to cross the Manchurian Plain and brought Russia into contact with China when this section was finished, 1903.

Vladivostok was not an ice-free port. Russia now looked for chances to get such a port elsewhere in the Far East.

6.4 The Sino-Japanese War, 1894–5

Some of the outlying parts of the Chinese Empire had already been acquired by Western powers. Britain seized Burma, and France took several provinces in what became French Indo-China (see below).

Korea was the part of China nearest Japan (Fig. 17.1). Japan wanted this region for her growing population and as a market for Japanese goods. Russia, already well established in Manchuria, also wanted Korea—and an ice-free port.

For some time the Japanese, in agreement with the Chinese, had kept a legation in Seoul, the capital of Korea. After a Korean revolt they got permission to keep soldiers in Seoul to guard the legation. In 1894 there was another Korean revolt. Both China and Japan sent in troops to put it down. The Japanese then refused to withdraw their forces. The Chinese sank a Japanese warship and war was declared. Japanese victories brought the war to a quick end.

THE TREATY OF SIMONOSEKI, 1895

Korea was to be independent of China. Japan was given southern Manchuria, the Pescadores, Formosa and the valuable Port Arthur on the Liao Tung peninsula (Fig. 17.1). Japan also got trading concessions in China itself.

6.5 The Western Powers and the Far East, 1895–8

JAPAN, 1895

Russia was alarmed at this Japanese advance. France and Germany saw Japan as a threat to their trading position in the Far East. The three nations threatened to make war against Japan if she did not rewrite the Treaty of 1895.

Japan was forced to give up her mainland possessions, including Port Arthur.

CHINA, 1895–8

The Western powers used the Japanese victory to force even more concessions out of the weak Manchu government. Germany seized and colonized Kiao-chow (1897) on the mainland (Fig. 17.1). Britain seized and colonized Wei-hai-Wei (1898) just to the north of Kiao-chow (Fig. 17.1). France extended her colonies in Indo-China, as did the British in Burma. It seemed that there might be a 'Scramble for China' as there had been for Africa (see Unit 5).

Russia seized Port Arthur (1898), and had her ice-free port.

6.6 Japan and Russia

Russia helped force Japan to hand back Port Arthur to China, then she seized it for herself.

Having taken Port Arthur (1898), Russia went on to occupy Manchuria in 1900, taking advantage of the weak position of the Chinese government during the Boxer Rising (see below). She linked Port Arthur with Harbin on the incomplete Trans-Siberian Railway.

Both countries expanded their trade in Korea. They agreed to the 39th parallel of latitude as the dividing line between their 'spheres of influence'. But competition was bound to increase the friction between the two countries.

Britain had been the most important of the countries trading with China. By 1900 she was alarmed, because Russia was increasing her activities in China. Britain had always opposed Russian power (see Unit 4). Also, Russia and Germany were friendly. Until 1890 they had been linked in the Dreikaiserbund (see Unit 8). Britain feared that they might try to dominate the Far East.

Japan was angry at the Russian seizure of Port Arthur. Britain was the one Western country that had not helped to drive Japan from that port in 1895.

BRITAIN AND JAPAN

They both feared Russia; both of them were naval powers. Britain feared an attack by Russia allied with Germany, while Japan was planning a war against Russia.

The Dual Alliance, 1902

Britain and Japan signed an alliance in 1902. They agreed that if either was at war with only one country (i.e. Russia) the other would remain neutral, but if one ally was at war with two countries (e.g. Russia and Germany), the other would join the war.

This was particularly valuable for Japan. But it also gave Britain an anti-Russian ally in the Far East.

THE RUSSO-JAPANESE WAR, 1904–5

The causes

The long term causes were rooted in that Japan and Russia had been opposed to one another over Korea and Manchuria. The Port Arthur affair increased that hostility. However the immediate cause was that in 1904 Japan put proposals to Russia about the military and trading policies of both countries in Korea and Manchuria. These were rejected by Russia.

Plehve, the Tsar's main adviser, wanted a 'short victorious war' (see Unit 3).

The course of the War

The Japanese attacked a Russian fleet in Port Arthur, February 1904. Port Arthur was besieged by Japanese forces and captured in January 1905. The Russian fleet in the Baltic sailed for the Far East in October 1904. Its inefficiency was seen in:

▶ the time taken to get ready to sail (eight months);
▶ its attack on the British herring fleet on the Dogger Bank—on the assumption that this must be the Japanese fleet;
▶ the sinking of a Russian ship by a Russian torpedo during this Battle of the Dogger Bank;
▶ its lack of preparation for the battle with the Japanese when finally the fleet got to the Far East;

At Tsushima in May 1905 the Russian fleet was destroyed by the Japanese, only a few small ships escaping.

On land the Japanese inflicted a heavy defeat on the Russians at Mukden in Manchuria when 90,000 casualties were suffered and 40,000 prisoners captured.

The Treaty of Portsmouth (USA), 1905

President Theodore Roosevelt of the USA called both sides to a peace conference. This is an indication of the late arrival of the USA on the international scene (see Unit 7).

The terms of the Treaty were:
▶ Russia had to take her troops from Manchuria;

▶ Japan acquired Port Arthur and the southern half of the island of Sakhalin;
▶ Korea was to be a Japanese 'sphere of influence'.

The effects of the War

Japan emerged as the most important country in the Far East. She planned further attacks on China.

Russia had a revolution (see Unit 3) which, though it failed, was a sign of the weakness of the Tsar's position.

China was shown to be incapable of handling its own affairs.

6.7 China

The Russo-Japanese war had been fought by two non-Chinese powers to decide the future of a part of China (Korea).

Even before this War, the Manchu government had been seen to be unpopular because of the increasing power of Western states in Chinese affairs. In the Treaty Ports, these countries built warehouses, offices, shops and other businesses – and walled their 'estates' to keep out the Chinese. In French 'estates' the streets had French names. German, British and French soldiers paraded the streets.

The Manchus were incapable of resisting the West. This was made clear by the colonization of Wei-hai-Wei by Britain and of Kiao-chow by Germany.

Western influence was increasing in other ways: Christian missionaries were trying to destroy the old religion and convert the people to Christianity.

Some Chinese opposed this Westernization and hated the government for allowing it. Others wanted the government to adopt Western methods and ideas. The Japanese had done so successfully.

In 1898 the Emperor announced a number of reforms (in the Hundred Days of Reform):

▶ naval and agricultural colleges were to be founded;
▶ Western-style examinations would be held to allow China's most able children to get on;
▶ the army would be modernized;
▶ a liberal-minded government would be set up.

The Emperor's aunt, the Empress Dowager, united all those who were opposed to such Westernization. Army officers arrested the reformers and imprisoned the Emperor.

THE BOXER REBELLION, 1900

Few peasants were involved in the arguments between the reformers and the traditionalists. They did, however, share the anti-foreigner attitudes of the traditionalists.

A semi-religious organization which taught the ancient form of self-defence, or boxing, became a centre for anti-foreign and anti-reform Chinese. In May 1900 the activities of the 'Boxers' led to widespread attacks on Europeans and their industries. The railway between Peking and Tientsin was destroyed, churches were burnt down, Christians—European and Chinese—were slaughtered.

An international army led by Admiral Seymour was defeated trying to get to Peking to relieve the foreign legations.

The Chinese government supported the Boxers and declared war on all foreigners (June 1900).

Another international force was gathered. Troops came from the USA, Britain, France, Germany, Austria, Italy and Japan. The commander-in-chief was a German.

The course of the War

On 14 July Tientsin was captured. On 14 August Peking was captured. In October, the last of the Boxers surrendered, and in September 1901 the Boxer Protocol was signed by twelve major governments. This forced the Chinese government to:

▶ apologize for the massacres and damage to Western property;
▶ agree to the execution of the leading Boxers;
▶ agree on compensation to be paid to the foreigners;
▶ accept the presence in the capital, Peking, of a foreign army to guard foreign legations.

China after the Boxers

Hatred of foreigners increased. It was also clear that the traditionalists would not be able to drive the foreigners out. However, many Chinese accepted the need for Westernization. This would be opposed by the Manchus. They would have to be replaced by a Western-style democratic government.

SUN YAT-SEN

Sun emerged as the leader of the anti-Manchu and pro-Westernization movement.

Born to a poor peasant family, he grew to dislike landlords who took so much from the peasants, and merchants and money lenders who cheated the peasants. As a child of a Christian family, he learned the benefits of Westernization, and a hatred for the Manchus.

His brother, an emigrant to Honolulu, paid for his education at a Chinese mission school and for his medical training in the English College in Hong Kong.

In 1892 Sun qualified as a doctor—one of China's first Western-educated doctors. He gathered around him other Chinese students who formed the Revive China Society (1894) and a revolutionary group who tried to seize Canton (1895). These were also the people who went to Japan, Hawaii and the USA, where Chinese emigrants supported them with money.

In 1896 Sun was in London. The Chinese government planned to kidnap him and return him to China for trial and death. He escaped, helped by the Foreign Office and Scotland Yard.

In 1905 Sun was in Japan, where he formed the Sworn Chinese Brotherhood. Later this became known as the Kuo Min Tang. At its first meeting Sun laid down the outlines for the future of the Chinese nation, the Three Principles of the Kuo Min Tang:

1 the Principle of Nationalism—the freedom of China from western domination;
2 the Principle of self-sovereignty (or democracy)—with the rights to elections and parliamentary control of government;
3 the Principle of the People's Livelihood—involving the question of the ownership of land and industry.

THE 1911 REVOLUTION

After 1905 Sun was accepted by all Chinese revolutionaries as the official leader of the revolutionary movement.

In 1908 both the hated Empress Dowager and the weak-willed Emperor died. The government of the three-year-old Emperor was controlled by the reactionary Prince Ch'un, who dismissed many officials. Many of these offered to help Sun.

A rising by peasants after a bad harvest in the Yangtse Province was put down by the army (September 1911). On 10 October ('Double Tenth') there were a series of risings by Sun's supporters in southern China. Many sections of the army supported the rebels. By the end of November the rebels had control of the country south of the Yangtse—including cities such as Canton and Shanghai, where anti-foreign feeling was high.

Nanking, the old capital of China, was taken in November 1911. In Nanking the rebels set up a Provisional Government for their republic. Their forces marched north to attack the Manchu capital of Peking.

Most army generals refused to march against the rebels, but in Peking the loyal section of the army was commanded by an energetic General Yuan Shih k'ai. He attacked the rebels and drove them south of the Yangtse. Then he opened negotiations with the rebels. He wanted to get rid of the Manchus, put off the reforming movement, and take power for himself.

SORTING OUT THE POSITION, 1911–12

On Christmas Eve 1911 Sun arrived in China from the USA. He was named the first President of the United Provinces of China.

Yuan forced the Manchu boy-Emperor to sign a declaration of abdication. The Manchu dynasty came to an end. The Nanking Assembly, which supported Sun, was afraid of a civil war in which Yuan with his army would defeat the republican forces. In 1912 Sun resigned his position and allowed Yuan to become the President of the Chinese Republic.

THE REPUBLIC BETRAYED

Yuan lived in Peking and not in Nanking—the home of the Assembly. He proved to be an autocrat: he expelled Sun's supporters (the Kuo Min Tang) from the Assembly, and in 1914 he dismissed the Assembly and declared himself sole ruler of China.

In July 1913 Sun organized a second revolution, but this was put down by Yuan's forces which captured Nanking.

Though Yuan was accepted by most Chinese as a successful leader, his position was not really that strong. He depended on the loyalty of other army leaders.

THE WAR LORDS

Many army generals were more powerful than the provincial governor appointed by the government. Their badly-paid, ill-dressed and poorly disciplined soldiers often attacked the peasants and townspeople. This was one way of getting the food and money which the government under Yuan did not send them.

Yuan died in August 1916, after he had failed to get himself declared Emperor. His successor, Li Yuan Hun, restored the Republic constitution of 1912 and recalled the Parliament dismissed in 1912.

But Li was unable to cope with the War Lords. Some of these fought with one another to try to gain control of the government. Others fought government troops to ensure that they alone controlled a certain region. In all this fighting the people of China suffered badly. Farms were ruined, millions died from famine. Town life became difficult—drains broke down, roads were destroyed, trade was interrupted. Millions died from the fevers and diseases following a breakdown in urban life.

6.8 Japan, China and the First World War, 1914–16

When the war broke out in July–August 1914, China declared herself to be neutral.

Japan, Britain's ally, declared war on Germany: she invaded Germany's Pacific islands and claimed the German colony of Kiao-chow on the Chinese mainland—but promised to return it to China. However, when asked to leave, Japan issued the Twenty-one Demands. These included:

▶ Japanese rights to former German colonies in China;
▶ extra mining and railway rights in China which would have given Japan the most powerful influence in China;
▶ that only Japan should be given new trading rights in China;
▶ that Japanese financiers and military experts be appointed to advise the Chinese government.

Yuan signed an agreement (May 1915) giving the Japanese most of what they wanted.

There was an outbreak of anti-Japanese activity in China. Japanese goods were boycotted; factory workers refused to work in Japanese-owned industries; Chinese servants refused to work for Japanese masters.

SUN IN POWER, 1917

The terrible conditions in China (see above) led Sun to call a meeting of the National Assembly in Canton. Most of the Kuo Min Tang members who had been expelled by Yuan met and declared themselves the government of China. Sun was elected President of China. His government controlled only Canton and part of the province of Kwangtung—and even there depended on a War Lord.

Elsewhere the War Lords were in charge. Nationalist feeling was strong (as was seen in the anti-Japanese outbreak in 1915). There was also a spirit of despair as trade died down, farming failed and disease killed off millions.

Foreign countries refused to recognize Sun as the President. They pretended that whoever was in power in Peking was the head of the government. The foreigners preferred the activities of the War Lords to the thought of an anti-Western and democratic government.

THE TREATY OF VERSAILLES, 1919

This treaty ended the war with Germany (see Unit 12). It confirmed Japan's claim to the former German colony of Kiao-chow on the Chinese mainland. This was against the spirit of at least one of Wilson's Fourteen Points (Fig. 12.1). It led to the outbreak of nation-wide demonstrations in China against foreigners in 1919. We will see the results of this in Unit 17.

Unit 6 Summary

▶ Europe and China, 1793–1870.
▶ The opening of Japan, 1853, and its industrialization.
▶ Japan versus China, 1894–5.
▶ Japan versus Russia: the War of 1904–5.
▶ Chinese rebellions, 1900 and 1911.
▶ Sun Yat-sen and the overthrow of the Manchus.
▶ Japan, China and the First World War, 1914–18.

7 THE UNITED STATES OF AMERICA, 1870–1917

European countries dominated the world during this period. They divided Africa amongst themselves (Unit 5). They dominated Asia, although the arrival of Japan towards the end of the period was a sign of things to come (Unit 6). The emergence of the United States was another sign that European powers would, one day, no longer control the world's affairs.

7.1 The American Constitution

In 1783 the original 13 colonies (Fig. 7.3) of British North America won their War of Independence. They decided never to be governed by a king. The USA is a republic; the head of state is a President.

A WRITTEN CONSTITUTION

Having won their independence in 1783, the leaders of the 13 colonies wrote out their Constitution and agreed on it in 1787. Several of the states (or former colonies) were unwilling to sign the original document. This led to the writing of Ten Amendments in 1791. There have been another fourteen Amendments since then. We will study some of these in this Unit.

Checks and balances

The leaders of the revolution against Britain believed that the King, George III, had too much power. When they wrote their Constitution they did their best to see that no part of their government would be too powerful.

The central government has three parts (see below). The writers of the Constitution made sure that these parts were kept separate. The powers of each part were carefully defined to make sure that no one part could become too powerful.

STATES' RIGHTS

The states freely entered into a federation (hence the Federal Bureau of Investigation, or the FBI). Each state had to give up some of the powers it had enjoyed before the formation of the Union. The federal (or central) government alone has the right to print money, declare war, make peace, decide on import and export duties and form an army.

On the other hand, the federalists (those who wanted a strong central government) had to please states which were reluctant to join such a union. For this reason every state has kept certain powers. From time to time there have been disputes between the central government and some state governments over states' rights. In the 1860s differences between central government and states of the South led to the Civil War. In more recent times, as we will see in Unit 32, there have been disputes about the treatment of black people in various states.

7.2 The Government of the USA

The government consists of the Legislature, Executive and Judiciary.

THE LEGISLATURE

This makes the laws (the Latin word *leges* means laws or rules). In the USA the Legislature is known as the Congress and is divided into two bodies:

The Senate

This is the Upper House and the more important of the two bodies making up Congress.

Senators

The voters of each state elect two senators to represent the state. Senators are elected for a term of six years. This gives them more independence than the members of the House of Representatives, who are elected for only two years. It also gives them the appearance of being more powerful than the President, who is elected for four years.

The House of Representatives

This is a much larger body than the Senate.

Congressmen

The members are elected on the basis of population. The more heavily populated states have more Congressmen than the lightly populated States. The House of Representatives is elected every two years. This pleases those who believe in democracy; the electors have much more control over a Congressman than over a Senator.

THE PRESIDENT

The President is elected for four years. In theory he is indirectly elected by an electoral college chosen by the people of the various states. In practice he is directly elected by the votes of the people. Presidential elections take place in the November of each leap year. The successful candidate takes office at the beginning of the following year.

Presidential powers

▶ The Cabinet: the President chooses his team of Ministers. Because of the belief in the separation of powers, none of these can have a seat in Congress.
▶ The President is Commander-in-Chief of the Armed Forces.
▶ Foreign policy: the President is responsible for the country's foreign policy. He can declare war and make peace treaties. But, in keeping with the belief in 'checks and balances', he has to get the approval of two-thirds of the Senate for his actions. We will see that Presidents did not always get that approval (Unit 14).
▶ Veto: the President can veto (or set aside) any Bill which comes from Congress. However, if such a Bill is passed again by a majority of two-thirds in both chambers of Congress, it automatically becomes law (see Unit 16).
▶ Higher appointments: while the President picks his own Cabinet and appoints the judges to the Supreme Court, he has to get the approval of the Senate for such 'higher' appointments. This limits his freedom.

THE EXECUTIVE

The body which has to carry out the laws passed by the Legislature (or lawmakers) is the President plus his ministers. In the USA the Executive is often called the Administration.

THE JUDICIARY

This is represented by the Supreme Court of the USA. This Court consists of a Chief Justice and eight associate judges. All these judges are appointed by the President. But they are appointed for life so that they may be independent of political pressure. Their task is to decide whether laws passed by Congress are in keeping with the spirit and letter of the original Constitution (and its Amendments). The Court has become known as 'the sacred Guardian of the Constitution'. Their decisions have to be obeyed by President, Congress and state governments.

7.3 The American 'frontier'

In Europe the word 'frontier' usually means the geographical boundary between countries. In the USA such a boundary (e.g. between the USA and Canada or the USA and Mexico) is known as the border. To Americans, 'frontier' means 'the limits reached by civilization'. Their early history is one of constantly pushing the frontier out to the west until the Pacific had been reached.

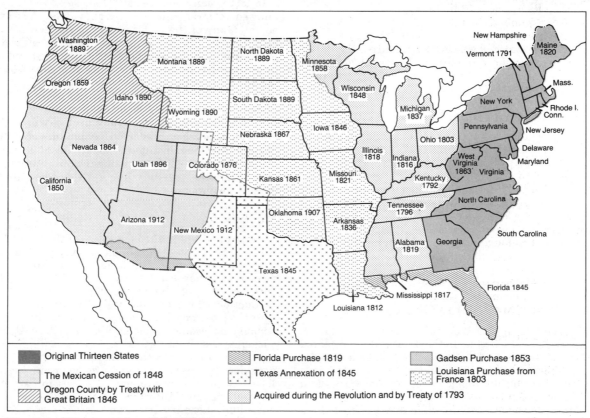

Fig. 7.3 The expansion of the USA

The 13 original states (still remembered in the stripes on the US flag) were strung between the eastern seaboard and the Appalachian mountains (Fig. 7.3). Some pioneers soon pushed through the mountains to the west. By 1800 the frontier had reached the Mississippi, and the town of St Louis was a frontier town.

THE LOUISIANA PURCHASE

In 1803 there took place the Louisiana Purchase (Fig. 7.3). In the reign of King Louis XIV of France, an explorer, La Salle, had explored the length of the Mississippi and had claimed the river basin for France under the name of Louisiana. This had gone to Spain at the Treaty of Paris (1763), ending the war in which Britain had driven France from Canada.

In 1800 Napoleon forced Spain to hand Louisiana as well as Florida to France. Napoleon dreamed of a large Empire in North America. However, the war with Britain needed all his attention—and money. He could not afford to fight the Americans as well, so in 1803 Napoleon sold to the US government the territory stretching from the Mississippi to the Rocky Mountains (and from the Gulf of Florida to the Canadian border) for fifteen million dollars. As the map shows (Fig. 7.3) the addition of a million square miles of largely unexplored territory doubled the size of the United States.

'GO WEST, YOUNG MAN, GO WEST'

1804–6

President Jefferson, who had arranged the Louisiana Purchase, sent out two explorers, Lewis and Clark. They followed the course of the Mississippi and went on to reach the Pacific, proving that the continent could be crossed.

1806–36

Fur traders and trappers moved west in search of the beaver, whose fur was needed for the hat trade. Pioneers opened up trails along which families could move into the almost unknown (Fig. 7.3).

New states were formed when enough settlers had made their homes in a particular region.

1845

A war with Mexico (during which there occurred the Battle of the Alamo) led to the acquisition of Texas, and further defeats led the Mexicans to cede the whole of the area from Texas to the coast in 1848 (Fig. 7.3).

1848

The discovery of gold in California led to a gold rush which took thousands of people to the Far West.

By the 1860s railways linked the east and west coasts of the continent. Industrial goods could be carried from the East; agricultural produce could be taken from the Far West and the Mid-west to the large towns and cities of the East.

So the 'frontier' was pushed ever westwards by a great westward migration. What would the Americans do once the frontier could no longer be pushed further westwards?

7.4 Problems of Internal Expansion

THE AMERICAN (RED) INDIANS

The original settlers in the 13 colonies fought several large wars and many battles against Indian tribes which resented the settlers' occupation of their tribelands. The moving of 'the frontier' to the west brought the 'immigrants' into further conflict with the Indians living on the Great Plain between the Mississippi and the Rockies. In 1851 Congress passed a law which forced the Plain Indians to live in reservations.

Between 1865 and 1876 Indian resistance to the white settlers increased. The Indians resented the mass slaughter of the buffalo, which was the basis of their economy. There were 300 major battles between Indians and the US army in this period.

Gradually the Indians lost the power and will to fight. The disappearance of the buffalo destroyed their main livelihood and source of meat and clothing. The better-armed soldiers of the US army won most of the pitched battles. Many Indians were tempted to side with the white settler—by bribery or out of fear.

In 1890 the last of the Sioux tribe were destroyed at the Battle of Wounded Knee. By 1900 there were only about 250,000 Indians in the USA.

THE CATTLE FARMERS

The clashes with the Indians had largely resulted from the expansion of the cattle ranching business. Some ranches led to the displacement of some Indians. When ranchers drove their cattle from Texas to markets in Illinois, Colorado and California (Fig. 7.3) the Indians attacked and destroyed the cattle. Ranchers naturally asked for US reprisals.

The development of the railway system led to the building of railway cattle terminals to which cattle could be driven (over a shorter distance) before being transported by rail to the industrial towns.

Driving cattle to the terminals often exhausted the animals. This led to the development of the open range. Graziers would buy young cattle, feed them on the range for three or four years and then sell them in the cattle markets.

The growth of industrial towns and of a large urban population led to increasing demand for meat. This led to an increase in the number of cattle prospectors on the range from Kansas to Montana (Fig. 7.3).

During the 1880s there were so many of these prospectors that the range became overcrowded and the price of meat fell. This led to the development of the homestead. Each grazier fenced in his holdings and grazed his own herd.

ARABLE FARMING

There was a spread of arable farming on the Great Plains.

In 1862 Congress passed the Homestead Act. Settlers were allowed to farm units of approximately 65 hectares (160 acres). Many of the governments of the new states offered land cheaply, or in some cases free, to attract settlers. Railway companies also bought land and offered it cheaply to prospective settlers in the hope that this would lead to increased use of the railway system.

The railway system opened up the country and made it easier for settlers to move. But more importantly, it increased the market for agricultural products. Perishable goods such as vegetables and dairy produce could be carried quickly over long distances. The system also carried goods cheaply. The cost of transporting the bulky produce, such as wheat, fell sharply once the railways had replaced the horse-drawn wagons.

Machinery

The early settlers in the new states of the Great Plains had few sources from which to get workmen. This meant that from the beginning US farming had to become more mechanized than European farming. Ploughs able to cope with the soil of the Great Plains led to an increased production of wheat. Machines for reaping, binding and threshing became increasingly efficient. In the 1880s the combine harvester enabled a farmer to harvest 28 hectares (70 acres) in a single day.

Science also helped the farmer. New strains of seed were developed to resist droughts, common in the Mid-west. Research helped to eliminate diseases in cattle and pigs. Laboratories in California showed how to grow fruit and vegetables successfully.

The agricultural boom led to huge increases in

production. Exports of wheat and other produce to Europe led to a sharp fall in food prices. This had a bad effect on European farmers, but it led to a rise in living standards for most Europeans.

Immigrants from Europe flocked to the 'new country'. Over five million arrived in the 1890s. Many of these became farmers; in the 1880s over 70 per cent of the people of Wisconsin (Fig. 7.3) were of foreign origin.

Between 1860 and 1900 the amount of land farmed doubled to over 800 million acres.

7.5 Industry in the USA

Most industry was in the north-east. Immigrants provided plenty of cheap unskilled labour.

Before the Civil War (1861–5) the USA was largely an agricultural country. It was the Civil War which led to the first expansion of the northern industry. There was a demand for coal, iron and steel to provide the munitions needed by the Northern armies. There was an expansion of the railway system to carry the Northern troops. This, too, led to an expansion of the coal, iron and steel and engineering industries.

By 1900 the USA was the world's industrial leader, producing more coal, iron, steel and railway lines than any other country. It had more and much larger factories than any other country.

INDUSTRIALISTS AND THE GOVERNMENT

After 1865, businessmen and industrialists gained control of the Congress. They organized the election of Representatives and Senators who were their friends, and paid special firms to supervise the passage of favourable legislation through Congress. They also bribed Congressmen and judges to favour industry in their laws and judgements.

Congress brought in laws which favoured industry and removed any existing laws which might have hampered industrial development. This was in keeping with the spirit of self-reliance to be found on 'the frontier'.

The Supreme Court helped industrialists by judgments which removed almost all barriers to private enterprise. Industrialists supported this belief in freedom:

Vanderbilt, the railway king, asked 'Can't I do what I want with my own?' Carnegie, the steel king, said 'What do I care about the law? Haven't I got the power?' Morgan, the financial king, when called to the White House by President Roosevelt, said, 'Mr President, I'll get my lawyer and you get yours.' Talking of the Supreme Court, one industrial 'king' told a President: 'You buy your judges and I'll buy mine. We'll see whose stays bought the longest.'

It is not surprising that conditions in US towns and factories were worse than those found in Britain in the early industrial revolution: hours of work, working conditions and wages were fixed by employers. Trade unions were small, weak and easily crushed. Towns grew up around the industrial centres with little care for sanitation. High death rates were common.

7.6 The Problem of the Southern States

CIVIL WAR

In 1861 eleven Southern states declared that they were leaving the 'union'. They formed their own Confederacy. They were afraid that President Lincoln might push through a constitutional amendment to abolish slavery.

Lincoln made war on the south, not in the cause of slavery, but to preserve the union of the states. The war lasted for four years, 1861–5. Its effects on the south were:

▶ agricultural devastation;

▶ loss of 600,000 men, one-fifth of the male population;
▶ starvation and the outbreak of disease;
▶ the ruin of the south's cotton industry.

ABOLITION OF SLAVERY

Lincoln announced (September, 1862) that all slaves would be free from 1 January, 1863. The Thirteenth Amendment, which abolished slavery, was passed by Congress on 18 December, 1865. There were many far-reaching effects of this abolition.

What were the freed blacks to do?

In Russia, Alexander II gave the freed serfs some land (Unit 3). Lincoln did not go that far. Congress set up the Freedman's Bureau, which set up special camps where blacks were given some assistance. But the death rate in these camps was high.

Who would govern the Southern States?

States which accepted the law on the Emancipation of Slaves were allowed to form their own governments again. But many of these introduced their own 'Black Codes' to prevent blacks owning land, working at skilled trades, serving on juries, carrying arms and, maybe most importantly, having the right to vote.

How did it affect the relationship between the Southern whites and the Northern whites?

The victorious North produced radical politicians who pushed through the Fourteenth Amendment which said: 'No state shall abridge the privileges of citizens of the United States nor shall any state deprive any person of life, liberty or property without due process of law.' If Southern politicians refused to accept this amendment they were unable to hold office.

SOUTHERN OPPOSITION

Some Southern politicians won back power and passed state legislation to hinder the progress of blacks. Other southerners formed secret societies such as the Ku Klux Klan to terrorize blacks trying to exercise their civil rights and whites who supported them.

In 1870 Congress passed the Amnesty Act to restore the political rights of all Southern politicians. There was an increase in intimidation of blacks. Southern whites elected to Congress called themselves Democrats, because it was Republicans under Lincoln who had abolished slavery.

The Supreme Court favoured the white racists. It ruled that the Fifteenth Amendment did not give anyone the right to vote (as it seemed to do: 'The right of citizens of the US to vote shall not be denied or abridged by the US or by any state on account of race, color or previous condition of servitude'). Governments in the Southern states took away the right to vote from blacks.

In 1877 the last Federal troops were withdrawn from the South. Southern whites had an even freer hand.

The South was to remain a problem in the twentieth century, as we will see in Unit 32.

7.7 The Giant Trusts

John D. Rockefeller was the leading industrialist in the USA in the period 1860–1900. He believed that the large firm (or corporation) which controlled all (if possible) of an industry was the natural outcome of private enterprise. It would have certain advantages:

▶ it would have great resources and be able to afford new developments and inventions;
▶ because it was so big, such a firm would be less likely to go bankrupt as many small businesses did.

Rockefeller made his first fortune in oil during the Civil

War before setting up the Standard Oil Company. By 1880 he controlled 90 per cent of US oil production as well as most of the world's market in oil.

Andrew Carnegie was the steel 'king'. He controlled most of the steel supply needed by the developing railway system. In 1901 a merger between his firm and other steel firms produced the United States Steel Corporation.

J. Pierpont Morgan was a financial 'king'. He controlled banks and other sources of investment and helped organize giant corporations. He paid Carnegie 250 million dollars for his share in the United States Steel Corporation in 1901.

These were the three leading capitalists of the time. Others included Philip Armour, the pork packer, Cornelius Vanderbilt, the controller of much of the railway system, and Averell Harriman, who controlled most of the rest of the railway system.

THE GOVERNMENT AND THE TRUSTS, 1885–9

The giant firms certainly 'delivered the goods'. The United States became the world's industrial leader. They made their owners very wealthy. Vanderbilt spent 2 million dollars in the building of a house—and 9 million dollars in furnishing it. Carnegie gave 400 million dollars to charities before he died. Rockefeller created a foundation which spent 530 million dollars on medical research.

But others suffered in the making of this wealth. Children worked 16 hours a day in factories; miners trying to form trade unions faced attacks by private armies hired by the trust owners.

Smaller industrialists and farmers also suffered. Some were forced to pay a very high freight charge on railways, while the powerful few were able to get much lower freight charges. Telephone and other companies charged the trusts a lower rate than that paid by the smaller firms.

'Muckrakers' was the name given to critics who attacked the 'robber barons'. These included journalists, pamphleteers and novelists such as Upton Sinclair whose book *The Jungle* (1906) exposed the horrors of Chicago's meat-packing industry.

President Cleveland (1885–9) was the first to try to gain some government control over the industrial giants. He set up the Interstate Commerce Commission in 1887. This could prevent railway companies from raising freight charges.

But the political power of the trusts was very great. The Supreme Court ruled in favour of the trusts when cases were brought before it. 'The best judges stayed bought' said one trust owner.

In 1896 the Republican McKinley became President and the Interstate Commission had its powers cut down.

THE AMERICAN TRADE UNION MOVEMENT

American workers were slow to form trade unions, largely because American industrialization was a new development. There was no history of craft societies as in pre-industrial Britain. Also, most American workers were immigrants, grateful for the political freedom they had and for the chance to get work. The constant flow of immigrants allowed industrialists to recruit non-unionized labour if workers formed unions. In addition, American workers shared 'the frontier' spirit and believed in the benefits of free enterprise.

In 1869 the National Labour Union was formed, but it collapsed a few years later. Also in 1869, the Knights of Labour were founded to form separate unions in the different states and to create some form of union co-operation. Then, in 1886 a bomb outrage in Chicago was blamed on the Knights and the organization collapsed.

In 1886 the American Federation of Labour for skilled workers was formed. While supporting free enterprise, it demanded a fair share in the new prosperity. By 1900,

however, only half a million of the 17 million factory workers were organized in trade unions.

THE TRUSTS UNDER FIRE, 1903

There was a business depression in 1903 when shareholders lost 600 million dollars. Trusts, it seemed, did not always manage their affairs well.

Congress investigated the depression. It found that many trusts used criminal means to get control. The investigation showed that trusts did not make new inventions or use those offered to them. This was the opposite of the claim made by Rockefeller. The investigation published reports on working and social conditions which showed that the attacks on 'the robber barons' had been justified.

Reforms

A number of reforming organizations were set up. These succeeded in pushing through important reforms. By 1914 there were child-labour laws in 43 states (but none in the remaining five states). Many states passed laws on compulsory school attendance—but others did not.

The electoral laws were changed. Presidential candidates in the political parties had now to go through a primary election in most states. The registered members of the political parties then had a direct vote in the adoption of candidates. This cut down the power of the 'robber barons' to influence the choice of candidates. This is still the system by which Presidents are elected.

THEODORE ROOSEVELT, 1901–9

Roosevelt became President when McKinley was assassinated in 1901. He was a colourful character, having been a boxer, bear hunter (hence the Teddy Bear toy), a friend of cowboys and leader of soldiers in the Spanish-American War (see below).

Both at home and abroad he believed that the government should wield 'the big stick' against its opponents. In 1904 he forced the break up of the Morgan-Rockefeller Northern Securities Corporation which controlled a large section of US industry. He made mine owners accept arbitration on demands by the United Mineworkers Union for better wages and conditions.

He set up the Bureau of Corporations to investigate and report publicly on the activities of the great trusts, and a Department of Commerce and Labour where civil servants could supervise industrial affairs. He also set up an anti-trust division in the Department of Justice where specially trained lawyers led the drive against the trusts. In addition, he increased the powers of the Inter-State Commerce Commission over railway freight charges.

He called for the development of programmes of social welfare. In this, as in much else, the USA lagged behind European countries such as Britain and Germany.

WOODROW WILSON, 1912–20

William Howard Taft, the Republican President, 1909–12, carried on with Roosevelt's policies of 'trust-busting'. Then Wilson, Democratic President 1912–20, pushed through the Clayton Anti-Trust Act (1914) outlawing many business practices of large companies. He cut import duties and exposed US industry to foreign competition, hoping that this would lead to lower prices and a rise in living standards. He set up special law enforcement commissions to see that factory legislation was obeyed. However, the decisions of successive Supreme Courts limited their power.

▆ 7.8 The Expansion of the United States after 1865

In 1867 the USA bought Alaska from Russia for one and a half million pounds. In the 1840s US politicians had watched the expansion of the European powers into Asia (see Unit 6). The US developed the theory that 'the American mission' was to help backward nations of the Pacific and South America as well as to protect American trading interests in China and Japan.

MAKING THE PACIFIC MORE AMERICAN

In the 1850s fifty small Pacific islands were brought under US control. These provided the fertilizer guano. Costa Rica was developed by the building of railways. Mexico and other South American countries were helped by the American development of copper and silver mines.

Samoa

This was a valuable staging-post for American ships on the trans-Pacific routes. In 1899 the USA gained the harbour of Pago Pago, leaving Britain and Germany to argue about control of the rest of the island.

Hawaii

In 1877 the US developed the Pearl Harbor naval base. The islands proved to be good for sugar growing and became important to the US. Agreements were made with the islands by which no other foreign nation was allowed to get trading rights with Hawaii. Between 1894 and 1898 there was a Hawaiian attempt to reassert its independence, but in 1898 the islands were annexed to the USA.

The US navy

In 1884 a Naval War College had been set up and its first president was the naval historian A. T. Mahan. Under his influence the US navy grew until in 1898 it was the world's third largest navy.

EXPANSIONIST POLITICIANS

In 1895 while McKinley was President there was a border dispute between Venezuela and British Guyana. Roosevelt, Assistant Secretary to the Navy, wanted the US to make war and drive the British from the American continent. Calmer counsels prevailed. The British Prime Minister, Lord Salisbury, submitted the case to international arbitration. The case was settled in Britain's favour in 1899.

THE SPANISH-AMERICAN WAR, 1899

In 1895 there were a series of risings by Cuban nationalists against Spanish rule. The Cuban rebels asked for US help. Roosevelt wanted the US to help the rebels.

In February 1898 the US battleship, *Maine*, was blown up in Cuban waters. There was no proof that the Spaniards were responsible for the sinking of the ship. McKinley wanted to keep out of the war. But the war party forced him into a declaration of war in April 1898.

The Spanish fleet was destroyed by the US navy in Manila Bay, in the Spanish-controlled Philippines. Troops landed in July and captured Manila.

In Cuba Roosevelt led a force of troops nicknamed 'the Rough Riders' who gained the surrender of Cuba in July 1898. The USA then announced the annexation of Cuba, the Philippines, Puerto Rica and Guam. In 1898 there was a Philippine revolt against US rule. This was not finally defeated until 1901.

Cuba remained under US direct rule until 1902, when it was allowed self-government again.

THE PANAMA CANAL

De Lesseps failed to build a canal across the Panama isthmus (see Unit 2). In 1880 Britain and the USA agreed that there would be no attempt to build a canal except as a joint British-US venture. In 1901 Britain surrendered her rights under the 1880 agreement. The USA was free to build a canal. The French Company had sold its rights in the Canal to the USA. The agreement said that the money due should be paid to the government of Colombia. To prevent such payments, the US supported a Panamanian rebellion which led to the separation of Panama from Colombia.

The construction of the Canal started in 1904 and the first ship sailed through the completed Canal in 1913. The Canal zone remained under US control, independent of the government of Panama.

THE US EMERGES AS A WORLD POWER

The US prevented European powers from arranging a division of China along the lines of the 'Scramble for Africa'. US forces formed part of the foreign army which crushed the Boxer Rising in 1900 (see Unit 6).

In 1905 Roosevelt helped arrange the Treaty of Portsmouth, New Hampshire, which ended the Russo-Japanese War (see Unit 6).

The US also took part in the discussions following the Moroccan crises (see Unit 8).

7.9 The US and the First World War, 1914–17

Wilson was President when the First World War broke out in 1914. He had to take account of widespread hostility to Britain:

▶ millions of Irish Americans hated Britain because of her ill-treatment of Ireland;
▶ millions of German Americans were loyal to the Fatherland;
▶ millions of Russian Jews had fled to America and hoped for a German victory over the hated Tsar;
▶ many Americans were opposed to Japanese expansion in the Pacific. Japan was one of the Allies in 1914.

It is not surprising that in August 1914 Wilson argued that the US had to remain neutral in Europe's 'Civil War'.

However, several things tended to make the US support the British and French causes: there was a long tradition of friendship with France which had helped the Americans against Britain in the 1770s, and large sums of money were loaned to the Allies to help them buy the war goods they needed from American industry. If the Allies lost the war, these loans would not be repaid.

German policy also turned US opinion in the Allies favour: the attack on neutral Belgium shocked many Americans. Submarine attacks on neutral vessels, including passenger shipping, also angered Americans. When the British ship, the *Lusitania*, was sunk in May 1915, 124 Americans were among the 1198 who lost their lives.

In 1916 Wilson was re-elected President on the promise that he would keep the US out of the war. German policy, however, again helped the Allied cause. In January 1917 the Germans announced their resumption of an unrestricted submarine campaign—against all shipping. In January 1917 the German Foreign Secretary, Zimmerman, sent a note to the German Ambassador in Mexico in which he proposed an alliance between Mexico and Germany and the declaration of a joint war against the USA.

In February and March 1917 Wilson tried to get the Germans to call off their submarine campaign. Their failure to do so led him to declare war on 2 April 1917. The USA now marched to the front of the world stage for the first time.

Unit 7 Summary

▶ The Constitution and government of the USA.
▶ The 'frontier spirit'.
▶ Problems of internal expansion: Indians; cattle farming.
▶ The industrialization of the USA: the growth of monopolies.
▶ Slavery and the Southern states.
▶ Government versus the industrial monopolies; trust-busting.
▶ US expansion in the Pacific: the Spanish-American War.
▶ The USA and the First World War, 1914–18.

8 INTERNATIONAL RELATIONS, 1870–1914

8.1 Bismarck's Foreign Policy and System of Alliances

OBJECTIVES

Germany was united as the result of three wars (see Unit 1). After 1871 Bismarck wanted peace.

The Catholic states had been reluctant to become part of the Prussianized Empire. They might have left if Germany had been involved in an unsuccessful war after 1871.

German industry also needed time to take advantage of the newly acquired Alsace-Lorraine coal and iron fields.

Other problems arose after 1871—the Catholics, the Socialists and the demand for colonies. Bismarck wanted time to deal with these internal problems.

Britain

To ensure Britain's friendship Bismarck was careful not to do anything to annoy her.

Colonies

He resisted the German demand for a larger Empire (Unit 1). He was afraid that looking for an Empire would bring Germany into conflict with Britain.

Navy

He did not try to build a German navy which Britain would have seen as a threat.

France

Bismarck realized that France would want a war of revenge to try to get back Alsace and Lorraine (see Unit 1). He did not fear France on her own, but he was afraid of a war on two fronts—against France and some French ally. So the main object of his foreign policy was to make sure that no one allied with France.

The isolation of France

Bismarck emphasized that republican France must be opposed to rule by monarchs. This propaganda* scared off Russia and Austria. He also urged France to look for colonies, since this would distract attention from the losses of 1871, and it would also push France into conflict with other countries.

Italy and France quarrelled over Tunisia—Tripoli (see Unit 5). Britain and France quarrelled over Egypt and the Sudan (Unit 5) and over colonies in Asia (Unit 6).

Austria and Russia were drawn closer to Germany.

THE DREIKAISERBUND (OR LEAGUE OF THREE EMPERORS) 1873

Austria was defeated by Prussia in 1866. How did Bismarck persuade the Austrian Emperor to link up with his old enemy?

Austrian expansion into the Balkans could only come about if Germany supported Austria. Prussia had treated Austria very leniently in 1866 and Austria was grateful for that, so in 1873 talks were held in Berlin. Russia heard about the talks and asked to be invited. Bismarck explained the danger from republican France (see above). The three Emperors agreed to be friendly to one another and guard against revolutionary activity by France.

France was now without friends.

AUSTRIA VERSUS RUSSIA

Russian and Austrian policies were in conflict in the Balkans (Unit 4 and Fig. 4.1).

At the Congress of Berlin Bismarck supported Austria. There were three reasons for choosing Austria:

▶ if he chose Russia, he would anger Britain;
▶ Austria would be easier to control than Russia;
▶ Austrian expansion into the South East would be good for German trade, as it would leave the River Danube open.

THE DUAL ALLIANCE, 1879

In 1879 Bismarck made a secret treaty with Austria. The terms of the treaty or alliance favoured Austria. If Germany were attacked by one country (e.g. France) Austria would remain neutral; if Germany were attacked by two countries, Austria would come in on Germany's side; if Austria went to war with Russia, Germany would come in on Austria's side.

The German Emperor, William I, did not like this alliance. He thought it was aimed against his nephew, Tsar Alexander II, but Bismarck overcame his opposition.

THE LEAGUE OF THE THREE EMPERORS, 1881 AND 1884

The League had been a friendly understanding in 1873. In 1881 it was strengthened. Bismarck persuaded the three Emperors to sign a treaty. They promised that none of them would help a fourth country (obviously France) if that country went to war with any of the three nations.

THE TRIPLE ALLIANCE, 1882

In 1881 France occupied Tunis (see Unit 5). Italy had ambitions in that area. Later on, in 1912, she took Tripoli (see Unit 4).

Italy was annoyed by the French occupation of Tunis. Bismarck got her to join Germany and Austria in a Triple Alliance. Italy insisted that she would never fight Britain. Her long coastline made an easy target for the Royal Navy.

THE EASTERN QUESTION AGAIN, 1885–7

In 1878 the Congress of Berlin had created a 'small' Bulgaria (Unit 4 and Fig. 4.1). In 1885 Bulgaria and Eastern Rumelia (Fig. 4.1) united under a nephew of Tsar Alexander II. In 1886 Serbia declared war on Bulgaria—and was defeated.

Russia organized the kidnapping of the Bulgarian ruler, hoping to force him to become more pro-Russian. Bulgaria refused to accept him as their leader. He was replaced by Prince Ferdinand of Saxe-Coburg in 1887. He followed an anti-Russian and pro-German line.

THE REINSURANCE TREATY, 1887

Russia was angered by this loss of influence. Austria was encouraged by the anti-Russian movement in Bulgaria and by the defeat of the Serbs. Bismarck was afraid that Austria might declare war on Russia and so drag Germany into a war.

In 1887 Bismarck made a secret treaty with Russia. In this

Reinsurance Treaty he promised German support for Russia's claims to influence in Bulgaria, and German neutrality in an Austro-Russian war, if Austria was the aggressor. This was contrary to the terms of the Dual Alliance with Austria. Bismarck had been driven to dishonesty. This became clear in 1888 in another row over the choice of the German Prince Ferdinand as ruler of Bulgaria. Bismarck published the terms of the Dual Alliance. Russia would have to fight Germany if she went to war with Austria.

WILLIAM II AND BISMARCK, 1888–90

In Unit 1 we saw how the grandson of William I came to the throne in 1888. He quarrelled with Bismarck over the question of the treatment of socialists, Germany and colonies, and the proposals for a German Navy.

He also differed with Bismarck on foreign policy: he wanted to come out strongly in support of Austria, and he wanted Germany, as well as Austria, to get control and influence in the Balkans.

We have seen that in 1890 Bismarck resigned.

8.2 The Franco-Russian Alliance, 1892–5

The Reinsurance Treaty of 1887 was not renewed in 1890. William II made it clear that he wanted Germany to become an important influence in the Balkans.

The Berlin-Baghdad railway was to go via Constantinople, capital of Turkey. It would lead to increased German trade in the Middle East. Austria supported the scheme. She was promised large territorial gains in the Balkans as a reward. Russia now felt as isolated as France was after 1871.

However, France and Russia were traditional enemies. They had fought each other in the Crimean War, 1853–6. France was a democratic republic, Russia an autocracy;* France had an anti-clerical policy (Unit 2); Russia was dominated by the Orthodox Church (Unit 3).

Economics helped draw the two countries together: France had recovered from the Franco-Prussian War, but Russia needed foreign loans to pay for the imports needed for her industrialization. France could arrange such loans. The navies of the two countries exchanged visits. The press in both countries wrote friendly articles.

The Franco-Russian Alliance was signed in 1892, confirmed in 1894, and strengthened in 1897. Each nation promised to help the other if attacked by Germany.

8.3 Britain and 'Splendid Isolation'

Britain was not a member of either Armed Camp. During the 19th century Britain had played only a small role in European affairs. She had not, for example, interfered in any of Bismarck's wars (Unit 1).

The Eastern Question was the one issue which involved British interference. Britain did all she could to block Russia's power in the Balkans.

BRITAIN'S OPPOSITION TO RUSSIA AND FRANCE

Britain feared Russian influence in the Balkans and in the Far East. After Russian expansion into Central Asia (Unit 6) Britain also feared Russian influence in Tibet and Afghanistan, as a threat to India. The growth of the French colonies in Indo-China led to British fears of French ambitions towards Burma. France and Britain clashed over Egypt and the Sudan (see Unit 5).

THE MEDITERRANEAN AGREEMENT, 1887

Britain, Austria and Italy signed this agreement in which Britain promised to help Italy, if she was attacked by France in the Mediterranean; and Austria, if she was attacked by Russia in the Balkans.

In 1897 Chamberlain, British Colonial Secretary, tried to arrange an alliance with Germany. He failed, because the Kaiser wanted Britain to join the Triple Alliance. Britain refused.

8.4 Trying to Outlaw War, 1899

In 1899 Nicholas II of Russia (Unit 3) called a conference to find ways of limiting the growth of armies and navies. This conference met at the Hague in Holland. However, no nation believed that the others would cut down the size of their armies or navies. William II of Germany in particular had just started to develop plans for a large German Navy.

The Conference did agree to ban the use of poison gas in wartime, and the launching of weapons from 'balloons or by similar new weapons'. During the First World War these agreements were disregarded.

An International Court was set up. Nations were to bring the causes of their disagreement to the court. Settlement might then be reached without war.

8.5 Britain and the Effects of the Boer War, 1899–1902

Britain took a long time to conquer the Boers (see Unit 5). What would Britain do in a major war?

Kaiser William II sent a telegram congratulating the Boers when the Jameson Raid failed. What might the Kaiser have done with a large enough Navy to take German troops to help the Boers?

THE ANGLO-JAPANESE ALLIANCE, 1902 (see Unit 6)

This was Britain's first formal alliance. It recognized Britain's need of Japanese help against Russia in the Far East, and was a by-product of the Boer War.

8.6 The Growth of Anglo-German Hostility

KAISER WILLIAM II

William was Queen Victoria's grandson and Edward VII's nephew. He was jealous of the size of the British Empire. His colonial ambitions led to his anti-British attitude. Meanwhile, Britain feared Germany's search for colonies. Germany replaced Russia and France as the major threat to Britain's interests.

THE GERMAN NAVY

In 1892 Admiral von Tirpitz persuaded William II that Germany needed a large navy. In 1897 the Reichstag passed the first Naval Bill, and in 1900 a Navy Law doubled the size of Germany's fleet.

The British feared that a German Navy would be used to fight Britain. Admiral Fisher led the British demand for an improved British Navy to safeguard Britain against Germany, and in 1906 a new battleship, the *Dreadnought*, was launched. It was faster and stronger than any battleship in the world.

The Germans built nine Dreadnought-class ships between 1909 and 1911. Britain finally built 18, although the popular cry had been, 'We want eight and we won't wait'. The Kiel Canal linking the Baltic and the North Sea was deepened and widened to take the new Dreadnoughts. It was ready exactly six weeks before war started.

GERMAN TRADE

By 1900 German industrial power was overtaking that of Britain. British exports fell because of competition from German goods—and there was a rise in unemployment. German imports to Britain led to a fall in the demand for British goods, and to more unemployment.

GERMANY AND THE BALKANS

By 1900 Germany had replaced Russia as the country to be feared in this region because of:
- The building of the Berlin–Baghdad railway;
- German offers to train the Turkish army;
- German support for Austrian ambitions (see above).

PROPAGANDA IN BOTH COUNTRIES

The German press demanded a German Empire, more trade, a larger Navy and, in 1899, military help for the Boers.

In Britain the press reported on the anti-British policies of the Germans—in building a Navy as a threat in the Balkans and in supporting the Boers.

The ill-feeling in both countries was used by the politicians as aids to their policies.

8.7 Britain's Ententes with France and Russia

THE ANGLO-FRENCH ENTENTE, 1904

France and Britain feared Germany. Both countries had almost come to war in 1898 (see Unit 5). Delcassé, French Foreign Minister, wanted Britain to join France and Russia in an anti-German alliance. Lansdowne, British Foreign Minister, knew that Britain needed a friend in the West, just as she had Japan for a friend in the Far East.

State visits by Edward VII to Paris and President Loubet to London created a mood of goodwill. In 1904 the two countries agreed to settle their past differences:
- France recognized Britain's control of Egypt;
- Britain accepted Morocco as a French zone of influence;
- long-standing disagreements about Newfoundland fisheries were settled and would not cause future dispute.

The Entente was not an alliance; it said nothing about what either country would do if the other went to war.

Military talks between the army chiefs of staff of both countries were allowed. These led to the discussion of how each country would use its armies in the event of a war—

with, of course, Germany. In this way the Entente changed its nature without politicians always being aware of the change.

THE ANGLO-RUSSIAN ENTENTE, 1907

Delcassé, having arranged the Entente in 1904, had also wanted Britain to become friendly with France's ally, Russia. Britain's fears of Russian power declined, because Germany and Austria were the new threat in the Balkans, and Russia's defeat by Japan in 1904–5 (Unit 6) lessened fears of Russian ability to affect British interests.

In 1907 an Entente was signed in which the two countries settled their past differences: in Afghanistan, Russia kept her trading interests but agreed not to threaten British India; in Persia the two countries agreed on their spheres of influence. Russia became the dominant influence in the north around Tehran. Britain had control of the south, including the rich oil deposits. There would be a neutral zone between the two—to lessen the danger of conflict.

As with the Anglo-French Entente, this one said nothing about what would happen in the event of a war.

8.8 Crises, 1905–11 (Fig. 8.8)

THE FIRST MOROCCAN CRISIS, 1905–6

William II was annoyed that Germany had not been consulted about the Anglo-French division of North Africa. In 1905, the first Moroccan Crisis, he went to Tangier and declared that Germany would help the Sultan of Morocco to resist French attempts to control his country. He demanded an international conference to reconsider the affairs of North Africa.

The French feared war. Delcassé resigned in protest when France agree to hold an international conference. In April 1906 the Conference met at Algeciras in Spain. Britain and the USA supported France. France was given control of the Moroccan Bank, the customs and excise system, the supply of arms and the maintenance of a police force.

The Entente was strengthened by this diplomatic 'victory' over Germany. Britain and Germany were even more hostile to each other.

THE EASTERN QUESTION, 1908

In Unit 4 we saw how Austria took advantage of Turkish weakness to annex Bosnia and Herzegovina. Russia was in

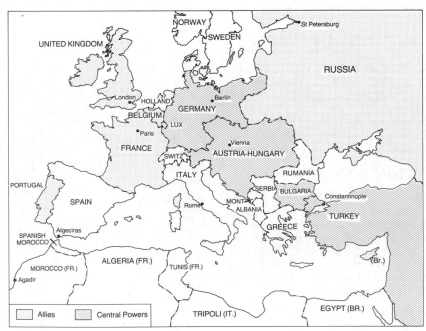

Fig. 8.8 European camps and crises

no condition to oppose her. France would not agree to a declaration of war over this issue.

THE SECOND MOROCCAN CRISIS, 1911

In 1911 there were a number of risings against the inefficient ruler of Morocco. France sent an army to Fez, the capital, to restore order. The Kaiser, fearing that France might annex Morocco, sent a gunboat, the *Panther*, to Agadir on the west coast. He claimed that he wanted to protect German businessmen in Morocco—but there were none there. He was testing the Anglo-French Entente again.

The British Foreign Minister, Grey, feared that Germany might be going to build a naval base at Agadir. The British Chancellor of the Exchequer, Lloyd George, declared that Britain might have to go to war to stop this threat to her naval and trading interests. The Germans demanded an apology for this warlike speech—but did not get one. The British navy was put on a war footing.

However, as in 1905, a Conference settled the issue. It met in Paris. France gave Germany a strip of the French Congo, and Germany agreed to France having a free hand in Morocco.

The Entente had once again been shown to work. Indeed, it became stronger. Talks were held between the chiefs of the naval staffs of both countries. It was agreed that:
► the French fleet should be concentrated in the Mediterranean to guard British and French interests;
► the British fleet should be concentrated in the North Sea to guard British interests and the northern coast of France.

You will see that this almost made the Entente into an alliance. Could Britain remain neutral if France were at war? If she did, what would happen to a German naval attack on the French ports on the northern coasts? The French fleet would not be there to guard French interests.

8.9 Events in the Balkans

In 1912–13, Balkan countries were involved in two wars (see Unit 4). These wars were settled by international conferences. They left Serbia and Austria hostile to each other.

AND SO TO WAR, JULY—AUGUST, 1914

The Austrian Archduke was killed at Sarajevo, 28 June 1914 (see Unit 4). Statesmen assumed this crisis would be settled by a conference. Austria wanted to use this as a chance to crush Serbia. On 5 July William II told Austria that she could count on German support in whatever she did. On 23 July Austria sent·a series of demands (an ultimatum) to Serbia. If accepted, they would have virtually ended Serbian independence. On 24 July Serbia accepted most of the demands and asked for time to consider the rest. She asked that the dispute be sent to the International Court at The Hague.

On 25 July Austria refused the Serbian request. Russia announced that she would have to start mobilizing her forces. On 28 July, Austria declared war on Serbia. On 30 July, Russia ordered partial mobilization. Germany demanded that this be called off. On 1 August Russia refused to do as Germany asked. Germany then declared war on Russia, which was followed by her declaration of war on France on 3 August.

8.10 Plans for the War

WAR BY TIMETABLE

The dates listed above indicate the almost inevitable way in which the nations went to war. This was less the fault of the politicians in 1914 than of the system they had allowed to be built up. Vast armies had been created in various countries. Plans for their use in the event of war had been made out.

Success in war depended on speed of attack. To achieve this speed, military plans were linked to railway timetables. Mobilization of forces meant that men had to travel to military centres by rail. Once mobilized, armies had to be got to the front as quickly as possible—also by rail.

Once mobilization had started, then the politicians were in the hands of their military staffs.

THE SCHLIEFFEN PLAN (Fig. 9.1)

Count von Schlieffen had been Chief of the German General Staff between 1891 and 1906.

The alliance between France and Russia forced Germany to plan for a war on two fronts. In 1905 Schlieffen drew up a plan to knock France out of the war in a few weeks before turning to fight Russia. German armies would advance into France through Belgium, which was largely undefended. They would then swing around Paris to link up with German armies attacking from the south.

BRITAIN AND BELGIUM

In 1839 Britain and other nations had signed the Treaty of London to maintain the neutrality of Belgium. Germany invaded Belgium on 3 August. Britain demanded a withdrawal, but Germany refused. The Kaiser and his Ministers could not believe that Britain would go to war over the 1839 Treaty. The German Chancellor, Bethmann-Hollwegg, dismissed it as 'a scrap of paper'. On 4 August Britain declared war.

BRITAIN AND FRANCE

Some Ministers wanted Britain to declare war as soon as France was involved. They argued that the results of the naval talks (see above) imposed a moral obligation on Britain. However, other Ministers did not agree. Indeed two resigned after the British declaration of war on 4 August and the invasion of Belgium. Many others might have done so if the government had gone to war in support of her French and Russian friends. Thus the Schlieffen Plan brought a united Britain to war.

Unit 8 Summary

► Bismarck's foreign policy and system of alliances.
► The Franco-Russian Alliance, 1892–5.
► Britain and the two 'Armed Camps'.
► The growth of Anglo-German hostility.
► Britain's ententes with France and Russia.
► Crises, 1905–11: Algeciras, Bosnia and Agadir.
► Sarajevo, 28 June 1914 and war by timetable.
► The Schlieffen Plan.

9 THE FIRST WORLD WAR, 1914–18

9.1 The Schlieffen Plan, 1914

Schlieffen had drawn up his famous 'Plan' for the quick defeat of France. He thought Russia could not become involved in any war for some months after its outbreak because of the time needed for full mobilization of the Russian army. He thought that Russian military administration was highly inefficient.

THE PLAN

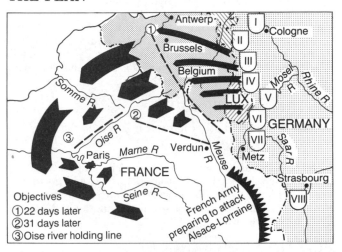

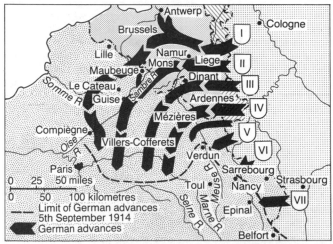

Fig. 9.1 The Schlieffen Plan

The French would want to take Alsace and Lorraine (see Unit 1). They would expect the main German attack to come from the Metz area of Germany. Verdun was made into a strongly fortified city to withstand a German advance.

Schlieffen's plan differed from French expectations:

▶ the main German attack would come from the north;
▶ seven German armies were to drive through Belgium and northern France, sweep around Paris (which would surrender) and link with armies advancing through the central region;
▶ Verdun would then be attacked from the front and rear—and would surrender.

There was a strict timetable to which each of the armies had to stick. This is illustrated in Fig. 9.1. The final link-up

between the various armies was to be completed within 48 days.

Once France was beaten, Germany would then switch armies to the Russian front and defeat that Eastern enemy. Moltke, chief of the General Staff in July 1914, had to put the Schlieffen Plan into practice.

THE FAILURE OF THE PLAN, JULY–AUGUST 1914

Russia mobilized more quickly than had been expected. Some German troops had to be transferred to the Eastern Front from the attack through Belgium, where Belgian troops fought bravely and checked the advance.

Britain entered the war on 4 August. The Schlieffen Plan had not taken that into consideration. Within days the British Expeditionary Force, commanded by Sir John French, was in Belgium. Its task, agreed with the French (Unit 8), was to defend Mons.

Mons was directly in the path of the German advance and here the British had their first taste of the War. British rifle fire was so rapid that the Germans thought the troops had machine guns. British losses were very high. Some regiments (e.g. the Cheshire) lost almost all their men. However, the German advance was delayed. British resistance at Mons and the slow retreat after the battle gave the French more time to prepare.

At Ypres another army, commanded by Sir Douglas Haig, made another stand in another bloodbath.

Kluck, the German commander in France, saw that he could not keep to the Schlieffen Plan. His armies (weakened when Moltke sent troops to Russia) had been too long delayed by the British resistance.

Kluck changed the plan of attack (Fig. 9.1): instead of going around Paris the Germans turned south (to the east of Paris). This left the Channel ports along the coast free from attack—and enabled British reinforcements to get to France.

Joffre was the commander of the French troops which rallied on the northern banks of the River Marne. Sir John French commanded the British who first held the Germans along the Marne, then drove them back—in some places across the River Aisne.

9.2 Trench Warfare, the Western Front

By December 1914 the opposing armies were dug in, and trenches ran from Switzerland to the Channel coast (Fig. 42.3B).

Life in the trenches was very hard. Rain turned the trenches into muddy pathways along which troops moved into positions. Men slept where they could in their uniforms. Cooking facilities were scarce—armies lived off tinned food. Dead bodies littered the space between the opposing trenches ('no-man's land'). Packs of rats attacked men—dead and alive—and their supplies.

Defending the trenches was fairly easy. Massed rolls of barbed wire were laid in front of the trenches. This made enemy advance very difficult and slow. Machine guns allowed gunners in the defending trench to wipe out large numbers of advancing troops.

Attacking the trenches was difficult and costly: an

artillery bombardment was made by large guns in the rear. Thousands of shells were fired on the enemy lines. It was hoped that this would frighten the enemy, smash the barbed wire and make advance easier. However, such bombardments only warned the enemy, who were then better prepared when the attacking troops jumped from their trenches and advanced across 'no-man's-land'. The advancing troops were normally weighed down with their packs, trenching tools, ammunition bandoliers, Mills bombs and other weapons.

GAINS AND LOSSES

The generals on both sides wanted to break through the enemy lines. Although their attacks never worked, they insisted on yet more. Major battles took place in 1915 at Ypres, Loos and Vimy Ridge; 1916 at Verdun (see below) and the Somme (see below); 1917 Ypres again (in the Battle of Passchendaele), Vimy Ridge, Cambrai (where massed tanks were first used) and Messines; 1918 the Marne (again) and St Quentin.

Verdun was the fortress town built for the defence of the Rhine (Fig. 9.1). It was of little real value once trench warfare had become the pattern of things. Indeed, the French ought to have abandoned it and straightened out their lines of defence. However, the French government refused to allow a withdrawal, fearing a panic if such a fortified town were handed over to the Germans. The Germans realized this and made a series of heavy attacks from 21 February 1916 to the end of June.

The Germans lost 281,000 men in these attacks; the French lost 315,000 men. The commander of Verdun, Pétain, became a national hero. His slogan, 'Ils ne passeront pas' ('They shall not pass'), became a popular declaration of French determination.

The Somme was Britain's most costly battle. It started on 1 July 1916; 60,000 men were killed out of a force of 100,000 men. Many more were seriously injured; still more drowned in the sea of mud created by the collapse of the drainage system under artillery bombardment.

The battle ended in the middle of November 1916. Britain had suffered 400,000 casualties in this 'graveyard of Kitchener's army'. German and French losses were equally heavy—and almost nothing had been gained.

9.3 New Weapons

To try to break the deadlock both sides introduced new weapons.

Poison gas was first used by the Germans at the second battle of Ypres (1915).

The tank was invented by the British. It was first used on the Somme in 1916. Travelling at about 3 miles per hour, most got bogged down in the mud, while others were easily destroyed by enemy artillery. Even those which broke through the enemy lines were captured by the Germans, because they had got too far ahead of supporting troops. Only in 1917 (at Cambrai) were tanks used properly; they proved to be a very effective weapon.

Mining of enemy lines by sappers (the nickname for engineers) was developed as an underground method of attack. Men burrowed beneath 'no-man's-land' and the enemy lines, where they planted loads of explosives. When these were blown up, the enemy trench system and the soldiers in it were destroyed. But such activities were often and easily discovered and the sappers killed before they could complete their work.

THE AEROPLANE

At the outbreak of war this was an inefficient, slow and unarmed machine which, at best, could only go at about 70 m.p.h. At first generals used aeroplanes to spot enemy movement, but at Verdun planes were used to support the German attack, and on the Somme they were used to bomb enemy positions.

In 1917 the Germans developed the first two-engined bomber. By 1918 both sides had developed aircraft industries to produce stronger engines, and by the end of the war there were four-engined bombers. In 1919, a British aircraft made the first Atlantic crossing.

The Germans were the first to work out how to fire a machine-gun through the revolving propeller. A Fokker EI was fitted with interrupter gear in 1915; by 1916 the British and French had also learned to do this and the aeroplane became slightly more efficient. But in general aircraft played little part in the War.

Five Zeppelins bombed eastern ports and London.

9.4 The Eastern Front

In August 1914 Russian troops invaded East Prussia (Fig. 1.2). Generals Samsonov and Rennenkampf won small victories and planned to march on to Berlin (see Unit 10).

German troops were withdrawn from France and defeated the Russians at the Battle of Tannenberg, where 90,000 Russians were captured. At the Battle of the Masurian Lakes the Germans again defeated the Russians and drove them from East Prussia.

At Lemberg the Russians defeated the Austrians, and many Slavs in the Austrian army surrendered without fighting.

In 1915–16, the Germans drove the Russians back. Two million Russians died as they retreated. In June 1916 Brusilov launched a series of attacks and defeated the Austrians—but lost a million men. These losses played a part in the movement against the Tsar (Unit 10).

GALLIPOLI

The Allies (Britain and France) sent munitions to Russia via the northern ports of Murmansk and Archangel.

Turkey entered the war on Germany's side (October 1914). This gave the German–Turkish allies control of the Dardanelles, linking the Mediterranean and the Black Sea. The Allies wanted to gain control of the Dardanelles so that supplies could more easily be sent to the Russians.

The naval attack, March 1915

A fleet of old battleships tried to get through the Dardanelles, but several were sunk by mines and the plan was abandoned. The Turks defending the Dardanelles had almost run out of munitions and might have given in to another attack.

The military attack, April 1915

A small force commanded by **Sir Ian Hamilton** tried to capture **Gallipoli** as a step to an attack on Constantinople from the rear. Hamilton delayed his attack, and the Turks had time to prepare. Mustapha Kemal led the Turkish defence.

In April 1915 British, Australian and New Zealand troops (the ANZACs) landed and tried to climb the steep cliffs of the straits. For eight months they made a series of costly attacks. Finally in December 1915 the government called off the venture and the troops were withdrawn from Gallipoli.

SALONIKA (Fig. 4.1)

The British failure led Bulgaria to enter the war on Germany's side (October 1915). She wanted revenge on Serbia for the defeats of 1913 (see Unit 4). Serbia was quickly defeated.

The Allies, having withdrawn from the Dardanelles, sent 600,000 men to Salonika to show they had not abandoned Serbia. This army suffered from a shortage of food and supplies and many men died of malaria and other diseases.

PALESTINE

The Turks threatened to invade British-controlled Egypt. The British attacked the Turks to prevent such an invasion.

The British advance into Mesopotamia was meant to protect British oil supplies on the Persian Gulf. At Kut-el-Amara the Turks defeated the British (1916).

T. E. Lawrence ('Lawrence of Arabia') played a part in bringing the Arab tribes on to Britain's side against their Turkish overlords. While their part in the fighting was useful, the British had to face the problem of paying the price which Lawrence had promised—Arab national independence (see Unit 13).

In 1917 the British and their Arab allies defeated the Turks in a series of battles. They captured Baghdad and, in December 1917, General Allenby captured Jerusalem. His entry into Damascus in September 1918 marked the end of fighting in this region.

9.5 The War at Sea

THE ROLE OF THE BRITISH NAVY

The navy was to ensure a free flow of goods and troops to and from Britain, to blockade enemy ports, to keep food and other supplies from reaching the enemy. Food shortages in Germany in 1918 played a part in the demand for an end to the war. The Navy was also intended to guard colonies and other possessions from attack, and to capture enemy colonies.

THE GERMAN NAVY

This Navy had been built as a challenge to Britain (see Unit 8).

The widening and deepening of the Kiel Canal allowed the Navy to get from its bases and into the North Sea and to escape back to its bases whenever it needed to.

The Germans won a victory at the Battle of Coronel (1914) off the coast of Chile but suffered a major defeat at the Battle of the Falkland Islands where Admiral Von Spee's fleet was almost wiped out.

THE BATTLE OF JUTLAND, 1916

There had been small battles in the North Sea. The Battles of Heligoland Bight (1914) and of the Dogger Bank (1915) were indecisive; neither side could claim victory.

The German High Fleet only sailed once into the North Sea. In one day's fighting at Jutland in May 1916 a British naval force led by Admiral Jellicoe had a running battle with the German fleet led by Admiral Scheer. Once again the battle was indecisive. Both sides claimed partial victory:

▶ the British argued that the German retreat to their bases marked a British victory—certainly the German High Fleet never came to battle again;

▶ the Germans claimed a victory because the British had suffered much heavier losses. Their fleet had better armour to protect their ships, better armaments which inflicted the damage on British ships, and better technical and naval awareness.

SUBMARINE WARFARE

The submarine (or underwater boat) was a weapon for attacking British and other Allied shipping. In 1915 the Germans declared an all-out submarine campaign. Their submarines sank not only Allied shipping but any ship suspected of trading with the Allies.

There were also attacks on passenger-carrying shipping. Perhaps the most important ship that was sunk was the British Cunard liner, the *Lusitania*, sunk off the coast of Southern Ireland; 1198 people died, including 124 Americans. The Americans protested, and the Germans called off their all-out campaign.

Attacks on Allied shipping continued. Various methods were tried to halt the success of the submarine. Echo-sounders were fitted to Royal Naval protection ships. It was hoped that these would then be able to discover the submarines before they could attack merchant shipping.

Ships were also fitted with equipment to fire depth charges, which exploded underwater and, if well-aimed, damaged or destroyed submarines.

Q-ships were merchant ships manned by Royal Naval crews and carrying hidden guns. These ships might tempt submarines to attack on the surface—when the naval guns could damage or destroy them.

9.6 The Second All-out Campaign, 1917

The German generals, led by Ludendorff, argued in 1917 that their government had to make a decisive push for victory. The heavy losses on the Western Front and the food shortages at home could not be allowed to continue for much longer.

In January 1917 the Germans announced the return to the all-out campaign. This was very successful. In February 1917, 266 ships were sunk; in March another 338 and in April another 430.

In April 1917 Britain had only six weeks supply of wheat (for flour) left. Britain might be starved into surrender.

The convoy system was forced on a reluctant Navy by Prime Minister Lloyd George. Instead of merchant ships sailing alone, they were organized into groups which could be guarded by Royal Naval destroyers. It was hoped that this would make it harder for submarines to attack merchant shipping.

This system succeeded. Fewer British ships were lost. By March 1918 German submarines were suffering very heavy losses; more were being sunk than were being built.

9.7 The USA Enters the War, April 1917

President Wilson had been re-elected in 1916 after a campaign in which he promised to keep America out of the war. It was the resumption of the all-out submarine campaign which helped to change American opinion in favour of the Allies.

Allied propaganda also changed American opinion: the Germans were shown as cruel attackers on small Belgium; stories appeared in American newspapers of the savage behaviour of German troops; the cruelty of the submarine campaign was highlighted: women and children passengers drowning as a result of an attack were shown to be victims of German barbarity. Also, cartoons drawn to show German savagery appeared in popular papers and magazines.

American troops did not play a large or immediate role in France. But America's entry into the war ensured a continual supply of food and the promise that, if the war went on, there would be a large number of fresh troops on the Allied side.

9.8 The Germans Defeated

In March 1918 the war was finely balanced. The Allies had gained the support of the Americans; the Germans had forced Russia out of the war and this allowed the transfer of troops from the Eastern Front. The submarine campaign was affecting life in Britain, while the British blockade was affecting life in Germany.

Heavy losses on the Western Front affected both sides. French troops mutinied after Verdun; German troops were badly affected by the gloomy news from home. Ludendorff, the German commander, decided to make an all-out attack in France to end the war quickly.

THE GERMAN ATTACK

On 21 March 1918 the British at Arras and Amiens were overrun but managed to regroup. By 31 March they were holding the Germans.

In April, the attack switched to the north. Again, there were battles in Flanders fields around Ypres. Again, the British held the Germans, and the breakthrough did not take place.

In May, the Germans attacked the French on the Aisne. Again they had initial victories—the French retreated to the Marne. The road to Paris was again open. But this attack was halted with the help of the American troops, a British army with an Australian corps led by General Monash, and French determination to resist.

THE ALLIED COUNTER-ATTACK

In July, Allied troops came under the control of a Supreme Commander-in-Chief, Marshal Foch. He ordered a series of counter-attacks along the front from the Marne to Amiens. For the first time the German army broke.

In August, at Amiens the British defeated the Germans—in what Ludendorff called 'the blackest day in the history of the German army'. In September, Allied attacks continued to succeed. The British won victories in Flanders around Ypres; the Americans won victories in the south around Verdun. The French won victories in the centre. The Germans were forced to give up their line of defences known as the Hindenburg Line.

GERMAN COLLAPSE

From Salonika Allied forces advanced into Bulgaria, Serbia and Austria. Bulgaria asked for peace on 29 September 1918, the Austrians on 3 November.

Allenby was victorious in the Middle East. In Italy the Austrian forces collapsed.

In Germany there were uprisings:

▶ on 4 October Ludendorff asked for a truce in the fighting on the Western Front. The Allied reply was Wilson's Fourteen Points (Fig. 12.1).
▶ fighting continued when Germany rejected these points.
▶ In Kiel, sailors of the High Fleet mutinied.
▶ In Berlin and other cities, people rose against the Kaiser's government which had failed to deliver the promised victories, and which, in 1918, could not provide food.

Further Allied victories led to a major change in Berlin. A new Chancellor, Prince Max of Baden, persuaded the Kaiser to abdicate (9 November 1918) in the hope that this would prevent a Bolshevik revolution in Germany. German representatives went to meet French representatives at Compiègne to discuss an end to the fighting.

THE ARMISTICE

The Germans hoped that the peace would be based on the Fourteen Points which they had earlier rejected. The Allies argued that this rejection allowed them to dictate a different set of terms.

The German fleet had to be surrendered and her army had to leave all occupied territory. The Allied blockade would continue until a Peace Treaty had been signed. The left bank of the Rhine had to be evacuated and the right bank of the Rhine had to be demilitarized.

A small minority of Germans wanted to fight on. However, Ludendorff and other army leaders did not want to see their forces humiliated. They advised acceptance of the harsh terms. Prince Max and other politicians did not want the civilian population to suffer any longer. They feared a Bolshevik revolution. They too advised acceptance of the harsh terms.

The Armistice was signed, and at 11.00 a.m. on 11 November 1918 the Great War came to an end.

▨ Unit 9 Summary ▨

▶ The failure of the Schlieffen Plan.
▶ Life in the trenches.
▶ Weapon development, on land, at sea and in the air.
▶ The Eastern Front: Gallipoli, Salonika and Palestine.
▶ The war at sea: submarine campaigns.
▶ The defeat of Germany: the Armistice, 11 November 1918.

---

10 RUSSIA, 1914–28

▨ 10.1 Russian Attitudes to War ▨

SUPPORT FOR THE WAR, 1914

The majority of the Tsar's ministers hoped that war would put an end to criticism of the government.

Most radicals welcomed war. They hoped that the Tsar, to gain the support of the people, would make concessions.

The Russian masses rallied to the support of 'the Little Father' in a wave of patriotic fervour.

OPPOSITION TO THE WAR, 1914

Agrarian reformers continuing the work of Stolypin (see Unit 3) wanted a period of peace. They remembered Stolypin's warning: 'Our internal situation does not permit us to pursue an aggressive foreign policy.'

Some ministers remembered the disastrous consequences of the defeat in the Russo-Japanese War, 1904–5 (see Unit 3).

Rasputin, 'the evil monk', warned the Tsar: 'With the war will come the end of Russia.'

The Bolsheviks, led by the exiled Lenin, opposed Russia's entry into the war, condemning it as 'a capitalists' war' which would bring no benefits to the working class.

▨ 10.2 Successes and Failures, 1914–16

SPEEDY MOBILIZATION AND IMMEDIATE SUCCESS

On 30 July 1914, the Tsar signed the order for mobilizing troops because Austria had declared war on Serbia. On 31

July 1914 posters appeared calling up Russian reservists, and on 1 August 1914 Germany declared war on Russia.

Russian troops were the first into action. Cossack regiments of the regular army invaded East Prussia. Victories were won at Stalluponen and Gumbinnen.

Many Russians imagined that, when the millions of reservists were called up in late August-September, the Russian 'steamroller' would trundle on to Berlin. Victory seemed certain.

DEFEATS

On August 26–28 the Germans defeated Samsonov at Tannenberg. About 90,000 Russians were captured. Samsonov committed suicide.

On September 9–12 the Germans attacked Rennenkampf at the Masurian Lakes and drove the Russians from East Prussia.

STALEMATE

The Austrians were less successful than the Germans. At Lemberg, superiority in numbers enabled the Russians to defeat the Austrians. Many Slavs in the Austrian-Hungarian armies deserted.

Hindenburg took command of German forces. Warsaw was attacked—but held by the Russians. As for Lodz, three German divisions were lucky to escape.

The Germans withdrew some of their best forces from France to help to end the fighting in the east.

1915–16

The Russians fought on a front 1300 km (800 miles) long. The peasants in the Russian army fought bravely against German artillery and machine gun fire. In retreating, the Russians lost 2 million men.

Russian industry managed to produce more war goods. Between 1914 and 1916 production of rifles increased by 200 per cent, of artillery by 400 per cent and of machine guns by 300 per cent.

THE BRUSILOV OFFENSIVE, 1916

In June 1916 General Brusilov counter-attacked. The Austrians lost many men in this attack. A million Russians died; another million deserted.

10.3 The Effects of War

The growth of criticism in 1916 was caused by Russian industry being less efficient than German industry and unable to produce weapons of the same quality or in the same quantities. Russian generals had also been incompetent, and younger officers became critical.

The Tsarina was seen as having too much power: when Prime Minister Kokovstov criticized Rasputin, the Tsarina persuaded the Tsar to sack him (January 1915). His 75-year-old successor lasted only until the middle of 1916. He was replaced by Rasputin's favourite, Stürmer, an incompetent and corrupt junior minister.

The Duma was led by Rodzianko, whose son was a junior officer under Brusilov. He asked the Tsar to form a ministry based on the Duma. This, he claimed, might gain wide support from the people. However, the Tsarina persuaded her husband to 'remember the autocracy' and to reject this offer of help from 'a democratic Duma'.

Generals were dismissed or changed to other posts because 'Rasputin has had a vision'.

THE RUSSIAN PEOPLE, 1916

Food shortages

Food supplies became scarce because the Ukraine, the largest corn producing area, was lost, and because the railway system could not cope. Many miles of line had been destroyed at the front. The army used it to transport munitions, soldiers, the wounded and food and other supplies; industry used it to transport raw materials and coal, finished products and munitions; farmers used it to bring in fertilizers, machinery and animal feed and to take away their food products; town merchants used it to bring in corn, meat and other farm produce.

Farms were less productive, because:

▶ many young workers had gone into the forces. The old and the women left behind could not do all the work.
▶ many farmers refused to sell their corn in the towns. What could they buy for the money they got?
▶ corn prices were fixed by the government. Other prices were free. The farmer resented being asked to pay higher prices for consumer goods.

Food price rises

The government was unable to control prices charged by merchants in towns. Skilled workers received higher wages—and could cope with the higher prices for food, but most workers were unskilled. They could not cope with the increases in rents and food prices. Thus for many people there was a fall in living standards as the cost of living rose more quickly than did wages.

The weather

November–December 1916 was unusually severe. This added to the misery of the millions of workers.

THE BEGINNING OF THE END, NOVEMBER 1916–FEBRUARY 1917

Shadow Ministries were set up with the Tsar's approval by members of the Duma. A Council of National Defence had Ministers of Industry, Trade, Fuel, Agriculture and Food Supplies, Transport, Navy and Finance. But these 'Ministries' had no member of the government on them. They had no real power.

The All-Russian Union of the Zemstvo (see Unit 3): delegates from various local zemstvos formed committees to try to help the war effort. They were in touch with similar committees set up by trade unions and local government officers. But all these had no real power.

Political criticism at meetings of these committees and 'Ministries' was aimed at the Tsarina's power and policies, Rasputin's influence and behaviour, the incompetence of the government, and the failure of the generals.

The Tsar, foolishly, left the capital for Mogilev, where he took control of the army. This gave the Tsarina even more power.

Food queues were commonplace. Occasionally there were riots when supplies ran out or prices were very high. Cossacks loyal to the Tsar put down these riots.

Rasputin was murdered in December 1916 by aristocrats who hoped to free the Tsar from 'the evil influence'.

Mutinies in the army became frequent. Men wanted to get away from the incompetent generals and the constant defeats.

10.4 The February Revolution and the Fall of the Romanovs

THE BACKGROUND TO THE FEBRUARY REVOLUTION

In 1751 most countries reformed their calendars to take account of the fact that, until then, there had been no leap years so that the world had, as it were, 'lost eleven days'. The Russians had not made that reform. This explains why the Russians write about the February Revolution and we write about a March Revolution.

18 February Strike at the large Petilov steelworks in Petrograd. Men demand a 50 per cent increase in wages.

19–21 February Many other workers join the strike.

23 February Rioting at bread queues; striking workers join in. Police and troops attack the rioters.

24 February Thousands demonstrate in Petrograd. Cossacks begin to show sympathy.

24–25 February The election of the first workers' councils (or soviets). Strikers joined by middle classes.

25 February Workers occupy factories; police do not always come on to the streets; Cossacks attack a mounted policeman attacking a flag-carrying demonstrator. Said one man: 'I knew then that the Revolution had started.'

25–26 February The Tsarina tells the Tsar (by letter) that all is under control except for a handful of rioters. The Tsar sends an order to army commander, Petrograd, to suppress all disturbances.

26 February Troops attack and rioters disperse; Prime Minister orders the Duma to dissolve.

27 February Duma remained in session. Meeting of the Petrograd Soviet consisting of delegates from factories, shops, offices, schools, and soldiers' and peasants' delegates. Duma and Soviet both in Tauride Palace.

27 February Kerensky, leader of the Peasant Party in the Duma, demands the Tsar's removal, by force if necessary. Soldiers join the demonstrators.

THE OVERTHROW OF THE TSAR

27 February Duma still meeting; Army commander, Petrograd, declares martial law—but staff cannot find glue to stick up the notices. Tsar's ministers meet at the Admiralty building but go home when electricity fails.

28 February The Tsar left Mogilev to return to Petrograd. Train diverted to Pskov 160 km (100 miles) from the capital. Generals and ministers tell Tsar that a revolution is taking place. The Tsar thinks of abdicating and naming his son as successor. On 2 March he signs a decree of abdication, naming his brother Michael as successor. Michael refuses the post.

3 March Tsar abdicates. This was the end of the Romanov dynasty.

The Duma chose a set of new Ministers: Prince Lvov, of the Union of Zemstvo, was Prime Minister; Miliukov, of the Cadets, was Foreign Minister; Kerensky was Minister of Justice.

The Petrograd Soviet continued to meet. It made no effort to take power, although it issued Soviet Order No. 1 saying that orders to soldiers had to be approved by the Soviet. Some of the 3000 members of the Soviet were also in the Provisional Government—Kerensky being Deputy Chairman of the Soviet.

■■ 10.5 The Provisional Government

The Provisional Government announced a programme for future reform, and decided to continue the war against Germany. Both actions showed that the Government was out of touch with the feelings of the people. The majority of soldiers did not want to fight; the town workers wanted immediate action on food supplies, prices, working conditions and wages; and the peasants demanded more land.

The feelings of the people were shown by:
▶ the revolt of sailors at the naval base at Kronstadt;
▶ mutinies in the army when officers were shot;
▶ attacks on noblemen's estates;
▶ strikes for an eight hour day (May 1917);
▶ an increased number of local soviets;
▶ growing hostility between the Government and the delegates at the Petrograd Soviet.

■■ 10.6 Lenin and the Bolshevik Revolution

LENIN'S RETURN, APRIL 1917

Lenin was in exile in Switzerland when the Tsar fell. Because the Germans wanted to get Russia out of the war, they paid him to return to Russia in a sealed train. His first speech called for a wider 'socialist' revolution.

On 7 April, in the Bolshevik paper, *Pravda*, Lenin outlined his policies. His April Theses urged his followers:
▶ not to support the Provisional Government;
▶ to try to create a Republic of workers' and peasants' Soviets;
▶ to work for the nationalization of all land, workers' control of all factories and farms and an end to the war.

THE BOLSHEVIKS VERSUS THE PROVISIONAL GOVERNMENT

The Bolsheviks were only a small group. They had been outvoted in the All-Russian Council of Soviets on the war issue.

From April onwards Lenin's followers went among the soldiers and people in Petrograd. The soldiers had to be shown that an immediate peace with Germany would be for their good; the people had to be won over by promises of 'bread' and social reform.

In June 1917 Brusilov launched another offensive against the Germans. By 2 July he reported failure and the loss of 40,000 men. These losses were the last straw. The army retreated in panic.

In Petrograd the news of the defeat led to widespread rioting ('the July Days'). Some members of the Petrograd Soviet wanted to take power. The non-Bolsheviks on the Soviet wanted to wait for elections to be held; Lenin and the Bolsheviks wanted things to get even worse before seizing power.

The government used the rioting as an excuse for an attack on the Bolsheviks. In July 1917 the Bolsheviks' HQ was attacked and *Pravda* closed down, Trotsky and other leaders were arrested, Lenin shaved off his beard and went into hiding.

At this point Kerensky became Prime Minister. A Menshevik (Unit 3), he was not a revolutionary; his war aims were supported by the middle class.

THE KORNILOV AFFAIR

Many officers thought Kerensky too weak a leader. When General Kornilov, Commander-in-Chief, marched his army against Petrograd, 'to hang the German supporters with Lenin at their head', Kerensky dismissed him (27 August).

On 7 September Kornilov demanded Kerensky's resignation. Kornilov continued his march to Petrograd. Kerensky appealed to the Bolsheviks for their help. They came on to the steets of Petrograd; some, working on the railway system, switched the trains carrying Kornilov's army into sidings. He never reached Petrograd.

Kornilov was arrested without any bloodshed. His plot and its failure put the Bolsheviks in a stronger position.

LENIN AND THE OVERTHROW OF THE GOVERNMENT

The Germans supplied Lenin with money to help to overthrow Kerensky—and to end Russia's part in the war.

Lenin got Trotsky to train a small, highly skilled body of Red Guards of former officers and soldiers. He also trained industrial workers to seize key points in Petrograd when he was ready.

Lenin published his campaign of 'Peace by your own feet', which called on soldiers to mutiny, and 'Land by your own hand', which called on peasants to riot.

Kerensky tried to take action against Lenin. But his troops refused to obey him; sailors on the cruiser, *Aurora*, came out in favour of Lenin and threatened to bombard the capital.

THE OCTOBER (NOVEMBER) REVOLUTION

25 October Orders were given for the Red Guards to take the telephone exchange and the State Bank. The Government met at the Tauride Palace.

25 October, evening The Bolsheviks demanded the surrender of the government. The *Aurora* fired blanks to frighten ministers and signal the Bolshevik revolution.

The government was guarded by a handful of Cossacks, some officer cadets and a battalion of women. But the Cossacks deserted, the officers surrendered and although the women were ready to fight, they were persuaded it would be useless.

26–27 October During the night the Bolsheviks attacked the Palace and arrested the ministers. During that night the 650 delegates of the All-Russian Congress of Soviets came together for their second Congress; 390 of these were Bolsheviks. The Mensheviks and others condemned the attack on the Provisional Government.

Trotsky, Commander of the Red Guards, told the Mensheviks 'You may go . . . to the garbage heap of history'.

LENIN IN POWER, 1917

The Congress of Soviets gave power to the 15 People's Commissars—all of whom were Bolsheviks: Lenin was chairman of the Council of People's Commissars. It passed a decree to seek peace with Austria and Germany. It proclaimed the nationalization of all land, seizing 540 million acres from private landowners and the Church.

Elections, called by the Provisional Government, were held in the autumn. In these the Bolsheviks won only a quarter of the votes; most support went to the moderate socialists.

The Constituent Assembly met on 5 January 1918. It rejected a Bolshevik statement of policy. On 6 January Lenin's Soviet Executive Committee dissolved the Assembly. Its members went home. Democracy had died.

THE CONSTITUTION

In January–July 1918 the Congress of Soviets considered Bolshevik proposals for a new form of government. Lenin's opponents accused him of wanting a dictatorship.

In July a Constitution was agreed. It created the Russian Soviet Federal Socialist Republic.

Supreme power was given to the All-Russian Congress of Soviets, whose members were elected in town and rural constituencies. This congress elected an executive committee of about 200 members, which in turn appointed the Council of People's Commissars. This council was dominated by the Central Politburo of the Bolshevik Party which had an inner group of five members. These five were dominated by Lenin—the dictator who argued that 'the will of a class is at times best realized by a dictator who sometimes can accomplish more by himself'.

10.7 The Treaty of Brest-Litovsk, March 1918

In December 1917 Lenin agreed to an armistice to end the fighting with the Germans and Austrians. Trotsky was sent to negotiate terms for a peace treaty.

The Germans refused to accept Trotsky's terms. The German army advanced further into Russia, and the Bolsheviks had to accept Germany's terms. Russia lost: Poland, Finland, Estonia, Latvia and Lithuania and, most importantly, the Ukraine, which became independent. She also lost one-third of European Russia, one-third of her ironworks, three-quarters of her coal industry and one-third of her population.

10.8 Lenin's Government in Action

In the early months of 1918 the government issued a number of reforming decrees. Education was to be free; everyone was to be covered by a system of national insurance which would provide pensions, a health service and assistance for the unemployed.

A campaign was launched against adult illiteracy. The calendar was changed to bring it into line with the rest of the world. The capital was shifted from Petrograd to Moscow. The decree on the press closed down all newspapers except those loyal to the Bolshevik Party and government.

A new secret police force, named (from its Russian initials) the Cheka, was set up. It was this force which organized the Red Terror in which critics were arrested, imprisoned, tortured and killed. The first to be attacked were the Liberals or Cadets; next to suffer were the non-Bolshevik socialists—the Mensheviks and the SRPs (Unit 3). Later Lenin was to use this secret force against the

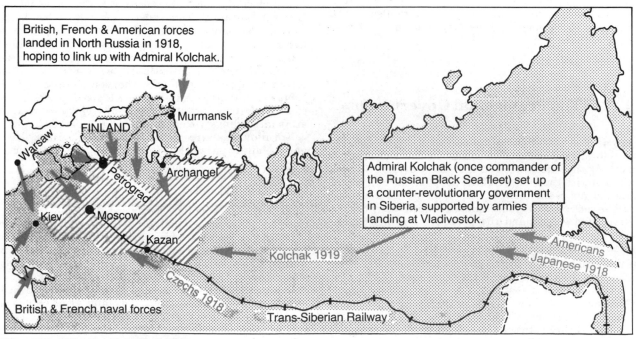

Fig. 10.8   The Russian Civil War

members of his own Party who became critical of his policies. It was the Cheka which murdered the Tsar and his family.

THE CIVIL WAR

Its origins (Fig. 10.8)

The Treaty of Brest-Litovsk shocked many Russians.

A Czech legion, of prisoners-of-war from the Austrian army, was making its way home from camps in the Far East across Russia. They looted as they went and had to be put down by the Red Guards.

In Siberia, Admiral Kolchak led a revolt. He wanted the restoration of the Tsar or the return of the Provisional Government.

In the north, based in Estonia, rebels were led by ex-General Yudenich. From the Crimea there were revolts led by Denikin and later by Baron Wrangel. In the Ukraine a peasants' army was led by the brilliant Makhno, who wanted independence for his people. From Turkestan came rebels financed by the British.

The Allies and the Bolsheviks

The Allies had sent masses of supplies to the Tsar. After Brest-Litovsk there was a danger that these might fall into German hands. British and French troops were sent to the Crimea, to Murmansk and to Archangel to guard the dumps.

British forces gave help to the northern rebels. The French helped the Poles and the rebels from the south (see Unit 18). Both Allies hoped to get a government which would fight the Germans.

The Reds victorious

The Bolshevik government had many problems to meet in its first year. There was massive unemployment in industry still trying to get back to producing non-war goods. Food was even scarcer than it had been in 1917. And there was the Civil War which started in 1918 and went on until 1922.

The anti-Bolsheviks contributed to their own defeat. Some of them wanted to bring back the Tsar. This did not appeal to the mass of the people. Some wanted to set themselves up as dictators and so there were divisions among the rebels. Some were getting help from foreigners—which offended the national pride of many Russians. Some wanted to abolish the earlier land reforms.

Trotsky proved to be a brilliant organizer and leader. He had the advantage that his forces were fighting in a unified command—unlike the divided commands of the Whites.

10.9 War Communism, 1917–21

The government nationalized all the means of industrial and agricultural production in the territory controlled by the Red Army. So much for 'Land by your own hands'.

Workers received ration cards so that they could get their wages in kind—in food and coal. This forced the unemployed to rob the peasants.

The peasants had to hand over all their surplus grain to the Soviet authorities at prices fixed by the government, ensuring peasant hostility to the government. Men could be forced to work in mines, on roads and canals.

1921, A YEAR OF CRISIS

The Kronstadt Rising

In 1921 the sailors at the naval base at Kronstadt were angered when Trotsky and the Cheka put down a workers' strike in Petrograd. They revolted and called for a 'third revolution'. Trotsky led the Red Army and the Cheka to put down this rising. Many sailors were massacred.

The Great Famine

The breakdown in transport and the almost constant fighting throughout the countryside meant that food supplies became continually scarcer. In 1921 things came to a head. Famine and sickness spread across Russia. Millions of people died. It was the American, Herbert Hoover, who organized the American Relief Administration to bring in wheat.

THE NEW ECONOMIC POLICY (NEP)

It was obvious that the Russian people were not willing to be communized. Peasants were not supplying enough food to the towns, where there were insufficient goods for them to buy for money received from food sales.

In March 1921 Lenin declared the end of War Communism and the onset of a New Economic Policy.

▶ Peasants would be allowed to keep part of their grain—for sale whenever they liked. They had to sell (at low prices) part of their output to the government.

▶ People were allowed to set up small profit-making businesses which, Lenin hoped, would produce the clothes and other consumer goods which might attract the peasants to sell their food in the hard-pressed towns.

▶ Some hard-working peasants built up profitable farms.

Many Bolsheviks saw this as a retreat from Communism.

10.10 Lenin's Death and Succession

In July 1918 a member of the SRP, Dora Kaplan, tried to assassinate Lenin. He survived, with two bullets lodged in his body—but he never really recovered.

In 1922 he had a stroke which left him paralysed and speechless, although he continued to rule the country. In 1923 he wrote his *Testament* in which he revealed that he was afraid of a quarrel among his followers when he died. On 21 January 1924 he died.

The apparatus left by Lenin was:

▶ The acceptance by most Bolsheviks of the dictatorship;

▶ A controlled Press;

▶ A secret police with great power and a grim record;

▶ A people who saw that they had got rid of one Tsar only to see him replaced by a stronger one.

TROTSKY—LENIN'S SUCCESSOR?

Lenin thought Trotsky the most able of his supporters. Most Bolsheviks admitted his intellectual superiority. He had travelled widely, written many books, led the Petrograd Soviet in 1905 (Unit 3) and organized the Red Army during the Civil War.

However, Trotsky did many things that raised suspicion. He argued (against Lenin) in favour of allowing free discussion within the Party about the problems facing Russia. Was he 'too soft' to lead?

He called for a war on the peasants as a way of solving the food crisis and rising prices—which was contrary to Lenin's NEP policy of co-operation with the peasant masses. Was Trotsky 'too harsh' to rule?

He condemned the NEP which allowed private enterprise—although this was Lenin's policy. Was he 'too arrogant' to be trusted with power?

Many Bolsheviks also suspected him because he seemed too clever for them: they would have liked someone more ordinary; and because he had joined them only in 1917. Before that he had been a Menshevik. Would he turn his coat again if he had power?

STALIN—LENIN'S SUCCESSOR?

After the February Revolution, 1917, Stalin became editor of *Pravda*. In 1917 Lenin made him Chairman of the Commissariat of Nationalities. During the Civil War he organized the defence of Tsaritsyn (later called Stalingrad and now Volgograd).

Later he went with the Cheka to lead the fight against

Kolchak (Fig. 10.8) and, later, Yudenich. In 'The Rape of Georgia'—his home state—he ruthlessly put down a band of rebels.

He became head of Orgburo, which organized the growing Bolshevik Party and, most importantly, became General Secretary of the Central Committee of the Bolshevik Party. This put him in touch with all the officials throughout the country. He could do small favours for them—and in return they helped to get his friends elected to various Congresses and Committees.

Lenin saw the danger of Stalin having got all this power in his hands. He thought Stalin 'too rude... intolerable...' and in his *Testament* urged his followers to 'think about a way of removing Stalin'.

10.11 The Struggle for Leadership, 1924–9

TROTSKY VERSUS STALIN—STAGE 1

Zinoviev was Party organizer in Leningrad and a member of Lenin's inner Cabinet. Kamenev ran the Party in Moscow and was another of Lenin's inner Cabinet. Both were opposed to Trotsky, partly for reasons suggested in 10.10 but also because Trotsky wanted to try to organize 'a world revolution'. They knew that they had enough problems in Russia.

In May 1924 at a Party Congress Trotsky called for a series of plans aimed at the more speedy industrialization of Russia. Stalin organized the opposition to this proposal, which was defeated. (It is worth noting that in 1929 this became Stalin's own policy.)

Trotsky wrote *The Lessons of October*, in which he showed that Zinoviev and Kamenev had opposed Lenin's plans for the revolution in that month. The angry 'bosses' sided with Stalin and helped to get Trotsky dismissed from his post of Commissar for War (December 1925). Stalin's friends at the Party Congress approved of this.

STALIN VERSUS ZINOVIEV AND KAMENEV—STAGE 2

The leaders of the big city parties now tried to use their power to make life easier for their supporters—the industrial workers. Under NEP, unemployment was rising,

workers went hungry, but peasants prospered. The workers wanted more investment in industry and government control of food prices.

Stalin argued that this was 'Trotskyism', condemned as early as 1924. Other members of the Politburo—Bukharin, Rykov and Tomsky—sided with Stalin against Zinoviev and Kamenev. The Party Congress denounced the two 'bosses', sacked them and approved the appointment of Kirov (to Leningrad) and Molotov (to Moscow)—both of whom were Stalin's allies.

In 1926 Trotsky, Zinoviev and Kamenev joined forces again Stalin and demanded the end of NEP, an attack on the peasants and a crash programme of industrialization. Stalin's friends controlled the Congress which jeered at the opposition.

Trotsky was expelled from the Politburo and the Central Committee of the Party. In 1927, on the tenth anniversary of the October Revolution, Trotsky tried to lead a revolt to overthrow Stalin. No one followed, as they had done in 1905 and 1917. Stalin announced that Trotsky was to be expelled from the Party; exiled to Alma on the distant Chinese border. In 1929 Stalin banished him from Russia altogether—by which time Stalin could claim to be the undisputed dictator.

By 1929 Zinoviev and Kamenev had apologized to Stalin and been allowed back into the fold—to be used at a later date against Bukharin and his supporters, when Stalin adopted Trotsky's policies of industrialization and a war on the peasants. We will study this in Unit 11.

Unit 10 Summary

▶ Russian attitudes to war, July–August 1914.
▶ Successes and failures, 1914–16.
▶ The effects of war on life in Russia.
▶ The February Revolution, 1917, and the fall of the Romanovs.
▶ The weakness of the Provisional Government.
▶ The Bolshevik Revolution, October 1917, and the death of democracy.
▶ The Treaty of Brest-Litovsk.
▶ Lenin in power: the Civil War and the secret police.
▶ War communism: the New Economic Policy.
▶ The struggle for leadership, 1924–9.

---

11 RUSSIA, 1928–41

11.1 Establishing the Stalin Dictatorship

Why was this possible?—Lenin created a dictatorship (see Unit 10). Rivals for power were also eliminated:

▶ Trotsky, the most able, was first isolated as an 'anti-Leninist' before being exiled;
▶ Zinoviev and Kamenev were first used against Trotsky, then shown up as 'Trotskyists' before they were forced, publicly, to apologize to Stalin.

These and other rivals were eliminated in the Purges.

THE SECRET POLICE

The Cheka was founded by Lenin in December 1917. He used it to kill the Tsar and his family at Ekaterinburg in July 1918. It was also responsible for killing thousands suspected of being opposed to Lenin and his policies.

The Cheka was abolished in 1922. It was replaced by the OGPU, part of the NKVD (the People's Commissariat for Internal Affairs). The OGPU broke away from the NKVD in

1923. It was the OGPU which was responsible for enforcing the collectivization programme (see below), when millions of people were killed. In 1934 the OGPU again merged with the NKVD, which acted as Stalin's instrument of terror during the Purges (see below).

A series of purges, in which millions were imprisoned without trial and thousands killed, terrorized the population. Stalin faced little opposition—and that was crushed by secret police agents supported by a terrified people.

11.2 The Great Purge

1934

On 1 December 1934 Stalin's ally, Kirov (see Unit 10), the city boss of Leningrad, was murdered.

Yagoda, head of the NKVD, organized the arrest and imprisonment of Zinoviev, Kamenev and other eminent Party members who might have been rivals for Stalin's position. Between 1934 and 1938 millions of people were arrested and imprisoned as possible supporters of Zinoviev and Kamenev.

During 1934 the number of Party members fell from 3.5 million to 2.7 million. By the end of 1935 there were fewer than 2 million Party members. Stalin, through Yagoda, had got rid of the remainder.

1936

In August 1936 Zinoviev, Kamenev and fourteen other prominent Bolsheviks were brought to trial. They had been with Lenin before 1914, and fought with him in 1917. Now, after years of 'treatment' by the NKVD, they 'confessed' to any charge brought against them. The sixteen were found guilty and shot.

1937

In 1936 Stalin had killed some of those who helped him against Trotsky. In 1937 the NKVD arrested Radek and sixteen other leaders who had helped Stalin against Kamenev and Zinoviev. Radek was put on trial, sent to a labour camp and, in 1939, shot.

1938

Stalin now turned his attention to others who had once sided with him against Trotsky. Rykov, Bukharin and Tomsky and eighteen other leaders were brought to trial and shot.

Yagoda, the head of NKVD, responsible for millions of arrests and executions, was arrested and executed. His successor, Beria, was even more subservient to Stalin and even more ruthless.

THE PURGE OF THE ARMY

In 1937 Stalin arrested Marshal Tukhachevsky and seven other generals, all 'heroes of the Civil War' (see Unit 10). Stalin feared they might use their power to end the rightful dictatorship. So he had them executed—after trials in which they 'confessed' to many (often impossible) crimes.

RESULTS OF THE PURGES

Almost all the delegates at the 1934 Party Congress had been executed. Almost all the 'old Guard' of 1914–17 had been executed; in their places Stalin had dependent supporters. Eight and a half million people had been arrested; one million had been shot. Seven million were in concentration camps. Many of these were industrialists and engineers. Their arrests helped slow down Russian industrial growth. The army lost more officers during the Purges than between 1941 and 1945 against the Nazis. Its efficiency suffered as a result.

11.3 Stalin and Industrialization

REASONS

At the Treaty of Brest-Litovsk (Unit 10) Russia lost a large percentage of its population, industry, coal and iron deposits. If Russia was to grow strong and richer, there had to be a programme to industrialize Russia.

Western countries (Britain, France and the USA) had opposed the Bolshevik government in 1917–21. Many Bolsheviks feared that they might try to attack Russia to get rid of the new form of government. Russia had to become militarily strong—and required industries to produce weapons.

Trotsky and others had talked of 'a world revolution'. Stalin had opposed such ambitious plans. However, he knew that Russia was the centre of world communism. Russian (Bolshevik) industrialization would be an advertisement for communism.

Unlike Trotsky, Stalin talked of 'socialism in one country'. If that 'socialism' was to produce results, Russian industry would have to be developed to produce the goods.

THE FIRST FIVE-YEAR PLAN

In his New Economic Policy (Unit 10), Lenin had allowed the return to some kinds of private enterprise. The State continued to control the major industries.

Trotsky had called for 'a crash programme of industrialization' but had been condemned in 1924. In 1928 Stalin adopted Trotsky's policies. A production schedule was drawn up for all major industries, and targets had to be achieved in five years.

Before the end of 1932 most targets had been beaten. Production in coal, iron and electricity generating industries had doubled. Huge projects had been completed. Among the more spectacular were the Stalingrad Tractor Works, the Volga–White Sea Canal and the Magnitogorsk metallurgical industry.

THE SECOND FIVE-YEAR PLAN, 1933

In 1931 Stalin insisted that 'the tempo must be increased' if Russia were to catch up with the industrialized West.

In European Russia there was a consolidation of industries. In Russia-beyond-the-Urals there was a huge increase in the number, size and output of factories far from the path of possible invaders from the West.

PAYING FOR THE INDUSTRIAL GROWTH

Foreign capital paid for Russia's early industrialization (see Unit 3). But Western capitalists would not help communist development. Russia had to pay for her industrialization from her own resources. Capital investment went up five times between 1928 and 1931 ('the heroic years'). Much of this investment came from the profits made on collective farms. Most of this went into heavy industries. There was little left for investment in consumer industries. Living standards fell below the level reached under the New Economic Policy.

LABOUR AND INDUSTRIALIZATION

Young communist 'shock workers' were sent to give other workers the example of hard, dedicated work. On 25 August 1935 a young worker, Alexei Stakhanov, produced fourteen times his usual output of coal. The government encouraged other workers to become 'Stakhanovites'. However, if they did, they received no more in wages—they simply had their 'normal target' increased. Workers who protested, those who failed to meet their targets and the managers whose factories or mines failed to fulfil their targets, were arrested as 'anti-government agents'.

The 1938 Decrees introduced fines for such failures and, for workers, loss of social security benefits. In 1940 the Decrees were strengthened. Anyone who was twenty minutes late on more than two occasions was to be sentenced to forced labour.

THE PEASANTS AND RUSSIAN INDUSTRIALIZATION

In the unrest of 1917 many peasants took land from their nearest nobleman's estate. Lenin nationalized all land in the name of war communism (see Unit 10). The peasants had to hand over all their surplus grain crop to the government. Many hid such surpluses; others even burnt them rather than hand them over to 'the townies'.

In March 1921 Lenin changed the law. Requisition of crops ended. Peasants had to pay their taxes in kind (crops or animals). The rest they could sell. Under this New Economic Policy many peasants prospered. Some bought horses to pull their ploughs (instead of using their wives and children); some bought extra land from the less ambitious. These kulaks or prosperous peasants did well out of the revolution.

Trotsky had said this made a mockery of Bolshevik claims to be communists. He had wanted a war on the peasants. Stalin used this as a weapon against him in 1926.

In 1928 Bukharin and other 'right wing' Bolsheviks took up the argument for an anti-peasant campaign, since Russia had to import machinery to help industrialization, and this could only be paid for by agricultural exports. The increasing labour force also had to be fed; the peasants would produce this extra food—and become richer. Industrialization, therefore, depended on the peasants.

Stolypin had argued that a prosperous peasantry would be the best safeguard against revolution (see Unit 3).

Stalin was forced to adopt Trotsky's policy because:

▶ he needed a continued increase in agricultural exports to help his industrialization plans (see above);
▶ there was no guarantee that a prosperous peasantry would produce enough—or at the right price;
▶ if they did produce and if he did pay what they wanted, then there would rise, in a seemingly communist country, a rich and free peasantry.

11.4 Stalin and the Peasants

Stalin attacked the kulaks as 'enemies of the state' who held the country to ransom. He knew that, if he got rid of them, the other peasants could be easily controlled.

COLLECTIVIZATION

In 1929 Stalin announced a plan for the collectivization of all farmland—by timetable; 'the lower Volga by the autumn of 1930, the central area and the Ukraine by the autumn of 1931...'

Collective farms took various forms. On state farms (or sovkhozy) workers got wages paid by the government official who ran the farm; on collectives or kolkhozy, which were more common, the land was granted to the peasants of the two or three villages which were united to form the collective.

Collectives

▶ The peasants were allowed private plots near their cottages to grow vegetables and keep chickens and other animals;
▶ The bulk of the land was managed by a committee elected by the peasants but chaired by a local Party official;
▶ The workers were divided into brigades of between 50 and 100 workpeople. The collective had to produce a certain amount of grain, chickens, pigs and so on each year;
▶ The government took approximately 15 per cent of the output at about one-eighth of the normal market price and

another 5 per cent at the market price. The government sold this at about 700 per cent profit. It was this which provided the money needed for investment in industry;
▶ Another 15 per cent went to the Machine Tractor Station;
▶ Some of the output would be set aside for seed and as reserves against a poor harvest;
▶ The rest, roughly one quarter of the total output, was distributed to the workers on the collective according to the number of workdays they had put in on the collective.

The collectives were not always successful, because:

▶ some workers put in too much time on their private plots and slacked at their collective duties;
▶ the machinery from the MTS was sometimes defective and no one was available to put things right.

STALIN AND THE WAR ON THE PEASANTS, 1929–33

In 1929 many peasants consumed all they produced. There was nothing left for the government to take. Many refused to hand their farms to collective committees. This led to clashes between government agents and peasants, and a shortage of food in the towns. There was bread rationing, food queues, high prices and the danger of the unrest which had led to the February Revolution in 1917.

The kulaks were to be dispossessed. Government agents were to round up over a million of them and announce the formation of collectives. This announcement led to the wholesale slaughter of animals by angry peasants determined to resist the government. The result of this was another Great Famine.

Stalin went ahead with his policy. The army was sent to help communist officials get rid of the kulaks. Most of these were deported to the icy wastes of Siberia or the burning deserts of Central Asia. About 13 million kulak families died.

But the committees and less-able peasants were unable to run the new, very large farms efficiently. Crop failure was common—which added to the famine.

When, as happened, bad weather also coincided with inefficiency, the result was even worse. At least three million people died of malnutrition during the Great Famine of 1932–3.

STALIN DRAWS BACK—IN SOME SUCCESS

The majority of peasants survived on food from their private plots.

Collectivization was called off when its failure became evident. However, by 1932 some two-thirds of farms had already been collectivized. The policy was resumed later in the 1930s, and by 1939 it was complete.

Collectives became more successful. In 1937 there was a record grain harvest. Millions of peasants learned to drive tractors.

The Motor Tractor Stations (MTS)

The first of these was developed to help the peasants around Odessa in 1928—before collectivization. Stalin developed more stations. They got a supply of tractors from industrial plants; drivers and engineers were sent to work them on the collectives. More importantly, lecturers and engineers went to train the collective workers who learnt to use these machines.

Unit 11 Summary

▶ Stalin's dictatorship: reasons and methods.
▶ The Purges, 1934–8.
▶ Industrialization and collectivization.

12.1 Preliminaries to the Versailles Treaty

WILSON'S FOURTEEN POINTS (Fig. 12.1)

President Wilson issued his Fourteen Points in January 1918. He hoped these would form the basis for peace.

The Germans rejected the Points. Ludendorff hoped for a complete victory in 1918 (see Unit 9). When, in November, the Germans surrendered, they hoped that the peace settlement would be based on those Points.

Program for the Peace of the World

By PRESIDENT WILSON January 8, 1918

I. Open covenants of peace, openly arrived at, after which there shall be no private international understandings of any kind, but diplomacy shall proceed always frankly and in the public view.

II. Absolute freedom of navigation upon the seas, outside territorial waters, alike in peace and in war, except as the seas may be closed in whole or in part by international action for the enforcement of international covenants.

III. The removal, so far as possible, of all economic barriers and the establishment of an equality of trade conditions among all the nations consenting to the peace and associating themselves for its maintenance.

IV. Adequate guarantees given and taken that national armaments will reduce to the lowest point consistent with domestic safety.

V. Free, open-minded, and absolutely impartial adjustment of all colonial claims, based upon a strict observance of the principle that in determining all such questions of sovereignty the interests of the population concerned must have equal weight with the equitable claims of the government whose title is to be determined.

VI. The evacuation of all Russian territory and such a settlement of all questions affecting Russia as will secure the best and freest cooperation of the other nations of the world in obtaining for her an unhampered and unembarrassed opportunity for the independent determination of her own political development and national policy, and assure her of a sincere welcome into the society of free nations under institutions of her own choosing; and, more than a welcome, assistance also of every kind that she may need and may herself desire. The treatment accorded Russia by her sister nations in the months to come will be the acid test of their goodwill, of their comprehension of her needs as distinguished from their own interests, and of their intelligent and unselfish sympathy.

VII. Belgium, the whole world will agree, must be evacuated and restored, without any attempt to limit the sovereignty which she enjoys in common with all other free nations. No other single act will serve as this will serve to restore confidence among the nations in the law which they have themselves set and determined for the government of their relations with one

another. Without this healing act the whole structure and validity of international law is forever impaired.

VIII. All French territory should be freed and the invaded portions restored, and the wrong done to France by Prussia in 1871 in the matter of Alsace-Lorraine, which has unsettled the peace of the world for nearly fifty years, should be righted, in order that peace may once more be made secure in the interest of all.

IX. A readjustment of the frontiers of Italy should be effected along clearly recognizable lines of nationality.

X. The people of Austria-Hungary, whose place among the nations we wish to see safeguarded and assured, should be accorded the freest opportunity of autonomous development.

XI. Rumania, Serbia and Montenegro should be evacuated; occupied territories restored; Serbia accorded free and secure access to the sea; and the relations of the several Balkan States to one another determined by friendly counsel along historically established lines of allegiance and nationality; and international guarantees of the political and economic independence and territorial integrity of the several Balkan States should be entered into.

XII. The Turkish portions of the present Ottoman Empire should be assured a secure sovereignty, but the other nationalities which are now under Turkish rule should be assured an undoubted security of life and an absolutely unmolested opportunity of autonomous development, and the Dardanelles should be permanently opened as a free passage to the ships and commerce of all nations under international guarantees.

XIII. An independent Polish State should be erected which should include the territories inhabited by indisputably Polish populations, which should be assured a free and secure access to the sea, and whose political and economic independence and territorial integrity should be guaranteed by international covenant.

XIV. A general association of nations must be formed under specific covenants for the purpose of affording mutual guarantees of political independence and territorial integrity to great and small States alike.

Fig. 12.1 Wilson's Fourteen Points

THE FOUR LEADERS AT VERSAILLES, 1919

Wilson hoped the Allies would accept the Fourteen Points. He pleaded for 'no annexations, no contributions, no punitive damages'. He did not understand the deep enmity between France and Germany.

Clemenceau, Prime Minister of France, was nicknamed 'The Tiger' because of his determination that France would not be defeated even when the Germans seemed to be winning in March 1918. He was determined to punish the Germans as harshly as possible, and to undo the damage done by the 1871 settlement (Unit 1). He was also determined that Germany would not be able to start another war.

Lloyd George, British Prime Minister since 1916, was, at first, in sympathy with Wilson. He realized a harsh treaty

would lead to German attempts at 'revenge'. However, the British public wanted to 'hang the Kaiser' and 'make the Germans pay'.

Orlando, Prime Minister of Italy, wanted to punish Austria and to make territorial gains for his own country.

THE CONFERENCE AT VERSAILLES, 1919

This was only one post-war peace conference. Others were at:

▶ St Germain, to arrange a peace with Austria, September 1919;

▶ Neuilly, to arrange a peace with Bulgaria, November 1919;

▶ Trianon, to arrange a peace with Hungary, June 1920;

▶ Lausanne, to arrange a peace with Turkey (see Unit 13), July 1923.

There were 70 delegates from 32 victorious countries. They had 60 committees of experts to help them. But the Conference was dominated by 'The Big Four' who met secretly and arrived at their decisions.

None of the defeated countries was represented at the various peace-making conferences. Russia, although an ally in 1914, was not represented. The Allies refused to recognize the Bolshevik government.

THE 'THREE' MAKE WILSON IGNORE HIS 'POINTS'

Look again at Fig. 12.1 and then note the following:

Point 1: the Allied leaders met in secret.

Point 2: Britain refused to give up its right to search shipping trading with an enemy during wartime.

Point 3: tariff barriers were retained—and increased (see below).

Point 4: there was no real attempt at disarmament (Unit 14).

Point 5: Britain and France increased their colonial holdings.

Point 6: the Allies sent troops to attack the Bolsheviks.

Point 9: the boundary of Italy was not settled.

Point 13: post-war Poland contained millions of Germans.

Point 14: the League of Nations never worked as Wilson had hoped.

12.2 The Treaty of Versailles, 28 June 1919

GERMAN LOSSES IN EUROPE (Fig. 12.2)

Alsace and Lorraine went back to France. Germany lost three-quarters of her iron deposits.

The Saar, an important coalfield, was to be governed by the League of Nations for 15 years, when France was to have control of the mines. At the end of that time its inhabitants would vote as to their future (see Unit 23).

West Prussia and Posen, with four million Germans, were given to Poland, one of the new states created at Versailles; small portions of German territory (and 48,000 German people) were handed to Czechoslovakia, another new state.

Danzig, once an important German port, and its 300,000 Germans, was named 'a Free City', to be governed by the League of Nations.

Memel, another important port, with 141,000 Germans,

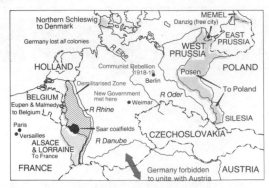

Fig. 12.2   German losses, 1919

was ceded to the new country, Lithuania, created by the Treaty (see Unit 14). Northern Schleswig (1.2) went to Denmark.

Note

Six and a half million Germans (or one tenth of the former population) lost their German citizenship and became citizens of other countries.

The Rhineland was not all lost. Eupen and Malmédy were handed to Belgium. The remainder of the Rhineland was named as a demilitarized zone. The Allies were to keep armies of occupation there for 15 years while the Germans were permanently forbidden to have armies or fortifications in this region.

GERMAN COLONIES

The League of Nations handed these to the Allies to run as mandates (see Unit 13).

▶ German East Africa (Tanganyika) went to Britain;
▶ the Cameroons went to France;
▶ German Samoa went to New Zealand;
▶ South-west Africa went to South Africa—which failed to carry out the terms of the mandate to help the local population prepare for independence.

GERMAN MILITARY STRENGTH

This was weakened:

▶ the air force had to be disbanded;
▶ the navy had to be surrendered to the Allies;
▶ the army was not to exceed 100,000 men—smaller than the Belgian army.

REPARATIONS

Germany was required to pay for the damage caused by the war. This followed the example set by Germany when she imposed such a punishment on France in 1871 (Unit 1);

▶ £6600 million was to be paid in cash (Unit 18);
▶ the merchant navy had to be surrendered to Britain;
▶ fixed quantities of coal had to be handed to France;
▶ a fixed number of cattle had to be handed to Belgium.

12.3 German Humiliation, Losses and Anger

WAR GUILT

The Germans resented the 'dictated peace'; they played no part in the negotiations on the terms of the Treaty. They had either to accept or reject them and face a continued blockade by the British and the threat of a military attack by France and Britain.

But above all the Germans resented Clause 231 of the Treaty, which blamed Germany for the outbreak of the war. Their delegates had to sign a Treaty in which Clause 231 stated: 'Germany accepts the responsibilities of Germany...for causing all the loss and damage...consequence of the war imposed...by the aggression of Germany and her allies.'

TO ACCEPT OR REJECT?

The fall of the Kaiser had led to a revolution in Berlin.

The first post-war government met at Weimar. When the terms of the Treaty were revealed, the government debated them for several days. In the end the Weimar government accepted the Treaty.

THE HALL OF MIRRORS: FRENCH REVENGE

In 1871, Bismarck had imposed the harsh Treaty of Frankfurt on France (see Unit 1). Before that Treaty was signed, Bismarck organized the proclamation of the creation of the German Empire. As an insult to defeated France, that proclamation took place in the Hall of Mirrors in the former royal palace of Versailles. On 28 June 1919 the Germans signed the Treaty of Versailles in that same Hall of Mirrors. France had her revenge.

12.4 The Treaty of St Germain— with Defeated Austria

Austria was separated from Hungary (with whom the Treaty of Trianon was signed in 1920). She became a small, landlocked country—a pale shadow of the country which had once dominated Europe (see Unit 1).

TERRITORIAL LOSSES

Yugoslavia was formed from the old Kingdom of Serbia and from Bosnia and Herzegovina. The Southern Slavs who had lived inside the pre-war boundary of Hungary were handed over to the new state.

Rumania was enlarged by Transylvania (from Hungary) and Bessarabia (from Russia).

Czechoslovakia was created from the old German kingdom of Bohemia, and from the Northern States of Austria-Hungary.

Poland gained Galicia from Austria.

Italy was given Trentino, Trieste and part of south Tyrol and Istria.

Austria was to be kept permanently weak, largely because Italy feared her emergence as a major power. In particular the Treaty forbade the union of Austria with Germany.

12.5 Criticism of the Peace Settlements

There were too many small states, unable to defend themselves from attack by any major power.

Each state imposed its own tariff barriers, contrary to Point 3 of the Fourteen Points. This led to a reduction in international trade, one of the reasons for the post-war depression.

Contrary to Point 12, the population of the new Poland was not entirely Polish. The presence of racial minorities—Germans, Hungarians and others—in Poland was matched by the presence of similar minorities in Czechoslovakia and Yugoslavia. This was to cause international unrest in the 1920s and 1930s.

Germany was angered by the loss of so much territory. It was almost inevitable that she would look for revenge.

The Allies ignored Bolshevik Russia and her legitimate interest in the future of the countries on her border.

The reparations imposed were too harsh—and were never paid. Keynes, a leading British economist and an adviser to Lloyd George at Versailles, argued against reparations. If they were to be paid, Germany had to export masses of materials and goods—and so ensure unemployment in other industrialized countries.

The French insisted on reparations being imposed. When Germany fell behind with her payments, the French occupied the Ruhr industrial region in 1923. This only ensured that Germany would fall even further behind in her payments.

MacDonald, Labour Prime Minister in 1924, helped to organize a plan named after the US minister, Dawes (see Unit 18).

Reparations were abandoned in 1932. By that time the Germans had only paid over the money borrowed from

America. But in 1932 the reparations problem had helped to create economic problems for the world. It had also helped Hitler to appear as the spokesman for the German hatred for the harsh reparations (see Unit 15).

Unit 12 Summary

▶ The Versailles Treaty, 1919.
▶ German humiliation, losses and anger.
▶ The Treaty of St Germain: Balkanization.
▶ Criticisms of the European peace settlements.

13 PEACEMAKING—TURKEY

13.1 The Break-up of the Turkish Empire

THE IMPORTANCE OF THE SÈVRES SETTLEMENT

The old Eastern Question (see Unit 4) was ended. The defeat of Turkey led to freedom for the Christians in the Balkans, and a new and successful challenge to the Sultan's rule.

A new, Westernized Turkey emerged. This was the work, above all, of Kemal Ataturk (see below).

Several Mandated Territories (see below) were also created. This provides us with a chance to examine this system of government.

The Sèvres settlement saw the beginning of the Palestine problem (see below). This problem was to become more important in the 1920s and 1930s (see Unit 22). In more recent times it has become better known as the Arab-Israeli problem (Unit 37).

If you are studying British history, you should note that this settlement played a part in the fall of Lloyd George.

THE TREATY OF SÈVRES, AUGUST 1920

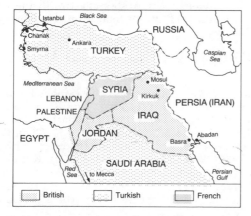

Fig. 13.1 Dividing up the Turkish Empire, 1923

Britain was anxious to safeguard her oil interests in Mesopotamia (now Iraq) and Persia (now Iran) (Fig. 13.1) and ensure control of one approach to India.

France wanted to gain influence in the former Turkish Empire. She already had a Muslim Empire in North Africa. She hoped to enlarge her empire by gains made in the Middle East.

Italy, with a small Empire in North Africa, hoped to extend it.

The three Allies tried to obtain 'spheres of influence' as part of this Treaty. The Treaty never came into force because of the Turkish revolution (see below).

THE GREEKS GAIN SMYRNA, AUGUST 1920

At Sèvres Greece was allowed to retain Smyrna (Fig. 13.1). A fleet of British, French and American warships guarded a Greek force which landed to take control of this port in mainland Turkey. Smyrna was then the scene of a massacre of Muslims.

This massacre united the Turks against the Treaty of Sèvres and the Sultan who had not been able to prevent it. It was also the signal for the revolution by Kemal.

13.2 Kemal's Revolution and Dispute with the Allies

In 1908 Mustapha Kemal had been leader of the Young Turks against the corrupt rule of the Sultan (Unit 4). They had deposed Sultan Abdul Hamid. Sultan Muhammad V came to the throne.

In 1915 Mustapha Kemal led the Turks in the Dardanelles campaign (Unit 9). This made him a popular hero.

In 1920 he helped to form a new Nationalist Party which pledged itself to the overthrow of the Treaty of Sèvres. He set up a nationalist government in Ankara in opposition to the Sultan's government in Constantinople.

KEMAL VERSUS THE ALLIES AND THE GREEKS

To try to defeat Kemal's revolution, an Allied force occupied Constantinople in March 1920. Nationalist leaders and supporters were arrested and deported.

Kemal's government had a great deal of popular support. The majority of Turks were tired of the corrupt government led by a Sultan who had been unable to avoid defeat by the Allies and the massacre of Smyrna. France and Italy realized this. They made agreements in which they recognized Kemal's government. Britain maintained a pro-Greek attitude.

By September 1922 Kemal's forces had defeated the Greeks and recaptured Smyrna and massacred the Christians (see above).

KEMAL VERSUS LLOYD GEORGE

Having driven the Greeks from Smyrna, Kemal decided to invade Thrace, and to re-conquer former European Turkey.

French and Italian troops were withdrawn from Chanak where they had been stationed to stop the Turks from entering South-eastern Europe (Fig. 13.1). Only British forces were at Chanak to face Kemal's Turks. Lloyd George appealed to the Dominions (Australia, Canada, New Zealand and South Africa) for help. They refused.

The danger of a renewed war was avoided when the British General Harrington did not deliver Lloyd George's ultimatum to Kemal telling him to withdraw, and Kemal did not order his forces to attack the British.

On 11 October 1922 both sides agreed a truce. The Chanak crisis was over. The problem of peacemaking remained.

THE TREATY OF LAUSANNE, 1923

This reviewed and changed the terms of the Treaty of Sèvres. Turkey retained part of Thrace, including Adrianople and the old capital, Constantinople (Istanbul). The Straits remained under Turkish sovereignty.

KEMAL REFORMS TURKEY

The last of the Sultans, Mohammad VI, was deposed in 1922. The Caliphate (headship of the Islam religion) was then given to a cousin of the Sultan. In 1924 the Caliphate was abolished. All members of the former royal family were banished from Turkey.

Mustapha Kemal, President of Turkey, was given almost dictatorial powers in the new constitution. He used these powers to try to modernize his country.

Religious reforms

Kemal thought that Islam was one of the major reasons for Turkey's decline from power. So Sunday was named the day of rest—and not the Islamic day, Friday. The fez, or hat, worn by men when praying, was forbidden. The chador, or veil worn by Muslim women, was abolished. In 1928 the Muslim religion ceased to be the official religion of Turkey.

Social reforms

Kemal wanted to westernize his country. So the alphabet was westernized and state elementary schools were established. Women were encouraged to play an active part in the country's life. In 1922 they were given the right to vote in elections for the National Assembly.

Political change

Free elections were held for a National Assembly in 1922. In 1924 Kemal carried out a purge of all the opposition, and Turkey became a one-party state.

Ataturk

In 1934 Mustapha Kemal officially changed his name. He took the name of Kemal Ataturk ('the father of the Turks').

THE END OF THE TURKISH EMPIRE

The Empire had stretched into South-eastern Europe, North Africa and, as you can see in Fig. 13.1, into the Arabian Gulf.

Britain had a great interest in the oil fields in Mosul, Kirkuk and Basra in modern Iraq and at Abadan in Persia.

Britain, France and Italy might have liked some parts of this Empire. That is what they, and others, had done in Africa (see Figs. 5.1 and 5.3). This would have run counter to their stated war aims of 'no annexations'. During the war, Britain and France had reached agreement on the division of this Empire between themselves. However, this Sykes–Picot Agreement (1916) never came into operation.

At San Remo in April 1920 the Allied Supreme Council devised a new system of government for colonies of defeated enemies.

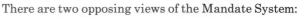 **13.3 The Mandate System**

There are two opposing views of the Mandate System:

▶ 'A disguise for colonial annexation...';
▶ 'An admission of a new sense of responsibility towards backward peoples.'

We have seen that the victorious Allies were unwilling to annex the former colonies of the defeated countries. The League of Nations set up a Mandate Commission to supervise the work of the Mandated Powers which administered the Mandated Territories on behalf of the League.

The Mandated Powers had to help their territories towards self-government and to promise not to use them as military bases. The League's Mandate Commission received annual reports from the Mandated Powers. It could offer them advice. In fact it had little power over the actions of the Powers. This is best seen in the case of South Africa, which refused to hand over its Mandate for the former German South West Africa to the United Nations and treated it as its own territory.

BRITAIN, ARAB NATIONALISM AND THE WAR, 1914–18

In 1914 Turkey planned to attack Egypt, hoping for support from other countries in the Muslim world. Britain rushed troops from India, Australia and New Zealand. British forces won victories at Ismailia and El Kantara. In 1915, British troops won a victory at Romani which guaranteed the control of the Suez Canal for Britain.

In 1916 the British switched to attack—on Palestine. Allenby won victories at Beersheba, Gaza, Askalon and Jaffa, and on 9 December 1917 entered Jerusalem.

In 1918 many of Allenby's forces were taken to France. The pro-British Emir Feisal supported the British. This support had been won by T. E. Lawrence ('Lawrence of Arabia'), and vague promises that after the war there would be a series of independent Arab states, to fill the vacuum that would be created by the final dismemberment of the Turkish Empire.

MESOPOTAMIA, DURING AND AFTER THE WAR

The defence of Mesopotamia was the responsibility of the government of India. In 1914 Basra and Kurna were captured, ensuring British control of the important delta.

The Turks suffered other defeats in 1915. Then General Townshend was ordered to attack Baghdad, with insufficient forces. Townshend was defeated at Kut-el-Amara (1916). Later General Maude took Kut (December 1916) and Baghdad (March 1917). The British went on to defeat the Turks in Persia and to capture Mosul, the great oil centre (November 1918).

Mesopotamia became a British Mandate after 1920. The

Arabs resented their new rulers and a serious revolt broke out in 1920. The British put down the revolt. However, they created the kingdom of Iraq under Feisal, who had been driven from Syria by the French.

In 1932 Britain recognized the independence of Iraq and secured her admission to the League of Nations.

THE POLITICS OF PALESTINE—ARAB HOPES

The first Arab chief to raise the flag of revolt against the Turks was Hussein, the ruler of the Hejaz. The Hejaz, the coastal strip running down the eastern bank of the Red Sea, was not a wealthy trading or farming state. It was important as it contained the Muslims' sacred city, Mecca.

Hussein hoped the British would help him win independence from Turkey. McMahon, the British representative in Cairo, reached an agreement with Hussein in 1915. This contained a vague promise of Arab independence for the traditional Arab lands.

One of Hussein's sons was Feisal. He went to Versailles in 1919 to claim 'the promised land'. But the hopes of the Hashemite family (Hussein, Feisal and his other brothers) and of Arabs generally grew less as the powers set up their Mandate System.

The French offered the crown of a united Syria (including Syria and Lebanon) to Feisal. But once he had accepted, the French drove him from Damascus. As we have seen he became ruler of the British Mandate, Iraq.

Another of Hussein's sons, Abdullah, went to Amman in 'British' Palestine (mandated to Britain in 1920) and was proclaimed King by Arab nationalists. In 1921 the British assigned the area of Trans-Jordan (or across the River Jordan from Palestine) for him to rule. Jordan remained under British supervision until 1956.

THE POLITICS OF PALESTINE—JEWISH HOPES

By 1914 many thousands of Jews from Europe and the USA had gone to live in Palestine, the Biblical home of their people.

The Zionist Movement had been founded by Theodore Herzl. It demanded the right of Jews to live in Palestine. In 1914 that movement was led by the British scientist, Chaim Weizmann, whose work on explosives was important for Britain. The movement had a great deal of American support. By 1917 Britain was anxious to gain the support of the USA. If she could please American Jews, they might get Wilson to help Britain.

In 1917 the British Foreign Secretary was A. J. Balfour. He wrote to the leader of the British Jews, Rothschild, in what has become known as 'the Balfour Declaration'. In this he promised that, after the war, Britain would ensure 'a national home for the Jewish people' in Palestine.

As the Mandated Power, Britain let a number of Jews into Palestine. This policy pleased no one. The leaders of world Jewry resented the limitations on Jewish immigration by the British. The Palestinian Arabs resented the influx of Jews.

McMahon had promised everything to the Arabs. Balfour had promised Palestine to the Jews. Here lay the seeds for future conflict (Units 22 and 37).

Unit 13 Summary

▶ The break up of the Turkish Empire.

▶ Ataturk's revolution and dispute with the Allies.

▶ The Mandate System: Palestine and the Jewish 'home'.

---

14 THE LEAGUE OF NATIONS

14.1 The Origins of the League

IDEALS

The League was an attempt to move away from the old power politics which had, in the past, led to war. Its supporters hoped that the League would solve the world's problems peacefully.

It had many weaknesses—but was a brave pioneering effort.

WILSON'S FOURTEEN POINTS

We have seen that most of Wilson's Points were ignored or changed in the hard bargaining at Versailles (Unit 12). His 14th Point (see Fig. 12.1) was secured.

14.2 The Covenant of the League

This was the constitution of the League. It had 26 articles dealing with such things as:

▶ arms reduction and the control of arms manufacturing;

▶ the duty of the League to prevent war;

▶ the duty of the member-states to take any disputes to the League for a decision. Once a decision had been given there must be no resort to war for three months;

▶ if war broke out the League would call on members to apply economic sanctions—to stop trading with the aggressor nation;

▶ if economic sanctions did not end the fighting, the League would order military action to be taken.

This Covenant was included in all the peace treaties signed after the war. This had several results: all nations appeared to accept the idea of the League, but the treaties were imposed on the defeated nations. The League appeared, at first, as an association of the victors.

14.3 The Organization of the League

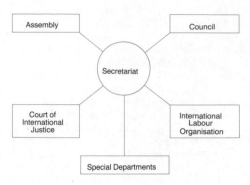

Fig. 14.3 The organization of the League

THE ASSEMBLY

This was a large body. Every nation had the right to send three delegates, although each nation had only one vote.

The Assembly met annually. It could be summoned to meet at other times for special reasons.

The rights of the world's smaller nations were recognized—they had the same voting power as the major powers.

For a decision to be reached, every member had to vote in its favour. This decision by unanimity was a weakness. Any member could block League action. In fact there was a surprising degree of agreement. Most matters were thrashed out in committees and when the final votes were taken those in the minority often preferred to abstain rather than block the will of the majority.

THE COUNCIL

This smaller body met at least four times a year and could be easily called together at times of crisis.

The victorious Allies (Britain, France, Italy and Japan), had permanent seats on the Council. The USA would have had a seat but the Senate refused to ratify the peace treaties (see below).

Non-permanent members were chosen from among the smaller member nations. In 1920 there were four non-permanent members. In 1922 this became six, in 1926 it became nine and by 1939 there were eleven non-permanent members chosen, by rotation, from the smaller powers.

Decisions of the Council had to be unanimous, which led to long arguments and slow progress in times of crisis.

The Council had no real power. It had, for example, no army at its disposal. It relied on the goodwill of members.

The Council supervised the work of a variety of Commissions. Some of these were very successful.

THE SECRETARIAT

This international civil service ran the League. Its members were drawn from the peoples of member nations. It had its permanent headquarters at Geneva, and was headed by a Secretary-General, the first one being an Englishman, Sir Eric Drummond.

Among the duties of the Secretariat were:
► to implement League decisions;
► to provide the factual information needed by the Assembly and Council on issues being discussed;
► to keep the records of the various Commissions.

THE INTERNATIONAL LABOUR ORGANIZATION (ILO)

At the League's headquarters, representatives of governments, employers and workers met in an annual conference. One of their aims was to work for the improvement of working and living conditions throughout the world. They also proposed new laws to the various governments. Each year the ILO provided information as to how governments were reacting to the decisions already published.

The ILO enjoyed a good deal of success:
► Member nations agreed that the working day should be no more than eight hours and the working week no more than forty-eight hours. This gave workers and employers a target at which to aim in their discussions in their separate countries.
► The principle that workers should have annual paid holidays was accepted. In Britain, for example, in 1938, this became part of the 'normal agreement' between employers and workers.
► The ILO decided that workers had a right to form trade unions. This became an important part of workers' campaigns in various countries. In the USA, for example, this right was denied by some employers in the 1930s (see Unit 19).
► The ILO decided that no one should be in full-time employment before the age of fifteen. Few countries had such a liberal view. In Britain the school-leaving age was 14 (1918). Only in 1947 was it raised to 15. But the ILO prodded governments into action.
► The ILO published information on the dangers arising from the use of some materials. It proved that the use of white lead in print manufacturing endangered the lives of workers in that industry. Trade unions could then argue with governments and employers to have such substances banned.

THE COURT OF INTERNATIONAL JUSTICE

This had been set up in The Hague in 1900 (see Unit 8). Few nations brought their disputes to the Court. Austria, for example, refused to allow its dispute with Serbia in 1914 to be taken before the Court.

In 1922 the Permanent Court of International Justice was formally established at The Hague. It had limited powers. It could not compel nations to bring disputes before the Court. Nor could it force states to accept its decisions.

By 1939 its 15 judges had settled 70 major cases and had helped arrange 400 international agreements.

THE COMMISSIONS OF THE LEAGUE

Smaller committees, or Commissions, were set up to deal with special problems or issues.

The Mandates Commission kept an eye on the good government of the Mandated Territories (see Unit 13).

The World Health Organization (WHO) campaigned for such things as the attack on preventable diseases.

The Drugs Commission drew attention to the danger of certain drugs and to methods of controlling the drugs traffic.

The Minorities Commission drew attention to the ill-treatment of various racial minorities and invited states guilty of such ill-treatment to mend their ways.

The Commissions for the administration of the Saar and of Danzig ensured that these territories were properly governed in the name of the League.

The Disarmament Commission got the greatest attention in the world's press—and was the one which had the least success (see below).

14.4 Successes and Failures

HOW DID THE NATIONS JUDGE THE LEAGUE?

It had its first meeting in Geneva in 1922, and 42 nations sent delegates to this meeting. However, none of the defeated nations was represented. Russia was not invited to join, because the Western Powers were still unwilling to recognize the Bolshevik government.

The United States

Wilson was 'the father of the League'. In the mid-term elections in 1918, the Republicans won majorities in the House of Representatives and the Senate. Thus Wilson, the Democrat President, was in a weak position because of this Republican opposition. He did not take a Republican with him to Versailles.

The Senate refused to ratify the peace treaties (see Unit 7). The USA therefore never became a member of the League.

France

France saw the League as an agency for enforcing the terms of the Treaty of Versailles, and in particular she wanted it to guard her security against the danger of fresh German aggression. She also hoped it would defend members' interests. When it proved not to be a strong body, France turned to other means of safeguarding her interests (see Unit 18).

Britain

She hoped that the League would help solve the world's problems peacefully, but Britain was not willing to send her forces to act on behalf of other people's interests. This was because pacifism was a feature of British life in the 1920s and 1930s. People's memories of the slaughters of 1914–18 were too fresh for them to be willing to engage in another war.

Generally

Nations followed their own self-interests rather than the interests of the wider world. This was made clearly evident by the actions of:
▶ Italy in 1923 (see below);
▶ Japan in 1931 (see Unit 17).

Both Japan and Italy were permanent members of the League Council. Their disregard for the League was particularly harmful to its claims to be an effective organization.
▶ Germany, which joined the League in 1926 but which, under Hitler, walked out when the Disarmament

quent defiance of the League showed it at its weakest.
▶ Russia, which joined in 1934, was expelled in 1939 when she invaded Finland.

In conclusion you should note that the power of national sovereignty was greater than the power of internationalism.

SOME EARLY SUCCESSES

Danzig

In spite of the rivalry between Poles and Germans, Danzig was established as an International Free City (Fig. 12.2).

Upper Silesia

In 1921, plebiscites confirmed the division of this coal-rich area (arranged by the League) between Poland and Germany. Although neither country was really satisfied by the division, they accepted it—and went on to make a trade treaty.

The Aaland Islands

In 1921 a dispute between Sweden and Finland over the ownership of these islands was settled, peacefully, in favour of Finland.

Austria

In 1922 the Austrian economy was on the point of collapse. The League organized financial help to save Austria.

Greece and Bulgaria

These were long-term rivals in the Balkans (see Unit 4). In 1925 the Greek invasion of Bulgaria was halted by the League, which forced Greece to pay compensation to Bulgaria.

The above issues involved only smaller countries.

SOME EARLY FAILURES

Vilnius

This was a town controlled by Lithuania but which Poland attacked. The League condemned the attack but was forced to allow Poland to hold on to it in 1923.

Memel

In 1923 Lithuania, which had lost Vilnius, invaded Memel and in spite of League protests, held on to it (see Unit 12).

Corfu

In 1923 an Italian on a League Commission was murdered on the Greco-Albanian border, where Italy wanted to expand. Italy did not take the issue to the League. It bombarded the Greek island of Corfu. The League Council wanted to refer the matter to the Permanent Court of Justice. The Allied Conference of Ambassadors instead allowed Greece to pay an indemnity. The League's most powerful members refused to support it.

FAILING MAJOR TESTS, 1931–9

The first major test of the League concerned Japan's invasion of Manchuria. We shall see that the League failed to prevent Japan succeeding in an aggression condemned by the League (see Unit 17). Japan left the League in 1933.

In the Abyssinian crisis of 1935 the League again failed to halt the aggressor or help the victim (see Unit 23).

Hitler went ahead with his aggressive policy in defiance of the Treaty of Versailles and the League (see Unit 23).

Disarmament Commission and Conference

In 1929 the world went through the first stages of the great depression in trade and industry. The League had no suggestions to make as to possible solutions to this major crisis.

The Covenant (see above) called for the nations to base their foreign and military policies on collective security (Article 10 of the Covenant). It also called, in Article 14, for the nations to disarm. The Allies refused to carry out their own decisions. There was no reduction in arms.

Originally the League had appointed a Military Commission to advise on disarmament. Later this was replaced by a Temporary Mixed Commission which had military and civilian members. No agreement was reached on anything. In 1925, plans were made for a World Disarmament Conference to meet in 1926. This failed even to agree on the definition of 'armaments' or how they were to be counted.

In 1930 Germany, now a member of the League, asked for a revision of the terms of the Treaty of Versailles; she wanted an army as large as the French and a navy as large as the British. Britain had some sympathy with the claims, but the French refused to accept them.

In 1932 the Disarmament Conference finally met in London. The Germans threatened to walk out if they were not given parity with France and Britain (June 1932). While the Conference was in session (1932–4) Hitler came to power in Germany (January 1933). By the summer of 1933 Hitler had made himself dictator of Germany (Unit 15). He withdrew from the Conference and resigned from the League.

In 1934, the Conference broke up, having reached no agreement.

SOME REASONS FOR THE LEAGUE'S FAILURE

The principle of nationalism was stronger than the idea of internationalism; nations were not ready (nor are they today) to put their own national self-interests after international interests. Today this can be seen in such issues as the refusal of the developed world to tackle the issue of underdevelopment (Unit 38). It can also be seen in the way in which even the newer nations use war as an instrument of policy.

Some major powers refused to support the League:

▶ the USA was never a member;
▶ Germany left when its interests seemed to be ignored (see above);
▶ Italy disregarded the principles of the League in the Corfu issue and proved the League helpless in the Abyssinian crisis (Unit 23).

The League had no army at its disposal. If its decisions were to be imposed, particularly against a major power such

as Italy, then Britain and France would have had to supply the forces required. Neither was willing to do so. Like the rest of the world they seemed to prefer peace at any price.

The diplomacy of the 1920s (Unit 18) and 1930s (Unit 23) was achieved by the Great Powers acting outside the League.

Unit 14 Summary

▶ The Covenant and the peace treaties.
▶ The League's organization and structures.
▶ Successes and early failures.
▶ 1931–9; why the League failed to stop the dictators.

---

15 GERMANY, 1919–33

15.1 The Weimar Government

UNREST, 1918–19

William II abdicated on 8 November 1918 amid unrest. Millions starved because of the British naval blockade. Revolutionaries were encouraged by Lenin's success.

A naval mutiny broke out in November 1918 (see Unit 9); socialists in the Reichstag had demanded the Kaiser's abdication in October–November 1918, and the government had little support among the people.

Ebert, a socialist, became Chancellor. The unrest grew. Soviets of workers and soldiers were set up on the Russian model. A Council of Commissars was created. Then a German Republic was proclaimed by the German communists, who claimed power for the workers' and soldiers' councils.

A socialist government versus communist soviets

The mildly socialist government was opposed to the soviet system. This split the socialist and working-class movement.

The Kaiser's civil servants and officials stayed in office. These were more concerned for the good government of Germany than for a communist-style revolution.

The communist revolt

The communists took the name Spartacists, after the leader of a slave revolt in ancient Rome. The Spartacists wanted a dictatorship on the Lenin model; their leaders were Karl Liebknecht and Rosa Luxemburg. On 6 January 1919 they led a mob of 100,000 on anti-government demonstrations in Berlin and seized control of the main buildings.

CRUSHING THE COMMUNISTS

Weimar

The unrest in Berlin forced the government to flee to Weimar, south-west of Leipzig (now in East Germany).

The Free Corps, a volunteer group of ex-soldiers, was opposed to the socialist government and, above all, to the

communists. The Weimar government asked the Free Corps to help put down the Spartacists. Berlin was retaken; many prisoners, including Liebknecht and Luxemburg, were murdered.

This had three main long-term results:

▶ it encouraged the Free Corps and other right-wing groups;
▶ it led to bitter enmity between communists and socialists;
▶ it made fears of a communist revolt seem justified and gave support to the idea that strong government was essential, even if that government ignored some civil or political rights.

THE GENERAL ELECTION

The Germans had a system of proportional representation. The vote was given to all over 21. In the election, the moderate Social Democrats emerged as the largest single party.

There were many other parties, from Communists on the extreme left to right-wing Nationalists of the old type. The Nationalists with 42 seats represented the views of the Prussian Junkers (Unit 1) and German industrialists. They still had the militarist and expansionist views which had led them to support the Kaiser before 1914. The Communists wanted a Russian-style revolution.

A COALITION GOVERNMENT

The system of proportional representation meant that it was almost impossible for a single party to have an overall majority. The Socialists, with the support of some of the smaller parties, formed a coalition.

A coalition (or collection) of parties has to try to agree on government policy and actions to be taken. This is very difficult; it tends to lead to governments which actually take very little action—and are 'weak' as a result (see above).

THE NEW CONSTITUTION

The President, the head of state, elected by direct election, had considerable powers:

▶ he could dissolve the Reichstag and order new elections;
▶ he could use the army to put down a revolution;
▶ he chose the Chancellor, usually choosing the leader of the single largest party in the Reichstag;
▶ he could suspend the constitution if he thought that unrest required this, and could rule with dictatorial powers (by decree).

These powers seemed to be a sensible and stable counter-balance to the possible weakness of coalition governments. But it put a great responsibility on the shoulders of the President, who would have to use care in his implementing of his great powers.

The Chancellor and his Ministers were, in normal times, answerable to the Reichstag for their actions. This was a more democratic system than under Bismarck and William II.

The Reichstag (or Lower House) was elected by the people. It had control over taxation—as the Liberals had hoped for in the Prussian Landtag in 1862 (see Unit 1).

The Reichsrat (or Upper House) represented the individual states of Germany. It could not hold up any proposals which had a two-thirds majority in the Reichstag.

Because the constitution-making Assembly met in Weimar, the new state became known as the Weimar Republic.

The first President was the socialist Ebert.

▉ 15.2 The Initial Problems of the Weimar Republic

THE 'STAB IN THE BACK'

Many Germans claimed that the army had not been beaten by the Allies (Unit 9). They argued that the politicians at home had demanded an end to the war. The army, they said, had been 'stabbed in the back'. This was the view of:
▶ ex-soldiers, many of whom joined the numerous societies and gangs which grew up in post-war Germany;
▶ Nationalists (see above).

THE 'DIKTAT', OR THE TREATY OF VERSAILLES

It had been 'dictated to them' (Unit 12). The Treaty's terms were very harsh. The Weimar government was blamed for this.

ECONOMIC PROBLEMS

Food shortages continued after the end of the British blockade. Millions of the under-nourished died in the influenza epidemic which swept through Europe in 1919–20.

Unemployment was very high.

OPPOSITION

The first enemies of the Weimar Republic were:
▶ The Nationalists—see above;
▶ the officer-class, which opposed left-wing governments;
▶ ex-soldiers who opposed the Treaty of Versailles;
▶ communists, who wanted a Russian-style revolution (see above).

Anti-Weimar risings

Communists led uprisings in the Ruhr and in Munich. These were put down by armed forces on Ebert's orders.

In March 1920 the Free Corps tried to seize Berlin. Their leader, Kapp, wanted to restore the Kaiser. Their rising was defeated by a general strike led by socialists and communists.

Elections were held during this unsettled atmosphere. The extreme right (Nationalists) and the extreme left (Communists) gained more seats. This added to the tensions of the time.

REPARATIONS AND THE WEIMAR REPUBLIC

Reparations were meant to punish Germany. In 1923 the Germans were unable to pay their yearly instalment to the French, so French and Belgian troops invaded the Ruhr.

German workers went on strike. This led to a further decline in German industry, a rise in unemployment and a greater scarcity of goods in shops. The scarcity of goods led to increased prices.

The great inflation of 1923 was caused in part by that scarcity. But it was also caused by the government's decision to print vast sums of money. This was intended to reduce the real value of reparations. The effect of this on the mark was devastating (see Fig. 15.2).

Inflation under the Weimar Republic

Nov. 1918 £1 = 20 Marks
Nov. 1921 £1 = 313 Marks
Jan. 1922 £1 = 1000 Marks
Jun. 1922 £1 = 1500 Marks
Dec. 1922 £1 = 50 000 Marks
Nov. 1923 £1 = 20 000 000 000 000 Marks

Munich Putsch
Nov. 1923

Fig. 15.2   Inflation under the Weimar Republic

The effect of the great inflation was very severe:
▶ pensions, fixed in pre-1923 days, were valueless;
▶ savings, in uninflated marks, were valueless;
▶ insurance policies were almost worthless.

The middle classes suffered most from the inflation. They were the people who had saved most and taken out most insurance.

▉ 15.3 Gustav Stresemann, 1923–9

In 1923 Stresemann became Chancellor and Foreign Secretary. He established a new mark. This did not help those whose savings had been wiped out. It did, however, help German industry and trade to recover.

In 1924 he persuaded the French to leave the Ruhr, and in the same year he negotiated a reduction in reparations.

In 1925 he got Germany accepted as an equal by other European countries which signed the Locarno Treaties (see Unit 18).

In 1926 he got Germany admitted as a member of the League of Nations, when she became a permanent member of the Council.

He persuaded American banks to make massive loans to help German industry to recover. Unemployment fell as industry recovered, and by 1928 Germany seemed to have recovered: unemployment was down, the mark was a stable currency, living standards were rising. At the same time, extremist parties became less popular.

THE WEAKNESS OF STRESEMANN'S 'SUCCESS'

False prosperity
Much of the improvement depended on American loans. What if those loans were recalled?

Few 'Weimarians'
The Germans enjoyed rising living standards and voted the moderate socialists, led by Stresemann, back to power. But few Germans were fervent supporters of the Republic. Nationalists, industrialists, communists and ex-soldiers would still have preferred some other system.

The army

In spite of the anti-militarist terms of the Treaty of Versailles, the army continued to be a major power in Weimar Germany. The High Command would use that power in its own interests—even if that meant a threat to the Republic. We shall see this more clearly later in this Unit.

THE 1929 COLLAPSE

In 1929 reparations were reduced by the Young Plan (see Unit 18).

In October 1929 the Wall Street Crash took place. We shall examine the causes and effects of that Crash in Unit 16. The immediate effects in Germany were:

▶ American banks recalled loans which propped up German industry and trade;
▶ many German banks were ruined;
▶ many industries closed down;
▶ the fall in American demand for goods led to a fall in German exports which led to other industries closing down;
▶ unemployment rose: by 1931 there were 6 million unemployed in Germany. It looked as if the Republic were going back to the harsh days of 1923 again.

In this atmosphere the extremist parties gained in popularity—one proof that support for the Republican government was very fragile (Table 15.5).

15.4　The rise of Hitler and the Nazi Party, 1921–9

ADOLF HITLER—EARLY CAREER

Hitler was born in Austria to middle-class parents. He worked as a sign painter in Vienna before 1914, and in 1914 joined the army, rose to become a corporal and gained the Iron Cross First Class.

In 1918 he was in hospital when the war ended. In his writings he told of his bitterness at the 'stab in the back' (see 15.2), and at the 'dictated peace' with its harsh terms.

In 1921 a small group in Munich founded the National Socialist (or Nazi) Party. Hitler became President of the Nazis in 1921–2.

The Nazis were just one of the many anti-Weimar groups of the period. The Spartacists had tried to seize power. So, too had the Free Corps led by Kapp. The Nazis also tried to seize power.

MUNICH, 1923

By 1923 Hitler had become the undisputed leader of the Nazis. He had got the party to adopt the crooked cross (or swastika) as its symbol, and he became the party's leading orator, proclaiming in fiery speeches that Germany's ills (in 1923) were the fault of Jews, communists, international bankers, foreigners and Weimar socialists.

To the unemployed he promised work in Nazi Germany, to the middle classes, ruined by the great inflation, he promised stability and a restoration of national pride.

He created a 'defence band' which dressed in brown shirts (the SA) under an ex-officer, Captain Roehm. This broke up left-wing meetings and defended Nazis from similar attacks by communist gangs. These rival gangs threatened law and order.

In 1923 the French marched into the Ruhr (see above).

Stresemann came under Nazi attack because of negotiating over reparations and with the French in the Ruhr. Hitler claimed that he would not pay reparations and would drive the French from the Ruhr.

On 8 November 1923 after a meeting in the Beer Hall in Munich Hitler attempted to seize power. He proclaimed himself the President of Germany. Ludendorff, once the hero of wartime Germany (Unit 9), supported Hitler in this conspiracy. But the commander of Hitler's own forces lost his nerve and went over to the government side.

The Bavarian government put down the attempted rising, arrested Hitler and, after a trial, sentenced him to five years in jail.

Mein Kampf (My Struggle)

In jail, Hitler wrote a book, 'the Nazi bible', entitled *Mein Kampf*. In it he set out his ideas on the superiority of the Aryan race, his hatred for Jews and other non-Aryans, and his plans for a Greater Germany which he would create by conquering other countries, particularly Russia; these conquests would provide extra living space ('Lebensraum' for the Germans). He also included his views on propaganda, which he said had to be used to win popular support. This he geared to the level of the least intelligent and said it could be as untruthful as was necessary. The 'big lie' was preferred to the 'little lie' because it would be more effective.

THE FORTUNES OF THE NAZIS, 1924–9

In 1924 the Party had 24 seats in the Reichstag. However, in the prosperous 'Stresemann period' the Nazis lost seats, and in 1929 they had only 12 seats in the Reichstag.

On his release from jail Hitler declared that he would never again try to seize power. He would work through the Republican constitution, even if that meant having to do 'deals' with the hated socialist, communist and Catholic members.

He also realized that he would have to get the support of German industrialists (to provide money to fund his Party) and of the Army (which could prevent him taking power).

15.5　The Crumbling of Weimar, 1929–30, and the Elections

On 3 October 1929 Stresemann died. Then 28 October 1929 saw the start of the Wall Street Crash and an economic crisis in Germany—banks closed, unemployment rose.

Chancellor Brüning proposed:

▶ to cut unemployment benefit (opposed by left-wing members of his coalition government—see above);
▶ to increase taxes paid by the rich to get the money needed to pay the increasing number of unemployed. This was opposed by the right-wing members of the coalition.

Brüning asked the President, Hindenburg, to use his powers and to rule by decree.

1930 ELECTION

The President ordered fresh elections. Hitler, funded by industrialists who feared communism, recruited (and paid) increasing numbers into his Party. Massive demonstrations attracted popular support, and his party gained a larger number of seats (see Table 15.5).

Table 15.5 Relationship between unemployment and party fortunes

		Seats in the Reichstag		Unemployment in millions
		Nazis	Communists	
May	1924	32	62	0.5
Dec	1924	14	45	0.5
	1928	13	54	2.5
	1930	107	77	4.0
July	1932	230	89	6.2
Nov	1932	196	120	6.0
Mar	1933	288	81	5.8

AFTER THE 1930 ELECTION

Brüning remained in power; the army kept him there. General Schleicher, head of the army, hoped to be able to use Brüning.

The Communists gained extra seats (Table 15.5). They argued that the capitalist system had broken down. Germany could be saved only by a Russian-style government.

The Nationalists, with 41 seats, were led by Hugenburg. This party of the extreme right wanted to see the undoing of the Treaty of Versailles. They would give their support to Hitler if needs be.

Brüning invited Hitler to join a coalition. He refused. Street violence increased. Nazi stormtroopers, led by Roehm, numbered 400,000; communists had their paramilitary force—the Red Banner. Clashes became increasingly violent and bloody. Millions of ordinary Germans were terrified.

Propaganda

Hitler had recruited Dr Goebbels to take charge of Nazi propaganda. In speeches, newspapers, posters and cartoons Goebbels tried to convince the German people to support Hitler.

THE PRESIDENTIAL ELECTION, MARCH 1932

In 1932 Hitler stood against the popular but ageing Hindenburg in the Presidential election. He polled 11 million votes as against the 18 million gained by Hindenburg and 5 million gained by the Communist, Thaelmann.

Hitler used this campaign as a chance to put over his ideas to the whole German people.

In April 1932, Brüning wanted to use the army to suppress the activities of Hitler's stormtroopers. Hindenburg refused to let the army get directly involved in 'dirty politics'. Brüning was dismissed and replaced by Papen, leader of the Catholic Centre Party.

ELECTIONS AND THE POLITICIANS, JULY–NOVEMBER 1932

Papen asked for fresh elections (July 1932), because his government was unstable. Unemployment was at its height (Table 15.5).

The Nazis and Communists gained seats. Papen asked Hitler to join in a coalition. He refused. He wanted total control of the government.

Roehm and other Nazis asked Hitler to imitate Mussolini (see Unit 21) who had won power by the threat of force. However, Hitler knew that the army could crush such a rising.

In November 1932 Papen called fresh elections. He hoped to win more seats so that his government could be more secure.

Unemployment was slowly falling (Table 15.5).

While the Communists won even more seats, the Nazis lost ground (Table 15.5) with 196 seats. Had the Nazi movement begun to run out of steam?

▓ 15.6 Hitler's Path to Power ▓

NOVEMBER 1932–JANUARY 1933

Terrorism by the stormtroopers was stepped up.

Schleicher, on behalf of the army, persuaded Hindenburg to sack Papen. Schleicher became Chancellor. However, the Reichstag refused to support Schleicher, and Hindenburg refused Schleicher's request to rule by decree. Papen, anxious to get his own back on Schleicher, advised Hindenburg to invite Hitler to become Chancellor.

In January 1933 Hitler became Chancellor and head of a government of Nazis and Conservative-Nationalists. Hindenburg, representative of Prussian militarism, seemed to give his blessings to the Nazis by appointing Hitler. Nationalists supported the anti-Treaty government, and Papen hoped that he and the 'old politicians' would be able to control the new, inexperienced Chancellor.

ESTABLISHING THE DICTATORSHIP, JANUARY–MARCH 1933

There were only three Nazis in the Cabinet in January 1933. Hitler called fresh elections, hoping to gain more seats.

The reign of terror, February 1933

The Nazis had taken control of a good deal of the German administration—even if not of the Cabinet.

Hermann Goering was the Nazi Minister of the Interior in Prussia, the largest state. He enrolled thousands of Nazis into the police force, which attacked and broke up opposition meetings.

The Reichstag fire

On 27 February 1933, the Reichstag building in Berlin was burned down. Hitler accused the Communists of planning this as a signal for an uprising.

The attack on the left, March 1933

Thousands of communists and socialists were arrested; communist and socialist newspapers were banned; violent attacks were made on Jewish property.

The election was held on 5 March 1933 in this atmosphere of crisis and violence. The Nazis gained increased support, while support for the Communists fell (Table 15.5).

ESTABLISHING THE DICTATORSHIP, MARCH 1933–AUGUST 1934

With their Conservative-Nationalist allies the Nazis had 341 of the 647 seats in the Reichstag—a slender majority. Terrorism continued; the Nazi-controlled police forced many opposition parties to dissolve themselves. They did not appear in the Reichstag.

The Communist representatives were expelled from the Reichstag by a vote of the Nazis and their right-wing allies. Socialist representatives protested against Nazi tactics.

Mass demonstrations by Nazi gangs and stormtroopers were organized around, and even in, the Reichstag building to frighten representatives into passing an Enabling Act. This Act, passed by 441 to 91, gave Hitler power to govern for four years without calling a meeting of the Reichstag. The dictatorship was almost ensured.

THE FÜHRER (OR LEADER)

Captain Roehm, commander of the stormtroopers, wanted Hitler to follow a radical, socialist policy. This had been the declared policy of the Nationalist Socialists. Hitler knew, in 1933–4, that the industrialists would not approve such a policy.

Roehm, an ex-army officer, wanted Hitler to incorporate the SA (stormtroopers) into the Regular Army (the Reichswehr). He hoped to gain more power for himself. However, the General Staff despised Roehm and the stormtroopers. They would have used their power to overthrow Hitler and the Nazis—as they had overthrown Brüning and Papen (see above).

Hitler made a deal with the General Staff:

▶ he would get rid of Roehm and the threat to the power of the General Staff;

▶ the Army would support him if, on Hindenburg's death, he became President.

Roehm and many of his supporters were assassinated on Hitler's orders on 30 June 1934 in what has become known as 'the Night of the Long Knives'.

Later in 1934, when Hindenburg died, Hitler became President (August 1934), although he never used that title, preferring to use the term 'Führer'. This gave him the legitimate control of the Armed Forces as the Commander-in-Chief. His power now was complete.

Unit 15 Summary

▶ The Weimer constitution: the search for stability.
▶ Initial weaknesses and problems: German reparations.
▶ Stresemann's success—and its limitations.
▶ The rise of Hitler and the Nazi Party, 1921–9.
▶ The crumbling of the Republic: the Elections, 1930–3.
▶ Hitler to power: establishing the dictatorship.

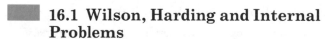

16 THE UNITED STATES OF AMERICA, 1917–32

16.1 Wilson, Harding and Internal Problems

PRESIDENT WOODROW WILSON, 1912–20

Before 1914 Wilson was a 'liberal' President (see Unit 7). Then he led the USA into the war in 1917 and in January 1918 he issued his Fourteen Points (Fig. 12.1).

At Versailles he was under great pressure from Lloyd George and Clemenceau (Unit 12). This prevented him from putting his ideals into practice.

The League of Nations (Unit 14) was his brainchild. In 1918 there were mid-term elections for the House of Representatives and one-third of the Senate. The Republicans gained control of both Houses of Congress, which voted against US participation in the League.

Wilson, a sick man, retired from politics in 1920.

PRESIDENT WARREN HARDING, 1921–3

Harding, a Republican, won the 1920 Presidential Election. His campaign had been summed up in the slogan 'Back to normalcy'. By 'normalcy' he meant:

▶ no foreign entanglements; America became 'isolationist';
▶ American efforts should concentrate on internal development—of industry and commerce—and a growth in prosperity.

Harding had been Senator for the State of Ohio. As President he took many of his friends with him to Washington. This 'Ohio Gang' held many important government posts. These businessmen-politicians were as corrupt as many American industrialists in the 19th century (see Unit 7), e.g.:

▶ the Head of the Veterans' Bureau stole millions of dollars given to him for the relief of disabled servicemen;
▶ the Attorney-General escaped prison on a charge of corruption because he destroyed his bank records before the trial.

The Teapot Dome Scandal

The US navy had oil reserves in fields in the Elk Hills, California and at Teapot Dome, Wyoming. Harding's friend and Minister of the Interior, Albert B. Fall, persuaded another Harding crony, the Secretary of the Navy, to lease those oilfields to the Department of the Interior.

He then leased out the fields to oil companies. One company 'boss' paid Fall 200,000 dollars and another paid him 100,000 dollars for these profitable leases. Fall was found out, sentenced to one year's imprisonment, and fined 100,000 dollars.

THE WORLD'S RICHEST NATION IN 1919–20

In 1914 the USA was a major industrial power (see Unit 7). In the years 1914–18 the US grew even more powerful:

▶ the Allies bought a great volume of munitions; coal, steel and engineering industries grew rapidly;
▶ after 1917 the US government spent a great deal of money on arming its own forces;
▶ there was a fall in British and German exports. US industrialists won a large share in world markets.

THE 'RED SCARE' 1918–20

The trade union movement was weak in 1914 (see Unit 7). However, during the war many workers joined unions. Republican politician-industrialists feared that the growing trade union movement might lead to a Bolshevik-style revolution such as had swept the Tsar from power in 1917 (see Unit 10). Politicians and newspaper editors warned Americans against the danger of 'international' trade unionism. In 'isolationist' America, 'internationalism' was a dirty word.

Industrialists employed gangs of ex-soldiers to break up trade union and/or socialist meetings. Mitchell Palmer, Harding's Attorney-General, organized a campaign against foreigners and 'internationalism': police and troops were ordered to raid magazine offices, public halls, private houses, union headquarters and meetings of any liberal organization, and in 1920 6000 people were arrested.

Violence bred violence:

bombs were placed in offices of leading businessmen;
▶ many factories were destroyed by gang activities;
▶ politicians received bombs in their mail;
▶ Palmer's own house was blown up.

Sacco and Vanzetti

On 15 April 1920, two men were murdered during a wages robbery. Police arrested two Italian immigrants, Sacco and Vanzetti; they were found guilty on 14 July 1920. During the years 1920–7 world-wide protests led to many court appeals, but in 1927 the men were executed. It is now generally agreed that the two Italians were innocent and victims of the 'Red scare' campaign.

16.2 Coolidge and the Prosperity of the 1920s

PRESIDENT CALVIN COOLIDGE 1923–8

Harding died in 1923; Vice-President Coolidge succeeded him. In 1924 Coolidge won the Presidential election. He said: 'The business of America is business' and argued that the American prosperity was the result of the freedom which Republican governments gave to industrialists.

GOVERNMENT POLICY, 1920–8

Tariffs were imposed on imported goods. In 1922 the Fordney-McCumber Act increased existing tariffs, then in 1930, at the start of the Great Depression, the Hawley-Smoot amendment further increased tariffs.

Industry benefited from the tariffs and from low taxation:

▶ industrialists and businessmen paid low taxes and had money for industrial and commercial investment;

▶ consumers paying low taxes had more money to spend on goods produced by industry.

Anti-trust legislation

Before 1914 governments tried to limit the power of large firms (see Unit 7). Then the Republican governments of the 1920s relaxed the laws. Industrialists could do as they wished.

Immigration

Most Americans were of immigrant stock (see Unit 7). However, in post-war America the government tried to limit the flow of immigrants.

In 1921 the Immigration Act limited the number of immigrants from any one country to 3 per cent of the number of that nationality living in the USA in 1910. In 1924 an amendment to the 1921 Act pushed back the base year to 1890. This allowed the immigration of many from Britain, Ireland and Germany but of few from Italy, Russia and Eastern Europe.

The trade union movement

Courts often declared union activities illegal, and in addition police and troops were often used to attack the strikers.

Foreign debts

US bankers and financiers had lent 10 billion dollars to the Allies to help them to buy supplies in wartime America. Britain had borrowed most of this money but had made even greater loans to her Allies—France, Italy and Russia. If they repaid their loans, Britain would be able to repay the Americans. However, repayment would have crippled the debtor countries, so Britain asked for all inter-Allied debts to be cancelled. Coolidge refused. Thus to get the money for such repayments, Britain had to sell goods in the USA. But this was made more difficult by the tariff policy (see above).

American loans were made in the 1920s to Germany to enable her to make her reparations payments and to help her industry to get back on its feet (see Unit 15).

Prohibition

During the war there was a growth in the temperance movement, and in 1919 Congress passed the Eighteenth Amendment to the US Constitution, making illegal the manufacture and sale of alcoholic drink anywhere in the USA. The Volstead Act 1919 implemented the 18th Amendment. Wilson tried to veto this legislation, but Congress overcame his veto.

Suffrage

Women were given the same political rights as men—by the Nineteenth Amendment to the Constitution.

Welfare

Before 1914 the US had started to develop a welfare system. Child-labour laws were passed (see Unit 7) and, though Theodore Roosevelt wanted a welfare programme, little had been achieved. The Republican politician-industrialists of the 1920s made no effort to develop such a programme. They refused to increase the taxes which would have been needed to pay for such a programme. They preferred a policy of low taxation.

ECONOMIC PROSPERITY, 1920–8

Basic industries

Some basic industries (coal and textiles) did not grow much, whereas others (steel) grew rapidly to provide the material needed by consumer goods industries (see below).

Consumer goods industries

▶ Widespread electricity supply led to the growth in the demand for many goods—radios, vacuum cleaners and other household gadgets. This led to the growth in the electrical engineering industry and in the industries producing these consumer goods.

▶ The film industry grew rapidly, its 'capital' being Hollywood. The invention of 'the talking pictures' in 1928 led to a further growth in this industry.

▶ Entertainment became a major industry in prosperous America; cinemas were built to show films, more dance halls were built where crowds of people learned such popular dances as the Charleston.

▶ The car industry: Henry Ford had introduced mass production methods into this industry in 1913. This assembly-line technique allowed the production of an increasing number of cars. In 1920 there were 9 million cars on US roads, but by 1930 this had risen to 30 million cars—and some four million new jobs had been created in the car industry alone. Ford's Model T or 'Tin Lizzie' was bought by workers in prosperous America.

Hire purchase

To help workers pay the 300 dollars for a car in 1926 (compared with 850 dollars in 1914) businessmen enlarged, or started, finance companies to lend money to prospective buyers who could then get a car (or other article). Weekly instalments repaid the loan and the interest on it. Such a system helped to:

▶ increase the demand for goods—and so helped industrialists to expand as well as helping to create jobs for many workers;

▶ raise living standards. Americans bought many things on hire purchase (H.P.)—cars, radios, furniture, as well as holidays away from home.

THE STOCK MARKET BOOM 1920–8

There was a rapid growth in company profits. Owners of shares in these companies received, each year, higher dividends—their share in the profits. Their shares became more valuable. If they decided to sell, they could get much more for the share than they had paid.

Hire purchase was used to buy consumer goods. In the 1920s many Americans used a similar system to buy shares in profitable companies.

The Wall Street Stock Exchange allowed a system of 'buying on the margin': people had to put down only 10 cents for each dollar's worth of shares they wished to buy. The rest of the money had to be paid within a few months. People hoped to be able to sell, at a higher price, the shares bought 'on the margin'. They expected enough to make their own final payment *and* a profit.

Banks made it easy for people to borrow money to buy shares. They accepted shares as guarantees for loans. If clients could not repay the loan, their banks could sell the shares.

Millions of Americans became shareholders.

16.3 Prohibition, Crime and Violence

After January 1920 a 'black market' in alcohol soon developed. Gangs got and sold alcohol, bribed police and judges and fought other similar gangs.

'Bootleggers' smuggled drink from Canada, Mexico and Europe. Criminal gangs controlled 'bootlegging', armed with machine guns. Motor cars helped them to raid other gangs' territories and to attack rivals' vessels and lorries.

Irishmen such as Dion O'Banion led the first gangs. Italians, usually Sicilians, such as Al Capone, ran the gangs which first destroyed the Irish gangs and then gained almost complete control of the illegal drink trade and other criminal activities.

Capone, based in Chicago, had an income of 60 million dollars a year from crime. This allowed him to bribe politicians, judges, police and other officials. He was sent to jail in 1931—but for the evasion of income tax, not his criminal activities.

THE KU KLUX KLAN

This secret society was originally formed to terrorize the freed slaves in the Southern States (see Unit 7). In the hysterical anti-internationalism of the 1920s the Klan grew rapidly. By 1928 it had 5 million members. It turned to targets other than the blacks. Jews and Catholics came under attack from the Klan, which supported the idea of a White Anglo-Saxon and Protestant people (WASP). Socialists and trade unionists were attacked for having links with international organizations.

The Klansmen in their long white, hooded cloaks set fire to property, attacked individuals and organized lynching parties in which 'guilty' people were hanged.

These activities were another of those outward signs of the violence in isolationist America.

16.4 The Agricultural Depression, 1921–8

During 1914–18 American farmers enjoyed a period of prosperity. Foreign imports almost ceased; nations bought American farm produce to make up for the lost output of war-torn countries.

American farms became more productive: new land was broken in and farmed, and new machinery was bought to help to increase output.

In 1920–1 this farming prosperity ended. European farmers began to produce again; their output, plus the increased output in America, led to over-production. This led to a drastic fall in farm prices. Prices slumped in 1922 and continued to fall; by 1929 wheat prices were lower than they had been for 40 years.

With very much smaller incomes, American farmers bought fewer goods. The future President, Harry S. Truman, owned a drapery store in Kansas City, the centre of a prosperous farming industry in wartime. In 1922 Truman found that he could not sell his goods to Kansas farmers—and he went bankrupt. This had a snowball effect: shops bought less from factories, which sacked workmen and announced lower profits.

Many farmers had bought their land with a loan from local banks. With lower incomes they could not make the mortgage repayments. Thousands of farmers were thrown off the land by banks, which then tried to sell the land to get back the money they had lent.

Banks which could not profitably sell the farms they had taken back had to declare falling profits. These banks failed—becoming 'bankrupt'.

CLOUDS ON THE HORIZON, 1928

Many companies had lower profits—and lower sales. Many farmers, evicted from their farms, were unemployed.

America's increasing wealth was unfairly shared out. The richest 5 per cent of the population earned one-third of all the money earned in America. The rich spent most of this money on luxuries and on investments in the stock market. They did not buy one-third of all the goods produced by US industry.

The rest of the people, with only two-thirds of the American income, could only buy, at best, two-thirds of all that was produced. This led to under-consumption; less was bought than was produced. Other people saw this as over-production; more was being produced than could be bought.

The result was a fall in prices of many goods.

16.5 Hoover and the Wall Street Crash

PRESIDENT HERBERT HOOVER, 1928–32

Hoover had played an important part in the American famine relief sent to Europe after 1918. He was Secretary of Commerce under both Harding and Coolidge. Honest and efficient, he was known as 'the Great Engineer'. Because of the prosperity of America under his Republican predecessors, he won the 1928 Election by a huge majority.

He claimed that 'the rugged individualism' of America was responsible for the growth of prosperity. He claimed that prosperity would increase. There would be 'a chicken in every pot and two cars in every garage'.

THE WALL STREET CRASH, 1929

Causes–past

Over-production and under-consumption (see above) led to falling prices, sales and profits and more unemployment. Falling profits made shares less valuable.

Causes–immediate

Banks had made loans to buyers of shares, and the shares bought with the loans were taken by the banks as guarantees (or collateral). In 1929 banks saw that the value of the shares they held was less than the loans made, so many asked clients to repay their loans. People then had to sell their shares, and, with millions trying to sell, share prices fell.

October 1929—the Crash

24 October (Thursday) First panic: 13 million shares for sale.
25 October Prices steadied (at a lower level than before).
28 October (Monday) Much heavier selling; prices fell steeply; many people announced heavy losses.
29 October 16 million shares 'thrown upon the market for what prices they could get'.

16.6 National and International Effects of the Crash

THE EFFECTS OF THE CRASH IN AMERICA

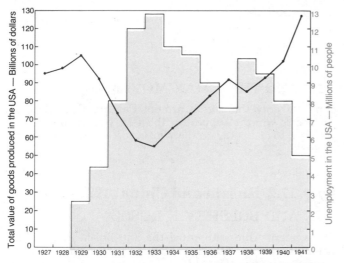

Fig. 16.5 The changing pattern of US industry, 1929–41

Many large companies were ruined. Factories and shops closed because employers had no money to pay wages and no hope of selling their goods.

Banks which had advanced loans could not recover their money. Many of them ran out of money. Savers could not get their money back from banks—and they, too, were ruined.

House buyers who had borrowed to buy their homes could not make the mortgage repayments. Many were evicted. There was a fall in the output from factories and other workplaces, many of which closed down.

Unemployment grew. The unemployed with meagre, if any, incomes could buy little if anything. This had a snow-balling effect on the demand made for goods from factories—and helps to explain part of the fall in output.

Those who had a job were unsure of the future. Would they lose their jobs? Should they hold on to the money they had?

The decline in the number of people willing to make hire purchase agreements led to a fall in the demand for cars, radios and other consumer goods.

Many farmers were evicted when banks tried to get back money loaned to them in more prosperous times. In Iowa, farmers fought off representatives from banks coming to claim their property. They had a slogan 'In Hoover we trusted, now we are busted'.

Thousands of unemployed marched to Washington to demand government action. They put up ramshackle shelters on the outskirts of Washington; in other cities and towns similar 'Hoovervilles' were built to shelter the evicted and unemployed. Troops and police tried to clear these camps. Some people thought that America was on the brink of a revolution.

Hoover and the Depression

At first Hoover claimed that 'prosperity is just around the corner'. He refused to spend money on the development of the Tennessee Valley (see Unit 19), and insisted that private enterprise would solve the problem. However, he set up the Reconstruction Finance Corporation (RFC). This government agency lent money to banks, railways and State governments willing to help schemes to provide work. But this body and some tinkering with interest rates did little to improve matters.

THE EFFECTS OF THE CRASH IN EUROPE

American loans helped European industry to recover (see above). Stresemann had depended on such loans (see Unit 15). In the winter of 1929 American banks demanded the immediate repayment of these loans.

Austrian, Italian, German and other national banks were forced to try to repay the money, if they could. Many were forced to close down, ruining millions of savers who had put their money into the banks. Thousands of industrialists were also ruined—forced to repay the loans on which they had depended.

The rise in American unemployment led to a fall in the demand for goods exported by Europe to America. This led to a further rise in European unemployment. Note that the high US tariffs also made exporting to the US very difficult.

The rise of Hitler to power was a major result of the Crash. The relationship between German unemployment and Nazi electoral success is illustrated in Table 15.5.

THE POLITICIANS AND THE CRASH

Hitler was one politician who benefited from the Crash. Mussolini also claimed credit for policies aimed at bringing down Italian unemployment (see Unit 21).

Huey Long, governor and virtual dictator of the State of Louisiana, argued for an American Fascist movement.

Franklin Delano Roosevelt

F. D. Roosevelt was Vice-Presidential candidate for the Democratic Party in the 1920 Election. In 1928 he was elected governor of New York State. The State Legislature was controlled by the Republicans. That Legislature did not pass laws which he proposed in 1928:

▶ to reduce the length of the working day;
▶ to provide compensation for men injured at work;
▶ to help the aged and sick;
▶ to help farmers affected by falling prices.

When New York was affected by the Crash he acted quickly:

▶ he claimed that it was the duty of government to step in to prevent starvation and hardship;
▶ he set up committees of industrialists, trade union leaders, economists and social workers to develop schemes for the unemployed in the State of New York;
▶ he persuaded the Republican legislature to pass a law to allow the spending of 20 million dollars to help the unemployed.

In 1930 Roosevelt ran for re-election as governor. His popularity was reflected in his increased majority. In 1932 he became the Democratic Party candidate in the Presidential Election. In June he promised 'a new deal for the American people'. He took office in March 1933, claiming that 'the only thing we have to fear is fear itself...'. We will study his work as President in Unit 19.

Unit 16 Summary

▶ Wilson, Warren Harding, Sacco and Vanzetti.
▶ Coolidge and the prosperity of the 1920s.
▶ Prohibition and crime; the Ku Klux Klan and the blacks.
▶ The agricultural depression in the 'roaring twenties'.
▶ Hoover and the Wall Street Crash, 1929.
▶ National and international effects of the Crash.

17 CHINA AND JAPAN, 1914-49

17.1 China and Japan 1914-19

A DIVIDED CHINA, 1914 (see Unit 6)

The Manchu dynasty was overthrown in 1911-12. Sun Yat-Sen inspired the revolution of Double Tenth. He allowed Yuan Shih-k'ai to become President in 1912, and Yuan set himself up as dictator. He had the support of War Lords, generals who controlled various regions in China.

CHINA AND JAPAN AND THE FIRST WORLD WAR, 1914-18

Yuan declared China to be neutral. Japan had been an ally of Britain since 1902. She declared war on Germany. Japan seized Germany's Pacific Islands colonies, and invaded the German-controlled province of Shantung on mainland China, including the port of Kiao-chow, promising to return this territory to China.

Yuan gave way to most of the Twenty-One Demands in May 1915 and started negotiating others. China was controlled by either Japan or the West. Anti-Japanese activity broke out.

Yuan died in August 1916. His successor, Li Yuan-hung restored the 1912 constitution and recalled the 1913 parliament. War Lords were too strong for Li; fighting each other, they made life very hard for the Chinese people.

Sun Yat-Sen, accepted as President of China by the Assembly which met in Canton (Fig. 17.1), was in a weak position:

▶ War Lords controlled most of China;
▶ even Sun depended on the support of a War Lord;
▶ foreign governments refused to recognize him as ruler.

JAPAN AND THE TREATY OF VERSAILLES, 1919

Japan was one of the victorious powers at Versailles. She was given a mandate (see Unit 13) over the former German Caroline, Marshall and Mariana Islands.

Shantung, including Kiao-chow (Fig. 17.1), was transferred to Japan.

CHINA AND THE TREATY OF VERSAILLES

China was angry at the gains made by Japan. The grant of Shantung was also against Wilson's principle of 'national self-determination'.

Movement of 4 May 1919

Peking students held anti-government demonstrations, and a boycott of Japanese goods was organized. Government forces arrested many students.

The anti-government, anti-Japanese and anti-Versailles campaign spread; students and workers in many towns joined in. The young Mao Tse-tung was one such recruit (see Unit 17.3).

The demands by the organizers changed. They asked for:

▶ constitutional government;
▶ Western-style education;
▶ the suppression of the War Lords;
▶ an end to corruption in official life;
▶ an exclusion of foreigners from Chinese trade and industry.

SUN AND THE 4 MAY MOVEMENT

Sun held only the region around Canton (Fig. 17.1). He decided to win the support of the 4 May campaigners and proposed to make war on the War Lords. For this he needed an army.

17.2 Russia and China, 1920-5

SUN AND BOLSHEVIK RUSSIA

The western Allies supported the anti-Bolsheviks against Lenin (see Unit 10). They also supported Japan's anti-Chinese campaign (Unit 17).

In 1920 Lenin gave up Tsarist claims on China. In 1921 the Chinese Communist Party was formed, but in 1922 it still had only 200 members.

In 1922 Sun refused Russian offers of help. Then his War Lord at Canton turned against him. He was saved from assassination by a young supporter, Chiang Kai-shek. In 1923 Chiang took Sun to Shanghai (Fig. 17.1) and his businessmen friends. The Russian agent, Joffe, met Sun and they agreed that Sun would accept the help of the Chinese Communists, and Russia would provide various forms of aid (see below).

RUSSIAN AID TO SUN

Blucher, a Russian general, set up a military academy at Whampoa near Canton (Fig. 17.1). It trained young officers for a Sun-controlled army.

Chiang Kai-shek was the first commandant; Chou En-lai, a Communist, was appointed political educational officer at the academy.

Borodin, a Russian agent, organized the Kuo Min Tang. He helped set up small cells in various towns, showed how to spread political ideas among the people, and helped Sun create an army, based on Canton, with Russian money, advisers and equipment.

A REVISED KUO MIN TANG (KMT)

In 1924 Sun restated the Three Principles (see Unit 6). He agreed to set up a small committee to make decisions. This, later, led to party dictatorship under Chiang Kai-shek.

Sun allowed Communists to join the KMT. They supported him—hoping for complete control later on. In 1925, Sun died.

17.3 Chiang versus Mao, 1925-30

CHIANG KAI-SHEK'S EARLY CAREER (TO 1925)

Born in 1887, son of a landowner, he had a private education; in 1905 he went to Manchu military academy, and in 1907 he was sent to Tokyo for further training. In 1911 he returned to lead the revolution in Hangchow (see Unit 6). Then in 1912 he returned from Japan to help Sun as chief-of-staff. Chiang and Sun travelled to Japan after the revolution failed. In 1917 Chiang was back in Canton as Sun's chief adviser.

In 1918 Chiang quarrelled with Sun's protecting War

Lord. He went to Shanghai (Fig. 17.1) where he made a fortune on the Stock Exchange. He also made many friends in the business community and was popular with the secret societies and gangs.

In 1921 he returned to Canton and in 1922 saved Sun from assassination (see above). In 1923 he was appointed commandant at Whampoa.

When Sun died in 1925, he became leader of the KMT.

MAO TSE-TUNG'S EARLY CAREER (TO 1925)

Born (1893) into a poor family, he went to Changsha High School in the capital of Hunan (Fig. 17.1). In 1911 he joined Sun's army, but fought no battles. Then in 1913 he went to Changsha Teachers' Training College where students opposed Yuan's submission to foreigners (see above). In 1918 he became assistant librarian, Peking University.

In 1919 Mao, back in Changsha as a teacher, led a students' strike in support of the 4 May Movement (see above). He edited a newspaper which was suppressed by the local War Lord.

In 1921 he formed the Changsha cell of the Communist Party and in July 1921 attended the first Party Congress, Shanghai. Then in 1922 he went to Hunan (Fig. 17.1) to organize workers to strike, to fight troops sent against them and to win higher wages for miners and railwaymen.

In 1924 he joined the KMT, and in 1925 he was in charge of propaganda for the KMT in Canton.

CHIANG'S KUO MIN TANG, 1925

Communists in the KMT were led by Borodin (see above). Right-wing businessmen and landlords wanted the expulsion of Western merchants and a restoration of order.

Moderate left-wing members distrusted the Communists. The Three Principles (Unit 6) led them to oppose the right wing. Sun's wife was a member of this group.

Chiang was distrusted by the Communists. He expelled all Communist officers from the army. He favoured the right-wing group.

Canton was Chiang's 'capital'; Western governments recognized the Peking government controlled by War Lords.

On 30 May 1925 there was an anti-Japanese demonstration in Shanghai (Fig. 17.1). Western police in the International Settlement arrested some demonstrators. Crowds demonstrated at the police station. A British officer ordered shooting. Ten were killed. The Peking government reacted feebly. The KMT called it an 'imperial agent'.

THE NORTHERN EXPEDITION, 1926

Chiang's aims

▶ to drive the war lords from Peking (Fig. 17.1);
▶ to unite China under a KMT government in Peking;
▶ to drive the foreigners from China.

His campaign

He led 100,000 men in attack on Yangtse valley. In October 1926 he took Hankow (Fig. 17.1); in March 1927 he took Shanghai (Fig. 17.1).

Political agents

These were under the control of Mao Tse-tung. They educated the peasants against landlords; they also educated town workers against foreign merchants.

THE SHANGHAI MASSACRES, 1927

Chiang had succeeded in the first part of the Expedition. The Communists had played a large part in this success. Mao had led the political agents. Chou En-lai formed a revolutionary committee in Shanghai.

However, Chiang's right wing resented their success. He suspected communists wanted to 'take over' the KMT. He

had many friends in Shanghai. With their help he arrested and shot many communists, expelled his Russian advisers, and smashed the Shanghai communists' organization. Five thousand were killed in Shanghai. More were killed in other towns, including Mao's wife, though Chou En-lai, Chiang's colleague at Whampoa, escaped.

Madame Sun thought Chiang had betrayed the revolution. However, her sisters, married to Chiang and to T.V. Soong, thought that he had done well by setting up a right-wing dictatorship.

THE NORTHERN EXPEDITION, 1927–8

1927

Chiang marched on to Peking, the accepted capital of China. The War Lords fled to Manchuria (Fig. 17.1).

The KMT army marched through Shantung and the port of Kiao-chow (Fig. 17.1) but Chiang ordered it not to fight the Japanese.

1928

Peking was captured, and Nanking (Fig. 17.1) was named as Chiang's new capital. It had been Sun's capital in 1912 (see Unit 6).

CHIANG IN POWER, 1928

The Three Principles were ignored (see Unit 6):

▶ there was no elected government, no Parliament;
▶ the rights of the peasants were ignored;
▶ foreigners were not driven out.

Chiang had a right-wing government of businessmen and landlords.

Western powers made some concessions to Chiang: they gave up their control of the tariff system, and they allowed China to control its postal system. However, they retained many powers. There were International Settlements in Shanghai and Tientsin (Fig. 17.1). Foreign gunboats patrolled the Yangtse (Fig. 17.1).

Communists under Mao held the region around Canton.

JAPAN—THE TANAKA MEMORIAL, 1927

Baron Tanaka was Prime Minister of Japan in 1927. His government issued a policy statement (Unit 42.3 Q.4). In this 'Memorial' Tanaka outlined policies for:

▶ the military conquest of Eastern Asia;
▶ the need to fight and defeat the USA, China's friend;
▶ the seizure of Manchuria and Mongolia (Fig. 17.1).

Fig. 17.1 China in the 1930s

MANCHURIA, 1928

Its ruler was War Lord Chang Tso-Lin ('the old Marshal'). Japan controlled its railway lines.

In 1928 Japanese forces assassinated 'the old Marshal'. His son, 'Young Marshal', succeeded him. He declared his loyalty to Chiang Kai-shek.

THE LAST WAR LORD

Most war lords had been defeated in 1927 and 1928. The 'Young Marshal' had accepted Chiang as ruler of China. General Feng, 'the Christian General' was the last war lord. Chiang attacked him, lost 150,000 men, but was victorious.

17.4 Mao and the Kiangsi Soviet

Chiang feared communism more than he hated the Japanese. The Shanghai Massacre (see above) started the war on communists.

Mao controlled Hunan province (Fig. 17.1). In 1928, 40,000 of the Red Army were killed by Chiang's men. In 1930, 2000 were killed in a communist rising in Changsha.

Mao led 10,000 to found a soviet in Kiangsi (Fig. 17.1). He changed the Communist Party line:

▶ the Revolution would not be based on town workers;
▶ Chinese peasants would lead the Revolution.

The Red Army was made up of peasants; other peasants hid, fed and helped Mao's forces. This was against the principles of the Party (and of Marx), which said that a communist revolution had to follow an industrial revolution and be based on industrial workers.

LIFE IN KIANGSI

Soviets were elected and a ruling soviet chosen. Living conditions were hard; but officers and men shared equal conditions. Political agents educated local peasants against landlords. They helped peasants to fight dishonest merchants.

Chiang attacked Kiangsi. Mao had four principles:

▶ 'the enemy attacks, we retreat;
▶ the enemy camps, we harass;
▶ the enemy tires, we attack;
▶ the enemy retreats, we pursue.'

CHIANG VERSUS MAO, 1930–1

In 1930 Chiang planned to wipe out the Kiangsi soviet. Peasants helped the Red Army. In 1931 Chiang had lost 23,000 men, and Mao was still in Kiangsi.

17.5 Japan and Manchuria, 1931

Japan controlled Shantung Province around Kiao-chow (Fig. 17.1) and the Manchurian railways.

She wanted control of Manchuria as:

▶ a market for her industries;
▶ a source of raw materials and minerals;
▶ extra living space for her growing population;
▶ the first stage of the Tanaka scheme (see above).

THE ATTACK, 1931

Part of the Japanese-controlled railway was blown up. Japanese officers in Manchuria blamed the Chinese; they attacked Mukden, capital of Manchuria (Fig. 17.1).

The 'Young Marshal' was driven south to China. Japan put a three-year-old ex-Manchu on the throne, and the region was re-named Manchukuo.

Chiang appealed to the League of Nations when Japan attacked. He did not try to fight the Japanese.

THE LEAGUE AND THE MANCHURIAN CRISIS

Japan was a permanent member of the League Council and had signed the Covenant (see Unit 14).

The League sent a Commission under the Englishman, Lord Lytton. The Lytton Commission's report (1932) condemned Japan. The League accepted the report and refused to recognize the re-naming of Manchuria. Japan, in anger, left the League.

The League did not take any further action. Japan held Manchuria, and it seemed that 'might is right'. This weakened the League.

17.6 The Long March

CHIANG VERSUS MAO, 1932–4

Chiang did not fight the Japanese when they invaded Manchuria (see above). He had fought three campaigns against Mao in 1930–1.

In a fourth campaign in 1932 Chiang sent a million men and an airforce of 200 planes under two German generals. Mao followed his first principle and retreated.

Chiang's army had encircled the communists by October 1934. Mao decided that, rather than accept defeat, he would lead his small band of followers to another, distant part of China.

OCTOBER 1934–OCTOBER 1935

On 15 October 1934, 120,000 men, women and children escaped from the Kiangsi region (Fig. 17.1). Mao hoped to found a new soviet in the north-west, but Chiang's forces were too strong: 4000 communists were killed before the Reds got to the Yangtse River (Fig. 17.1).

Mao then decided to go to north China, where Chiang's rule was at its weakest. This meant a march of 9600 km (6000 miles) which lasted for 368 days. During the march they were attacked by Chiang's forces, by War Lords and by bandit gangs.

They reached Yenan (Fig. 17.1)—20,000 of them.

MAO IN YENAN

In the mountains, Mao set up a new soviet. Industry was developed—partly to manufacture arms. Peasant farmers were helped by a fixing of fair rents. The landless got farms created from formerly unused land. New farming techniques helped improve output.

Mao and his leading supporters lived, like everyone else, in homes made in caves. Everyone worked—in the fields, as political agents in the locality or in the small industries.

Propaganda was used to win people's support—plays, operas, newspapers, cartoons and posters all being employed.

An army was trained, because, said Mao: 'Political power grows out of the barrel of a gun'.

17.7 Chiang's Government, 1930–5

The War Lords had been wiped out or had accepted Chiang's rule. The communists had been driven from Kiangsi to the Japanese-controlled northern region. Chiang's government controlled most of the vast country.

Western businessmen came back to the southern ports which enjoyed growing prosperity (Fig. 17.1). Shanghai, 'the Queen of the East', was the wealthiest city and controlled half of China's foreign trade. New factories were built—by foreigners and Chinese.

An extended railway system, new roads and airlines made transport easier. Postal services, telecommunications and other public services encouraged Western businesses to develop and make China more industrialized. Western firms had special privileges, 'extra-territorial rights' and angered Chinese who remembered Sun's Principles (see Unit 6).

Landlords were Chiang's main supporters. Chiang's government did little for the peasants, which angered Sun's followers.

THE SOONG FAMILY

Madame Sun (widow of Sun Yat-sen) was critical of Chiang's government from 1927 onwards. One of her sisters had married Chiang; another had married a rich business-man, T. V. Soong. The Soong family prospered in Chiang's China. The family got many top jobs in government; others got contracts which allowed the growth of their businesses. T. V. Soong owned banks, factories, airlines and shipping companies. He was a very Westernized Chinese, out of touch with the ordinary people.

He and his brother-in-law Chiang did little for:
► the 6 million peasants who died in the famines of 1929–32;
► the 20,000 who died of starvation each year in Shanghai;
► the regular flooding by China's main rivers which each year devastated the countryside and made millions homeless.

Chiang governed with a small inner group of party faithfuls. This ignored the Principle of People's Democracy (see Unit 6). Chinese intellectuals grew critical of Chiang's government which favoured the few, ignored the peasants and allowed corruption by the Soongs and others to spread.

CHIANG, THE COMMUNISTS AND THE JAPANESE, 1936

The Japanese had got control of five northern provinces. Chiang refused to attack them.

He sent the 'Young Marshal' to wipe out Mao in Yenan. Mao appealed that 'Chinese ought not to fight Chinese'. In November 1936 the 'Young Marshal' signed a truce with Mao and agreed to join him to fight the Japanese.

THE SIAN INCIDENT, 1936

Chiang flew to Sian to undo the truce. On 12 December the 'Marshal's' men arrested Chiang.

Chou En-lai was sent by Mao to negotiate. He saved Chiang from assassination by some of the 'Marshal's' men. Chou and Chiang agreed to unite to fight the Japanese. On 25 December Chiang was released.

In January 1937 the war against the communists was called off, and in February 1937 Chiang was proclaimed head of a government of 'The United Front'. Yenan was called 'the autonomous border'.

▮ 17.8 Japan and China, 1932–9 ▮

At Versailles, Japan had gained the Shantung Province. In 1931 Japan had conquered Manchuria and extended her control from Shantung over five northern provinces. Western powers, including America, saw the Japanese expansion as a barrier against Russian advance.

The Japanese shared with the Western nations many extra-territorial privileges (see above).

SHANGHAI, 1932

Western nations had a large International Settlement; Western police patrolled this area. A Japanese was killed during a riot outside the area.

The Japanese government sent a naval force to Shanghai, and Japanese armed forces moved into Charpei, north of the International Settlement.

The Chinese resisted, and in January 1932 the crowded area of Charpei was bombarded. Chiang did nothing; Western countries approved Japan's military defence of Western privileges over the Chinese.

THE START OF THE CHINESE-JAPANESE WAR, 1937

The aims of the Tanaka group were partly realized by the conquest of Manchuria and the extra-territorial rights enjoyed in the five northern provinces. However, the Japanese wanted more. They decided to act before the United Front got to work (see above).

On 7 July 1937 Japanese troops were on manoeuvres near Peking. At the Marco Polo Bridge (a railway junction near Peking) Japanese troops clashed with Chinese troops.

Japanese forces bombarded the city of Wanping, near Peking. They demanded the right to search the city for those who had 'attacked' their forces. The Chinese refused.

On 28 July, the Japanese launched a full-scale war by air and land and massacred the 29th Chinese Army guarding Peking.

THE WAR, 1937–9

The Northern War

Japanese troops landed at Tientsin (Fig. 17.1), where there was little Chinese resistance. Japan soon controlled most of northern China.

Conquering the Yangtse region

The Yangtse River valley was the richest region in China. Shanghai was the starting point for an attack on the valley. In August 1937 a Japanese naval force and land army attacked Shanghai. Chiang's forces resisted for three months. Then on 3 December 1937 the Japanese organized a victory parade through Shanghai. Their forces conquered most of the Yangtse valley.

On 12 December 1937 Japanese troops took Nanking, the capital of Chiang's China (Fig. 17.1).

Chiang's policy

Chiang's forces had resisted in Shanghai, and been beaten, so he decided to 'trade space for time'. He retreated and allowed the Japanese to gain more territory. He hoped that America would, one day, come to his aid.

Mao's policy

The Japanese took the cities and towns, but they found it almost impossible to control the countryside.

The communists used guerrilla tactics and created 'liberated areas' which communists ruled. In these areas they collected taxes, and reduced rents to gain the support of the peasants.

In Japanese-controlled areas they organized guerrilla resistance and won the support of patriots who hated the Japanese. The position in 1939: Chiang had retreated to a new capital, Chungking; the Japanese controlled most of the Chinese coastline; the Communists controlled most of the north and north-east and were the leaders of the anti-Japanese movement.

▮ 17.9 China, Japan and the Second World War, 1939–45 ▮

After December 1941 the Chinese-Japanese War became one part of the wider war (Units 25 and 26).

The USA became China's ally. General Stilwell went to Chungking to help organize the Chinese resistance to Japan. He condemned Chiang's forces. They refused to fight, and their men were short of food. Wounded men were allowed to die because of shortages of medicine and doctors. Also, officers were cruel to their men. He summed things up with 'corruption, neglect, chaotic economy, hoarding, black market, trading with the enemy'.

However, Stilwell approved of Mao's forces: 'reduces taxes, rents, interest: raises production and standard of

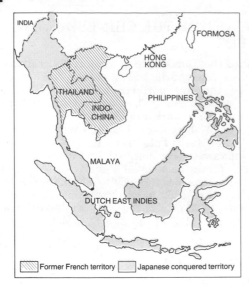

Fig. 17.9 Japanese conquest of South East Asia, 1941–3

living, people participate in government, practise what they preach'.

 17.10 Chiang and Mao, after the Second World War

1945–6

Chiang's advantages

He received massive aid from the USA, and was one of the Big Four Allied leaders. He replaced the Japanese occupation forces in the cities and towns in north and east China.

Chiang's weaknesses

Intellectuals opposed him because of the dictatorial rule and its inefficiences as reported by Stilwell (see above). Businessmen suffered from raging inflation; peasants had been ignored at best and ill-treated generally by Chiang's ill-disciplined forces. Patriots resented the small part Chiang had played in the anti-Japanese war. His army was disloyal. Men sold their arms to the Reds and deserted rather than fight.

Mao's advantages

He had won the support of the peasants by his land policies. Intellectuals admired the honesty of his government; businessmen admired the rule of law which he established; patriots admired his persistent resistance to the Japanese.

THE FIRST CLASH–MANCHURIA

The communists controlled this area when the Japanese surrendered in August 1945. The USA advised Chiang not to re-occupy Manchuria, but he decided to do so—and face a war with Mao.

However, General Marshall of the USA persuaded Chiang and Mao to work together. On 10 October 1945 ('Double Tenth') they signed an agreement to work together. Nevertheless, Chiang was really unwilling to consider the spread of communism with its programme of land reform, and Mao was prepared to work in a coalition government—but only as a stage towards communist control of China. So in June 1946 Chiang launched a full-scale attack on communist centres in Central China.

THE CIVIL WAR, 1946–9

The Kuo Min Tang controlled China south of the Yangtse (Fig. 17.1) and held most of the cities in the north and in Manchuria. The communists controlled the countryside, so that contact between KMT forces had to be by air.

June 1946—Spring 1947

Chiang launched a three-pronged attack—towards Shantung, Yenan and Manchuria. He promised that the Reds would be defeated in six months.

The communists retreated from Yenan, made their way to the south and set up a base in the Tapeh mountains.

Using guerrilla tactics, the communists controlled the route to the north from the Yangtse and threatened the rich Yangtse valley region (Fig. 17.1).

1948

Having gathered and trained a peasant army, Mao went on to the offensive. Armed with Russian weapons and American arms sold by corrupt leaders in Chiang's army, Mao drove Chiang's forces into town bases.

By January 1949 the Communists had captured every city north of the Yangtse. Many cities surrendered without fighting. Chiang's men deserted in their thousands. Many of Chiang's generals wanted to negotiate a deal with Mao.

Communist success

In the winter of 1948–9 the Communists won three major battles in Manchuria. They then marched to take Peking on 31 January 1949. Other Red forces crossed the Yangtse and made their way south (Fig. 17.1).

Red armies drove Chiang's armies into Nanking and Shanghai. In these cities inflation destroyed the savings of the middle class whilst nationalist executioners were busy killing suspected opponents of Chiang's crumbling régime.

Rule by War Lords, destroyed by Chiang in 1926 (see above), had reappeared under his leadership. The advance of the Reds was welcomed by most Chinese anxious to have honest, efficient and disciplined government.

Shanghai and Nanking were taken in April–May 1949. Chiang's army held out at Canton for a short while before fleeing to Formosa (Taiwan) in December 1949 (Fig. 17.1).

THE CHINESE PEOPLE'S REPUBLIC

On 1 October 1949 Mao appeared at the Gate of Heavenly Peace of the Imperial Palace in Peking to read his address which inaugurated the People's Republic of China. He promised to raise living standards and to work for world peace. In Unit 33 we will study China under Mao and after.

Unit 17 Summary

▶ China, Japan and the First World War: the Treaty of Versailles.
▶ Russia and China, 1920–5.
▶ Chiang Kai-shek versus Mao Tse-tung, 1925–34.
▶ Japan's attack on China, 1931; the failure of the League.
▶ Mao and the Kiangsi Soviet: the Long March; Yenan.
▶ Chiang's government, 1930–5.
▶ The Sino-Japanese War, 1937–45.
▶ Civil War, 1946–9: the communists' victory, 1949.

18 INTERNATIONAL AFFAIRS, 1919–29

 18.1 Pacifism and Optimism in the League of Nations

INFLUENCE OF THE FIRST WORLD WAR

There was a widespread desire to avoid another major war. France feared German revenge for her defeat. Germany wanted a revision of the Treaty of Versailles (see Unit 12). Reparations were a major problem. Britain believed that the Treaty had been too harsh.

The Covenant contained anti-war agreements. Nations still looked for ways of enforcing 'collective security'.

The League's supporters hoped it would ensure peace (see Unit 14).

All member nations had denounced war as a policy.

THE LEAGUE AND THE REAL WORLD

To Germans the League appeared as an association of victors and part of the hated 'dictated peace'. It had no real power and national self-interest proved too strong (see Unit 14).

Diplomatic activity continued outside the League framework.

THE GENEVA PROTOCOL, 1924

The League had had its early failures (see Unit 14). League supporters claimed that one reason for failure was the difficulty of defining who was 'an aggressor'. To do this, they drew up the Geneva Protocol. According to this, any country which refused to accept arbitration in a dispute was to be labelled the aggressor, and every nation in the League would act against an aggressor.

However, the British Dominions were unwilling to accept this—they feared being drawn into a number of European wars. The British government under the Conservative, Baldwin, refused to accept the Protocol in 1925. It never came to anything.

18.2 German Reparations, 1920–9

France and Belgium were the most insistent on their payment. Germany failed to pay in 1922. The Ruhr was occupied by French and Belgian troops, in 1923. This helped cause the great inflation in Weimar Germany (see Unit 15).

1924, A NEW CLIMATE

Briand replaced Poincaré as French Prime Minister. He was more sympathetic to Germany's problems. Stresemann, the new German Foreign Minister, proved to be a good negotiator. MacDonald, Labour Prime Minister of Great Britain, wanted to solve the reparations problem. The USA gave Germany loans to help industrial recovery.

THE DAWES PLAN, 1924

Dawes, an American general, had a new plan for reparations; he proposed that the amount paid would depend on what Germany could afford each year. This was an attempt to balance two objectives:
▶ to ensure that France, in particular, got something out of reparations;
▶ to ensure that Germany's economic recovery was not hindered by over-heavy reparations.

Dawes proposed that the reparation charges should be met from money paid by the German customs, railways and industry. The reparations payments would be paid through the State Bank, and foreign nations would have representatives on the Bank's board.

German recovery was helped by huge American loans and by the production of a new German currency supported by the Allies.

THE YOUNG PLAN, 1929

In 1925–9 there was more agreement among European nations:
▶ the Locarno Treaties of 1925;
▶ the Kellogg Pact of 1928 (see below). This was the result of personal friendship between Briand, Stresemann and Austen Chamberlain, and it led to a further change in the reparations scheme.

Young, an American financier, knew that Germany had been in arrears with her payments since 1921. He devised a new scheme which reduced the amount of yearly payments, so that Germany had to pay £50 million a year. Stresemann accepted the terms, but Hitler and the Nazis campaigned against acceptance.

Stresemann died and the Nazis came to power (see Unit 15), so the plan never came into operation. Hitler stopped all reparations payments.

18.3 Russia and Europe, 1919–29

The Allies had intervened in the Civil War (see Unit 10). Poland gained parts of White Russia and of the Ukraine by the Treaty of Riga, 1921.

Russia was not allowed to join the League. But in 1921 many countries, including Britain, made trade agreements with Russia.

Russia and Germany were 'outsider' nations. However, the Treaty of Rapallo, 1922 brought them together. They renounced reparations, agreed to resume diplomatic relations, and resumed economic relations. Germany helped to build Russian industry, while Russia allowed Germany to train an illegal army and an illegal airforce on Russian territory.

Britain, under a Labour government in 1924 recognized the Bolshevik government, provided loans for Russian economic development, and signed a trade treaty with Russia.

18.4 France and Germany, 1919–25

Clemenceau had been largely responsible for the harsh terms of the Treaty of Versailles (see Unit 12). In 1922 Poincaré became Prime Minister. He had no sympathy with German complaints about the Treaty, and in 1922–3 he was responsible for the occupation of the Ruhr by French and Belgian troops (see above).

In 1924 Briand became Prime Minister. He was more sympathetic to Germany's complaints.

Stresemann became Chancellor and Foreign Minister of Weimar Germany in 1923 (see Unit 15). He was critical of the Treaty, and understood French fears of German militarism. Stresemann proved willing to negotiate with the Allies.

18.5 Treaties and Pacts, 1925–9

THE LOCARNO TREATIES, 1925

These Treaties were largely the result of personal friendship between:

▶ Stresemann of Germany (see Unit 15), who was concerned about the 'encirclement of Germany by France and the Little Entente' (see below);
▶ Briand of France, who wanted to have a friendly Germany on the French border;
▶ Austen Chamberlain, British Foreign Minister, anxious to bring Germany and France closer together.

They were signed by Britain, France, Germany, Belgium and Italy.

Germany's western frontiers

The frontiers with France, Belgium and Italy were accepted as drawn by the Treaty of Versailles. Britain and Italy guaranteed to maintain those frontiers. This pleased France, fearful of German militarism.

Germany's eastern frontiers

At Locarno the powers accepted treaties signed between Germany and Poland and Germany and Czechoslovakia. But they did not offer to guarantee Germany's eastern frontiers. This suggested willingness to see Germany take action to change them—which would have been contrary to the Treaty of Versailles.

Germany agreed not to use force against any of her neighbours.

The powers agreed to a Conference on Disarmament (see Unit 14).

FRANCE AND GERMANY'S EASTERN NEIGHBOURS

In August 1920, Czechoslovakia and Yugoslavia were 'created' at Versailles from lands taken from Germany and Austria-Hungary (see Unit 12). Rumania was enlarged by the Treaty. In August 1920 the three signed an Entente*. France made an agreement with this 'Little Entente', agreeing to supply its members with military aid.

Poland was another 'new', or rather, re-created, country which had gained territory from Germany and Austria as well as Russia. In 1921 France made an alliance with Poland.

In 1925 these agreements and the alliance were re-affirmed. At Locarno it was agreed that these treaties should continue. Germany saw this as a French plan to encircle her (see above).

France, by seeking such agreements and treaties, showed that she had little faith in the League.

THE KELLOGG PACT, 1928

In 1927 the League adopted an Assembly resolution to prohibit wars of aggression.

Note: you should ask yourself why such a resolution was needed—the Covenant (Unit 14) already had all the nations agreeing to renounce war. The resolution (1927) was an indication that few people believed in the Covenant. Why, then, should they have had any more faith in their 1927 resolution?

Kellogg was the American Secretary of State in 1928. He had the support of Briand of France (see above) in his search for peace.

Sixty-five nations signed the Kellogg Pact, including the USA, Russia and Japan. They agreed that for five years (1928–33) they would not go to war except in self-defence.

Again, the existence of this pact was a sign that the nations disregarded the League, its aims and constitution. A weakness of the Pact was that no one defined 'self-defence'.

THE POSITION AT THE END OF 1929

Locarno (see above) should have made France feel secure. Those Treaties had also brought Germany back into diplomatic life. She joined the League in 1926. Reparations had been twice re-negotiated (see above), which suggested Franco-German co-operation and a desire for peace.

The Kellogg Pact once again, had had the nations 'outlaw war', which suggested a desire for peace. The Disarmament Conference was under way (see Unit 14), suggesting that nations were willing to 'turn swords into ploughshares'.

The Rhineland was evacuated five years ahead of the date fixed at Versailles (Unit 12), showing that France and Germany were willing to live on friendly terms.

But there were major weaknesses. Briand hoped that Germany would now be content with the changes made since 1919. In fact Germany wanted more changes. Stresemann had hoped, in 1929, that France might give even more concessions (on reparations, on German rearmament). In fact, France had made concessions in the 1920s with much ill-will. Briand was not universally popular in France. The French people still distrusted Germany—hence the plans to build the Maginot Line.

Hitler was not yet in power. But Stresemann had died in 1929; this left a major vacuum in German politics. Hitler was going to fill that vacuum and would have a more forceful policy—towards Versailles, reparations (Unit 18), the Rhineland (Unit 23), German rearmament (Unit 14) and the League (Unit 14).

Unit 18 Summary

▶ Pacifism and optimism in the League of Nations.
▶ German reparations.
▶ France versus Germany, 1919–25.
▶ Locarno Treaties: the Kellogg Pact.

19 THE UNITED STATES OF AMERICA, 1932–41

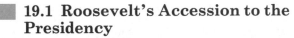

19.1 Roosevelt's Accession to the Presidency

THE 1932 PRESIDENTIAL ELECTION

Hoover, the President since 1928, was the Republican Party's candidate. In 1928 he had praised the 'rugged individualism' which, he claimed, had created the prosperity of the 1920s, and promised 'a chicken in every pot, two cars in every garage'.

The Wall Street Crash, 1929 (Unit 16), had wrecked the American economy. Hoover did little until 1932. By then many banks had gone out of business, millions of people having lost their invested savings, and more banks were threatened as their clients rushed to take out their savings. The unemployment level also soared.

Franklin Delano Roosevelt, Governor of New York State (see Unit 16) was the Democratic Party's candidate. He came from a wealthy family, had been educated at one of the best schools and universities, and was assistant Secretary for the Navy in Wilson's government and Vice-Presidential candidate in 1920.

Roosevelt was crippled by poliomyelitis, which gave him time to study and to develop that strength of character that enabled him to fight his way back into public life. In 1932 he made a 'whistle-stop tour' of the States, partly to show himself to the people and assure them that he was fit enough to be President, partly to tell them his policies.

THE 'LAME DUCK' PRESIDENCY

The Presidential election took place (and still does take place) in November of each leap year. The incoming President was not due to take office until the next June. The outgoing President was in office but had no real power. Hoover agreed that Roosevelt should take office in March to deal with the many problems facing the country.

19.2 The Hundred Days, 4 March–16 June

THE NEW DEAL

Roosevelt had promised a New Deal in June 1932. In his first hundred days in office, he persuaded Congress to pass a great deal of legislation (below).

The Emergency Banking Act

Roosevelt declared 4 March to be a bank holiday. This gave time for experts to examine the accounts of the nation's banks. The Emergency Banking Act was passed on 9 March. This forced weak banks out of business. It allowed the government to help stronger banks. In a broadcast, Roosevelt assured the people that their money was safe in their banks and invited them to put their money (wages, savings, profits) into the banks.

The Banking Act gave the government more control over banking. It set up the Federal Deposit Insurance Corporation which insured deposits in banks, forbade banks to use clients' money in investment on the Stock Exchange and gave people more confidence in the banking system.

The Federal Emergency Relief Administration (FERA) was set up and given 500 million dollars for cash relief for the poor, and help to local authorities with their poor relief schemes. Roosevelt also used the RFC set up by Hoover (see Unit 16).

The Economy Act reduced the pensions and salaries of state employees, to take into account the fall in prices.

Prohibition was swept away and the eighteenth amendment was repealed.

The Civilian Conservation Corps (CCC) was set up to provide work for the unemployed. Anyone between the ages of 18 and 25 was allowed to join for six months to work on afforestation schemes and other work. They received 30 dollars a month—and had to send 25 dollars home to parents and wives. In 1933 some 300,000 people joined the Corps; by 1940 two million had done so, many rejoining after their first six months. Many found work after six months. Employers welcomed the effort they had made by joining the Corps.

The Civil Works Administration (CWA) was set up under Harry Hopkins to provide work for unemployed on public works schemes, such as the building of roads, schools and other publicly-owned utilities. Four million registered with the CWA in 1933. In 1935 it was replaced by the Works Progress Administration (see below).

The Agricultural Adjustment Administration (AAA)

This was set up to aid farmers, the first to suffer (see Unit 16). It invited farmers to set up co-operative marketing schemes, and gave loans to stop evictions.

Advisers went to help farmers improve soil and methods. Farmers were also asked to cut production because of the effects of overproduction on prices. Those who did so were given a subsidy which came from new taxes:
▶ a tax on cotton-spinning subsidized farmers who gave up cotton production on their land;
▶ a flour-milling tax subsidized those who cut wheat production.

The National Industrial Recovery Act (NIRA)

This Act set up the Public Works Administration as an extension of the CWA (see above). It provided money for public works schemes undertaken by the government or local authorities. Similarly, the National Recovery Administration (NRA) was formed to draw up rules or 'codes' for industrial relations:
▶ it abolished child labour, shortened the working week and fixed minimum wages;
▶ employers who accepted the 'code' could display a 'Blue Eagle' and the government invited people to buy from such firms;
▶ it gave workmen the right to form trade unions.

THE TENNESSEE VALLEY AUTHORITY (TVA)

This was set up during the 'Hundred Days'. It deserves to be studied carefully.

The Tennessee River runs through seven states. The Valley was one of the most backward areas in the USA. Agriculture in the Valley suffered from:
▶ soil erosion owing to overcropping, with winds taking away dusty top soil;
▶ floods, which washed away remaining topsoil and ruined many of the poor farmers.

There was very little industry, so there was little alternative employment for the children of the poor farming families.

In 1930 Senator Norris asked Hoover to set up an Authority to tackle the problems of the Tennessee Valley. It would:

▶ tackle problems too big for any single state to tackle;
▶ build dams to prevent flooding while also providing hydro-electricity which would attract industry and provide employment;
▶ set up factories to produce fertilizers to help farmers to improve their soil.

Hoover refused. Roosevelt set up the TVA during his 'Hundred Days'. It provided immediate employment for thousands, cut across the rights of seven states, and built 16 new dams and enlarged five others. It also made the river navigable. In 1928 only 48 ton-miles of traffic was carried on the river; in 1941, 161 million ton-miles travelled through the locks. The dams ended the damage previously done by floods, and provided cheap electricity for farm houses, industries and towns which had never had it before.

THE NEW DEAL–STAGE 2

The rush of legislation and the creation of so many agencies gave evidence of Roosevelt's wish to tackle America's problems.

The Works Progress Administration, 1935

This agency was set up to replace the CWA (see above). It paid people to do various public works—e.g., building roads, dams, airports, schools, hospitals and playgrounds, and it provided work for artists, actors and writers. The Federal Theatre Project sent touring companies to perform plays in major cities. The agency provided work for over four million people, enabling them (as wage earners) to buy goods, which created more employment. It also provided America with schools, hospitals and the like, which otherwise might not have been built. The Hoover Dam across the Colorado River was one such public work.

The Wagner Act, 1935

This replaced that part of the NIRA which had dealt with trade unionism (see above). It forced employers to recognize trade unions to which their workers belonged, and forced them to negotiate with these unions in matters of dispute and over wages. It forbade employers to interfere with workers' rights to join unions, and set up the National Labour Relations Board to which workers took their complaints.

The Social Security Act, 1935

This provided pensions for the old and widowed. It provided a state unemployment insurance scheme, each local state being free to adopt the scheme as it thought best. This still left America a long way behind European states as regards social security.

19.3 The Growth of Opposition to Roosevelt's Policies

In 1936 Roosevelt stood in the Presidential elections—and was re-elected for a second term of office.

'Revolutionary' was one accusation by his opponents. They knew that for fifteen years there had been no reforming legislation under Harding, Coolidge and Hoover (Unit 16).

Hoover attacked four years of the 'New Deal'. It was an attack on free institutions; employers were forced to pay minimum wages, recognize trade unions; they were forbidden to employ young children. The NRA, said Hoover, favoured 'big business' and harmed 'the little man' with its

price-fixing and codes; the AAA compelled farmers to do as they were told. Planning (as in the TVA) was said to be Marxist.

The spending of vast sums of public money or 'priming the pump' was the idea of the British economist, Keynes, whose ideas had been rejected in his own country. Some of the schemes had proved to be unworkable and had to be amended and improved. This suggested that Roosevelt acted without enough thought.

Some critics thought that the power of the Federal government had been increased too much.

Unemployment had not fallen by very much. The country was still locked into a great depression in 1936 (see Fig. 41.3B).

ROOSEVELT VERSUS THE SUPREME COURT, 1932–9

The Court is 'the Sacred Guardian of the Constitution' (see Unit 7). It hears cases brought by people who think that an Act passed by Congress is invalid under the Constitution.

In 1932 seven of the nine judges had been appointed in the 1920s by Republican Presidents. Roosevelt could not change things until a judge died or retired; few were willing to retire, although by 1936, the average age of the nine judges was 71 years.

In 1935–6 the Court ruled against Roosevelt:

▶ the NRA and the AAA were declared invalid. Several other lesser measures were also declared invalid. This confirmed the opinions of those opponents who thought that Roosevelt's work was 'unconstitutional'. This angered Roosevelt and those who thought that what he was doing was to try to get America back to work and so avoid the danger of a revolution (see Unit 16).

In 1937, after his sweeping victory in the 1936 election, Roosevelt sent a proposal to Congress asking for laws which would enable him to get a more favourable Supreme Court:

▶ judges should be encouraged to retire when aged 70;
▶ if any judge decided not to retire then, Roosevelt wanted the right to appoint an extra judge although the total number of judges should not exceed 15.

Congress refused. Members were conscious of the importance of the 'separation of powers' of the President, Congress and the Court. They did not approve of Roosevelt's attempt to 'fiddle' with the composition of the Court.

However, the Court seemed to have learned a lesson. There were no more rulings against Roosevelt's work.

HOW SUCCESSFUL WAS ROOSEVELT?

Millions of people had jobs, even if only for a short period, because of one or other of his agencies. Labour relations were improved, although many employers resisted the introduction of trade unionism into their firms. Trade unions grew. In 1933 only 7 per cent of workers were in a union; by 1938 this had grown to 21 per cent.

It has been argued that Roosevelt saved American business or capitalism from more revolutionary policies as favoured by Long and others (see Unit 16). However, although unemployment fell by 1937 it increased again after that. Very little was done for the most deprived—the black population.

19.4 America and the Outside World, 1933–41

America was not a member of the League of Nations (see Unit 14). She took little part in world affairs in spite of the Japanese attack on China, Mussolini's attack on Abyssinia (Unit 23) and Hitler's breaking of the Versailles Treaty (Unit 20 and Unit 23).

THE NEUTRALITY ACT, 1935

This Act forbade the sale of munitions to warring countries, and it forbade the lending of money to countries involved in war. The USA seemed determined to avoid getting trapped into going to war in defence of its loans as it had done in 1917.

The Nazi invasion of Poland saw the outbreak of the Second World War (Unit 23). Roosevelt broadcast to the American people promising to keep them out of the war.

The Neutrality Act was amended to allow the supply of arms to Britain and France.

CASH AND CARRY

A plan was approved which allowed the British and French to buy arms in the USA provided that they paid for them in cash and took them away in their own ships.

The sweeping victories gained by Hitler in 1940 (Unit 25) led Roosevelt to ask Congress to approve the spending of millions of dollars on American rearmament.

THE FOUR FREEDOMS

In January 1941 Roosevelt, in a broadcast, spoke of the four freedoms for which Britain, now alone, was fighting. These were freedom (a) of speech; (b) of worship; (c) from want; (d) from fear of other nations.

LEND-LEASE

Early in 1941 Britain ran out of money to buy arms from the USA. Roosevelt proposed (and Congress passed) a scheme by which the USA would 'lend' the arms to Britain who would 'lease' them for the duration of the war and 'return' them if unused. Roosevelt argued that if they were used, then America had been guarded from the danger of attack by Hitler—and there would be no charge for the arms.

THE ATLANTIC CHARTER

In August 1941 Roosevelt met Churchill on board the American warship, *Augusta*, off the coast of Newfoundland. They discussed the lend-lease scheme, the possibility of Japan's coming in on Germany's side, and the possibility of developing an atomic bomb. They also issued a statement christened 'the Atlantic Charter'. This said that (a) neither power would try to increase its own power by seizing land from any other country or in any other way; (b) people throughout the world should be given the right to choose their own government, and that countries conquered by force should be given their independence. This was meant to be an answer to the threat posed by Germany and Japan. But the idea that people should have the right to self-government was seized upon by the colonial countries of the Third World and became an important stage in the growth of the demand for freedom from colonial rule; (c) after the 'final destruction of Nazi tyranny' the nations of the world should join together to ensure greater prosperity and a lasting peace.

AMERICAN ACTION

RAF men were trained in the USA. Also, Royal Navy ships were repaired in US shipyards. From July 1941 US warships were ordered to escort British convoys as far as Iceland— which saved many British lives and freed the Royal Navy for other duties elsewhere.

Germany regarded this as an act of war. In September 1941 a German submarine fired on a US destroyer. In October 1941 a US destroyer was sunk, although officially the USA was not at war.

For America's part in the Second World War see Units 25 and 26.

Unit 19 Summary

▶ The Hundred Days: the Tennessee Valley Authority.
▶ The New Deal; aims, methods and opponents.
▶ Roosevelt versus the Supreme Court.
▶ Isolationism and the Second World War, 1939–41.

---

20 HITLER'S GERMANY, 1933–9

20.1 Establishing the Dictatorship, January–March 1933

In January 1933 Hitler was democratically elected and appointed Chancellor (see Unit 15). In February 1933, during the run-up to fresh elections there was a Nazi 'reign of terror' and an anti-left campaign to weaken the opposition.

In March 1933 the election gave the Nazis more seats. In a fresh anti-left campaign many opposition parties were dissolved and communists were expelled from the Reichstag.

On 23 March, the Enabling Act gave Hitler dictatorial powers.

WINNING THE ARMY FOR THE DICTATORSHIP, JUNE–AUGUST 1934

Roehm, socialist leader of the SA (see below), wanted a socialist policy and the SA to be an important part of the Regular Army (see Unit 15). However, Hitler was afraid of Roehm as an enemy inside the Nazi Party. He also feared the loss of support by industrialists, and the power of the Army General Staff.

On 30 June 1934 Hitler got rid of Roehm, and in August 1934 Hitler succeeded Hindenburg as President, but used the title Führer instead. The post of President made him Commander-in-Chief of the Armed Forces, all of whose members took an oath of loyalty to him.

20.2 Nazi Organizations and Leaders

HITLER'S CHIEF MINISTERS

Hermann Goering

Goering was Minister of the Interior in Prussia. This was the largest and most important state in Federal Germany (see Unit 1). He was the first commander of the Geheime Staatspolizei, or Gestapo, a politically-dominated police force (see below). He organized the reign of terror against Hitler's opponents during 1932 and 1933. Following the Reichstag Fire he led the anti-left campaign (see Unit 15). His men were partly responsible for the assassination of Roehm and his associates. In 1934 he was in charge of German industrial development, and during 1939–45 he was in command of the German Air Force.

Joseph Goebbels

A former journalist, Goebbels was the Party's best propagandist. In 1926 he was made Party leader (Gauleiter) for Berlin. Then in 1927 he founded a Berlin daily paper, *Der Angriff*. In 1928 he was elected to the Reichstag (Table 15.5), in 1929 he was made chief of party propaganda, and in 1933 he became Minister of Propaganda and Enlightenment in Hitler's government.

Heinrich Himmler

Himmler was an early member of the Nazi Party. In 1929 Hitler appointed him leader of the SS (see below), and he later succeeded Goering as head of the Gestapo.

Himmler was responsible for:

▶ the assassinations of June 1934 (see Unit 15);
▶ the suppression of opposition inside Hitler's Germany;
▶ the attacks on the Jews (see below);
▶ the running of the concentration camps.

Hjalmar Schacht

In 1918 Schacht was partner in a bank at Bremen, and in 1924 he devised the plan for the restoration of a stable currency by means of issuing a new Rentenmark (see Unit 15). In 1924 he took part in the conference which led to the Dawes Plan (Unit 18) while he was head of the Reichsbank. By 1933 he was an active supporter of the Nazi Party and of Hitler's accession to power in January 1933, and during 1933–7 he was Hitler's Economics Minister.

As Economics Minister, Schacht:

▶ devised a scheme to pay for German rearmament (see below);
▶ supported public spending to reduce unemployment;
▶ arranged trade and currency deals with countries in Central and Eastern Europe which helped to develop trade and get important imports.

On 2 January 1939 as President of the Reichsbank he wanted Hitler to reduce spending on armaments so that the budget could be balanced and inflation stopped. He was sacked.

MAJOR NAZI ORGANIZATIONS

The Nazi Labour Front

All workers were enrolled in this organization, and trade unions were abolished. The Nazis claimed that these were socialist or communist organizations. Strikes were forbidden as anti-State activities.

The Hitler Youth organization

This had been formed in the 1920s, and through it the Nazis won the support of the young.

Boys 'played' at being soldiers in the 1920s—having uniforms, camps, 'battles' at week-ends. In the 1930s, these former boys were fervent supporters of Hitler's policies.

All other youth organizations were banned after 1933.

The Sturmabteilung (SA)

Hitler built his own private army, infantry and cavalry, the SA—commanded by Captain Roehm. The money for this force was provided by industrialists who were afraid of the rise of communism (see Unit 15). The force had brown shirts for its uniform. It took part in the street fighting in the late 1920s.

In 1930 the two million stormtroopers were used to:

▶ win support as they marched through the streets;
▶ disrupt opposition meetings and so help Hitler to power;
▶ terrorize the opposition, January–March 1933, and so help Hitler to establish the dictatorship.

Once in power, Hitler got rid of Roehm (see Unit 15).

The Schutzstaffel (SS)

Hitler and his powerful ally, Roehm, did not always agree. In 1934 this led to Roehm's assassination (see Unit 15).

Hitler organized a special detachment to be his own political executive: the Schutzstaffel (or protective squadron) in their black-shirted uniform was set up in 1928, rival to the SA.

It had a military organization like the SA but included artillery sections. One SS regiment consisted of Hitler's Life Guards. Like the SA, there were many full-time professional members of the SS. But as with the SA, most members served in their spare time. There were about 500,000 in the SS. In 1929 Hitler appointed Himmler leader of this army.

The SS was the force used in the Night of the Long Knives when the leaders of the SA were assassinated (Unit 15).

The Geheime Staatspolitzei (or Gestapo)

We have seen that one of Lenin's first acts was to set up a secret police force, the Cheka (Unit 10). In 1933 Hitler set up the Gestapo as his secret police force.

Himmler took control from Goering. The SS (above) and the Gestapo were under one man's control. The Gestapo was responsible for infiltrating every anti-Nazi organization, and by terrorism it stamped out opposition to Hitler.

It had secret files on every prominent German, including the leading Nazis. Himmler was able to use these to blackmail many people and so gain even more power for himself.

It was Himmler's men who led the anti-Jewish campaigns (see below) and ran the concentration camps.

20.3 Opposition and Support

OPPOSITION TO HITLER'S RULE

Most opposition was crushed. The separate Parliaments of the various States (see Unit 1) were abolished in 1934 by a decree under the Enabling Laws (see Unit 15). The Reichsrat, or second House of the German Parliament, 'disappeared' with the abolition of the separate States. This gave political power to the Reichstag which, by the Enabling Law, gave Hitler dictatorial powers for four years.

All political parties, except the Nazi Party, were declared illegal. Those that had not been smashed simply went out of existence—Nationalists, Catholics, Conservatives. Trade unions were also declared illegal (see above).

The Catholic Church and Hitler

Hitler claimed that it was impossible to be a good German and a Christian. However, in 1933 Hitler made a Concordat (or agreement) with the Pope which allowed the Catholic Church to run schools and newspapers, and to maintain its churches and cathedrals. Many Catholics saw this as Papal approval for Hitler.

The persecution of the Jews (see below) led to a quarrel

with the Catholic Church. In 1937 the Pope issued an Encyclical (or Papal Letter), entitled *Mit Brennender Sorge* (*With Burning Anxiety*) which condemned Hitler's racialist theories and practices.

Some Church leaders, such as the Cardinal Archbishop of Munich, preached and wrote against Hitler and the Nazis. However, many priests and the majority of Catholics went along with Hitler's policies because they seemed to be successful.

The Protestant (Lutheran) Church and Hitler

Many Lutherans supported Hitler, who had given the Germans a new pride and hope. Nevertheless, some opposed his anti-Jewish policies. Pastor Niemöller led this opposition. He and others were sent to concentration camps.

SUPPORT FOR HITLER

The German middle class

They remembered the inflation and chaos of 1923 (Fig. 15.2), and in 1931 they feared a repeat of that chaos (see Unit 15). They provided leadership for Roehm's Brownshirts (see above) and welcomed the strong, firm government provided by Hitler.

Anti-communists

Hitler claimed that he saved Germany from Bolshevism (see Unit 15). By signing an anti-communist pact with Italy and Japan he claimed that he would save the world from Russian Bolshevism. This was welcomed by:

▶ industrialists who feared the loss of their property;
▶ the Church, afraid of anti-clerical Bolsheviks;
▶ the middle class, which most feared Bolshevism.

Industrialists

Germany had recovered under Stresemann (see Unit 15) and by 1930 Germany was the world's second most powerful industrialized nation. Industrialists, such as the 'steel barons' Thyssen and Krupps, provided much of the money to finance the Nazi Party. They also supported the Party in newspapers which they owned. They benefited from German rearmament after 1933. Rearmament proceeded as follows:

▶ half a million men were conscripted into the Wehrmacht (Army);
▶ thousands of Panzerkampfwagen (armoured fighting vehicles) or tanks were built;
▶ the Luftwaffe (Air Force) bought thousands of aircraft;
▶ the German Navy was enlarged and hundreds of U-boats built. In 1936 the *Admiral Graf Spee* was launched, a revolutionary kind of fighting 'pocket-battleship' which could outgun any ship fast enough to catch her and was speedy enough to escape from conventional battleships which would have outgunned her.

This rearmament led to an expansion of the iron and steel, coal and engineering industries. These and other industries also benefited from Hitler's (and Schacht's) development of public works, the building of miles of motorways (or autobahns), schools, houses and hospitals.

The army

The traditional officer-corps helped Hitler's rise to power. Ludendorff had taken part in the 1923 putsch (Unit 15). Schleicher had used his influence politically in 1932–3 to help Hitler but had been assassinated along with Roehm in June 1934. The officer corps welcomed the expansion and rearmament after 1933. They supported Hitler's demands for a tearing-up of the Treaty of Versailles and for equality for Germany compared with other European nations. They hoped that they would have the same control in Hitler's Germany as army leaders had had when Bismarck control-led Germany after 1870 and when Kaiser William II allowed Schlieffen and the army to determine foreign policy (see Unit 1).

Hitler was aware of the opposition he might get from this traditional officer class, because:

▶ he was Austrian by birth; most officers were Prussian;
▶ he had been only a corporal in 1914–18;
▶ they despised his Brownshirts and terrorist tactics;

Hitler made them take an oath of loyalty to him as Head of State in 1934 (see above). However, they opposed his plans for an expansionary foreign policy (Unit 23). The success of that policy from 1935 to 1940 made it even less likely that the officer class would provide opposition to the Führer.

The working class

Employment was provided for millions after 1933 by:

▶ conscription of 500,000 soldiers;
▶ rearmament, and industrial expansion;
▶ public works such as the building of the autobahns;
▶ aid to agriculture to help Germany become economically independent;
▶ aid to industrial development. The German car industry produced the 'people's car' or Volkswagen. Radio and other industries were also developed.

Nationalists

Nationalists from all classes welcomed the evident growing strength of the Armed Forces, the regaining of the provinces lost at Versailles (Unit 12) beginning with the Saar in 1935, and the new confidence in Germany as the economy boomed.

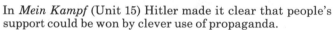 ## 20.4 Propaganda

In *Mein Kampf* (Unit 15) Hitler made it clear that people's support could be won by clever use of propaganda.

By 1922 onwards Goebbels was in charge of party propaganda. In his own speeches, Hitler used propaganda against:

▶ Jews;
▶ communists;
▶ socialists, such as Stresemann;
▶ foreigners, who had forced Versailles on Germany.

He also promised:

▶ law and order in place of 'Bolshevik unrest';
▶ an expanding economy instead of unemployment;
▶ a 'Greater Germany' instead of one downtrodden by the Treaty of Versailles.

Goebbels was another clever orator able to rouse the masses. But as Minister of Propaganda and Enlightenment (see above) he also used:

▶ radio, which was government-controlled and put out pro-Hitler propaganda in plays, stories and news bulletins;
▶ the press, also government-controlled and censored. Only items favourable to Hitler were allowed to appear;
▶ marches, demonstrations and rallies in which thousands of men sang their songs, chanted their slogans and carried their banners with the sign of the swastika;
▶ sporting events and personalities. Max Schmelling's victory over the Negro, Joe Louis, for the world heavyweight championship in 1936 was highlighted as victory for 'the Aryan race'. The 1936 Olympic Games were held in Berlin and became a means of spreading Nazi propaganda.

EDUCATION

Teachers had to accept Nazi doctrine, and textbooks were rewritten to fit into Hitler's views of history and racial purity.

Children were recruited into the Little Fellows at six, the Jungvolk at ten, and the Hitler Youth at fourteen. Boys swore loyalty to Hitler as 'the saviour of our country'. Girls, in the League of German Maidens, were taught that the mothering of future soldiers was to be their highest aim.

Teachers, even at universities, who were lukewarm in their support were sacked. Books which the Nazis disliked were destroyed; in May 1933 there was a public burning of such books in city squares and the grounds of universities.

Behind this propaganda there was also the fear of the Gestapo, and the concentration camps.

20.5 Hitler and the Jews

In *Mein Kampf* Hitler 'showed' that the Jews were responsible for the defeat of 1918 and the economic collapses of 1923. During 1929–32 the Jews were blamed for the economic collapse (see Unit 15). They were the bankers and financiers responsible for the Wall Street Crash and the banking collapses in Germany.

Die Stürmer, a Nazi newspaper, specialized in anti-Jewish attacks.

On 1 April 1933 Hitler decreed a boycott of all Jewish shops, business houses, lawyers and doctors. Stormtroopers plastered Jewish shops and offices with notices warning the public not to enter; others stood as guards outside such buildings.

By Spring 1933 Jews were not allowed to enter universities. Later on they were to be banned from certain professions.

In September 1935 there was a special meeting of the Nazi-packed Reichstag at Nuremberg. The Nuremberg Laws said:

▶ Germans of Jewish blood were deprived of citizenship;
▶ marriages between Aryans and Jews were forbidden under pain of death;
▶ Jews had to wear a yellow patch (in the form of a star) on

their clothes. This marked them off from other people.

Concentration camps were built to house Jews and other potential opponents of the Nazis. The first, near Munich, was completed in April 1933 and housed 5000 prisoners.

Many Jews went into exile, including theatre and cinema producers such as Max Reinhardt, scientists such as Einstein, writers and university teachers.

9–10 November 1938

On 7 November a German Jewish refugee killed a member of the German Embassy in Paris. In reprisal the Nazi government organized a mass attack on German Jews. Synagogues, businesses and homes were destroyed. During this Crystal Night thousands of windows were smashed in Jewish property, and 200 synagogues destroyed. Thirty-five Jews were killed in these attacks. About 20,000 were arrested for 'resisting the forces'.

The Final Solution

The final solution to the Jewish problem was ordered in 1942 as Hitler decreed the killing of all Jews throughout Europe by mass executions in specially designed gas chambers in the concentration camps. Six million Jews had died in this way by 1945.

Unit 20 Summary

▶ Establishing the dictatorship.
▶ Nazi organizations and leaders.
▶ Opposition to and support for Hitler.
▶ The importance of propaganda.
▶ Hitler and the Jews.

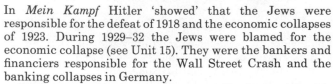

21 ITALY, 1919–39

21.1 Italy's Problems, 1870–1920

A NEW AND DIVIDED COUNTRY

Italy had completed its unification only in 1870.

Social problems

Social problems in this new country included:

▶ widespread poverty in a country with no coal and little raw material resources as aids to industrialization;
▶ peasant poverty in the rural south and in the Lombardy Plain, the result of centuries of over-cultivation which had lowered the quality of the crop and made the regions liable to flood damage and erosion;
▶ governments which paid no attention to these problems.

The religious problem

This was the result of the powerful position of the Catholic Church in Italy, as well as the Church's opposition to the government, which had taken the Papal States in 1860–1 and

Rome in 1870. The Pope's refusal to recognize the Italian government while he was 'the prisoner in the Vatican' also added to the problem. It was compounded by socialism of the Marxist and non-Marxist variety among industrial workers in the cities of the North such as Turin and Milan. These were centres of strikes and discontent. Socialism was opposed by important sections of the community:

▶ the Church, fearing anti-clericalism;
▶ landowners and industrialists;
▶ the majority of the professional middle classes.

Discredited politicians and a despised democracy

The system of proportional representation led to the appearance of many small parties in Parliament, as in France (see Unit 2). These parties ranged from:

▶ right-wing Conservatives wanting the King to be more powerful;
▶ centre parties, often Catholic-based, anxious for lower taxes;

▶ moderately left-wing Liberals supporting increased democracy;
▶ radical left-wing socialists willing to work with the King;
▶ extreme left-wing communists waiting for a Bolshevik Revolution.

Forming a government meant winning support from several of these parties. This led to weak policies. Also, the politicians were more interested in the in-and-out of government-forming than in solving the country's problems.

THE WAR, 1914–18

Italy was a member of the Triple Alliance and its membership excluded war with Britain (see Unit 8). In 1915 Italy joined the Allies against Germany–Austria. Then in October 1917 the Italians suffered a major defeat by the Austrians at Caporetto. Austrian–German armies took large portions of N.E. Italy.

The Allies had to send troops, although already involved in savage fighting on the Western Front (see Unit 9). In October 1918 Austria signed an armistice while still in occupation of parts of N.E. Italy.

Inflation was the result of the printing of paper money to pay for the war—munitions, soldiers' pay and the rest.

THE TREATY OF VERSAILLES

The Italians hoped to gain some or all of the province of Istria—in former Austria-Hungary—including the ports of Trieste and Fiume, part of the Dalmatian coast around Zara, Albania, created by Austrian power in 1913 (Unit 4), and the province of Trentino-Tyrol to the north of Italy.

Actual gains were much smaller. Italy gained a part of Istria, including Trieste but not Fiume, and Trentino-Tyrol.

During the war as many as 600,000 Italians had been killed. Italian gains brought 500,000 Croats and Slovenes and 250,000 Germans into Italy, leading to racial problems.

DISCONTENT, 1919–20

Inflation affected the middle class, whose savings were wiped out, and workers, whose wages did not keep pace with rising prices.

Unemployment followed from the end of government orders for munitions, the demobilization of millions of servicemen, and less spending by the unemployed and the demobilized.

Social unrest was caused by 150,000 ex-soldiers who roamed Italy, living on charity or banditry.

In the years 1918–22 there were five governments, none of which lasted long enough to begin to tackle the problems.

THE DISCONTENTED ORGANIZE AND ACT

The Blackshirts were gangs of ex-servicemen. The Blueshirts were nationalists opposed to the Treaty (see above). The Greyshirts were Liberals who wanted efficient government. The Red Guards were the Bolsheviks.

Violence was commonplace:
▶ workers went on strike for higher wages;
▶ employers locked out workers seeking higher wages;
▶ riots took place in industrial towns and cities;
▶ the police and troops sided with employers;
▶ rival gangs attacked each others' meetings.

21.2 Benito Mussolini's early career

Mussolini was born in 1883, the son of a socialist blacksmith. He went to a training college for priests from which he was expelled for stabbing a fellow pupil. He then worked as a schoolmaster and as a journalist.

In 1912 Mussolini was editor of the socialist paper, *L'Avanti* (*Forward*). In 1914 he left the socialist party when it opposed Italy's entry into the war against the Germans and Austrians. He founded a paper, *Il Popolo d'Italia* (*The Italian People*), and in 1915 he joined the army but was invalided out, injured while practising with grenades—not by the 'war wounds' he spoke of.

By 1919 he was critical of the government which failed to deal with Italy's problems (see above). He formed the Fascist Party.

THE FASCIST PARTY

Fasces were the bundle of rods around an axe carried in ancient Rome as a symbol of magistrates' authority. 'Fascio' is Italian for a group or a squad. It was used in 1919 to describe various gangs fighting socialists and communists. Many anti-left gangs were supported by wealthier Italians.

In 1919 Mussolini founded a Milan Fascio. It won only two per cent of the votes in a Milan constituency. Then in 1921 he founded the National Fascist Party. Members wore a black uniform and greeted each other with the Roman salute. In industrial towns and cities his men attacked gangs of socialists and communists. This gained Mussolini the support of the wealthy landowners and industrialists, as well as middle class professional people—teachers, lawyers and so on.

Fascism did not have a worked-out political doctrine. Mussolini and other leading Fascists 'invented' ideas and principles as the need arose. Generally it can be said that Fascism taught that:
▶ there was a need for strong, centralized government;
▶ the individual had to submit his or her interests and will to the interests and decisions of the government;
▶ Mussolini (Il Duce) was always right;
▶ communism was a threat to be fought;
▶ Italians could take a pride in their nation and State.

GABRIELE D'ANNUNZIO

D'Annunzio was a one-eyed poet and orator, who in 1919 led an attack on, and captured, Fiume. He held it for 15 months before the Italian government helped to drive him out. He taught Mussolini the idea of strong action in the name of the Italian people's nationalistic pride.

THE PATH TO POWER, 1919–22

In 1919 Mussolini's Fascio won only 2 per cent of the votes in a Milanese constituency. Then during 1919–21 his growing movement adopted a policy of violence. Meetings of socialists and communists were attacked. This won him the support of the wealthy, the frightened and the anti-communists.

In 1921 Mussolini's Fascist Party (see above) won 35 seats in the Italian Parliament. He demanded a seat in the government. This was refused, but no government was formed, as politicians squabbled for position and power.

In 1921–2, while Italy had no government, Mussolini's supporters won control of several local councils, including Milan.

21.3 The March on Rome, 28 October 1922

In July–August 1922, socialists organized a general strike in protest against government failure to deal with unemployment. In response, Mussolini's supporters occupied many public buildings in towns in northern and central Italy. They organized public services in many of these towns, something which the government ought to have done but was unwilling to do in face of the general strike. The Fascists also attacked left-wing organizations and burnt the printing press of the *Avanti* newspaper.

Early in October, King Victor Emmanuel III invited Mussolini to become Prime Minister. He refused, not wishing to appear to be merely another politician of the 'ordinary' kind.

On 28 October 1922, about 30,000 Fascists 'marched' (by train) from various parts of Italy, threatening to take over the capital, Rome. Mussolini, fearing arrest, stayed in Milan. Liberal and left-wing politicians wanted the King to order the army and police to move against the Fascists, but the King refused to act. He feared that to arrest Mussolini would suggest that he favoured the socialists and communists. He also thought that Mussolini was just the 'strong man' that the divided and violent country needed, and, again, he invited Mussolini to form a government.

21.4 Establishing a Fascist Government

MUSSOLINI'S FIRST GOVERNMENT, 1922–4

There were only three Fascists in the Cabinet. This was only a temporary expedient, needed to soothe the right-wing politicians. All decisions had to receive Mussolini's approval. He soon replaced with Fascists anyone opposing his ideas.

He founded the Voluntary Fascist Militia for National Security, which was a private army for his own use.

In 1923 Mussolini proposed that the party which got the largest number of votes in the next election should take two-thirds of the seats in Parliament. His blackshirted army filled the galleries in Parliament. The Electoral Law was passed by the frightened members.

In 1924 during the election there was a great deal of violence, including armed fighting. Fascists got 65 per cent of the vote.

THE SECOND GOVERNMENT, 1924–5

Socialists demanded an enquiry into the election violence. Matteotti, a leading socialist, led the attack on Mussolini. He showed that opposition newspapers had been attacked, printing presses smashed and newsprint burned. He also named individuals who had been attacked.

His campaign won a good deal of support.

Within a week, Matteotti was brutally murdered. Mussolini may not have given the order for this murder, but he stood to gain from the removal of his opponent.

There was widespread demand for Mussolini's dismissal. However, the King refused to sack him. Opposition members left Parliament and held meetings elsewhere. Mussolini then attacked other opponents.

FASCIST 'STABILITY'

Mussolini decreed that Italy needed time to forget the Matteotti affair. Fascist gangs closed the offices of opposition parties, papers and clubs. Opponents were attacked, imprisoned and tortured. Remaining independent papers were taken over by Fascists.

Local government was changed: Fascists replaced existing mayors. Central government was changed: Mussolini became responsible to the King alone and not to Parliament.

The electoral system was also changed. Lists of possible candidates were drawn up by workers' organizations. From these the Fascist Grand Council chose the final list. Electors could only accept or reject the list as a whole. In 1929 and 1934 the Fascist list was accepted.

University teachers had to take an oath of loyalty to Il Duce. Anti-Fascists were arrested and exiled to the Lipari Islands. Everywhere organized bands of Fascists terrorized opposition.

THE FASCIST GRAND COUNCIL

Before 1924 membership of the Party had been small. After 1924 a Party card was essential for anyone wanting an official job or an army post. Ninety-six Provincial Secretaries appointed by Mussolini ran the Party throughout the country.

The Fascist Grand Council consisted of 22 representatives from the various Corporations (see below). The Council met when Mussolini ordered it to do so.

The Secretary-General of the Party had a powerful post. We have seen how Stalin used such a position to win power for himself (Unit 10). In 1925 Mussolini appointed a loyal supporter, Farinacci, to the post—and he organized the reign of terror. Later, Mussolini dismissed Secretaries—to ensure that none of them stayed long enough to become too powerful.

THE CORPORATE STATE

Thirteen (later 22) Corporations were set up to organize various industries and occupations. There was a Corporation for steel, another for teachers, another for the theatre and so on. Employers and workers were represented on the Corporation, which settled pay, working conditions and the running of industry. A Minister of Corporations supervised the Corporations.

Members of each Corporation were taught to put the interests of the State before their self-interest. Trade unions were abolished as unnecessary. Strikes were illegal—disputes were settled by the Corporation. Lock-outs by employers were banned. This appeared to make workers and employers equal; in fact the Corporations were controlled by the wealthy and influential. Mussolini claimed to have abolished class warfare by uniting employers, workers and managers in the Corporations.

In 1938, representatives of the 22 Corporations replaced Parliament through the Assembly of Corporations.

THE DICTATORSHIP

The Corporations controlled economic life. Then, in December 1925, Mussolini took away the King's right to appoint or dismiss Ministers, and in January 1926 all decrees signed by Mussolini became law.

The Fascist Party controlled local government (see above). Propaganda convinced many of Mussolini's success (below).

PROPAGANDA

The media

Opposition papers were closed down (see above). Many independent papers were controlled by Fascist editors. All papers had to submit everything to a government censor.

Books had to be approved by the government. Many were banned.

Radio was government-controlled.

Education

This was strictly controlled.

University teachers had to take an oath of loyalty, and school teachers had to be Party members (see above). Syllabuses were drawn up by Fascist officials. Textbooks were written to fit in with Fascist ideas.

Speeches by Mussolini to organized demonstrations roused great enthusiasm and won him a good deal of popular support.

Mussolini was presented as an example to his people of the spirit of Fascism. His office light was kept on until late in the evening, to give the impression of hard work. He was often photographed in sporting scenes and clothes to present the image of health and vitality.

21.5 Domestic Policies

ECONOMIC 'BATTLES'—AND SOME SUCCESSES

Unemployment was tackled by government spending.

The Pontine Marshes were drained, and provided work

for thousands. Being near Rome this scheme was an advertisement for the system.

Railways were electrified, providing more work. Autostrade (or motorways) were built, as were many public buildings—sports stadiums, railway stations, blocks of flats. Hydro-electricity schemes were developed.

The Battle of the Lira

In 1925 the lira was over-valued, with large American loans, and in 1929 the Wall Street Crash led to the recall of those loans. Thus the value of the lira fell. Mussolini decided to force its value back up. One method was the halving of wages. This led to a fall in living standards and, because people had less to spend, a rise in unemployment.

The Battle for Grain

Mussolini wanted to cut wheat imports to help the lira. So farmers were subsidized to produce more wheat, and land suitable for growing olives and fruit was ploughed up. Wheat production rose; other production fell. Overall, the cost of subsidizing farmers was very high.

The Battle for Births, 1934

Mussolini wanted a population increase from 40 to 60 million by 1950. Thus large families were encouraged, and bachelors were heavily taxed. Larger families often led to greater poverty.

THE LATERAN TREATIES, 1929

The Church had opposed the Italian government since 1870 (see above). Mussolini made a Concordat (or agreement) with the Church in 1929. The Church gained by the Concordat. Catholicism was recognized as 'the official State religion'. Bishops and priests received State salaries. The Church was free to preach and run schools. The Vatican, in Rome, was recognized as an independent State and the government paid for Papal lands lost before 1871 (see above).

Mussolini also gained. The Church recognized the government. Bishops and priests were to take an oath of loyalty.

The propaganda value of these various Treaties was great. Many Italians assumed that the Pope was a Mussolini-supporter. Foreign governments saw Fascism as 'respectable'.

21.6 Mussolini's Achievements?

Under Mussolini, there was much less freedom than in the past (see above). The rich did better than the less well-off. Living standards fell. His successes were, in reality, very few. Most of his achievements (e.g., making the trains run on time) were superficial and not long lasting. There were few measures which made radical changes in the nature of Italy's problems. His achievements were in the fields of morale and national pride rather than in any economic miracle, and in prestige projects rather than in long-term solutions.

WHY WAS HE SO POPULAR?

Opposition was violently crushed and could not express itself. Propaganda made him appear a success. The Church appeared to support him—and many priests actively did so because of his anti-communism.

Law and order was imposed and appeared better than the violence which had been common between 1919 and 1925. The Mafia was attacked and partly suppressed.

His foreign policy appeared to be 'glorious'. His propaganda machine was successful and convincing.

FOREIGN POLICY

In 1923 Mussolini defied the League over Corfu (see Unit 14), and in 1924 he gained Fiume and Zara when giving up Italian claims to Dalmatia (see above).

In 1934 he stopped a German invasion of Austria and in 1935 was a member of the Stresa Front (Unit 23).

In 1935 he launched an attack on Abyssinia, in 1936 helped Franco in the Spanish Civil War (see Unit 24) and in 1939 he invaded Albania (see Unit 23).

HIS FALL AND DEATH, 1945

In May 1940 Mussolini entered the war as France collapsed (see Unit 25). During 1940–3 Italian troops had varying fortunes in North Africa (Units 25 and 26). Then in July 1943 the Allies invaded Sicily (Unit 26). In August 1943 the King dismissed and imprisoned Mussolini.

A new government asked for an armistice. Hitler poured troops into Italy. Paratroopers rescued Mussolini and set him up in government again.

In April 1945 Mussolini and his mistress were captured by anti-Fascist Italians. Their bodies were hung upside-down in a square in Milan where Mussolini had begun his march to power (see above).

Unit 21 Summary

▶ Italy's problems, 1914–20: Mussolini's early career.
▶ The 'March on Rome', 1922.
▶ Domestic policies: the Lateran Treaties, 1929.
▶ Fascism: origins, structures and weaknesses.

22 THE BRITISH EMPIRE, 1918–39

22.1 The Dominions and the Statute of Westminster

THE EMERGENCE OF THE DOMINIONS

Independent colonies

Canada

The British North American Act 1867 united four Provinces (Quebec, Ontario, New Brunswick and Nova Scotia) in the Dominion of Canada. It left each Province its own local Parliament, and created a Union Parliament for the whole Dominion, with more power than the local Parliaments. The Act also made provision for the expansion of the Dominion. British Colombia joined in 1871.

Australia

The Commonwealth of Australia Act 1900 created a Federation from six self-governing colonies (New South Wales, Victoria, Western Australia, South Australia, Queensland and Tasmania). It left each colony its own local Parliament, and created a central government, with an elected Senate and House of Representatives, to deal with defence, commerce, postal systems, railways, immigration and currency.

New Zealand

New Zealand refused to join the Commonwealth of Australia. In 1907 it was given the status of Dominion.

South Africa

The Union of South Africa, 1910, was created from two self-governing British colonies (Cape of Good Hope and Natal) and two former Boer republics (Transvaal and the Orange River Colony).

Imperial unity proposals, 1900–14

Prime Ministers of the independent colonies met in London in 1887 and 1897 during Queen Victoria's jubilees. Chamberlain, Colonial Secretary, 1895–1903, wanted to create an Imperial 'Zollverein' (see Unit 1). Australia and New Zealand—the most distant—were most in favour; South Africa and Canada (with racial minorities) were against. Chamberlain's Tariff Reform suggestions, including Imperial Preference, were rejected in Britain in the 1906 Election.

Unity and war, 1914–18

The Dominions were brought into the War by the King's declaration on 4 August 1914. They had no choice. In 1917 there was an Imperial War Conference which tried to agree on closer unity—on defence costs and trade. The Dominions lacked the will to agree, fearing also the costs which would fall on the colonies (for an Imperial army and navy). Distance and the problem of communications would have led to a British-dominated Empire. The Dominions opposed this.

Searching for greater independence, 1919–25

At Versailles in 1919 Lloyd George represented the Empire at the Treaty. Each Dominion took part in policy-making discussions. Australia and South Africa received Mandated Territories (see Unit 13).

In 1921 the Prime Ministers' Conference, London, tried to work out means whereby the Empire could act in common policy. However, in 1922 over Chanak (Unit 13) the Dominions refused to support Lloyd George's war-like policy, and in 1923 at Lausanne (Unit 13) the Dominions did not sign this Treaty.

In 1924 the Empire Exhibition at Wembley was staged to encourage the mutual buying of 'Empire' goods to help employment.

In 1925 the Dominions did not sign the Locarno Treaties concerned with European frontier agreements (see Unit 18).

DEFINING DOMINION STATUS, 1926–31

In 1926 a report by former Prime Minister, Balfour, defined the Dominions as 'autonomous Communities within the British Empire, equal in status, in no way subordinate one to another in any aspect of their domestic or external affairs, though united by a common allegiance to the Crown and freely associated as members of the British Commonwealth of Nations'. This gave the Dominions that freedom in foreign policy which they had not had in 1914 but had acquired by accident in the 1920s (see above).

In 1931 the Statute of Westminster was passed by the British Parliament to implement the Balfour Report.

22.2 Indian Independence and Gandhi

THE DEMAND FOR INDIAN INDEPENDENCE, 1900–19

In 1833 the Whig MP, Macaulay, talked of India becoming self-governing 'in some future age'.

Middle-class dissatisfaction

Western-style education had created an Indian middle class. However, there was little industry for them to work in. They were not allowed into the higher ranks of the Indian Civil Service.

In 1885 the dissatisfied middle class held the first Indian Congress, in which there were more Hindus than Muslims, partly because the Hindus were, in general, richer and more successful than the Muslims, but also because there were more Hindus than Muslims throughout India. The Congress also contained moderates, who wanted social reforms to help the less well-off and changes in law to allow greater opportunities for the better educated. They hoped that peaceful campaigning would persuade the British to change the law. There were also extremists, who thought that an armed rising would have to be organized to force the British out of India.

Reforms

In 1909 John Morley (Secretary of State in the Liberal Government) and Lord Minto (Viceroy of India) were responsible for reforms. The Imperial Legislative Council (or central Council of India) was enlarged from 21 to 60 members. Of these, 27 were elected by Indians; the majority were appointed by the British government. For the first time,

Indians were to be elected to the provincial councils.

The franchise (or right to vote) was based on a property qualification. The Muslims were, generally, not as rich as the Hindus. To overcome this problem there was separate representation for Muslims, which pleased the Muslim League, formed in 1906.

Factors promoting independence

During the First World War (1914–18), Indian troops fought in Europe and the Middle East (see Unit 9).

Indian reformers, in Congress and the Muslim League, pressed for further reforms, promised for 'after the war'. Extremists gained control of Congress.

In 1917 the Russian Revolution (see Unit 10) was seen as an example of how an unpopular government could be overthrown, and during 1918–19 the disappearance of the Austro-Hungarian Empire showed that Empires could be divided up. Wilson's Fourteen Points (Fig. 12.1) were also a strong moral factor in support of Indian nationalism.

In 1917 Montagu, the Secretary of State, said that British policy was to involve Indians in the government of their country and to lead India to self-government within the Empire. By this the British meant 'at some distant future' such as 500 years, while Indians thought it meant immediate independence.

1919 The Montagu–Chelmsford reforms

The Central Legislative Assembly was to consist of 106 elected members and only 40 nominated by the British government. An Upper House, or Council of State, was created to represent the Princes and large landowners in British India. A Chamber of Princes was created for rulers of states not in British India but who had certain matters of common concern with the British Indian government.

At least 70 per cent of the members of provincial councils were to be elected, and provincial ministers, usually British, were responsible to the largely elected provincial councils.

The franchise was greatly extended, but still based on a property qualification. Five million voted for elections to provincial councils; one million for the Central Legislative Assembly and about 17,000 for the Council of State.

Dyarchy (dual control) was instituted. Some powers, concerning such matters as health, education, industry and agriculture, were exercised by ministers responsible to provincial councils. Others (on law and order, police, terrorism) were reserved to non-elected executive councils, governors and, ultimately, to the Viceroy. The Central Executive Council (a Viceroy's Cabinet) had three Indians out of its six members. The Viceroy still had a deciding vote.

Reaction to these reforms

The British thought they had been generous in bringing Indians into the system, and sensible in giving them some control while not giving them complete freedom—which would come 'in the future'.

Indians thought that the reforms had not gone far enough.

INDIAN UNREST, 1919

The Rowlatt Bills allowed judges (usually British) to try cases of terrorism without juries and gave provincial governments (usually British) the power of internment without trial. Gandhi (see below) called on the people to protest at this by a hartal. In the Punjab there was widespread rioting, put down by firm action by Brigadier-General Reginald Dyer. In the Sikhs' holy city, Amritsar, four Europeans were murdered. The provincial government banned all meetings in the hope that the unrest would die down.

On 18 April 1919 an illegal gathering took place (peacefully) in a square which had only one narrow exit. Brigadier Dyer commanded the troops sent to disperse the gathering. The crowd could not (or would not) disperse. Troops opened fire and 379 people were killed and 1200 wounded.

In 1920 a commission of inquiry condemned Dyer. But in the debate in the House of Commons he received a good deal of support, while the House of Lords passed a resolution in his favour. Indians, on the other hand, never forgot Amritsar. Relations between the British and Indians were never the same as they had been.

MAHATMA GANDHI

Early career

Gandhi was born in 1869 to a wealthy and religious family. In 1888 he went to London University to qualify as a barrister. In 1891 he practised as a barrister in Bombay. Then in 1893 he went to South Africa on business, and stayed for some years. There he led Asian opposition against harsh racial laws. In 1899 he organized an Indian Red Cross for the Boer War, and in 1903 he founded a paper, *Indian Opinion*, in Durban. In 1906 he led a demonstration against racial laws. By 1914 many of the worst racial laws were removed.

Gandhi was frequently imprisoned because of his activities. Many extremists in his own side also attacked him because of his non-violent policies.

In 1914 he went back to India. When war broke out he went to London to organize an Indian ambulance corps. Like many Indians, he hoped that the Indian part in the war would persuade the British to make major concessions.

Gandhi and Indian politics, 1914–22

Gandhi was the religious leader of the nationalist movement until 1920, when he also became the political leader. His political followers called him Mahatma, which means 'Great Soul', in recognition of the religious nature of his political power. His non-violent policy (see below) was known as satyagraha, or soul force.

On 6 April 1919 he called a hartal, a day for Indians to fast and pray, and not to do any work. This would draw British and Indian attention to the demand for independence.

In spite of Gandhi's appeal for non-violence, many Indians rioted against the British government which, in turn, led to violent behaviour by the government.

Gandhi also supported the Muslims in their protest at the treatment of Turkey by the Allies (see Unit 13) and Indian Muslims supported his non-cooperation with the government by:

▶ refusing to obey 'unfair' laws;
▶ refusing to pay 'unfair' taxes ('civil disobedience');
▶ boycotting British imports. This led to the fostering of home industries, such as making cloth on small spinning-wheels. This cut the imports of Lancashire cloth into India.

Violence was widespread as strikes and riots took place (1921) when Gandhi supervised the burning of foreign goods in Bombay. Violence led to looting, and Gandhi called off the non-cooperation policy. He was given almost dictatorial powers by the Congress. Although he had called off the policy of non-cooperation and civil disobedience, he was arrested in 1922 and sentenced to six years in jail for 'preaching disaffection'.

Gandhi and the independence movement, 1924–35

After an operation for appendicitis in 1924, Gandhi was released from jail. He played little part in affairs for three more years. In 1927 he was elected President of Congress—but refused to accept the post, leaving it to his lieutenant, Motilal Nehru.

In 1928 the Simon Commission visited India to see how the 1919 reforms (see above) were working. Gandhi boycotted the Commission, which had no Indian members, an omission which confirmed the suspicions of Congress. That body had already adopted the recommendation of Jawaharlal Nehru that it should accept nothing less than complete independence.

The Round-table Conference

The British Labour government proposed a conference in London to discuss Indian politics. Gandhi asked if this would lead immediately to Dominion status. When the British said this was their 'ultimate' aim, he refused to go to London.

In March–April 1930 he made his march from Ahmedabad to the sea, where he distilled salt from sea-water. This was to show opposition to the salt tax. In May 1930 he was sentenced to an indefinite term of imprisonment. However, in January 1931 he was released from jail, having promised to attend the London Conference. He called off the civil disobedience and boycott campaigns.

The Round-table Conference took place in 1932. Gandhi took Muslims with him when he went to London. The Conference failed to reach any agreement; Indians demanded more progress than Britain wanted to make.

In 1933, back in India, he called another campaign of non-cooperation. During the unrest that followed he was, again, arrested, jailed and released. He retired from politics to live in his retreat (ashram) at Wardha. He was discouraged by Hindu-Muslim enmity. He hoped to lead a united India to independence. Religious bigotry often led to riots by one group against another. He was also discouraged by extremists in Congress, led by younger men such as Jawaharlal Nehru, who wanted more direct action against the British. Nehru was elected President of Congress in 1936.

THE GOVERNMENT OF INDIA ACT 1935

This Act promised India Dominion status 'in the future'. Provincial councils were given more powers, suggesting the future creation of a federal system, such as in the USA (Unit 7) or Germany (Unit 1).

Provinces were given direct aid through income tax, and the system of dyarchy (see above) was swept away. Local ministries were made responsible to the electors.

The franchise was extended. Thirty-five million people had the vote—on a property qualification. New provinces were created, and separate representation for minority religious groups—Hindus and Sikhs—continued with 're-served seats'.

The weaknesses of the proposals were:

▶ they did not provide Dominion status;
▶ the conservative Indian princes were given one-third of the seats in the Lower House of the Central Legislature and two-fifths of the seats in its Upper House;
▶ dyarchy was retained by central government. Only certain ministers were responsible to the Legislature.

The Act proposed the creation of a Federation of provinces. This would be compulsory for the states in British India; it would be optional for the Princely States. This section of the Act would come into operation when half the Princely States joined. They never did. Federation never came into effect.

Under the Act, the Indian government had no control over Indian foreign policy.

PROGRESS AND FAILURE, 1936–9

Although Gandhi had 'retired', he still 'ruled' Congress, whose leaders felt they had to consult him.

In 1936 the Congress took a full part in the elections, and in 1936–9 Congress formed the governments in seven out of eleven provinces. This gave many Indians experience in government—but only at a provincial level.

Muslims

They were in a minority (see above). They were disappointed by the results of the 1936 elections. Hindu majorities governed provinces in which there were large Muslim minorities.

Muhammad Ali Jinnah

Jinnah asked that there should be Hindu–Muslim governments in some provinces. Congress rejected this. This led Jinnah and the Muslim League to develop demands for a separate state for Muslims. This was to become Pakistan (see Unit 34).

22.3 Palestine

1919–39, THE SEEDS OF FUTURE CONFLICT

In 1918, Arab leaders hoped that a series of independent Arab states would be created out of the Turkish Empire (see Unit 13). Britain had proposed the division of much of that Empire with France. The Sykes–Picot agreement came to nothing.

In November 1917 Britain issued the Balfour Declaration, promising 'a national home for the Jewish people' in Palestine. Palestine was mandated to Britain, and in the 1920s some 10,000 Jews entered Palestine each year. Arabs protested, although the British assured them that what had been promised was 'a home for the Jewish people' and not 'a Jewish national state'.

In 1929 Arabs rioted and attacked Jewish homes and property, and in 1933 Jews rioted because of British restrictions on immigration.

Hitler's attacks on German Jews (see Unit 20) led to increased numbers trying to enter Palestine. By 1937 there were 400,000 Jews in Palestine. Many of them were better-educated than most Arabs. They were also supported by money from world Jewry. This, and their own ability, enabled them to buy up land, set up businesses and prosper. Arab guerrillas attacked Jewish farms, homes and businesses.

In 1937 a commission, under Lord Peel, recommended the partition of Palestine into:

▶ an Arab state;
▶ a Jewish state;
▶ a British Mandate for Jerusalem and Bethlehem.

Partition was rejected as an idea by Jews and Arabs. It was also condemned by the Mandates Commission (see Unit 13).

In 1938 another Commission, under Sir John Woodhead, said that Arabs and Jews were so tangled up that partition was impossible.

In 1939 a round-table conference was tried—in spite of the failure of the Indian experiment (see above). This failed too.

In May 1939 a White Paper (or outline of future policy) promised an end to Jewish immigration once another 75,000 had been admitted. This meant that the Balfour Declaration was to be abandoned in the face of Arab hostility and violence, and Britain's belief that she needed the friendship of Arab states, with their oil fields and strategic ports.

22.4 Egypt

Before 1914, Egypt was 'a British sphere of influence' in which a British Consul General really ruled the country (see Unit 5). In 1914 Britain kept 250,000 troops in Egypt to guard the Suez Canal from Turkish attack. On 18 December 1914 Britain declared Egypt to be a British protectorate. The Khedive was deposed and his uncle made Sultan.

In 1919 there was an increase in Egyptian nationalism and a demand for complete independence. The leaders of the movement were exiled: rioting followed, which was put down by Allenby (see Unit 9), the specially-created High Commissioner.

On 28 February 1922 Britain recognized Egypt as an independent sovereign state but reserved some points for later settlement:

▶ security of the Canal;

▶ the defence of Egypt from outside attack;
▶ the protection of European interests, mainly financial.

The question of the Sudan

The Sudan had once been part of Egypt but had been separately governed since its reconquest by Kitchener (see Unit 5).

On 19 November 1924 the British High Commissioner of the Sudan, Sir Lee Stack, was murdered by Egyptian nationalists. The British insisted on the withdrawal of Egyptians from garrisons in the Sudan.

In spite of Egyptian demands for the inclusion of Sudan in a larger Egypt, Britain went ahead with preparations for the emergence of an independent Sudan. In 1936 an Anglo-Egyptian Treaty was signed. Egypt recognized Britain's

special interest in the Suez Canal zone. British troops were to be based in that zone for twenty years.

Nationalism continued to develop. It was accompanied by the emergence of a guerrilla movement which attacked British troops—the symbol of Britain's control of an apparently independent Egypt.

> ### Unit 22 Summary
>
> ▶ The Dominions and the Statute of Westminster.
> ▶ The movement for Indian independence; Mahatma Gandhi.
> ▶ Palestine: Arabs versus Jews.
> ▶ Egypt.

23 INTERNATIONAL RELATIONS, 1930–9

23.1 The Uneasy Background

The League was meant to abolish war (see Unit 14). However, 'might is right' was shown in Corfu (Unit 14) and Manchuria (Unit 17). The failure of the League was due, largely, to its over-dependence on Britain and France, neither of whom was willing or able to take a strong line against aggression (Unit 14). Many Western statesmen thought Bolshevism and Russia was the real menace. They were unwilling to fight right-wing aggressors.

Hitler had left the League (Unit 14) and started to rearm (Unit 20).

23.2 The Saar, 1935 (Fig. 23.8)

This was under French rule during 1919–24 (Fig. 12.2). It then came under the rule of a League Commission (see Unit 12). It was an important industrial centre.

In January 1935 under the terms of the 1919 Treaty, there was a plebiscite—a vote on a simple issue. Nine out of ten voted for reunification with Germany. Following this success, Hitler announced his plans on conscription and rearmament (see Unit 20).

23.3 Austria, 1934 (Fig. 23.8)

The post-war Treaties forbade Austria's union with Germany.

In 1932 a right-wing Chancellor, Dollfuss, came to power. In March 1933 he suspended parliamentary government and attacked left-wing housing centres and organizations. In July 1934 Dollfuss was assassinated by Austrian Nazis who tried to take over power. They asked for German help. Schuschnigg, the new Chancellor, appealed to Mussolini, who did not want a strong Germany–Austria on his frontier. Italian troops were rushed to the Brenner Pass, and Hitler called off his plans.

Peace and the terms of the Treaties had been maintained—but by the threat of force and not by League action.

23.4 The Stresa Front, April 1935

Mussolini met the Prime Ministers of Britain and France. They signed an agreement to resist attempts to revise the terms of the Treaty of Versailles. This was obviously aimed against Hitler's Austrian plans. If people had believed in the League, such an agreement would not have been needed (see Unit 14).

23.5 The Anglo-German Naval Agreement, June 1935

The British Foreign Secretary, Sir Samuel Hoare, and Hitler's 'roving Ambassador', Ribbentrop, signed this agreement.

The German navy was to be 35 per cent the size of Britain's. This was contrary to the Treaty of Versailles (Unit 12) and against the Stresa Agreement. It angered Italy and France, both of which feared Germany.

France signed a defensive alliance with Russia to offset the Ten Year Pact signed between Germany and Poland, France's ally (see Unit 18).

This naval agreement was the first act of appeasement.

23.6 Abyssinia

By 1890 Italy had conquered Eritrea and part of Somaliland on the east coast of Africa. In 1896 she tried to unite these regions by conquering part of Abyssinia. Defeat at Adowa put an end to that plan. In 1925 Mussolini proposed Abyssinia for League membership.

In 1934 there were clashes between Italians and Abyssinians on the border. Mussolini demanded financial compensation and Abyssinian territory. The Emperor of Abyssinia, Haile Selassie, appealed to the League. He was advised to negotiate with Mussolini. In 1935, Italian troops moved to Somaliland and Eritrea.

In October 1935 Italian troops invaded Abyssinia. With

modern weapons (aircraft) and chemicals (poison gas) they defeated the Abyssinians. The League decided that Italy was an aggressor, so economic sanctions were to be applied under Article XVI of the Covenant (see Unit 14). Coal, steel and oil were excluded. Austria and Germany ignored this decision. American firms also sold arms to the Italians.

Britain and France allowed Italy free passage through the Suez Canal—a sign of appeasement of their 'Stresa friend'.

In December 1935 Hoare (see above) and Laval, Foreign Minister of France, signed a Pact by which Italy would get two-thirds of Abyssinia, including the coast, and landlocked Ethiopia (as Abyssinia became known) would have a corridor to the sea. There was a public outcry and Hoare resigned. The Plan was dropped and the Italian conquest went on.

By May 1936 the conquest was completed. Haile Selassie went into exile. Italian East Africa consisted of Somaliland, Eritrea and newly-conquered Abyssinia.

THE EFFECTS OF THIS VICTORY

The League had been proved a failure—again. Sanctions, weakly applied, did not halt the aggressor. The Stresa Front was weakened by Anglo-French criticism of Mussolini. In 1937 he withdrew from the League. Mussolini was drawn into an alliance with Hitler, who used the crisis to further his own aims (see below).

In 1935–6 France made an alliance with Russia. They promised to aid one another if attacked.

23.7 The Spanish Civil War, July 1936

In Unit 24 we will see how Hitler and Mussolini used this war to strengthen their friendship and train their forces.

23.8 German Expansionism

Fig. 23.8 Hitler's expansionist policy, 1933–8

THE RHINELAND (Fig. 23.8)

This region had been de-militarized in 1919 (see Unit 12). This was further agreed in the Rhineland Pact signed at Locarno, 1925 (see Unit 18). Then in March 1936, Britain and France (signatories of Locarno) were involved in the Abyssinian crisis.

German troops marched into the Rhineland. They were outnumbered by better-armed French troops. Hitler gave orders that they were to withdraw if opposed.

Britain and France were unwilling to stop Hitler. The region was described as 'only his own backyard', and neither country was militarily prepared for war. Germany spent on arms double the amount spent by Britain and France combined. Her industrial power was greater than that of the two possible Allies.

German generals had opposed Hitler's plan. They feared war. However, Hitler's success illustrated his claim to be 'always right'.

THE HOSSBACH MEMORANDUM, NOVEMBER 1937

Japan's expansion was forecast in the Tanaka Memorial (see Unit 17).

Hitler's expansionist policy was summarized in the memorandum prepared by his adjutant, Colonel Hossbach. In November 1937 Hitler called a meeting of military advisers. He told them of his plans for expansion (Fig. 23.8). Expansion had to be won 'at the lowest cost', and it had to 'solve the German space problem at the latest by 1943–5'.

'The first aim had to be to conquer Czechoslovakia and Austria'. He told his generals that Britain appeared ready to 'give up' both of these countries. His two leading generals, Blomberg and Fritsch, pointed out that we should 'not run the risk of making England and France our enemies'. He overruled them, as in 1936.

HITLER'S GROWING CONFIDENCE, 1937

In November 1936 Hitler signed the Anti-Comintern Pact with Japan. In November 1937 Italy joined the Pact. All three aggressor-nations were now linked in this anti-Russian Pact.

Russia was weakened by the Stalinist purges (see Unit 11). German industrial and military power was growing rapidly.

In November 1937 Lord Halifax (later to be Foreign Secretary) visited Hitler and suggested that Britain would not oppose German moves to occupy Austria and the Sudetenland (Fig. 23.8).

AUSTRIA: THE ANSCHLUSS (Fig. 23.8)

In January 1938 Seyss-Inquart led an Austrian Nazi attempt to seize power. Schuschnigg prevented this. In February 1938 Hitler summoned Schuschnigg to Germany. In a stormy interview he threatened to make war unless Seyss-Inquart was made Minister of the Interior (controlling the police forces in Austria).

Schuschnigg proposed a plebiscite to see if the Austrians wanted to unite with Germany. Hitler, fearing a negative vote, rushed troops to the border, threatening an invasion if Schuschnigg did not resign. Schuschnigg resigned, and Seyss-Inquart became Chancellor.

On 12 March Seyss-Inquart 'invited' Hitler to occupy Austria and to ward off 'a communist plot', and on 14 March Austria became a province of a larger Germany.

A plebiscite showed that 99 in every 100 Austrians favoured this union with successful Germany. Opposition was crushed; many were imprisoned, others murdered. The Jews also came under attack. In June 1938 they were made to strip in public and to crawl around on all fours.

THE SUDETENLAND (Fig. 23.8)

In 1919–20 this region was taken from Austria-Hungary to help to form the new state, Czechoslovakia (see Unit 12). It had 3 million Germans. Its inclusion in Czechoslovakia ignored the notion of 'national self-determination'.

The Sudetenland provided the new state with valuable mineral deposits and heavy industry, the means of producing one-third of her exports, and manageable and defensible frontiers.

In 1933 Henlein led Sudeten Nazis who complained of ill-treatment by Czechs and demanded self-government for the Sudetenland. In 1938 Hitler seemed ready to intervene.

Neville Chamberlain, Prime Minister of Great Britain, thought it possible to arrange things in peaceful discussions. Eden, his Foreign Secretary, resigned; Halifax (see above) succeeded.

Czechoslovakia betrayed, 1938

In August 1938 Chamberlain sent Lord Runciman to examine the Sudetenland problem and to persuade President Beneš of Czechoslovakia to give in to Henlein's demands. Beneš agreed to Sudeten self-government. Hitler was not satisfied. He described Czechoslovakia as an 'artificial state' 'in alliance with Russia'.

On 15 September 1938 in Berchtesgaden Hitler, Chamberlain and Daladier (of France) met. After talks they told Beneš that the Czechs would have to make 'sacrifices' by giving up regions where 50 per cent of the population was German. However, on 22 September 1938 in Godesberg the Czechs refused to the demands made on them. Chamberlain flew to Godesberg to ask Hitler not to invade until he had another try at persuading the Czechs to give in.

Was this conflict going to spark off a war? In France military reservists were called up, in Czechoslovakia the army was mobilized, and in Britain the Fleet prepared for action. Air raid shelters and trenches were built or dug, gas masks issued and anti-aircraft barrage balloons appeared above towns and cities. Chamberlain, 'the peacemaker', complained of the stupidity of being involved in 'the quarrel between people in a faraway country of which we know nothing'.

Chamberlain flew to Munich. On 29 September 1938, he met Daladier and Mussolini. The Russians were not invited to the meeting (although they were allies of Czechoslovakia). The Czechs were left waiting in a nearby hotel and did not take part in the discussions about their future. The statesmen decided that Germany should take the Sudetenland. A Commission would decide exactly which areas were to be handed over.

Would this agreement lead to peace? On 30 September Hitler signed a piece of paper expressing his hopes and confidence in 'consultation' as a means of avoiding war. Chamberlain flew home. He waved the paper as the sign of 'Peace in our time'. Few people believed Churchill, who saw the Munich agreement as a 'disaster of the first magnitude for Britain and France'.

Czech losses

The loss of the Sudetenland meant the loss of a good deal of Czech industry and source of raw materials, and easily defended boundaries.

In October 1938 Hungary took advantage of the crisis to take part of Slovakia with its ore deposits and sugar beetfields. In November 1938 Poland joined in 'the rape of Czechoslovakia' by taking part of Moravia with its coal deposits and steelworks.

After Munich

Beneš resigned; Hacha became President of the smaller state. Slovakia and Ruthenia demanded independence. Hacha produced a federal constitution. Czechoslovakia would consist of the states of Bohemia, Moravia, Slovakia and Ruthenia, each with its own provincial government.

Hitler took no notice of 'Peace in our time' or Hacha's constitution. On 13 March 1939 Hitler summoned Hacha to Germany. He made him agree to special rights for any Germans still under Czech rule. Then, without waiting for action, Hitler ordered the invasion which brought most of Czechoslovakia under German rule. Hungary acted quickly to occupy Ruthenia.

The Versailles-created state, Czechoslovakia, died.

23.9 Poland (Fig. 23.8)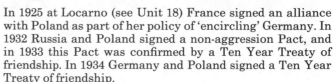

In 1925 at Locarno (see Unit 18) France signed an alliance with Poland as part of her policy of 'encircling' Germany. In 1932 Russia and Poland signed a non-aggression Pact, and in 1933 this Pact was confirmed by a Ten Year Treaty of friendship. In 1934 Germany and Poland signed a Ten Year Treaty of friendship.

In April 1939 Britain gave a guarantee to Poland promising to come to her help if she were attacked. Also in April 1939 Mussolini invaded and conquered Albania, one of the gains Italy had hoped for in 1919 (see Unit 21).

In May 1939 Hitler and Mussolini signed the Pact of Steel. Danzig (Fig. 23.8) had been made an International City in 1919 (Fig. 12.2), and Poland was given part of Prussia as a corridor to the sea (Fig. 23.8). Hitler wanted to get both Danzig and the corridor which separated East Prussia from the rest of Germany.

23.10 Stalin's Foreign Policy

Litvinov, the Russian Foreign Minister, arranged a non-aggression Pact with Poland in 1932, and in 1935 a defensive treaty with France and Czechoslovakia. Stalin was angered when, at Munich, Russia was not consulted about the future of her Czech ally. In May 1939 Litvinov was sacked.

Molotov, the new Foreign Minister, and Stalin thought that Munich marked one (if important) stage in the policy of appeasement. This gave the right-wing dictators (Mussolini and Hitler), as well as anti-communist Japan, whatever they could grab.

In July 1939 Molotov held talks with Hitler and with Britain. Britain was hesistant in its approaches. Then on 23 August 1939 the Nazi-Soviet Pact amazed the world, because it was 'an association of criminals' who crushed enemies, and 'an association of opposites'.

In this Pact the Communists and Nazis agreed not to fight one another. Hitler was free to take on Britain and France. He would not have to fight on two fronts as the Kaiser did in 1914 (see Unit 9). They also agreed to divide Poland between their two countries. Russia would regain lands lost in 1917–21 (see Unit 10).

23.11 And so to War, 1939

On 1 September Germany invaded Poland, and on 3 September Britain and France declared war on Germany. Then on 15 September Russia invaded Poland, met the German troops, and the country was divided between the two countries.

Russia then invaded the Baltic countries lost in 1917: Estonia, Latvia and Lithuania. Only Finland offered any resistance in a war which began in November 1939 and ended in Russian victory in March 1940.

In a futile gesture, the League expelled Russia.

Unit 23 Summary

▶ The Saar votes to return to Germany, 1935.
▶ The Austrian crisis, 1934 and the Stresa Front, 1935.
▶ The effects of the Anglo-German naval treaty, 1935.
▶ The Abyssinian war, 1934–6: failure to halt Mussolini.
▶ Hitler's re-occupation of the Rhineland, 1936.
▶ The effects of the Spanish Civil War.
▶ The Anschluss: German takeover of Austria.
▶ The Czech crisis, 1938: Munich.
▶ The outbreak of war, 1939.
▶ Stalin's foreign policy, 1935–9.

24 SPAIN, 1919–39

24.1 Problems and Unrest, 1917–23

PROBLEMS

Economic

In 1898 Spain lost her Empire in Cuba and the Philippines (Unit 7). The loss of these markets led to increased unemployment and, for those in work, low wages.

Agricultural

The majority of Spaniards were peasants. Rich landowners had huge estates (latifundias), many of which were left unused. Other parts were rented out, and tenant farmers paid high rents to landowners. There were also $2\frac{1}{2}$ million landless peasants, some working for low wages, many often unemployed, all frequently suffering from starvation.

Political

The great division between rich landowners and poor peasants was reflected in Spain's political system. The right-wing parties supported the idea of a strong monarchy. They were supported by the wealthy, the Church, the police and the army. Left-wing parties included:

▶ socialists, who wanted a strong central government to bring in such things as land reform (see below);
▶ communists, who wanted a Russian-style revolution, the overthrow of the monarchy and the Church, and the end of the economic power of the wealthy landowners;
▶ anarchists, who were opposed to any form of government;
▶ syndicalists who, as in France (Unit 2), wanted workers to take control of the industries in which they worked. Their main support was in industrial centres—the Basque region and Catalonia (with its port of Barcelona) (Fig. 24.4).

UNREST

In 1917 industrial workers held a general strike which was crushed by the army.

In 1917–23, as in Italy (Unit 21), the Spanish Parliament (the Cortes) contained many small parties. As their leaders jockeyed for power, there were frequent changes of government: 12 in six years. This political instability was one reason for little being done to tackle Spain's problems.

24.2 Primo de Rivera, 1923–30

De Rivera was a general in the Spanish army. The army had been a powerful force in Spanish politics in the 19th century, as in Spanish America today. In 1923 the army acted to defend 'the national interests' against 'parliamentary imperfections'. General de Rivera was installed to set up an efficient government.

He had the support of the right wing (see above) and the King, Alfonso XIII. The Church's support was also important in this Catholic country. A left-wing rebellion was easily crushed.

The army and its supporters (nationalist-patriots) approved de Rivera's decision to fight Moorish rebels in Spanish Morocco (Fig. 24.4). But this was a heavy drain on Spain's scarce resources.

In 1929 Spain, like other European countries, was affected by the depression following the Wall Street Crash (see Unit 16). Exports fell, unemployment rose and living standards went even lower.

In 1930 de Rivera quarrelled with King Alfonso XIII and resigned.

24.3 The Spanish Republic, 1931–6

THE FALL OF THE MONARCHY, 1931

The King had shared in de Rivera's popularity, which was the result of financial stability—until 1929, and increased agricultural output following on massive irrigation schemes in some $1\frac{1}{2}$ million hectares of Spanish soil.

The Depression ended that popularity, while it also increased the long-standing hostility of industrial workers who worked a 9- or 10-hour day and had low wages which made overtime essential, and radical intellectuals angered by press and postal censorship.

When de Rivera resigned, the Opposition became more outspoken. In April 1931 Alfonso XIII abdicated, and left.

THE SECOND REPUBLIC

1931–3

Elections were held for a new Cortes which was to write a new constitution for republican Spain. The voters elected a large number of liberal and radical intellectuals. These had little political experience. They also had little contact with ordinary people. They were not sufficiently progressive to appeal to the socialist and communist extremists, and they were too revolutionary to gain the support of the industrial and commercial middle class.

The coalition government under Prime Minister Azaña included the trade unionist, Largo Caballero, as Minister of Labour. His inability to push through industrial and social reforms led him to resign in 1933 when he said, 'the only hope of the masses is social revolution'.

The right-wing members of the Cortes and their supporters in the country outside were opposed to Azaña's government, Caballero's attempted reforms and the new constitution.

The new Constitution, December 1931

Women were given the right to vote. This 'radical' reform provided the right-wing with increased support; women were more under the influence of the Church than were men.

The Church

It was to be an ordinary association subject to general laws like any other association. State grants to the clergy were abolished. Convents and monasteries were dissolved; their property was nationalized. Religious orders were forbidden to teach in primary and secondary schools.

This section of the constitution angered the right wing. The outcry led to modifications: religious orders were allowed to remain—but not the Jesuits. However, they were still forbidden to run schools.

This 'step backwards' angered the left-wing Republicans.

However, even after this modification the right wing (landowners, Church, army and police) rallied in defence of the Church against the Republic. Education suffered from a shortage of schools and teachers, and in 1933 over one-third of the children were not in school. The Republic became increasingly reliant on the support of the industrial working class—based in the few towns and cities.

ATTEMPTED REFORMS, 1932–3

Trade unions pressed for wage increases. Also, in 1932, land reform was set in motion. Wage labourers were entitled to an 8-hour day. But this did nothing for the millions of unemployed peasants. Tenant farmers were given the right to appeal against rent increases, and tenants were to be given a chance to buy their farms by a massive programme of expropriation of the latifundias (see above).

This land reform had very little success, because it was costly. Owners were to be compensated for their 'lost' land. But Spain did not have the resources to make such payments. The reform was also slow. Officials in local and central government offices tended to be more conservative than their political 'masters'. They put obstacles in the way of reforming ministers and delayed expropriation schemes.

The promise of 'land for all' had roused peasants' expectations. When the government failed to deliver quickly enough, the peasants squatted on owners' estates. They had to be driven from their illegal 'squat' by police and army. This brought the radical republicans into more disfavour—with the peasants.

The Church owned a great deal of land in Spain. Angry peasants attacked Church property (May 1931) because it symbolized all that they thought was wrong with Spain.

The economy which had slumped in 1929–30 continued to decline. By 1933 exports were only one-quarter of the 1930 level. This led to increased unemployment in industrial Spain.

THE FALANGE, 1933

In January 1933 Hitler came to power in Germany (see Unit 15). About the same time de Rivera's son founded the Falange, a Spanish Fascist party. In the troubled Republic it got support from the right wing (see above).

ELECTIONS

In the 1933 elections, there was a great swing to the right. Too little had been done for some voters—peasants, workers, educational reformers (see above). Too much had been done to anger others—Church, landowners and industrialists. They owned many newspapers and had the support of priests preaching to the Catholic Spanish people.

The extreme left (symbolized by Caballero) began to believe that democracy could not bring the needed reforms.

Women voters were conservative.

The 1936 elections, however, saw a swing to the left. A popular front government (of radicals, communists and socialists) was set up under Azaña.

Azaña was too moderate for some. He was nicknamed 'the Spanish Kerensky' who would be overthrown by the left-wing Caballero, 'the Spanish Lenin' (see Unit 10 for Lenin versus Kerensky in Russia).

In 1936 the political success of the left led to a wide outbreak of church-burning and priest-killing. This angered the right wing and alarmed even moderate republicans. Also in 1936 peasants seized land rather than wait for reforms.

Many Spaniards shared the view, 'we cannot live with anarchy'.

24.4 The Civil War

JULY–DECEMBER 1936 (Fig. 24.4)

The Nationalists was the name taken by the rebels. Franco was Chief of the General Staff. The government had sent him to the Canary Islands because they feared a revolution. In July he flew to Morocco to take charge of the rebellion.

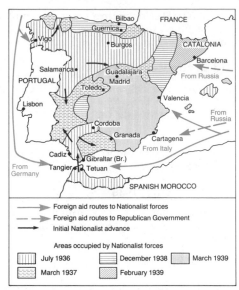

Fig. 24.4   The Spanish Civil War, 1936–9

The army in Morocco (see above) was angered by the anarchy on the Spanish mainland. The army in Spain played the 'traditional' role (see above). Its headquarters at Burgos (Fig. 24.4) was the rebel 'capital'.

The Nationalists, or rebels

The Falange (see above) supported the right-wing rebellion. Church authorities sided with Franco's rebellion, and landowners hoped for an end to land seizure.

Advantages

The Nationalists quickly gained control of the major wheat-growing areas and so could feed their troops. They had the better-qualified military leaders, and they had the important support of the Church.

The Republicans, or government forces

The Popular Front politicians had, after all, been democratically elected in 1936, so industrial workers supported 'their' government (see above). The Spanish navy and air force remained loyal.

Advantages

The Republicans had the industrial centres which supplied them with arms and munitions. Nationalists had to import most of theirs. They also had the support of industrial workers who might have made a strong army. But they were poorly led; the easy way in which Cadiz and Seville fell was proof of inefficient command.

The League and the Civil War

'Liberal' opinion in democratic countries called for aid to the Republicans. However, Eden, British Foreign Secretary, and Blum, Prime Minister in a French Popular Front government, urged non-intervention. They wanted no aid to be given to either side. Germany and Italy ignored this plea and aided the rebels; Russia ignored the plea and aided the Republicans.

Foreign aid to Nationalists

Salazar, dictator of Portugal, sent 20,000 troops to help the rebels and to help conquer central Spain (Fig. 24.4).

Hitler sent 10,000 soldiers through Vigo (to help Franco in the north) and Cadiz (to help in the south) (Fig. 24.4). He also sent the Condor Air Legion, which was stronger than the Spanish air force. The war provided a chance for Hitler's growing air force (see Unit 20) to put its training to the test.

Mussolini sent 50,000 soldiers through Cadiz and Valencia. These were not well trained and were often defeated. Italy suffered economically from the cost of this venture.

Foreign aid to the Republicans

Russia sent troops, advisers, munitions and food through Barcelona in Catalonia (Fig. 24.4). These were often the cause of bitter fighting inside the Republican ranks (see below).

An International Brigade of 40,000 volunteers from many countries went to fight with the Republicans. Many of these were poorly trained.

The course of the war, 1936

By the end of 1936 Franco's men had gained control of about one-quarter of Spain (Fig. 24.4), and in October 1936 Franco was named Chief of State.

THE COURSE OF THE WAR, 1937–9

Franco's forces in Cadiz and the north made slow progress and were separated from each other by a Republican centre (Fig. 24.4).

Parts of the Basque country were taken. The bombing by the Germans of the Basque town of Guernica (April 1937) was particularly savage.

From Seville (Fig. 24.4) Franco advanced to take the region around Granada in the south and, at the same time, advanced north towards Madrid.

Catalonia, the region based on Barcelona (Fig. 24.4), was the scene of a bitter struggle between Stalinists and non-Stalinist communists. Many Republicans were killed in this 'second civil war'. The Stalinists won; Caballero was forced from office and replaced by the Stalinist, Negrin.

In October 1937 Franco was proclaimed as El Caudillo (as Hitler was Führer and Mussolini was Il Duce).

More progress, 1938

Franco's men pushed through to the south and the Mediterranean. They by-passed Madrid, leaving it under siege. Four columns took part in that siege. Their commander said that he also had the help of 'a fifth column' of anti-Republicans inside Madrid itself.

The end, March 1939

In February 1939 Catalonia was conquered by the Nationalists. This was, in a sense, the end of the Republic. On 28 March 1939, after a year's siege, Madrid fell.

REASONS FOR FRANCO'S VICTORY

Internally he had the support of powerful groups. Army officers and the Civil Guard had the advantages of having been better trained and were better armed than the irregular forces of the Republicans. The aristocracy and rich middle class provided the money to finance his war, and the Church gave him its moral backing.

Aid from Germany, Italy and Portugal (troops, advisers, planes and munitions) outweighed foreign aid to the Republicans in total and in quality.

The neutrality of Britain and France worked in favour of the Nationalists. It put the elected government (Republicans) and the rebels on an equal footing, and it denied the government the aid it might have expected from other elected governments.

The Republican forces were not united: Communists and anarchists fought each other.

Russian aid was limited; Stalin did not want to get fully involved and he did not really want a Republican (non-communist) victory.

Franco provided the Nationalists with strong and united leadership. His rivals were suppressed, while his skilful planning of the campaign won him increased support.

The League's embargo on arms stopped the Republicans from receiving aid but did not prevent Hitler and Mussolini from sending aid to Franco.

SOME EFFECTS OF THE WAR

Three quarters of a million people had died. One quarter of all homes and one third of all animals had been destroyed. £3 billion had been spent, equal to 16 years of the Spanish national income. Italy and Germany had had 'practice' at war. Democracy had received another defeat.

FRANCO IN POWER

Franco's government was harshly anti-communist. Many communists were imprisoned, executed or exiled. He was also harshly repressive to all who fought for the Republic.

The Church enjoyed a special place in the nation's life.

The Falange was only one part of Franco's coalition government. Spain did not become as fascist a state as Italy or Germany.

The rich and powerful benefited most from his rule—the Church, landowners and industrialists.

He allowed a Cortes to be elected in 1942 but it had no power.

He did not help Hitler as the Führer had hoped. Gibraltar was not attacked; the Mediterranean was that much safer during the War.

In 1947 Franco became Chief of State for life, with the right to name his successor.

◼ **Unit 24 Summary** ◼

▶ Problems and unrest, 1917–23.
▶ De Rivera's dictatorship, 1923–30.
▶ The policies and problems of the Republic, 1931–6.
▶ The Civil War, 1936–9; why Franco won.

25.1 Poland and the Phoney War

THE GERMAN BLITZKRIEG (OR LIGHTNING WAR)

Six Panzer divisions (heavily armoured but mobile forces) poured into Poland on 1 September 1939. The Luftwaffe also pounded the country from the air and carried paratroopers behind enemy defensive lines. On 27 September Warsaw was battered into submission, and on 3 October Poland capitulated.

Jews were herded into ghettos. Three million were to die.

Russia entered eastern Poland two weeks after the attack from the west. Poland was divided up (see Unit 23).

THE 'PHONEY WAR'

Britain and France could not save Poland. German generals were unwilling to attack France. France, secure behind the Maginot Line, was not militarily prepared to attack Germany and its Siegfried Line. Britain was even less prepared.

Both countries shared varied hopes. They hoped that peace terms might still be arranged. The 'Munich mentality' dominated most British and French thinking. Also, a naval blockade might bring Germany to her knees, as in 1917–18 (see Unit 9). In addition, time was needed to build up British and French forces.

Few hostilities took place in the winter of 1939–40 (but see Unit 23, section 11).

25.2 German Victories, 1939–40

THE NAVAL WAR

U-boats were used to attack merchant and passenger shipping such as the *Athenia*, sunk on the day Britain entered the war. U-boats also attacked the naval base at Scapa Flow, sinking the *Royal Oak*.

German surface raiders, notably the *Graf Spee* (see Unit 20) attacked shipping in the Indian and Atlantic Oceans. The *Graf Spee* was scuttled in Montevideo (20 December 1939) after a running fight with three British cruisers in what became known as the Battle of the River Plate.

'Hotting-up' the naval war, April 1940

Britian and France thought of sending help to Finland (see Unit 23.11). Norway lay along the route to Finland, and Swedish steel came south on this route to Germany.

Churchill, First Lord of the Admiralty, acted. Mines were laid in Norwegian waters to hinder the Germans. The German ship *Altmark* was chased into a Norwegian fiord and boarded from the British ship, HMS *Cossack* (February 1940).

Britain planned to invade Norway to capture its coast.

THE GERMAN CONQUEST OF SCANDINAVIA, APRIL 1940

Hitler forestalled British plans, and on 9 April Denmark and Norway suffered a blitzkrieg. Denmark surrendered on the same day, whereas Norway held out with British help. British forces landed near Trondheim. South and central Norway fell to the Nazis, partly because of a Norwegian

'fifth column' under Quisling. British help was withdrawn when Nazi forces attacked Holland, which made German conquest of the rest of Norway easier.

Hitler gained control of Norwegian iron ore, the entrance to the Baltic and many naval and air bases.

Norway's defeat was a bad blow for Britain and led to criticism of Chamberlain's government. On 7–9 May 1940 after a major debate in Parliament, Chamberlain got only a small majority. He tried to form a coalition with Labour and Liberal leaders but failed.

On 10 May Germany invaded Holland and Belgium. Also on 10 May Chamberlain resigned, and Churchill became Prime Minister.

THE GERMAN CONQUEST OF THE LOW COUNTRIES

Belgium, Luxembourg and Holland were invaded. A blitzkrieg led to Holland's speedy surrender. On 10 May Rotterdam airfield was captured and the city devastated by low-level bombing. Utrecht was threatened with the same fate, and the government surrendered. The Queen and her ministers fled to Britain.

Belgium

German forces struck through the Ardennes, and paratroopers dropped behind Belgian forces defending the Albert Canal, making Belgian outer defences useless. Panzer divisions drove speedily to cut off troops in the north of Belgium. On 20 May the Germans reached the coast, pushing back British troops defending Belgium.

FRANCE

Panzer troops cut across the northern edge of France. On 20 May Abbéville was taken, and on 24 May Dunkirk came under attack.

Dunkirk 24 May–3 June 1940

The bulk of the British army was driven back to Dunkirk. About 200,000 British and 140,000 Allied troops were attacked by German land and air forces. However, Hitler called off a final onslaught. Did he want to allow the Luftwaffe a chance to finish off the British? Goering boasted that it could. Did he hope to persuade Britain to negotiate peace?

The 'Miracle of Dunkirk' was the description of the heroic story of hundreds of ships, of all sizes, which sailed to Dunkirk and brought back the besieged men. The RAF provided what cover it could. The Luftwaffe with its superior forces launched almost countless dive-bombing attacks.

The fall of France, June 1940

For France there was no such miracle. The fall of Belgium made the Maginot Line irrelevant. French troops were scattered and in retreat. People fled from German-occupied areas and Paris. German dive-bombers attacked the crowded roads. On 14 June the Germans took Paris.

General Weygand advised the government that the Germans could not be stopped. Prime Minister Reynaud resigned. Marshal Pétain (the hero of Verdun—see Unit 9) became head of government. He asked for an armistice.

Hitler insisted that the railway carriage in which the Germans had signed the armistice on 11 November 1918 be brought from a French museum. At Compiègne in 1940 (where the Germans had signed their surrender in 1918) Hitler gave France an armistice. The shame of 1918 (see Unit 9) had been wiped out.

Mussolini had not entered the war in 1939. In June 1940, confident of German victory, he declared war on Britain and France. He attacked France, made a separate armistice and gained a slice of French territory.

Vichy France

Pétain took the title of Head of the French State. His government had its headquarters at Vichy.

The armistice gave Germany the western coast and northern France. The Vichy government agreed to bear the costs of this occupation. German refugees in Vichy France were returned to the Nazis. French prisoners of war stayed in German hands. The French fleet came under Vichy control, but most of it was destroyed by British action to keep it out of German hands.

The Vichy government with its belief in 'authority, law and order' became fully fascist in 1944. Hitler distrusted Vichy politicians. In 1942 he ordered the occupation of the whole of France.

The Free French set up an alternative to Vichy collaboration. In 1940 General de Gaulle escaped to London and called on French people to continue the struggle.

OPERATION 'SEALION'

Germany now dominated Europe. She had gained her success in little over two months.

Hitler expected Britain to make peace, but she refused. Operation 'Sealion' was the plan for a seaborne invasion of Britain. Thirteen divisions were assembled in northern France. The Luftwaffe was sent to destroy the RAF to ensure control of the Channel.

25.3 The Battle of Britain, July–September 1940

STAGE 1: 10 JULY–7 AUGUST

Coastal convoys, vital inland targets and some cities were attacked and river estuaries mined. The Germans lost more planes than they had expected.

STAGE 2: 8–23 AUGUST

Large scale attacks on RAF airfields and on radar stations might have succeeded in knocking out the RAF but Goering switched targets. Hitler hoped to defeat Britain by cutting off her supply routes before he attacked Russia (see below).

STAGE 3: 24 AUGUST–6 SEPTEMBER

The Germans bombed factories and military targets defended by the RAF.

STAGE 4: 7–30 SEPTEMBER

All RAF fighters were based in the south to protect the country against an invasion. Huge raids by day ended after the Battle of Britain, in which German losses totalled 1733 planes. These raids were called off and the Germans went back to bombing airfields and, at night, London.

The RAF lost over 900 planes, and 700 pilots were killed or wounded.

25.4 The 'Blitz', 1940–1

Night-bombing attacks saw the dropping of high-explosive bombs, incendiaries which caused widespread fires, and parachute mines which demolished streets of houses.

The civilian population was partially protected by Anderson shelters set in the earth and covered with soil, Morrison shelters which were indoor steel boxes, communal shelters, and underground stations.

Heavy damage and many casualties led to an increased communal spirit, and an increase in volunteers for voluntary services.

Coventry was raided three times, starting on 14 November. Ports were attacked constantly. The attacks on Merseyside lasted for eight nights in May 1941, during which 2000 people died.

Churchill discovered that the 'blitz' damaged morale but only for a time. But he insisted that the RAF should prepare a huge bomber force, under 'Bomber' Harris, to attack German towns.

25.5 The Battle of the Atlantic

Hitler called off Operation 'Sealion' and decided to attack Britain's convoys. These brought food and raw materials, as well as foreign war materials. Convoys were organized from the start of the war (see Unit 9). Crossing the Atlantic took about 15 days.

U-boats, in 'wolfpacks', waited until the convoys had little cover from air or surface vessels, then attacked. Condors (German heavy bombers) also attacked convoys in British waters. Mines in British waters were a final obstacle.

The battleship *Bismarck* and the cruiser *Prinz Eugen* came into the Atlantic from the Baltic (May 1941). They were attacked by the *Hood* (the 'pride of the Navy'), the *Prince of Wales* and the aircraft carrier *Ark Royal*. The German ships sank the *Hood*; only three survived of the crew of 1429. They also drove off the *Prince of Wales*. However, the German ships were attacked by Swordfish planes from the *Ark Royal*, which crippled the *Bismarck* and left her an easy target for the *Rodney* and the *Duke of York*, battleships which had joined the battle.

The *Bismarck* was sunk by torpedoes from the *Dorsetshire* (27 May), but the *Prinz Eugen* escaped.

WINNING THE BATTLE OF THE ATLANTIC

Many ships were lost: in 1941 and 1942, 800,000 tons of shipping was lost each month.

Escort vessels became better equipped with asdic and radar which located the U-boats, and bomb-throwers armed with more effective depth charges.

Better-quality escort vessels appeared in the shape of faster frigates and corvettes which could ram or otherwise destroy submarines when they came on the surface.

Bomber planes played their part in 1942 and 1943.

In 1943 the number of U-boats being sunk rose sharply from an average of 10 a month (1942) to over 50 a month (1943). At the same time the losses of shipping went down sharply with an average monthly loss of less than 100,000 tons.

25.6 The Extension of the War

ITALY

On June 1940 Italy declared war on the Allies (see above), and on October 1940 Mussolini invaded Greece. Greece defeated the Italians and invaded Albania (see Unit 23).

Mussolini asked for German help. Hitler agreed, seeing a chance to gain influence in the Balkans. In November 1940 Hungary and Rumania signed alliances with Germany to provide food and oil, and in March 1941 Bulgaria signed an alliance with Germany. Then, in April 1941, Germany invaded Yugoslavia and Greece. About 60,000 British troops were rushed from North Africa to Greece. However, in May 1941 the British were defeated, Greece surrendered and

British troops retreated to Crete. A German airborne assault captured that island.

The Balkans were under German control.

ABYSSINIA

Italian troops invaded British Somaliland. From Libya Italian troops attacked Egypt.

▨ 25.7 Hitler and Russia ▨

OPERATION 'BARBAROSSA' (Fig. 25.7)

Why did Hitler attack Russia? He wanted to destroy communism, and he believed that the Slav people were 'sub-human', fit only to work for German industry and Empire. He also needed:

▶ *Lebensraum*, living space for Germans (see Unit 23);
▶ Ukrainian wheat;
▶ the oil from the Caucasus.

Conquest of Russia would provide a link with Japan (see below).

With most of Europe and Russia under his control, Hitler would be able to ignore Britain and the USA. He would also be able to launch attacks on Africa and the Middle East with its oil supplies and the route to India.

The attack

The invasion was delayed because troops were sent to help Italy in Greece (see above). On 22 June 1941 a five-pronged invasion was launched by 153 divisions and 2000 aircraft. Hungary (3 divisions) and Rumania (15 divisions) supported the invasion:

▶ the northern prong drove for Leningrad;
▶ a north-central prong drove towards Moscow;
▶ the central prong drove into the Ukraine;
▶ a south-western prong drove towards Stalingrad;
▶ the most southerly prong made for the Crimea.

Speedy success

The Luftwaffe caught the Russian Air Force by surprise and destroyed hundreds of fighters parked on runways. The Wehrmacht's panzers rolled in their blitzkrieg, supported by dive bombers and fighter aircraft. Thus western Russia was speedily overrun; many Ukrainians welcomed their release from Bolshevik rule (see Unit 10).

In July 1941 Smolensk was captured. The German army moved into the Ukraine. In September 1941:

▶ Germans at the outskirts of Leningrad completed the land blockade of this northern 'capital';

▶ in the Ukraine, they took Kiev, having destroyed 5 Russian armies.

October 1941 saw widespread German advances:

▶ from Smolensk they moved towards Moscow. The government was evacuated to Kuibishev. At the end of the month there was the first offensive against Moscow—which failed;
▶ from Kiev further advances were made into the Ukraine. After a major battle Kursk fell on 3 November;
▶ in the Crimea, Odessa (once the centre of revolution) was captured and Sebastopol came under siege.

In November 1941:

▶ the sieges of Leningrad and Sebastopol continued;
▶ a second offensive against Moscow failed;
▶ Timoshenko led a counter-offensive which led to the recapture of Rostov;
▶ Russia launched a counter-offensive on the Moscow front.

In December 1941 the Russians' capture of Tikhvin saved Leningrad.

A slower progress, to May 1942

The Wehrmacht had been 'invincible' in the summer–autumn of 1941. The Russian winter brought progress to a halt. Further but slow progress was made in 1942:

▶ in July 1942 Sebastopol surrendered;
▶ in September 1942 Stalingrad came under attack. The capture of this city would have opened the Caucasus to the Germans.

We now know that this was the limit of German success and we will see more of this in Unit 26.

HITLER'S MISTAKES IN RUSSIA

Hitler delayed the invasion and lost six weeks of good weather. German attacks took place on too wide a front. The German generals wanted an all-out drive to Moscow. Hitler preferred an attack on the Caucasus with its oil fields. The dispersed attack fell between two stools; neither objective was achieved.

From November 1941 'General Winter' came to the help of the Russians. Fuel, for tanks, aircraft and other motorized vehicles, froze. Men had not been supplied with the necessary clothing; many died of frostbite. Supplying forces deep in Russia proved difficult.

Russian patriotism was roused by the inhuman treatment shown to the population by the conquering invaders.

Stalin called up memories of Peter the Great and other Tsarist heroes. The Russians were asked to fight 'a patriotic war' in defence of 'Holy Russia'.

A 'scorched earth' policy was followed by the retreating Russians. Everything of value was destroyed—homes, factories, animals, crops in the fields. The Germans were unable to live off the land.

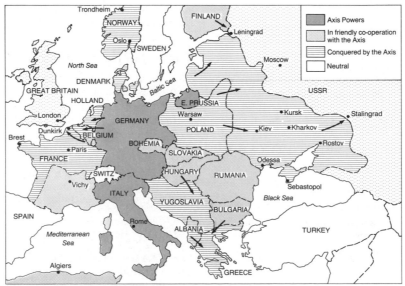

Fig. 25.7 The Axis powers in victory, 1939–42

25.8 North Africa, June 1940–May 1942

1940

In September Italian troops advanced from Libya to Egypt. Britain rushed in reinforcements, South African, Australian and Indian. Tanks were sent from Britain, itself facing threat of invasion. In November six Italian battleships were sunk at Taranto.

1941

In February Wavell, commander of the British forces, drove Italian forces from the border of Egypt to Benghazi. In March German troops were sent to support the Italians. The British Navy won another battle at Matapan. In August in East Africa British troops liberated British Somaliland, and Haile Selassie was restored to the throne of Abyssinia (see Unit 23).

1942

Rommel, a brilliant German general nicknamed 'the Desert Fox', drove the British from all of Libya, except Tobruk. Auchinleck, a brilliant British general, with much less equipment than the Germans, drove them back again. He captured Cyrenaica and relieved Tobruk. Rommel suffered a shortage of supplies because of the demands of the Russian front (see above).

British supplies were affected by the bombing of Mediterranean convoys by enemy planes based in Italy. Malta was under constant air attack.

MAY 1942

Rommel received extra supplies. He launched a massive attack against weakened British forces, drove them from Libya and deep into Egypt. This threatened the Suez canal, the route to India and British oil supplies from the Middle East. We now know that this was the limit of Rommel's success. The Battle of El Alamein in July 1942 marked a turning point (see Unit 26).

25.9 The USA and the Far East

THE UNITED STATES AND THE WAR, 1939–41

Roosevelt had been determined to keep out of the war in 1939. He sold supplies to whoever had gold to buy them (see Unit 19).

By December 1940, Britain had no more gold. Then Roosevelt persuaded Congress to pass the Lend-Lease Act (see Unit 19). This permitted lease or lend of supplies to any government whose defence was thought to be vital to the USA. The Act was applied to supplies for Britain alone, until Russia entered the war, when it was extended to Russia.

Roosevelt had earlier (January 1941) spoken of 'four freedoms' (see Unit 19). The Atlantic Charter was drawn up at a meeting between Roosevelt and Churchill off the coast of Newfoundland (Unit 19).

JAPAN AND THE WAR, 1939–41

Japan was already at war with China (see Unit 17). The Tanaka Memorial had outlined Japanese plans for the 'Co-Prosperity Sphere' southwards.

Summer 1940

The defeat of France left Indo-China exposed, and the defeat of Holland left Indonesia exposed.

Britain's weak position meant that she was not anxious to take on another enemy. Japan 'persuaded' Britain to close the Burma Road and cut off supplies to China.

The tripartite Axis, a new treaty between Japan, Germany and Italy, turned the Anti-Comintern Pacts (see Unit 23) into a joint defence pact against any power 'not already engaged in war'.

Japanese advance

Troops moved into the north of Indo-China. In July 1941 the Vichy government (see above) agreed to a joint protectorate with Japan over the whole of Indo-China. Japanese troops landed in the south.

The USA and the Japanese advance, July 1941

In July 1941, when Japan occupied Indo-China, the USA stopped the sale of oil to Japan. She had earlier cancelled trading agreements between the two nations. Britain and Holland took similar steps. Japan was dependent on the West for oil and certain metals such as copper. The USA said that before trade could be restored, Japan had to evacuate Indo-China and China.

General Tojo replaced the civilian Prime Minister of Japan. He believed that Japan should use force to get what it needed. Japanese negotiators went to Washington to discuss a settlement, while preparations were made for a Japanese attack on American forces in Asia.

THE EXTENSION OF THE WAR TO THE FAR EAST, DECEMBER 1941 (Fig. 26.2)

On 7 December 1941 Japan launched an attack on Pearl Harbor, Hawaii, where they crippled the American Pacific Fleet. At the same time they attacked American airfields in the Philippines and British bases in Malaya, Singapore and Hong Kong.

Reasons for Japan's immediate successes

America was ill-prepared for war. It took time to mobilize men and resources. Britain had made little preparation for war in the East. The air force was run down, land forces ill-equipped.

The extent of Japan's advance, May 1942

Armies seized Hong Kong, Thailand, Malaya and Singapore, Indonesia and the Philippines, defeating British, Dutch and US forces. They invaded New Guinea and threatened Australia, then invaded Burma and threatened India.

The end of the expansion

We now know that in May 1942 Japanese advance reached its furthest limit. Evidence of that was provided by:

▶ the Coral Sea where (May 1942) the US won a naval action to the south of New Guinea. American and Australian troops prevented the total conquest of New Guinea itself;

▶ Midway Island, where the Americans won another victory to the east of Japan (June 1942);

▶ the British 'Forgotten Army' held the frontier between India and Burma. The Japanese conquest of Burma was the limit to the extent of their victory in this theatre of war.

THE PART TO BE PLAYED BY THE USA

The USA might have come into the war eventually, to help defeat Hitler's Germany. The attack on Pearl Harbor brought her into war against Japan and, because of the Tripartite Pact, against Germany.

The USA became the 'arsenal of the free world' because it:

▶ built new factories and adapted existing ones for producing war materials;
▶ developed new, better-built and better-armed ships, planes and tanks in large numbers;
▶ sent men to fight in North Africa and Europe (see Unit 26) as well as against Japan;
▶ never faced difficulties of supplies or threats to its own security—unlike the other Allied countries.

Unit 25 Summary

▶ 1939–40: blitzkrieg in Poland; phoney war in the west.
▶ 1940: German victories in the Baltic, Low Countries and France.
▶ The Battle of Britain and the blitz.
▶ The Battle of the Atlantic.
▶ The German invasion of Russia.
▶ The war in North Africa.
▶ The USA, Japan and the start of war in the Far East.

26 THE SECOND WORLD WAR FROM 1942 TO 1945

26.1 Turning Points in the War

MAY–JUNE 1942: THE PACIFIC

May 1942, the Battle of the Coral Sea (Fig. 26.2)

A Japanese fleet approached Port Moresby, New Guinea. It was defeated by an American fleet. Thus the immediate threat to Australia was removed.

June 1942, the Battle of Midway Island (Fig. 26.2)

The Japanese had even heavier losses.

In both battles most damage was done by carrier-based aircraft—a new development in warfare. These defeats weakened the Japanese. The Americans could begin their advance (see below).

JULY–OCTOBER 1942: NORTH AFRICA

Both sides had made dashes across hundreds of miles (see Unit 25). In May 1942 Rommel and the German Afrika Korps drove deep into Egypt. However, in July 1942 he was checked at the first battle of El Alamein, 130 km from Alexandria. Then in August 1942 he was defeated at Alam Halfa. On 23 October 1942 Montgomery defeated Rommel at the second battle of El Alamein. He drove Rommel from Egypt, across Libya and into Tunisia.

JANUARY 1943: RUSSIA

In the summer of 1942 the Germans were within sight of the Caucasus Mountains and 85 per cent of Russia's oil supplies. In September 1942 there was fighting in the streets of Stalingrad.

German weaknesses

They failed to defeat Russian guerrilla forces; their supply lines were over 4800 km long. There was also Hitler's vanity. He insisted on 'no surrender' when withdrawal would have saved thousands of lives.

Stalingrad

This city was attacked and partly occupied by 240,000 Germans untrained in street fighting. Russian forces surrounded the Germans who suffered:

▶ shortages of food and medical supplies;
▶ from the savage winter with 30 degrees of frost.

Hitler tried to relieve his armies—and failed. Because of his order of 'no surrender', 140,000 died. On 2 February 1943 Paulus, the German commander, finally surrendered with his 90,000 men. Hitler called him 'a coward'.

THE AIR

Increased output from British factories and from the USA (see Unit 25) led to Allied air superiority.

Halifax and Lancaster bombers attacked German towns, cities and industrial regions by night. American Fortresses and Liberators bombed by day. Thunderbolts and Mustangs were developed as escort fighters.

26.2 Allied Victories

TURNING TO ATTACK: RUSSIA 1943–4

Behind the Urals the Russians made surprising industrial development and produced vast quantities of the IL-2 Sturmavik ground-attack aircraft which inflicted heavy casualties on panzers, and the T-34 tanks with diesel engines, sloping sides and powerful guns.

Russia was provided with massive Allied aid:
▶ 8.7 million tons came through Vladivostock and on the Trans-Siberian railway to the Ural industrial area of Magnitogorsk;
▶ 4.2 million tons came via Persia, partly Russian-occupied;
▶ 4.0 million tons came via the Arctic route in spite of heavy damage inflicted on convoys by U-boats and torpedo bombers.

This aid included 10,000 tanks, 18,700 planes, 427,000 trucks and 1100 locomotives.

In July 1943 at Kursk (Fig. 25.7) Zhukov won the largest-ever tank battle and shortly afterwards freed Orel. In June 1944 the Germans were driven over the Russian border. In December 1944 Rumania and Bulgaria were liberated, and in January 1945 Hungary was liberated. Then in February 1945 Poland was liberated. But this had followed:
▶ 1 August 1944, the Warsaw Rising, as Poles tried to gain their own freedom, independent of Russian aid;

▶ the crushing of the Poles by the Germans, the Red Army waiting on the Vistula and not interfering. The deaths of so many leading Poles made it easier for Russia after 1945;
▶ the destruction of Warsaw by German troops. In March 1945 Russian troops entered eastern Germany, and in April 1945 Russian troops reached Berlin.

TURNING TO ATTACK IN THE PACIFIC

Fig. 26.2   The defeat of Japan

US forces had an 'island-hopping' campaign (Fig. 26.2) in which they captured certain islands, leaving the Japanese in control of many others. Each attack was very costly because of the fanatical defence put up by the Japanese. The capture of Tarawa (Fig. 26.2) cost 3000 American casualties and 5000 Japanese deaths.

1944
Slim's 'Forgotten Army' won the important victory at Kohima, which ensured Indian freedom. Australian troops began the clearing of New Guinea; Guam and the neighbouring Mariana Islands were taken. From the airfields in Guam, Superfortresses flew 2000 km to bomb Tokyo.

Back to the Philippines
General MacArthur, commander of US forces in the Pacific, had been driven from the Philippines in 1942 but had vowed that he would return at the head of victorious troops.

He commanded the troops engaged in 'island-hopping'. The US navy won the Battle of Leyte Gulf and sank most of the Japanese navy (Fig. 26.2). In spite of Japanese defence, the Americans captured most of the Philippines in 1944 and MacArthur entered Manila in triumph in February 1945.

1945
In February the Americans captured the island of Iwo Jima (Fig. 26.2) after a month's bitter fighting and 20,000 casualties.

Okinawa (Fig. 26.2) was taken after 40,000 casualties. Japanese kamikaze (suicide) pilots mounted attacks on the US fleet engaged in the attack on Okinawa.

Heavy bombing of Japan continued. There remained two million Japanese soldiers and 5000 kamikaze pilots to be defeated.

The end
The USA planned two invasions of Japan. Southern Japan was to be taken in 1945 and Honshu in 1946. The expected casualties would be very high.

Japan rejected peace proposals made at Potsdam (see below). On 6 August 1945 a B-29 dropped the first atomic bomb on Hiroshima, wiping out vast areas of the city; 80,000 people died.

On 8 August 1945 Russia attacked Japanese-held Manchuria and Korea. Stalin knew that his men would not have to fight for very long, but Russia would gain influence in the Far East.

On 9 August 1945 the second atomic bomb was dropped on Nagasaki. 40,000 were killed.

On 15 August 1945 the Japanese surrendered.

TURNING TO ATTACK IN NORTH AFRICA

Operation 'Torch' was the Anglo-American attack on North Africa in November 1942. Eisenhower's forces captured Casablanca. They drove through Morocco, and captured Oran in Algeria.

Hitler sent orders that there was to be 'no surrender'. The Nazis sent tanks and troops in six-engined planes.

On 7 May 1943 Montgomery's Eighth Army captured Tunis. Rommel was caught in a pincer-movement, and on 14 May 1943 the Afrika Korps surrendered.

THE RAID ON DIEPPE
August 1942

Hitler had strengthened his hold over 'Fortress Europe'. On the northern coast of France the Germans had built the heavily fortified West Wall to prevent or hinder invasion.

Operation 'Jubilee' was an Allied attack on Dieppe. About 6000 men, mainly Canadians, took part in the raid, and 3379 Canadians died in the disastrous failure.

The Allies learned from the disaster that a heavily defended port could not be taken without too heavy casualties. This led the Allies to develop their own port, the Mulberry Harbour (see below). They also learned that defenders had an easier time than attackers. Their defences would have to be bombed or by-passed. At Dieppe many people had been killed on the beaches. In an invasion a strong beachhead would have to be established, or invading forces would be annihilated.

THE ATTACK ON ITALY

In July 1943, from North Africa, the Allies crossed into Sicily which was captured in August. Then in September 1943 the Allies crossed into mainland Italy. At Salerno a major battle provided the necessary port.

Italy was regarded as the 'soft under-belly of the Axis'. Many Italians changed sides; the King dismissed Mussolini and put him in jail. A government under Marshal Badoglio sought an armistice.

Hitler rushed troops south to check the Allied advance which began in September. German paratroopers freed Mussolini from jail and set him up with a new Fascist government in the north of Italy.

It was difficult to conquer Italy because its many mountains and rivers made invasion difficult, and the Germans fought fiercely.

In June 1944 Rome was taken, but the north of Italy was not conquered until April 1945.

In April 1945 Mussolini, captured by Italian resistance fighters, was killed, then hung upside down with his mistress beside him in a square in Milan, where his career had begun (see Unit 21).

THE MAIN ATTACK ON FORTRESS EUROPE, 1944

Rommel was commander of the German defences against invasion. **Operation 'Overlord'** was the name of the Allied plan for invasion. Thousands of US troops were trained and stationed in southern England, and Eisenhower was given command of the invasion.

Many new 'weapons' were designed to help:
▶ US factories produced thousands of landing craft;
▶ British engineers produced an artificial harbour (**Mulberry**) to be towed across the Channel and through which Allied troops could pour into France. The lesson of Dieppe had been learned;

▶ a pipe line under the ocean (**Pluto**) was to take the much-needed oil from Britain to Europe.

Diversionary attacks in the Calais area persuaded Hitler and Rommel that this was the main target. On 6 June 1944 130,000 men crossed the Channel. They landed on several beaches in the Normandy area, which was more lightly defended by the Germans. Rommel still believed that Calais was the main target.

The Allies had command of the seas, so that no vessels came under attack; they also commanded the skies—unlike in 1940 (see Unit 25).

The beaches were taken; men pushed inland quickly. The ports of Cherbourg and Calais were taken, making invasion easier. A million men poured into northern France. The invading forces were helped by French resistance fighters, who hindered German attempts to stem the advance.

In August 1944 the Battle of the Falaise Gap broke the German resistance. The way was open for a rapid mobile advance through Western Europe.

Air power

Allied fighter-bombers ruled the skies, attacking German convoys, troop-trains and even solitary German cars.

Other weapons

There were bridge-carrying tanks, a new form of (Bailey) bridge which made river-crossing easier, flame-throwing tanks and flail-tanks to destroy minefields.

Paris and Arnhem

On 25 August Paris was taken. De Gaulle (Unit 25) led Free French forces on a triumphal entry.

In September British paratroopers landed at Arnhem to try to take a bridge across the Rhine. They were not sufficiently protected and panzer forces destroyed them.

German weapons

At this late stage in the war the Germans produced V1 flying bombs and V2 rockets which fell on Britain until the bases from which they were launched were captured or destroyed.

The Ardennes

At Christmas 1944 Hitler launched a counter-attack in the Ardennes. German troops broke through American lines but were halted, before being rolled back in January 1945.

Victory

On 24 March 1945 Allied forces crossed the Rhine, and in April they linked up with the Red Army (see above).

On 30 April Hitler committed suicide in Berlin. On 7 May Doenitz, the new head of state, surrendered German forces. The European war was over.

26.3 Wartime Conferences of Allied Leaders

Churchill met Roosevelt before the USA entered the war (see Unit 25).

WASHINGTON, DECEMBER 1941

Churchill and Roosevelt met and agreed that Germany and not Japan was the main enemy. Many Americans wanted to concentrate on defeating Japan. The two leaders also agreed to set up machinery for united action—by industry and by the armed forces.

MOSCOW, AUGUST 1942

Churchill explained Anglo-American plans to Stalin and got him to agree to Operation 'Torch' and not (as Roosevelt and Stalin wanted) to demand the immediate implementation of operation 'Overlord' (see above).

CASABLANCA, JANUARY 1943

Following the success of 'Torch', Churchill and Roosevelt met at Casablanca. Here they agreed on the invasion of Italy rather than of northern France, and on the demand for unconditional surrender by the Axis powers. This would mean that after this war the Germans would not be able to complain of a 'stab in the back' or a dictated peace (see Unit 12).

QUEBEC, AUGUST 1943

Churchill, Roosevelt and Mackenzie-King (Canada) agreed on the strategy for the defeat of Japan.

CAIRO, NOVEMBER 1943

Churchill, Roosevelt and Chiang Kai-shek agreed on the strategy for the defeat of Japan.

TEHRAN, NOVEMBER 1943

Churchill, Roosevelt and Stalin agreed that the Western Allies would open a Second Front in France, and that the Russian attack from the east would be co-ordinated with the Allied attack from the west. They also agreed that they would set about forming an international organization to replace the League of Nations, and that Russia would declare war on Japan 'at some suitable moment'.

YALTA, FEBRUARY 1945

Roosevelt, Churchill and Stalin met in this Crimean town. They agreed:
▶ on the temporary division of Germany into four zones (one of them French) after Germany's surrender;
▶ on the punishment of war criminals;
▶ that Germany would have to pay reparations;
▶ that German military power would have to be paralysed;
▶ to organize a conference in San Francisco to launch the United Nations Organization;
▶ to reaffirm the principles of the Atlantic Charter (see

▶ to liberate conquered nations and Axis satellites;
▶ to prepare the way in these countries for free and democratic elections;
▶ that Russia would declare war on Japan 'within a few months of the defeat of Germany'.

POTSDAM, JULY–AUGUST 1945

The war in Europe was over (see above), but Japan was still fighting.

Stalin represented Russia as he had done at other Conferences. Truman replaced Roosevelt, who had died in April 1945. Churchill came to the start of the Conference, bringing the Labour leader (and Deputy Prime Minister) Attlee with him. Attlee became Britain's representative after the Labour victory in the General Election, 26 July 1945.

Stalin, Attlee and Truman agreed that the Oder-Neisse line should be the new boundary between Germany and Poland. They agreed to divide Germany into four zones of occupation, and that Germans living in Poland, Hungary and Czechoslovakia were to be repatriated to Germany to avoid such minority problems as the pre-war Sudetenland (see Unit 23). A Conference of Foreign Ministers would settle the problems of a peace treaty.

In later Units we will see how the UNO was set up and worked and how successful, if at all, the Foreign Ministers were.

26.4 Why Did Germany Lose the War?

Germany, like Japan, had an efficient military machine and won easy victories at the start of the war. However, Germany overreached herself. The conquest of most of Europe and a good deal of Russia created the problems of supplying the conquering forces over vast distances (see Unit 25), providing forces to hold down the conquered peoples, and the creation of a coalition of hostile powers outraged by German greed and cruelty. In addition the Nazis were hampered by many resistance movements.

In 1940 Hitler failed to destroy the British army at Dunkirk and Britain's determination to resist. He underestimated the commitment of the British and their Commonwealth Allies.

In 1941 Hitler attacked Russia, hoping for speedy success because:

▶ he had a contempt for the 'sub-human' Slavs (see Unit 25);
▶ he assumed that Stalin's purges had weakened the Russian power;
▶ he had seen Russian difficulties in the attack on Finland (Unit 23);
▶ he underestimated the Russian will to survive and defend 'Holy Russia' (Unit 25).

In 1941, when Japan declared war on the USA, Hitler need not have done so. His decision to do so brought the power of the USA to Britain's aid.

The British Navy succeeded in winning the Battle of the Atlantic, which kept supplies coming. By the summer of 1943 the U-boat campaign was almost at an end. On the other hand, the British naval blockade affected supplies to Germany, making her dependent on supplies from conquered Europe. This made the conquered peoples even more anti-German.

Air superiority had been proved, in part, at the Battle of Britain. By 1942 British and US forces were bombing Germany. The almost total destruction of towns such as Hamburg and Dresden was a symbol of that superiority.

Scientists in the free world provided Allied leaders with many and varied weapons. Mulberry and Pluto (see above) are examples. Whittle invented and developed the world's first jet aircraft. Barnes Wallis invented the 'bouncing bomb' used by the Dambusters to attack the Mohne Dam which provided hydro-electric power to much of German industry.

UNCONDITIONAL SURRENDER

Once the Allies had decided on this harsh policy, there was no chance of a negotiated peace. Hitler had to fight on in the face of overwhelming odds.

DIVISIONS IN GERMANY

There had always been a small opposition to Nazi rule (see Unit 20). When, by 1944, it was clear to most people that Germany was going to be defeated, plots for Hitler's assassination were developed. The most famous was the attempt of Colonel Stauffenberg and the plotters of 20 July 1944 when a bomb was taken into the meeting at Hitler's HQ. The failure of the plot led to massive arrests and executions. It was, however, a sign of deep division in Germany, showing there was not the same determination to win as there had been in Britain even in 1940.

Unit 26 Summary

▶ Turning points in the Pacific, North Africa, Russia and the air.
▶ Allied victories in Russia, the Pacific and Western Europe.
▶ Wartime conferences and decisions.
▶ Why Germany lost the war.

---

27 THE UNITED NATIONS ORGANIZATION

27.1 Origins and Aims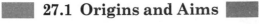

ITS WARTIME ORIGINS

In January 1941 Roosevelt spoke of 'four freedoms' (see Unit 19). In August 1941 the Atlantic Charter issued by Roosevelt and Churchill declared that basic human freedoms were to be respected, and that after the war no territory should change hands except with the consent of the inhabitants.

In January 1942, 26 nations involved in the war against Germany agreed at Washington to accept the Atlantic Charter, and in November 1943 at the Tehran Conference (see Unit 26) Allied leaders agreed to set up an international organization.

In August–November 1944 a conference of delegates from Allied countries at Dumbarton Oaks, near Washington, agreed the basic framework for the proposed organization.

In February 1945 at Yalta (see Unit 26) the Charter of the United Nations was agreed, and in June 1945 at San Francisco representatives of 50 nations approved the Charter. Finally, on 24 October 1945 the Charter came into effect on what has become known as United Nations Day.

THE AIMS OF THE FOUNDERS OF UNO

Their aims were to provide:
▶ a replacement for the League of Nations;
▶ world peace (Article 1 of Charter);
▶ all peoples with equal rights to self-determination;
▶ cultural, economic as well as political co-operation;
▶ no interference in the internal affairs of member states, except to enforce measures approved by the Security Council (Article 2);
▶ freedom for local collective action against aggression (Article 51). Regional organizations—e.g. NATO and the Warsaw Pact—claim to act under the terms of this Article.

27.2 How UNO Differs from the League of Nations

Russia and the USA were founder members of UNO (see Unit 14). Voting in the General Assembly is by simple majority or by a two thirds majority in certain cases. No member has the veto possessed by members of the League Assembly.

The Security Council is in permanent session, unlike the League Council.

None of the peace treaties referred to the UNO. In 1919–23 all the Treaties included an article on the League.

None of the members has withdrawn permanently. Some members have withdrawn for short periods:

▶ in 1950 Russia withdrew when the other members refused to admit Communist China as a member;
▶ in 1958 France withdrew in anger at the UNO resolutions about her war with the Algerian rebels;
▶ in 1965 Indonesia withdrew during her war with Malaysia. But each returned to the UNO. This was different from the experience of the League (see Unit 14).

The Charter gave the Security Council the right to raise an armed force to be used to resist aggressors and to maintain peace (see below). The League had no such power.

As countries in Africa and Asia gained independence, they became members of UNO. The creation of an Afro-Asian group (or bloc) created many problems (see below), but it made the UNO more representative of world opinion than the League had been.

The aims of the UNO were at one and the same time more realistic than the highly idealistic aims of the League, and so were more likely to be achieved, as well as much wider than those of the League, which had been almost entirely concerned with political objectives.

Its headquarters are in New York and not in Geneva. The Rockefeller family made a gift to the UNO of the site on which stands the 39-storied building which houses the Secretariat and the smaller building where the Security Council meets.

27.3 The Structure of the UNO

THE GENERAL ASSEMBLY

Each member nation has one vote in this Assembly, although it may send up to five delegates to its meetings. It normally meets in September and for a few weeks only, and it chooses its own President and controls its own agenda. It elects the non-permanent members to the Security Council (see above), and the members of other Councils and Committees. The number of members increased from the 50 who met at San Francisco to over 150 today.

The 'new' nations were mainly from Africa and Asia, but included West Indian countries. They had many things in common:

▶ a struggle against colonialism before independence;
▶ low standards of living and a need for aid.

They formed the Afro-Asian 'bloc' and tend to vote together on most issues. Although they depend heavily on aid from and trade with Western countries, they have often used their votes against the interests of the USA and her Western friends. While they claim that they are 'non-aligned' with either the West or the Russian East, they have tended to give support to Russia in their votes in the UNO.

Uniting for peace

During the height of the Cold War (Unit 28) Russia's use of the veto paralysed the organization. In other circumstances other permanent members might equally obstruct the work of UNO. The Assembly took things into its own hands in November 1950. By 50 votes to 5 it agreed:

▶ if the Security Council was unable to work because of the veto, then the Assembly could act;
▶ any seven members (i.e. a majority) of the Council or a simple majority of the Assembly could call for an emergency debate by the Assembly;
▶ at the same time a UN Observation Commission was set up and UNO observers sent immediately to crisis areas.

This resolution turned out to be very important in practice and was used in connection with the crises in Hungary (1956), Suez (1956) and the Congo (1960).

Voting in the Assembly is by a simple majority or, in serious cases, by a two-thirds majority. No country can hold up the Assembly's work by its veto.

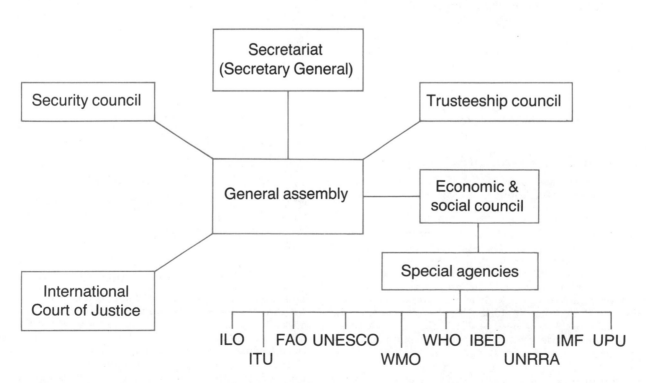

Fig. 27.3 The organization of the United Nations

THE SECURITY COUNCIL

This Council is in permanent session. It has five permanent members: Britain, Russia, the USA, France and China. Until 1971 the Chinese seat was occupied by the Nationalist Government in Taiwan (Formosa). Although China was governed by Mao's communists (see Unit 17), the USA used its veto to prevent communist China from being voted into the UN. In 1971–2 there was 'a thaw' in the relations between China and the USA (see Unit 33). The USA agreed to allow China to take the Chinese seat in the Security Council.

The non-permanent members of the Council

At first there were six, elected for a period of two years, but as the number of member-states in the UN grew, the size of the Council was increased. There are now 10 non-permanent members. By general agreement these non-permanent members are chosen to represent various regions and 'blocs'; two always come from the Latin American countries; two from the West, five from among the African countries; one from Eastern Europe.

The Council's powers

The permanent members have the right of veto. They gave themselves this power as a safeguard against a vote of small nations. Russia abused the veto, using it over 100 times before 1950. Since then every permanent member, except the USA, has used this power to protect its own interests. This has weakened the power of the Council, but this has been partly overcome by the Assembly's 'uniting for peace' decision (see above).

The Council has a military staff committee and has power to raise an armed force under UN control. This armed force was used in Korea (Unit 28), the Congo (Unit 36), Palestine (Unit 37) and Cyprus.

The Council may also order the imposition of economic sanctions against offending nations. This power was used against South Africa (Unit 36) and Rhodesia (Unit 36).

The Council controls the election of the Secretary General and the admission of new members, and it has power to send Commissions to investigate problem areas such as Kashmir (Unit 34) and Indonesia (Unit 35). It also has responsibility for organizing plans for world disarmament. In fact most talks on disarmament have taken place outside the UN.

THE SECRETARIAT

The Secretariat or 'International Civil Service' draws its 5000 members from every nation. It runs the headquarters in New York, implements the decisions of the Assembly and Council, brings problems before the Council, draws up an annual report of the organization's work, and runs the technical aid schemes and funds for the many specialized agencies (see below).

THE SECRETARY GENERAL

The Secretary General is appointed by the Assembly on the recommendation of the Council for a period of five years.

Trygve Lie of Norway was the first holder of this office. He supported UNO action against Russian aggression in Korea (Unit 28) and showed himself to be pro-western in other ways. The Russians showed that they would not support a proposal to re-elect him and he resigned in 1952.

Dag Hammarskjöld of Sweden took up the post in 1952. He helped to make the job of the Secretary General both more important and better-known. He played a major rôle during the Suez crisis of 1956 (Unit 37) and during the Congo crisis of 1960–61 (see Unit 36). He was killed in a mysterious air crash while engaged on a mission in the Congo, 1961, where he was trying to bring peace to that war-torn country.

U Thant of Burma succeeded Hammarskjöld. He showed that he was angry and disappointed at the many failures of

the UN and it was only with great reluctance that he allowed himself to be re-elected to the post in 1966.

Kurt Waldheim of Austria succeeded U Thant in 1971 and has since been succeeded by Perez de Cuellar.

THE INTERNATIONAL COURT OF JUSTICE

This is the successor to the League's Permanent Court of Justice (Unit 14). Its 15 judges from various nations meet in The Hague. It has had only limited success, because few states accept its decisions. In 1965 it decided in favour of South Africa in the dispute over that country's Mandate over South West Africa (see below).

THE TRUSTEESHIP COUNCIL

This Council consists of the five permanent members of the Council plus six members elected by the General Assembly. It took over the work of the Mandates Commission of the League (Unit 14) and is responsible for the mandated territories named after the First World War, and for the eleven territories taken from Italy and Japan after 1945. Most of these countries have achieved their independence, and now only some Pacific Islands and New Guinea remain as trusteeship territories administered by Britain, Australia, New Zealand and the USA.

The Council has been an improvement on the League's Commission, because people from the Trusteeship territories have the right of direct appeal to the Council. Many hundreds of such appeals were considered by the Council or by the Assembly. Also, the territories are visited by inspectors every three years.

South West Africa

However, the Council has failed in respect of this region, known by Africans as Namibia. It was administered after 1919 by South Africa (see Unit 13), but after 1945 South Africa refused to hand it over to the UN. After 1950 South Africa agreed to allow UN inspectors to visit the area, but refused to give them adequate information. The principle of apartheid (see Unit 36) was extended to the region, and in 1960 South Africa refused to allow UN inspectors to visit it.

In 1960 Ethiopia and Liberia, representing African countries with an interest in Namibian independence, brought the case of that country's administration to the International Court. In 1962 the court decided that it had a right to hear the case. In 1966 it reversed this decision, so that South Africa retained its hold over Namibia. The development of the revolutionary South West African People's Organization (SWAPO) is one result of this failure by the Court and the Trusteeship Council.

THE ECONOMIC AND SOCIAL COUNCIL

This Council consists of 18 members appointed by the General Assembly. Its rôle is to supervise the work of the many specialized agencies and their use of the funds voted by the UN (see below).

THE SPECIALIZED AGENCIES

Each agency is organized like the main body of the UN: it has an Assembly, a Council, a Secretariat and a Director-General or Secretary-General. The success of their work depends on the co-operation of people from various nations. Each calls on experts and resources from every country.

Food and Agricultural Organization (FAO)

This has its headquarters in Rome. It is mainly concerned with world food supplies and agricultural development in backward countries. Some of its more important projects have included the combating of locusts in South America, the introduction of school meals in Greece, the development of irrigation and improved farming techniques in South-East Asia and the introduction, in 1961, of an experimental world food programme to deal with chronic malnutrition and food emergencies. In 1969 it worked out a new world plan for agricultural development to benefit a billion people by 1985. In 1970 its World Food Programme was helping $4\frac{1}{2}$ million people in 75 countries, and there were 385 food-producing projects in 78 countries being paid for by contributing nations.

International Bank for Reconstruction and Development (IBRD)

This is also called the World Bank. It works by:
► making loans from its own funds, raised by the sale of stock to member countries and from the issue of bonds in the world's financial centres;
► guaranteeing loans made by private investors.
Its ability to help in development is limited by:
► the need for any project helped to make a profit;
► the insistence that it must not compete with private investment;
► its lack of technical personnel to oversee the schemes on which its money is being spent.
In spite of these limitations it has provided over £4 billion in loans to underdeveloped countries.

The International Development Authority (IDA)

This was set up in 1960 to make loans at low rates of interest as a supplement to the work of the IBRD.

The International Finance Corporation (IFC)

This was set up by the IBRD in 1956 to act as a spur to private investment in underdeveloped countries.

The International Monetary Fund (IMF)

This was set up in 1946 to provide the money needed to help countries which had balance of payments problems. Member nations put a quota of their own currency into the Fund; they are allowed, when in difficulty, to draw up to four times that amount in gold whenever they have a balance of payments crisis. In 1984 discussions took place to increase the amount of money at the Fund's disposal and to allow it to play a more active rôle in the world's financial affairs.

International Labour Organization (ILO)

This is one of the institutions taken over from the League of Nations. As examples of its work, it has produced agreements on such matters as the proper inspection of labour conditions in agriculture, paid holidays, minimum wages, youth employment and training schemes for industrial development. The ILO Assembly meets every year at Geneva with two government delegates, one employers' delegate and one workers' delegate from each member state.

Educational, Scientific and Cultural Organization (UNESCO)

This has its headquarters in Paris. It co-ordinates educational research and promotes international scientific and cultural co-operation. It aims to establish a minimum world standard of education including knowledge about agriculture, handicrafts, health, citizenship and world affairs as well as the basic skills of reading, writing and numbers. Through exchange scholarships, international conferences and the exchange of cultural collections, it works to foster international understanding.

International Children's Emergency Fund (UNICEF)

This often works in collaboration with some other agency—FAO or WHO. It has provided aid for children:
► suffering because of war, e.g. in Nigeria and Vietnam;
► suffering from epidemics and hunger;
► suffering from preventable diseases. It has organized the vaccination of 280 million children against tuberculosis and the treatment of 32 million against malaria;
► in deprived countries it has set up over 40,000 health centres and so helped the work of the WHO.

United Nations Relief and Work Agency (UNRWA)

This is the descendant of the earlier United Nations Relief and Rehabilitation Agency (UNRRA). This was set up in 1943 to provide relief in countries liberated from Germany. It existed from 1943 to 1947 and helped in the provision of clothing, food and medical supplies as well as in the rehabilitation of agriculture and industry in Europe. UNRWA has taken the work outside Europe. It has had to cope with the problem of refugees in the Middle East following from the Arab–Israeli conflict. It also works with the refugees in Africa where civil wars and unrest in Nigeria, Uganda and Chad have created a major refugee problem.

World Health Organization (WHO)

This is another agency trying to reduce human suffering and so increase the sum of human happiness. You should remember that half of the world's children cannot read or write; that three-quarters of the world's people still have little chance of getting to a doctor when ill and even less chance of visiting a dentist. The WHO provided the staff, the centres and the equipment, medicine and drugs which have been used against cholera epidemics in Egypt (1949) as well as providing aid for starving and sick children (along with the FAO and UNRWA), attacks on preventable disease (with UNICEF) and the spreading of knowledge and medical skills among people in the underdeveloped world (with the help of UNICEF and UNESCO).

Other agencies deal with such things as telecommunications, trade, human rights, weather forecasting and civil aviation. These too have played their part in increasing international understanding and co-operation.

 ## 27.4 Actions, Failures and Successes

THE POLITICAL ACTIVITY OF THE UNO

This has brought the Organization into most major international problems since 1945. In 1946 UNO played a major rôle in getting Soviet troops out of Persia (Iran). However, in 1946 it failed to overcome Russian opposition to a UN settlement of the Greek problem (see Unit 28). In 1946–9 it helped to solve the problems following on the demand of Indonesia for independence and Dutch resistance to let go of her colonial possessions. Indonesian independence (1949) owed a good deal to UN influence.

In 1947 UNO failed to help India and Pakistan to resolve the Kashmir problem (Unit 34). In 1948 it inherited the Palestine problem from Britain (see Unit 37). Its proposals for the partition of Palestine were rejected by both Arab and Israeli. The UN mediator, Count Bernadotte, was assassinated by Jewish terrorists. His successor, Ralph Bunche, arranged an armistice in 1949.

In 1948–9 the UN played no part in the Berlin Crisis (Unit 28). In 1950 the outbreak of the Korean War (Unit 28) led to the Uniting for Peace Resolution (see above) and the despatch of UN forces under US commanders (Unit 28).

In 1956 the Suez Crisis (Unit 37) saw the UN paralysed by the vetoes of France and Britain. The Assembly's demand for an end to the fighting was, fortunately for the UN, accompanied by similar demands from Russia and the USA. Also in 1956 during the Hungarian uprising (Unit 30) the UN condemned Russia's invasion of Hungary—but failed to prevent Russia from continuing with her action.

In 1960–2 the Congo crisis (Unit 36) saw the raising of a UN force of 20,000 men trying to bring peace to the country torn by a series of civil wars and the attempted secession by Katanga. In 1962 the UN supervised the handing over of Western Irian (New Guinea) to Indonesia when the Dutch were finally persuaded that colonialism was dead.

In 1963 UN forces kept the peace in Cyprus.

In 1965 another force was sent to Kashmir to restore peace between India and Pakistan (Unit 34). The solution to the Kashmir problem only came when Kosygin of Russia acted as mediator (Unit 34). Also in 1965 UN sanctions were imposed on Rhodesia when that 'colony' declared UDI (Unit 36). There is no evidence that sanctions had much effect. There is evidence that many member-states ignored the sanctions' resolutions and continued to trade with the 'criminal' nation.

In 1967 UN forces which had been stationed between Arab and Israeli forces were withdrawn at Arab demand. The victory of Israel in the ensuing war and its occupation of more Arab land led to a resolution in 1967 demanding Israeli withdrawal. The continued unrest in the Middle East is a sign of UN inability to enforce its resolutions.

THE FAILURES OF THE UNITED NATIONS

Causes

A major cause was the unwillingness of the major powers to give up their 'rights'. Russia (in Hungary, 1956), Britain and France (in Suez, 1956) and America (in Vietnam) have all been guilty.

Also, the hostility between East and West weakens the UN, making it incapable of effective action in certain disputes such as the situation in the Middle East where Israel is a 'client state' of the USA, and Syria and the PLO are 'clients' of Russia. That hostility led to a weakening of the original resolve that the UN should have an army at its disposal. Russia feared that it would be a 'capitalists' army' and so vetoed proposals for such a force. UN forces have to be cobbled together in certain crises—but only when the major powers agree to such a formation. When they do not agree (as in Vietnam and the whole area of Indo-China since 1975) then wars continue.

Evidence

In the USA–USSR confrontation over Cuba, 1962, neither country took its case to the UN. Both seemed prepared to risk a world war. The crisis was settled outside the UN.

Over Vietnam, Russia and China aided one side and the USA the other in a war in which the UN had no part. Neither did the UN have any part in the peace-making sorties by Henry Kissinger on behalf of US President Richard Nixon (Unit 32).

Disarmament was to be one of the main aims of the new organization. In fact world armaments have increased alarmingly since 1945. Such proposals as are made for disarmament are made by the major powers, in bilateral discussions (such as the SALT discussions—see Unit 32).

ITS SUCCESSES

Some political successes have been achieved (see above). Many social successes have followed the work of some agencies (see above).

More people are now conscious of the interdependence of the countries of the world than was the case before 1939.

UNO still exists in spite of its weaknesses and failures.

Unit 27 Summary

▶ Origins and aims.
▶ The UNO compared to the League of Nations.
▶ Structure and agencies.
▶ Actions, failures and successes.

---

28 INTERNATIONAL RELATIONS, 1945–53

28.1 The Iron Curtain and the Cold War

UNEASY ALLIES, 1939–45

Russia had signed a pact with Hitler in 1939 (Unit 23). Britain had wanted to help Finland against Russia (Unit 23). Stalin had been suspicious of Allied failure to open the Second Front in France in 1942 and 1943.

Roosevelt wanted to see the break up of the British Empire. He also made concessions to Stalin—and angered Churchill.

Stalin did not enter the war against Japan until his spies (including Fuchs) told him that the atom bomb was to be dropped. He knew, then, that the war would soon be over—so he joined in.

THE 'IRON CURTAIN' FALLS

In August 1945 Stalin met Allied leaders at Potsdam (see Unit 26). The Allies had suspicions of Russia's behaviour in Eastern Europe (see Unit 30).

Poland was seen as a Russian-dominated government set-up. The Polish government-in-exile, which had fought in the West, was imprisoned when it returned to Poland (Unit 30).

Bulgaria, Rumania, and Albania were liberated by Russian troops and Russian-dominated governments set up (see Unit 30).

Churchill drew attention to what was happening. In a telegram to President Truman in 1945 he wrote, 'What is to happen about Russia? An iron curtain is drawn down upon their Front. We do not know what is going on behind.' Then in March 1946 in his speech at Fulton, Missouri, he said, 'From Stettin in the Baltic to Trieste in the Adriatic, an iron curtain has descended across the continent.'

WHY DID PEOPLE TALK OF THE 'COLD WAR'?

It was not a real (or 'hot') war. There was no declaration of war between Russia and the USA. When they did fight (in Korea—see Unit 28), they did so under 'assumed' titles. However it was certainly not a real peace. The struggle between the two super-powers was carried on by the build-up of armed forces and by propaganda. In their own countries they attacked the enemy in articles, cartoons, interviews and speeches. In neutral countries they tried to 'win friends and influence people' by the activities of their diplomats and countrymen. Economic aid was offered to win friends here; military aid was offered to keep a friend in power there. Since the powers' armed forces had nuclear weapons, there was fear that a Third World War might break out and destroy humankind.

Even when the 'war' seemed to lose some of its heat (after 1953) there seemed little chance of peaceful co-existence for the two power blocs.

GREECE

The Cold War flares up

At Yalta and Potsdam Greece was named as a British sphere of influence. After the German withdrawal from Greece in 1944, British troops fought communist guerrillas to keep a monarchist government in power. Then in 1946 the communists rose again, helped by supplies from their Russian-controlled neighbours.

In February 1947 Britain decided that she could no longer afford to pay for the defence of Greece. She asked the Americans to help.

28.2 The Truman 'Doctrine'

Truman had quickly come to distrust Stalin. He feared that Russia would gain control of Greece, and persuaded Congress to accept an American commitment to 'free' Europe.

In March 1947 Truman spelled out his policy. America would support free peoples resisting aggression by armed minorities and outside forces.

Congress voted 4 billion dollars to pay for American forces to be sent to Greece and Turkey. There was to be no 'return to isolationism' as in 1920 (see Unit 16). However, America would not try to 'roll back' communism. It recognized the principle of co-existence. It would not allow it to advance further; this was the principle of containment.

28.3 The Marshall Plan

In 1945–7 America provided essential aid for war-torn Europe through the United Nations Relief and Rehabilitation Administration (UNRRA). This came to an end in 1947. However, Europe had not completely recovered. On 5 June 1947 the US Secretary of State, George C. Marshall, announced that the USA would be willing to provide massive aid to help European recovery to go on. European countries should get together to decide how this aid might be spent. Stalin announced that no Russian-controlled country would take this aid.

Ernest Bevin, British Foreign Secretary, persuaded other European countries to form the Organization for European Economic Co-operation. Sixteen countries joined the OEEC, with the western part of Germany as an associate member.

In April 1948 Congress voted 5.3 billion dollars for aid to Europe under the Marshall Plan. In fact, by mid-1952 over 13 billion dollars of aid had been given. Food, fuel, machinery, raw material and essential manufactured goods bought with this money helped Europe to get back on its feet. Stalin saw this as an American attempt to dominate Europe.

28.4 Czechoslovakia—a Special Case

This was the most industrialized state in Eastern Europe. Between 1919 and 1939 it had been a liberal democracy.

During the war the communists had played a part in the resistance (guerrilla) movement against the German occupation.

In 1945 President Beneš was anxious for Russian help. He agreed to help the Communist Party to gain increased power. Thus he agreed to the banning of the Agrarian Party as the price to be paid for communist participation in the government, with communist Gottwald as Prime Minister. He also agreed to appoint communists to the important ministries controlling the police, communications (including the radio) and the armed forces. In 1947 Beneš allowed a purge of the non-communist Czech Social Democratic Party, so that a communist sympathizer became its leader.

Russians rejected the Marshall Plan (see above). They insisted that this American offer of aid should be rejected also by their satellites. The Czech government was divided on this issue. There was need of economic and financial aid, but the communists insisted on following the Stalin line. Several ministers resigned and the government became even more strongly communist-dominated. There were student demonstrations against this government, put down by the army and police.

1948, THE YEAR OF DECISION

In March 1948 the elections were postponed because of communist fear of popular opposition. Dr Beneš rejected widespread demands that the communists should be dismissed and replaced by 'popular' ministers.

Communist strong-arm gangs occupied the offices of non-communist ministers. Jan Masaryk, son of the founder of the state in 1919, 'fell' from the window of his ministry and died.

Elections were held in May. The voters were offered a single list of candidates which they could vote for or against. There was an overwhelming victory for the communist-controlled National Front.

Beneš, who had become increasingly opposed to communist tactics, resigned. Gottwald became President. The communists had 'taken over'. Gottwald ordered a purge of the Czech Communist Party. Anyone opposing the Stalinist line was arrested, tried, imprisoned or executed. Among those killed was Slansky, the Secretary of the Party.

THE CATHOLIC CHURCH

Archbishop Beran had been an inmate of a Nazi concentration camp. He led the Church's opposition to the communists.

The government insisted that all priests should take an oath of loyalty to the state. Beran rejected this. In 1950 most Church property was confiscated and monasteries closed. Then, in 1951, seven bishops were arrested and Beran was exiled.

28.5 Germany

THE DANGER OF A RENEWED WAR

At Yalta the Big Three (Unit 26) had agreed to divide Germany into four zones of occupation; there was to be a joint administration for the whole country. Berlin was also divided into four zones of occupation.

At Yalta it was agreed that Russia would take reparations from Germany to compensate for the over-running and destruction of the country.

The four powers co-operated to bring the leading Nazis to trial at Nuremberg. Elsewhere, lesser Nazis were brought to trial, often before German judges.

In 1945, conditions in Germany were very hard. Thousands were homeless; there was a shortage of food and fuel. The currency system collapsed. The stream of refugees from Poland made these problems worse.

In 1946 the Americans drew up plans for the reconstruction of Germany; neither the Russians nor French would agree.

In 1946–7 the winter was unusually severe, and conditions in Germany became even worse than they had been.

In 1947 the British and Americans agreed to unite their two zones to help Germany get back to normal. A new currency was introduced to help economic life get started. American and British aid poured into their zones of Germany.

France merged her zone with the US and British zones. The Russians refused to co-operate. They also refused to allow Western officials into their zone to see how it was being governed.

In 1948 the Marshall Plan was applied to 'western' Germany, and in 1949 West Germany was granted an occupation statute. A German Parliamentary Council drew up a new constitution. At the same time the Russians proclaimed the foundation of the German Democratic Republic in their former zone.

BERLIN: THE COLD WAR FLARES UP

In February 1948 the Russians announced that the whole of Berlin was part of their zone of occupation.

In June 1948 the London Agreement provided for the formation of a federal government in West Germany (see below).

The decision to create a new currency in the western zones led the Russians to claim that this was against the principles of the Potsdam agreement—that all four powers should co-operate in the government of the whole of Germany. Russia forbade the circulation of the new currency in its zone. This meant that it did not circulate in Berlin, which is inside the Russian zone.

In June 1948 Russia closed all the land links between Berlin and the western zones. Russia hoped to make it impossible for the Western powers to supply and govern their zones of Berlin. The city would then have 'fallen' to the Russians.

The Allies replied by a massive airlift. For almost a year, fuel, food and other supplies were flown every day from airports in the western zones across the Russian zone to the airport in the British zone in Berlin.

In May 1949 Russia finally lifted the blockade and Berlin could be supplied by rail, road, river and canal—more easily and more cheaply than by air.

28.6 The North Atlantic Treaty Organization (NATO)

In March 1947 Britain and France signed the Treaty of Dunkirk aimed against a revived Germany. Then in March 1948 the 'Dunkirk Powers' were joined by Belgium, Holland and Luxembourg (the Benelux countries) in the Treaty of Brussels, which guaranteed mutual aid against both German and Russian aggression.

The Brussels Powers could never have hoped to hold off a Russian attack; they had only 12 divisions of men as compared to the 250 divisions of Russian forces. The blockade of Berlin and the communist takeover in Czechoslovakia made everyone more afraid of the danger of a Russian attack.

In April 1949 the five Brussels Powers allied with the USA, Canada, Norway, Iceland, Denmark, Italy and Portugal in NATO. They were later joined by Greece and Turkey (1952) and West Germany (1955).

The USA provides about three-quarters of the cost and the military power of the alliance, and has complete control of the nuclear weapons inside the alliance.

28.7 Korea

THE COLD WAR FLARES UP AGAIN (Fig. 28.7)

Stalin's attempt to extend Russian power was halted by:
▶ Yugoslavia's break with the Eastern bloc (see Unit 30);

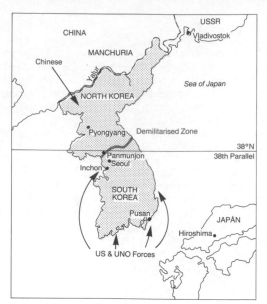

Fig. 28.7 The Korean War

▶ the failure of the Berlin blockade;
▶ the creation of NATO.

He then turned his attention to the Far East. There were Russian-backed risings by local communists in Malaya and Indonesia in 1948–50. These, too, failed.

Korea had been annexed by Japan in 1910 (see Unit 6). In 1943 at the Cairo Conference (see Unit 26) it was agreed that independence should be restored to Korea after the war.

After the surrender of Japan in August 1945 Korea was occupied by Russian troops (in the north) and US troops (in the south). The dividing line between the two zones was the 38th parallel.

In 1948 Russia set up the communist Korean People's Republic. The Americans then set up the Republic of Korea in the south. Russia and the USA withdrew their forces. A series of border clashes took place.

In 1948 the UN tried to organize national elections, but failed.

In June 1950 North Korean troops crossed the 38th parallel, overran South Korea and pushed her forces back to a small region around the southern port of Pusan.

Russia was boycotting the UN because of its refusal to admit communist China as a member. However, the USA got the Security Council to condemn the North Koreans as aggressors and to agree to send a UN force to drive them back. This force was mainly American, although soldiers from 15 other nations (including Britain) also took part in the fighting. It was commanded by General MacArthur (Unit 26). The UN forces were driven back into the area around Pusan.

MacArthur organized an amphibious landing at the port of Inchon behind the North Korean lines and drove the invaders back across the 38th parallel. He then planned to drive them north to the Yalu River. China warned the world that if that happened she would join in the war.

MacArthur carried out his plan. The Chinese then entered the war. UN forces operating far from their supply bases were often defeated and quickly driven south again. MacArthur asked permission to drop the atomic bomb on China. The USA's allies were alarmed at this threat to extend the war which might easily have become the Third World War. President Truman was persuaded to sack MacArthur.

The war continued with heavy casualties on both sides, with neither side able to win a major victory. The 'see-saw' across the 38th parallel saw refugees being driven to the south, and peasants having their lands destroyed.

In June 1951 Russia proposed at the UN that there should be an armistice. Discussions went on—but so did the fighting.

In 1953 a truce was finally agreed and signed at Panmunjon. A truce commission was set up to deal with problems between the two Korean states, who still have not signed a peace treaty. A demilitarized zone separates the two halves of Korea.

THE EFFECTS OF THE KOREAN WAR

There was massive destruction in Korea itself. The bitter enmity between the USA and China was intensified. The Cold War thus spread into Asia. Anti-communist feeling in the USA allowed Senator McCarthy to gain a great deal of support (see Unit 32).

The South East Asia Treaty Organization (SEATO) was set up in 1954 as the Asiatic attempt to imitate NATO and to provide an obstacle to communist aggression in the Far East.

 28.8 1953: a Thaw?

In March 1953 Stalin died. He had led Russia since 1924, having taken part in the Bolshevik revolution of 1917 and the Civil War. During that war he had seen Western powers helping the anti-Bolsheviks (Unit 10).

He had led Russia against Hitler after 1941, having seen how the Western powers had appeased Hitler—even excluding Russia from the Munich Conference which decided the fate of Czechoslovakia, Russia's ally (see Unit 23).

He had taken part in the Yalta and Potsdam Conferences and won for Russia a great deal of control over Eastern Europe (Unit 30). He had tried to extend that control over Berlin and in Korea (see above).

Stalin's successor, Khrushchev, was a different sort of person. He did not have the sort of power that Stalin had had inside Russia, nor did he seem to have Stalin's ambitions to extend Russian power abroad. He was prepared to accept the Truman idea of co-existence.

The change of leadership in Russia led to a 'thaw' in East-West relations, and 'the road to détente' (Unit 39).

> ### ▨ Unit 28 Summary ▨
>
> ▶ The Iron Curtain and the Cold War.
> ▶ The Truman 'doctrine' and the Marshall Plan.
> ▶ Czechoslovakia, 1948.
> ▶ The German problem and the airlift to Berlin.
> ▶ NATO.
> ▶ The Korean War, causes, courses and effects.
> ▶ 1953: a thaw?

29 RUSSIA, 1945–88

▨ 29.1 Stalin's Domestic Policies, 1945–53

THE POSITION IN 1945

Much of Russia had been devastated. The main food-producing regions had been ruined. There were food shortages; food riots had to be put down by the Army and Beria's MVD.

President Kalinin warned that 'only Hitler's Germany has been defeated', suggesting that the rest of the capitalist West was waiting to destroy Russia. In February 1946 Stalin also warned of the dangers from the West. This fear helps to explain his policies in Eastern Europe (Unit 30) where he wanted to create buffer states.

Contact with foreigners was limited. Russian soldiers returning from service in the West were 're-educated' so that they 'forgot' the evidence of the higher standards of life in the West. Many were imprisoned, others sent to work in Siberia.

In 1947 Russia was a closed society. Her people were not allowed contact with the West; few were allowed to travel, few westerners were allowed in. Churchill's 'iron curtain' had come down.

INDUSTRIAL RECOVERY

Stalin returned to the pre-war policy of building up Russian industry. His success can be seen in the output figures:

	1945	*1953*
Coal	149 million tons	320 million tons
Steel	9 million tons	38 million tons
Oil	19 million tons	53 million tons
Electricity	43 billion kWh	133 billion kWh

One result of this development was the build-up of new industrial centres, many behind the Urals. Sverdlovsk grew from being a village to having 350,000 inhabitants.

Weaknesses of the development

Little attention was paid to new industries such as plastics. Russia remained an old-fashioned industrial country. In agriculture she continued to use heavy tractors which spoiled the soil, ignoring the development (in the West) of new, lighter tractors.

Military spending continued at a high level. In July 1949 Russia exploded her first atomic bomb.

EVIDENT PROBLEMS

There was widespread inflation. By 1951 food prices were double what they had been in 1940. Stalin was forced to revalue the rouble in an attempt to check this rise in prices.

The new towns grew very rapidly; there was always a shortage of housing, families sharing a single room.

The high spending on weapons and arms development was one cause of the constant shortage of consumer goods.

29.2 Policies, 1953–6

THE LEADERSHIP, 1953

On 5 March 1953 Stalin died. At that time, several people occupied leading positions. Malenkov was Prime Minister, Bulganin was Deputy Prime Minister (1947–55) and represented the power of the Russian army, Molotov was the long-serving Foreign Minister, and Krushchev was First Secretary of the Communist Party. None of these wanted the powers which Stalin had had. All of them were anxious to pursue policies which would lead to an improvement in Russian living standards and an easing in world tension.

EVIDENCE OF THE CHANGE IN ATTITUDES

Beria, the head of the MVD, was murdered in June or July, 1953. None of the 'collective leadership' wanted the secret police to keep its old powers.

The official agency, Intourist, tried to attract foreign tourists to Russia—although foreigners' journeys inside Russia were carefully controlled.

Malenkov was dismissed from the post as Prime Minister in 1955. He was not assassinated, as might have happened in Stalin's time. In 1958 he was sent to manage a generating station in far-away Kazakhstan.

Bulganin became Prime Minister. With Khrushchev he formed a duumvirate, sharing joint authority, although Khrushchev was, in fact, the dominant partner.

In 1957 the army became concerned at the growth of Khrushchev's power. An anti-Party campaign was led by Bulganin. This failed and Bulganin was demoted, before being expelled from the Central Committee. He then lived in retirement near Moscow.

Khrushchev became Prime Minister in 1958, so that he was the supreme ruler—of Party and government.

AGRICULTURE: RUSSIA'S MAJOR PROBLEM

Continuing food shortages proved that collectivization was not an efficient way of farming.

Khrushchev led the campaign for the use of the 'Virgin Lands' of Siberia. About 250,000 volunteers from the Young Communist League (the Komsomol) were recruited to farm in these regions, and 120,000 tractors were sent. Two and a half million hectares of Siberia and Kazakhstan were ploughed in the first year. By 1955 it was planned that 13 million hectares would have been brought under the plough.

Opposition to the plan was led by Malenkov, who argued that it would be better for Russia to import food, paying for it by exports of industrial goods. Khrushchev argued that in addition to the increased output of wheat there would be increased output of maize. This could be fed to cattle and pigs, so providing more meat for the workers.

Success

There were two good harvests which seemed to prove Khrushchev right.

Failure

Soil erosion led to the creation of dust bowls as the valuable top soil was swept away by the wind.

Food imports

Russia, once the granary of Europe, now had to import grain from Canada, Australia and, later, the USA. Bread rationing was also introduced, indicating a further lowering of living standards for the Russian people.

A CHANGE IN FOREIGN POLICY

Khrushchev supported the policy of co-existence (see Unit 28) which had been first put forward by President Truman in 1947. He argued that communism did not need a military victory over the capitalist West. It would 'crush' the capitalists by its very success as a system. This led to more contact between Russian and Western politicians and to more peaceful policies.

Bulganin and Khrushchev visited Britain and other countries, and Khrushchev, when in complete power, toured the USA. Summit Conferences were arranged, although they rarely led to far-reaching changes in policies. In 1954 Russia took part with the USA and Britain in talks at Geneva which led to the withdrawal of French forces from Indo-China. The 'spirit of Geneva' was the description of the way in which the East and West could work together. In 1955 the wartime Allies signed a peace treaty with Austria and withdrew their forces.

However, suspicion of the West remained a feature of Russian policy, even under Khrushchev. In 1955 the Warsaw Pact was created as a Russian alternative to NATO (Unit 28), particularly when West Germany was admitted as a member of that Organization. Albania, Czechoslovakia, East Germany, Hungary, Poland and Rumania joined Russia in this Pact. Comecon (the Council for Mutual Economic Assistance) had been created in 1949—the Russian alternative to the OEEC (Unit 28). In 1959 it was strengthened, as Russia wished to show its hostility to the recently created European Economic Community or Common Market (see Unit 31).

29.3 De-Stalinization

THE TWENTIETH PARTY CONGRESS, 1956

This was supposed to be a secret meeting of communist representatives from all over the USSR. There were non-Russian communists from Western countries at the Congress—as observers. It was these who brought out the reports of what Khrushchev said in a major and surprising speech. He attacked the memory of Stalin (whom he had served for so long). He attacked:

▶ Stalin's autocratic rule;
▶ the purges of the 1930s;
▶ the mistakes made by Stalin in the early years of the war;
▶ the quarrel with Tito (see Unit 30).

THE EFFECTS OF THIS 'DE-STALINIZATION'

Many people imprisoned by Stalin were released. The memories of many who had been killed were rehabilitated. They were shown not to have been the 'monsters' Stalin had claimed.

There were similar policies throughout Eastern Europe. We will see in Unit 30 what effects that relaxation had.

Some communists argued that there were different roads which might be followed to the same object—Socialism.

China, under Mao, became critical of Russia (see below).

IMPROVEMENTS IN KHRUSHCHEV'S RUSSIA

There was an increased production of consumer goods. The secret police had less power (although they still had some). There was a fall in the number of people sent to labour camps—although there were still many who were sent to these 'gulags'.

Russia seemed to be beginning to enjoy the fruits of the massive industrialization policies of the 1930s and 1940s. The launching of the first Sputnik (1957) and of Vostok 1 manned by Yuri Gagarin were signs of technological advance.

29.4 Khrushchev and Germany

Khrushchev was anxious to get the West to recognize East Germany's independence. If this were granted, East

Germany could stop travel from the West and West Berlin. He also wanted to halt the flow of refugees from East Germany. Since 1949 over 2 million had gone, via West Berlin, to the West. This led to a labour shortage in East Germany.

In 1958–9 Khrushchev told the Western Allies that they had six months in which to leave West Berlin. Then in September 1959 Khrushchev visited President Eisenhower in the US President's 'retreat' at Camp David. He withdrew his threat over Berlin.

In May 1960 a Summit Conference was held in Paris. Khrushchev had announced his intention to sign a separate peace treaty with East Germany. But the Russians shot down an American 'spy' plane piloted by Gary Powers. This led to Khrushchev's walking out of the Summit.

In June 1961 Khrushchev met Kennedy in Vienna. Again he threatened that the West had only six months to get out of Berlin.

THE BERLIN WALL

The constant threats to cut Berlin off from the west led to an increase in the numbers seeking to escape. Over 1000 a day were getting out of East Germany. On 13 August 1961 two Soviet divisions of tanks were ordered to combat readiness in East Germany. Truckloads of East German Police (the Vopos) lined the boundary between the Soviet and Allied sectors of Berlin. On 17 August 1961 workmen began to erect a wall across Berlin. The 'Iron Curtain' now had physical form.

After the building of the Wall

About 60,000 East Berliners lost their jobs in West Berlin. The flood of refugees was halted. People trying to escape to the West now have to take tremendous risks. They still try, however.

There was little chance of further crises in Berlin, although there was the 'Checkpoint Charlie affair'. In October 1961 ten Soviet tanks turned their guns on ten US tanks at the crossing point between East and West Berlin. But nothing happened.

29.5 The Cuban Affair, 1962

In 1958 Fidel Castro's guerrillas overthrew the American-supported government of Batista, and attacked American-owned capitalist enterprises, which Castro blamed for the inequalities in Cuban life.

The USA refused to recognize the Castro government. She refused to trade with Cuba from which she had bought most of the sugar crop. She took in, and gave support to, anti-Castro refugees.

Castro responded by taking over more American investments in Cuba. Russia bought the sugar crop and became Castro's major supporter.

Russia, Castro and the USA saw the new government as a model communist government in the Caribbean. Castro and Russia hoped, while the US feared, that other countries in Latin America might imitate Castro's example and set up communist governments.

In April 1961 President Kennedy of the USA allowed a CIA-backed invasion by Cuban exiles. This was a fiasco and both worsened USA hostility and encouraged Castro's supporters in Cuba (see Unit 32).

In October 1962 American 'spy planes' brought back photographs showing that there were Soviet missiles in Cuba. President Kennedy announced a naval blockade of Cuba until these missiles were removed. He threatened that if a missile were let off, then US forces would retaliate.

Khrushchev said the missiles were to defend Cuba from the threat of an American-supported invasion by anti-Castro forces. He also claimed that there was no difference between Russian missiles in Cuba and US missiles in Turkey.

Kennedy said that Castro did not need missiles to defend

himself. He argued that the missiles were intended to threaten the USA. The US air force and Polaris nuclear-carrying submarines were put on a war footing.

A Russian convoy was approaching Cuba (22–8 October). Would it challenge the US blockade—and so lead to war? Would it turn back—and indicate a climb-down by Khrushchev?

On 28 October Khrushchev announced that the ships would turn back—except for an oil tanker which Kennedy quickly decided could be let through. Khrushchev also announced that the missiles would be removed.

Note that throughout this crisis the USA had forces on its naval base at Guantanamo in southern Cuba.

29.6 Khrushchev and China (See also

Unit 33)

Stalin had not supported Mao Tse-tung in the 1930s and 1940s. Mao's 'revolution' was based on support from peasants. Marxism taught that the revolution had to be based on industrial workers.

In 1950 Russia and China co-operated in Korea (see Unit 28). After 1950 Russia sent technicians and material to help in China's industrialization.

Mao had been angered by Khrushchev's attack on Stalin. It was 'impossible' said Mao, for such a 'monster' to have led the world's first communist state.

In 1957 Russia supplied aid for Mao's 'Great Leap Forward' (see Unit 33), but then became angered when Mao's system of communes did not follow the Russian model.

During 1957–60 Mao accused the Russians of being 'revisionists', of wanting to ignore the teachings of Marxism-Leninism, of being more concerned with developing consumer industries than with creating a communist state. Russia, he argued, was trying to imitate the West in its search for material affluence.

In 1960 the Russians withdrew their aid teams and sent no more material aid to China.

In 1964 China exploded her own nuclear bomb. Mao could now claim to be, at least, equal to Russia. In fact, he claimed to be superior because of the purity of the doctrine which he followed in revolutionary China.

Border disputes were the result of Russian expansion in the 19th century into the Amur basin and Central Asia. She shared a 6400-km long frontier with China. Clashes between civilians and armed forces led to a weakening of the relationship between the two communist 'giants'.

As Russia tried to work out peaceful co-existence with the USA, Mao put himself forward as the only real communist leader.

29.7 Khrushchev's Fall, 1964

Political power in Russia was shared by the army, represented by Bulganin until 1957 when he was demoted by Khrushchev, and by the Communist Party, of which Khrushchev was First Secretary.

Khrushchev lost the support of the leading members of the Party, because he seemed to be creating for himself that 'cult of personality' for which he had denounced Stalin. He also made organizational changes in the Party structure which proved to be unsound and clumsy.

He then lost the support of the hard-liners in the Army and the Party by his Cuban policy (see above). His Berlin-German policy had not led to Western recognition of East Germany.

During his trips abroad Khrushchev often behaved in what some saw as 'honest', others as 'boisterous' and others as 'foolish' ways. Some leading Russians thought he was discrediting the system.

However, Khrushchev's major failures were:

▶ his agricultural policy in the 'Virgin Lands';
▶ the continuing lack of consumer goods;
▶ the clash with China.

In October 1964, while he was away on holiday, there was a meeting of the Party praesidium (or governing body). Khrushchev was dismissed from both his posts.

On returning to Moscow he tried to undo what had happened—but failed. He was succeeded by President Podgorny, Prime Minister Kosygin and Party Secretary Brezhnev.

29.8 Khrushchev's Career

This is a popular examination question.

Khrushchev was born in 1894 to a peasant family, and worked in the Donetz Basin, where he joined the Communist Party in 1918. He worked his way up the ladder of Party organization. In 1934 he was Second Secretary of the Moscow Party organization; in 1935, First Secretary; and in 1938, First Secretary of the Party in the Ukraine.

During 1934–40 Khrushchev helped Stalin to carry out the great purges (see Unit 11). In 1939 he became a member of the Politburo, and during 1941–5 he was a high-ranking political commissar in the armed forces.

During 1945–53 Khrushchev was the Party's main agricultural expert, and in 1953–4 he ousted Malenkov and became First Secretary of the Party.

In 1955 he was the most prominent member of the collective leadership. In 1956 he condemned Stalin, and in 1957 he rid himself of his rivals, Malenkov, Kaganovich, Molotov and (army leader) Zhukov. Then in 1958 he rid himself of Bulganin and became Prime Minister.

The following are also important:

▶ his 'Virgin Lands' policy (see above);
▶ his relations with foreign powers: the USA, including the Summit meetings, Western Europe, including the question of Berlin, and China;
▶ his fall from power (see above).

29.9 Agriculture 1964–85

It was evident that the Russian system was a failure. It employed 40 million workers compared to the 4 million in US farming. Yet it could not supply enough for the Russian people.

Kosygin and Brezhnev announced an increase in wages for farm workers, and freedom for collectives to decide on what crops to grow. During 1966–71 the changes seemed to work. There was a series of good harvests.

However, in 1971–2 the harvest was ruined by a severe frost which killed off the winter wheat crops, and a drought which killed off the main crop. Russia was forced to buy food from the USA and Canada. This had the following effects:

▶ it took a good deal of gold out of Russia and so made it more difficult for her to buy the industrial equipment she needed to continue her modernization plans;
▶ it pushed up world prices, and was one of the causes of the 'great inflation' which occurred after 1973;
▶ it made it more likely that there would be more contacts between Russian and US officials and so helped détente (see Unit 39).

29.10 Industry 1964–85

Russian industry was not up to Western standards, as shown by its inefficiency and low productivity per worker. Kosygin and Brezhnev realized that state-run organizations had to change.

Higher wages were allowed for workers who worked harder and produced more. This was the Western-style system of bonus payments—and the end of 'to each according to his needs'. These higher wages would increase demand for consumer goods—and so, it was hoped, would stimulate industries producing those goods.

To achieve increases in productivity, Russia bought industrial machinery from the USA, and got Fiat of Italy to re-organize the Russian car industry. In May 1973 Brezhnev also went to West Germany (the 'arch-enemy') and asked for technical aid and capital investment by the successful Germans.

To help increase Russia's wealth Brezhnev and Kosygin proposed the exploitation of the vast gold, copper and oil deposits in Siberia. They found it difficult to recruit Russian workers to go to the inhospitable wastes of Siberia.

Note that, in spite of its backwardness, Russia has produced the Mig 21, at the time the world's most successful jet fighter, and Sputnik 1, the first man-made satellite.

29.11 The Government and People

Brezhnev was the most important of the triumvirate (see earlier). Podgorny was ousted, and Brezhnev, Party Secretary, also became President of the USSR.

During 1975–82 Brezhnev suffered from ill-health but continued to develop that 'cult of personality' which was favoured by Stalin and Khrushchev. Brezhnev helped his friends and supporters into positions of power in the Politburo and dismissed possible rivals. One result of this process was that Russia was governed by a group of ageing 70-year-olds who had lost whatever 'fire for revolution' they may ever have had.

Corruption became fairly commonplace; several senior officials were executed for smuggling, currency offences, dishonest selling or buying on a massive scale.

In the relaxed atmosphere of the Khrushchev years, critics and dissidents had become more outspoken. Brezhnev's government cracked down on these. Writers such as Daniel, Sinyansky, and Solzhenitsyn were punished by exile or imprisonment. Critics who passed on duplicated copies of critical works were punished severely. In addition, scientists such as Sakharov became critical of the government's policies concerning personal freedom. These dissidents were imprisoned (often in psychiatric 'clinics').

Critics drew attention to the way in which the government failed to honour its commitments to human rights as outlined in the 1975 Helsinki Agreement (see p. 160). Orlov and other such critics set up 'Helsinki' committees to supervise the government's record. They, too, were punished.

In old-fashioned Russian tradition, the government attacked the Jews, making it difficult, if not impossible, for those who wanted to leave to get to Israel or the West.

Andropov (1983–4) had been head of the KGB (1967–82) and, in 1956, Khrushchev's agent in the suppression of the Hungarian rising. Some people in the West thought that he would provide a 'new, liberal face to the system'. He died in February 1984 before he had time to prove whether they were right or wrong. Certainly, he wished to improve the Soviet system. He wanted it to be more efficient and productive, and he proposed a series of reforms in industry and agriculture which were similar, in aims and methods, to those proposed earlier by Khrushchev and Kosygin. He also used the knowledge gained while head of the KGB to root out some of the more corrupt Party leaders and officials. In addition, Andropov drew public attention to the problems of alcoholism, absenteeism, low productivity and shoddy work.

Gorbachev became General Secretary only after the 73-year-old Chernenko (1984–5) had been brought to power by supporters of Brezhnev who were opposed to Andropov's reforming zeal. When Chernenko died, Gorbachev was quickly installed as Party Secretary by a combination of Party leaders, army chiefs and leaders of the bureaucracy.

29.12 Gorbachev's Inheritance, 1985

HIS PROBLEMS

Gorbachev was appointed immediately on Chernenko's death: Russia's leaders were anxious to tackle the many problems facing the country. He was known as 'Andropov's man', one willing to push through the badly-needed reforms of agriculture, industry and the political system.

Russia was, and is, a military super-power, able to challenge the USA, to control Eastern Europe, to fight a war in Afghanistan, and to support Cuban-led aggression in parts of southern Africa. However, in many respects, the Soviet Union had, and has, the appearance of a Third World country. The problems the Soviet Union had to face, and still faces, were many and various:

▶ Its people consumed only one-third of the goods and services consumed in the USA, and only one-half as much as was consumed in most East European countries. For how long would the Soviet people put up with this low living standard?

▶ The annual growth in the Soviet economy was only about one-third that of the USA and less than one-quarter that of the Japanese and other economies. For how long could this relatively declining economy manage to support the military and aggressive policies of the government?

▶ In spite of, or because of, 70 years of communist rule, agriculture continued to be a failure. Russia had to import about one-sixth of its grain needs from the USA and other capitalist countries. As its earnings from oil sales fell (as oil prices fell) Russia had to find a way to earn the foreign currency needed to pay for those imports.

▶ Because of food shortages, Russia had to have a rationing system, in spite of which people had to queue for hours to buy the food when it appeared in the shops. There were similar shortages of, and queues for, most consumer goods.

▶ In 1985 Soviet housing did not meet the minimum standards for health and decency set by Stalin in 1928.

▶ Soviet doctors reported that five key diseases were out of control – polio, diphtheria, scarlet fever, whooping cough and measles. They also reported that infant mortality continued to rise and life expectancy continued to fall.

▶ Russian technological development was incapable of absorbing or exploiting modern information technological change.

▶ Defence spending was 25 per cent higher than that of the USA, in spite of the crippled nature of the economy.

GORBACHEV'S SUPPORTERS, 1985

His call for *perestroika*, or the *restructuring* of the economy, was welcomed by:

▶ some defence chiefs who hoped that an improved economy would produce improved weaponry;

▶ some Party leaders who wanted to prove, after 70 years of failure, that 'communism works';

▶ some of the millions of Party workers hoping that, in an improved economy, they would have more power and influence;

▶ some dissidents who hoped for an improved living standard for the mass of the people.

GORBACHEV'S OPPONENTS, 1985

▶ Some defence chiefs feared that cuts in military spending might lessen their influence;

▶ some Party leaders claimed that *perestroika* in industry and agriculture would lead to demands for political restructuring and, perhaps, social unrest;

▶ many of the millions of Party bureaucrats feared that, in a changing economy, they might lose power and position.

29.13 Gorbachev's Reforms, 1985–88

A NEW STYLE

Like Khrushchev, but unlike most of his other predecessors, Gorbachev went to meet the people. He heard of their problems (and his) and argued for his reforms. This policy of *glasnost*, or *openness*, suggested, to Western observers, that he was 'a liberal'.

With his attractive wife, he also visited many Western countries, talking of the need for arms control and détente (Unit 39) and seeking Western capital and aid.

A NEW TEAM

He sacked corrupt local leaders, some of whom were put on trial. He dismissed aging members of the Politburo along with a younger, dangerous rival, Romanov. At regional and district level, he promoted younger, more ambitious and, he hoped, more efficient men to positions of power.

THE NEW AGRICULTURE

Farmworkers were allowed to have larger private plots on which they could grow food for sale in local markets. Some collective farms were partly broken up and tenant farmers allowed to rent land on 50-year leases. One result was an increase in food output: although only about 5 per cent of the land was privately farmed, this produced about 30 per cent of the food output. Gorbachev found that, as in Britain, 'privatization works', much to the dismay of hard-line Marxists.

A NEW CONSTITUTION, 1988

In 1977, Brezhnev had produced a new Constitution. This recognized 15 Union Republics, of which the Russian Republic was the largest, as well as about 20 National Areas. Each Republic was supposed to be a voluntary member of the Union from which it could, in theory, withdraw.

Figure 29.13 illustrates the political structure.

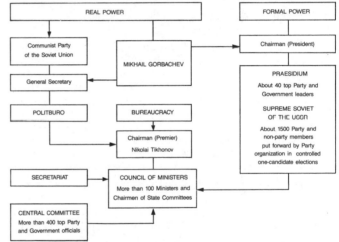

Fig. 29.13 The unreformed power structure, 1988

In theory, power belonged to non-Party political organs, the main one being The Supreme Soviet, 'the highest representative body of the people and supreme state authority'. It had two Chambers: The Soviet of the Union, which had 740 members; and The Soviet of Nationalities, which had 32 members from each of the National Areas. Delegates used to be nominated by local Party-controlled organizations and elected as the sole candidate for each constituency.

In 1988 Gorbachev's reforms provided for:

▶ elections at the local level with candidates being allowed to campaign against one another;

▶ the right of certain named organizations (e.g. Union of Writers, Union of Scientists) to put forward candidates.

The Supreme Soviet met for only a few days each year to approve items presented by the Party Secretariat. Gorbachev's reforms included the creation of a smaller body drawn from the Supreme Soviet to meet more frequently and have more powers.

The Supreme Soviet elected the Praesidium of 39-40 members, all of them major figures in either the Party or the Government. Gorbachev's reforms included one which enabled him to become Chairman of the Praesidium and President of the Soviet Union. However, he also put a limit on his growing power: another of his reforms limited his term of office, as President, to five years after which he would stand for re-election.

Real power, even after Gorbachev's reforms, was still exercised by the Party and not by the Government bodies. Every five years the Party Congress elected a Central Committee of some 400 Party officials, generals, judges and others. This in turn elected the Politburo of 15 or so members, from a list of names presented to the Committee by the General Secretary (now Gorbachev), who had power to dismiss members of this small body which, in every way, was his 'creature'.

In September 1988, as part of his reforming process, Gorbachev showed his 'tough' side:

▶ he sacked six leading members of the Politburo who were opposed to his 'liberalism';

▶ he demoted others, including the former head of the KGB and his main opponent, Ligachev, both of whom were given less important posts than they had held previously;

▶ he also lessened Party control of the economy. Previously, there had been 100 Party departments which had supervised (and really controlled) the economy and social life: for each government department (health, finance, housing, etc) there had been a similar Party 'ministry'. After his reforms there are now only six such Party 'shadow ministries': the plan is for the Government to be freer of Party control and to become more subject to the demands of the people.

29.14 Gorbachev's Russia, 1988

UNREST

Critics who feared that his reforms would lead to demands for even greater change pointed to:

▶ Baltic unrest. Estonia, Latvia and Lithuania were seized by Russian invasion in 1940. In 1988 there were major nationalist demonstrations and, even, local communist government decisions to throw off Soviet control of their affairs. The people of these countries had a higher standard of living than do people in Russia itself, but they had become increasingly resentful of the arrival of many Russians (looking for a better life) and by Soviet control of their Parliaments. In Lithuania, nationalist feeling included the demand for the restoration of the Catholic Church.

▶ Armenian unrest. In 1988 there were a series of clashes involving the Christians of Armenia and the Muslims of neighbouring Azerbaijan which has a large Armenian minority. Soviet troops had to be rushed to the southern states to try to restore an uneasy peace.

▶ Georgian unrest. In Georgia there were growing demands for greater freedom from central government control.

Hardline Party leaders claimed that Gorbachev's *glasnost* had encouraged such 'old-fashioned' nationalism. They argued that if such nationalist movements were not crushed (as they had been in the past), then the Ukraine and other Republics might begin moves to withdraw from the Union and the Russian 'empire' would start to break up.

PARTY CONTROL

Gorbachev had been careful to maintain Party control of the economic, social and political life of the country. His reforms had made small, if significant, changes so far. One result of this continued Party control was that the bureaucracy, transport systems and agriculture remained largely unaffected by his reforms. Late in 1988 the Politburo debated the reasons why up to 70 per cent of food output arrived at markets in a rotting state, and why, although Russia produced more potatoes than China, the USA, both Germanies and Britain, there were not enough potatoes in the market. In February 1989 a special Central Committee meeting discussed this problem which, said Gorbachev, 'is the most important question of internal policy'.

DEPENDENCE ON THE WEST

If his *perestroika* was to succeed, and if Russia was to be modernized, Gorbachev needed Western support.

▶ German, Italian and Japanese firms were encouraged to build factories and plants in Russia.

▶ German, French and British banks were persuaded to lend, in 1988, over 40 billion dollars to pay for the imported technology, raw materials and food.

Western critics wondered whether it was wise to aid the development of Communist Russia; they said that:

▶ In spite of his reforms and 'liberalism', Gorbachev was the leader of a Marxist-Leninist state; it remained this state's belief that the rest of the world had to be brought under control and no one had yet dismissed the Marxist-Leninist belief in world revolution.

▶ If the West did not provide the essential aid to make life easier for people in Russia, Gorbachev would have to cut military spending. This would make the world a safer place. But, if the West provided him with the aid, there was less need for him to cut plans for the modernization of the Soviet defence system. Was the West was wise to pay, indirectly, for the improved efficiency of Russia's military machine?

THE WESTERN DILEMMA

After three years, Gorbachev's reforms had not produced much evidence of real change in Russian economic life. This was not surprising: there was a great deal of backwardness to overcome. However, there were two groups inside Russia, about whom the West was concerned, who showed different responses to Gorbachev's 'failure':

▶ Hardliners claimed the failure of the economy to respond to Gorbachev's reforms was a sign that *perestroika* will not work. They also claimed that his policy of *glasnost* led to increasing unrest, particularly in states on the periphery (the Baltic, Georgia, Ukraine and Armenia). His critics claimed that this weakened the Soviet state and made it more easily a prey to Western aggression.

If such hardliners gained increasing influence in the Party leadership, they might be able to replace Gorbachev with a more hardline leader: Khrushchev, an earlier 'reforming liberal', was replaced by such hardliners. What might be the response of such a 'tougher' government to the failure of the system to produce the food, raw materials and technology needed to run a modern society? Would its difficulties push such a government into, say, invasion of Iran to obtain oil, or of Germany to get technology?

▶ Other critics claimed that *glasnost* and *perestroika* could not be confined within narrow limits as Gorbachev hoped: the unrest in the peripheral states as well as the growth in the activity of Russian dissidents suggested that, as people came to enjoy some freedoms (in economic life, in local elections) they would demand other freedoms in other aspects of life. Would the Marxist leadership of the Soviet Union be able to accommodate the demands of people for greater political freedom? Would it be able to allow people the sorts of human rights which it had voted for in the European Conference in 1988 (Unit 39)?

GORBACHEV'S OWN REPORT, January 1989

In January 1989 the Soviet government published its economic report. This showed that:

▶ neither industry nor agriculture was producing enough: grain imports from the USA, EEC and Australia had to be greater in 1989 than ever, if famine was to be avoided;

▶ wages were growing faster than productivity so, for the first time, inflation was acknowledged as a problem;

▶ local party leaders were still not trying hard enough to promote efficiency in their regions and districts.

For recent developments in the Soviet Union see Unit 40.

29.15 Détente and Human Rights

See Unit 39.

Unit 29 Summary

▶ Stalin's domestic policies, 1945–53.
▶ 1953: the beginning of change in leadership, agriculture and foreign policy.
▶ 1956: the attack on Stalin's record.
▶ Khrushchev and Germany, 1953–61; the Berlin Wall.
▶ The Cuban crisis, 1962.

▶ Khrushchev and China, 1953–64; from ally to enemy.
▶ The fall of Khrushchev.
▶ Agriculture, 1964–86; Russia's major problem.
▶ Industry, 1964–86; the demand for modernization.
▶ Changes of leadership.
▶ The treatment of dissidents and of corruption.
▶ Gorbachev's Russia.

---

30 EASTERN EUROPE, 1945–86

The Questions to be Asked

▶ How, and over which countries, did Russia extend her control?
▶ Why did Russia wish to have this satellite 'empire'?
▶ How, and where, has anti-Russian feeling been expressed?
▶ How did Russia deal with this 'nationalist' development?

30.1 Which Nations Were 'Taken Over', 1945–6?

POLAND

In autumn 1939 Poland's pre-war leaders set up a Free Polish government-in-exile (London). Many Poles got to the West (some via Russia) to fight for the Allies.

Within Poland, Polish resistance fighters formed the Home Army. Their loyalty was to the government-in-exile in London. After 1941 Stalin sent agents to help to organize resistance by a Polish Workers' Party loyal to Russia.

Before the Russians were driven from Poland (December 1941) they massacred, in Katyn, 4000 Polish army officers who might have led post-war opposition to communism in Poland.

In 1944 the Russian army re-crossed the Polish border. The nationalist Home Army rose in revolt in Warsaw. The Red Army waited for the Germans to destroy the nationalists before it defeated the Germans.

A National Council of the Homeland was set up by Stalin's agents on 1 January 1944. On 31 December 1944 this communist organization decided:

▶ its National Committee of Liberation would form the post-war government of Poland;
▶ its chairman (Bierut, educated in Russia and head of the Polish section of the NKVD since 1936) was to be the new President.

In Yalta, February 1945, it was agreed that:

▶ the Polish borders would be changed. In the west Poland would be pushed westwards to the line of the Oder–Neisse rivers. This gave Poland what had been German Silesia. In the east, the Poles would give up some of their territory to Russia;
▶ Poland was to have a 'free and independent government' which would include members of the Free Polish government-in-exile.

In March 1945 Stalin invited 16 leaders of the nationalist Home Army to visit Moscow—and then put them in prison. Stalin also refused to honour his Yalta promises. Poland did not have the 'free and unfettered election' agreed on. A Russian-controlled communist government was imposed on Poland.

RUMANIA, BULGARIA AND HUNGARY

These were treated as defeated countries, former 'allies' of Hitler's Germany. They were conquered by the Red Army, welcomed by local people as 'liberators' freeing them from rule by the hated Germans.

The Russians then set up governments in each country. Stalin borrowed a phrase from Tito (see 30.3) and called these governments People's Democracies. Socialists, leaders of peasants parties and communists formed co-alitions in Popular Front governments. Some communists hoped that this gave them a chance to form a nationalist form of communism. Gomulka of Poland said 'Our democracy is not similar to the Soviet system'.

Gomulka and others were wrong. The Red Army brought:

▶ agents of the Agitrop Brigade to spread communist propaganda in the newly liberated countries;
▶ agents of the NKVD to recruit local agents for a local secret police.

Within a short time the communists abandoned their socialist and peasants' party allies. Some were imprisoned, others kept under house arrest.

The Bulgarian Communist leader, Dimitrov, showed the intention of the Stalinist agents when he said: 'The Soviet régime and the Popular Democratic régimes are two forms of one and the same system.' They were neither popular (they had not been elected) nor democratic (they used all the trappings of Stalinist autocracy to keep themselves in power).

ALBANIA AND YUGOSLAVIA

In these countries communist partisans had freed themselves from German occupation with little or no help from the Russians. In both, the communist leaders set up the People's Democracy-form governments—but without the burden of Russian agents always behind them.

30.2 Why Did Russia Want a 'Satellite' Empire?

Western leaders were angered at the extent of Russian control over Eastern Europe. Churchill's 'iron curtain' references indicate Western thinking (see Unit 28). They were led to fear further Russian expansion:

▶ into Western Europe. The crises over Czechoslovakia and Berlin (see Unit 28) proved their points;
▶ into Asia. The war in Korea (Unit 28) and Russian-inspired revolutions in Malaya (Unit 35) and Indonesia (Unit 35) proved the case.

Western leaders also tried to think up means of halting this expansion. The 'Truman Doctrine' and the formation of NATO (Unit 28) were attempts to halt Russia.

Stalin claimed that Russian control of Eastern Europe was essential to Russia's own safety, because:

▶ the Western allies had aided the Whites during the Civil War after 1919 (see Unit 10). The American decision to feed the starving Germans and to rebuild West Germany were, to Stalin, proofs of Western hopes of launching fresh attacks on the Soviet Union;
▶ the communist-controlled Eastern Europe would provide a buffer between Russia and this 'expansionist' West.

Russia had been devastated by the war; its economy and agriculture lay in ruins. Stalin intended to use the resources of the satellites to rebuild Russia, so that, in his terms, global communism would be protected.

GIVING FORM TO THE RUSSIAN CONTROL, 1947–9

The West showed its opposition to Russia by the announcement of the 'Truman Doctrine' and the declaration of the Marshall Plan (see Unit 28).

Stalin called all communist leaders to Warsaw in 1947 to set up the Communist Information Bureau (Cominform). Zhdanov, speaking for Stalin, said that the Truman Doctrine and the Marshall Plan were twin parts of the American policy of putting Europe under American control. Cominform would rally not only the communist states of Eastern Europe; it would also rally the support of communists in Western Europe, Vietnam, Indonesia, Egypt and Syria.

In October 1947 the US Assistant Secretary of State said that the formation of Cominform was 'a deadly serious challenge to the free peoples of Europe and the USA which would have to be met.'

Economic control, 1949

The Marshall Plan had led to the formation of OEEC (see Unit 28). Stalin set up the Council for Mutual Economic Assistance (Comecon). Russia provided technical and industrial aid to its satellites to help them to develop their economies. However, these economies had to be run to benefit Russia's own development, supplying the 'mother country' with the materials which she most needed.

EXTENDING COMMUNIST CONTROL, 1947–51

Poland

In 1947 the People's Party (representing the peasants) was suppressed. Other political parties were broken up. A National Front of the Workers Party (communist-controlled) was the only party allowed to function. There were also purges. Some Polish communists were more Polish than communist. Stalin's agents expelled 75,000 from the Party. In 1948 Gomulka, Stalin's First Secretary of the Polish Communist Party, had to resign. He was 'too Polish'. In 1951 Gomulka was arrested and imprisoned.

The Catholic Church had the support of about 90 per cent of the Polish people. The uneasy 'peace' between the Church and the government ended in 1951 when the government abolished papal control of the dioceses in the areas taken from Germany. Cardinal Wyszynski, head of the Polish Church, was arrested in September 1953 and not released until October 1956.

Hungary

In 1945 a coalition government was set up and the leader of the Small Farmers' Party became Prime Minister. In 1947 all non-communist members of that government were attacked by Stalin-like purges organized by the communists. Imre Nagy, the then Prime Minister, resigned.

Also in 1947, the elections gave the communists a majority of the votes, although there was a 35 per cent anti-communist vote. The communists put pressure on the non-communist parties.

In 1949, in the fresh elections, there was a list of candidates and voters could either support or reject the list. Ninety per cent voted for the Communist-inspired list.

The Catholic Church also had an important rôle. Russian troops were stationed in Hungary and political trials and purges were frequent. Cardinal Mindszenty led the anti-government campaign in defence of Church schools and against the closure of Catholic papers and organizations. He was arrested, tortured, put on trial and imprisoned. The government set up a National Church, independent of the Pope and under communist control.

Czechoslovakia came under Communist control in 1948 (see Unit 28).

30.3 Tito, a Communist Rebel

Tito's career is a popular examination question.

Josip Tito, born 1890, of peasant stock, first worked as a farm labourer. After the First World War he became a communist, and frequently visited Moscow.

In 1928 he was arrested in Zagreb. After release he went to Moscow and attended the Lenin School for two years. In 1934 he became a member of the Yugoslav Politburo and in 1937 General Secretary of the Yugoslav Communist Party. He dissolved the Party, ordered all members to re-register and ensured that his supporters formed the leadership.

During the War he organized resistance to the Nazis. The conquering Germans divided Yugoslavia into:

▶ a nominally independent Croatia which was Catholic and industrialized and contained the major city of Zagreb;
▶ an occupied zone, Slovenia, around the major city of Ljubljana. Here, too, the people were mainly Catholic;
▶ an occupied zone, Serbia, an agricultural area; the majority were either Orthodox Christians or Muslims.

Tito recruited his partisans from peoples of all the regions and all the religions. He had to fight not only the Germans but also another resistance movement led by General Mihailovitch. Mihailovitch's movement was entirely Serb and spent a good deal of time fighting Tito's communists— even collaborating with the Germans for that purpose.

By 1944 Tito had become the undisputed leader of the anti-German movement, getting aid from the Western allies as they advanced through Italy. However, Stalin wanted a return of the Yugoslav monarchy driven into exile by Hitler. He gave no support to Tito.

In 1945 Tito headed a communist government. But he had not been brought to power by Russian 'liberators'. He was independent.

TITO'S BREAK WITH STALIN

In 1945 Tito held elections, abolished the monarchy and set up the Federal People's Republic of Yugoslavia. His constitution was based on the 1936 Stalin constitution. He had his own secret police, purged critics and imprisoned dissidents. In this way he was very much a communist hard-liner, but he refused to obey Stalin's orders. He would not allow the resources of his country to be used as Stalin wished.

On 28 June 1948, Stalin ordered the Cominform (see above) to expel Tito because he was not willing to make Yugoslavia 'a Russian colony'.

AFTER THE BREAK

Russia ordered the Cominform to break all trade relations with Yugoslavia, and she stopped sending economic aid. Tito made trade treaties with Western countries and received economic aid from Britain, France and the USA. In 1953 he made a state visit to Britain, the only communist leader to feel free enough to do so.

STALIN'S ATTACK ON 'TITOISM'

Stalin was afraid that others might follow Tito and find 'a national road to socialism'. He rid himself of most of the very men whom he had appointed to head the governments of his satellites:

▶ Dimitrov (Bulgaria) died in suspicious circumstances in 1949;

▶ Gomulka (Poland) and Dej (Rumania) were dismissed from their posts of First Secretaries of their local Parties;

▶ Anna Pauker (Rumania), Rajik (Hungary), Slansky and Clementis (both of Czechoslovakia) were all executed by the MVD between 1949 and 1952;

▶ Prime Minister Nagy (Hungary) was on holiday in Switzerland. He resigned by phone.

All these former leaders were replaced by lesser-known Russian nominees and trusted Stalinists.

30.4 Expressions of Anti-Russian Feeling

THE FIRST ANTI-RUSSIAN RISINGS, 1953

In March 1953 Stalin and the Stalinist leader of Czechoslovakia died at about the same time. These deaths were the signal for a series of anti-Russian risings in Eastern Europe. (See Fig. 30.4.)

Fig. 30.4 'Colonial' revolutions against Russia

East Germany

The People's Democratic Republic was set up in 1949; a Stalinist, Ulbricht, headed the government.

Russia took material and machinery worth £7 billion to help in its own rebuilding. East Germany remained much poorer than West Germany, which was helped by Marshall Aid. Wages were very low while prices rose. Each month a flood of refugees fled to the West.

In May 1953, the government announced that while wages would remain the same, every worker had to produce 10 per cent more than in the previous year. On 16 June 1953,

building workers went on strike. In the evening a mass of workers marched through the streets of East Berlin demanding 'bread and freedom'. On 17 June 1953, over 100,000 people crowded the streets of East Berlin demanding freedom and improved living standards.

The government's response was to send military police to disperse the crowds. When they failed, Russian tanks were brought out. By nightfall the streets were cleared. However, during the next two days there were anti-communist demonstrations in over 300 villages and towns. Prisons were attacked and people released. Nevertheless, within a few days the power of the Russian-supported army and police restored order. East Germany sank back under the rule of its unpopular government.

Czechoslovakia

Workers in the Skoda factory in Pilsen rioted and demanded freedom and better living standards. But they were quickly crushed.

A MORE SERIOUS UPRISING, 1956

Khrushchev's condemnation of Stalin (see Unit 29) led to two serious challenges to Russian control of Eastern Europe.

Poland

On 28 June 1956 car workers at Poznan went on strike for better wages and living conditions. This strike, which gathered increasing support, quickly became a political demonstration. The crowds in various towns chanted anti-Russian and anti-Party slogans. Pitched battles were fought with police, troops and tanks; 60 people died.

The Russians were forced to make some concessions:

▶ Gomulka was restored as Party Secretary;

▶ he was allowed to follow a more 'liberal' line. However, Gomulka was careful not to break with Russia over foreign policy as laid down by the Warsaw Pact (see Unit 29).

Hungary

News of the Polish rising led to a similar rising in Hungary. The Hungarians, traditionally anti-Russian, demanded:

▶ a better standard of living;

▶ an end to the rule by Rakósi, the Party Secretary who had tied Hungary to Russia economically and politically;

▶ the abolition of the secret police which terrorized the people.

In July 1956 the Russians deposed Rakósi, hoping that this would be enough to satisfy the Hungarians. However, news that Gomulka was back in power in Poland led to Hungarian demands that Imre Nagy should be appointed Prime Minister. Students demonstrated in Budapest in favour of Nagy. Party Secretary Gero agreed to his appointment.

Nagy announced negotiations to get the Russians out of Hungary, and on 26 October 1956 Russian tanks and troops left Budapest, where they had killed over 600 people.

New freedoms were given to press, radio and television. Politicians were allowed to form non-communist parties. Statues of Stalin were smashed, hundreds of secret police were lynched.

Nagy announced that Hungary was going to withdraw from the Warsaw Pact and would become a 'neutralist' state with no allegiance to East or West. The Russians then sent their troops and tanks back into Budapest to crush the revolution. On 4 November Budapest was bombed from the air. Artillery and tanks fired on the rebel-held radio stations, newspaper offices and university. About 20,000 Hungarians were killed in ten days, and a further 200,000 Hungarians fled to Austria.

Nagy took refuge in the Yugoslav Embassy in Budapest. When all resistance was over, he and his colleagues surrendered to the government of János Kádár, who had come back with the Russian tanks. Kádár promised Nagy his freedom. But he was kidnapped, taken to Russia and executed in 1958. Khrushchev had a Stalin-like attitude towards some dissidents.

CZECHOSLOVAKIA'S 'COMMUNISM WITH A HUMAN FACE', 1968

In 1953 there was a small rising in Pilsen (see above). In 1956, in the wake of the Twentieth Party Congress, Gottwald's police were denounced and political prisoners freed. But under the hardline President Novotny, Czechoslovakia continued to be a Stalinist-like state.

In 1967 Dubček became Party Secretary. He took a 'liberal' line towards workers' demands for an increased supply of consumer goods and intellectuals' demands for greater freedom of expression and an end to censorship.

In January 1968 Novotny was forced to resign. The new President, Svoboda, co-operated with Dubček to bring in major reforms:

▶ public meetings were allowed;
▶ political parties could be formed;
▶ press censorship was abolished;
▶ local assemblies in Bohemia and Slovakia were given greater powers;
▶ political prisoners were released;
▶ travel outside the country was allowed;
▶ the activities of the secret police were limited.

Dubček began negotiating a treaty with West Germany.

The Russians then took action. On 20 August 1968 Russian troops and tanks, supported by forces from all the Warsaw Pact countries, invaded Czechoslovakia. They entered all the main cities and quickly took control. Resistance, particularly in Prague, was strong - but of little value against the tanks and troops. Dubček was arrested and taken to Moscow.

President Svoboda refused to negotiate with the Russians without Dubček. Both 'liberals' then negotiated with the Russians, who forced the Czechs to give up most of their reforms and to allow Russian troops to stay in Czechoslovakia.

Dubček's men were removed from office. In 1970 an anti-Dubček government, under Husak, was in power.

RUMANIA: A SPECIAL CASE

In 1941 a pro-Nazi government was in power. In 1944 Rumania was 'liberated' by the Red Army and a communist-dominated government installed in power.

Between 1949 and 1952 the Rumanian Communist Party was purged by Stalin's agents. Anna Pauker, party leader, was executed.

The economy was run in Russia's interests until 1956, when Khrushchev abolished a series of trade agreements inside the Warsaw Pact countries. Rumania's leaders rejected the 'inferior' position which Russia wished Rumania to occupy under Comecon's plans. They would not agree to abandon some industries which might operate more cheaply elsewhere inside Comecon countries. In 1963 Rumania carried this independent attitude to a Titoist extreme by signing a trade treaty with the USA. In the 1970s Russia wanted the Warsaw Pact countries to agree to an extension of that Pact to include countries in the Far East such as Vietnam. This would have involved Eastern European forces in Russia's quarrel with China. Rumania led the opposition to this suggestion.

But Rumania still followed, internally, an authoritarian, almost Stalin-like policy. It was only in her relations with Russia that she appeared to be 'liberal'.

HUNGARY: 'PEOPLE'S CAPITALISM', 1956-86

Kádár remained in power after 1956 (see above). He persuaded the Soviet Union to end its pillaging of his country's economy and to increase its aid to help its economic development. By 1963 Hungarian real income had risen by 36 per cent over that of 1956.

In 1965, Kádár introduced a series of economic reforms:

▶ state investment was made on the basis of profitability rather than of Party ideology;
▶ foreign investment was encouraged;
▶ peasants were allowed to spend more time on their private plots. By 1986 some 30 per cent of agricultural output came from such profit-making private plots.

The result was a rise in living standards as shown by the quantity and quality of food, clothing and cars available to the people, and the development of private initiative, self-improvement and self-enrichment. Workers were encouraged to work overtime and professional people were allowed to have private practices – as doctors, lawyers, accountants and so on.

Soviet observers feared that the development of this 'mixed economy' would affect the foundations of the totalitarian economic and social structure. However, there was no evidence that the Hungarians sought the overthrow of the system which provided them with the highest living standard in Eastern Europe in 1986.

POLAND, 1970–86

In 1970 the Russians could congratulate themselves on the removal of Dubček from power in Czechoslovakia. But in that year Poland became a centre of discontent. Younger people were dissatisfied with the crushing burden of bureaucracy and officialdom. Even the controlled press demanded more freedom.

The economy was in a poor condition. State planning led to the production of goods for which there was no demand. There was, on the other hand, a serious shortage of everyday goods. Low agricultural production led to the need to import food from Russia, Canada, the USA and West Germany. Food shortages and rationing were commonplace. Government revenue did not meet government's costs.

In December 1970 the government announced price rises in food, fuel and clothing, ranging from 8 to 60 per cent. This led to widespread rioting.

On December 15 rioters set fire to the Party headquarters at Gdansk. Rioting spread to other industrial centres, and heavy fighting took place with police and the army.

Gomulka was replaced by Gierek. He cancelled many of the recent decisions: food prices were frozen for two years, and large wage increases were ordered for the lower-paid. Gomulka toured the country inviting discussions of the faults of Polish society.

The Church played an active role in these discussions, denouncing methods used by hard-liners to put down discontent. It also demanded democratic freedom of discussion in the press and throughout the country.

Gierek's government in Poland, 1971-8

Younger and more democratic people were given positions in state organizations – many of them not even being Party members. Industry was given more freedom; productivity improved. Western firms were allowed to open factories in Poland while Polish firms borrowed Western capital to help their development.

In 1973 real wages rose by 24 per cent, industrial production by 33 per cent and agricultural production by 19 per cent.

In 1976 the government tried, again, to increase basic prices. This led to widespread resistance, and the government was forced to modify its demands.

In October 1978 Cardinal Wojtyla, Archbishop of Cracow, was elected Pope of the Catholic Church. He took the name of Pope John Paul II.

Poland, Catholic or communist?

In May 1935 Laval of France asked Stalin to allow more freedom for Catholics living in Russia. This, said Laval, would please the Pope. Stalin's reply was: 'The Pope! How many divisions has he got?'

In various parts of the world the Catholic Church has emerged as a centre of opposition to tyranny. This has been clear in Poland since 1978.

The election of Pope John Paul II led to the formation of a number of free trade unions by Polish workers under the general heading of Solidarity. It was the Solidarity movement which led the campaigns for freedom, better wages and working conditions in Poland from 1978.

This created a series of problems for the Polish and Russian governments. How far could democratic freedom (of press, trade unions and expression) be allowed by a totalitarian system? How far could a Communist government go in allowing the powerful Catholic Church to have the freedoms it demanded – to preach, teach in its own schools and universities and to have its own uncensored newspapers?

When the demands of some extremists in Solidarity showed the Poles might be led to demand free elections and freedom to form non-communist political parties, the Russians intervened. General Jaruzelski was appointed as head of government; martial law imposed. Solidarity leaders were arrested or driven in to hiding and Solidarity was banned.

In 1986 the position in Poland was unclear. Former Solidarity leader Lech Walesa was freed and allowed to return to his workplace in the Gdansk dockyard. But Solidarity was not re-established in spite of Church demands. Only the future would tell what was to happen in Poland.

In November 1983, the government announced that, in the New Year (1984), food prices would have to be increased. It was such increases which had led to rioting in 1970 and in 1976 (see above). It is important to note that, in November 1983, the government promised that there would be 'more consultations' before the price rises were finalised in 1984. Some said that this showed that the government had learnt a lesson from the unrest led by Solidarity; others believed that 'more consultations' would prove to be worth nothing.

For recent developments in Eastern Europe see Unit 41.

Unit 30 Summary

▶ Poland: imposition of communism, 1945.
▶ Red Army 'liberation' of Rumania, Bulgaria and Hungary.
▶ People's Democracy in Albania and Yugoslavia.
▶ Russia's 'Satellite' empire.
▶ Anti-Russian risings in Eastern Europe.

31 WESTERN EUROPEAN INTEGRATION

 **The Issues to be Studied**

▶ European unity.
▶ German recovery.
▶ The growth of friendship between France and Germany which owed much to the work of Adenauer of Germany and de Gaulle of France.

 **31.1 European Unity: Early Attempts**

WHY SHOULD EUROPEAN COUNTRIES COME CLOSER TOGETHER IN 1945?

In 1939 Europe was the centre of the world's affairs. In 1945 it was a devastated no-man's land between two super powers. There were 25 million people living in refugee camps, or cellars of bombed out buildings; commerce, industry and transport had been almost destroyed. No country could rebuild on its own. Europe had to develop as 'the European family', as Churchill said.

Europe had only 2 per cent of the world's land surface. But it had 10 per cent of the world's population, which was the most literate, the most experienced in trade and industry, and from a common cultural background.

The various states could form the richest and most powerful bloc in the world. However, without unity, Europe would become just a collection of semi-important states squeezed between Russia and the USA.

A MILITARY AND DEFENCE PATH TOWARDS CLOSER UNITY

In 1947 Britain and France signed the Treaty of Dunkirk, aimed against the revival of German power. In March 1948 the Dunkirk powers were joined by the Benelux countries in the Treaty of Brussels against Germany and Russia.

In April 1949 the five Brussels powers allied with seven other nations to form NATO (Unit 28). For those seeking to bring about 'a United States of Europe', the formation of NATO was an important step, because the alliance had a close political structure, and its members put part of their national forces under international commands. Each country gave up part of its sovereignty to a supra-national (or above-nation) authority.

The European Defence Community, 1952

In May 1949 the German Federal Republic was set up (see Unit 28). By 1952 the West Germans were rebuilding their economy. For European statesmen this raised some problems:
▶ Was an increasingly rich Germany to be excluded from contributing to the cost of Europe's defence against Russia?
▶ Could Germany be allowed to re-arm as part of that contribution towards Europe's defence?

French fears of Germany led them to oppose German rearmament. In 1951 Pléven of France proposed the formation of a European army, including German troops. Britain refused to pool her forces in this international army. Because of the British refusal, the French vetoed their own plan, fearing Germany might become the dominant power in a non-British European army.

The European Defence Community, which might have provided a major push towards closer unity, did not live up to expectations. Britain, for her own reasons, and France, for her own reasons, were still hesitant about European unity.

The Western European Union, 1954

This alliance of Britain, France, West Germany and the Benelux states allowed Germany to become a member of NATO and to control her own conventional weapons. This showed that the various nations could work together and that Germany could become part of a 'United Europe'.

AN ECONOMIC ROAD TOWARDS CLOSER UNITY

Until 1947 aid to Europe was provided by UNRRA, and in 1947 the Marshall Plan was proposed (see Unit 28). In 1948 16 countries set up the OEEC (Unit 28) with West Germany as an associate member. For those seeking a 'United States of Europe' the formation of OEEC was an important step. It had a permanent administrative staff and a number of specialist advisory committees to deal with co-operation in trade, agriculture, power supplies, fisheries and transport. It also distributed the billions of dollars of aid and helped bring about the economic rebirth which could not have been achieved by individual countries working alone.

However, the OEEC was limited by national sovereignty. Each decision by OEEC had to be approved by the individual governments.

A POLITICAL PATH TOWARDS CLOSER UNITY

In 1945 Britain was, economically and politically, the most important of the European states. Unconquered for centuries, she had, for a time, stood alone against Hitler, provided a home for governments-in-exile and aid to resistance movements.

Churchill, even after July 1945, was accepted as the most important European statesman. In 1946 at Zurich, Churchill called for the re-creation of 'the European family... with a structure under which it can dwell... a kind of United States of Europe.'

In May 1948 political leaders from ten European states met at The Hague and produced a plan for a European parliament. Many wanted this to be a true parliament, its members elected directly by the people. But in 1948 Britain, in particular, was unwilling to see the creation of such an important body. What powers might it demand? Would it become a too powerful rival for the national parliaments? Would it lead to the creation of a European Cabinet, a government of Europe?

The Council of Europe was the weak result. Members were appointed by national parliaments. It met three or four times a year at Strasbourg, but it had no powers to propose legislation; power remained with the individual parliaments. This made it little more than a debating society.

Britain, France, the Benelux countries, Norway, Denmark, Sweden, Italy and Eire were the original members of the Council. Later Greece, Turkey, Iceland, Austria, Cyprus and West Germany joined.

THE FUNCTIONALIST ROAD TO UNITY

Those who believed in European unity were disappointed with the failure to unite the continent. However, they could point to some successful attempts at closer unity.

In 1944 the exiled governments of Belgium, the Netherlands (Holland) and Luxembourg agreed to form a customs union, Benelux. This came into being in 1947. It started by being an agreement on tariffs; it went on to develop closer economic integration between the three states. In 1960 they set up the Economic Union allowing the free movement of people, capital and goods between the three states. People of three countries could live almost as one to get the benefits of economic unity.

In 1948 the OEEC also showed that economic benefits brought states together.

Leaders from several countries saw that unity might be achieved by joining the nations in an ever-increasing number of specialist organizations. This functionalist approach was advocated by Monnet of France ('the father of the Common Market'), Spaak (Belgium), Adenauer (Germany) and de Gasperi (Italy).

The first successful project took its name from the French Minister who first proposed it—Robert Schuman.

31.2 Internationalism

THE SCHUMAN PLAN, 1950

Schuman proposed that France and Germany should pool their resources in coal and steel under a joint authority independent of the governments of both countries. Other nations could be invited to join.

France would benefit. She could allow the development of the great industrial areas of the Ruhr and the Saar, without fearing that they would supply arms against France as they had done in the past.

Europe would benefit. The larger coal and steel industries of the 'community' would be more efficient. The larger market would encourage the use of the most up to date methods; larger, more efficient units could be created and the inefficient forced to modernize or to go out of business.

Schuman hoped that Britain would join; she was the largest coal producer in Europe and the second largest producer of steel. But Britain was afraid of the powers to be given to the controlling commission (see below). In 1951 a Labour government rejected an invitation to the discussions; in 1952 Conservatives, under Churchill, the 'great European', refused to join the new community which came into being in July 1952.

THE EUROPEAN COAL AND STEEL COMMUNITY (ECSC)

France, Italy, West Germany and the Benelux countries were the members of this Community. The High Authority was at the head of the Community. Its nine experts were appointed by the six governments for a period of six years. Once appointed, they were not responsible to the governments as ministers would be. They had to think as 'members of a community' and not as Germans or Frenchmen.

A permanent secretariat administered the Authority's orders. A Court of Justice of seven international lawyers was set up as a Court of Appeal against decisions of the Authority. A Consultative Assembly was made up of the representatives of the six countries at the Council of Europe. This could hand on recommendations to the Authority. It could also dismiss the Authority—by a two thirds majority. A Consultative Committee of 51 delegates of employers and workers in heavy industry would represent their interests to the High Authority.

The significance and success of the ECSC

The High Authority was a major innovation. It had real international control. Each member-state of the Community handed over to the Authority its sovereign right to control its coal and steel industries. The Authority had the right to interfere in the economic life of the countries involved:

it could close down a section of an industry in one state and spend money on the development of a section in another. It would be guided not by national but by Community interests;

it could rule as illegal the subsidy given to the coal or

steel industry of a member government if it gave the industry of the state involved an unfair advantage.

The Authority had its own income from dues paid to it by the industries involved, not by the governments. Foreign and Economic Ministers from the member-states were forced to consult and work closely with the Authority. Their Council of Ministers could not block Authority decisions.

Jean Monnet was the Authority's first chairman. The success of the Community was very evident: it stimulated output in steel, it helped old-fashioned firms to modernize, and it widened its scope to take into account the housing and social security for workers in the heavy industries. As people moved freely across national boundaries, there had to be supra-national decisions about housing and welfare benefits.

Until 1956 the Authority stimulated coal output to meet growing demand. In 1956 coal was hit by competition from cheap oil and natural gas. The Authority lessened the hardship that the fall in coal production caused. It provided aid to depressed areas affected by the closure of uneconomic pits.

EURATOM

Russia and the USA could afford the high costs of nuclear research. No independent European country could. Only through co-operative action could European countries keep pace with the super powers. Britain was the most advanced European state in this field. But, as with the ECSC, Britain refused to co-operate with Europe.

In 1957 the six members of the ECSC set up the European Atomic Energy Community (Euratom). This was a High Authority on the ECSC model. It had powers to:

▶ hold stocks of fissile material;
▶ set up reactors;
▶ promote research into the peaceful uses of atomic power.

This Authority was advised by:

▶ a Council of Ministers;
▶ a scientific and technical committee;
▶ a social and economic committee.

▰ 31.3 Konrad Adenauer and the German 'Economic Miracle'

Adenauer was born in 1876 and became a lawyer in Cologne. He was Lord Mayor of Cologne, 1917–33, a member of the Catholic Centre Party, but was dismissed by the Nazis when Hitler came to power (see Unit 15). He made little secret of his dislike of the Nazis. He was imprisoned for short periods in 1933 and 1944, when he was sent to a concentration camp.

In 1945 he became Lord Mayor of Cologne after Germany's defeat. However, in 1946 the Allied Military Government dismissed him.

Adenauer was a founder-member of the Christian Democratic Union, a conservative party, and its president in the British zone, 1946–8. In 1948–9 he represented North Rhine Westphalia in the parliamentary council of the three Western zones and was president of the council for most of this period. In 1949 the Western Allies created the Federal Republic (see Unit 28).

In the elections of August 1949 Adenauer's party won the most seats in the Bundestag. He formed a coalition with other conservative parties, the main one being the Christian Social Union. The CDU-CSU coalition provided a strong and stable government. The opposition was led by the Social Democrats.

ADENAUER'S AIMS

Adenauer wanted to create a stable and democratic Germany. This was no easy task, because:

▶ Germany had had very little experience of democracy. There was no guarantee that Adenauer would be more successful than the politicians of Weimar had been after 1919;
▶ the majority of adult Germans had co-operated with the Nazis; many had been actively working for them. There was no guarantee that they would co-operate with a less exciting form of government.

Adenauer also wanted to restore the German economy so that the people could enjoy a decent standard of living. This was no easy task in war-devastated Germany, where the millions of homeless were increased by the flow of refugees from the east. In 1949 there were some 15 million unemployed in West Germany. To get these back to work would call for 'a miracle'.

He aimed to get Germany accepted in the 'concert of powers': this was no easy task, with the memories of the war still fresh and with the truth about concentration camps and the slaughter of 6 million Jews becoming clearer as time went on.

He also aimed to re-unite divided Germany and to end the traditional hostility between France and Germany, a difficult task following the war in which the French had suffered conquest and occupation.

POLITICAL STABILITY

Extremist parties were banned. A Nazi-style Socialist Reich Party had recruited many ex-Nazis. Adenauer abolished this and similar parties. Werner Naumann recruited ex-soldiers into a Freikorps; he was arrested and his organization made illegal. In 1956 the Communist Party was banned. Adenauer then pushed through an electoral law: no party could gain seats in the Bundestag unless it had 5 per cent of the national vote. This prevented the rise of a mass of local parties.

Democratic measures?

Some of Adenauer's actions appeared to be autocratic. Was it 'democratic' to make extremist parties illegal? However, Adenauer argued that he had to avoid the mistakes of the Weimar Republic. This democracy had been overthrown because it could not produce a stable government.

THE GERMAN ECONOMY AND THE 'ECONOMIC MIRACLE'

Evidence of success

Adenauer's government supervised the rebuilding of Germany. Work was found for the unemployed, for refugees from the east. In the 1960s Germany faced a labour shortage. Foreign workers, many from Turkey, were drawn to work in prosperous Germany.

Reasons for success

▶ Allied investments, particularly Marshall Aid, provided the stimulus to the rebuilding of West Germany.
▶ Wartime destruction created the need for new building—industrially and commercially. The West Germans therefore had the most modern and efficient industry.
▶ The Minister for Economic Affairs, Erhard, supervised the 'economic miracle'. Low interest rates stimulated investment; government aid was provided to ensure industrial, commercial and social investment (e.g. schools and universities).
▶ German workers had a tradition for hard work. They helped German recovery by good labour relations and willingness to accept low wage increases negotiated by their industrial unions.
▶ For several years the Germans spent little on armaments. This released resources for industrial investment.

Enjoying the miracle

By 1963, when Adenauer retired, the German standard of living was the highest in Europe. West Germany and

Britain have roughly the same population. By 1963 Germany was building twice as many houses as Britain. Germans had higher wages, shorter working hours, higher pensions, better social benefits and longer holidays than British workers.

GETTING GERMANY ACCEPTED

Adenauer ensured German participation in:
▶ NATO (see Unit 28);
▶ OECC (see Unit 28);
▶ ECSC (see above);
▶ EDC (see above);
▶ Euratom (see above);
▶ EEC (see below).

He lost some support, particularly among trade unionists when, in 1957, he insisted on military conscription, the result of German participation in European defence arrangements.

TO RE-UNITE GERMANY

In 1955 Adenauer visited Moscow and arranged for the repatriation of German prisoners still held in the Soviet Union.

As Foreign Minister (as well as Chancellor) until 1955, Adenauer campaigned for the unification of Germany. At the same time he insisted on West German participation in Western economic political and military systems (above).

The Russians refused to talk of unification while West Germany was, in their eyes, 'the creature of the USA'. Adenauer failed in this part of his policy.

TO CREATE A FRANCO-GERMAN UNDERSTANDING

Germany worked closely with France in the various political, military and economic systems which we have so far examined. Adenauer wanted to build still closer relations with France. In March 1950 he called for economic union between France and Germany—before the ECSC had been formed, and in September 1958 he met President de Gaulle. During 1958–62 Adenauer ensured that, at meetings of Ministers of the EEC countries, Germany normally supported de Gaulle. He did not oppose de Gaulle's veto on Britain's application to join the EEC in 1962 (see below).

In January 1963 relations between France and Germany reached their high point with the signing of the Treaty of Co-operation. In this treaty the traditional enemies agreed:
▶ on exchanges in the field of education and youth so that young people would get to know each other better;
▶ that their foreign policies would follow the same line.

GROWING UNPOPULARITY, 1963

By 1963, the 'economic miracle' seemed to have run out of steam. Europe was suffering an economic recession. Germans blamed their government for the slow economic growth.

A new, younger breed of politicians, journalists and voters resented Adenauer's autocratic behaviour. They wanted their politicians to be more under popular control. Specific incidents such as his attempt to curb the activities of the hostile paper, *Der Spiegel*, raised doubts about his belief in democracy.

Some people resented Germany's being France's junior partner in the EEC; others were annoyed at his hostile attitude to Willy Brandt, the Mayor of West Berlin and a member of the Socialist party. Some thought that Brandt might be able to work out a plan for German re-unification with the Russians.

Adenauer retired in October 1963.

▇ 31.4 The European Economic Community (EEC)

SETTING IT UP, 1955–7

The success of the ECSC led to demands for ways of improving this economic union. Paul-Henri Spaak, Foreign Minister of Belgium, was giving the task of working out plans for a wider economic union. Meetings were held at Messina in Italy, and in 1956 the Spaak Committee completed its work.

On 25 March 1957 the Treaty of Rome set up the European Economic Community. The 'Six' Community countries were Belgium, France, Holland, Italy, Luxembourg and West Germany.

THE IMMEDIATE AIMS OF THE EEC

It was a customs union; by 1967 all tariff barriers between member states would be abolished. There would be a free movement of capital, labour and goods inside the Community. There would be a uniform and low external tariff on goods coming into the Community. To ensure that there were no hidden tariffs or subsidies, the central authority would have to interfere in the social and economic policies of the member countries.

Member states would be handing over more and more sovereignty to a supra-national organization. This, claimed some, would lead to political unity.

THE STRUCTURES OF THE EEC

The European Commission

The Commission runs the Community's day-to-day business. Initially it had nine members appointed by the governments of the member states but owing them no responsibility. Its first chairman was a German, Walter Hallstein.

The Commission was not as powerful an Authority as that of the ECSC. Its decisions had to be approved by the Council of Ministers and, thus, by the individual governments. However, its activities were much broader than that of the Authority of the ECSC. In 1967 it was agreed to merge the ECSC and Euratom in the EEC.

The Council of Ministers

Member states sent their foreign, finance or agricultural ministers, depending on the issues being discussed. The Council had to approve Commission decisions.

The Court of Justice and the Assembly coincided with those of the ECSC and Euratom, and the final merger of all three Communities in 1967 was an indication of the creation of a European Community.

THE ADVANTAGES OF THE EEC

A vast new market had a population of 170 million, so Europe's resources could be used more efficiently.

An Investment Bank with a fund of one billion dollars was set up to help the development of the more backward regions of the Community, such as southern Italy and the declining industrial areas like the Ruhr and southern Belgium.

A Common Fund was set up to help the movement of labour and to provide migrant workers with social security benefits.

An Overseas Development Fund was set up to provide investment in the overseas dependencies of the six member states.

The Community provided a third force in world politics—dependent on neither Russia nor the USA.

THE SUCCESS OF THE EEC

Trade between member states increased rapidly. In 1960–1 it increased by 29 per cent. Trade barriers were lowered, leading to lower prices. Common prices were fixed for agricultural products. Living standards improved.

The German mark became the world's leading currency and it was to Germany that the world's financiers turned for help in periods of crisis in 1968, 1974 and 1978.

DIFFICULTIES

The Common Agricultural Policy (CAP) caused problems— see below.

Areas furthest away from the centre of the Community gained least and became relatively poorer.

31.5 Britain and the EEC, 1955–62

Britain had been invited to the Messina talks (see above). The six members of the ECSC sent senior ministers; Britain only sent a second-grade civil servant. Britain believed the talks would fail.

Britain welcomed the customs union and the abolition of tariffs between member states. She would be willing to join in such a free trade scheme, but she could not join the proposed EEC.

About half of Britain's trade was done with the Commonwealth countries. This pattern could not be easily fitted into the tightly-knit system proposed for the EEC. Also, membership of the EEC leads to a loss of sovereignty, of control of one's own affairs. Britain was opposed to giving up such control.

The Common Agricultural Policy would lead to a rise in British food prices. In addition, Britain already had its depressed areas, in Scotland, Northern Ireland, the North-East and Wales. It was feared that these, being furthest away from the centre of the Community, would suffer even more rapid decline. Hugh Gaitskell, leader of the Opposition Labour Party, declared that to join the EEC would be to reject 'a thousand years of British history'. Isolationism was strong in Britain.

THE EUROPEAN FREE TRADE ASSOCIATION

Britain appreciated the benefits of industrial free trade. While the Messina talks were going on, she proposed the setting-up of a free trade area with no internal tariff barriers. She proposed that the EEC could be treated as a single-member state of such a free trade area. Britain wanted to exclude agricultural goods from the proposed free trade area—because of the cheap food imports she received from New Zealand and Australia. She proposed that there should be no common external tariff—so that she could maintain her imperial preference system. There would be no Commission or High Authority and no loss of sovereignty.

The EEC rejected these attempts to 'sabotage Europe'. In December 1959 Britain, Norway, Sweden, Denmark, Portugal, Austria and Switzerland formed the European Free Trade Association (EFTA).

This was a limited success. It increased trade between the members. But its population was much smaller than that of the EEC—and was not as rich. It was also a less natural and less compact unit. Its success, even limited, depended on Britain, whose trade with EEC countries increased faster than did her trade with EFTA countries.

BRITAIN TRIES TO JOIN THE EEC, 1961–2
(Fig. 31.4)

The evident success of the EEC (see above) led many in Britain to wish that Britain would become a member. EEC countries were becoming richer more quickly than was Britain. Living standards were higher in Europe.

In 1961 Prime Minister Macmillan appointed Edward Heath to lead the British negotiating team. He tried to get the EEC countries to agree to Britain's right to safeguard her special interests—Commonwealth trade. He wanted adjustments in the Common Agricultural Policy. He also

Fig. 31.4 Macmillan tried to change EEC rules

wanted to make arrangements to cater for the other EFTA countries.

While these negotiations were going on Macmillan met President Kennedy and he arranged an Anglo–US arms deal. The USA would provide Britain with Polaris nuclear submarines.

General de Gaulle saw this as a sign of Britain's dependence on the USA. De Gaulle feared that Britain might replace France as leader of the EEC and change the organization. He announced a veto on the British application. None of the other EEC states challenged the President's power.

31.6 De Gaulle

Charles de Gaulle was born in 1890 and entered the military academy at St Cyr in 1910. At 21 he was commissioned in the 33rd Infantry Regiment. His commanding officer was Colonel Pétain (see Unit 9). In 1914–8, at Verdun, he was captured by the Germans. After the armistice he went back to St Cyr as professor of military history before being sent to the French staff college, where he became aide to Pétain, the commander-in-chief.

In 1932 he became general secretary of the Committee of National Defence. He campaigned for a change in military thinking, because the next war would be a mechanized war; tanks would be more important than old-fashioned infantry-men. That war would also be a war of movement; there would be no place in it for such massive defences as the Maginot Line. The French ignored his work; Guderian, of Germany, profited from it and became an outstanding tank commander.

CAREER DURING THE SECOND WORLD WAR

In 1937 de Gaulle was given command of the 507th Regiment of Tanks, rising to become colonel and commander of the tank brigade of the 5th Lorraine Army. On 15 May 1940 he became brigadier general in command of the 4th Armoured Division. He tried to persuade Reynaud and Weygand to allow him to defend the Marne, the Seine or Paris. But the government had decided to capitulate (see Unit 25).

De Gaulle escaped to London, set up a French National Committee and assumed the title of leader of all Free French people. He organized a French army and navy in Britain. He failed to seize Dakar, but brought Chad and French Equatorial Africa over to the Allies. He was commander-in-chief of the Fighting French Forces and, after 1943, President of the Committee for National Liberation.

Churchill and Roosevelt did not invite him to any of the

wartime conferences (see Unit 26). The Allies allowed him to lead the force into liberated Paris, where he became Head of the French Provisional Government in 1944, and Chief of the Armed Forces.

POST-WAR CAREER

The elections of 1945 confirmed him as President of the government, Minister of National Defence and head of the armies. He resigned in 1946 because the politicians could not reach agreement about the future for French industry and economy. In 1947 he founded the Rassemblément du Peuple Français, a right-wing movement for the re-generation of France, rather than an ordinary political party. It believed in strong government, sharing de Gaulle's belief that the President should have very great powers. He withdrew from the RPF in 1953 and in 1956 it lost most of its seats.

THE 1958 CRISIS

In 1958 France was in a political crisis. Since 1946 there had been 22 short-lived governments, none able to deal with France's problems. She had lost her empire in Indo-China in 1954. In May 1958 French settlers in Algeria rebelled because of the tottering French government's inability to defeat the Muslim rebels who wanted Algerian inde-pendence. With the help of the army they set up a Committee of Public Safety in Algiers. They spread the rumour that paratroopers were going to make an airborne assault on Paris to overthrow the government.

Many people thought de Gaulle could save the country:
▶ the army thought that he would put down the Algerian Muslims and save it from being shamed as in Indo-China;
▶ the French settlers thought that he would help the army put down the Muslims and preserve a French Algeria;
▶ French people hoped that, while doing his colonial 'trick' he would provide political stability at home. They were tired of the too frequent changes in governments.

THE FIFTH REPUBLIC

When he came back from retirement, de Gaulle became Prime Minister only on condition that he was given a free hand to take drastic measures to restore the French economy and secure acceptance of his policies by referendum.

A new constitution was promulgated for a Fifth Republic. The President, elected by direct popular elections after 1962, could dissolve the Assembly and rule by decree in times of crisis. This would provide France with the much-needed 'strong government' so desired by the RPF, so lacking since 1946 (see above). The Prime Minister was to be appointed by the President, although he had to be responsible to the Assembly. Ministers appointed by the President could not be members of the Assembly. This resembled the US system (see Unit 7).

A referendum approved the new Constitution. In the elections which followed, the Socialists won only 40 seats and the Communists only 10. The new Gaullist Union won 188 seats and had the support of several right-wing groups.

In January 1959 de Gaulle became President. He appointed Michel Debré as Prime Minister; in 1962 he was succeeded by M. Pompidou, who became President in succession to de Gaulle in 1969.

HIS ALGERIAN POLICY

Once in power, de Gaulle began negotiations with the Muslim rebels.

Colonists and dissatisfied army officers formed the Organisation de L'Armée Secrète (OAS), an extreme right-wing group. Using terrorist methods they tried to retain French hold on Algeria, to assassinate de Gaulle (the 'great traitor') and gain influence for their kind. However, de Gaulle ignored these attempts at terrorism. He made peace with the Algerian Muslims in 1962 (see Unit 37).

HIS IMPERIAL POLICY

In 1958 de Gaulle offered the states of French Africa the choice of independence or of being associated with France in the French Community. The Community gave them self-government, but France had some control of their foreign policies. France provided aid to former colonies.

By 1960 the whole of the French African Empire had chosen independence. France would have no more costly colonial wars.

HIS FOREIGN POLICY

De Gaulle distrusted the USA and Britain because of his wartime experiences. He insisted on an independent French policy. This led to:
▶ withdrawal from NATO;
▶ the creation of a French nuclear force;
▶ opposition to British entry into the EEC;
▶ good relations with Russia, Eastern Europe and China;
▶ refusal to sign the Test Ban Treaty of 1963.

HIS INTERNAL POLICY

The government controlled the radio and television. This ensured control of news items. De Gaulle held frequent referendums to get popular approval for his policies.

He revalued the franc. The end of the outflow of money to fight colonial wars made France economically stronger. In 1963 the French balance of payments problem was finally solved. France began to accumulate huge reserves of gold, industrial production increased; wages and prices were government-controlled, to prevent inflation.

1968, THE YEAR OF CRISIS

Russia's attack on Czechoslovakia (see Unit 30) showed that there was a good reason to fear Russian aggression. De Gaulle's confidence that he could deal with Russia seemed misplaced.

In May 1968 students rose in rebellion, largely because of the inefficient university system. This snowballed into a general rising. Workers took over factories. They had be-come increasingly dissatisfied with wage control. Rioters took over the streets. Some of these were 'out' against government control of the media; others because of de Gaulle's right wing and authoritarian system of government.

De Gaulle showed courage and self-confidence in view of this widespread hostility:
▶ he appealed on television for national unity;
▶ he promised workers some social reforms and gained their support against the extreme left-wing students;
▶ he called a snap election and destroyed the opposition in the Assembly. He appeared to be stronger than ever.

But there was a third crisis in the autumn of 1968. The concessions over wages and social reform had to be paid for. The first result was an adverse balance of payments in the autumn of 1968. This led to an outflow of gold, and this, in turn, led to a run on the franc by foreign speculators. Many French people speculated against their own franc and bought the stable currency, the German mark.

De Gaulle had to ask for massive international loans to help him out. It seemed that he would have to devalue the franc. Rather than take this humiliating step he imposed severe restrictions at home. This created more industrial unrest and led to a further run on the franc.

1969, THE YEAR OF DEFEAT AND RESIGNATION

De Gaulle put his proposals to the people and, foolishly, turned the referendum into one of confidence in his government. He lost. And he resigned.

Gaullism lived on. In the ensuing election Pompidou, de Gaulle's 'man', won an overwhelming victory for the presidency.

31.7 The EEC, 1967–86

BRITAIN AND THE EEC, 1967

Labour's Prime Minister, Harold Wilson, and the Foreign Secretary, George Brown, campaigned throughout Europe to win support for a new application to join the EEC.

Once again de Gaulle vetoed the application, although Britain was prepared to enter without any of the pre-conditions on which Heath and Macmillan had insisted in 1961–2.

BRITAIN JOINS THE EEC, 1973

President Pompidou objected less to Britain's entry than had de Gaulle. Heath, now Prime Minister, made another application for membership.

On 1 January 1973 Britain, Denmark and Eire joined at the same time. The 'Six' became 'Nine'.

Norway, another member of the EFTA, held a referendum and the people rejected the idea of membership of the EEC.

Many people in Britain demanded a referendum, because:
▶ some objected to the loss of sovereignty;
▶ others feared a loss of jobs;
▶ others were opposed to the threat of regulation of wages, prices, working conditions and the like from Brussels which, they claimed, would lead to higher prices and a lowering of prosperity;
▶ trade unions came out against entry, claiming that the EEC was a producers' club with no benefit to workers.

In 1975 the new Labour government held a referendum and by a majority of two to one the British people came out in favour of Britain's continued membership of the EEC.

THE EEC 1973–86

In spite of the world recession following OPEC's increase in oil prices, the EEC continued to grow richer. Britain alone, because of internal policies, did not share fully in that increasing prosperity.

Greece, Spain and Portugal all became democracies and became members in January 1986.

Lack of progress

The EEC has not produced the political union for which its founders had hoped. France continued to 'go it alone' in defence. Britain, the only oil-bearing member of the Community, regarded the oil as 'her own' and not Community property. Also, almost all members squabbled over fishing rights. Germany, Belgium, France and Britain quarrelled over which of them should shut down steelworks as the world demand for steel slumped.

THE COMMON AGRICULTURAL POLICY

The aim of the policy is to make Europe self-sufficient in food as far as is possible. Farmers get a guaranteed and agreed price for their products, the price being fixed at an annual review by the Ministers of Agriculture of the member states.

The political influence of farmers in France, Germany and Holland is very strong. Their ministers have to try to get as high a price for their products as they can. This has led to massive over-production. There are 'mountains' of meat, butter and fruit, and 'lakes' of milk and wine held in storage. The cost of storage is high, taking about half the total cost of the CAP.

Food-importing countries—and especially Britain—resent this system which leads to higher prices and higher taxes.

A good deal of the surplus food produced each year is sold off at vastly-reduced prices to Russia and countries in Eastern Europe. While this does not do away with the 'mountains' or 'lakes', it causes resentment in Britain and the countries which pay most into the Agricultural Fund.

Attempts have been made to limit the money spent on food production. Britain, in particular, has called for an end to the system which encourages farmers to produce more, and more expensive, food. However, in spite of some verbal agreements at various ministerial meetings, the politicians of France, Germany, Ireland, Denmark and other food-producing countries are unwilling to risk the opposition of their farmer-voters. In 1986, in spite of some lowering of quotas for wheat output and milk production, the cost of the CAP threatens the EEC with bankruptcy. Only the future will show how this problem will be tackled: recent history suggests that the politicians will vote to increase the size of the CAP budget rather than vote for limitations on output and/or price levels.

THE EUROPEAN PARLIAMENT

Until 1978 the European Parliament had little power:
▶ its members were appointed by the member governments;
▶ it had little control over the Commission and the Council of Ministers;
▶ it was a mere debating chamber.

Not surprisingly, few eminent politicians sought to become members of the 'talking shop'.

However, in 1978 things changed. Each member state held elections for Members of the European Parliament (MEP). Each member state was allocated a number of seats depending on the size of population. Britain, for example, had 81 constituencies, as had France, Germany and Italy; the smaller countries got fewer seats. In France and Germany, but not in Britain, leading politicians became candidates and were elected.

In the European Parliament the MEPs sit in their political groupings: socialist, conservative, liberal and communist. They do not sit as British, French, German or whatever Members. They have already begun to demand that they should be treated as a true Parliament. This would give them powers over the Commission and the Council of Ministers. It is too soon to say what success they will have. It may be that this Parliament may see the next step being taken along the road to European integration.

For recent developments in the EEC see Unit 40.2.

Unit 31 Summary

▶ Formation of NATO, 1949.
▶ The OEEC: its aims.
▶ Increasing European co-operation.
▶ The German 'economic miracle'.
▶ Formation of the EEC, 1957.
▶ British membership of the EEC.

32 THE UNITED STATES OF AMERICA, 1945–88

32.1 Truman's Problems, Policies and Successes

THE EFFECTS OF THE WAR ON THE USA

After 1941 the USA was the 'arsenal of democracy'. Most Russian transport in 1941–5 was provided by the USA; Chiang's armies were equipped by America (see Unit 17); Britain received planes and all sorts of equipment; 16 million US servicemen fought throughout the world.

US workers had a vast increase in incomes. Trade unions were more important (see Unit 19). Black people and other minorities got jobs more easily and became more conscious of the need for social reform. American bankers became the world's bankers. Industry did not suffer from aerial bombing.

THE TRUMAN ADMINISTRATION, 1945–52

Truman had run a draper's shop in Kansas City until the low incomes of the US farmers drove him into bankruptcy. He was one of the millions who suffered from the depression in the 1920s.

He was 'taken up' by the political boss, Prendergast, who 'ruled' the Democrats in Missouri and got Truman elected as Senator in 1934. In 1944 he was a surprise choice for the Vice-Presidency, and in April 1945 Roosevelt's sudden death brought him to the Presidency.

DOMESTIC PROBLEMS, 1945

There was inflation, because of too high government wartime spending. Militant and strong trade unions were seeking higher wages, with nation-wide strikes to back up wage demands.

The switch from war to peace went smoothly. Twelve million servicemen were demobilized, industry got back to making civilian goods, and US farmers sold their output at home and abroad. They were helped by the US money given to UNRRA (Unit 28).

There was a demand for an extension of Roosevelt's New Deal, and a growth of anti-communism.

The great gulf in living standards between the rich and the very poor—the majority of whom were black—was very noticeable.

THE CONGRESSIONAL ELECTIONS, 1946

In September 1945, in his 21 Points Truman promised:
▶ more social security, including a National Health Service;
▶ more jobs, largely through public works, including low-cost housing for the less well-off;
▶ legislation to improve working conditions.

The elections showed a swing to the right. Why was this? Voters were frightened by inflation and the strikes which were evidence of labour unrest. The effect was that the Republicans gained a majority in Congress.

DOMESTIC POLICY, 1946–8

Truman's Bill on working conditions was vetoed by Congress. Almost all his other social legislation was thrown out.

The right-wing Congress pushed through the Taft-Hartley Act 1947, to restrict the power of unions. Truman vetoed the Bill. His veto was overriden by the combination of anti-unionists in the Congress.

The Act provided for:
▶ the abolition of the closed shop;
▶ a 60-day 'cooling off' period before a strike could take place;
▶ power for the President to impose a further 90-day period if strikes threatened the national interest.

The Act did not prevent the growth of union membership.

THE PRESIDENTIAL ELECTION, 1948

Truman was expected to lose to Dewey. The 1948 elections showed a swing against Democrats. Congress had thrown out his proposed social reforms. Dewey was a popular New York Attorney-General, fighting against crime and communism.

Truman went on a whistle-stop tour (by rail), meeting millions of ordinary people. The result proved all the polls wrong. Truman won. The Democrats also won majorities in Congress.

TRUMAN'S 'FAIR DEAL'

This extended Roosevelt's New Deal:
▶ government-financed public works to provide jobs;
▶ low-cost housing to help the poorly housed;
▶ more social security legislation to include an extension of the old age pensions scheme.

Truman proposed to promote civil rights for blacks (see p. 121), but he failed. Southern Democrats allied with Republicans in Congress to reject his proposals. He was also hampered by the growth of anti-communism (see p. 121).

TRUMAN'S FOREIGN POLICY, 1945–52

Truman was an active President and avoided the mistakes made by Wilson in 1918–20. His delegate at the preliminary meeting of UNO was a leading Republican.

Truman persuaded Congress to vote 3 billion dollars for UNRRA (Unit 28) and 5 billion dollars for other aid. He had less faith in the Russians than Roosevelt. His Truman Doctrine was the basis of later policy.

Truman was responsible for Marshall Aid and ensured US membership of NATO.

In the Far East, he sent aid, but not men, to help Chiang against Mao (see Unit 17). He committed the USA to membership of UNO and used that membership to fight communist aggression in Korea (see Unit 28). He helped in the rehabilitation of Japan (Unit 35).

THE PRESIDENTIAL ELECTION, 1952

Truman did not run again and Eisenhower was the Republican candidate. Eisenhower was a wartime hero and leader, the commander-in-chief of NATO forces, and had no party affiliation but could be made to appeal to almost everyone (anti-communist, 'strong man', peace-keeper who would 'bring the boys home from Korea').

Eisenhower won; the first Republican President since 1932. He did not share the isolationist views of some Republicans and continued most of Truman's policies. His foreign policy was the work of Secretary of State, John Foster Dulles.

32.2 Eisenhower's Domestic and Foreign Policies

EISENHOWER'S FOREIGN POLICY, 1952–9

Eisenhower benefited from the 'thaw' in the Cold War (see Unit 28). He sent the US Seventh Fleet to deter China from attacking Chiang's forces on Formosa (later Taiwan). He also ended the war in Korea (see Unit 28).

In 1952–4 the French lost their Empire in Indo-China; North Vietnam became communist-controlled under Ho Chi Minh (see Unit 35).

Dulles developed the 'Domino Theory'. If one state went communist in South East Asia, there was a danger of a 'knock-on effect'. In 1956 he opposed the Anglo-French Suez policy (Unit 37).

The Eisenhower Doctrine, 1957

This was an updating of the Truman Doctrine (Unit 28). The US would ensure peace with justice throughout the world. The difficulty was in the definition of 'justice'.

The US was prepared to get involved anywhere. In 1958 US Marines were sent to Lebanon to stop a coup by supporters of Nasser. In 1954 Dulles set up SEATO as an alliance to halt communist aggression in South East Asia. Four billion dollars was given to aid NATO and SEATO.

Dulles developed the principle of 'brinkmanship'. This meant that Dulles (and the US) would appear to be willing to go to the edge (or brink) of war in defence of a policy, hoping that the threat would lead the communist enemy to withdraw. This policy failed in 1956 when Russia savaged Hungary (see Unit 30).

Dulles could not stop Castro's successful revolution in Cuba.

Was the foreign policy a success?

US generosity was said, by enemies, to be a form of 'dollar imperialism', giving the US control of its allies.

The growth of independent states in Africa (Unit 36) and Asia saw the creation of states committed to neither the US nor USSR. Dulles did not understand neutralism: 'those who are not with me are against me'.

The US tended to support right-wing governments as the best barriers to communism. Their failings were often good advertisements for communism.

Batista in Cuba, and Trujillo in the Dominican Republic, were typical of the dictators maintained in power by US aid.

Distrust of the US was increased by the work of the CIA. In 1954 it helped overthrow a left-wing government in Guatemala.

The right-wing attitude of Dulles allowed Russia to appear as the 'champion of popular opposition to colonialism'.

Khrushchev's visit to Camp David was of some value, although nothing was decided there or at the Paris Summit in 1960 (see Unit 29).

EISENHOWER'S DOMESTIC POLICY

Eisenhower was a 'moderate' with no 'Deal', although he let Roosevelt's and Truman's legislation stand.

He chose 'eight millionaires and a plumber' for his Cabinet. They tried to:

► reduce government activity and spending;
► reduce taxation, to leave more for private spending;
► increase the scope for private enterprise.

Their policies could be seen working in:

► cuts in spending by the Tennessee Valley Authority (Unit 19);
► reduction in company taxation;
► handing over to private enterprise of atomic energy plants.

The USA became more prosperous because of the low taxation and laissez-faire policies, and because of lower military spending with the end of the Korean War, and the fall in world prices in the 1950s.

Eisenhower's success could be judged by:

► the total output of goods—three times that of 1939;
► agricultural output—up by one-third in 1960 compared to 1952;
► the number of cars—one for every three people;
► half US families had incomes of over 2000 dollars a year.

However, in 1960 there were domestic problems. Inflation, a world wide phenomenon, was rising, unemployment was high: $4\frac{1}{2}$ million or 6 per cent of the workforce was out of work, and taxation had to increase to pay for the high level of military expenditure. In 1959–60 the government spent more than Truman had spent during the Korean War. Vast sums had to be spent to pay farmers to take their land out of cultivation as a means of avoiding crop surpluses.

Eisenhower had to contend with two major problems— McCarthyism and the demand by blacks for civil rights (see below).

CIVIL RIGHTS, 1945–60

Since the 1860s there has been no slavery in the USA. American blacks were, however, second-class citizens. In the southern states, where black people form a large proportion of the population, white politicians passed state laws to prevent them enjoying equal social, educational and political rights. Violent groups, such as the Ku Klux Klan (see Unit 7) frightened them from taking advantage when these barriers were broken down by federal legislation.

Blacks had to take the lowest jobs and the worst housing, and use separate schools, hotels, transport, public lavatories. In the northern cities blacks lived in slum ghettoes where they had poorer education and fewer job prospects.

Truman tried to end the segregation in the army, in which there were separate units for black servicemen.

In 1954 the Supreme Court decided that enforced segregation of blacks and whites in state schools was illegal, and Eisenhower supported this all-important decision. Then in 1957 at Little Rock, Arkansas, nine black children tried to enrol in an all-white school. The state government encouraged the mob violence which supported its decision not to de-segregate their schools. Eisenhower sent federal troops to enforce the law.

Other states still refused to comply with the law. Black parents were afraid to bring their children to white schools.

In 1955 blacks in Montgomery, Alabama, began to protest against segregation in public buses. Their refusal to use the public transport system forced the authorities to de-segregate.

Martin Luther King emerged as the leader of a peaceful but active Civil Rights Movement. In 1957 the Civil Rights Act protected the rights of blacks to vote in state and national elections. In 1960 there was a demand for government supervision of elections so blacks were not frustrated by mob violence.

By 1960 blacks were more vocal in their demands, wanted reform to take place more quickly, and were moving from the south to the industrial mid-west and north. Here they would create an urban problem.

McCARTHYISM

The USA had had anti-communist hysteria in the 1920s (see Unit 16). After 1945 the spirit of the Cold War increased US suspicions of Russia and of communists.

During Truman's presidency the Republicans took up an anti-communist attitude. They claimed that:

► Roosevelt had been 'soft to Stalin';
► Truman failed to halt Russian aggression in Europe;
► the Civil Service was riddled with communists;
► Mao's victory in China was aided by US communists in the State Department.

In 1949 Truman set up a system of loyalty checks for

government employees—his response to Republican attacks.

In 1948 the Un-American Activities Committee had been appointed by Congress to investigate the activities of potential Nazi enemies of US democracy. Now it was used against communists, socialists and liberals.

The trial of Alger Hiss, in 1949, added to the anti-communism. Hiss, an official in the State Department, had advised Roosevelt at Yalta and had made arrangements for the San Francisco meeting of the UNO (see Unit 27). Accused of spying for Russia, he was found guilty of perjury for having denied that he passed secrets to the Russians.

In 1950 Congress passed the Internal Security Act. This restricted the activities of known communists and banned the entry into the US of anyone known to have been a member of a communist organization.

The Korean War increased the suspicion of communism.

Senator Joseph McCarthy, junior senator from Wisconsin, saw how to use the Un-American Activities Committee as a way to win popularity and, maybe, higher political office. He bullied witnesses who appeared before the Committee, accusing them of knowledge of, or part in, some Russian-inspired organization. Many had belonged to anti-Fascist movements in the 1930s or had supported the anti-Franco International Brigade (see Unit 24). McCarthy made this appear as un-American. He smeared, without proof, organizations, universities, politicians and officials in statements to the committee. McCarthy claimed, without giving evidence, that there were known communists in the State Department. The numbers of such 'traitors' changed with each speech he made. He won the support of the Churches by seeming to be the champion of opposition to atheistic communism.

The 1950 Internal Security Act was one response to McCarthy's growing power. In 1951 the government decided civil servants could be dismissed if there was 'reasonable doubt' of loyalty.

Eisenhower's victory in 1952 was due in part to McCarthy, and the President tolerated McCarthy's activities because he needed Republican support in Congress.

In 1953 McCarthy became Chairman of the Senate's Permanent Committee of Investigation. He got the atomic scientist Robert Oppenheimer sacked from his government post on flimsy evidence, and organized the burning of 'subversive books' by leading US writers. He also managed to get an unofficial censorship imposed on literature and the film industry.

In 1954 a Senate Committee denounced McCarthy's smear attacks on members of the Senate. Also in 1954 he accused army leaders of being 'commie-sympathizers'. Fortunately for democracy, sanity returned. TV commentators showed him at work in the Committee and pointed out how un-democratic he was. The Senate removed him from his post. He died in 1957.

McCarthyism did not completely die. The John Birch society carries on similar anti-communist witch hunts.

THE PRESIDENTIAL ELECTION, 1960

The Democratic candidate was John Fitzgerald Kennedy. His millionaire father, US Ambassador to Britain in the 1930s and 1940s, had opposed US entry into the war. Kennedy was an Irish-American and a Catholic. Many thought that his religion could lead to his defeat in 1960.

The Republican candidate was Richard M. Nixon. He had won a Congressional seat in 1946 by a vicious smear campaign in California against his rival. He had also played a major part in the uncovering of Hiss (see above). He had supported McCarthy's activities and had been Eisenhower's Vice-President.

Kennedy won by a narrow majority.

32.3 Kennedy's Problems and Policies

The domestic economy was a problem. The US was suffering from inflation and unemployment (see p. 121). Urban poverty was largely the result of that unemployment. It was particularly a black problem. Blacks and other minorities such as Puerto Ricans had a low standard of living and little chance of state aid.

KENNEDY'S DOMESTIC POLICY: THE NEW FRONTIER

Kennedy had a young, intellectual Cabinet, but he achieved little. Some people think that he would have achieved more in a second term, if he had lived. In his presidency, plans for a health service for the old were rejected by Congress, as was a scheme to provide government money to the state schools. Kennedy did help blacks (see below) but failed to get approval for a housing bill aimed at massive slum clearance. Congress refused to extend New Deal legislation on social security for the unemployed.

In 1962 the Democrats lost seats in the Congressional elections. Kennedy's task became even harder. He was assassinated in Dallas on 22 November 1963.

KENNEDY AND CIVIL RIGHTS, 1960–3

Southern schools were still mainly not integrated: in five states not one school was integrated.

The Congress of Racial Equality (CORE) was formed by blacks impatient with other long-established black organizations. Kennedy appointed the first black federal judge, the first black ambassador and the first black commander of a US warship. His brother, Robert, as Attorney General, used his legal powers to help blacks get their voting rights.

In 1962 a black student, James Meredith, tried to enrol at the 'whites only' college at Oxford, Mississippi. Whites rioted; several people were killed. Kennedy sent federal troops and marshals to restore order because the state governor refused to act.

In Alabama and other southern states, white police used brutal methods against civil rights workers—black and white. Many students were killed, more arrested. Anyone who attacked them got a sympathetic trial from all-white juries.

Kennedy's civil rights legislation was held up in Congress by a combination of Republicans and southern Democrats. His death was greeted with applause in many southern states violently opposed to black emancipation.

KENNEDY'S FOREIGN POLICY

Lesser points

In 1961 he set up the Peace Corps to allow young volunteers to give assistance to underdeveloped nations. By 1980 the Corps had 12,000 Americans at work in over 50 countries.

In 1961 he signed the Alliance for Progress with Latin America for economic co-operation and to raise living standards.

In 1962 he persuaded Congress to make large tariff cuts to give encouragement to greater international trade. This led to the 'Kennedy Round' whereby the nation-members of the General Agreement on Tariffs and Trade (GATT) made reductions in many tariffs. Kennedy believed that more trade would be the 'New Frontier' method of lessening world poverty.

In 1963 he signed the Nuclear Test Ban Treaty.

Russia

In 1961 Kennedy met Khrushchev in Vienna, but the two leaders failed to make any progress on Berlin and nuclear disarmament. The Berlin Wall was built after the Vienna meeting (see Unit 29). In 1963 Kennedy visited the Wall and attacked Russian fear of freedom for the people of the east.

Cuba

In 1961 he approved a CIA scheme for an invasion of Cuba by Cuban refugees. This force was wiped out soon after landing in the Bay of Pigs. In 1962 there was the Cuban crisis (see Unit 29). Following that crisis Kennedy and Khrushchev agreed to the opening of a 'hot line' between the USA and USSR so that leaders might easily be in touch in times of crisis.

Europe

In 1961 Kennedy attacked the building of the Berlin Wall (see Unit 29), and in 1962 he agreed to supply Britain with Polaris (Unit 31).

Vietnam

It was under Kennedy that the USA became totally involved in Vietnam (see Unit 35).

Space

Kennedy saw Russia's sputnik as an aid to Russian foreign policy. He took the USA into the space age.

32.4 President Lyndon Baines Johnson, 1963–8

Johnson was Kennedy's Vice-President and succeeded him in 1963. He was a more astute politician than Kennedy. He used the sympathy which followed Kennedy's killing to push through the social legislation begun by Kennedy. He had always been a dedicated social reformer.

The Great Society was his hope for the USA, and he pushed through a good deal of Kennedy's legislation:

▶ money for rebuilding inner cities was provided by the Development Act, 1964;
▶ federal money was provided for educational expansion;
▶ a Social Security Act provided medical care for the old ('Medicare');
▶ minimum wages were raised and extended to more industries;
▶ a start was made on providing aid for the unemployed.

In 1964 Johnson crushed the Republican candidate, Goldwater, in the 1964 presidential election. This election also helped the Democrats to win more seats in Congress, which made Johnson's task easier. However, southern Democrats and Republicans still worked against him. A liberal trade union law to replace the Taft-Hartley Act (see above) was blocked. Congress passed a stringent Immigration Act to make the admission of immigrants more selective.

Johnson's presidency saw the increase of US action in Vietnam (see Unit 35).

JOHNSON AND CIVIL RIGHTS

Although Johnson was from Texas, he had always opposed the southern Democrats. In 1965 a Civil Rights Act provided black people with equal rights of admission to cinemas, theatres and shops, and a guarantee of their right to vote. This still meant that blacks had to face white mobs when they registered and voted.

However, basic inequalities remained—in jobs, education and housing. Younger, better educated blacks turned to extremism. The Black Muslims demanded a separate state for US blacks. They taught their followers to respect women, hard work and education. Black Power movements decided that even the Muslims would not succeed or would only succeed after a long time. They adopted more violent methods. In 1965 the Watts district of Los Angeles was almost destroyed by fire during a battle with the police, and in 1966 similar riots and arson attacks turned Chicago, Newark, New Jersey and Detroit into scenes of violent conflict.

In 1968 the assassination of the moderate leader, Martin Luther King, seemed to many Black Power leaders the best answer that whites could give to calls for moderation. Also in 1968 the assassination of Robert Kennedy was seen by blacks as an indirect attack on their equality campaign.

THE EFFECTS OF THE VIETNAM WAR ON THE USA

We will study the causes and course of the war in Unit 35, but we can examine some of the effects of that war now.

Inflation grew because of vast spending on armaments. The USA had a severe balance of payments problem. The war led to increased spending overseas. Exports did not rise at the same rate. The dollar had been the world's leading currency. The continuing balance of payments problem led to a weakening of the dollar. This was to lead Nixon to devalue it in 1971–2 (see below).

Dissension grew and became widespread. Students became opposed to the war in which they might have to fight. Students rioted in anti-war demonstrations; some were killed by anti-riot police. The year 1968 saw a world-wide students' movement. In the USA it was marked by a wave of anti-war demonstrations and by students demanding the right to 'participate' in their own education—to write course contents, to decide on the ability of lecturers and to share in College government.

Blacks became more violent. There was a high proportion of black servicemen in Vietnam; on return they would be expected to go back to the unequal state they had left to go to war. Many refused to do so and joined Black Power movements. In the 1968 Olympic Games black US athletes gave Black Power signs from the victors' rostrum to draw world attention to their frustration and rebellion.

The violence was so great that Johnson announced that he would not stand for re-election in 1968 in the hope that a new president would be more acceptable to the people. The Republican Nixon won the election.

In 1968 Johnson signed the Nuclear Non-Proliferation Treaty to try to limit the spread of nuclear weapons.

32.5 Nixon's Foreign and Domestic Policies

FOREIGN POLICY

Vietnam

After a series of failures and disastrous switches in policy (see Unit 35), Nixon signed a peace treaty in January 1973.

China

Nixon had made his political mark attacking State Department advisers who, he said in 1949, had helped Mao to victory. In 1971 he helped China to take her seat at the UNO (see Unit 33). His visit to China marked a major stage in détente.

Russia

The Nixon Doctrine, 1969 (see Unit 39), expressed the US commitment to resist communist aggression. But the reality was different, as we have seen above. As regards Russia, Nixon visited Moscow, strengthened by the fact that China was now more friendly to the USA than to the USSR, and he started off the Strategic Arms Limitation Talks (SALT) which came to fruition in 1972 (see Unit 39).

DOMESTIC POLICIES

These were less successful.

In 1971 the dollar was devalued; the German mark and the Japanese yen were stronger currencies. By 1973 following the vast increases in oil prices (see Unit 38) the dollar was further weakened.

Nixon's Council for Urban Affairs tried to tackle the problems of the cities. For much of the period 1968–72 there was less unrest. Unemployment rose to 4 million, in spite of the work-creation involved in arms spending. Inflation continued to rise. Nixon imposed an unpopular freeze on wages and prices.

Watergate may be, unfortunately, the thing for which Nixon is best remembered. In the 1972 presidential election Nixon crushed his democratic opponent, George McGovern. During the campaign some of his supporters broke into the Democratic headquarters in the Watergate Building. In a series of court trials it was shown that Nixon may not have known of the plot to break in. But he played a part in the attempt to pervert justice to get people out of trouble. More and more of his senior officials were tried and sentenced to various fines and/or imprisonment. Finally he was forced to resign—to avoid the shame of an impeachment and trial.

Nixon's Vice-President, Agnew, had already been imprisoned. Gerry Ford became President.

32.6 'Jimmy' Carter's Presidency

HIS INHERITANCE, 1976

The Democrat, Carter, defeated the Republican, Ford, in the Presidential Election of 1975, and took office in January 1976. He faced a series of difficulties:

▶ Congress, after Nixon's presidency, had a new, bolder, critical attitude towards the White House.

▶ Carter, formerly governor of Georgia, had no 'bloc' in Congress, unlike Johnson and Kennedy before him.

▶ The balance of payments crisis became worse because of oil price increases in 1973–4, and was to become worse after further price increases in 1979 (Unit 38). The dollar went down in value, and inflation (4 per cent in 1976) rose to 10 per cent in 1979.

Carter wanted to reduce the size of the budget and the amount of government spending. He hoped to tackle urban poverty, but left this to city governments. As city taxes rose to pay for this, white taxpayers moved out into low-tax country areas. This worsened the urban problem. Carter also wanted to reduce unemployment, particularly among the blacks. But during his presidency, it rose.

CARTER'S FOREIGN POLICY

Major aspects of his foreign policy are examined in Unit 39. However, the following aspects of his policy are important, and should be seen as having a more than usual impact on domestic affairs and his own popularity.

Central America

In 1978 he signed the treaty to hand over the Panama Canal to Panama by the year 2000 (see Unit 7). In the hope of gaining access to a cheaper source of oil, he became more friendly to Mexico.

The Middle East

Carter brought together Sadat of Egypt and Begin of Israel at his presidential retreat, Camp David, where they arranged their bilateral peace agreement (see Unit 37).

In 1979 the Shah of Iran was forced into exile by an Islamic uprising against his Western-style and autocratic government. A religious leader, Ayotollah Khomeini, returned from exile and roused the people to even greater anti-Western fervour. He described the USA as 'the Great Satan' responsible for the Shah's evil policies. Iranian students seized the US Embassy in Teheran and held 50 Americans hostage for over a year: they tried to bargain for the return of the Shah to stand trial for 'crimes against the people'. Carter had first welcomed the Shah to the USA but domestic and international pressure forced him to persuade the Shah to leave. In efforts to get the hostages freed, Carter tried:

▶ economic sanctions against Iran. This had no effect on the fanatical régime, prepared to ruin its oil industry rather than sell fuel to 'the wicked West';

▶ a military raid to rescue the hostages. Its dismal failure made the USA a laughing stock, and was the single most important reason for Carter's defeat in the 1980 Election.

FOREIGN POLICY AND DOMESTIC POLITICS

In 1979–80 Carter came under increasing attack because of his failure in Iran (above), and his inability to halt Russian aggression in Afghanistan and Africa (Unit 39). Opinion polls in the USA showed that people demanded a tougher policy:

▶ some people wanted to see the bombing of Iran;

▶ Senator Jackson proposed a ban on the sale of US grain to Russia unless the Russians changed their policies towards dissidents and Jews. However, Carter could not afford to offend US farmers and so the sale of grain went on.

32.7 Ronald Reagan's Presidency, 1981–89

HIS INHERITANCE, 1981

Reagan defeated Carter in the 1980 Election mainly because he appeared to be 'tougher' than Carter. When he took office:

▶ inflation was over 10 per cent a year, there was 7 per cent unemployment, and interest rates were above 20 per cent.

▶ abroad, Russia seemed to be free to act as she wished;

▶ the USA's prestige was low following the Iranian affair.

FOREIGN POLICY

This will be examined in Unit 39. However, because of the impact of certain aspects of his foreign policy on domestic affairs, the following should be noted:

▶ Reagan built up US defence forces (at great cost to the economy) and forced Russia to negotiate arms reductions;

▶ he ordered US troops into the British Commonwealth island of Grenada in the West Indies in 1983 to overthrow a Cuban-supported Communist government and to restore some form of democratic government;

▶ he ordered the bombing of Tripoli, the capital of Libya and the seat of Colonel Gaddaffi, in the belief that Gaddaffi had supported terrorist offensives against the USA (see Unit 37).

ECONOMIC POLICY

In 1980-81 Reagan adopted a monetarist policy, similar to that followed in Thatcher's Britain, in an attack on inflation. Government spending and taxes were cut, in an attempt to balance the budget. However, these policies increased unemployment and so racial tension, since blacks suffered from severe unemployment and cuts in welfare spending.

After 1982 Reagan adopted a more 'Keynesian' policy. The government spent much more than it collected in taxation. Some effects of this new policy were:

▶ increased employment, since people had more money to spend. By 1988 some 20 million new jobs had been created;

▶ increased budget deficits–the difference between government income (from taxes) and government spending. In 1985 the deficit was a massive 211 billion dollars.

▶ increased imports, particularly from Japan, to meet the demands of prosperous Americans. This led to massive deficits in the US balance of trade: 123 billion dollars in 1984 and 150 billion dollars in 1988.

Meeting the deficits

The budget deficit forced the government to borrow money–from people in the USA and from foreigners–by the sale of bonds and other government securities on which interest had to be paid. The balance of trade deficit was met by borrowing from foreigners; but interest had to be paid on these borrowings. As the deficit continued year after year, the US government had to push up the rates of interest it was willing to pay. This made the dollar attractive for foreign lenders, but it lead to US exports being over-priced (as the dollar held its high value) while US imports were under-priced. This led to:

▶ even higher volumes of imports, mainly from Japan;

▶ further falls in US exports;

▶ increased unemployment in some US industries;

▶ the call in the USA for some form of protection against foreign (mainly Japanese) goods.

Finding a cure for the problem

Reagan refused to raise taxes – which would have been one way of limiting the budget deficit. He also insisted on increasing defence spending which tended to increase the deficit while Congress, the other partner in policy-making, refused to accept cuts in welfare spending, which might have been one way of limiting the deficit.

In December 1985 Reagan accepted a Congress-supported proposal by which the budget would be brought into balance by 1991. The idea was that, year by year, the President and Congress would agree, or be forced to agree, to annual cuts in the size of the deficit. By 1989 there was little sign that this was more than a pious wish. In 1986, for example, while agreeing to the need for cuts in spending and/or rises in taxation, Congress refused to accept Reagan's proposals for cuts in spending while he campaigned for more cuts (rather than increases) in taxation.

High interest rates in the USA meant that international interest rates had to be high. Such high interest rates affected investment possibilities, mortgage rates and employment levels. In 1985, the leading five industrial nations ('the Group of Five'– USA, Japan, West Germany, Britain and France) agreed to cooperate to bring down interest rates. In 1985, 1986 and 1987 this policy succeeded in bringing down overall rates. However, such falls made the dollar a less attractive currency to foreigners, so the Group of Five agreed to cooperate to ensure a steady reduction in the value of the dollar. The US government welcomed the fall in the value of the dollar against, in particular, the Japanese yen: it fell from 270 yen in 1984 to 160 in 1986 and to 120 in 1988. This led to increased prices for Japanese exports to the USA and a lowering of the prices of US exports.

Another effect of the dollar's falling value was that it became easier (and cheaper) for foreign firms (mainly British and Japanese) to buy US companies and sections of industry. Although this ensured employment in the USA, it also meant that profits/dividends had to be paid, which added to the US balance of payments problem, but gave a boost to the overseas earnings of Britain and others.

In 1973, Nixon had signalled the end of the post-war system in which the dollar had been the world's major currency. By 1989, it was clear that the Japanese yen and the German mark had become, at least, equal partners with the dollar, a sign of their countries' economic performance. The USA is now the world's leading debtor nation, owing hundreds of *trillions* of dollars to foreign lenders. In October 1987, there were fears that the foreigners might call a halt to the lending: one result of this was the panic which hit the US Stock Exchange (Wall Street) in which share prices fell to half their previous values. There were subsequent falls in share prices throughout the world – a sign that, in spite of its performance, the USA is still a most important player in the world economy.

32.8 George Bush's Inheritance

Reagan was the first President since Eisenhower to be elected to two terms of office. In the 1988 Election his Vice-President, Bush, defeated the Democratic candidate, Dukakis. This was the first time that a party had won three elections in a row. Reagan's success in office was a key factor in Bush's victory. Bush governed a country in which:

▶ unemployment was close to a 14-year low;

▶ the trade deficit seemed to be shrinking, slowly;

▶ the dollar had stopped falling in value;

▶ inflation was lower than some had feared it would be;

▶ the economy continued to expand;

▶ growing exports were providing employment in the USA;

▶ most Americans felt a pride in their country again;

▶ the Democrats had lost their role as 'natural' rulers.

For recent developments in the USA see Unit 42.1.

Unit 32 Summary

▶ Truman's problems, policies and successes.

▶ Eisenhower's domestic and foreign policies.

▶ Civil rights, 1945–61.

▶ McCarthyism.

▶ Kennedy's problems and policies; civil rights, 1960–2.

▶ Johnson's 'Great Society': civil rights, 1963–8.

▶ The effects of the Vietnam War on the USA.

▶ Nixon's domestic and foreign policies.

▶ Carter's domestic and foreign policies.

▶ Reagan's domestic and foreign policy; the decline in the relative power of US industry, trade and currency.

---

33 CHINA, 1949–86

33.1 The Chinese People's Republic, 1949–56

On 1 October 1949 in Peking, Mao Tse-tung proclaimed the Chinese People's Republic.

Unlike Lenin in 1917, Mao had fought a civil war before gaining power. The new government was widely accepted in China and by Russia and her satellites.

Fourteen political parties were at the Constitutional Congress. Two played a major role and gained places in the government: the Left Kuo Min Tang which had broken with Chiang Kai-shek, and the Democratic League of middle-class intellectuals.

FOREIGN POLICY

In December 1949 Mao went to Moscow. Stalin had provided

little help to Mao before 1949. In 1949 he gave a military security pact, technical and economic aid.

The USA had wanted Mao and Chiang to work together (see Unit 17). Once Mao had tied himself to Russia, the USA broke with China. She refused to recognize the Communist government, and re-equipped Chiang, now on Formosa (Taiwan). She also sent the Seventh Fleet to guard the straits between Formosa and the mainland to prevent a communist invasion, and she vetoed China's membership of the UNO.

The Korean War led to increased hostility (see Unit 28) and led to the formation of SEATO and ANZUS as anti-Chinese organizations.

In 1955 the Chinese, like the Russians, took a softer line towards the USA and the West. They also tried to win friends among the uncommitted nations in Africa and Asia. Chou En-lai led Chinese delegates on foreign tours, and won friends such as Nasser, Nehru and Sukarno.

This policy operated at the Afro-Asian Conference, Bandung, 1955. Russia was not invited to the Conference. Nehru tried, but failed, to get a united Third World which would be neutral towards both Russia and the US. Nasser tried, but failed, to get the Conference to accept Egypt as the focal point for the three 'Worlds' of Arab, African and Muslim peoples. China and India confirmed their friendship which had been endangered because of the Indo-Chinese dispute over Tibet.

India and China share a 3000 km-long frontier, and in Tibet, Russian, Chinese and Indian influences meet. Britain had invaded Tibet in 1904; China always claimed sovereignty over Tibet, which claimed independence.

In 1950 China invaded Eastern Tibet. In 1954 India reached an agreement with China, giving up her policy of regarding Tibet as a buffer state (see below). Nehru outlined an Indian policy of co-existence. China and India agreed to mutual non-aggression.

In 1956 Mao went to Moscow to advise Khrushchev on policy in Eastern Europe following the unrest in Hungary (see Unit 30).

DOMESTIC POLICY, 1949–52

Theory and industry

Mao wanted broad agreement for his policies and the help of millions of non-communist technicians and officials.

The property of leading nationalists was seized. The state took control of banks, gas and electricity supply, railways and heavy industry such as coal and steel. This nationalization was done slowly and former owners received compensation.

Middle-class support had to be won. Mao tried to ensure that this class (of intellectuals and officials) would be 'purified' of the corruption practised under Chiang. Thus the Three-Anti-Movement (against corruption, waste and government inefficiency) was launched to re-educate people, and the Five-Anti-Movement was aimed at wiping out bad practices in government and industry. It aimed at abolishing tax evasion, theft of government property, theft of industrial secrets, bribery and fraud.

In this unspectacular way China began to recover. In 1949 China produced one-third less than in 1935, and in 1952 China produced one-sixth more than in 1935.

Agriculture

China was, largely, a poor agricultural country. Mao had gained his greatest support from the peasants.

June 1950 Land Reform

Landowners had to give their property to the peasants although they, as 'people', were allowed to have their share of the estate. About a million landlords were killed by peasants with bitter memories.

The peasants were encouraged to form marketing and producers' co-operatives to help them become efficient.

Other changes

Women were completely emancipated. Education was extended to children of every class. Europeans lost all their privileges and their investments in China were seized. Only Russian investment escaped.

PURGES, 1949–52

As Mao settled into power, he rid himself of some supporters. Some had joined Mao only in the latter years of the struggle with Chiang. Some of these were expelled from the party by 1952.

During the Korean War there was a purge of the faint-hearted who had not wanted to challenge the giant USA.

Communists took over existing youth groups to gain the young for the government.

There were anti-religious campaigns. Priests and other ministers were imprisoned or expelled from China.

Propaganda campaigns, largely through huge wall posters, tried to brainwash the people against foreigners and Christianity and to support Mao and the government.

About a million people were killed as 'enemies of the people'.

THE FIRST FIVE YEAR PLAN, 1953

This aimed at increasing the output by heavy industry. It was, in some ways, like Stalin's Plans (see Unit 11), but China started from a lower industrial base than Russia and wanted to move more quickly than Stalin had. This meant that the people had to work harder while getting almost no benefit from their increased output.

Private industry in these heavy industries was abolished. Slow workers and the critics of the Plan were purged.

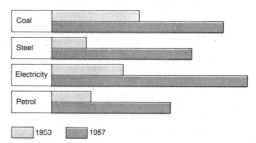

Fig. 33.1   China's first Five Year Plan

Figure 33.1 illustrates the success of this first Plan.

The first Chinese-built lorries appeared in 1956; the first oil-tankers and aircraft in 1957. But even after this 'success' China only produced 5.3 million tons of steel compared to 20 million tons produced in Britain and 100 million tons in the USA.

COLLECTIVIZATION, 1953

In 1935 the grain harvest was 140 million tons; in 1949 it was only 108 million. An increased output was essential to save spending of valuable foreign currency on food imports, but the peasants did not earn enough to pay for investment in machinery. So Mao followed the Stalin path of collectivization (see Unit 11). This was done in three stages.

Communist teams (cadres) tried to persuade peasants into Mutual Aid Teams of about ten families. Each retained their own land but all pooled their animals, equipment and labour.

This led to a greatly increased output, but it gave rise to a Chinese form of kulak or rich peasant, likely to be more of an individualist and less likely to support communism.

The cadres were therefore sent out again to persuade several Mutual Aid Teams to combine to form a co-operative:

▶ all the land of the co-operatives would be sown and harvested in one operation;
▶ a committee elected by members of the co-operative would decide on the crop to be grown, the work to be done and where the crop was to be sold;
▶ profits would be shared among the co-operative members.
Again, this led to increased output. China's towns and cities were now, for the first time, free of famine.

Cadres encouraged peasants to form collective farms. All private property was abolished and peasants were paid for the work they did on the much larger collective farm.

Not surprisingly the peasants resisted this process. They had been taught, in 1950–2, that they had a right to own property. They had enjoyed the benefits of individual hard work, and they resisted attempts to drive them into being wage-earning workers on collectives.

There were local uprisings against enthusiastic cadres, and the government recognized the danger. Collectives were broken down into smaller units. People worked in smaller groups, they could organize their own work, provided it fitted into the party plan for the collective as a whole, and each peasant was given enough land for the growing of vegetables and the rearing of a few pigs and hens.

These concessions were enough to win the support of the peasants. By 1957 almost all land had been collectivized. However, even the increased output was barely enough to keep pace with the 2 per cent annual increase in population.

▪ 33.2 Domestic Policies, 1957–67 ▪

THE HUNDRED FLOWERS CAMPAIGN, 1957

Mao was satisfied with the industrial progress and with the collectivization process. He decided to allow free discussion of China's problems. 'Let a hundred flowers bloom and a thousand schools contend' he said, inviting comment on China's progress.

He was surprised by the volume of criticism. Such criticism had led to crises in Europe (see Unit 30), so he put an end to the freedom and purged the more important of his critics.

THE GREAT LEAP FORWARD, 1958 (the Second Five Year Plan)

Mao decided to take a giant stride towards the socialist society, making the great changes needed in a few years. Industry was to increase output by 30 per cent a year. Steel output was to double each year by extending traditional steel mills and industries, and 'backyard furnaces' which ordinary people would set up. Thus every man would become a part-time steel maker.

Agriculture was to be reformed to produce the food needed by the growing population and to pay for essential imports: the 750,000 collectives were reformed into 24,000 communes, each covering about 4000 hectares. Private plots (see above) were abolished.

The commune would be not only a farming unit. It was to be something like an Israeli kibbutz. It provided common dining rooms, dormitories, nurseries and schools; it provided its own welfare schemes and local government. The individualism of the peasant was to be wiped out: the commune would produce a new breed of people.

The success and failure of the commune

Output

A million town workers were driven into the countryside to become commune workers. Crops were sown on wider areas. But the result was disappointing. The government had hoped for a harvest of 375 million tons; only 250 million tons were produced in 1958. In 1959, 1960 and 1961 a series of floods and droughts made matters worse. In 1962 only 175 million tons were harvested. The government had to import grain from Canada and Australia.

Attitudes

Peasants resented the loss of their private property. They took less care of 'communal' tools and machinery than they had of their own property.

Industrial failure

Most 'backyard steel' was useless.

The government steps back

Mao had not taken into account the need to prepare the people for the vast changes proposed by the Great Leap. He had hoped to be able to do without the technicians and bureaucrats who were concerned more with efficiency than with the purity of ideological thought. He had hoped to bring the people to accept the need for 'permanent revolution'.

Changes

▶ Mao stepped down from being head of state and concentrated his attention on being Chairman of the Party.
▶ Liu Shao-chi became head of state. With the Prime Minister, Chou En-lai, he concentrated on saving the economy more than on promoting party ideology.
▶ The communes were partly broken down. On 75,000 new communes peasants were given back houses, gardens and plots. The commune retained control of overall planning and of machinery. The day-to-day running of the commune was given to teams which ran individual villages and to brigades which ran groups of villages.

Benefits of the Great Leap

Many people had had their first industrial experience in the 'backyard furnaces' scheme: millions of Chinese, particularly the young, caught some of Mao's enthusiasm for change and permanent revolution. The commune, even changed, remained a feature of China.

THE THIRD FIVE YEAR PLAN, 1962–7

This started from a broader and deeper base than existed when Mao launched his first plan in 1952. There were many new industries—machine tools, motor vehicles, aircraft and electrical equipment. Many industries had grown—coal, steel, chemicals and cement.

There were many new industrial centres. In 1952 industry had been concentrated in Manchuria and around the southern ports. By 1962 there were major centres throughout China and a new railway system linked them together.

This Plan was hampered by the sudden withdrawal of Russian aid and technicians (see below). But it was successful. China became the world's second largest coal producer, she surpassed Britain in the production of machine tools, and her steel industry matched those of the USA and the USSR.

One external sign of her growth was her explosion of nuclear weapons (1964) and of a hydrogen bomb (1967). Other signs of progress were in the improved standard of living. Within 20 years of taking power the communists had:

▶ abolished usury and the power of money lenders;
▶ ended starvation and famines;
▶ made government officials more honest.

The individual Chinese is now better fed and clothed, fully employed and enjoys well-developed welfare services.

China stills remains largely an agricultural country, able to identify with other underdeveloped countries, while also being able to offer them the technical aid they need.

33.3 China and Russia

LONG-STANDING HOSTILITY

In the 17th century Russia occupied the Amur Valley, and in the 19th century there were clashes over Mongolia. Then in the early 20th century they clashed over mineral-rich Sinkiang, bordering on Kazakhstan.

In 1945–6 Russia stripped Manchuria of its industrial goods. In 1946–9 Stalin did not aid Mao in his war with Chiang. In 1949–56 Russia provided less aid than she gave to India.

Russia did not share her atomic power secrets with China.

IDEOLOGICAL DIFFERENCES

After Stalin died, Mao thought of himself as communism's 'elder statesman'. The Russians did not agree. Khrushchev claimed that an atomic war would destroy not only the capitalist west but the communist world. There would always be millions of Chinese survivors of such a war, said Mao.

The Great Leap Forward was criticized by Russia as not following the 'Russian path'.

A GROWING RIFT

By 1960 the dispute had become much fiercer. Mao accused the Russians of wanting to become more like the West. Khrushchev's visits to the USA and his meetings with Eisenhower and Kennedy were dismissed as attempts to lessen communist commitment to socialism. 'The goulash society' was Mao's description of Russia as it concentrated on material growth.

At the 22nd Party Conference, 1960, the quarrel became an open one. Russia withdrew the 1390 technicians working in China and cut off technical aid, hampering Chinese development.

In 1962 China accused Khrushchev of cowardice in the Cuban crisis (see Unit 29). In 1963 she refused to take part in the negotiations which led to the Test Ban Treaty.

In 1964 Khrushchev planned a meeting of all communist leaders to get them to throw China out of the communist 'club'. In fact it was Khrushchev who fell from power (see Unit 29).

Russia became even more hostile to China during the chaos of the Cultural Revolution (see below). China described Russia as 'a paper tiger' anxious to make peace and détente with the West.

In 1971 it was a major surprise when China changed her attitude towards the USA in particular and the West in general. It began when China allowed Western teams into China to play table tennis, a game at which China excelled. 'Ping pong' diplomacy, allied with Nixon's wish for world-wide détente, brought speedy results:

▶ the USA ended its veto on China's application to join the UN. Taiwan was expelled to make room for China;
▶ Nixon visited Peking and started the diplomatic contact between the two countries.

In 1973 Chou En-lai warned the 10th Party Congress to be on their guard against a surprise attack from the USSR. Border clashes on the Kazakhstan-Sinkiang border took place in 1968 and 1969. Russia had moved her mobile missile launchers into Mongolia to threaten China. The USSR saw the aggressive Mao as an Asian Hitler, whereas Mao spoke of the 'anti-Chinese atrocities of the new Czars...Fascist heels trample on the Motherland.'

33.4 The Cultural Revolution, 1966–71

REASONS

There were tensions between Mao, who wanted 'continuing revolution', and Chou En-lai and Liu Shao-chi who wanted to improve the economy. Mao was concerned about his successors. Would they take the Russian line and become too concerned with materialism? He was also afraid that the West would attack China. Would the new generation, without experience of the Long March (see Unit 17) and guerrilla war, be able to defeat such an attack?

AIMS

Mao aimed to purge the party of the unreliable, and to drive from office and power the 'functionaries'—the technical experts, more interested in results than in revolution, and the party bureaucracy, the officials more interested in holding on to positions of power and to developing their own careers than in revolution. He also wanted to get the Chinese people used to the idea of 'continuous revolution'.

COURSE OF THE CULTURAL REVOLUTION

In 1967 Mao's main supporter was Defence Minister, Lin Piao. He started a massive propaganda campaign to ensure that a 'revolutionary' army would guarantee Mao's success.

Mao launched a series of attacks on writers, historians and intellectuals who disagreed with him. This attack on the country's cultural leaders gave the movement its name. Mao undertook his famous Great Long Swim in the Yangtse River to prove that, aged 72, he was still strong enough to lead.

He urged the young to form militant Red Guards. Millions of young workers and students went on a nation-wide rampage:

▶ religion came under attack: temples and statues were smashed;
▶ government ministers were attacked and humiliated. Peng Chu, Mayor of Peking, was denounced and forced to resign. Liu Shao-chi, Head of State, was expelled from the party he had helped to victory in the 1930s and 1940s. Teng Hsiao-ping, the Communist Party General Secretary, was forced to resign;
▶ the Red Guards commandeered trains, took over radio stations, arrested anyone showing 'Western tendencies'— by wearing lipstick or expensive clothes or owning some small luxury;
▶ teachers, university professors, journalists and commentators all suffered at the hands of the rampaging mob. Waving the 'Little Red Book' containing 'The Thoughts of Chairman Mao' they dominated Chinese life for several years.

EFFECTS

Little, if any, work was done. Workers were forced to listen to lectures or to take part in demonstrations.

Some leaders managed to avoid arrest. But Chou had to watch while nine tenths of the government was overthrown. Some leaders tried to put an end to the chaos.

CIVIL WAR, 1971–3

Lin Piao, once named as Mao's successor, tried to get the army to stop the revolution which he had started. Mao discovered this 'treachery'; Lin died in an air crash as he was trying to escape to the West.

Teng Hsiao-ping argued that Mao could not be the only leader of China. The leadership ought to be collective. Teng and others saw that China was going backwards economically.

Army commanders, in seven out of China's eleven military regions, opposed the Red Guards. Workers in Wuhan and Shanghai fought pitched battles with the Red Guards; severe fighting took place in other cities and communes. Finally the army stepped in and drove the Red Guards back to the classrooms and workplaces.

THE END

Mao was still Chairman—until his death in 1976. However,

Chou, supported by the army, the bureaucracy and those responsible for running the economy, emerged as the real leader.

Teng Hsiao-ping was reinstated in 1973 when he became Deputy Prime Minister to Chou. This was the real sign that the Cultural Revolution was over.

Not everyone came back. Liu was not reinstated; the number of officials running the country was reduced from 60,000 to 10,000.

Some 'Maoists' were included in Chou's Politburo—the sign that Chou had to take account of the Revolution.

33.5 China after Mao

THE END OF MAOISM

Mao's wife campaigned against Chou's revisionism. But Chou had enough support to resist even this powerful lady.

Madame Mao managed to get her ageing husband to drive Teng Hsiao-ping from office when Chou died in January 1976.

Mao died in September 1976. This removed his powerful influence which had helped his wife and the 'perpetual revolutionaries'. Madame Mao and her leading supporters were arrested. The army put down pro-Maoist risings in various provinces. Fighting went on into 1977. Millions were killed.

Teng Hsiao-ping came back to power. Very quickly he became the real ruler of China. This was the sign that economic realism had proved stronger than revolutionary fervour.

Khrushchev waged war on Stalin's memory in 1956. Teng and his supporters have similarly tried to abolish the myth of Maoism.

'FREE-MARKET SOCIALISM'

The adoption of a new economic system marked the end of Maoism and acceptance of the fact that the Cultural Revolution had been a disaster. The move to the new system was led by Teng, who (1985) forced the retirement of many old leaders and their replacement by younger, more pragmatic, men.

Agriculture, China's major industry

Peasants were allowed large private plots on which to grow whatever they wanted. They were free to sell this produce, for profit, in the open market.

Since 1980 there has been a sharp increase in peasants' incomes and in food output—although both are low by Western standards. The state has built many new houses in the villages where the 'rich' peasants can enjoy a better life style.

Industry

Teng encouraged foreigners to invest in China. Many Special Enterprise Zones, some around the main ports, were set up as tax-free regions where industry (much of it foreign-owned) could develop. Japan, in particular, took advantage of these schemes to build up its industrial holdings in China.

There was an increase in industrial output and more consumer goods were available for the better-off.

Problems

The rush for economic growth led to banks providing too much credit for investors, to sharp rises in prices (inflation) and to demands for wage increases.

Many urban people resented the way in which the peasants became much better off.

Many officials were found guilty of corruption; a sign, said some critics, of the inevitable failure of free-market systems.

In spite of the increased output by industry and agriculture, living standards are still low. Most townspeople live in overcrowded housing and have too low an income.

Some of China's leaders have shown that they are not completely behind Teng's reforms: they might prefer a more centralist and socialist system.

33.6 China and the Outside World

THE USA

For Chinese–US relations during 1946–9, see above. In 1950, their relations worsened during the Korean War (Unit 28), and in 1971 their relations changed abruptly (Unit 33).

INDIA

China annexed Tibet in 1950 (see above). The Dalai Lama, the traditional ruler, was forced to flee after an unsuccessful revolution in 1959. In 1965 Tibet became a self-governing region of China.

India was alarmed at China's Tibetan policy, but remained benevolently 'neutral' to China until 1960. In 1960 China absorbed the Burmese province of Wa, a sign that she had 'imperialist ambitions'. Then in 1962 China challenged Indian claims to sovereignty in some parts of the Himalayas. The border was ill-defined. China claimed Ladakh and other regions which India regarded as hers.

The Indo-Chinese war, 1962, ended in Chinese success. Indian troops withdrew. China claimed another 39,000 square kilometres of territory.

HONG KONG

China made no attempt to seize the island, ceded by the Manchus in 1842 following the Opium War, nor did she try to take back areas of the mainland (Kowloon and other New Territories) leased by the Manchus to the British in 1898. She also left alone the Portuguese colony of Macao.

There were good economic reasons for this 'friendly' attitude towards 'western imperialists':

▶ through Hong Kong and Macao, China had access to the markets of the West, and to the financial markets which she used to get the money needed for her development;

▶ she could have taken them when she wished. This knowledge kept some countries inclined to be friendly to China.

In 1983 the British and Chinese began negotiating the future of Hong Kong and the New Territories—which provide the overcrowded island with living space and, above all, water supplies. China agreed to recognize Hong Kong as an especially privileged part of China with a special and recognized relationship with the West.

Unit 33 Summary

▶ 1949–56: domestic and foreign policies; purges and collectivization.
▶ 'A Hundred Flowers'; Great Leap Forward and Cultural Revolution.
▶ China and the USSR.
▶ China after Mao; 'free-market socialism'.

34 THE INDIAN SUB-CONTINENT, 1939–86

34.1 Wartime India

THE POSITION IN 1939

There had been some progress towards self-government in India (see Unit 22). The Congress Party had become increasingly active. Congress had won majorities in many provincial assemblies.

Jinnah, leader of the Muslim League, was anti-Congress, because he feared the creation of a Hindu India and called for a separate Muslim state. Congress did not take this threat very seriously.

INDIA AND THE WAR, 1939

The Viceroy, Linlithgow, declared war on Germany on behalf of India without consulting Congress. Congress saw the war as 'a European affair'. If India was to get involved, Congress demanded immediate independence.

The British promised Dominion status (see Unit 22) 'at the end of the war'. Congress then opposed Indian participation in the war.

Many leaders were arrested and imprisoned without trial. Gandhi, a pacifist, was arrested for opposing the war effort, and, in the Provinces, Congress ministers resigned in protest.

The more warlike Muslims supported the war effort. Muslims held on to their posts in provincial governments, and in 1940 the 'loyal' Muslims put forward their policy for a separate Pakistan; 'Pakistan or perish' was their slogan.

THE WAR, 1941

The Japanese took Burma and got to the borders of India. Gandhi and Congress argued that the only reason to fear a Japanese invasion of India was because of the British presence. If the British 'quit India', Japan would leave her alone.

A minority of Hindus, led by a Congress leader, Chandra Bose, went to fight for the Japanese. His Indian National Army was made up of some who left India and others recruited from Hindus in Japanese prisoner-of-war camps.

THE CRIPPS MISSION, 1942

Britain needed Indian support for the war against Japan. Cripps was a socialist minister in Churchill's coalition. He was sent to consult with Congress and to promise:
► Dominion status at the end of the war;
► the right to leave the Commonwealth if they wished;
► the right to work out their own constitution.

Nehru wanted to accept this offer, but Gandhi was opposed to it. He proposed a campaign for mass civil disobedience.

The 'Quit India' campaign forced the government to put Congress leaders back in jail, as a threat to Indian security.

MUSLIM PROGRESS, 1940–5

Congress's refusal to co-operate was a mistake, because it could have had many important posts in government, and it would have won the sympathy of the British.

It provided Muslims with unexpected opportunities:
► in the Punjab, a key state, the Muslim League shared the government with British officials;
► in Bengal, a Leaguer was Prime Minister;
► there were League governments in Sind and Assam;
► in the North West Frontier Province, Congress Muslim leaders had been arrested. Leaguers then formed the government.

This growth of Muslim power showed that Congress did not speak for 'all Indians' as it claimed.

THE SIMLA CONFERENCE, 1945

Wavell, a new Viceroy, called a Conference of the released Congress leaders and the leaders of the Muslim League. He put forward, again, the Cripp's proposals (see above). Congress claimed that, since it included some Muslims, it had the right to nominate Muslim members of a central government. Leaguers, with their wartime experience (see above), denied this.

Hostility between the leaders wrecked the Conference.

34.2 Towards Independence

THE PETHWICK-LAWRENCE MISSION, 1945–6

The new Labour government in Britain had promised Indian independence. A Cabinet Mission, headed by Lord Pethwick-Lawrence, and including Cripps, was sent to try to get agreement.

The Mission offered:
► immediate Dominion status without any partition of India;
► increased powers to provincial governments—which would help Muslims in states where they were in the majority;
► the right for groups of provinces to form a union within a Federal India. There would have been a Muslim Union of Sind, the North West Frontier Province and the Punjab.

The leaders of Hindus and Muslims agreed, but the agreement was wrecked when Congress refused to give the League the right to appoint all Muslim members of the proposed central government.

This was the last chance of achieving a united and independent India for which Gandhi had worked.

UNREST, 1946–7

Wavell, the Viceroy, asked Nehru to form a government.

Jinnah, head of the Muslim League, joined the government. But he also declared that Muslims would no longer follow constitutional methods to get their separate Pakistan. This encouraged local leaders to use violent methods to show their opposition to Congress and the Hindus. Racial and religious rioting led to wholesale massacres of Hindus, Sikhs and Muslims. Provincial governments, themselves dominated by religious differences, were unwilling or unable to stop the killings. Jinnah and other Muslim League ministers did all they could to make it impossible for Nehru's government to function.

THE MOUNTBATTEN MISSION, MARCH 1947

The Labour Prime Minister, Attlee, sent Lord Louis Mountbatten to replace Wavell as Viceroy of India. He was related to King George VI. Attlee hoped that this would gain British support for his policies. He had been Supreme Commander South East Asia in the war against Japan. Attlee hoped this would gain him the support of Indians.

Attlee and Mountbatten announced that Britain would leave India in June 1948. They hoped to force Indians to agree. Attlee hoped to maintain a united India. Mountbatten quickly realized this was not possible.

On June 1947 Mountbatten agreed to the partition of India. He fixed an early date for independence, 15 August 1947.

THE VIOLENT BIRTH OF TWO NEW NATIONS

Having decided on the creation of two states, Mountbatten set up Commissions to deal with the transfer of power.

The problem of boundaries was illustrated in the Punjab. The Punjab was to be divided between India and Pakistan; this would divide Sikh from Sikh. Amritsar, the Sikh 'holy place', was to be in India, cutting off the Sikhs in Pakistan from their 'holy place'.

In March 1947, while the boundary commission was being set up, Muslims wrecked the Hindu bazaars in Amritsar, burning Hindu homes and murdering the Hindu people. The warlike Sikhs prepared to take action against Muslims on the other side of the proposed boundary. The police, themselves divided racially, did not take action or join in the rioting.

Other problems of partition

The religious massacres in the Punjab were only the first. Other, and worse, massacres were to follow.

Irrigation schemes were 'partitioned'. Would Hindus allow 'their water' to flow into the Muslim areas? And vice versa?

The army and navy contained men of all religions. These All-India forces had to be 'partitioned'. How?

The Civil Service was predominantly Hindu but contained people of all religions. This had to be 'partitioned'.

The railway system was another All-India system. Would separate governments provide an All-India service?

The massacres

The technical problems (see above) had been foreseen and most of them solved before partition in August 1947. However, no one had provided for the transfer of millions of people from one new state to another in areas which were religiously divided. Bengal and the Punjab were particularly affected:

▶ 5 million Hindus left West Pakistan for India;
▶ 5 million Muslims left India for West Pakistan;
▶ 1 million Hindus left East Pakistan for India.

The scale of killing was horrific. As many as 500,000 were killed before they left their original homes, and at least 1 million were killed as they made their way by train or on foot to their new homes.

It was ironic that the man who tried to stop this religious slaughter—Gandhi—was himself to be assassinated in 1948. It was, perhaps, fortunate that his murderer was a Hindu fanatic who thought that Gandhi had been 'soft on the Muslims'.

The princely states

There were 570 states in India where native princes ruled. In theory, Mountbatten's agreement with Hindus and Muslims allowed these princes to choose their future. Most of them were small and had to join one of the new 'giants', depending on their religion. Some, notably the Maharaja of Hyderabad, were rich enough to remain independent. They felt betrayed when Britain did nothing when India took Hyderabad by force in 1948.

Kashmir provided a long-standing problem (see below).

THE PROBLEMS FACING THE NEW STATE OF INDIA

Mass illiteracy

How would this affect the world's largest democracy?

Starvation

In agricultural India millions lived below an acceptable 'poverty line'; thousands died each each week of starvation. How would the independent government cope with this problem, resulting largely from religious problems?

Religion

Hinduism taught India's millions to accept their fate. Would they make efforts to raise living standards? It taught them to honour the 'sacred cow'. How would this 'worship' affect attempts at agricultural reform?

Caste

Hindus are divided and sub-divided into hundreds of social castes. Caste determines a person's job, marriage-partner, political loyalty and educational opportunity. Would a government be able to break down these traditional religious divisions?

Economic inequality was the result of the caste system. Would independent India, under socialist Nehru, be able to alter this inequality?

Women were regarded as inferior. Would a male-dominated and Hindu-dominated government try to 'modernize' India?

Population

There were 400 million Indians in 1947. The population increased by about 2 per cent a year after that.

Agriculture

There were to be frequent reports of a 'green revolution' by which India had become self-supporting in food. In fact there were regular failures in agriculture. The output in 1964 equalled that of 1961 (but then there were 28 million more mouths to be fed). The output in 1966 was lower than that of 1964.

Food imports were essential in most years. But if India was also to import machinery (for industrialization) she could not afford such food imports.

34.3 Nehru's India

It was the world's largest democracy, with 170 million voters in 1947.

Congress won the first election. Opposition parties were created by communists, eager for a social revolution, the Jan Sanga, representing Hindu traditionalists and opposed to any policies which offended their religious beliefs, and other groups, such as that representing the lowest social caste known as Untouchables.

Nehru was Prime Minister from 1947 until his death in 1964.

In 1950 India became a Republic but remained in the Commonwealth.

POLITICAL DIFFICULTIES

Congress was a much divided Party, split by:

▶ regional differences;
▶ caste;
▶ economic interests. The mill-owning millionaires dominated Congress to the detriment of social reform.

There was a great gulf between the rich ruling élite and the majority of Congress supporters. Corruption was also a fact of Indian life. Even foreign aid was often syphoned off by corrupt officials so that it never achieved what was intended.

NEHRU'S FOREIGN POLICY

Nehru adopted a neutralist stance. India would favour neither the capitalist West nor the communist East. He wanted to be an 'honest broker' standing between the two rivals in the Cold War. He played a major role in bringing the two sides together in Korea where he helped arrange a truce (see Unit 28), and in Geneva, 1954, where he helped end the fighting between France and the Vietnamese (see Unit 35).

India and China

They quarrelled over Tibet, 1950–9 (see Unit 33). Nevertheless, Nehru tried to get the 1955 Bandung Conference to accept China as the 'natural' leader of the Third World (see Unit 38). In 1959–62 there were many border clashes along the ill-defined frontier—particularly in the Himalayan area.

In 1962 during the Sino-India War India received aid from both Russia and the USA. For this war see Unit 33.

Goa

In 1961 India sent troops into Goa to take this Portuguese colony on the Indian mainland. Many people were shocked by this use of force by the 'pacifist' Nehru.

ECONOMIC DEVELOPMENT

To help in her modernization and industrialization, India has received a great deal of aid from both East and West. This has allowed her to develop economically much faster than would have been the case if she had been forced to stand on her own feet.

Five Year Plans, the first of which was produced in 1951, have been adopted to try to stimulate industrialization. A Planning Commission was set up to produce the Plans and supervise their implementation. Basic industries were nationalized. Emphasis was placed on the development of steel, cement and hydro-electricity, essential for industrial progress.

By 1961 output of industrial goods had almost doubled. But still only about one per cent of the population worked in industry.

Caste

Nehru tackled this problem. Discrimination, particularly against the Untouchables, was made an offence.

Illiteracy

The constitution laid down that free and compulsory education was planned for all children up to the age of 14. This has never been achieved.

Agriculture

Poor farmers cannot provide the savings needed for investment. Even with foreign aid there has only been small progress. The 25 per cent increase in output achieved by the first Five Year Plan was almost wiped out by the increase in population.

Foreign aid

This has helped Indian development. But it has been mainly in the form of loans on which interest has to be paid. This is a burden on India's balance of payments.

Legal changes

In spite of opposition from traditionalists, Nehru pushed through two important Acts. The Hindu Marriage Act, 1955, made monogamy (one wife, one husband) the law and provided for maintenance for Hindu widows and for wives separated from husbands. The Hindu Succession Act, 1956, gave women equal rights with men to hold and to inherit property.

Evidence of success—even limited

Thousands of villages got an electricity supply, millions of new jobs were created, and agricultural yields went up as irrigation schemes and local co-operatives helped some regions to improve.

The population problem

In 1956 Nehru introduced an intensive programme to encourage birth control. But this had little success. The majority of the illiterate peasants did not understand what they were told, and could not 'read the instructions'. Also, many religiously orthodox people were offended by the interference with nature—as they saw birth control.

34.4 Lal Shastri, 1964–6

Nehru died in May, 1964. There was no real struggle for power on the death of India's 'founder', a proof that democracy had taken firm root.

Lal Shastri had a long record of service to India: he had been imprisoned for 9 years for civil disobedience, he had been a minister under Nehru, and he had had particular responsibility for laws against discrimination, part of the social revolution.

As Nehru's successor he was opposed by the right-wing (traditionalists) of the Congress. To please them he went to war over Kashmir (see below). However, they resented his attempts at peace in Kashmir. They also wanted him to make India a nuclear power.

In January 1966 Shastri died suddenly.

34.5 Indira Gandhi

Mrs Gandhi was Nehru's daughter, and a surprising choice in a male-dominated country which needed a firm government to cope with its many problems.

SUCCESS

Her government won majorities at elections in 1967 and 1971. Between 1967 and 1971 she fought the Syndicate, the party bosses who dominated Congress. Most of them were corrupt and had none of Nehru's idealism; they assumed they could 'run' Nehru's daughter. She fought them, splitting Congress. Her left-wing group won majorities in most states in the election of 1971, and she remained as Prime Minister.

HER PROBLEMS

Mrs Gandhi had to cope with India's long-standing problems (see above), and she had also to cope with new problems:

▶ Communists won power in West Bengal in 1967. Rioting there and in other states forced Mrs Gandhi to bring in decrees allowing direct (presidential) rule 'in times of crisis'.

▶ The Naxalites were Maoist agitators who imitated the Red Guards (see Unit 33) and tried to rouse the masses to revolution.

HER POLICIES

Economic planning continued on the lines laid down by her father.

Hindi was established as a common language to promote national unity.

The fourth Economic Development Plan aimed to increase Indian wealth by 6 per cent a year, to provide 19 million jobs and to raise average incomes by 25 per cent. The Plan was a partial success: it still left the mass of Indians in great poverty, and in 1966 inflation forced the government to devalue the currency in the hope that this would help Indian exporters.

ECONOMIC SETBACKS

In 1967 there was a general food shortage; Bihar state suffered a famine. Thousands died.

In 1971 the coast of Orissa was struck by a tidal wave; thousands died in this one storm alone.

SOCIALISM—AND APPROVAL

Mrs Gandhi, like her father, was a socialist. She nationalized the banks and, after the election of 1971, the insurance companies.

Education

She planned to give every Indian child at least five years' schooling by 1975.

In the 1971 Election her party gained 100 more seats and held nearly 350 seats. The Opposition was bitterly divided.

BANGLADESH

The flood of refugees from Bengal increased India's problems; so, too, did the war with Pakistan (see below).

POPULATION

Nehru had failed to develop a family planning programme. Mrs Gandhi tried to hurry the programme along:

▶ male vasectomy was advocated and, in some regions, insisted on by government officials;

▶ attempts were made to compel women to accept mechanical methods of birth control.

Mrs Gandhi's opponents used this as an excuse to attack her and her government.

IN AND OUT OF POWER, 1975–84

In June 1975 Mrs Gandhi was found guilty of corrupt practices and disqualified from holding electoral office for six years. In 1975–7 she ignored the decision and declared a state of emergency, giving herself power to rule without Parliament. In this period thousands of opponents were imprisoned.

In March 1977 she was replaced as Prime Minister by Mr Desai, but in November 1978 she re-entered Parliament as the leading member of the Opposition. She had shown that she had retained a considerable personal and political following. The anti-Gandhi faction of the Congress Party proved unable to govern. Then, in 1979, Mrs Gandhi became Prime Minister again.

THE PUNJAB

Sikhs wanted some form of political independence. Extremists, led by Bhindranwale, demanded an independent Sikh state. Mrs Gandhi would not accept this threat to the break-up of India. Moderate Sikhs, in the Akali League, were opposed to the militant policies of the extremists with their demand for a Sikh Khalistan.

The extremists seized the Golden Temple in the Sikh holy city of Amritsar. Here they stored arms and called for a military rising against the Gandhi government. In June 1984 Mrs Gandhi ordered the army to attack the Golden Temple in Amritsar. This shocked many moderate Sikhs.

In October 1984 Mrs Gandhi was assassinated by a Sikh member of her own bodyguard—a sign of Sikh anger.

34.6 Rajiv Gandhi, 1984–

He was Mrs Gandhi's younger son; the elder, Sanjay, had been politically active before his death in an accident; Rajiv had been an airline pilot and not an active politician. He was persuaded to succeed his mother as leader of the Gandhi faction of the Congress Party and to become Prime Minister.

In December 1984 Rajiv Gandhi called Parliamentary elections, in which he gained widespread popular support. He negotiated with the moderate Sikhs, hoping to find a solution to the problem of Punjab.

In October 1985 he called for elections for State governments but found that the Sikhs and other opponents did better than he had expected.

Extremist Sikhs refused to accept his moderate policies or the leadership of the moderates. In mid-1986 they were again using Amritsar as a base for storing weapons and planning militant campaigns against Rajiv's government.

SRI LANKA

Rajiv became involved in the tribal struggle which threatened Sri Lanka (once known as Ceylon). The Sinhalese majority in Sri Lanka dominated the island-state's economic, social and political life. The Tamil minority—descendants of Indian immigrants—resented this domination and demanded reforms. Extremist Tamils formed armed gangs which organized terrorist attacks on Sinhalese people and property. The Sinhalese government used the army to try to restore order. Their actions often drove moderate Tamils to support the extremists.

Many Tamils demanded that Rajiv should intervene on their behalf; they were, they claimed, 'Indians in exile'. They hoped that he might force the Sinhalese government to allow the creation of an independent Tamil state in the north of the island. In mid-1986 there was no solution in sight.

34.7 Pakistan

THE PROBLEMS FACING PAKISTAN, 1947

Common problems

Pakistan shared with India a number of problems (see above). She also had her particular ones.

An unreal nation

Pakistan had no historic roots. Its two separate parts were divided by 1600 km, and the people of the two regions were racially and linguistically different.

East Pakistan's jute-growing industry was cut off from its main outlet, Calcutta, now in Indian Bengal.

Political policies—the lack of

The League had developed no policies, except for the creation of the separate state of Pakistan.

Jinnah *was* Pakistan. His death shortly after independence (1948) was a major loss. The assassination (1951) of Pakistan's first Prime Minister, Liaquat Ali Khan, was another disaster. These deaths left lesser men squabbling for power.

AYUB KHAN'S GOVERNMENT

In 1956, following India's example, Pakistan became a republic. In 1957 the army decided to put an end to the political unrest. The army commander, Ayub Khan, seized absolute power. He promised to clean up the administration before handing power back to 'the politicians'.

In 1960 Ayub was elected President and ruled without Parliament. In 1965 he was re-elected, defeating Miss Jinnah in the Presidential election.

Ayub won the presidential election, 1965, but he had less support in East than in West Pakistan. He was blamed, unfairly, for the floods and famines which affected East Pakistan.

He announced plans for 'basic democracy':

▶ there would be elections for local councils;

▶ there would, later, be elections for councils to send MPs to a central Parliament.

▶ Ayub would retain control of the government until Pakistan and its politicians had gained political experience.

Many suspected that he intended to hold on to power. Politicians, released from prison, whipped up opposition: Ayub was accused of corruption and favouring his family; the religious leaders (mullahs) criticized his lack of religious fervour; communists argued that he favoured the rich industrialists; landlords complained that he favoured the poor.

AYUB'S INTERNAL POLICIES

Ayub had a programme for economic development, with Five Year Plans for expansion and attacks on corruption and inefficiency.

There were many improvements:

▶ communications were developed;
▶ house-building expanded;
▶ hydro-electric schemes were built;
▶ there was increased output of jute, carpets and leather goods.

RELATIONS WITH INDIA

Ayub reached agreement on the River Indus, but Kashmir remained a problem (see below).

In March 1969 the commander-in-chief, Yahya Khan, forced Ayub to resign. He imposed martial law. He promised that 'when the country was ready' he would restore democracy.

PAKISTAN'S FOREIGN POLICY

Unlike 'neutralist' India, Pakistan favoured the West. In 1954 she signed a Mutual Assistance Pact with the USA, joined SEATO—against Chinese aggression, and joined other Muslim states (Iraq, Iran and Turkey) in the Baghdad Pact—against Russian aggression in the Middle East. Nehru condemned this as a 'step towards war'.

Ayub became increasingly friendly to Russia and China. In 1965 he went to Moscow to get technical aid. With China he settled peacefully frontier disputes over the 300-km border between Pakistan and China.

34.8 The River Indus

The headwaters of the rivers feeding the Indus are in India. India wanted to divert these rivers for irrigation schemes. However, the Indus is vital to West Pakistan's irrigation schemes.

The dispute between the two new states was temporarily settled by a truce arranged by the World Bank. This led to a treaty (1960) which allowed for the joint development of the Indus waters: new dams would be built in both India and Pakistan; both countries would be guaranteed sufficient water for irrigation development.

34.9 Kashmir

In 1947 this was a princely state (see above). Its Maharaja was a Hindu; his people were mainly Muslim. There was a good deal of communal killing in 1947. Muslims from the North West Frontier Province invaded.

India was asked to send troops to put down this invasion. The Maharaja applied to join his state to Hindu India. Pakistan then invaded the state.

The UN arranged a temporary truce. Pakistan was allowed to 'govern' the mountains, India the valleys. The UN proposed to hold a plebiscite.

Nehru (a Kashmiri) claimed the state for India. It is worth noting that Nehru refused to accept a plebiscite as a means of settling this dispute—although, in other cases where there was a Hindu majority, he insisted on plebiscites.

He held elections there which his friend, Sheik Abdullah, won. But the Sheik declared Kashmir independent—and Nehru imprisoned him.

In 1964 a meeting was planned between Nehru and Ayub to try to settle the dispute. Nehru died before it could be held. In 1965–6 the war broke out again.

In January 1966 Prime Minister Kosygin of Russia arranged a meeting between Ayub and Shastri (see above) at Tashkent. They made another truce. But the Kashmiri problem remains unsolved.

34.10 Yahya Khan's fall

In 1969 Yahya announced a new Economic Plan and promised elections. In December 1970 elections were held. The People's Party, led by Ali Bhutto, won a majority of seats in West Pakistan.

In East Pakistan the Awami League, led by Sheik Mujibur Rahman, won an even greater majority of the seats and an overall majority in the Pakistan Parliament.

The West Pakistanis refused to accept rule by Easterners. Bhutto announced that his party would boycott Parliament. Yahya visited the East, hoping to arrange a compromise. Bhutto demanded a government which would satisfy both East and West. The Awami League's electoral policy had been to free East Pakistan from control by the West. Sheik Mujibur would not agree to any compromise; 'the League had won'.

34.11 Bangladesh

In March 1971 Yahya outlawed the League and asserted the power of his military government over both regions of Pakistan. Rebels in East Pakistan proclaimed independence for Bangladesh. The military government arrested Sheik Mujibur, but civil war was inevitable.

Bengali refugees poured into India from East Pakistan, escaping from the savagery of the West Pakistan forces. This put a great strain on India's resources. Eight million refugees had to be fed, housed and otherwise cared for.

Frontier incidents were frequent; India and Pakistan started fighting again in Kashmir. In December 1971 India and Pakistan went to war. Indian troops, aided by Bangladesh freedom fighters, routed the Pakistanis. At the end of 1971 Yahya was forced to resign, and Bhutto became President of West Pakistan. Sheik Mujibur, released from prison, took control of Bangladesh.

The Simla Conference, July 1972

Russia had supported India during the short war, China had given lukewarm support to Pakistan, and the USA had been very critical of India's action. After the victory, Mrs Gandhi was anxious to reach a settlement. In July 1972 an agreement was reached at Simla:

▶ all troops would be withdrawn from occupied territory;
▶ 90,000 Pakistani prisoners-of-war would be repatriated;
▶ the status quo would be maintained in Kashmir.

However, Bhutto refused to agree to recognize the existence of the new state, Bangladesh. Because of this refusal, India refused to honour the Simla agreement.

34.12 Pakistan, 1972–86

Bhutto tried to form a new constitution, but his People's Party was not very popular; many Pakistanis resented their defeat by India and the creation of Bangladesh (see below).

China had provided Bhutto with too little help during the war and he looked elsewhere for support while announcing Pakistan's withdrawal from the Commonwealth, which had recognized Bangladesh.

In 1973 Pakistan's many economic problems were worsened by the vast destruction caused by floods in the Indus valley.

Bhutto became increasingly autocratic, while his government proved to be corrupt and inefficient.

In July 1977 General Zia led an army revolution and overthrew Bhutto, who was arrested. Elections were promised for October 1977, November 1979 and March 1985. The first two elections were never held.

In April 1979 Bhutto was hanged in Rawalpindi jail.

In February 1981 Opposition parties formed the Movement for the Restoration of Democracy. In March 1981 Zia launched his own constitution with a nominated (and not elected) Parliament. Miss Benazir Bhutto (daughter of the dead leader) was put under house arrest. Later she was allowed to leave Pakistan to live in Britain.

In August 1983 Zia announced plans for a 'controlled return to democracy'; the opposition launched a country-wide agitation against his regime and his scheme.

In September 1983, local elections were held, and in December 1984 a referendum confirmed Zia in office for five years.

In February 1985, elections to a new Parliament were held—although no party was allowed to campaign.

In December 1985 Zia announced the end of martial law, although he retained power to arrest political activists and to imprison them without trial. The Opposition parties denounced his scheme as 'a farce'. In April 1986 Miss Bhutto returned from Britain to lead the Opposition.

34.13 Bangladesh, 1972–86

PROBLEMS FACING THE NEW COUNTRY

There was wartime destruction in an already poor country.

Inflation and food shortages caused severe problems.

Racial tension was high in this new, small, poor, flood-ridden state:

▶ Muslims hated Hindus;
▶ Bengalis hated Biharis, who had fought for Mujibur.

There was political unrest: Sheik Mujibur and most of his family were assassinated in August 1975 when General Assad seized power. In 1977 Assad and several of his successors as President were assassinated before General Ziaur Rahman emerged as President.

ZIAUR'S PROBLEMS

In 1978 an influx of Muslim refugees from Burma put a strain on a fragile economy. In time, most of these returned to Burma.

In 1979 Muslim anger was roused by the Russian invasion of Afghanistan and the imposition of an irreligious pro-Soviet government in that country (see Unit 29).

Many Muslims, including many in Bangladesh, were affected by the development of a new, more strict, 'fundamental' Muslim faith. While this fundamentalism was best seen at work in Khomeini's Iran (see Unit 32) it is also evident in Gadaffi's Libya, and in Pakistan and Bangladesh.

POLITICAL INSTABILITY

Ziaur maintained the traditional pro-Western and anti-Soviet attitude previously followed by Pakistan, in Bangladesh. Both states received considerable aid from Arab oil-producing countries which did something to lessen their enormous economic problems. Politicians refused to unite against Ziaur. Some 18 political parties were formed, while 65 candidates were put forward for a presidential election. This political division contributed to the continuing weakness of the state's economy.

In March 1982 General Ershad seized power and became President. He promised to hold parliamentary elections and formed a party (Jatiyo) to represent his views.

Mujibur Rahman's daughter led the main Opposition Party, the Awami League. In March 1985 Ershad banned all political activity in the hope that peace might be restored to the state.

In May 1985 local elections were held and Ziaur's party won most seats in state governments.

In May 1986 parliamentary elections were held. Outside observers confirmed that violence, ballot-rigging and other forms of corruption were commonplace. In spite of this, Ershad feared the loss of power; while votes were still being counted he announced the temporary halt to the electoral process.

Unit 34 Summary

▶ 1939–45: wartime India: Gandhi, Cripps and Wavell.
▶ Mountbatten and the partition of India: Nehru and Jinnah.
▶ Nehru's India: problems, policies and progress.
▶ Indira Gandhi: problems, policies and opposition to.
▶ Rajiv Gandhi.
▶ Jinnah's Pakistan: problems weaknesses and failures.
▶ Military governments from Ayub to Zia.
▶ The problem of Kashmir.
▶ Bangladesh: origins and problems: military government.
▶ Bhutto: aims and failure.
▶ Zia's Pakistan.

35 THE FAR EAST, 1945–86

35.1 The Post-War Period

Japan had taken the European colonies (see Unit 25) and her defeat led to changes in these colonies.

The Dutch East Indies became Indonesia (see p. 136).

Malaya became independent and, enlarged, became Malaysia (see below).

French Indo-China was divided into three countries, but only after bitter fighting which, later, involved the USA (see p. 140).

Perhaps the most surprising feature of this period in this region has been the rehabilitation of Japan.

35.2 The Rehabilitation of Japan

THE GROWTH OF DEMOCRACY

General MacArthur led an army of occupation into Japan. MacArthur wanted to:
▶ break the power of the zaibatsu, the huge industrial combines whose leaders had often disrupted Japanese political life;
▶ end the power of the militarists. Japan was to have no army;
▶ create a genuine democracy in the country;
Under the Constitution of 1947:
▶ both houses of the Japanese Parliament are elected;
▶ universal suffrage gives women the vote;
▶ the government is responsible to Parliament (as in Britain), and not to the Emperor, as in pre-war Japan;
▶ there is no official state religion (religion had been one cause of aggressive nationalism);
▶ the Emperor Hirohito remained as ruler but was no longer regarded as a divine being, as he had been.

Political parties

MacArthur encouraged the formation of political parties and legalized the Communist Party.

ECONOMIC REFORM UNDER US OCCUPATION

Land reform

Four million peasants were given their own land. This led to increased agricultural output, the end of starvation and provided greater stability in the countryside.

Trade unions

These were encouraged, and strikes legalized.

JAPAN AND THE COLD WAR, 1945–53

The US needed a strong Japan as a barrier to communism, so the Communist Party was made illegal. Then in 1950 MacArthur set up a Japanese police force which soon had its own tanks—and soon grew into an army. In 1951 the USA and Japan signed the Treaty of San Francisco which led to the withdrawal of US forces from the mainland. The US held on to Okinawa until 1972. In 1960 the USA and Japan signed a security treaty in which the US guaranteed Japan's defence.

JAPANESE POLITICS, 1952–86

The 1947 Constitution led to stable governments. Most governments have been conservative in character.

Violent battles often took place between the riot police and well-organized demonstrators, protesting at times about US influence in Japan, the government's military stance, the danger of Japan becoming a nuclear power and the pollution caused by mass industrialization. However, election results continued to show that most voters were satisfied with their government.

ECONOMIC EXPANSION, 1948–86

Japan has, again, become the most industrialized nation in Asia. The Japanese 'economic miracle' is visible in:
▶ shipbuilding, electronic and motor vehicle industries;
▶ the continued rise in the volume of exports;
▶ the rise in living standards;
▶ 1966: Japan's leading part in the planning for an Asian Development Bank;

▶ the International Trade Fair, Expo 70, an advertisement for Japan's success;
▶ Japan's membership of the 'Group of Five', the world's leading industrial nations;
▶ the USA's continued trade deficit (largely with Japan) and its financing by overseas borrowing (mainly by Japanese lenders);
▶ the continued strength of the Japanese yen; in mid-1986 it had risen by over 50 per cent in value against the US dollar.

The main reasons for Japan's growth are:
▶ modernization and willingness to adopt modern technology;
▶ heavy investment in modernization and in new industries;
▶ a willingness to work hard;
▶ good industrial relations: trade unions encourage loyalty to employers who, in turn, look after their workers;
▶ private competition, which encourages modernization;
▶ Japan has spent little on her defence;
▶ an unusually high tendency to save rather than to spend; Japanese people save some 40 per cent of their income, which allows for a plentiful supply of money for capital investment, as well as reducing the demand for domestic and foreign goods.

SOCIAL PROBLEMS

Social problems follow from industrial expansion.

A shortage of building land leads to a housing shortage and overcrowding. Towns provide problems of sewage and refuse disposal, and pollution of the atmosphere and water supplies. Large firms give high wages and welfare benefits. Most Japanese work for small firms which do not have the capital to adopt such paternalistic attitudes. Low wages are the norm.

FOREIGN POLICY

Trade with **China** fell after the war. Since Mao's death things have improved. Japan has easier access to the vast Chinese market and helps China's industrial development.

The USA maintained close links with Japan, providing her with much of the early investment. Recently the USA has become concerned at the effects of Japanese exports on US employment.

Europe also suffered from massive imports of Japanese goods. Negotiations about limiting those imports and increasing imports into Japan have had little success.

Russia was not invited to sign the San Francisco Treaty. She resents the growth of an American-backed economic giant.

The UN

Japan gained admission to the UN in 1956.

For recent developments in Japan see Unit 40.5.

35.3 Indonesia

In 1939 the 7000 islands of the Dutch East Indies supplied half the world's rubber and pepper.

An Indonesian Nationalist Party, founded in 1927, had an engineer, Sukarno, as one of the leaders. Sukarno spent 13 years in prison; few Indonesians supported him. Most feared rule by the Javanese if the Dutch left.

THE SECOND WORLD WAR

Japan overran the islands and tried to win support. Nationalist leaders were released from prison. Indonesians could fly their 'national' red and white flag. In 1943 Sukarno was given some political power, within the framework provided by the Japanese conquerors, and an Indonesian resistance movement was secretly encouraged and helped by Sukarno.

THE JAPANESE DEFEAT, AUGUST 1945

The Japanese gave Sukarno's Party an administrative experience denied by the Dutch. Towards the end, Japan fixed a date for Indonesian independence, hoping to gain support against the Allies.

Japan surrendered on 15 August; Sukarno proclaimed independence on 17 August, before Allied forces arrived.

THE BRITISH AND SUKARNO, SEPTEMBER 1945

Sukarno had six weeks of 'power' before British forces arrived. He formed an army, its weapons taken from the Japanese. In the Republican constitution he named himself as President and Jakarta as the capital.

The British wanted only to hand back the colony to Holland. This led to fighting with the nationalists, leading the government to take the Mountbatten line—to get the Dutch to negotiate independence.

THE DUTCH AND SUKARNO, 1945–7

A small number of Dutch soldiers and officials returned; Holland hoped to regain full control over its colony. This determination led to clashes with Sukarno's forces. In November 1946 Holland agreed to a small change:

▶ Java, Madun and Sumatra were formed into a nationalist-governed republic;

▶ they set up a Federation of the United States of Indonesia, consisting of the Republic, Borneo and the Great East (the other islands).

The Dutch set up separate governments in the small islands of the Great East. These puppet governments would ensure Dutch control of the Federation. They supported an independence movement in West Java, which was under Republican control.

THE DUTCH VERSUS THE REPUBLIC

Sukarno was angered by Dutch policy (above); the Dutch were angered by his attempts to get the world to recognize his Republic as a separate country.

In July 1947, the Dutch attacked the Republic. Parts of Java and Sumatra were captured. The Republic appealed to the rest of the world. Australia and newly-independent India helped the Republic's case to the UNO, which showed that UNO recognized the Republic's independence.

Security Council negotiations led, in January 1948, to an agreement giving Holland the right to rule Indonesia until a plebiscite was held. The Dutch held their own plebiscite, set up separate governments in many islands and set up a Federal government which did not contain anyone from the Republic.

STALIN AND THE REPUBLIC, 1948

In September 1948 Stalin ordered a series of world-wide risings.

A communist rising in the Republic was put down by Sukarno's nationalist forces.

In December 1948 the Dutch then launched their own attack, bombing Jakarta and capturing many Republican leaders.

INDEPENDENCE

The UN called for a cease-fire. The USA cut off all economic aid to Holland.

In August 1949 a conference was called at The Hague. In November 1949 agreement was reached. The Republic of the United States of Indonesia was to comprise the whole of the former Dutch East Indies.

On 30 December 1949 the Republic came into being as part of a meaningless Netherlands Indonesian Union in which the Republic was equal partner with Holland and the Queen of Holland was the Head of the Union. This Union was dissolved in 1954.

INDONESIA AFTER INDEPENDENCE

In 1954 the Union was dissolved (see above). In 1957 all Dutch citizens were expelled from Indonesia and their property confiscated. In 1962 West Irian, (part of New Guinea) which was retained by the Dutch, was placed under UN administration. In 1963 it was handed to Indonesia.

Sukarno

Sukarno had confronted the Dutch in West Irian. In 1963 he quarrelled with Malaysia, which claimed British possessions of Sarawak and Sabah in northern Borneo (see below).

Indonesian guerrillas fought against Malaysian forces in Sarawak and Sabah; parachutists invaded Malaya.

Sukarno was condemned by the UN, from which he withdrew in 1965. But in 1966 he gave up the anti-Malaysian struggle.

Many Indonesians resented Sukarno's autocratic methods. The 1950 Constitution provided for democratic government, but until 1955 the provisional parliament was appointed, not elected, although political parties were formed. In the 1955 elections the four main parties won roughly the same number of seats. There could be no stable government. Sukarno said that Western democracy did not suit Indonesia.

In 1956–7 clashes between Javanese and the people of the smaller islands and between right-wing and Communist groups made the shaky government even more unworkable.

In 1960 Parliament was dissolved and replaced by a National Front, with a People's Consultative Congress and a Supreme Advisory Council. In fact Sukarno was a dictator.

In October 1965 a communist rising was crushed by the army. Sukarno may have organized the rising to allow himself even greater powers—and without communist opposition. In anti-communist rioting 87,000 people were killed. In January 1966 students rioted when Sukarno included pro-communists in his government.

In March 1967 the army overthrew Sukarno and put General Suharto in power.

35.4 Malaya becomes Malaysia

MALAYA, 1945–63

During the war Malayan Chinese formed a guerrilla movement. This was under communist control.

In 1948 Stalin ordered a communist rising. This was not put down until 1960. Few Malays joined the rebels.

In 1957 Malaya became independent. Malay and Chinese leaders co-operated in negotiations leading to independence.

The first Prime Minister of Malaya was Tunku Abdul Rahman who remained in power until his retirement in 1970.

In 1963 Britain handed over her colonies in Borneo. Brunei opted out; Sabah and Sarawak joined the Federation of Malaysia.

MALAYSIA, 1963–5

Malaysia had a long struggle with communist guerrillas in the north. She also had a war against Indonesia (see above). She was unable to keep Singapore in the Federation of Malaysia because the population of Singapore was mainly Chinese, and Lee Kuan Yew, leader of Singapore, was afraid that the Malays in the Federation would pass anti-Chinese laws. Also, the Malays feared that the thrustful Chinese would dominate the Federation's economy. Singapore wanted free trade, the Federation wanted a tariff system to protect infant industries. In 1965 Singapore left the Federation and became independent.

 35.5 French Indo-China

1939 (Fig. 35.6)

Cochin-China, around Saigon, was a French colony. Annam and Tonkin (which, with Cochin-China make up modern Vietnam) were only French protectorates. Cambodia and Laos were two other protectorates.

The five states known as French Indo-China were run for the benefit of France:

▶ Asiatics were treated as second-class citizens;
▶ they could not form trade unions or political parties;
▶ education was provided for Asiatics to help them run the French-controlled government and French-owned industry;
▶ but the educated minority were allowed only less important jobs, and got lower salaries than Europeans in similar posts.

A nationalist movement, the Vietminh, had been formed by the leading nationalists. It was particularly strong in the three states making up modern Vietnam. In 1939 its leaders were Ho Chi Minh and Vo Nguyen Giap.

Ho Chi Minh

Ho left Vietnam in 1911 to work as a cabin boy. Later he worked as a labourer in Paris and as a dishwasher in a London hotel. In 1920 he became a communist and went to Moscow to study. He met Lenin, Stalin and Trotsky. In 1930 he founded the Indo-Chinese Communist Party.

Vo Nguyen Giap

Giap had been eduated in the French system in Indo-China. He qualified as a history teacher and, later, as a lawyer. Because of his political activities the French had imprisoned him. His sister had been executed and his wife had died after two years in prison.

INDO-CHINA AND THE WAR, 1939–45

Ho and Giap led the guerrillas in night-time campaigns; they fought in the rice fields, mountains and jungle. Like Mao (Unit 17), the Vietminh gave land to the peasants in areas which they controlled and received help from them.

The Japanese wartime government united Annam, Tonkin and Cochin-China into one region (Vietnam); Cambodia and Laos were governed as two separate regions.

Ho's Vietminh were particularly strong in Vietnam.

There was a gap between the Japanese surrender (15 August) and the return of the colonial 'rulers' (3 October). Ho declared Vietnam independent in August 1945 and united all the nationalist groups in his government.

THE FRENCH AND THE CLAIM TO INDEPENDENCE, 1945–7

The returning French hoped to rule Indo-China as in 1939. Terrorist raids on the French suburbs of Saigon persuaded them to negotiate with Ho's 'government'.

Ho wanted an independent Vietnam with strong links with France. He wanted a form of Dominion status (see Unit 22). In March 1946 negotiations in Indo-China agreed on an independent North Vietnam as part of a Federation of Indo-China.

In June-September 1946 Ho was in Paris negotiating the details of this agreement with the French government. In Vietnam, Giap's guerrillas, extremists and nationalists, denounced Ho for collaborating with the French. The French refused to accept Ho's moderate claims.

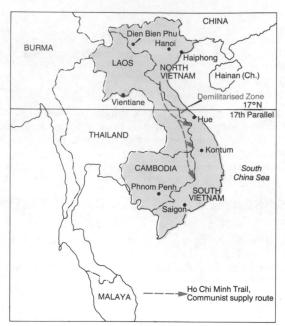

Fig. 35.6   The war in Vietnam

THE FRENCH TRY TO IMPOSE 'INDEPENDENCE', 1947–50

In 1947 the French decided to destroy Ho's 'government'. They got aid from the USA.

The Domino Theory

The USA thought that if one state (e.g. Vietnam) fell under communist control, other neighbouring states would also fall to communism—*either* from internal aggression encouraged by the success of the first 'domino' *or* by external aggression from that newly-independent state.

Bao Dai

He had been Emperor of Annam before 1941. Until 1947 he was Ho's political adviser. In December 1947 France invited him to become President of a new Vietnam. They hoped to win the Vietnamese away from Ho.

In 1948–50 the French wasted time in fruitless negotiations. Bao Dai became President and Head of State. He refused to carry out French policy. Like Ho, he was a Vietnamese nationalist.

Ho and Giap continued their guerrilla war against the French.

THE FRENCH LOSE INDO-CHINA, 1950–4

Ho's forces were strongest in North Vietnam. The French set out to destroy Ho's power. Their army was stronger and better-armed than Ho's guerrillas led by Giap, who received some aid from China, now under Mao.

The French could capture towns and hold on to them by leaving behind a large force, but they failed to conquer the countryside and mountains. They built fortified blockhouses to try to prevent Vietminh movement, but by night the guerrillas passed such posts. They were aided by the peasants in the mountains.

By 1953 the French had lost 12,000 soldiers, 12,000 members of their Foreign Legion and 14,000 Indo-Chinese soldiers. The war was costing 600 billion francs a year—more than the value of all French investments in Vietnam. Many people wondered whether it was worth fighting.

DIEN BIEN PHU, 1953–4

Around Saigon the war was one of terrorism and ambush. Further to the west Giap seemed to be planning to invade Laos and to extend the war.

General Navarre, the new French commander, decided to trap Giap into a pitched battle which he was confident he would win.

In November 1953 French paratroopers took Dien Bien Phu, deep inside Vietminh-held territory. Navarre built up the garrison supplied by air from Hanoi. Giap's men captured the surrounding hills.

In March 1954 the battle of Dien Bien Phu started. Guerrilla forces captured French outposts. The French air-force failed to destroy Giap's positions. Giap's men advanced, using captured French material against the besieged garrison.

France asked the USA for more help. The US Secretary of State, John Foster Dulles, talked of dropping 'one or two atom bombs'.

The USA agreed to a British proposal for a conference to discuss the Indo-China problem.

On 7 May 1954 Dien Bien Phu fell.

THE GENEVA SETTLEMENT, 1954

It was an accident that the conference opened on 8 May, the day after the fall of Dien Bien Phu. The USA, Russia, Britain and France attended the conference.

France agreed to withdraw from Indo-China completely. Cambodia and Laos became independent. Vietnam was divided by the 17th parallel of latitude into:

▶ a communist-dominated North Vietnam;
▶ a 'free' south under Bao Dai.

The agreement provided for elections to be held throughout Vietnam in 1956 to choose a government for the whole country. The USA refused to sign this part of the agreement, fearing that the communists would win the elections.

Many of Ho's guerrillas were still inside South Vietnam. It was these who formed the core of the Viet Cong (see below).

35.6 The US and Vietnam

THE EISENHOWER YEARS, 1952–60

Eisenhower and his Secretary of State, Dulles, had an anti-communist line. The main reasons for this were:

▶ Eisenhower's experience in NATO during the Cold War (see Unit 28);
▶ the growth of McCarthyite anti-communism in the USA (see Unit 32);
▶ Dulles's belief in the Domino Theory (see above);
▶ Dulles's rejection of neutralism (see Unit 32).

Until 1954 the USA was indirectly involved in Indo-China: they had sent aid to the French. The USA helped to make the Geneva agreement.

In October 1955 the USA supported the South Vietnamese plot in which Bao Dai was overthrown. As Ho's former adviser (see above) he was 'soft on communism'.

In October 1955 South Vietnam became a republic, with Ngo Dinh Diem as President. His government became increasingly unpopular because he did not hold the promised elections in South Vietnam, and he was a Catholic, whereas the majority of Vietnamese were Buddhists. They protested at his government's tyranny. He attacked, imprisoned and killed religious fanatics who wanted a Buddhist state, and left-wingers who wanted social reform.

In 1960 the National Liberation Front was set up by Ho's supporters still in the south (see above) and by other opponents of Diem. The guerrilla forces of the NLF became known as the Viet Cong.

THE KENNEDY YEARS, 1960–3

Laos was divided between rival factions and the north of the kingdom fell under the control of the communist Pathet Lao.

Cambodia's Prime Minister, Prince Sihanouk, became increasingly critical of US involvement in Indo-China. He hoped to put off a communist take-over by this anti-US policy.

South Vietnam was involved in a civil war with the 20,000 Viet Cong rebels getting aid from the North and from Russia.

Kennedy sent an increasing number of 'advisers' to help Diem. In 1962 the number rose from 5000 to 15,000, and with them came military equipment including helicopters.

The unpopularity of the Diem government led Kennedy to agree to a CIA plot to overthrow Diem, who was assassinated to make way for a military administration.

US military aid and the number of military and technical 'advisers' was increased.

However, the Viet Cong had the support of the majority of the peasants. By the time of Kennedy's assassination (November 1963) the Viet Cong controlled about 40 per cent of the countryside. They also terrorized the urban population by bombing campaigns.

THE JOHNSON YEARS, 1963–8

Johnson continued Kennedy's policy and increased the number of advisers.

The Tonkin incident

In August 1964 the war escalated: communist torpedo boats attacked US warships in the Gulf of Tonkin; US carrier planes bombed northern naval bases.

In the south the Viet Cong attacked the American base at Bien Hoa near Saigon, destroying many parked Canberra jets.

Johnson sent US troops to South Vietnam. By 1967, 400,000 troops were involved there.

The Viet Cong received an increasing volume of aid from the North. Russian material came from the North to the Viet Cong along the Ho Chi Minh trail through Laos and Cambodia (Fig. 35.6).

Much of the war was fought between Viet Cong guerrillas and US forces armed with sophisticated weapons. Part of the war consisted of pitched battles between US battalions and battalions of Viet Cong, both using modern weapons.

The peasants suffered from both sides: US forces believed that the peasants supported the guerrilla forces—and destroyed villages; the Viet Cong sometimes gained the support of the peasants by terrorist methods, killing headmen suspected of being sympathetic to the US-supported government.

Bombing the North

As US forces failed to defeat the Viet Cong, Johnson ordered the bombing of North Vietnam. This increased the number of Vietnamese who died in the war. About 3000 a month died in the south, victims of Viet Cong and of US firepower. Thousands more died in the north from the bombing of Hanoi, supply bases and ports.

The Hanoi government demanded an end to the bombing. The US demanded an end to the use of the Ho Chi Minh trail.

In January 1968 the Viet Cong launched devastating attacks in the south. In this Tet Offensive they captured, for a short time, 75 per cent of the main towns in the south, including for a time, parts of Saigon. This was in spite of the 750,000 men of the South Vietnamese army, 500,000 US servicemen and 50,000 men from various allied forces aiding the US.

Johnson calls a halt, 1968

There was increasing US criticism of Johnson's policy. Some 'liberals' opposed the bombing of the North because of its effects on innocent people; some deplored the brutalizing effects of the war on the US forces. Many men became drug users; others attacked their officers. There were reports of massacres of civilians such as the one at My Lai. Some liberals were worried at the effects of the war on the US economy. Increased government spending led to inflation and an outflow of dollars, a large deficit on the US balance of payments and a demand from Germany and Japan in particular for a devaluation of the proud dollar.

1968 was the 'year of the students' in France (Unit 31) and elsewhere. US students led anti-war demonstrations; there was widespread anger and puzzlement at the failure to beat the Viet Cong.

In the autumn of 1968 Johnson ordered an end to the bombing of the North. In return the North agreed to attend preliminary negotiations in Paris with the representatives of South Vietnam, the Viet Cong and the US.

Johnson did not stand for re-election in the 1968 Election won by Richard Nixon (see Unit 32).

THE NIXON YEARS, 1968–74

The talks in Paris made very little progress: President Thieu of South Vietnam could not agree with the Viet Cong on fair elections for South Vietnam; the US and North Vietnam could not agree on a formula for the mutual withdrawal from the South.

In November 1969, at Guam, Nixon announced the end of the Truman Doctrine (see Unit 28). The US would not accept a world-wide responsibility and would withdraw from south-east Asia.

Vietnamization

Nixon wanted the South Vietnamese to take over their own defence to allow the withdrawal of US forces. By the end of 1970 their number was halved.

Increased bombing

Nixon could not face the prospect of a Viet Cong victory. He resumed the bombing of the North.

Cambodia

In 1970 the army had overthrown Prince Sihanouk. His successor, General Lon Nol, attacked communist bases in Cambodia. The communists fought Lon Nol and seemed about to overthrow him. To save Lon Nol and to hinder the passage of supplies from the North, Nixon ordered the bombing of 'neutral' Cambodia.

Laos

In March 1971 South Vietnamese troops invaded Laos in an attempt to destroy communist bases there—and were driven into a disastrous retreat.

Withdrawal

In 1971 another 100,000 US troops were withdrawn, while the bombing of the North was increased.

The Viet Cong launched a major offensive in March 1972. They threatened Thieu's troops near Hue, around Kontum and around Saigon (Fig. 35.6). The US sent massive supplies to Thieu's troops who, like Chiang's men in 1945–9 (Unit 17) had little stomach for the fight.

Nixon increased the bombing of the North and of the Ho Chi Minh trail. The ports of North Vietnam were mined to try to cut off Russian sea-borne aid.

Cease fire

In January 1973 the USA and North Vietnam agreed on a ceasefire. President Thieu reluctantly agreed; areas in the south, controlled by the Viet Cong, came under a communist Provisional Revolutionary government. The 17th parallel was accepted as the line of demarcation. More US forces were withdrawn, although fighting between North and South continued.

The North Vietnamese captured more towns, built new bases and consolidated their power in their one-third of the country.

Nixon's involvement in Watergate, his resignation and the accession of President Ford weakened US concern for Vietnam.

The end of the war

The North Vietnamese launched a major offensive in 1975 and over-ran a series of South Vietnamese strongholds. The coastal towns fell quickly.

In May 1975 communist forces took Saigon, and in 1976 the two halves of Vietnam were united in a single Socialist Republic. In 1977 Vietnam was admitted to UNO, after some opposition from the USA. In 1978 Vietnam joined Comecon (see Unit 29), its membership sponsored by Soviet Russia but criticized by some East European governments.

35.7 'Indo-China' after the War, 1975–86

Russia had provided most of the aid to the North and the Viet Cong. China saw a united Vietnam as a Russian puppet in a part of the former Chinese Empire.

In 1978, Chinese forces invaded Vietnam, claiming that Vietnamese troops had invaded China. The Chinese were quickly defeated by the Russian-armed Vietnamese. They withdrew and there is an uneasy peace.

Cambodia was drawn into the war in 1970 (see above). A small communist party, the Khmer Rouge, opposed this involvement. After 1975 the Khmer Rouge defeated the US-supported government of Lon Nol.

Pol Pot headed a Khmer government which in 1978 slaughtered about 3 million of the 7 million Cambodians, thought to have been loyal to the old régime. In the ensuing chaos another 2 million died from disease and famine, the twin tragedies which marked the re-naming of the country, now called Kampuchea.

In January 1979 the Vietnamese, once the allies of the Khmer, invaded the country to help an ex-Khmer Heng Somrin to take power. The Khmers took to the hills and waged a guerrilla war in which the Vietnamese invaders were supported by Russia (see Unit 29).

Vietnam under a communist government has persecuted those who served the US-supported government. A mass exodus of people trying to escape death in 1978 and 1979 led to the existence of the 'boat people' seeking refuge overseas.

A CYNICAL WORLD

In the 1960s, and particularly in 1968, there were world-wide demonstrations against the part played by the US in the war. Students led chants of 'Ho, Ho, Ho Chi Minh, the Viet Cong are going to win'. These 'liberals' are surprisingly silent in the face of the cruel effects of the victory they wished for.

■ Unit 35 Summary ■

▶ Japan, the new industrial giant.
▶ Indonesia: independence under Sukarno and Suharto.
▶ Malaya becomes Malaysia; war with Indonesia.
▶ French Indo-China, 1949–54.
▶ The USA and Vietnam, 1952–74.
▶ 'Indo-China' since 1975: wars and genocide.

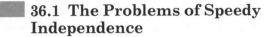

36.1 The Problems of Speedy Independence

In 1945 South Africa, Egypt, Liberia and Abyssinia were independent. In 1986, almost all states in Africa are independent. This speedy change has brought several problems:

► democracy, developed over many centuries in Europe, has generally failed in Africa;
► expectations: many African leaders promised too much to their followers in the struggle for independence. The poor states, mainly agricultural, have not been able to satisfy expectations;
► tribalism: most Africans have more loyalty to their tribe than to the nation-state. This has caused much discontent;
► corruption: many leaders saw independence as a chance to enrich themselves and their families;
► interference by outside countries and powerful economic interests has often made problems worse;

Third World problems will be examined in Unit 38. Here you should note that African countries suffered from some or all of the following:

► harsh climate, shortage of water and prevalence of disease;
► overdependence on one crop, of which the price fluctuates;
► lack of natural resources;
► lack of economic and social infrastructure such as roads, skilled workforce and technically qualified people;
► low incomes which make local investment difficult.

36.2 Ghana

THE GOLD COAST BECOMES GHANA, 1945–57

Colonial government under a 1946 constitution

A British colonial governor appointed an Executive Council. In the Legislative Council of 31 members, 13 were chosen by the Council of African chiefs, 11 elected democratically and 7 appointed by the governor.

Black politics was dominated by the United Gold Coast Convention Party (formed 1941). In 1947 Kwame Nkrumah was brought back from studies in the USA to become secretary of this party. In 1948 there was popular rioting against the new constitution.

In 1949 Nkrumah founded the Convention People's Party and demanded full independence.

In 1951 a new constitution (under which Nkrumah's party won 34 of the 38 seats in the larger Legislative Council) did not give full independence. During the election campaign Nkrumah was arrested for organizing anti-government strikes. Freed after the election, he became the first black Prime Minister (1952) and led his country to full independence (1957).

GHANA SINCE 1957

In March 1957 Nkrumah became President of his renamed country.

Industrial development included developments in cattle-rearing, forest industries, fishing and improved water supplies to villages. It also included the Volta River Project,

1961, which aimed to produce electricity and power for an aluminium smelter built in 1964, and increased irrigation.

Social development

Nkrumah had promised full employment, free primary education and a national health service. He had a crash programme to build schools and hospitals.

Prestige development

New government buildings, a television station and broadcasting station were built in Accra, and a rarely-used motorway was built linking Accra and Tema.

Private investment often took un-African forms such as the building of Western-type hotels in Accra.

Paying for the development

Nkrumah borrowed heavily. Ghana found it difficult to repay her debts, even when prices of her main export, cocoa, were high. When prices fell in the 1960s, repayment was impossible.

Political instability

Unrest because of the government's failure led to an army plot to overthrow Nkrumah in 1958. This failed but it led to a Preventive Detention Act (1959) allowing the imprisonment without trial of opponents, including Opposition MPs; the purging of Nkrumah's party to get rid of critics; and the deportation of Muslim leaders.

In July 1960 Ghana became a republic with Nkrumah as President. A plebiscite showed about 90 per cent approval for the change.

Nkrumah became even more autocratic. The Chief Justice was sacked for not convicting three of Nkrumah's party accused of plotting against him. The Constitution was changed to give the president power to overturn decisions of the Supreme Court. A referendum agreed with his decision to set up a one-party state.

Pan-Africanism

Nkrumah had ambitious ideas for African development throughout the continent. He called the first conference of independent African states in Accra in 1958. When the OAU was set up in Addis Ababa in 1963, he spoke in favour of the political unification of all Africa.

Changes in leadership

Nkrumah's overthrow, February 1966, was due to increasing discontent with his rule: the economy was in ruins and Ghana could not pay her debts. Politicians opposed to his autocracy combined with the army to overthrow him while he was visiting Peking. He was not allowed to return and died in exile in 1972.

In 1969 a new democratic constitution was proclaimed and elections saw the return of a Progress Party led by Bassia. However, an economic recession in 1971 led to further unrest and again the army intervened. In January 1972 Colonel Acheampong arrested the civilian government, withdrew the 1969 Constitution and ruled by decree through a Supreme Military Council.

In 1978 General Akuffo led another army coup because of the corrupt and inefficient way in which Acheampong's government failed to deal with Ghana's problems made worse by the oil price increases.

In 1979 Flight Lieut. Rawlings organized a coup in which Akuffo and Acheampong were executed. Rawlings promised a return to civilian government. Dr Hilla Limann was installed as President after an election in a country with a collapsing economy, aggravated social tension and little faith in politicians. It was a far cry from the optimism of 1957.

36.3 Uganda

In this largely agricultural country the tribal chiefs, led by the Kabaka of Buganda, had opposed British attempts to give Africans a share in the government of the country. The Kabaka was exiled in Britain between 1953 and 1955.

Black politicians had formed many (largely tribal) political parties. In 1960 the two largest combined to form the Uganda People's Congress, led by Milton Obote.

In 1962 Uganda became an independent state, a federation in which Buganda was one state. Milton Obote was the first Prime Minister.

In 1967 Uganda, Tanzania and Kenya formed the East African Community, an African form of the EEC (see Unit 31).

Tribal rivalries led to many clashes. In 1971 Idi Amin led an army coup against Obote and replaced him as head of state.

Ugandan Asians had a good deal of economic power while most of them refused to give up their British citizenship. Obote had wanted to limit their powers and give Africans chances to get on. In 1972 Amin announced that all Asians not having Ugandan citizenship had to leave within 90 days. This was condemned by Kenya and Tanzania. Many Commonwealth countries took in the former Ugandan Asians. Many settled in Britain, which, in 1973, passed a new immigration Act giving the government power to refuse to accept such 'refugees' even with British passports.

THE OVERTHROW OF AMIN, 1979

Nyerere of Tanzania was angered by the tyranny of Idi Amin. This gave black Africa a poor image throughout the world:

▶ there was the ill-treatment of the Asians (see above);
▶ there was, in 1975, the threatened execution of Mr Denis Hills, the British author of an unpublished book which criticized Amin;
▶ in 1976 there was the 'disappearance' of Mrs Dora Bloch during the raid on Entebbe by the Israelis (see below);
▶ in 1977 there was the sudden death of the Archbishop of Uganda, who had attacked Amin's corrupt and tyrannical rule.

Tribal groups inside Uganda were angered by Amin's rule, which favoured the Muslims of northern Uganda (from whom he had originated) at the expense of other tribes and national groups.

Border clashes took place between Ugandan troops and troops from Tanzania and Kenya. Tanzanian troops finally invaded Uganda to help rebel tribes. Amin was defeated and in April 1979 he fled to Libya.

THE RETURN AND DEPARTURE OF MILTON OBOTE

Obote who had been overthrown by Amin in 1971 (see above) returned with the victorious Tanzanian forces. But his government did not bring much peace to Uganda. The small section that had benefited from Amin's rule now found itself under attack. Tribalism remained a powerful and divisive force.

Obote's rule was marked by economic decline, further tribal fighting and the continuation of terror which Amin had practised. Exports of coffee, cotton and copper almost ceased; medical and other services collapsed. Obote's harsh, corrupt and inefficient rule was opposed by a National Resistance Movement led by Museveni. In the ensuing guerrilla war conditions declined further. Obote was forced to flee from the country in 1985, leaving behind a state where even children formed part of guerrilla armies.

36.4 Zaire

THE BELGIAN CONGO, 1945–60

This mineral-rich region contained 150 tribes. There were poor communications inside this very large state.

The Belgians had made no preparations for independence: there were no elections until 1957, when only local councils were elected. There were no African political parties; there was no African in a leading post in the Civil Service and few Africans trained in administration. There were no African army officers, and almost no African graduates and doctors.

In 1957–8, affected by the movement to independence in Ghana and other countries, Patrice Lumumba, a post office clerk, founded the Congolese National Movement, seeking early independence.

In 1959 large-scale unemployment led to widespread rioting. The Belgians panicked and in January 1960 announced that from June 1960 the country would be independent.

In June 1960 President Kasavubu named Lumumba as Prime Minister of a country whose first parliament contained 50 parties.

THE CONGO BECOMES ZAIRE

Immediate problems facing the country included:

▶ tribalism: tribes in the richer provinces did not want to share their wealth with the poorer regions;
▶ the army mutinied soon after independence. Many Europeans were attacked and killed;
▶ the Belgian government and the mine-owning Union Minière encouraged tribes in mineral-rich areas to seek self-government.

Lumumba was from the Batatele tribe, hated by the Kasai and the people from Katanga. He was also hated by the Belgians because he was a socialist who threatened to nationalize their mines.

In July 1960, one month after independence, the Kasai and people from Katanga declared their regions to be independent. The Belgians rushed in troops to defend their mines. Lumumba appealed to the UN for help.

The UN and the Congo

The UN wanted to maintain the unity of the Congo. It formed an army from small, 'neutral' countries, but it had no power to interfere in the internal affairs of a country. The dispute between Lumumba and Katanga was said to be an internal affair. This led Lumumba to ask for Russian help. An angry Kasavubu then sacked Lumumba, who was captured and slain by forces from Katanga.

Moise Tshombe was declared head of the independent state of Katanga and received military and technical aid from Belgium.

UN Secretary-General Dag Hammarskjöld went to the Congo to try to sort out affairs (September 1961). He was killed in a mysterious air crash. UN forces were rushed in to try to end the independence of Katanga (which had made the issue an external and not only an internal affair).

After many clashes between UN forces and troops from Katanga led by European mercenaries, the Katanga rebellion ended early in 1963.

Towards independence

In July 1964 Kasavubu named Tshombe as Prime Minister of the Congo. But there were many tribal rebellions against his rule. He used European mercenaries to put these down.

A food shortage made him unpopular in the Congo, while his subservience to European capitalists made him unpopular throughout Africa. In October 1965 he was dismissed by Kasavubu.

Tshombe went into exile, but was condemned to death in his absence. In 1967 he was imprisoned in Algeria when his aircraft was hijacked. He died in 1969.

Mobuto had been a corporal in the Belgian army who became a general on independence. In October 1965 after Tshombe's sacking he overthrew Kasavubu and became President. He used the army to put down more resistance from Katanga.

In 1968 he cleared the country of mercenaries, nationalized the mines and ended Belgian influence. In 1970 he was confirmed in office as President and in 1971 he re-named the country Zaire.

PROBLEMS IN ZAIRE

In 1977 Katanga was invaded by troops from Angola, seeking revenge for Zaire's earlier intervention in that country's affairs. They were supported by the Soviet Union, which resented the USA's influence in Zaire. This invasion was put down with the aid of troops from Morocco, Egypt, France and Belgium.

Zaire suffered because of the trade recession which followed the increase in oil prices in 1973 and 1979. There was a sharp fall in world copper prices (Zaire's major export), while a drought forced the country to import huge quantities of expensive food. These economic difficulties led to political and tribal unrest. Mobuto became increasingly dictatorial; international agencies condemned him for his ill-treatment of political prisoners. Mobuto assumed ever grander titles ('President-for-Life') and amassed a personal fortune while the country sank further into economic decline.

▨ 36.5 Kenya ▨

Kenya was a major exporter of tea, coffee and sisal but there was little industrial development before 1945. Arabs, Asians and a multiplicity of African tribes were ruled by a whites-only government aiming to please, mainly, the Europeans who had settled in the towns and, particularly, in the Highlands where they ran large farms.

Africans were discontented in 1945. Large-scale unemployment and low wages led to low living standards for townspeople. The educated Africans resented the bar which prevented them holding jobs reserved for Europeans. Many tribes, but particularly the Kikuyu, claimed that Europeans had 'stolen' their land in the past. As nomadic farmers they were used to leaving land 'free' to recover. Europeans had moved on to this unoccupied land.

KENYATTA AND THE KIKUYU

The Kikuyu were the largest tribe. They had their own Kikuyu Central Association to run their affairs. In 1929 Jomo Kenyatta was a delegate to this Association which sent him to London to take part in a commission examining the land question. In 1930 Kenyatta returned to Kenya but almost immediately went back to London to study (1930–2). He also studied at Moscow University (1932–4) before settling in London. He married an English woman in 1942.

In 1946 he returned to Kenya as Principal of the Kikuyu Independent Teachers' Training College. He formed the Kenyan African Union (KAU) to replace the Kikuyu Central Association outlawed by the white government.

Kenyatta led his people's demand for a share in the government of their country. In 1954 six Africans were brought on to the previously all-white council governing Kenya. But this was too little and too late.

THE MAU MAU TERRORISTS

In 1948 members of the banned Kikuyu Association formed a secret society called Mau Mau. This became a mass movement in which the Kikuyu were bound together by terrifying oaths.

In 1952 attacks were made to terrorize Europeans and thousands of Africans who refused to join the Mau Mau. In October 1952 Kenyatta and 130 leaders were arrested. The violence increased. Farms were burnt, animals crippled and slain, hundreds of 'loyal' Africans murdered.

In March 1953, after a massacre of Kikuyu by the Mau Mau, many turned against the society and helped the British to fight it.

INDEPENDENT KENYA

The war went on until 1960, by which time 10,000 Mau Mau were killed and the government had tried to improve the constitution. In 1956 each tribe was allowed its own political party—but there was to be no national party. This was condemned by the OAU, by Africans at the UN and by the Labour Opposition in Britain. But Africans had their first chance to put their representatives into the Legislative Assembly.

In 1960 Britain produced another constitution which denied Africans control of the Legislative Assembly. This was widely condemned—particularly by black Kenyans whose leaders were imprisoned as Mau Mau terrorists.

In April 1961 the KAU agreed to form a government, provided that the government built a home for the still-imprisoned Kenyatta in the Kiambu district where he was exiled. In August 1961 Kenyatta was freed; he became, again, the main political leader of the Africans.

In December 1963 Kenya became an independent republic within the Commonwealth, with Kenyatta as its first Prime Minister.

In independent Kenya tribalism was avoided, as Kenyatta chose ministers from more than one tribe and all Kenyan citizens were treated equally. Many Europeans stayed on to help run the country.

Kenyatta declared the country a one-party-state—both to avoid the emergence of tribal parties, and to check the growth of opposition. He imprisoned one of his former supporters, the Mau Mau leader, Oginga Odinga, for trying to form an opposition.

Kenyan Asians who refused to take out Kenyan citizenship were driven from the country in a policy of Africanization. In 1968, 60,000 former Kenyan Asians arrived in Britain with their British passports.

In 1978 Kenyatta died, leaving behind a state with a stable government and a thriving economy. His successor, Daniel arap Moi, was unfortunate; he became President as Kenya began to suffer from the effects of the oil-induced trade recession. A sharp fall in world prices for coffee and tea (which form 60 per cent of Kenya's exports) and increases in the prices for Kenya's imports led to deficits in the balance of payments. A poor harvest (1978–9) led to food shortages and increased prices which provided opportunity for some ministers and officials to indulge in corrupt practices. Moi's attacks on such corruption marked Kenya out as one of the few examples of an independent African government seeking to provide honest rule.

▨ 36.6 Tanzania ▨

TANGANYIKA, 1945–61

This largest country in Africa is underpopulated because of the harsh climate and the ravages of the tsetse fly. It was a British Mandate from 1920 to 1947 (Unit 13) when it came under the UN Trusteeship Council (see Unit 27).

Successive colonial governors had brought Africans into the Legislative Council while always allowing the chiefs to retain some power in the system of indirect rule.

Black politics were dominated by the Tanganyikan African Association formed in the 1920s. In 1954 this became the Tanganyikan African National Union (TANU) with Julius Nyerere as president.

Constitutional progress was marked by important changes. In 1947 the Legislative Council had 15 'official' members and 14 'unofficial' members. All were appointed by the British government. Three of the 'unofficials' were Asian and four were African. In 1955 a new constitution gave ten 'unofficial' members to each of the three racial groups. The government ensured control by its appointment of 31 'official' members.

In 1957 Tanganyika was given ministerial responsibility— government ministers were responsible to parliament. In 1958, in the first elections under the new constitution, TANU won every seat in spite of strong opposition from British-supported parties. This success was repeated in 1959 and 1960.

In 1960 Nyerere negotiated self-government and in December 1961 Tanganyika became independent.

AFTER INDEPENDENCE

In December 1962 Tanganyika became a republic with Nyerere as President. In 1964 she united with Zanzibar to form Tanzania.

Problems included the poverty of the country with its few natural resources and its 'front line' position in the black struggle with Rhodesia (see below).

Nyerere provided his country with political stability without any of the tribal violence common elsewhere. He initiated a peasant-based form of socialism, avoiding Russian-like steps towards industrialization. He taught the people that progress would be slow and would have to be earned. He insisted on austerity for himself and his ministers so that there has been none of the family-based corruption common elsewhere.

Economic planning has been undertaken by the National Economic Development Corporation which manages most of the economy. Nationalization was widespread. In 1964 an economic plan was drawn up in union with the two partners in the East African Community. Industries were to be sited in each country by the Community and not by decisions of the separate governments. The Community Service Organization controls the currency, customs, postal services, railways and harbours of the three states.

Nyerere, like Nkrumah, was a leading member of the OAU. He called on Africans to develop, in unity, the vast resources of their continent with its market of 250 million people.

From 1965 onwards, Tanzania was one of the 'front-line' states in the African's struggle against the illegal regime in Southern Rhodesia (see below). This brought Nyerere into dispute with Britain and was economically very costly. As the war wound down, the country was affected by the oil price increases of 1979 which pushed up her imports bill, by falls in the world prices for tea and coffee (her main exports) which drove down her overseas earnings and by the effect of the war against Amin which cost Tanzania at least £1 billion.

In 1980 Nyerere was forced to ask the IMF for a loan of £100 million which many of his critics claimed as proof that his high-minded ideals had not worked. They claimed that his impractical ideas coupled with the corruption of many of his ministers and officials had led Tanzania deeper into poverty.

In 1985 Nyerere retired.

36.7 Zambia

THE CENTRAL AFRICAN FEDERATION, 1953–63

In February 1953 Britain set up a Federation of three colonies—Northern Rhodesia (Zambia), Nyasaland (Malawi) and Southern Rhodesia (Zimbabwe), which had been self-governing since 1923. The Federation was supposed to achieve independence.

The main problem was racial. Was the Federation to be governed by whites only (as was S. Rhodesia) or by a black majority? Godfrey Huggins of S. Rhodesia was the first Prime Minister of the Federation. He intended that the whites would rule.

Black Congress Parties were led by Kenneth Kaunda (in N. Rhodesia) and by Hastings Banda in Nyasaland. Huggins had both arrested.

Black rioting in 1955 led to two British-appointed commissions examining the problems of the Federation. Both said that the Federation would fail because of black opposition. The British government refused to send an army to hold it together by force. In December 1963 the Federation was dissolved.

ZAMBIAN INDEPENDENCE

Zambia (Northern Rhodesia) became independent in July 1964 with Kaunda as its first President. It contains 75 different tribes. In the late 1960s the Vice-President, Kepwepwe, planned to set up a separate Bemba state in the north. Kaunda sacked him.

Zambia's main export is copper, whose price on world markets swings up and down depending on world demand.

In 1973 Kaunda declared Zambia a one-party state, hoping to avoid the rise of tribal factionalism.

After 1965 Zambia was another of the 'front line' states in the struggle with Rhodesia. Kaunda supported the policy of sanctions against Rhodesia, even though this harmed his own trade, dependent as it was on the rail link through Rhodesia to Beira on the coast (see below).

The Chinese-built Tan-Zam Railway has provided another link to the coast and helps Zambia's trade.

36.8 Zimbabwe

RHODESIA

The break up of the Central African Federation (see above) left S. Rhodesia as a self-governing colony where a white minority held total political power. The whites became more right-wing in their views.

Prime Minister Todd was dismissed in 1958 for trying to legalize trade unions and to give blacks some greater freedom. His successor, Whitehead, lost power when he condemned some forms of racial discrimination.

In 1962 Winston Field led the right-wing Rhodesian Front Party to electoral victory. White Rhodesians demanded independence—already given to Zambia and Malawi, their black partners in the Federation. The British Conservative government refused to give power while only 5 per cent of the population had political control. Africans had only 15 of the 65 seats in parliament, and African political organizations were banned.

SMITH AND UDI

Field was sacked to make way for Ian Smith. Rhodesians hoped he would force Britain to give way. Britain refused to grant independence 'before majority rule'.

In 1964 Wilson's Labour government came to power in Britain. Smith began to talk of making an illegal declaration of independence. On 11 November 1965 Smith announced the Unilateral Declaration of Independence (UDI) and named the country Rhodesia. To ensure peace, he imposed press censorship and banned African political meetings.

Britain and the UN imposed trade sanctions on the illegally-governed state. Various businesses in Europe and the USA and several states in Africa (South Africa and the Portuguese colonies) provided Rhodesia with access to international markets.

To try to stop oil getting in, the British navy patrolled the

Beira coast. Oil got in via South Africa. In the meantime, Zambia, which had imported its oil via Beira, suffered until the Chinese built the Tan-Zam Railway (see above).

Zambia and Tanzania were 'front line' states in the blacks' fight against Smith. Freedom fighters trained in these states, from where they invaded Rhodesia in guerrilla attacks.

Talks were held between Smith and Wilson of Britain in 1966, 1968 and 1970 without producing agreement.

A new Conservative government (1970) tried to get a settlement. It sent out the Pearce Commission to seek African opinion of the proposed constitution. Black Rhodesians rejected the scheme.

Slowly sanctions had an effect. More seriously, the Portuguese gave independence to Angola and Mozambique (see below), leaving Rhodesia even more isolated.

In 1975 Smith tried to negotiate a deal with Nkomo, the leader of the Matabele section of the guerrilla movement. He probably (and rightly) thought that Nkomo would be less demanding and less extreme than Mugabe.

TOWARDS INDEPENDENCE

In 1978 Smith announced a new constitution: blacks were to vote in parliamentary elections and could stand as candidates; if blacks gained a majority they would hold office; the whites would reserve 25 seats in the small parliament, so having the ability to prevent the passing of important laws, which would have to have a two-thirds majority. Whites would retain control of the army, police, foreign office and other important posts.

Bishop Abel Muzorewa became the first black Prime Minister.

Militant blacks led by Joshua Nkomo and Robert Mugabe (the leader of the Mashona section of the guerrilla movement), continued their guerrilla war on a government in which whites still held control.

Talks were held between Smith, Muzorewa, Nkomo, Mugabe and British ministers to try to find a solution. In 1979 a new constitution was worked out, giving blacks more power. The guerrilla war was called off. Robert Mugabe became the Prime Minister in 1980. He brought in a number of socialist reforms, limiting white power, giving government more control of the economy. Mugabe then quarrelled with his former partner, Nkomo and tribal violence developed, with many Matabele being killed.

Many Europeans moved out of what is rapidly becoming a one-party state.

36.9 Nigeria

This large state contained 56 million people from 150 separate tribes. It is rich in resources, including oil.

Regionalism was a fact of Nigerian life and was enshrined in early constitutional progress. In 1946 a constitution recognized three self-ruling regions:

▶ the northern region was dominated by the Hausa people, agricultural by occupation and Muslim by religion;
▶ the western region (including Lagos) was dominated by the Yoruba tribe, many of whom were Christian in religion;
▶ the eastern region was dominated by the Ibo, the most Christian and best-educated of the Nigerian tribes.

The Yoruba and the Ibo tended to dominate the commercial, industrial and official life of the country.

Regional politicians fought for independence. Nmandi Azikiwe ('Zik') was an American-educated Ibo who founded several Nigerian newspapers to preach nationalism. Awolowo formed the Yoruba-dominated Nigerian Youth Movement as a vehicle for his brand of nationalism. 'Zik' founded the National Council of Nigeria and the Cameroons, which from 1944 to 1957 was the dominant party. The Northern People's Congress (NPC) party was formed by the Hausas to express their kind of nationalism.

In 1951–60 under a new constitution there were separate Houses of Representatives for each of the regions. The NPC won 80 of the 92 seats in the Northern House; the Ibo and Yoruba had similar majorities in the Eastern and Western regions.

In the Central House of Representatives:

▶ 64 seats were reserved for the north;
▶ 34 seats were assigned to each of east and west:

The Council of Ministers had 4 members from each region. In 1960 Nigeria became an independent Federal State, and in 1963 it became a republic with 'Zik' as President and a northerner, Abubakar Tafewa Balewa, as Prime Minister.

THE CIVIL WAR

In 1964 there was acknowledged dishonesty at the elections: 78 candidates were declared 'unopposed', even though there had been opposition candidates.

The Yoruba resented the power of the Hausa. Balewa ordered the arrest of Awolowo, the Prime Minister of the Western Region.

In November 1965 in the Western Region elections the Yoruba complained of Ibo manipulation of the results. Two lists of elected candidates were published—one by the Ibo, one by the Yoruba. Widespread rioting left 2000 dead at the end of 1965.

In January 1966 the unrest spread. Prime Minister Balewa, Yoruba leader Akintola and the Northern Premier, the Sardauna of Sokoto, were all murdered. The Ibo general, Ironsi, announced that a military government had replaced the civilian government. He promised to divide the country into many provinces, hoping to end the regionalism. The northern Hausa feared the loss of their power. They massacred Ibos living in the north.

In July 1966 a northerner, General Gowon, led a rising which overthrew Ironsi. Between 10,000 and 30,000 Ibos were murdered in the north in September.

In May 1967 Colonel Ojukwu, military governor of the Eastern (Ibo) Region announced that the Eastern Region was seceding under the name of Biafra. This war lasted until January 1970 when Biafra surrendered.

POLITICAL INSTABILITY

After the war Gowon's government faced many problems:

▶ large-scale unemployment because of the chaos;
▶ increased tribal hatred by and for the Ibo who make up one-fifth of the population and are the best educated;
▶ the need for a constitution which would limit, if it could not end, the regional differences.

In 1975 Gowon's military government was overthrown by a military coup led by Brigadier Murtalla Muhammad, another Northerner. He set himself two main tasks:

▶ to create a new constitution, in which there might be less room for the regional divisions to show themselves. Nigeria was, for electoral purposes, divided into 19 states;
▶ to root out the corruption which had led to some leaders and officials becoming very wealthy and which had been one of the reasons for Nigeria's economic backwardness.

In 1975 Murtalla was assassinated within six months. His government continued under the leadership of Lieutenant General Olusegun Obansanjo, who worked steadily towards the 1979 elections, which re-launched Nigerian politics under a new United States-style constitution.

The year 1979 was a landmark in African and Nigerian politics. The military leadership handed back power to civilian politicians and organized an election. Shehu Shagari, a northern Muslim, became Nigeria's first US-style executive President, after the first elections to be held for 13 years.

1983 saw another general election in which, again, Shagari was returned to office. There were, however, doubts as to his ability to hold on to power. The 1983 elections had been the occasion of a great deal of well-publicized corruption and violence. There were too many Nigerians who were not happy with the outcome of this election. Corruption had not been attacked; indeed, it had grown so that the life-styles of the leading ministers and chief officials had become too much for suffering Nigerians to bear (see below).

The continued economic problems (see below) led to attempts to cut government spending and to cut imports. These attempts led to:

▶ increased unemployment, particularly among the un-skilled who had been attracted to the cities and towns during the 'boom' days from 1973 to 1979 (see below);

▶ higher taxes, imposed by the government in efforts to make it more difficult for people to buy imported goods. These higher taxes (on incomes and on goods) led to a fall in living standards for the majority of Nigerians;

▶ even more corruption, as officials and ministers sold the permits and licenses needed to do certain work or to import certain commodities. The rich life-style of the corrupt officials was in stark contrast to the much harder lives lived by the majority.

In December 1983 Shagari announced a fresh budget. This was intended to cut living standards even further, since taxes were to be further increased and government spending to be cut in another effort to cut the budget deficit which was to be, in 1984, double that which had been forecast—and that would have meant a government overspending of £11.4 billion.

Shagari's government was overthrown in what was Nigeria's fifth military coup since independence. Many people had expected the military to stage a coup at the time of the August 1983 elections. In fact they waited until December 1983. Led by Major-General Buhari the army set up a fresh government and promised, as all governments have promised in Nigeria, to root out corruption, to heal the tribal divisions and to restore the Nigerian economy.

NIGERIA'S ECONOMIC PROGRESS AND DECLINE, 1973–86

Nigeria was rich in oil resources. OPEC's sharp rises in oil prices after 1973 made Nigeria a very rich country. She planned to sell 3 million barrels of oil a day at 1979 prices of 35 dollars a barrel. Her economic plans were based on those figures. She contracted for major developments—harbours, roads, urban development, steel, chemical and cement industries and much social development—the provision of schools and hospitals for example.

Since 1979 there has been a fall in world demand for oil and yet a rise in oil production. This has led to Nigeria being able to sell only 1½ million barrels a day at 27 dollars a barrel.

Nigeria, in 1983, went through a serious economic crisis. She had no financial reserves, a heavy overseas debt and many unfinished projects. This caused tensions which, in Nigeria, took the form of tribal hostility.

The sharp fall in oil prices in 1986 increased Nigeria's economic and social problems. With oil at between 10 and 15 dollars a barrel, Buhari's government became increasingly incapable of living up to its promises. In the face of widespread opposition Buhari adopted repressive tactics, including the jailing of opponents and the use of military tribunals rather than civil courts to dispense justice. In August 1985 General Babangida organized Nigeria's sixth coup and seized power. He freed most political prisoners, negotiated a loan from the IMF aimed at lessening the effects of the continued fall in oil prices and promised a return to civilian government by 1990.

▓▓ 36.10 South Africa ▓▓

The Union of South Africa was created in 1910 (see Unit 5) as the British tried to win the friendship of the Boers. The policy of Union governments was always 'whites only government'. In 1936 Africans in the Cape Province were

taken off the electoral roll; their position was worse in 1936 than in 1900. Also in 1936 other non-whites (Asians and Coloureds) could vote—but only for white MPs.

In 1948 the Afrikaaners (Boers) won the election, Malan succeeding the 'liberal' Smuts as Prime Minister.

APARTHEID

Apartheid (the separate development of the Africans) was the official policy of all succeeding Afrikaaner (or Nationalist) governments. The black Africans were to have their own Native Reserves, where they could have their own industries and institutions. This was an unreal policy, because European industry in African towns needed the blacks to work at various levels—skilled and unskilled, highly qualified and less so, and because European homes needed the labour of black servants.

The Asian and Coloured voters were removed from the common electoral roll in 1956.

Verwoerd, Prime Minister in 1958–60, explained apartheid as a policy aiming to allow blacks and whites to live, each in their own 'states', as good neighbours. In practice this meant that Africans living in towns have become second-class citizens. They have to carry passes or identity cards issued only to essential workers but not to their families. Passes have to be shown whenever police ask; anyone not carrying a pass or having an out-of-date pass is imprisoned before being deported to a Reserve.

Bantu Education Acts ensured that African children had only a low level of education, fitting them only for poorly-paid jobs. African housing was separate from white, and black housing was always liable to be pulled down by white local authorities. Jobs, particularly those carrying responsibility, were only open to whites.

Some Africans had to be allowed to live in towns. But as many as possible were forced to move into the reserves under the Group Areas Act. An Immorality Act made it a crime for whites to marry or have sexual relations with blacks.

A Suppression of Communism Act was used to crush African efforts to form political parties or to develop campaigns against apartheid.

When Lower Courts failed to condemn blacks, the government created a new and ever-reliable High Court of Parliament.

Verwoerd was shot by a white farmer; he recovered, only to be stabbed to death in 1966.

His successor, Johannes Vorster, further developed the policy of apartheid and the creation of Bantustans (see below). He also strictly enforced petty apartheid, the laws by which blacks are forbidden to use 'whites only' cafés, public utilities, doors into post offices and hotels, beaches and other leisure facilities.

Bantustans

These were created first by Verwoerd. Eight regions were set aside to become self-governing black African states.

Although black Africans make up about four fifths of the population of South Africa, the Bantustans were to take only 14 per cent of the land mass of the Union.

The first Bantustan was the Transkei. Its Prime Minister was Chief Matanzima, who soon demanded that the whites leave the Transkei and went on to demand more land for his people.

TIGHTENING THE WHITE GRIP

In 1953 it was made a crime for African workers to strike.

In 1952 Chief Luthuli, a moderate, tried to organize a resistance to the segregation laws. He was deprived of his chieftainship.

A new law permitted flogging of anyone breaking existing laws.

In March 1960 at Sharpeville thousands of Africans gathered to protest peacefully against the pass laws; 67 were killed when police fired on the crowd.

BREAKING THE GRIP

In 1960 South Africa became a republic and had to apply for continued membership of the Commonwealth. In 1961 this application was opposed; Verwoerd withdrew it and South Africa left the Commonwealth.

The OAU and the UN constantly condemned apartheid.

In 1962 the UN imposed a trade boycott on South Africa. Not all countries followed this boycott, preferring to benefit from trade with the rich country which produced most of the world's gold. Sanctions have proved totally ineffective.

In 1968 the South African government refused to allow the coloured cricketer, Basil d'Oliveira, to enter the country as a member of the MCC team. The tour was cancelled. In 1968–69 radicals in Britain tried to stop the tour of Britain by the South Africa rugby team – but failed. In 1970 the clashes during the rugby tour led the British government to enforce the cancellation of the proposed South African cricket tour. Other Commonwealth countries followed this example; Australia cancelled a tour proposed for 1971.

Other international sports organizations took similar action so that South Africa was barred from all international sport. One result of this was attempts in South Africa to change the petty apartheid laws as far as they affected sport. White teams played coloured and black teams; some black sportsmen were chosen for national sides; white schools played games against black schools.

However, this was not enough to persuade the world that South Africa was ready to be welcomed back. Black sportsmen had few facilities and black schoolchildren poorer chances than white. Even if black and white sportsmen were allowed to mix during and immediately after a game, they were not allowed to have any more contact until the next game.

The effects of apartheid on sport could not be removed until the whole policy was swept away.

WHITES LOOSEN THEIR GRIP

In 1978 P W Botha became Prime Minister when Vorster became President of the Republic of South Africa. Botha was under pressure form white businessmen who needed both a supply of educated black labour and access to a developing black market. He was also aware of the growth of anti-government opinion both inside and outside the Republic. In particular he was conscious of the attitudes of black governments to the north which had aided Angola and Mozambique in their struggle and were, in 1978, helping Mugabe and Nkomo in their struggle against Smith.

Botha's government abolished some aspects of apartheid. Job discrimination declined; companies were allowed to end the segregation of toilet, dining and other facilities in factories and offices; black trade unions were legalized and became a focal point for black activists seeking improved social and economic conditions; some multi-racial theatres, hotels and restaurants were opened. In this more 'liberal' atmosphere, white industrialists encouraged black education and training, and, in 1986, forced the government to abolish the 1959 Universities Act.

In 1984 Botha's government introduced a new constitution. This provided for a segregated three-chamber Parliament for Whites, Coloureds and Asians. Only people of the appropriate racial group were elected to each chamber, while only people of that racial group voted for them. The constitution was rigged, the wishes of the majority in the white chamber always prevailed. However, the grant of the franchise to two of the non-white racial groups only increased resentment among blacks and heightened their political awareness.

In 1985 the Mixed Marriages Act and most of the Immorality Act were abolished, although mixed couples were still subject to other apartheid laws, such as those affecting where they lived, for example.

In September 1985, white industrialists from the Republic went to Zambia to meet leaders of black guerilla movements. They wanted to try to build bridges between white and black leaders indicating their belief that the future of the Republic lay with black leaders.

In elections held in 1981 and 1985 Botha's party was returned to power. However, there was increasing white support for extremist right-wing groups who opposed Botha's slow dismantling of apartheid.

At the same time there was increased activity among blacks. Some had campaigned for the release of the jailed leader of the African National Congress, Nelson Mandela. He was seen, by many whites and many blacks, as the real leader of black of opinion in the Republic. Others, impatient with the lack of success of the ANC, took to militant action. In black townships such as Soweto and Alexandra, younger blacks, such as Steve Biko, worked among schoolchildren and young blacks to raise their political consciousness. In spite of the killing of Biko, the constant presence of the army and the police, and the many imprisonments, the evidence was that black opinion was hardening, becoming more confident and demanding.

The abolition of the Pass Laws, the cause of the unrest in Sharpeville (see p. 146) failed to satisfy black opinion. Blacks had moved a long way from the relatively moderate position they occupied at the time of Sharpeville. Here was another example of a government which had done too little too late.

For recent developments see Unit 44.

36.11 Angola and Mozambique

These Portuguese colonies were among the larger states. By the mid-1960s they were, with Rhodesia and South Africa, symbols of white supremacy as other states gained their independence.

In 1964 Portugal signed an agreement for economic co-operation with South Africa. She also played a major role in helping Ian Smith to resist British attempts to break his illegal régime.

Guerrilla movements by black nationalists developed in Angola in 1961, while the Mozambique Liberation Front (Frelimo) was founded to organize the anti-colonial struggle there.

Portugal was helped in her anti-terrorist campaigns by white mercenaries from Britain, the USA, West Germany and South Africa.

The right-wing government in Portugal refused to enter into negotiations about self-rule.

In 1974 after the death of the autocratic Salazar in Portugal there was a revolution which led to the establishment of a democratic system in Portugal. In 1975 the new government granted independence to both Angola and Mozambique, which now became front-line states in the black struggle against South Africa, the last remaining white bastion.

Unit 36 Summary

- ► Africa's problems.
- ► Ghana: Nkrumah's policies and failure.
- ► Uganda: from democracy to Amin and Obote.
- ► The Congo: UNO involvement: Mobutu's dictatorship.
- ► Kenya: Mau Mau and independence under Kenyatta.
- ► Tanzania: Nyerere's problems and failures.
- ► The Central African Federation; origins and break up: Banda and Malawi; Kaunda and Zambia.
- ► From 'Rhodesia' to Zimbabwe.
- ► Nigeria; civil war; economic growth and collapse.
- ► South Africa; the white 'tribe' under pressure.
- ► Angola and Mozambique.

37 NORTH AFRICA AND THE MIDDLE EAST, 1945-86

37.1 Algeria

Algeria was the largest of the French colonies in N. Africa. For many years French settlers had lived in comfort and had done little to help the Muslim Algerians, most of whom lived in poverty.

In the 1930s a number of Algerian nationalist movements were founded. The North African Star was founded by Muslim exiles in Paris and was meant to defend working-class interests. By 1936 this had become the (La) Partie Populaire Algérienne. Muslim intellectuals, such as Ferhat Abbas, campaigned in Algeria for the extension to Muslims of civil and political rights. The Association of Algerian Ulama set up Algerian schools to give Arabic education to the 90 per cent of children ignored by the French colonial school system.

The years 1939–45 saw an increase in nationalist activity. Some Algerians welcomed the Germans, hoping for freedom from French settler rule. Others fought in resistance movements, hoping to win French sympathy.

In 1945–50 Abbas proposed to de Gaulle (see Unit 31) that he should allow an Algerian Republic to be set up in which French and Arab would be equal. De Gaulle allowed only equal opportunities for French and such Arabs as could get on, and the formation of an Algerian Assembly of 120 representatives elected by Algerian Muslims. This had no real power.

1954–62

France was fighting and losing a war in Indo-China (see Unit 35).

Muslims in Pakistan, Arabs in Egypt and blacks in Ghana had or were winning their independence.

In 1954 the FLN (or National Liberation Front) was founded by Ben Bella to fight a guerrilla war against French rule. This was helped by aid from Egypt and Russia.

The French settlers supported the French army of 600,000 which was determined not to lose this colony as it had Vietnam. In 1955 the UN proposed that Algeria should be independent, but the war continued, with Muslim guerrillas attacking French property in the countryside and towns.

In 1958 the army feared that the politicians might make a deal with the Muslims. General Salan led an army revolt which led to the overthrow of the Republic and de Gaulle's return to power (see Unit 31). De Gaulle realized that the French could not win and began negotiations with the rebel leaders.

French officers and settlers formed the OAS, a French terrorist organization aimed at preventing the handover of Algeria (OAS from the French term Organization de l'Armée Secrète). This was ruthlessly suppressed by de Gaulle.

In l962 an agreement was reached which ended the fighting. Ben Bella, the first President of the Algerian Republic, was replaced by Boumédienne (1965) who described Bella as a despot.

The French gave independence to Morocco and Tunisia with much less trouble (see Unit 40.8).

37.2 The Arab League

Britain had had a great deal of power in the Middle East through its control of Egypt and its Palestinian Mandate. In October 1945 Britain helped the formation of the Arab League. Egypt, Iraq, Syria, the Lebanon and Saudi Arabia were the first members of the League, which was intended to be an obstacle to Russian progress in this region.

As other Arab states gained independence they joined, and by 1983 the Sudan, Algeria, Morocco, Tunisia, Libya, Oman, South Yemen, Kuwait and Bahrein were members of the League.

The 36 million Arabs shared a common language and culture; most of them were Muslims and all of them had shared a hatred of colonial rule. They also had similar economic problems. Even the countries rich in oil had a mal-distribution of wealth 80 that here, and in the non-oil countries, there was a great disparity between the very rich (few) and the very poor (majority). The population of these countries was expanding and there wag little chance of them being able to provide decent living standards for their peoples.

Above all else these Arab countries were opposed to Israel.

37.3 Palestine, 1923–47

Palestine became a British Mandate after 1923. Wartime promises had led to the growth of Arab expectations and to Jewish hopes for a national home (see Unit 13).

The Zionist Movement had been started by a Viennese Jew, Theodore Herzl. At the first Zionist Congress in 1896 he had proposed the idea of a national home for the world's Jews. The Balfour declaration (Unit 13) seemed a British commitment to that idea.

In the 1920s 810,000 Jews arrived each year to settle in Palestine. This alarmed the Arabs, who saw Jews as representing Western imperialism. In 1922 Winston Churchill tried to pacify Arabs by saying that the British promised only a national home and not a Jewish state. In 1929 Arabs rioted on a large scale against the 100,000 Jewish settlers, who provided themselves with their own security force, the Hagannah.

THE 1930s

To pacify the Arabs, Britain imposed restrictions in 1933 on Jewish immigration. This led to Jewish riots against the British. 1933 was the year when Hitler came to power (see Unit 15) and the demand for entry into Palestine increased. In 1936 some 60,000 Jews were allowed in. By 1937 there were 400,000 Jews in Palestine; by 1939 some 600,000, facing a hostile 1,000,000 Arabs.

The Jews became more prosperous because of their hard work, technical skills and aid from abroad. They bought land from Arabs and watched 'the desert bloom'.

In 1937 a major rising by Arabs ('the Arab Revolt') led to the Peel Commission which reported that the Mandate could not work and that Palestine ought to be divided. The Arabs rejected this suggestion of a Jewish state.

THE SECOND WORLD WAR AND AFTER

During 1939–45, with the persecution of the Jews by Hitler, many tried to get to Palestine. The British restricted the numbers allowed in so that thousands tried to get in illegally.

In 1945-7 there was a world-wide sympathy with the Jews once the news of the concentration camps became better known.

Bevin, British Foreign Minister, wishing to please the Arabs, tried to restrict the numbers allowed into Palestine. The Arabs, angered by the continuous wave of illegal immigrants, attacked Jewish settlements. The Hagannah defended these. Some Jews also organized terrorist gangs, the Irgun and the Stern Gang, which used the tactics used by partisans fighting against German occupation. Police stations, army posts, and government buildings were attacked by bombs and gunmen.

The British were giving their Indian Empire its independence. They were also (1947) withdrawing from Greece (Unit 28) and it is not surprising that they felt unable to maintain their control of Palestine.

Truman, President of the USA, fighting an election campaign (Unit 32) asked the British to admit more Jews. This would have been a last straw as far as the Arabs were concerned.

Bevin handed the problem to the UNO and on 14 May 1948 Britain withdrew her forces from Palestine. The Jews immediately announced the creation of their own state and named it Israel. The UN suggestion was a division of Palestine (giving Israel the portion shaded horizontally in Fig. 37.4(a)). This was rejected by the Arabs, who preferred to try to drive the Jews out.

37.4 The First Arab–Israeli War, 1948

The fighting had begun before the British left.

Arab armies attacked from Jordan, which sent the Arab Legion under British General Glubb, Egypt, under officers including Neguib and Nasser, and Syria and Saudi Arabia.

The Jews were surrounded and outnumbered. President Weizmann and Prime Minister David Ben Gurion appealed to the world for help–but little came.

UN mediators tried to end the fighting. Count Bernadotte was murdered (September 1948) by Jewish terrorists.

The Arabs failed to defeat the Jews. Their leaders were at odds with one another, each seeking to gain an advantage from the war. Their armies had no co-ordinated plans; the Jews could concentrate on defeating first one and then another. Their armies were badly led, officers and men fleeing in times of difficulty.

The Jews, on the other hand, had the technical skills of British-trained officers, and the determination of a people which had no option other than to fight to the bitter end.

In February 1949 the War ended. Israel gained more

territory than had been alloted to it by the UN proposal of 1948 (Fig. 37.4).

Over 1,000,000 Arabs fled from Palestine to live in refugee camps in Syria, Jordan and Egypt.

AN UNEASY PEACE, 1949–56

A UN commission had helped to end the war. A UN Truce Supervisory Commission was needed to police the new frontiers.

Jerusalem was divided between Israel and Jordan. Israel claimed the Gaza Strip and only tolerated Egyptian possession of the Strip as a temporary arrangement.

There were frequent Arab terrorist attacks on Jewish property and Jewish attacks on the camps which harboured the terrorists.

Russia had originally supported Israel in the hope of winning a base in the region. When Israel proved to be a 'client' of the USA, Russia turned to support the Arabs, providing them with arms.

37.5 Nasser's Egypt

Gamal Abdel Nasser was an army officer who fought against Israel in 1948–9. In July 1952 Nasser was one of the leaders of the coup d'état which overthrew the corrupt King Farouk. He was Deputy Prime Minister to General Neguib, 1952–4, whom he overthrew and replaced.

Nasser saw himself as playing many roles:

▶ the Egyptian leader who would free his country from the last remnants of British control. He negotiated the withdrawal of the 90,000 troops stationed in the Suez Canal area. These left in 1954–5;

▶ the socialist leader who would provide his people with better living standards. A series of land reforms took land from rich landowners for use by peasants. Social reforms in education, housing and health legislation improved the quality of Egyptian life;

▶ the reforming leader who, with foreign aid, would build the Aswan High Dam to control the waters of the Nile and provide better irrigation for Egyptian farmers;

▶ the Arab leader who would unite all the Arab peoples in an Arab Union—and not only against Israel. He formed the United Arab Republic with Syria in 1958 only for it to break up in 1961, to be re-formed (and to include Iraq) in 1963 only for it to break up again.

Nasser's ambitions were viewed with alarm by other Arab

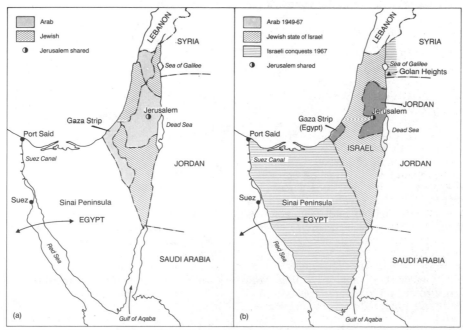

Fig. 37.4 The expansion of Israel, 1949–67

leaders, notably the Kings of Iraq, Jordan and Saudi Arabia. Nasser helped General Kassem to overthrow and murder King Feisal of Iraq (1958), but then faced him as a rival for leadership of the left-wing Arab future.

The USA, Britain and France feared both a Nasser-led Arab Union and, more importantly, a Russian-controlled, if Nasser-led, Middle Eastern Union. France, fighting her war in Algeria, was angered by Nasser's aid to the Muslim rebels, whom he also sheltered when they fled.

37.6 The Baghdad Pact

In 1954 Turkey and Pakistan signed a mutual defence pact. Then in 1955 pro-Western King Feisal of Iraq also joined that pact. In 1956 Britain and Persia joined the pact and the USA gave economic aid to its members.

In 1958 Iraq and Jordan formed the anti-Nasser Arab Federation.

The Western powers hoped that King Hussein of Jordan would now join the Pact. Nasser, fearing this, put pressure on him while also engineering the downfall of Feisal of Iraq. Jordan never joined the Pact.

In 1959 the Western powers thought that they had created a powerful bloc, first called the Baghdad Pact, then, in 1959, re-named the Central Treaty Organization (Cento).

37.7 The Suez Crisis, 1956

Nasser received aid from the USA and Britain to help to build the Aswan High Dam.

In 1955 he asked for more aid to help buy weapons. The US refused because Egypt would not be able to afford the repayments for both forms of aid. More importantly, the US feared that Egypt might attack Israel—her 'client state'. Nasser then got the arms from Russia and Czechoslovakia. In 1956 an angry US then cut the aid for the Dam and forced Britain to do the same.

In July 1956 Nasser announced the nationalization of the Suez Canal Company, claiming that the revenue from the Canal would pay for the building of the Dam.

Eden, Prime Minister of Britain, thought that he had got the support of President Eisenhower and US Secretary John Foster Dulles for his scheme to overthrow Nasser. Eden saw Nasser as another Hitler or Mussolini who would go from one conquest to another if he were not stopped.

The French, part-owners of the Canal Company, were already angered at Nasser's aid to the Algerian rebels.

The Israelis were angered by Egyptian-supported terrorist attacks from the Gaza Strip.

37.8 The Second Arab–Israeli War, 1956

Britain and France agreed with Israel for a joint attack on Egypt. In October 1956 Israel attacked the Gaza Strip and occupied most of the Sinai Peninsula (Fig. 37.4).

In November 1956 Britain and France called on Egypt and Israel to withdraw all forces from the Canal Zone. This would have meant only an Egyptian withdrawal—and from their own territory. Nasser refused. British and French forces attacked. The Egyptian Air Force was destroyed on the ground; troops landed at Alexandria to occupy the Canal Zone.

The US and Russia united to condemn the Anglo-French action. The forces were withdrawn, but only after Arab countries had threatened to cut off oil supplies, Nasser had blown up ships to block the Canal, the British and French had been made to appear as aggressors and as failures—which led many Afro-Asian states to turn to Russia for leadership.

37.9 An Uneasy Peace, 1956–67

A UN peacekeeping force moved in to clear the Canal and to keep peace on the old Israel–Egypt border. It also had a post at Sharm el Sheik at the entrance to the Gulf of Aqaba which ensured that Israeli ships could sail through to the port of Eilat.

Israel still faced terrorist attacks from the Gaza Strip.

Nasser, having gained a diplomatic victory with the humiliation of Britain and France, become more popular in the Arab world. He was also more anti-Israel than before. Syria, his partner in the United Arab Republic, shelled Israeli settlements from military posts on the Golan Heights.

In 1957 the US Seventh Fleet was sent to prop up a pro-Western régime in Lebanon in the face of Muslim (pro-Nasser) riots.

In 1958 the pro-Western Feisal of Iraq was assassinated and a left-wing (pro-Russian) government installed.

In 1959 General Kassem took Iraq out of the Baghdad Pact.

Local nationalists were supported by Egypt in their struggles to get rid of British influence in the Gulf, Aden and the South Arabian Federation.

GROWING HOSTILITY, 1967

In spring 1967 there was an increase in terrorist activity led by the PLO (see below). Syria also increased its shelling of Israel from the Golan Heights.

Syria had left the United Arab Republic in 1961 and was now outbidding Nasser in the demand for a united Arab attack on Israel.

Iraq, under the left-wing Kassem, was claiming to be more socialist than Egypt and staking its claim to be the leading Arab state.

Saudi Arabia was aiding the anti-Nasser forces in the Yemen and claiming the leadership of the less radical Arab states.

Nasser felt that he had to take some action to try to regain his former position as the outstanding Arab leader.

Jordan, under pressure from the PLO (see below), signed a military pact with Nasser on 4 June 1967.

37.10 The Third Arab-Israeli War 1967 (The Six-Day War)

Moshe Dayan, hero of the 1956 War, was appointed Minister of Defence in Israel. He argued that attack was the best defence. On 5 June 1967 Israel launched attacks on all Arab airfields. Israeli troops drove Egyptian forces across the Sinai, advanced to the Jordan River against the Jordanians and routed the Syrians on the Golan Heights (Fig. 37.4).

On 8 June Hussein of Jordan capitulated, and on 11 June 1967 both Syria and Egypt surrendered.

Israel refused UN pleas for a return to the old borders. Egypt was occupied as far as the east bank of the Suez Canal, Syria was partly occupied, including the Golan Heights, and the West Bank of the Jordan remained in Israeli hands (Fig. 37.4). Sporadic frontier fighting continued until the UN arranged a cease-fire in 1970.

37.11 The Palestine Liberation Organization

This was an organization which contained a number of groups aiming to 'drive Israel into the sea' and to get Palestine back for the Arabs who had fled in 1948–9. Yasser Arafat emerged as its main leader and spokesman, although more militant groups followed their own line.

In 1960 Kassem of Iraq formed the Palestinian Army.

The PLO was most active in Jordan where, in the 1960s, it forced Hussein to abandon his moderate line and to seek an alliance with Nasser (see above).

PLO terrorists drew world attention to their case by

frequent raids into Israel and hi-jacking aircraft, many of which were forced to land in Jordan where they were blown up. Then in 1972 PLO terrorists gunned down 100 people at Lydda Airport, Tel Aviv. At the 1972 Munich Olympic Games the Black September Group of PLO terrorists kidnapped Israeli hostages, who were killed during a gunfight between German police and the terrorists.

The Israelis always took 'an eye for an eye' in revenge attacks on terrorist camps, hoping to frighten Arab governments from giving refuge to the PLO.

In September 1970, Hussein of Jordan turned on his fellow-Arabs in the PLO when it tried to overthrow him and to run his country. The organization then found most help in Syria.

In 1972 Sadat, Nasser's successor in Egypt, sent Russian advisers home, which displeased Syria and created another rift in the Arab world.

 ## 37.12 The Fourth Arab-Israeli War, 1973

Egypt wanted to get Israel from the Sinai; Syria wanted to regain the Golan Heights. In spite of their different opinions over the PLO and the advantage of Russian aid (see above), they agreed to attack Israel.

6 October 1973 was a Jewish holy day (Yom Kippur). On that day Syria attacked the Golan Heights and received help from Jordan, Iraq and Saudi Arabia. Egypt attacked across the Canal and broke through the Israeli defensive Bar-Lev line.

The surprising attack was, at first, successful. Russia supplied aid and technical advice to the Arabs, while the USA was, at first, reluctant to aid Israel.

Once US aid arrived—planes and artillery—Israel drove the Arabs back. The Syrians were pushed back towards Damascus. The Israeli army drove through Sinai and captured the west bank of the Canal, leaving the Egyptian army surrounded east of the Canal and in Port Said.

UN mediators and the US Secretary of State, Kissinger, arranged a cease-fire. UN forces were sent to separate the Israeli and Egyptian forces, although Israel held on to her gains in the Sinai and on the Golan Heights (Fig. 37.4).

37.13 The Organization of Petroleum Exporting Countries (OPEC)

OPEC was founded in 1961, largely at the initiative of Venezuela. Its first aim was to help the oil-owning countries in their negotiations with the multi-national oil companies which, at that time, developed each country's oilfields, paying a relatively small sum to the country concerned.

By 1972 the foreign oil companies had lost their control of the industry and were forced to deal with well-educated and able ministers.

Saudi Arabia, Kuwait, Libya, Bahrein and Iraq were the leading Arab members of OPEC. Having failed to defeat Israel (and her Western allies) by force, the Arabs decided to use OPEC in their fight. In 1972–3 they pushed up oil prices so that by 1974 they were four times as much as they had been in 1972. This resulted in:

▶ a flow of money to the Arab world;
▶ quickening inflation in the Western world;
▶ a slow-down in world trade as countries tried to solve their balance of payments problems.

The Arabs also used their oil as a weapon: they threatened to cut off supplies to any country supporting Israel—Holland being the first sufferer.

But even in the oil world, the Arabs were divided: the 'royalists' such as Saudi Arabia and Kuwait were not as militant as anti-monarchist Libya wanted; Iraq found itself at war with Iran so that it was, itself, short of oil.

 ## 37.14 The Lebanon, Stage 1, 1975–6

In Lebanon the Christians and Muslims had lived in uneasy peace, with political power being shared by the two groups.

In 1975 right-wing Christian groups tried to break the power of left-wing Muslim groups. There was bitter fighting, in which the capital, Beirut, was devastated.

In 1976 the PLO had supported the Lebanese Muslims—hoping to find a new home for itself after being forced out of Jordan (see above). Then Syrian and other Arab forces entered Lebanon to try to restore peace—and Syrians fought the PLO while Christians looked on.

Israel kept a watchful eye on Lebanese affairs (see below).

37.15 The PLO again, 1976, and Entebbe

In June 1976 PLO terrorists hi-jacked an Air France plane containing many Jewish passengers and forced it to fly to Entebbe in Uganda. Amin (see Unit 36) allowed the terrorists to use the old airport as a prison in which they kept Jewish passengers as hostages. They demanded the release of Palestinian guerrillas held in Israel and other prisons.

The Israelis mounted a rescue operation, flying in an airborne force which rescued nearly all the hostages, killed most of the hi-jackers and the Ugandan guards placed by Amin around the airport.

 ## 37.16 Egypt–Israeli peace, 1977

In October 1977 President Sadat of Egypt flew to Jerusalem, where he met Prime Minister Begin of Israel and addressed the Israeli Parliament (the Knesset). Sadat asked that the two countries should arrange a peace.

Begin made a return visit to Cairo. Sadat was condemned by the Russians, most Arab countries and the PLO for 'betraying the Arab cause'.

Sadat could not arrange a total peace; no other Arab state would agree to one. So he made peace on behalf of Egypt. Israel withdrew her forces from the Sinai and handed the territory back to Egypt. Egypt allowed free access to Eilat through the Gulf of Aqaba. Israel promised that, in time, she would withdraw from the Gaza Strip. Religious fanatics and Israeli nationalists were opposed to this.

 ## 37.17 The Lebanon, Stage 2, 1976–86

There are numerous internal divisions. For example, among the Christians there are at least twelve different (and warring) Christian groups.

CHRISTIAN DIVISIONS

One way of looking at these divisions is to consider them from the point of view of religious belief. So, there are Greek Orthodox, Russian Orthodox, Roman Catholic and other groups. The most important group are the Maronites.

Another way is to consider the family grouping. Over the years, certain families have become accepted as leaders of some Christian groups. So, there are Christians who support the Franijeh, Gemayel and Chamoun families.

It is important to note that these groups have their own private armies, their own bases in various parts of towns and cities such as Beirut and in the country as a whole. So, part of East Beirut has become popularly known as Marounistan, an area controlled by the Maronites.

These different groups war with each other to try to gain more political and territorial power. They make allies of whoever will help them—Muslims, PLO, Israelis and Syrians. But they will as quickly turn against their former ally if this suits them.

MUSLIM DIVISIONS

Muslims are also divided into various groups.

The Shia Muslims are those who believe that when the Prophet Mohammed died in 632 his son-in-law, Ali, became the successor. This is the opinion of a minority of Muslims.

The Sunni Muslims, who form the majority, believe that the Prophet did not name a successor. They claim that the Muslims as a whole have the right to decide who is to be the leader at any one time.

The Druzes are a small group, followers of people who broke away from mainstream Islam and who have their own 'secret book', read only by chosen leaders who control the Druze community. They live, mainly, in mountain villages—so that the region is often referred to as 'the Druze Mountains'.

Some Muslims are left-wing in politics and accept the leadership of Syria. Others, the better-off, fear a communist take-over. The Druzes, hated by both Shia and Sunni groups, have taken on a left-wing stance. Led by the Jumblatt family, the Druzes have become the most warlike of the anti-Christian groups.

OUTSIDE INFLUENCES

Until 1975, the various groups had lived in an uneasy peace with one another. Political power was shared out (see above), and each of the important groups had its own power base and its own method of raising money. Many of them had their own ports, through which they handled the money-making drug traffic.

This uneasy peace was broken in 1975 (see p. 151, and the PLO tried to take advantage of the situation in 1976.

The dominant Christian groups accepted help from Muslim and left-wing Syria, which intervened to break the power of the independent Yasser Arafat and the PLO (see p. 150). This led to a long period of bitter civil war. From 1976 to 1982:

▶ Christian groups fought each other to try to gain leadership of the whole Christian community. In 1978 heads of several of the leading Christian families were assassinated by other Christian groups;
▶ the Lebanese government forces, a mixture of Christian and Muslims, fell apart as members tended to drift into the camps of the warring Christians and Muslims;
▶ Israel took advantage of the situation to attack PLO and other bases in South Lebanon, from which Muslims launched raids into Northern Israel;
▶ Israel launched a full-scale invasion in 1976 but was forced to withdraw by US pressure;
▶ in 1981 Syria defeated the Christian armies—the armies of those who had, initially, invited Syria to play an active part in Lebanon (see above).

THE ISRAELI INVASION, 1982

In 1981 Begin formed a new government. Many of its members were hard-liners, such as Sharon, the Minister of Defence.

Many Israeli leaders wanted to take advantage of the Lebanese war to wipe out the bases from which raids were launched into Israel. However, others seemed to want to expand Israeli territory by occupying (permanently, perhaps) South Lebanon. There was a real fear among Israelis that a Syrian-dominated Lebanon would be a major threat to Israel.

THE 1982–3 WAR

The Israelis advanced through Lebanon and reached Beirut. They were helped by various Christian forces, anxious to get Syrian forces out of Lebanon.

As a result of this war, the PLO was defeated—by the Israelis and with the connivance of the Syrians, who made little attempt to help Arafat and the PLO. The PLO forces were driven out of Lebanon. Some went to Syria; Arafat and others went to Algeria and Jordan. There then took place an internal struggle inside the PLO:

▶ Arafat was condemned by some who wanted a more warlike attitude towards Israel. Arafat himself seemed to have realized that it would be necessary to negotiate a deal with Israel if the Palestinians were to get any sort of recognition;
▶ in spite of the earlier agreement to withdraw from Lebanon, Arafat and other PLO forces returned in 1983. They then had their own PLO civil war in which Syrians finally defeated Arafat. He was driven away again, and left to find a new home in Egypt.

Israeli and Syrian forces were then engaged in a war for control of Northern Lebanon. Syrian forces were driven back into the northern valley. Israeli and Druze forces fought their own war, which goes on with Druze forces in control of the northern mountains. Under international pressure, Israel agreed to withdraw its forces to South Lebanon. It also agreed that, if Syria withdrew her forces from the North, Israel would withdraw completely from Lebanon.

THE US INTERVENTION, 1983–4

Syria gained increasing control of Lebanese affairs;
▶ she had defeated the PLO, which had withdrawn;
▶ she had defeated the Christians in 1981;
▶ she was supplied with Russian weapons and advisers;
▶ in 1983 she had forces which occupied the North and maintained the struggle against a weak Christian government under Gemayel.

Reagan had succeeded in overthrowing a communist régime in Grenada (see Unit 32). He sent 1500 US soldiers, an American fleet and aircraft to 'invade' Lebanon. He claimed that he was acting as the peacemaker. As proof of this he had the support of Britain, France and Italy who sent forces as part of the multi-national peace-keeping force. In fact, events proved that this was an anti-Syrian force which came under attack from Syrian, Druze and Muslim forces. This allowed public opinion to label the US and other forces as 'pro-Israeli' forces.

There was a threat to world peace, and Syria was backed by Russia. If US forces clashed with Syrian forces, would the Russians stand by and see their client-state defeated? Or would they, too, send forces into troubled Lebanon?

In 1984–6 terrorist attacks on the US Embassy in Beirut and the slaughter of many US Marines forced Reagan to order the withdrawal of US forces. Israel, too, withdrew her forces from the war-torn country in which Christians of the various groups and Muslims (see opposite) continue to fight each other. The PLO forces which had once withdrawn returned to add further to the country's troubles.

37.18 Iran versus Iraq, 1979–86

In 1979 Saddam Hussein took control of the government of Iraq. He wanted to assert Iraq's position in the Gulf, where his chief rivals were Saudi Arabia and Iran. Since both of these were supported by the USA, Saddam turned to the USSR for support, although he also made an agreement with France for the supply of a nuclear reactor, while Italy agreed to train his naval personnel and to sell him armed vessels.

1979 saw the fall of the Shah of Iran from power and the accession of the radical Ayatollah Khomeini and his fundamentalists to power.

In 1980 Iraq attacked Iran because of:
▶ the apparent weakness of Iran in the wake of the unrest caused by the fall of the Shah;
▶ the dislike of the Sunni Muslim Hussein for the radicalism of the Shia Khomeini, who called on the Shia majority in Iraq to rise against their ruler;
▶ the fear that Khomeini might persuade the Kurdish minority in Iraq to rise against Hussein and so threaten Iraq's oil interests in the Kirkuk region;
▶ rival claims to territory in the Shatt-el-Arab waterways which formed part of the frontier between the two countries.

The Shatt is Iraq's only outlet to the sea, while it also carries

Iranian traffic to the ports of Khorramshahr and Abadan. In 1969 Iraq had claimed the whole of the Shatt; Iran's support for the Kurdish revolt forced Iraq to accept a deal in 1975 by which the Shah abandoned the Kurds while accepting that the frontier between the two countries ran down the middle of the waterway. In 1980 Hussein declared this agreement at an end and claimed the whole of the Shatt.

The war dragged on, with both sides claiming 'victory' at various times. The Soviet Union aided Iraq in the hope of gaining influence in the Gulf – which also explains Soviet interest in Afghanistan (see Unit 35).

Western-oriented Arab states, such as Jordan and Saudi Arabia, supported Iraq because they fear the victory of Khomeini's radical government. Syria, Libya, Algeria, Yemen and the PLO tend to support Iran because they wanted Iraq to give up the war and concentrate on a war against Israel.

In November 1980 a summit of Arab leaders failed to heal the breach, and the war continued.

37.19 State Terrorism

In May 1986 US forces attacked military bases in various parts of Libya. Britain became involved because US planes took off from bases in Britain to attack Libya. Reagan and Thatcher claimed that this attack was a Western response to the terrorism emanating from Libya. Examples of such terrorism were:

▶ the murder of a London policewoman by Libyans inside the Libyan People's Bureau
▶ the hijacking of an American ship and the murder of one of the passengers by PLO terrorists based in Syria and Libya;
▶ the bombing of airports, notably in Athens and Vienna, in which many people were killed;
▶ the attempt to put a bomb on board an El Al plane in Heathrow, London, by an Arab who had been trained and financed by the Libyan government.

While most Western governments condemned Reagan and Thatcher, they were nevertheless driven to co-operate with the USA and Britain to draw up a series of agreements on methods of coping with 'state-aided' terrorism. For recent developments see Units 45.

Unit 37 Summary

▶ Algeria's war of independence.
▶ Arabs versus Jews, 1923–47.
▶ Arabs versus Israel since 1948; the four wars.
▶ Nasser's Egypt; the Suez Crisis, 1956.
▶ Lebanon, the 'cockpit' of the Middle East since 1972.
▶ Iran versus Iraq.
▶ State terrorism.

---

38 THE THIRD WORLD AND SOME OF ITS PROBLEMS

38.1 Definitions and Perceptions

WHAT DO PEOPLE MEAN BY THE 'THIRD WORLD'?

International relations

The term 'Third World' describes countries not allied to either the capitalist West or the communist East. These non-aligned countries come, mainly, from Asia and Africa.

Political

The term describes countries which have won their independence from some colonial power. These emergent nations come, again, from Asia and Africa.

Economic

The term describes countries with a low standard of living and which are trying to become more industrialized or developed. Such countries have a low average income per head, as can be seen from Table 38.1 which lists the average income per head of population for selected developed and 'Third World' countries.

Geographic

Most of these poor countries are south of the Equator (see below).

BECOMING AWARE OF THE 'THIRD WORLD'

The Colombo Plan, 1950 was devised by the Foreign Ministers

Table 38.1 Comparisons of per capita income

Country	Population (millions)	Per capita income (US dollars)	Main exports (% of whole)	
USA	211	6670	Machinery	27
West Germany	62	6260	Machinery	29
United Kingdom	56	3590	Machinery	28
Zambia	5	520	Copper	95
Ghana	10	430	Cocoa	64
Uganda	11	240		
India	595	140	Jute	13
Bangladesh	76	100		
Somalia	3	90		

of the Commonwealth to help the development of South and South-East Asia (see p. 157).

The UN had from the start a number of agencies whose main aim was to help to overcome the poverty of Third World countries (see p. 156).

Former colonial powers, such as France, took a special interest in the development of their former colonies.

Germany, perhaps because of its wish to wipe out memories of Hitler, has been especially generous in its aid to poorer countries.

Many private agencies exist in Britain (Oxfam, Cafod, War on Want and so on) and in other countries to channel aid to poorer countries.

In 1955 at Bandung the Afro-Asian Conference tried to set

up an organization in which Third World countries could unite, aloof from the Cold War.

In 1973 in Algiers there was a meeting of leaders of Third World countries, angered by the failure of the developed countries to give sufficient attention to their plight.

In 1976 in Ceylon the leaders met again but, once more, failed to arrive at any real solution to their problem of making the developed world more aware of the increasing gulf between rich and poor countries.

Reports by UN agencies, by groups of politicians (such as the Brandt Report) and by the Commonwealth Secretariat ('The North-South Dialogue') have shown how little has been done to bridge the gulf between the richer countries (mainly in the northern hemisphere) and the poor (mainly in the south).

THE EFFECT OF POLITICAL UNREST

Wars and civil wars have made matters worse for many poor countries. Money, material and men have been used in wars instead of in economic and social development. Examples of countries affected in this way are Uganda, Somalia, Pakistan-Bangladesh, India, Nigeria and Zimbabwe.

In 1984–5 the world became aware of the effects of the continuing civil war in Ethiopia. Largely because of the publicity given to the plight of refugees by British TV and because of the activities of pop star Bob Geldof, a series of efforts were made to help the suffering millions (see below).

Tribal conflicts have often led to unrest, rioting and an interference with a country's development. Examples of places affected in this way include Sri Lanka, where in 1983 the minority Tamils were once again attacked by the majority Sinhalese; Uganda, where both the overthrow and later return of Obote were accompanied by horrendous massacres of rival tribes; the Congo; Nigeria with its Biafran war; and, in 1984, Zimbabwe where the minority Matabele were attacked by the majority Mashona led by Mugabe.

Freedom fighters have used terrorist tactics to draw attention to their plight—but have hindered the economic and social development of the country for which they claim to be fighting. Among such 'fighters' are the PLO (see Unit 37), the IRA, the South West African People's Organization (SWAPO) which wants an independent Namibia, and Frelimo (see Unit 36).

Urban guerrillas in developed countries have claimed to be trying to overthrow a Western-dominated capitalist system in the hope that some better system may, somehow, be created. Among these are the Baader–Meinhof gang in West Germany, the Red Brigade in Italy, various Black Power groups in the USA where there was also the Symbionese Liberation Army, and the Angry Brigade in Britain.

Increased consciousness

In 1984–5 the suffering of the people of Ethiopia (see above) and neighbouring Sudan received worldwide publicity. This started with TV pictures of the millions of hungry people living in refugee camps. The publicity grew because of the actions of Bob Geldof, who won the support of many of his fellow pop stars. They developed Band Aid, and their major concerts and records gained over £50 million from people all over the world. Geldof used this money to provide immediate relief for the starving and to provide some long-term help.

Stars in other fields followed the pop stars' example: there were aid programmes organized by opera singers, schoolchildren and, in May 1986, by sportsmen around the world. While all these helped raise vast sums of money for relief, they also increased people's awareness of the problem of poverty in Africa.

 ## 38.2 The Problems of the Third World

ECONOMIC INSUFFICIENCY

Production and incomes

As can be seen in Table 38.1, Zambia and Ghana are heavily reliant on one commodity. This is typical of under-developed countries. The price they get for that commodity varies according to the level of output and the level of world demand. The supply of such items as coffee, sugar, cocoa, wheat and rubber may be very high in a good year and low in a bad year. If world demand is down when supplies are high, prices fall sharply and so does the income of the people and of the country.

Table 38.1 also shows the low incomes received by the people of some under-developed countries. This may be the result of the poor quality of their work (and equipment or tools); it may be the result of over-production of their principal commodity. But the results of that low income include:

Lack of money for private investment

Too few people in under-developed countries earn enough to save; savings are the source of investment. Since there are not enough savings, there is also too little local investment in machinery, buildings, equipment and so on.

Lack of money for public investment

The US government can tax its people with their incomes of around 6670 dollars a head (Table 38.1). With these taxes the government can build schools, roads, harbours, hospitals and all the economic and social infra-structure which helps a developed country to function. Governments in India or Uganda can only collect a low volume of taxation from their already poor people. This leads to lack of spending on infra-structure so that the possibility of economic development is even further limited.

Lack of spending by consumers

Consumers have little money. There is little encouragement to merchants and others to build factories because they have little chance of selling their product at home.

A low standard of living is measured in such things as clothing, food and housing, and reflected in such things as level of education, ability to work and to buy goods.

CLIMATE

Many under-developed countries suffer from the climatic problems explained in Unit 36.

TRADE

The economic and trading development in industrialized countries also makes things worse for developing countries.

Malaya used to export natural rubber. The demand for this has gone down with the development of synthetic rubber. Other synthetics (rayon, nylon and various plastics) affect world demand for such raw materials as wool, copper, cotton, tin and zinc.

Some developing countries have begun to produce goods which compete with goods produced by industrialized countries. This ought to be welcomed because it will raise incomes, living standards and the social life of the country. But many industrialized countries (including Britain) resent such competition and try to prevent imports from developing countries (by tariffs, quotas or bans on such imports).

POPULATION GROWTH SINCE 1945

Perhaps the most serious problem for developing countries is the continuous and rapid growth of their populations.

Asian countries

In India, the population is increasing by 2.6 million every year and there will be 800 million in India by AD 2000.

Asia generally now has half the world's population living on only one fifth of the world's land surface. In 1973 there were 2 billion Asians; by 1990 there will be 3 billion.

The main cause of this increase is not an increase in the number of babies born (the birth rate) but the sharp fall in the number of babies and other people dying each year (the death rate).

The main causes of the fall in the death rate include:

▶ the introduction of Western scientific and medical knowledge. DDT spraying reduced deaths in Ceylon from 22 per thousand to 12 per thousand in seven years during which period the malarial mosquito was wiped out. Drugs such as penicillin, vaccines for former 'killer' diseases such as diphtheria have allowed people to live, whereas formerly they might have died;

▶ improved food production in countries such as India has lessened, although not ended, the numbers dying of starvation each day;

▶ social reforms in such areas as sanitation, education and washing facilities have helped to lower the death rate.

Among the major effects of this increase in population are:

▶ the problem of feeding, housing and employing the larger number of people;

▶ the economic problem of paying for the imports needed to feed and clothe the people;

▶ the slow rise (where there is one) in the per capita income because even increased output fails to match the increased population.

Developed countries

These are the richest countries in the world, and their populations are rising only slowly.

The US population is rising by about 1 per cent a year, and the populations of most European countries, including Britain, are rising by less than one per cent a year.

In these countries there has been a sharp fall in the death rate and people are living much longer than used to be the case. This ought to have led to increased populations. But while the death rate has fallen, the birth rate has fallen even more sharply. The causes of this fall are:

▶ the changing roles of women in Western society. An increasing number of women wish to follow a career and do not want to have their jobs and careers hindered by child-rearing;

▶ the greater expectations of Western men and women. They expect to have an ever rising standard of living. These expectations can often be met only if both husband and wife are working;

▶ a greater knowledge of and willingness to use one of a wide variety of contraceptive methods of birth prevention;

▶ the Abortion Acts which, in an increasing number of countries, allow pregnant women to get rid of their unwanted babies.

African countries

The populations of many of these countries are rising even more sharply than the population of India. The causes of these rises are:

▶ economic development, although often slow, leads to higher living standards. Many people see this as an opportunity to have larger families. Only in Western countries do increased living standards lead to a fall in family size;

▶ urban development, a result of economic development, provides both increased job opportunities (and the ability to maintain a family) and housing (in which to shelter that family).

The problems following from these rising populations are similar to the problems facing India.

Some general observations

Food supply

In 1966 Mrs Gandhi, Prime Minister of India, asked all her people to eat a little less so that fewer of their fellow Indians would starve to death.

In 1966 the US government was paying out millions of dollars either to destroy crops or to compensate farmers who agreed to take land out of cultivation. In 1986 the EEC controls vast 'mountains' of unbought wheat, beef and other meat, as well as 'lakes' of unwanted milk and wine.

It might seem simple to transfer the 'unwanted' food of Europe and the surplus crops of the USA to the starving of the Third World. Unfortunately, the economic system is not that simple. The question we have to ask is: can the poor afford to buy this 'unwanted' or surplus food? Since the answer is 'No', then we have to ask whether the taxpayers in the rich countries would agree to make the payment needed to get the food transferred? Again, regretfully, the answer, for the time being, is 'No'.

Birth control

Western societies have accepted a variety of methods of contraception. However, in most countries in the Third World it is still regarded as being socially desirable to have large families. In these societies, too, there are strong religious objections to birth control. A notable example of successful birth control policy being implemented is China, where there is now a strict 'one child per family' policy.

It is also difficult to educate people in the Third World in methods of family planning because most adults are illiterate and there is a great shortage of doctors and clinics.

In India, Mrs Gandhi and her son, Sanjay, tried to make sterilization compulsory. Widespread objection to this 'dictatorial' behaviour was one reason for Mrs Gandhi's fall from power in 1977.

The gap between the rich West and the poor Third World is growing wider—in spite of international aid and economic development. The main reason for this 'slippage' is the ever-rising population in Third World countries.

38.3 World Poverty and Aid

STEPS TAKEN TO TRY TO SOLVE THE PROBLEM

Population control

This has been advocated by advisers from the West. It has been accepted as policy by some leaders in Third World countries. But, as Mrs Gandhi discovered, it has not been accepted by the majority of people in these countries.

Commodity agreements

Third World countries depend on the money earned by their exporting of raw materials or food (Table 38.1). Brazil depends on coffee exports; Ghana on cocoa exports; Zambia on copper exports. The prices of these goods (or commodities) depend largely on the demand from Western countries. If the Third World countries increase their output (to try to get their economy moving) while Western countries do not increase their demand, the prices of these goods will fall sharply. In many Third World countries these commodities are produced by international companies—largely controlled by Western interests.

Until the 1960s the oil-producing countries gained little benefit from the development of the oil industries in their countries. The formation of OPEC (see below) and the gradual expansion of its control of the world's oil supply showed how control of a vital commodity could enable poorer countries to get more of the world's wealth.

Brazil tried to organize a commodity agreement with the small number of coffee-producing countries. It was hoped that by controlling supply, the world price could be held at a level which would provide the Brazilians with a better income. The agreement had a short term success, largely because a heavy frost wiped out the Brazil coffee crop in 1972–3. Coffee prices rose—but fell sharply when, in the following year, there was a better than average crop.

Other countries have tried to organize commodity agreements covering lead, tin, copper, wool and bauxite. There has been little success to report; the Western countries have been able to limit the effects of such agreements by:

► using influence to persuade one or more members of such an agreement to 'break ranks' and fall in with Western needs;
► providing a substitute for the commodity concerned, e.g. synthetic rubber helped to offset the rubber agreement;
► threatening to use force. In 1972 the USA tried to seize Chilean copper shipments in protest at the nationalization of that country's copper production. US statesmen such as Henry Kissinger have suggested that the West might have to use force against a continued Arab control of the world's oil prices and supplies.

Increased trade

It is clear that if Third World countries are to 'grow' and provide more of their people with a good standard of living, then they will have to be able both to produce and to sell more goods. The world recession, which has now lasted since 1973 and has become even deeper since 1979, has led to a fall in world demand for many raw materials. Third World countries have therefore had an even lower income. But there are success stories to report. Among newly-developed and successful countries are Singapore, Korea, Taiwan and the Philippines. These formerly under-developed countries are now among the world's leading trading nations and their peoples have a rising standard of living.

Increased development aid

'If you provide a man with a fish, you keep him alive; if you teach him to fish you help him to improve his own life.' A good deal of international aid has been of the 'fish' variety; Western countries have helped Third World countries in times of famine or other natural disaster. But there is also a good deal of 'teach him to fish' aid (see below).

INTERNATIONAL DEVELOPMENT AID

Underdeveloped countries need help to develop.

Economic infrastructure

Economic development depends, very largely, on a country having such things as:

► good power supplies: a country needs things such as dams to help to create hydro-electricity, or generating stations to provide fuel-generated electricity;
► good transport systems: there is little point in increasing agricultural output in country farms if there are no roads to allow the transport of the output to towns and ports;
► harbours, to allow the speedy turn-around of ships bringing imports of industrial necessities and taking away exports. In the 1970s the development of Nigeria and Saudi Arabia was hindered by the poor harbour facilities in these countries. Ships had to wait for up to 6 months to be unloaded—which increased costs, led to a good deal of wastage as food rotted and other goods deteriorated.

Social infrastructure

As a country becomes developed it needs a larger and better trained workforce at all levels. This increases the need for schools, colleges and universities. In 1976, when it was the world's leading oil producer, Saudi Arabia reported that 75 per cent of its population was illiterate. High figures of adult illiteracy are also reported by other developing countries.

Agricultural progress

We have seen that one of the problems facing the Third World countries is that of feeding their populations. If money has to be spent to import food, then the country will have a balance of payments problem and will be unable to afford the imports of machinery and other goods essential to industrialization. It is important that the developing countries should be helped to increase their food output. This leads to the need for agricultural colleges as well as of machinery and improved strains of seeds.

Industrial progress

Industrialization provides a nation's people with better job prospects, higher incomes, better living standards and higher spending by government on social welfare schemes. To achieve this industrialization the Third World countries need help to:

► buy the essential capital equipment;
► construct the necessary factories and works;
► manage and operate the new industries.

We have seen that they are unable to provide the investment needed from their own resources.

We should also note that, if their industrialization is to succeed, they have to be allowed access to Western markets. Too many Western countries are unwilling to allow them such access (see above).

Methods of giving development aid

Grants may be made by western governments to governments in Third World countries. These do not have to be repaid and they do not require any interest payments on the amount given.

Loans are made by governments, by UN and other agencies, and by banks to help governments and/or companies in Third World countries to develop. Such loans have to be repaid in time (usually in 10 or 20 years). They also carry an interest charge which is adjusted every six months depending on whether western interest rates have risen or fallen in that period. There are many problems following from giving (and getting) loans:

► A developing country may be persuaded to take more loans than it can really afford. In the 1970s Western bankers had to try to cope with the huge influx of money from Arab oil-producing countries. They had to pay interest on the money put into their banks by the Arabs; they wanted to get that interest (and a profit) from lending the money out. Many Third World countries agreed to take loans which, in the 1980s, they are unable to repay.
► Interest rates can be varied—usually in an upward direction. Any Third World country which agreed in 1972 to take a loan at a rate of 6 per cent a year found in 1980 that the interest rates had shot up to 15 per cent a year.

The Third World country taking the loan assumed that it would be able to pay the interest and repay the capital out of export earnings. In the 1980s many countries have found that their exports have not matched earlier expectations. This had led them into increased difficulties, as can be seen below.

The Nigerian experience, 1970–83

Oil production in Nigeria expanded rapidly in the period 1970–5. Output reached 3 million barrels a day. Oil prices rocketed from 2 dollars a barrel (1973) to 35 dollars a barrel (1978).

Nigeria's income rose sharply. She embarked on a massive programme for development. This led to borrowing at rates of interest around 6 per cent a year. There was every expectation that this interest could be paid and the capital repaid out of the expected oil earnings.

In 1983 Nigeria was in deep trouble. The world demand for oil fell—and Nigeria sold only 1–1½ million barrels per day. Oil prices fell and Nigeria received between only 27–8 dollars per barrel for her oil. At the same time interest rates rose and Nigeria had to pay 15 per cent on her large loans. You will see why this drove her into financial difficulty. Such problems also affect developed countries whose industries may have invested in the country only to find difficulty in getting paid for their goods and investments.

Expectations

3 million barrels at 35 dollars a barrel = 105 m dollars

Reality

1 million barrels at 27 dollars a barrel = 27 m dollars

The Commonwealth and aid

Scholarships and training schemes help to provide education for Third World Commonwealth countries.

Teachers, doctors, engineers and experts of all kinds provide varied help.

Organizations operate a variety of schemes of aid:
▶ the Commonwealth Development Corporation (CDC);
▶ the Special Commonwealth African Assistance Plan (SCAAP):

The Colombo Plan

The Colombo Plan (see above) was devised by the Foreign Ministers of the Commonwealth in 1950 to help the development of South and South East Asia. A Council organizes training, research, economic development and better health services. The Plan receives help from non-Commonwealth countries such as Japan, and from the UN.

In 1958 the ideas behind the Plan were extended by the introduction of Commonwealth Assistance Loans. In 1959 in a further development a scheme of Commonwealth Scholarships was introduced.

The UN and aid

From the outset the UN has played a major role in providing aid for people in need.

In 1943 the United Nations Relief and Rehabilitation Administration (UNRRA) coped with the problem of refugees and emergency relief in the wake of advancing forces.

In 1943 the Food and Agricultural Organization (FAO) was set up to study the problem of world food supplies and to encourage the development of agriculture in poorer countries.

In 1944 the International Monetary Fund was set up after Anglo-US discussions at Bretton Woods. It gets its funds from contributions by member states and uses those funds to help countries which are in balance of payments difficulties and so helps to promote world trade.

In 1944 the International Bank for Reconstruction and Development, generally known as the World Bank, was started. It lends money to promote economic development.

The Economic and Social Council (Ecosoc) has set up a number of regional Commissions—for Europe, for Asia and Latin America and for Africa which compile annual Economic Surveys and act as advisers for countries in various regions.

The United Nations Children's Emergency Fund (UNICEF) has links with Ecosoc and provides aid for a wide variety of schemes aimed at helping children in the Third World. It has organized campaigns against illiteracy and attacks on diseases which particularly affect children.

The World Health Organization (WHO) and the UN Educational, Scientific and Cultural Organization (UNESCO) play roles in providing particular forms of aid to developing countries. As such they are part of the overall UN aim of trying to implement one of the pledges made by Roosevelt and Churchill when they signed the Atlantic Charter (see Unit 19) in August 1941: 'that all men in all lands may live out their lives in freedom from fear and want'.

SOME OF THE PROBLEMS CONNECTED WITH AID

Many countries providing aid insist that the recipient country has to spend the money in the donor country. This tied aid limits the freedom of the developing country. It also helps the economic well-being of the donor country which may see aid as a means of self-help and not of help to the Third World.

The USA and Russia in particular use aid as a weapon of foreign policy. Each provides aid only if the recipient government agrees to follow the 'party' line in foreign policy. Thus it is possible to link Korea, Pakistan, Israel and others with the USA and Cuba, North Korea and others with Russia.

Too many recipient countries have wasted a good deal of aid. Some have spent the money on arms; others have spent it on glamorous projects such as the building of huge sports stadia (Nigeria) and government buildings.

A country's development may be helped by the activities of one of the world's multi-national firms. The opening of a Ford car plant, an Esso refinery or an ICI chemical plant will provide employment, increase spending power and so help development. But there are many cases of such companies using their economic power to try to control government policy. Latin America has suffered from the activities of US companies; the Middle East suffered, before the formation of OPEC (see below) from the activities of the giant oil companies.

Third World countries need aid all the time—but may need even more aid when the world goes into recession. It is at such periods that their export prices fall so that their income declines. But it is at precisely such periods that developed nations provide less aid ('we have to help our own people who are unemployed') and try to cut down on imports from Third World countries.

The sad fact is that there has been little switch of resources from the rich countries (which get richer each year) to the poorer (which get richer only slowly, if at all).

 38.4 Oil and a Modern Crisis, 1972–83

Industrialized countries consumed ever increasing quantities of oil in the 20th century. Oil was often used to generate electricity—it was cheaper than coal. Oil drove most of the modern machinery in factories. Oil, or oil-based products, powered most of the modern transport systems—lorries, cars, ships and planes. Oil was used to heat our homes.

Third World countries also used a good deal of oil: most poor families cooked by paraffin stoves, and most poor countries had no electricity system. People relied on oil lamps to light their homes, shops and offices.

Until 1972 oil was a cheap product. Exploration for oil and exploitation of oil fields was controlled by large international oil companies. Most of these were American-owned, e.g. Esso (or, in the USA, Exxon), Texaco, Sonaco.

Britain has been involved in oil exploration from the start. Its interests were safeguarded by the two giant companies, Shell (an Anglo-Dutch company) and the Anglo-Persian Oil Company, later renamed as British Petroleum.

These companies paid small sums to the governments of the countries in which they exploited oilfields. Before 1945 these countries were:

▶ Persia, now known as Iran;
▶ Iraq, which as Mesopotamia had been 'created' by Britain (see Unit 13);
▶ small sites on the Persian Gulf—e.g. Kuwait and Bahrein;
▶ Mexico, which had, however, nationalized its oil industry following a communist revolution;
▶ Venezuela;
▶ various states in the Dutch East Indies, now called Indonesia.

It is worth noting that the giant oilfields in Saudi Arabia had not been properly investigated.

CHALLENGES TO WESTERN CONTROL

In 1951 the first challenge to the control of the oil companies ('the Seven Sisters' of the industry) was made by the radical Persian (Iranian) politician Dr Mussadeq. He nationalized the huge Anglo-Iranian Oil Company and evicted the British from Persia with its huge Abadan oil refineries.

The British and Americans responded by increasing oil output from other countries, mainly Kuwait. With only small sales of Persian oil, Mussadeq's government brought Persia to the edge of bankruptcy. In 1953 Mussadeq was driven from power in a rising organized by the American Central Intelligence Agency, and in 1954 the development of Iran's oilfields was taken over by a consortium of British, French, Dutch and US companies. The British had lost their total control.

In 1954–6 other Arab countries, notably Saudi Arabia, did not imitate Mussadeq by trying to expel the oil companies. However, they did force the companies to make more generous payments than had been made previously.

Oil companies resented being forced to pay what they saw as high prices for oil. To limit any one government's ability to force them to pay such a high price, the companies would threaten to lower production in the 'greedy' country, knowing that they could get what they wanted from another, less 'greedy' country.

OPEC

In 1962 Venezuela became aware of the fact that her oil deposits would dry up around 1988. She needed an increased income from her existing oilfields to get the money needed to build up an alternative economy which could provide her people with work after 1988.

The Organization of Petroleum Exporting Countries (OPEC) was founded when Venezuela persuaded other oil-producing countries that they should act together against the oil companies.

It took time for the Organization to understand its real power and for Arab countries, in particular, to train ministers able to hold their own in negotiations with the oil companies and with western governments.

The Yom Kippur War, 1973

This war (see Unit 37) proved to be a turning point in the history of OPEC.

The USA and most European countries had supported the Israelis, supplying them with weapons and other aid. Egypt and Syria, financed by the oil-producing Arab countries, were heavily defeated.

The Arabs decided to use oil as a weapon in their fight against Israel and its Western allies. Arab members of OPEC cut their supplies of oil to America and countries which had provided aid to the Israelis (notably Holland). OPEC, guided by Arab interests, announced a doubling (and later a quadrupling) of oil prices.

THE OIL CRISIS

The cuts and the increased prices led to a series of crises in the Western world in particular, and throughout the rest of the world in general.

There was a shortage of oil in the USA (which imported about 20 per cent of its oil from the Middle East) and in Europe, which depended on the output from the giant Dutch refineries at Rotterdam. Factories had to shut down, industrial output declined; transport became more expensive.

The increased oil prices led to increases not only in the price of petrol and higher charges for transport. There were also increases in the price of all oil-based products from plastics to drugs, from record-sleeves and discs to clothes and motor cars.

All industrialized countries had to pay much more for their oil imports than had been the case. This increase could not be matched by increased earnings from exports. This created world-wide balance of payments problems. Every country tried to put its balance back to rights by cutting other imports. But one country's imports are another country's exports. Cuts in imports by the world's industrialized countries led to falls in exports by other industrialized countries. This created large-scale unemployment throughout the world.

The countries of the Third World suffered in two major ways:

▶ they had to pay more for their oil imports. These had already taken a high proportion of their people's incomes. Now, with higher oil prices, spending on oil became an even higher proportion of the spending by poor people. This led to a fall in living standards, because people had less money to spend on other things;

▶ their exports to industrialized countries fell because of the fall in the total of world trade. The poor countries became even poorer than they had been. Higher oil prices led to price increases in almost every industrial product. This inflation harmed the industrialized countries because it led to a drop in demand for products and so to unemployment. But it harmed the Third World countries even more. They had to pay higher prices for the things they imported. These imports included machinery and other products needed for development. They found that their development aid bought fewer goods than had been expected before 1972. So their development was checked.

RESPONSES TO THE CRISIS

New sources of oil were hastily developed to try to limit the power of the Arabs. Britain was fortunate in discovering oil in the North Sea. Nigerian oil deposits were also developed, as were new fields in Indonesia, Alaska, the Sahara and Ecuador. These new sources were to provide their own problems later on.

New sources of energy were also developed. Britain, for example, after years during which its coal industry had been allowed to run down, now developed a new giant coalfield under the sea at Selby in Yorkshire and began the process of opening a new coalfield near Belvoir in Derbyshire. Scientists were asked to investigate the possibility of developing the production of energy from the sun, tide, wind and even sewage.

In 1984 the world still lived with the effects of the increases in oil prices. The first increases in 1972–3 were followed by a series of increases throughout the 1970s so that by 1979 oil, which in 1972 had been sold at 2 dollars per barrel, was selling for 35 dollars per barrel. In particular the world in 1984 had to try to cope with:

▶ inflation or rising prices. Government attempts to cope with this problem led to massive unemployment in the western world;

▶ balance of payments problems. To try to limit, if not end, the deficits on balance of payments, countries cut their imports — and so increased unemployment in exporting countries.

One unexpected effect of the increased prices was a fall in the demand for oil. As industry went into recession there was a drop in demand for oil for industrial purposes. Fewer people flew—so that some airlines were driven into bankruptcy (Braniff in the USA and Laker in Britain). This drop in demand for air tickets led to a drop in the demand for oil by airlines. People became more energy-conscious ('Save it', said the slogan) and used less fuel in cars and at home.

At the same time there was an increased supply of oil from new fields, largely in Nigeria and Indonesia. This led, unexpectedly, to a fall in oil prices since 1979. Oil sold at about 27 dollars per barrel. This upset the economic forecasts of oil-exporting countries.

The effects of this were, perhaps, most clearly seen in the case of Nigeria (see above). But the collapse of Nigerian development plans had effects in countries which had hoped to sell machinery and other goods to expanding Nigeria. World unemployment rose following the collapse of such development plans.

38.5 A New Oil Crisis, 1985–6

The world slump and the consequent drop in the demand for oil led to a crisis in OPEC itself. Some OPEC countries (Nigeria, Iraq and Venezuela) would like to sell more of their oil. They need the extra income they would hope to get from such increased sales. But if they increased their sales of oil, the demand for oil from other OPEC countries would fall. At the same time, their increased sales would increase the supply of oil and, in the face of falling demand, would lead to a fall in prices.

Saudi Arabia, the largest supplier of oil, cut back its output in an attempt to bring some better balance between the supply of oil and the world demand. However, Nigeria, Iraq and Venezuela took advantage of this cut back to further increase their output. At the same time, non-OPEC producers (Britain, Norway and Mexico) increased their output or, at least, maintained output at a high level.

In 1985–6 Saudi Arabia tried to force OPEC and non-OPEC countries to reach an agreement on each country's volume of output of oil and on the prices they would charge. To try to force countries to reach such an agreement, Saudi Arabia increased its output, forced down oil prices and hoped that falling prices would drive the oil-producing countries to reach agreement.

For oil-importing countries and for consumers in general, the result was beneficial. Prices fell—at one time to less than 10 dollars a barrel. This fall was reflected in cheaper petrol for motorists, cheaper oil for industry (which allowed electricity boards to cut prices to consumers) and a fall in the rate of inflation. The oil price increases of the 1970s had led to a fall in living standards in consuming countries. The fall in prices in 1984–6 led to a rise in living standards in the industrialized countries.

These improved living standards led to increased imports from Third World countries (the reverse of the situation following oil price increases: see above). Mexico, Brazil and other countries enjoyed surpluses on their balances of trade.

In May 1986 the price of oil climbed back to $15 a barrel, which is much less than the world had to pay during OPEC's heyday in the 1970s. Only the future will show whether the world will continue to enjoy this relatively cheap oil which allows low rates of inflation and rising living standards for most countries in the world.

Some OPEC countries have suffered badly because of the fall in prices. Saudi Arabia has asked that the industrialized countries (the main gainers from the fall in prices) should treat the Middle East (with its Arab members of OPEC) as a 'disaster area': Saudi Arabia asked for some form of Marshall Plan (see Unit 28) by which the industrialized West would help limit the harm done to Arab economies by falling oil prices. It is doubtful if the world will see this as something that needs to be done.

Unit 38 Summary

▶ Definitions of the 'Third World'.
▶ Third-World problems.
▶ Population control.
▶ Development aid.
▶ The oil crises.

39 THE ROAD TO DÉTENTE

39.1 Khruschev and the 'Thaw'

Stalin's death in 1953 and Khrushchev's accession to power saw Russia accept the USA's idea of co-existence (Unit 28). While this was an improvement on the warlike atmosphere of the Cold War (Unit 28), it still left the super-powers suspiciously hostile to each other. In 1955 Khrushchev organized the signing of the Warsaw Pact; Germany remained a problem as was shown by the failure of summit meetings in 1960 and 1961; and in 1962, Khrushchev's Cuban policy brough the world to the brink of war while his policy towards China led to border clashes (see Unit 29).

39.2 Brezhnev's Russia and the Outside World

EASTERN EUROPE

Eastern Europe remained united in the Warsaw Pact, but there were two major signs of unrest in this 'empire':
▶ Czechoslovakia's 'Dubcek Spring' in 1968 (Unit 30);
▶ Poland's constant Catholic-nationalism (Unit 30).

ASIA

China was increasingly hostile to Russia as shown by the clashes along the Manchurian border in 1969.

While Russia remained more friendly to India than to Western-oriented Pakistan, Kosygin and Brezhnev helped settle the Indo-Pakistan dispute over Kashmir (Unit 34).

Russia supported Vietnam in its war with the USA (Unit 35). After 1975 she supported Vietnam in its dispute with Kampuchea (Units 35 and 40).

Afghanistan had become a republic after a coup in July 1973. In April 1978 a Russian-supported Revolutionary Council seized power, but proved to be insufficiently submissive to Russia. On Christmas Eve, 1979, Russian troops invaded Afghanistan, allowed the President to be murdered and a puppet government to be set up. Afghan guerillas waged war against the Russians and their government, relying on aid from Pakistan and the West.

AFRICA

Russia supported Cuban aid to Angola (Unit 36), and in the 1970s Russian and Cuban forces supported the communist government of Ethiopia led by Mengistu. He had initially also received aid from the USA which had hoped to neutralize Russian influence in the Horn of Africa. In 1977, the Carter government withdrew its forces and aid, fearing that it might be drawn into a Vietnam-type humiliation if it backed Mengistu in his struggle with Eritrean guerillas and Somali insurgents, both of whom were opposed to the Marxist government of Ethiopia. The US withdrawal allowed Russian influence to grow in this strategically important part of Africa.

MIDDLE EAST

Russia supported Syria in her campaign against Israel which led to US involvement in the Lebanon in 1983–84 (Unit 37).

39.3 US Response to Brezhnev: 1968–76

Brezhnev declared that 'the class struggle between the two systems will be continued', a sign that, while he had power, Russia would have an aggressive foreign policy and would seek to extend her influence around the world.

In 1968 Nixon became President of the USA. He had been seen as a hard-line anti-communist. However, once in power he changed the nature of US foreign policy:

▶ In 1969 he proclaimed what became known as the 'Nixon Doctrine' which promised that the USA would continue to oppose communism, but which demanded that Asian states would learn to defend themselves. This was much less ambitious than the 'doctrines' stated by Truman and Eisenhower (Unit 32).

▶ In 1971 he supported communist China's claim to a seat at the UNO, a surprising turnabout for the man who had once attacked Truman for being soft on communism (Unit 32). In 1971–2 he visited China and Russia, so making the contacts which helped détente on its way (see opposite).

▶ In 1973 he signed the treaty which ended US participation in Vietnam's struggles (Unit 35).

SALT, 1969–72

Both Russia and the USA were concerned at the cost of the arms race, and both knew the destructive effects of modern weapons. They had achieved Mutual Assured Destruction (MAD): both countries had enough weapons to wipe out the other, which would, however, have been given sufficient time to launch its weapons before being destroyed.

In November 1969 both countries began talks aimed at limiting defensive anti-ballistic systems. In May 1972 they signed the Strategic Arms Limitation Treaty (SALT), by which they agreed to make some reductions in anti-ballistic missile systems and to hold further talks aimed at further arms reduction.

39.4 Carter and Brezhnev, 1976–80

Carter seemed to be dominated by concern for Israel and Iran (Unit 32) and by hopes for world peace. He agreed to a second round of SALT negotiations which led to agreement by both sides to limit the number of nuclear missiles which they possessed. However, the US Senate refused to ratify this Treaty when it was debated late in 1979, when Senator Jackson called for the halting of grain aid to Russia (Unit 32). To many Americans it seemed as if Russia was taking advantage of Carter's weakness when her forces invaded Afghanistan in December 1979. Carter's lack of response seemed to prove that his US critics were right:

▶ he ordered US athletes to boycott the 1980 Moscow Olympics and asked other nations to follow his example;

▶ he called for an economic boycott of Russia – while he continued to allow US grain to be sold to Russia.

INCREASED RUSSIAN CONFIDENCE

The USA withdrawal from Vietnam was, in essence, a Russian victory. At great economic cost, Russia built up her nuclear forces so that, by 1980, she had achieved superiority over the USA. Her own forces and those of her Cuban satellite won increasing control in Angola, Ethiopia and Afghanistan. It is not surprising that Brezhnev believed that he could do anything he wanted to. This was to be shown by his cynical attitude towards talk of détente and of human rights.

39.5 Defining Détente

Western statesmen believe that détente means:

▶ that both East and West have common interests;

▶ understanding can be increased and improved by contact;

▶ arms controls are essential;

▶ trade agreements forge links between the two sides.

Russians seem to believe that détente means:

▶ a lowering of tension and a lessening of the risk of war;

▶ a continuation of the struggle between communism and capitalism in a more peaceful world;

▶ that trade, cultural and other links are of no real importance, unless they help to promote Russian self-interest. Russia welcomed US grain, German technology, Western financial aid and chances to sell goods in Western markets. However, she rejected any notion of the West being free to criticise Russia's internal policies, such as her treatment of dissidents. This was revealed by her response to the Helsinki agreement.

39.6 Helsinki and Human Rights

Willy Brandt's Ostpolitik

Brandt became Chancellor of West Germany in 1969, having been Foreign Minister from 1966. He wanted to improve relations with Russia, East Germany and Eastern Europe as a whole. In 1972 West Germany signed treaties with Poland and Russia recognizing the existing Polish boundaries and the loss of former German land to Poland (Unit 30). Brandt urged other Western countries to improve their relationships with the Eastern bloc countries.

While Brandt was pursuing his new policies, Russia and the USA were engaged in the SALT negotiations (see 39.3). This helped Brandt's campaign for improved East-West relations.

The European Security Conference, 1973-75

This Helsinki Conference was attended by delegates from the USA, Canada and 33 countries from Europe. Their negotiations led to the Helsinki Agreement (August 1975):

▶ it recognized the frontiers of Eastern Europe, and Soviet domination over that region;

▶ West Germany gave up its claim to be the only true German state, so officially recognizing East Germany;

▶ Russia promised to give 21 days notice before holding military manoeuvres near another national border;

▶ Russia promised to help reunite divided families in Europe, to allow more freedom to Western journalists working in the USSR, and to encourage more East-West visits;

▶ Russia also seemed to agree to allow outside inspection of her record on human rights which encouraged Russian dissidents to compile records of ill-treatment by the government;

▶ Russia agreed to buy US wheat and to export oil to the US. Business, it seemed, backed détente.

39.7 Human Rights, Stage 1

In August 1941, Roosevelt and Churchill signed the Atlantic Charter (Unit 19) which, among other things, spoke of the four freedoms which people should have: of speech, of worship, from want, and from other nations. It also said that, when the war was over, people everywhere should be given the right to choose their own governments, while countries conquered by force should have their independence restored.

Stalin accepted the terms of this Charter when Russia was drawn into the war, and reaffirmed his support for this version of civil liberties, or human rights, at Yalta (see Unit 26). He also signed the UN Charter, June 1945, which aimed

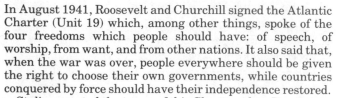

at creating 'respect for the principles of equal rights and self-determination of peoples, to reaffirm faith in fundamental human rights . . .'.

1948 witnessed the UN's Universal Declaration of Human Rights which attempted the seemingly impossible as it tried to spell out people's rights without suggesting who, or what, had the duties of ensuring the achievement of those rights. The UN document noted the right of people '. . . to work, free choice of employment, favourable conditions of work, to equal pay . . . other forms of social protection . . .'. This extended the concept of human rights beyond those noted in the Atlantic Charter from the civil, legal and religious fields into social and economic fields. Some saw this as progressive; others asked what difference such words made to the lives of people in underdeveloped countries.

In 1975 some Western optimists hoped that Brezhnev's signing of the Helsinki Agreement would lead to an extension of human rights throughout Russia and Eastern Europe. They also hoped that the 'linkage' of the economies of East and West would allow Western influences to promote demands for improvements in the Russian record in this regard. Brezhnev had other ideas. He saw the Helsinki Agreement as merely 'a scrap of paper'. Its purpose, as he saw it, was to limit military expenditure and so provide a chance for the Soviet economy to improve. The rest of the package was only acceptable if beneficial to the USSR. When Jackson tried to amend a proposed US-USSR trade deal with clauses concerning Russian treatment of Jews (Units 32 and 39), Brezhnev cancelled the deal.
Jews (Units 32 and 39), Brezhnev cancelled the deal.

The Agreement changed nothing in the Soviet Union or in Eastern Europe. Dissidents were still harassed: the Czech government attacked members of the Charter 77 group set up to monitor Czech adherence to the Agreement; in Russia Sakharov and others came under increased pressure. In 1975, President Carter, under pressure from a more confident Congress (Unit 32) affirmed US 'commitment to human rights as a fundamental tenet to our foreign policy'. Brezhnev condemned this as 'an attempt at interference with our internal affairs'. It is not surprising that subsequent reviews of the Agreement took place in a climate of hostility and consisted largely of each side attacking the other. Representatives of the Helsinki powers failed to reach any agreement at Belgrade (1978), Madrid (1981) when Afghanistan also appeared on the agenda, Ottawa (1985), Belgrade (1985) and Berne (1986). At all these meetings Western delegates condemned Russia's record on human rights which, for their part, the Russians condemned as interference with their internal affairs. Many western observers believed that their governments had been outmanoeuvred and hoodwinked by the Russians. Perhaps this indicated a more realistic attitude than that which had prevailed in 1975.

39.8 Reagan and Gorbachev

We have seen (Unit 32) that a major reason for Reagan's victory in the 1980 election was a widespread feeling in the USA that Russia had become too strong while US foreign policy was too weak. We have also seen how Reagan adopted a more active and aggressive foreign policy in the case of Grenada, and as regards Gadaffi's Libya (Unit 32). To back up this policy, Reagan also built up US defence forces, allowed research into the Strategic Defence Initiative (or 'Star Wars') to go ahead, and, as we shall see, increased and improved US nuclear weapons in Europe. We have seen that, at the same time, Gorbachev was being forced to reconsider Russia's military posture and defence spending (Unit 29). He realized that it was economic and military madness to spend 20 per cent of Russia's national output on defence equipment while shops were either empty of goods, or had such small supplies that people had to queue for basic items such as bread, meat, soap and so on. Reagan's determination to make the US powerful again combined with Gorbachev's need to cut military spending has enabled large strides to be made

down the road to détente. Carter had hoped for this, but his weakness was perceived as such by Brezhnev; if Gorbachev has become more peacefully inclined it may be because he has come up against new realities at home and a new reality in the USA, including 'the Reagan Doctrine' which increased US defence power and led to a more aggressive foreign policy.

39.9 Arms Reduction, Stage 1

There was an optimistic atmosphere in international relations in 1973 because of US withdrawal from Vietnam, the success of the SALT talks, Brandt's Ostpolitik, and the opening of the Helsinki conference. To take advantage of this, Nixon and Brezhnev agreed to a conference on Mutual and Balanced Force Reduction (MBFR).

The conference opened in Vienna in January 1974, its aim being to reach an agreement on the reduction in the number of troops and weapons held by East and West in the various countries in Central Europe. The Soviet delegates took a hard line from the outset, refusing to reveal the size of the forces of the Warsaw Pact countries, and making clear their determination to maintain their superiority over NATO. In view of this less-than-flexible approach on the Eastern side, and, on the Western side, the realization that the Soviet Union seemed to have no real interest in détente, it is not surprising that the bored delegates achieved nothing after 12 years of discussions, except the designing of a club tie.

In 1981 the climate of Western opinion was very different from the unmerited optimism of 1973. Reagan was in power in the USA, determined to increase defence spending. He was supported by Thatcher in Britain who saw that if the US drift to arms reduction (evident under Nixon and Carter) was ever put into effect, NATO would be helpless in the face of a Soviet attack. This made her anxious to ensure that either there were genuinely mutual and balanced reductions (to which the Russians wouldn't agree) or that there would be a European system able to stand up to Russian attack. Reagan's hard-line coincided with European fears. He made available, and many European countries willingly accepted, new, modernized US missiles – Pershing 2 and Cruise in particular, in spite of a European-wide protest by supporters of the Campaign for Nuclear Disarmament. By 1986 these weapons were in place.

In the face of this development, the Russians offered a reduction in their arms, if the Europeans would agree not to instal the new weapons. They insisted that, if the weapons were brought in, Russia would have to modernize and increase the number of Soviet missiles targeted on Western Europe and so increase the danger of war. NATO offered a 'zero option' under which both sides would dismantle all their long-range theatre weapons – but not their intercontinental ballistic missiles. The Russians rejected this proposal which would affect only short range or 'intermediate' missiles.

39.10 Arms Reduction, Stage 2

Gorbachev came to power in March 1985, and Reagan won the 1984 Presidential Election, largely because of approval for his strong foreign policy.

While Brezhnev had controlled Russia there were no apparent hopes for arms reduction. The MBFR talks had failed to reach any agreement on Intermediate Nuclear Forces reductions; and Reagan had ordered the plans to make a neutron bomb, a new B-1 bomber and a new Trident nuclear submarine. New missiles were being installed by both East and West in Central Europe while ongoing Strategic Arms Limitations Talks (or SALT 2) were stalled.

Within hours of Gorbachev's accession to power, Reagan invited him to the USA 'at a mutually convenient time'. Some of his critics feared that Reagan's commitment to 'summitry' would lead to further Russian diplomatic victories: the smooth Gorbachev was seen as more than a match for 'an aging actor'.

The first Reagan-Gorbachev summit was held in Geneva

in November 1985 where they reached no new agreements other than to promise another summit in 1986. Subsequently, Gorbachev announced that if the US went ahead with SDI, there would be no fresh talks – but, in spite of continued SDI research, talks did go on and arrangements finalized for another meeting. To smooth the way for that meeting, Reagan used conciliatory language about Gorbachev ('a modern man') and arms control ('my determination to keep the momentum going'). In an exchange of letters, Gorbachev asked for a halt to SDI research which Reagan refused, to which Gorbachev responded by promising to match US spending '. . . however much it costs our people'.

In spite of this apparent hostility, and of the failure of a hastily-arranged and badly-organized summit in Iceland, arms negotiators on both sides continued to meet and, finally, produced an agreement in December 1987 which became the Intermediate Nuclear Forces Treaty (INF). Both sides agreed to abolish their intermediate missiles, so 'at a stroke' doing away with a whole branch of nuclear weaponry.

39.11 Arms Reduction, Stage 3

Many Western commentators gave more credit to Gorbachev than to Reagan for the successful conclusion of the INF talks. This may be a reflection of an anti-US bias: it may be that they were bemused by the 'new' Russian and his 'attractive' wife – a change after the hard faces of Brezhnev and Gromyko and the bulk of most Russian leaders' wives.

Gorbachev won even more credit when he came to a third summit in Washington in December 1988. Here he called for cuts in conventional forces as well as the abolition of half of each side's strategic nuclear weapons. He chose his time well: Reagan had only a few more days in power, and was in no position to respond; Bush had not yet been installed in office and was constitutionally unable to respond. So the West perceived an apparently open-handed Gorbachev being met with stolid US response to his generous proposals.

Under his plans, the Soviet army would lose 5000 tanks from East Germany, Hungary and Czechoslovakia, and another 5000 in the western part of the Soviet Union; it would also lose 800 combat aircraft, 500 000 men and 85 000 artillery pieces. Soviet capacity to mount a sudden armoured thrust into West Germany would be sharply reduced.

However, the deputy chief of the Soviet general staff painted a slightly more aggressive picture when in London for four days of talks. While promising that, for the first time, the Russians would be forthcoming about the size of their forces and of those of the Warsaw Pact countries, he also pointed out that, in 1988:

▶ all Soviet forces had been modernized;

▶ the Warsaw Pact countries would still have twice as many tanks as NATO, three times as much artillery and five times as many surface-to-air missiles;

▶ while NATO was stronger in some areas, such as attack aircraft, the gap between the two sides was widening in favour of the Warsaw Pact countries.

It appeared that Soviet defence chiefs had not yet fully accepted Gorbachev's demand for a shift in Soviet thinking: instead of training for an aggressive war, Gorbachev had announced that the military would only have 'reasonable sufficiency' to defend the homeland.

39.12 Gorbachev: Peacemaker

Gorbachev's pursuit of arms reductions has been imposed on him by the continued failure of the Soviet economy (see Units 29 and 39). So, too, his search for peace and a lessening of defence spending in:

Afghanistan (Unit 39);

Angola (Unit 40.7);

Kampuchea (Unit 40.6);

China (Unit 40.3). In January 1989 talks were held to prepare for a possible Sino-Soviet summit later in the year.

▶ Eritrea. Here Russia has supported the 300 000 strong Ethiopian army in its war against 'freedom fighters' from Eritrea and Somalia. In November 1988 Gorbachev announced his wish for a peaceful settlement to this 27-year-long war, which is a drain on Soviet resources.

39.13 Human Rights, Stage 2

As part of the new-found search for détente, the countries involved in the Helsinki meetings (Unit 39) held a new series of meetings in Vienna beginning in 1986. Delegates from 35 NATO, Warsaw Pact and neutral European countries worked for two years before reaching agreement in January 1989 on human rights and conventional arms negotiations. As a result of this, there will be a new round of 23-nations arms talks on Conventional Armed Forces in Europe (CAFE). More immediately, the 35 countries signed an agreement on human rights which requires the Soviet Union and its allies:

▶ to observe wide-ranging standards of freedom of religion and the press;

▶ to respond within three months or less to requests from citizens for visas;

▶ to the reuniting of families divided by the Iron Curtain;

▶ to ban the jamming of radio signals, so permitting 'freedom of the air'.

This is a major breakthrough in the field of human rights, which seems to promise more than was achieved by the Helsinki Agreement. Gorbachev's support for these proposals was influenced by his wish to host a Human Rights Conference in Moscow in 1991: Western countries refused to discuss the possibility of such a historic conference unless Russia accepted their proposals on existing human rights.

39.14 Cautious Optimism

Even as their delegates were signing the Vienna agreement, the Czech government (Unit 40) along with the governments of Rumania and Bulgaria were showing their opposition to Gorbachev's policies. So too, were some defence chiefs in the Soviet Union, where Sakharov and others argued that 'Gorbachev will be out by the summer'. It is not surprising if some Western leaders, notably Mrs Thatcher and President Bush, call for caution in Western approaches to the Soviet Union, which, as we have seen:

▶ modernizes its forces and retains a superiority over NATO;

▶ may use western economic and technological aid to maintain that modernizing superiority.

This explains why:

▶ the USA has gone ahead with the production of a new radar-escaping Stealth bomber;

▶ NATO is discussing the modernization of its forces.

It is significant that Western leaders have, once again, homed in on Berlin as a symbol of division and potential source of dispute. British, US and other statesmen have called for the dismantling of the Berlin Wall which, they claim, is an affront to human rights' talks. Only the future will show if demands for its dismantling will succeed.

Unit 39 Summary

▶ 1953–68.
▶ 1968–76.
▶ 1970–80.
▶ Defining détente.
▶ Helsinki, 1975.
▶ Human Rights, 1975.
▶ Reagan and Gorbachev.
▶ Arms reductions – in stages.
▶ Human Rights, 1989.

40 FROM SOVIET UNION (USSR) TO THECOMMONWEALTH OF INDEPENDENT STATES (CIS) 1989–92

40.1 Electing Parliament, March 1989

Under Gorbachev's new constitution (see 29.13), the Soviet Union held its first relatively free elections. The new Parliament had 2250 members: 750 of these were elected by Party agencies (trade unions, the army, etc.), 530 by the professional organizations (see 29.13). Only 950 were to be elected by the people generally. But in 565 constituencies the Party used its 'influence' to ensure that only one name (a 'favourite son') appeared on the ballot paper. This meant that there were genuinely free elections in only 395 seats: the Party, and Gorbachev, tried to ensure that it held on to power. They used the March 1989 election as an attempt to 'disguise Party control and the old system in democratic clothing'.

Boris Yeltsin, Gorbachev's appointee as 'boss' of the Moscow Communist party, had quarrelled with Gorbachev: he was the spokesman for those who wanted more reforms than Gorbachev seemed willing to make (see 29.14). Gorbachev had sacked him from the ruling Politburo (Fig. 29.13) but left him in his Moscow post. Here he fought corrupt old-timers, called for greater reforms, won a lot of publicity – and a seat in the new Parliament.

40.2 Continued Economic Failure

In 1913 Tsarist Russia had a real income per head about four times that of Japan, a life expectancy equal to America's and was emerging from serfdom into fast economic growth (see 3.4 and 3.8). After seventy years of Communism, a Soviet citizen was less likely to own a car than was a black South African and had a life expectancy similar to an inhabitant of backward Third World countries (see 29.12).

Under Gorbachev the Party continued to control the economy. His attempts at reform (see 29.13) were blocked by Party officials at national and local level: they feared a loss of privilege and influence if the free market was allowed to operate.

However, his political reforms and the relatively free elections led to an increased demand for economic reforms. Gorbachev and his advisers agreed that Stalin's industrial and agricultural reforms (see 11.3 and 11.4) had created a huge bureaucracy which used its power to serve its own interests and not to provide what the people wanted.

In April 1989 Gorbachev sacked 110 leading 'conservatives' from the Central Committee (Fig. 29.13), the Party's policy-making body, so continuing a process he had begun in September 1988 (see 29.13). These 'conservatives' and their supporters criticized Gorbachev's dictatorial ('Stalinist') use of power whilst attacking him as a 'liberal' for allowing greater freedom to the media – TV, radio and press. They feared that Gorbachev was moving towards allowing the Soviet Parliament (see 40.1) to become the State's major policy-making body.

40.3 Parliament Meets, May – June 1989

The meetings of the first relatively 'free' Parliament were watched by millions of TV viewers. In spite of Gorbachev's attempt to ensure party domination (see 40.1), there were many critics of the 'old methods' of running the economy, and of the use of the army to put down nationalist demonstrations in Georgia (see 29.14). People saw and heard members of Parliament attacking the long-time Party philosopher, Ligachev (see 29.13), the activities of the KGB, of the army and of corrupt officials. They heard members criticizing not only Gorbachev but even the Party itself. And while the Party could win votes inside Parliament, the liberal critics won increasing support among people outside.

A leading liberal member of Parliament was the once-imprisoned scientist, Andrei Sakharov (see 29.11). The Party had tried to exclude him from Parliament; widespread criticism in the now more free media and in the West forced Gorbachev to allow Sakharov to be a candidate and he was elected. In Parliament he criticized Gorbachev for not being willing to reform quickly enough, and he asked Western countries to refuse Gorbachev's pleas for assistance (see 29.14): he wanted Gorbachev to introduce a free market economy as the price for such aid. He showed that Gorbachev's government was running a huge and inflationary budget deficit as people were paid far more than they produced, that agricultural output was failing and that state enterprises were losing £12 billion a year – while shops remained empty and people queued, even in Moscow, for basic goods such as soap and meat. Sakharov called for a speedy move towards private ownership of arms and industries and warned of the danger of an anti-Gorbachev *coup* by the Army and the threat of another civil war (see 10.8).

40.4 Call for End of Party Rule

By August 1989 about 330 members of Parliament had formed a solid Opposition to continued Communist Party rule. They called for a new constitution which would legalize political parties and guarantee basic human rights. They wanted a democratically elected government free from Party control, and they asked Gorbachev to decide whether he wanted to become leader of their political reform movement or whether he wanted to remain head of a corrupt and discredited Party.

40.5 Gorbachev–Bush Meeting, December 1989

Gorbachev met Bush in Malta in December 1989. Bush welcomed the increasing liberalization taking place in the Soviet Union and in Eastern Europe (see Unit 41). He called for speedy and widespread disarmament as a means of freeing economic resources for use in Soviet consumer goods' industries. He offered Gorbachev some assistance – financial credits to allow the Soviets to buy in badly needed machinery, food supplies to ease the shortages of basic foods and cheap loans to allow the Soviets to buy goods elsewhere than in the USA. Bush wanted Gorbachev to remain in power and to push through his promised economic and political reforms.

Gorbachev knew that economic reforms were essential. He knew that 1000 out of 1200 consumer goods were in short supply: in July he had faced a strike by Siberian miners angry at the shortage of soap: doctors were reporting evidence of widespread malnutrition because of the shortage of bread and meat (see 29.14). He knew that the Soviet economic infrastructure was crumbling – that the railways were inefficient, the roads left unrepaired and so the transport of goods was hampered: he knew that in some cities the water supply was turned on for only six hours a day because of lack of maintenance of piping and reservoirs.

Both Bush and Gorbachev knew that there were liberals (led by Yeltsin) who wanted wider, deeper and speedier reforms, and, on the other hand, conservatives (led by army officers) who wanted a slow-down in the reform process which, they said, would lead to higher prices, unemployment and, perhaps, social unrest.

40.6 Questions for East and West, December 1989

▶Did Gorbachev really want a free market and privatization? If he did, then he had to end central planning and Party control of economic power. Or did he merely want to approve such economic liberalism for Poland, Hungary and other parts of what was still his 'outer Empire'?

▶ Did he really want political liberalization, with multiple parties, elections and the rule of law? If he did, then he could not argue for a continuation of Party control of elections, Parliament and the levers of political power. Or, again, was he merely willing to approve of such moves towards democracy in Poland and elsewhere?

▶ Was he really willing to cut the power of the army (which had been humiliated by the withdrawal from Afghanistan (see Unit 39))? If he was, would he end Soviet aid to Cuba, Nicaragua, Libya and Iraq? And would he pull Soviet troops from their forward positions in East Germany, Czechoslovakia and elsewhere? And if he was so peace-minded, would the army and the Soviet 'nationalists' allow him to act?

For the West, the questions continued to be two-fold:

▶ Should they provide all the help that Gorbachev wanted, even though his reforms seemed half-hearted? Would such aid lead, perhaps, to a stronger Marxist state with its aim of world domination still in place?

▶ Was the ramshackle Soviet Union capable of using whatever aid the West provided? Or would such aid be a case of throwing money away? Would a Party-controlled system allow Western economists, bankers, industrialists and businessmen to come in and help create the economic and social infrastructure which would be needed if aid was to be fruitful?

40.7 The Effects of the Eastern European 'Revolution', March 1990

In Unit 41 we shall see that major changes took place in Eastern Europe in the winter of 1989–90. These liberal-nationalist movements had encouraged similar movements in the Soviet Union. In particular the three Baltic states (see 29.14) declared themselves independent, while the unrest in Georgia and Armenia (see 29.14) continued to gather momentum. Could the centralized Soviet State continue? Soviet Liberals, who watched on their TVs the triumph of Eastern European reformers, became increasingly critical of Gorbachev's hesitant approach to both political and economic reform.

40.8 Gorbachev's Reactions, March 1990

Gorbachev had to face three major problems:

▶increasing criticism because of the continued failure of his half-hearted economic reforms to produce goods;

▶ the possible collapse of the Soviet Union because of nationalist movements;

▶ the possible collapse of the Communist Party. Some leading Communists announced that they were seceding from the Party: rank and file members appeared on TV as they tore up their Party cards.

He proposed to bring forward a meeting of the Parliament (in which the Party controlled 87% of the seats). He said that this Parliament would elect a State President who would have increased powers and that it would consider replacing Party officials in some top State jobs. Yeltsin and other reformers feared that the new President (probably Gorbachev) would have Stalinist powers – to declare a state

of emergency, to veto Parliamentary legislation and to govern by decree when he saw fit. The weakness of Gorbachev's position was highlighted in June 1990 when elections had been held for Parliaments in the various individual Republics in the Soviet Union. In spite of increased Party activity, Yeltsin was elected President of the largest Republic (Russia), defeating Gorbachev's nominee by a huge majority. Yeltsin could now claim to speak with the support of the people. Gorbachev, on the other hand, never submitted himself to a free election. His position, even after the meeting of the new Parliament, depended on the votes of Party activists only: he had no popular mandate for any reforms he proposed.

40.9 The Union of Sovereign Soviet States, June 1990 – August 1991

After he had been elected President of the Russian Republic, Yeltsin met the Lithuanian President who had led the campaign for independence and had had to suffer an economic blockade by Gorbachev's government. Yeltsin proposed a trade treaty between Russia and the Baltic states – so defeating Gorbachev's attempts to force the Baltic states to stay in the Soviet Union. Many other local governments followed Yeltsin's liberal example. Gorbachev had been publicly humiliated.

To try to regain the initiative, he called a meeting of the newly created Council of the Federation. This consisted of himself and the elected Presidents of the 15 Republics. He asked this Council to approve a new Treaty of the Union which would redefine the powers of the Republics and of the Central Government. The USSR would be replaced by the Union of Sovereign Soviet States – socialist no longer. Each Republic's independence would be recognized, but there would be a Union which Gorbachev hoped would keep the country together. He wanted to keep foreign policy, defence and some economic powers for himself and he hoped that some of the Republics would give many powers back to the centre: he accepted that some, like the Baltic Republics, would give back none. Indeed, even as Gorbachev invited the Republics to consider his new treaty, Estonia and Latvia announced steps towards complete independence. Discussions on the proposed new treaty, and a new Constitution which would be needed, went on through the following year. It became clear that Gorbachev was proposing the death of the Soviet Union, the end of 'seventy years on the road to nowhere' and of Marxist-Leninist government. Power would clearly pass from Moscow to whichever Republics agreed to join the new USSS – and only ten appeared to be willing to do so.

Old-time Marxists, some army leaders and many bureaucrats were opposed to such a denial of all that they believed in. In August 1991, while Gorbachev was on holiday in the Crimea, some members of his own government tried to organize a *coup*: they told the world that Gorbachev was ill and that they were taking over the government. Events showed that they had not prepared things properly: they did not arrest Yeltsin, who defied the *coup* leaders, called on the people of his Russian Republic to demonstrate and himself appeared at the Russian Parliament to call for the overthrow of the *coup*. Nor had the diehards ensured complete support from the army, although the Minister of Defence was one of the *coup*'s leaders: local army commanders refused to obey orders, allowed demonstrations to take place and announced that they supported Yeltsin and the 'rule of law'. Within a short time the *coup* had crumbled as some leaders flew to the Crimea to try to placate the imprisoned Gorbachev, others tried to flee, while others stayed to meet Gorbachev when he was flown back to Moscow.

Now events showed clearly that power had slipped from Gorbachev to Yeltsin. When he met the Russian leader and his Parliament, Gorbachev foolishly ignored the opportunity to praise Yeltsin and the Russian people for their opposition to the *coup*. He also failed to note that the leaders of the *coup* were all Party members, and men whom he had appointed to office. He called for the maintenance of Party control and power. He was humiliated by Yeltsin who demanded that he sign a decree abolishing the Communist Party.

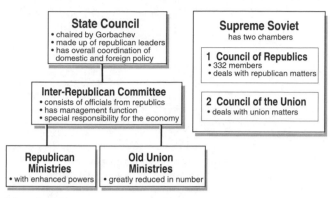

Fig. 40.9 The new Soviet hierarchy

In September 1991 a much weakened Gorbachev introduced his new constitution (Fig. 40.9). Gorbachev's power depended on his position as Party leader. Unlike Yeltsin he had not been popularly elected – as had the other 'republican leaders' (Fig. 40.9). Some of these emerged as being both popular with their own people and outspoken critics of centralization. They were clearly not going to be puppets in the hands of Gorbachev. Indeed, following the example of Yeltsin's Russia, the leaders of Georgia, the Ukraine and other Republics demanded that they have their own armies and make their own economic decisions in the interests of their people, so weakening the power of the State Council and its subordinate structures (Fig. 40.9).

The economic future of the new USSS was not very bright. Would the separate Republics be willing to submit to any economic control, even from a slimmed-down centre? The Ukraine, for example, threatened to ban the sale of grain to Russia, so that its own people might have enough food. In return, Yeltsin threatened to ban the export to the Ukraine of much needed Russian oil and gas. Would the economy of the USSS sink even further into the mire?

40.10 The Fall of Gorbachev, December 1991

An increasingly confident Yeltsin accepted the advice of his leading economists and took a series of decisive and necessary actions. He announced that his Russian government would take control of the former Soviet bank and offices in the Kremlin; he introduced a series of reforms aimed at ending price control and he promised further reforms aimed at helping the creation of a free market.

On the other hand, Gorbachev wasted days in fruitless negotiations with the ambitious leaders of the Republics. He warned of the dangers of the break up of the old Union into 'warring Republics'. But few listened to the man who had failed to act decisively enough when he had power and opportunity.

On 8 December 1991 Yeltsin signed an agreement with the Presidents of the Ukraine and Belorussia which created a Commonwealth of Independent States. The three Presidents invited the leaders of other Republics to join them. On 12 December 1991 Gorbachev announced that with the democratic and constitutionally correct creation of the CIS his work was finished and he would resign from office.

40.11 The Commonwealth of Independent States (CIS)

In March 1992 it is clear that the CIS as a whole, and the individual Republics which have formed it, face major problems.

PROBLEMS FOR THE CIS

▶ Can the various Republics agree on economic restructuring? In the old Soviet Union, because of Stalin's industrial policies, each Republic was the major provider of one or two basic items: 85% of all textile goods were produced in one Republic, while 80% of all engineering products came from another. Will it be possible to work out a system whereby production is economically dispersed? Or will the Republics have to continue their present systems of exchange by barter?

▶ Can the CIS (and the individual Republics) find the people to develop the needed infrastructure if reform and privatization are to operate?

▶ Will the CIS (and the individual Republics) be able to weed out the corrupt officials who ran the system in the past and who are still in place?

▶ Can the CIS accommodate the dominant position of the Russian Republic – the largest geographically, the most populated and economically the richest of the Republics? Or will the Russians rediscover the old imperialism which led Tsars to extend Russian power over eastern regions?

▶ Will the Muslim Republics of the south develop links with fundamentalist states such as Iran and so threaten the creation of an anti-Russian 'federation of Islamic states'?

PROBLEMS FOR THE SEPARATE REPUBLICS

▶ Will people put up with the huge price increases that have been put in place and are threatened? Food prices rose fivefold in the winter of 1991–2 and oil prices are set to rise threefold in the near future. Such increases are needed if the over-supply of money is to be cut back: but the resulting hardship may be more than the people can bear.

▶ Do the Republics have the structures needed to use wisely the aid demanded from the West? Or will a deal of such aid be siphoned off, as it has been, by a Mafia-like group of corrupt outlaws?

Unit 40 Summary

▶ Gorbachev's new constitution, 1989.
▶ The rise of Yeltsin.
▶ Liberalization versus conservatism.
▶ The formation of the USSS.
▶ The attempted *coup*, August 1991.
▶ Self-determination in the Baltics: the CIS.

41 THE EAST EUROPEAN REVOLUTION OF 1989

41.1 Common Problems

The former governments of Eastern Europe derived their power from the ideologies imposed by the Soviet army as it advanced in 1944–45 (see 30.1–30.2). Then, and until recently, the Communists claimed that they 'represented the future', that 'Marx knew best', that capitalist governments had 'failed the people' and that the Soviet Union, on which they all depended, 'best understood Marx'. As members of the Warsaw Pact (1955) they used 'the dangers from the West' as an excuse for the need for strong, centralized, Soviet-controlled governments.

All those arguments were undermined by developments which took place in the mid-1980s:
▶ Gorbachev admitted that Marxism had failed: he turned to capitalism at home and aid from capitalists abroad;
▶ the threat from the West diminished with détente;
▶ old-fashioned nationalism emerged in the eight 'independent' countries of Eastern Europe.

The failure of Marxism and Gorbachev's reforms created problems for the Soviets and their satellites:
▶ Could they move from 'party dictatorship' to more open forms of popularly accepted government?
▶ Could they have much needed economic reforms without creating a demand for political reform?
▶ Could they find the people (other than old-time Communists) to lead their countries along the road to reform?
▶ How would these countries, freed from Soviet control, deal with their racial problems?

In 1989 there took place what observers called the 'Great European Revolution of 1989'. Dictators were overthrown: Communism was rejected and Marx, Lenin and Stalin were thrown into 'the garbage heap of history' (see 10.6).

41.2 Poland 1987–92

President Jaruzelski was a 'liberal' communist (see 30.4). With Rakowski as Prime Minister he tried to deal with the problems (inflation, shortages, unemployment and a huge foreign debt) of a country which, in spite of years of repression, was still strongly Catholic and supportive of the still outlawed Solidarity movement.

Early in 1989 Jaruzelski held discussions with Solidarity with a view to that movement being legalized, provided that it agreed to cooperate with the Communist government in solving the country's problems.

In April 1989 Jaruzelski signed an agreement with Walesa, the leader of Solidarity. This 'historic compromise':
▶ legalized Solidarity as a trade union, along with Rural Solidarity and independent students' unions;
▶ allowed greater press freedom (and the emergence of Solidarity newspapers) and the Opposition's right to one hour a week on state radio and state TV every week;
▶ gave the Church the right to operate its schools;
▶ provided for the ending of state subsidies on food and other consumer goods; workers would be compensated by a form of wage indexation, although they would not be fully compensated for the expected price increases. Hardline Communist unions opposed this section of the deal and accused Solidarity of 'selling the workers out';
▶ set June 1989 as a deadline for partially free elections and the creation of a new constitution. Under this there would be:
(i) A President, to be chosen by the two houses of a new Parliament. He would be responsible for foreign affairs and defence and have the right to dissolve Parliament and to veto any legislation passed by it. This first President was to serve for six years after which a successor would be chosen by popular vote.
(ii) A lower House of Parliament (or *Sejm*) with 460 seats. 299 of these would be controlled by the Communists – but for one Parliament only. Later, these seats would be open to free contest. In June 1989 there would be free elections for the remaining 161 seats.
(iii) An upper house (or Senate) of 100 members which would be freely elected. The Senate was to have the right to veto laws passed by the *Sejm* but a two-thirds majority in the *Sejm* could override that veto. Clearly this Senate, popularly elected, would have great moral authority.

Not everyone welcomed these proposals:
▶ Hardline Communists accused Jaruzelski of giving too much away. He argued that his proposed reforms would 'buy time' for the Party to solve the country's problems and to regain its lost popularity among the people.
▶ Radical members of Solidarity claimed that Walesa had given too much away and that the Communists would still control the political system.

In the June elections Solidarity won all 100 seats in the Senate and all the 161 contested in the *Sejm*. The Communist party suffered total rejection. There were widespread students' demonstrations following these elections with demands for changes in a discredited constitution. Jaruzelski resigned in July 1989, although he remained the leader of the Communist Party. Because his former Prime Minister had failed to win 50% of the votes in one of the uncontested seats, he too resigned and another Communist, Kizcak, took charge. He invited Solidarity to take some Cabinet posts and help form a coalition government. Walesa refused, saying that the Party had to take the blame for the country's continuing economic decline, the rises in living costs and the fall in living standards.

In August 1989 the last Communist government resigned to make way for the first non-Communist government in Eastern Europe. A Solidarity leader, Mazowieki, became Prime Minister while Walesa was elected as President. It was Mazowieki's government which had to grapple with the country's economic problems. He negotiated a deal with the International Monetary Fund which provided a loan of $700 million to allow Poland to buy foreign goods. In return the government was forced to bring in a set of economic policies which:
▶ would abolish all subsidies of consumer goods;
▶ would allow privatization of old state industries;
▶ kept down wage increases so that, with prices going up, there would be a fall in living standards;
▶ gave Poland's currency a fixed exchange rate – which meant that foreign banks could exert pressure on the Polish economic and governmental decisions.

By February 1990 this programme of harsh austerity led to increasing unemployment. Some liberal democrats questioned the move towards economic liberalism. Was the price too high? Disputes between Walesa and the Prime Minister led to the latter's resignation. Solidarity 'lost its political innocence' as it tried to deal with the practical problems of governing. Other parties emerged: there was a right-wing, Catholic group and a centrist group which joined Solidarity in a coalition under Prime Minister Olszewski. In March 1992 this government failed to win approval for its plans to ease the austerity by pumping money into the ailing economy as a means of overcoming the effects of the world-wide recession.

41.3 Hungary 1987–92

Gorbachev's reforms in the Soviet Union (see 29.13–14) led to increased demand for more reforms in Hungary. In May 1988 Kadar was replaced by a 'liberal' Communist, Grosz, who hoped that a mix of reforms and repression would work. He had to deal with:

▶ economic unrest due to 22% inflation, a 20% fall in living standards and rising unemployment;

▶ political unrest among people who had enjoyed economic freedom (see 30.4) and now looked for more political freedom.

In November 1988 the government agreed to allow the formation of a non-communist political party. The emergence of this opposition party in January 1989 led to anti-communist demonstrations and government anxiety as to whether it could maintain Communist control in a multi-party state. Inside the party a growing group of 'liberals' pushed for further economic and political reform:

▶ more industry was privatized along with more state farms;

▶ a small Stock Exchange was opened to allow private investment in the private industries;

▶ the Party said that it would give up power if it were defeated in any free elections;

▶ a start was made on writing a new constitution which would be offered to the people in a referendum and lead to free elections in 1990.

In July 1989 Grosz was replaced by the more 'liberal' Poszgy whilst another 'liberal' Communist, Nyers, became Party Secretary. The new government took down the barbed wire fencing marking the boundary with Austria and allowed free travel to Austria – and to the West. Many East Germans, Czechs and other Eastern Europeans took advantage of this break in the Iron Curtain (see 28.1) to flee to the West.

In October 1989 the Communist-controlled Parliament approved a new constitution which:

▶ said that no single party or body should ever again be allowed to have sole control over the state;

▶ promised democracy;

▶ allowed freedom of conscience, religion, the press, the right of assembly and the rights to reside anywhere within the country and to travel abroad.

This brought to an end more than forty years of Stalinist government and paved the way for elections in March 1990 which saw the formation of democratic government. As part of its preparations for those elections, the Party:

▶ changed its name to Hungarian Socialist Party;

▶ denounced the past rule by the Party and, in particular, condemned the Party's role in 1956 (see 30.4).

41.4 The End of East Germany, 1987–90

In 1971 Erich Honecker had ousted Ulbricht as Party Secretary (see 30.4). In 1987 he refused to publish Soviet articles about Gorbachev's reforms which he attacked; he accused Gorbachev of 'revisionism' (see Glossary). And while Poland and Hungary went through some process of reform before 1988, Honecker maintained complete control of his country, largely through the activities of a hated secret police (the *stasi*).

In June 1989 Gorbachev visited East Germany: he was greeted by huge crowds which showed their approval of his reforming work. He spoke of the Berlin Wall 'coming down when circumstances permit it' and condemned Stalin's division of Europe as 'his greatest error'. The East Germans knew that their economy, perhaps the best in Eastern Europe, was continuing to fall behind that of West Germany: even younger Communist leaders saw the need for change.

On 7 October 1989 Gorbachev went to East Germany to help celebrate the fortieth anniversary of the founding of that state (see 30.4). Crowds cheered the 'reformer' leader. But in Dresden, Leipzig and other cities, students demonstrated, and others used the Churches as centres around which to hold anti-Honecker meetings; they demanded that their country be allowed to enjoy the sort of changes that were taking place in the Soviet Union, Poland and Hungary.

Then on 18 October 1989 in the most surprising development, Honecker resigned as General Secretary of the Communist Party. His successor, Krenz, was equally unpopular with the Church groups and student demonstrators: he had been a long-time member of Honecker's government and had been groomed to succeed the Stalinist ex-Secretary.

During the following month, demonstrations increased in size, in number and in confidence. On 10 November 1989 some demonstrators attacked the Berlin Wall and made new crossing points through which thousands of East Germans crossed into West Berlin. Since 1961 (see 29.4) the Wall had been a brutal symbol of the division of Germany, the Cold War and of Soviet domination of its satellite 'empire'. Now it was coming down and neither Gorbachev nor Krenz tried to prevent its destruction.

On 10 November 1989, the Krenz government announced:

▶ a promise of free elections;

▶ an immediate limitation to the power of the secret police;

▶ freedom for people to travel to the West.

Demonstrations continued against the Communist government in which Modrow was Prime Minister. Faced with such evidence of unpopularity, the whole Politburo resigned. Gorbachev, whose reforms had started the movement for change in Poland and Hungary, indicated that he accepted the changes in East Germany and the knock-on changes in Bulgaria (where the Stalinist Zhivkov had resigned on 10 November 1989) and in Czechoslovakia, where there were signs that unrest was growing. Kohl, of West Germany, welcomed the increased freedom given to East Germans. However, in December 1989, he showed no wish to have Germany united: he saw that this would raise fears in Poland (where millions of Silesian Germans lived under the Polish government), and in the Soviet Union, which might be alarmed by the collapse of the Warsaw Pack's strength. He urged that East Germany 'be allowed to find its own destiny and its own political and social order'. Krenz announced that 'only approved parties' (dominated by the Communists) would be allowed to contest the promised elections. Could he impose Communism in this way? Would Gorbachev back him? Would they use force against the demonstrators? Or would Krenz be forced into another humiliating climbdown?

On 27 November 1989, Modrow announced in the Communist controlled Parliament that 'the Communist party would give up its leading role in the state'. He chose a new Cabinet which included eleven men from minority (non-Communist) parties. He also further cut the power of the hated secret police (*stasi*) and allowed TV programmes to show the luxurious living conditions enjoyed by the Communist leaders.

There was widespread talk about German re-unification in both East and West Germany. Many East Germans:

▶ wanted East Germany to be a 'Middle European state', independent of West Germany;

▶ approved the socialwelfare state although they opposed the harsh rule by the Communists;

▶ feared that, in a re-united Germany, they would be dominated by 'the money mad Westerners' and that, in the free market economy of a united Germany, they would have to suffer mass unemployment, higher prices and a fall in the scale of the 'socially free' goods they enjoyed under Communist rule.

On 28 November 1989 Kohl told the West Germans that:

▶ he wanted unity only after the East German elections, scheduled for 6 May 1990, had taken place;

▶ he offered East Germany massive economic aid;

▶ he feared an influx of poor refugees from the East.

In January 1990 there were continuous demonstrations against the continued power of the Communists (now called the Socialist Unity Party), its control of TV, radio and the press, and the continuing existence of the *stasi*. However, the opposition had:

▶ no united policy about the future economy;

▶ no policy regarding German re-unification;

▶ no dominant leader (like Walesa, or, in Czechoslovakia, the playwright Havel);

▶ no real organization throughout the country.

In February–March 1990 Kohl led West German discussions about the currencies of the two Germanies. In July 1990 it was agreed that there should be a 1:1 exchange rate. This was part of an East German move towards the acceptance of a freer market economy. Now its run down industries and poor infrastructure had to face competition from the West: unemployment climbed to 15% of the workforce; prices rose and living standards fell. By this time East Germany had had its elections (brought forward to March 1990). The Communist Party was humiliated as the vast majority of people voted for the Conservatives who had been backed by Kohl, or for the Social Democrats who enjoyed the support of West Germany's leading opposition party.

This led to further talks on German re-unification. Kohl wanted to wait until West Germany had had its own elections in December 1990. In July 1990 he signed a treaty on economic and industrial unity for the two separate Germanies. He asked for '2 plus 4' talks in which the two Germanies would be joined by the four wartime Allies (USA, UK, USSR and France) to consider the question of unity. These talks led to:

▶ a decision to hold all-German elections in December 1990 or January 1991;

▶ the affirmation that a united Germany would be a member of the Western alliance, NATO (see 28.6);

▶ German acknowledgement of the existing Polish boudary behind which millions of Silesian Germans lived.

But, in fact, Germany was re-united on 3 October 1990, less than a year after the fall of Honecker and the start of the destruction of the Wall.

41.5 Rumania

In August 1989 the *Economist* noted that the megalomaniac leader, Ceausescu, and his wife seemed to have their country 'well under control', largely because of the activities of the secret police and the imprisonment of their critics and in spite of:

▶ harsh economic conditions – shortages of food and other essential goods;

▶ stringent laws which, for example, said that all typewriters had to be registered with the police, and that no one was allowed an electric light bulb of more than 60w strength;

▶ the decision to centralize the economy by the creation of industrial complexes in the Stalinist mould;

▶ the destruction of most villages to make way for the creation of large communes.

In March, six Communist veterans wrote to Ceausescu to ask that there ought at least to be freedom of debate inside the party: they were imprisoned. In April there were anti-Ceausescu demonstrations on the twenty-fourth anniversary of his accession to power, and Communist Hungary asked the UN Commission on Human Rights to condemn Rumania because of attacks made on ethnic Hungarians inside Rumania.

However, as the *Economist* had noted, there seemed no chance that the dictator would be overthrown: there were no Church groups (as in Germany) or Charter 77 groups (as in Czechoslovakia) to draw attention to the continuing export of grain (while people starved) or the deterioration of the medical services (which saw thousands of children 'imprisoned' in large institutions deprived of money).

But Rumania could not be totally isolated from the winds of change blowing through the Soviet Union and Eastern

Europe. On 20–21 December 1989 there were demonstrations throughout the country: students, members of ethnic minorities, professional people and workers united in protest against the harshness of the government. They were attacked by the army and the secret police in a series of street battles which led to increased hatred for the government. In a televised broadcast, Ceausescu and his wife were booed off a platform and, on 22 December, they fled from Bucharest. They were arrested by armed militiamen, and, while fighting continued throughout the country, the dictator and his wife were executed on 25 December 1989.

In the anarchy which followed, Communists continued to control central and local government, while the opposition was divided and small: the army threatened to take power in a *coup*.

When elections were held in May 1990, a President, Iliescu, was chosen, along with a Parliament in which there were representatives from many parties. While the government halted the export of food (so that Rumanians could be better fed), it also acted against demonstrators. In this it was supported by militant miners who marched to Bucharest to fight against the students and others who were calling for more reform. Like Bulgaria and Albania, the country suffered from the absence of an organized, educated, anti-Communist group which could take control of the failing economy and the levers of power at national and local level. Meanwhile, weak governments have had to try to deal with the problems created by the presence of ethnic Hungarian and German minorities. Western help flooded into the country after TV had shown the terrible conditions in which so many children and sick and handicapped adults were living. But it is clear that there is no short cut to Rumanian economic, social or political recovery.

41.6 Yugoslavia Falls Apart

Yugoslavia was made up of six semi-autonomous regions (Slovenia, Croatia, Bosnia and Herzegovina, Montenegro, Macedonia and, the largest, Serbia) and two autonomous regions (Volvodina and Kosovo). Most of this region and its people had once been part of the Turkish Empire (Fig. 4.1): as that Empire broke up, Serbia had hoped to become the centre of a new state (see Unit 4.5).

After 1945 Tito had held these regions and their racially mixed peoples together. But after his death no strong successor appeared and, at the time, the shaky state faced many problems:

▶ high inflation and constantly rising unemployment;

▶ a repressive Communist government which used the army and secret police to quash dissidence;

▶ the emergence of a variety of nationalisms: the Serbs claimed the right to rule over the two autonomous regions; Croats, Slovenes and others feared that Serbs might try to develop a 'greater Serbia' and take power from their semi-autonomous governments;

▶ religious differences became a factor as Serb Orthodox Christians attacked the growing Muslim minority in Serbia who, in Kosovo in particular, attacked Christians: Croatian Catholics were opposed to any sign of increased power by Serbs.

All these problems crystallized in 1989–90 around the Serb leader, Milosevic, President of the Serbian Republic and leader of the Yugoslavian Communist Party. He wanted to extend Serb control of the whole country: in Kosovo he used the Federal (mainly Serb) army to attack the two million Albanians who outnumbered Serbs by 2:1.

In Slovenia and Croatia the reaction to Milosevic's threat to extend Serb power was the emergence of locally based nationalist parties. These campaigned for an increase in the power of the governments of their Republics and a halt to Milosevic's policies of Serb aggrandizement. In these two Republics the once-dominant Communist Parties agreed to allow the formation of non-communist political parties. In April 1990 both Republics held elections in which non-communists gained power and formed governments.

Milosevic claimed that these 'nationalist' governments ill-treated Serb minorities inside their borders. He armed the Serb minorities who declared parts of the two Republics to be Serb enclaves: he sent the Federal (mainly Serb) army, navy and air force against Croatia and Slovenia in what was a vicious civil war.

Both the EEC and the UNO tried and failed to organize an end to the fighting in 1991. In January 1992 the German government persuaded the EEC to recognize Croatian independence and to cut off relations with Milosevic's 'Yugoslavian' government. In March 1992 a large UN peace-keeping force was sent to the war-torn country: it is not clear, yet, what the borders between Serbia and Croatia and Slovenia will be, nor what the Croats and Slovenians will do about their large Serb minorities. Meanwhile the second largest Republic, Bosnia, voted for independence. Here the Catholic Croats and the Muslims allied against the Serbs who wanted to retain some form of federalized Yugoslavia under Serb control. Milosevic must now either accept the collapse of the old federation or make war against Bosnia. If he chooses war then the result will be horrors even greater than those which afflicted Croatia and Slovenia in 1990 and 1991.

41.7 Czechoslavkia: a Cause for Hope

In 1988 Milos Jakes replaced Husak as Party boss and head of state. His hardline government had to deal with:
► continuing economic problems – inflation and shortages of food and other goods;
► demonstrations linked with the twentieth anniversary of the 1968 'Prague Spring' (see 30.4).

The government's uncertainty was shown by:
► allowing demonstrations in memory of Jan Palech, the student who had burned himself to death when Soviet forces invaded in 1968 (see 30.4);
► using armed force against demonstrators demanding economic and political reform. In 1989 the government signed the Vienna Declaration on Human Rights (see 30.13) even as armed forces were attacking a Prague demonstration.
► attacks on supporters of Charter 77; the author, Vaclos Havel, was imprisoned along with other leaders of the opposition; children of dissidents were punished by loss of jobs and non-admission to higher education. In 1989, news

of the Polish elections (see 41.2) led to increased activity by anti-communist Czechs and to widespread demands for reform. In November the government freed Havel. He helped to organize a Civil Forum which consisted of intellectuals, Church groups and students, and which organized discussion groups which debated the need for reform and recognition of human rights. Massive demonstrations took place to support Civil Forum's demands for change; Dubček (see 30.4) came out of retirement to lend his support to the movement. From the Soviet Union, Gorbachev urged the Czech Party to come to terms with people's demands and not to use force as it had in 1968: clearly he was not going to send Soviet forces to the aid of the beleagered Czech government.

On 3 December a new government was formed which included non-communists and which organized elections to be held in January 1990. Twenty two parties fought these elections which saw Havel elected as President who promised to bring in a new constitution. Havel's government has gained from:
► a strong democratic tradition among Czechs who had had their independence between 1919 and 1938 (see 12.4);
► an economy which, in spite of its problems, was better than those of most Eastern European states;
► the proximity of the country to the West – in a geographical and spiritual sense.

However, Havel has to try to deal with:
► the enmity between Protestant Bohemians and Catholic Slovaks;
► the existence of a large Hungarian minority;
► people's high expectations that from reform will come higher living standards.

In June 1992 elections will be held for:
► a 300 member Federal Parliament;
► separate National Councils for Bohemia and Slovakia.

Unit 41 Summary

► Moves towards reform in Eastern Europe.
► Walesa's presidency in Poland.
► Hungarian liberalism; the break with Communism.
► German re-unification.
► Execution of the Ceausescus and unrest in Romania.
► Yugoslavia divides in a bloody civil war.
► Havel's Charter 77 group takes power in Czechoslovakia.

42 WESTERN DEMOCRACIES 1987–92

42.1 President Bush

FOREIGN POLICY

Bush benefited from the collapse of the Soviet Union and the weakness of the CIS (see Unit 40).
► He was able to get agreements for wider and deeper arms cuts than had previously seemed possible (see 39.1).
► He saw Gorbachev abandon Castro's Cuba (see 29.5). While Castro maintains his loyalty to Communism, he is less of a threat to the USA than he has been.
► He saw the collapse of Soviet-backed movements in Angola (see 39.2) and Latin America.
► He got Soviet support at the UNO for armed intervention against Iraq after the invasion of Kuwait (see 45.6).
► He won a high popularity rating in early 1991 after the defeat of Saddam Hussein of Iraq. However, he lost popularity in 1992, as Saddam not only continued to rule Iraq but also resisted UN demands for the destruction of nuclear and chemical weapons.

DOMESTIC POLICY

► The world-wide trade recession (1989–92) led to a fall in US exports and to rising unemployment.
► Meanwhile foreign firms (mainly Japanese) continued to export to the USA which led to more unemployment.
► In the recession, tax revenue fell so that the budget deficit (see 32.7 rose to $200 billion in 1992. The Democratic-dominated Congress refused to cut spending (and voted to increase it). Bush was forced to increase some taxes in spite of his election promise not to do so.
► He gave no firm leadership on some major issues – the environment, race relations and women's rights.

THE 1992 ELECTION

► In the primary elections (March onwards) he faced strong opposition from a right-wing Republican, Buchanan, who offered a Reagan-like policy and won about 30% of Republican voters' support.
► In the run-up to the election (November 1992) support for the Democrats continues to grows because of the weak economy.

42.2 A Single Europe, 1992

In 1987 the members of the European Community signed the Single European Act which came into operation in 1992. Its supporters hoped that it would lead to a unified Europe: Britain, and others, had a more limited view.

It will create a single, internal market: goods, people and capital will move as freely across boundaries as inside countries. Britain believes that this will be as much as Europe can cope with. More pro-European leaders believe that there will have to be common policies in many other fields:
► tax systems will have to be unified to prevent one country having an advantage over others;
► welfare systems will have to be unified to give all Europeans equal advantages, and equal tax burdens;
► a common currency, and a European Bank, will be needed to ensure common pricing and to make trading easier;
► the European Parliament, with a Cabinet responsible to

it, will have to develop to ensure the application of these, and other, changes.

42.3 A Common Currency?

► By 1990, eleven countries (but not Britain) had joined the European Exchange Rate Mechanism (ERM) which imposed very strict rates of exchange between their currencies. This led to stable rates and to stable domestic prices as countries were forced to adopt anti-inflationary policies.
► In 1991, after the dismissal of Mrs Thatcher, Britain joined the ERM. This limited the Chancellor's freedom to lower interest rates which would have eased the effects of the recession.
► Delors, President of the European Commission, wanted to push through a series of treaties which would lead to (i) common economic and social policies; (ii) a common currency.
► For a while it seemed as if Britain alone was opposed to this move towards European federalism. However, by March 1992, it was clear that there was opposition from:
(i) France and others who feared that their currencies would have to be linked too closely to the German mark and to German interest rates;
(ii) several countries which feared that the Commission might get the power to dictate economic policies and so lessen national sovereignty.

42.4 Delors' Social Charter

► Delors had gained the support of eleven countries for his initial proposals for a common currency; they agreed, it seemed, to bring in such a currency by 1997. However, by 1992, only four countries still supported such a move. Britain, it proved, had not been the only opponent.
► Delors also gained eleven countries' support for a Social Charter which enshrines workers' rights on many issues – seats on companies' boards, equal wage rates for women workers, minimum wages for all workers, rights to strike, etc. Britain refused to accept this Charter, arguing that on some issues (e.g. rights to a Health Service) Britain was in advance of other countries while some of the terms of the Charter would revive trade union powers and might lead to an increase in the number of strikes and poorer industrial relations.

The debates over the Charter and the common currency showed that there were two competing groups of Europeans.
(i) Euro-federalists wanted to create a United States of Europe, build trade barriers against non-European imports and create a powerful, centralized system which would limit the rights of member states.
(ii) Free marketeers, led by Britain, wanted international free trade and saw the need for individual countries to retain their national rights.

In 1992 Delors and the Commission asked that the rich countries of the Community make large contributions to a budget which would allow the Commission to pay massive subsidies to the poorer members in an attempt to raise living standards in these countries. Britain opposed this centralizing move. Many Germans, too, in spite of apparent support of federalism, argued against this financial demand: they already pay heavily for the restructuring of the old East Germany and do not want to be burdened by having to pay for attempts to bring living standards in Greece, Portugal, Spain and others up to German standards.

42.5 EC and GATT

In 1988 the USA claimed that EC tariff policies limited the free sale of US grain in Europe. In retaliation it proposed to exclude some European goods from the USA. This led to an EEC ban on the import of US beef on the grounds that US cattle were fed with hormones banned in the EC. To try to resolve this trade 'war', countries in the General Agreement on Tariffs and Trade (GATT) held a series of meetings in the hope that the USA and EC and other countries (notably in South East Asia) would reach an amicable arrangement. They had not done so by March 1992.

42.6 A Wider Community?

▶ When Britain joined the EC in 1973 (see 31.7) she ceased to belong to EFTA (see 31.5). By 1992 several remaining members of EFTA had applied to join the EC and, in time, will probably be admitted.

▶ The increasing wealth of EC countries had played a part in making Eastern Europeans discontented with their Communist governments. With the collapse of the old order (see Unit 41), some countries – e.g. Poland and Hungary – applied for membership of the EC. Western countries have welcomed the changes in the East and have been willing to provide aid for and encourage investment there. However, these states will have to make major economic changes and improvements before being exposed to the harsh realities of a wider free market.

42.7 A Common Foreign Policy?

▶ Some countries, notably Britain, hoped that the Western European Union (WEU) (see Unit 31.1) might provide an increasingly united Europe with the means of developing a common defence policy. In 1988 Spain and Portugal joined the WEU which seemed to gain importance as the USA talked of withdrawing forces from western Europe. However, the WEU failed to act at the time of Iraq's invasion of Kuwait: individual countries maintained their sovereign right to act as they saw fit.

▶ Some people had hoped that the WEU might help the development of a European foreign policy. The absence of, but need for, such a common policy was shown by the failure of Europe to act against Iraq. In 1992 the EC, and not the WEU, took the lead in recognizing the independence of Croatia (see 41.6) and in calling for the formation of a European armed force to be used to impose peace on the warring factions in Yugoslavia. Only the future will show whether Europe can develop a united foreign policy: will Britain give up the right to act unilaterally as she did in the Falklands in 1982? Will the smaller countries be willing to see a powerful Germany taking the lead in foreign affairs?

Unit 42 Summary

▶ Bush and the USA 1989–92.
▶ Changes in the EC: the ERM and the Social Charter.
▶ The EC and foreign policy.

43 CHINA 1987–92

43.1 Reform's Problems

In 1987 Hu Yaobang, under Deng Xioping's leadership, took the credit for the economic reforms which had such good effects (see Unit 33.5). But he also had to take the blame for the evident corruption, the widening of the gulf between rich and poor, and for the student unrest which flared up in 1987 – a by-product of Chinese *glasnost* (openness). Hu Yaobang was replaced by another Deng man, Zhao Zi Yang, as Chairman of the Politburo. China's economy continued to grow: private enterprise was allowed to flourish in industry, agriculture and housebuilding, while the state created a better infrastructure with new roads and harbours.

But there were many highly-placed critics of these new policies. A leading critic was the Prime Minister, Li Peng. He pointed to less favourable results of the new freedom: the corruption of many officials, the growth of self-centred individualism and the growth of Westernized habits in ports such as Shanghai.

In March 1989 the government produced a new Five-Year Plan aimed at:
▶ checking inflation and curtailing price increases;
▶ slowing down the rate of growth;
▶ encouraging people to save so that resources would be available for investment and for exports;
▶ increasing the output of consumer goods;
▶ tackling the problem of corruption.

43.2 On to Tiananmen Square

On April 16 1989 Peking students organized a demonstration to mark the anniversary of the death of Hu Yaobang, who had fallen from power after similar demonstrations in 1987 (see 43.1). Their example was followed by students in many other cities throughout China – a sign of the growing confidence of educated Chinese and of the economic growth which underpinned the growth in educational provision. The students pointed to the widespread reforms which Gorbachev had introduced into the Soviet Union's political system (see 29.13) and they criticized Li Peng's attempts to halt economic development and his crack-down on political dissidents.

The students' demonstrations continued for the month leading up to Gorbachev's visit to Peking on 15 May 1989. Both he and China's leaders hoped that this visit would heal the rift between their two countries. Student leaders saw the visit as an opportunity to draw attention to their admiration for the Soviet leader and his reforms. They demanded similar reforms for China: a free press, free speech, the arrest of corrupt officials including Communist chiefs, and a move towards democracy. On 4 May, with the Gorbachev visit coming up, the government ordered the students to end their demonstrations. They refused: instead they gained increasing support for their demands: workers came out on strike and joined the many unemployed in anti-government protests, while the population fed and helped the millions of demonstrating students. The police, too, seemed unwilling to take any action to break up the mass movement which greeted Gorbachev when he arrived in Peking.

After that visit the students' demands grew more radical: they called for Deng's removal from power. The size of the demonstrations grew: on 18 May there were two million on the streets of Peking as civil servants and public officials (such as doctors) joined the students. Some students went on hunger strike to draw attention to their demands: Western TV and press reporters, who had gone to China for the Gorbachev visit, now reported the student unrest.

On 21 May Li Peng proclaimed martial law but found that he could not rely on Peking's army commanders to break up the demonstrations. He and Deng then sent for army groups from 'loyal' areas.

43.3 The Tiananmen Massacre

On 4 June these army groups attacked the students in the Square. In front of Western TV cameras, students were massacred. For another week there were widespread protests, particularly in university cities. Western statesmen protested and governments withdrew their diplomats and threatened to cut off relations with China.

43.4 And Now?

After the massacre, Deng was apparently back in control – because of his control of the 'loyal' army. The arrest, imprisonment and deaths of thousands of dissident leaders and a clamp-down on the press brought an uneasy calm to China. Meanwhile, in spite of politician's protests, Western industrialists and businessmen in Asia continued to invest in China.

Deng welcomed such foreign investment, in spite of the dangers that might follow – such as had led to the fall of Hu Yaobang in 1987 (see 43.1). Deng wanted to take China on 'a long march out of poverty' and if Western aid provided the means to that end, Deng welcomed it: the share of industrial output from the old-fashioned state-owned industries fell from 85% of all output (1986) to a mere 15% (1992) as new, privately owned firms flourished. In 1991 foreign trade was worth $135 billion – about one-third of China's total output. Multinational firms noted the success of small privately owned firms and giants such as Proctor and Gamble opened large factories in China.

Some of Deng's colleagues saw this as anti-Communist heresy. He, on the other hand, argued that 'it doesn't matter whether a cat is black or white so long as it catches mice': if Communism works and ends poverty, fine: if, on the other hand, private enterprise helps to end poverty, then, equally, fine.

China's old leadership hopes that its children (called 'princelings' in China) will have the ability to maintain a reformed Marxist-Leninist policy which incorporates economic change and that they will be able to avoid the sort of reforms which have rocked the old Soviet Union (see Unit 40) and Eastern Europe (see Unit 41). Time will tell.

43.5 China and the Outside World

THE SOVIET UNION

Before going to Peking in May 1989, Gorbachev had offered to withdraw a large section of Soviet forces from the Chinese border. This was taken as an attempt to create better relationships between the twin Communist giants (which were then in the process of reform). However, that May 1989 visit failed to cement the relationship. Gorbachev was critical of the Chinese leaders' refusal to allow political reform to march hand in hand with economic reform (although he failed to see that he, inside the Soviet Union, had brought in only political reform).

Gorbachev's fall and the collapse of the Soviet Union have confirmed the Chinese leaders' belief that only they have 'the truth' according to Marx and Lenin.

TAIWAN

In December 1949, as Mao's forces gained control of China, Chiang Kai Shek fled to the island of Formosa or Taiwan (see 17.10 and Fig 17.9). Here, with military and economic support from the USA (see 33.1), Chiang and his successors claimed to be the rightful ruler of mainland China which, they said, they would reconquer. In 1971 Nixon's rapprochment with Mao's China saw an end to US support for Taiwanese pretentions to form the government of a future China (see 33.3).

However, it did not end Taiwan's economic growth. Indeed, with its emphasis on private enterprise and with the ability of Chinese businessmen, together with a growing population, Taiwan became one of the world's economic giants. By 1992 Deng's China was encouraging better relations with this giant which could provide mainland China with investment capital as well as a market for Chinese goods. Taiwan's government, for its part, has soft-pedalled the notion of reconquering the mainland so that there is a relatively peaceful relationship between the two Chinese states.

HONG KONG (see 33.6)

Britain and China negotiated the agreement by which this colony will come under Chinese rule in 1997. Britain and the majority of Hong Kong's Chinese population hope that China will honour the promise to allow Hong Kong to be a 'special area' in which economic freedom will be allowed. It was this freedom which made Hong Kong one of Asia's 'economic giants' and the source of much investment capital for the mainland.

Britain refused to allow Hong Kong people the democratic freedom which their leaders demanded: the Governor (appointed by Britain) continued to dominate the island's political system. While Britain allowed the election of some members to a legislative council, it did not create an independent and democratic government. Some people argued that this was because Britain was afraid of offending China (which would have resented this latter-day creation of an independent Hong Kong). Others claimed that Britain was only being realistic: China could have occupied Hong Kong whenever she wished and, if angered by a move to independence, might have invaded the island; the negotiated agreement, it is hoped, will ensure the survival of a semi-free Hong Kong after 1997.

Unit 43 Summary

▶ Deng's leadership; economic growth.

▶ The Tiananmen Square Massacre.

▶ China's relationships with Russia, Taiwan and Hong Kong.

44 SOUTH AFRICA 1988–92

44.1 Botha's Problems

Botha's whites-only government had taken some steps to make South Africa a more liberal country (see 36.10). His problem was whether he should go further down the 'liberalizing' road. This was what world opinion and diplomatic pressure demanded, as South Africa became more isolated in the face of trade boycotts, with sports organizations refusing contact with South Africa and with social and cultural organizations drawing world-wide attention to the evils of apartheid.

While the government was trying to make up its mind, black leaders in the ANC (see Abbreviations and Glossary) and in the Zulu-led Inkatha, claimed that any such 'liberal' action would be 'too little, too late'. They wanted a system of one man, one vote. On the other hand, many whites belonged to Afrikaner neo-Facist groups and claimed that Botha was giving 'too much, too quickly' to the blacks.

44.2 Local Elections, 1988

These elections (November 1988) followed the principles laid down in the 1984 Constitution (see 36.10). Blacks objected to the system of segregated voting and to the qualifications needed for enfranchisement:
▶ only about 8% of blacks were entitled to vote;
▶ black leaders called for an electoral boycott and black extremists led violent attacks on black candidates;
▶ only about one-quarter of the blacks entitled to vote did so (about 2% of the black population). Botha claimed this as a triumph, but it was clearly a setback for his hopes of winning black support for his limited reforms. On the other hand, his party lost seats to hardline white parties, which suggested that further moves to reform might lead to the fall of the government.

44.3 F W de Klerk

In March 1989 Botha suffered a stroke. In his absence a reforming group in his Party managed to get a 'liberal' nationalist, de Klerk, appointed as Party leader. In the past the Party's leader had also been State President. But when Botha returned from illness, he refused to resign. He was supported by the neo-Fascist Afrikaners led by Terreblanche who, though opposed to Botha's reforms, were frightened that de Klerk would do even worse from their point of view. However, Botha faced growing opposition inside his government and Party. In the hope of regaining full control he called national, whites-only elections for August 1989. This campaign and the election results showed that the majority of whites wanted reform to proceed more quickly. Botha resigned from office and de Klerk became State President.

44.4 Black Development

De Klerk and his supporters, as well as white businessmen in South Africa, had accepted that black people were an increasingly important part of the social and economic scene and that they would have to be given some share of political power:
▶ half of all secondary schoolchildren were black;
▶ blacks bought over half of all goods in South Africa;

▶ one-third of middle managers were blacks;
▶ black trade unions played an important role in winning better wages and conditions for black workers;
▶ black demands for reforms were supported by the outside world's boycotting of South Africa: businessmen were most affected by the increasingly powerful trade boycott.

44.5 Nelson Mandela

The founder-leader of the ANC had been imprisoned in June 1964 under the Suppression of Communism Act. He was a member of the Xhosa tribe who made up the majority of black South Africans. They, and the Zulu-led Inkatha movement, saw Mandela as a symbol of their position in white-dominated South Africa. Their campaigns for his release were supported by world-wide organisations. In 1988 Botha suggested that, if Mandela renounced violence, he might be released. Mandela refused to do so, claiming that his people had none other than violent ways of expressing their opposition to apartheid. Botha did free some ANC leaders, but made it illegal for them to take part in political activities, give interviews to the media or to hold meetings. Many fled to neighbouring African states where they helped organize resistance movements inside South Africa.

Mandela was freed from solitary confinement so that he could get treatment in a hospital for a serious illness. Angry whites protested at this 'leniency' and showed Botha that he would not be able to free this 'black martyr'. De Klerk had more courage. In February 1990 he freed Mandela who agreed to hold negotiations with de Klerk with a view to the framing of a new constitution for South Africa. Mandela, although only Vice-President of the ANC, was, in fact, accepted as its leader – by blacks and whites in South Africa, by black leaders throughout Africa and by white political leaders in the West, whom he visited on a series of semi-state visits. In August 1990 he called off the ANC's militant anti-apartheid campaign which had seen bombings and murders become commonplace. However, he was unable to prevent the outbreak of savage 'warfare' between ANC supporters and their black rivals in the Inkatha movement. This led to thousands of deaths and to the growth of fear among some whites that 'black government would mean bad government'.

44.6 A New Constitution?

De Klerk and Mandela negotiated the setting up of a Convention for a Democratic South Africa in which leaders of all parties and groups met to hammer out a new constitution. Hardline whites resigned from the Nationalist Party to form a new Conservative Party: others had already formed the neo-Facist Afrikaner Party which had a militant and armed wing, the Afrikaner Resistance Movement.

In March 1992 de Klerk called their bluff. He held a whites-only referendum on the simple issue of whether or not the whites supported his reforms and his promises of further reform. Nearly 70% of whites voted 'Yes' in his support. Right-wingers of all hues won less than one-third of the voters' support. De Klerk called this a victory for common sense and progress, but while black leaders see it as another step along the road to 'one man, one vote' democracy, hardliners say that they will now prepare to make war against any government which hands power to the black electorate.

On a lighter note, de Klerk's reforms won increasing approval around the world, and although trade sanctions continue in a minor way, South Africa has been allowed to emerge into the world of sport, as was shown by its team's part in the World Cup cricket competition in March 1992.

 Unit 44 Summary

▶ Botha's fall, 1989.
▶ De Klerk's Presidency; Mandela free; relaxation of boycotts.
▶ The Convention for a Democratic South Africa; right-wingers object to reforms.

45 NORTH AFRICA AND THE MIDDLE EAST, 1987–92

 ## 45.1 North Africa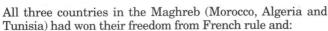

All three countries in the Maghreb (Morocco, Algeria and Tunisia) had won their freedom from French rule and:
▶ looked forward optimistically to the future;
▶ enjoyed a high level of self-sufficiency;
▶ believed that economic growth needed state intervention and control of the economy.

By the beginning of 1988, optimism had vanished as:
▶ state intervention led to wasteful overemployment in some industries and in the civil service;
▶ the inefficient state system and the collectivization of agriculture took too high a proportion of the countries' resources and hampered economic growth;
▶ each country borrowed heavily from abroad to finance the building of heavy industries, which governments had hoped to finance from the export of oil;
▶ falling oil prices (see 38.5) made it difficult, if not impossible, for governments to finance their foreign debts and, at the same time, pay for imported raw materials and spares for industrial machinery;
▶ high birth rates led to growing populations (see 38.2);
▶ unemployment increased, especially among young people.
In all three countries governments reacted to their growing problems by:
▶ following China's example (see 33.5) of allowing free markets to run more of the economy (see 43.4). This reduced the importance of state-run industries and state control of the economy;
▶ accepting the need for more democracy;
▶ calling for a united Maghreb and united policies to solve common problems.

MOROCCO

The conservative King had to face the demands of a growing middle class for a share in the political system. However in this, the poorest of the three countries, and the one with the heaviest burden of foreign debt, the King managed to keep democracy at bay with the help of a well-paid army.

TUNISIA

Bourguiba, who led the country into independence, had a paternalistic approach as ruler of a country with a strong economic base. However, his 'statism' wasted much of that base, so that Tunisia, once a food exporter, had to import food. In November 1987, following riots by students and the unemployed, he was deposed. He had attacked the growing influence of fundamentalist Muslims who had been encouraged by the success of Khomeini's revolution in Iran (see 32.6) and who had whipped up support among those who were discontented with Bourguiba's policies. Ben Ali, the new ruler, while opposed to fundamentalism, tried to negotiate with its leaders in an effort to create a more democratic Tunisia.

ALGERIA

Boumédienne's government had enjoyed the benefits of a strong economic base and well-developed agricultural system (see 37.1). It further gained from high oil prices in the 1970s (see 38.4). However, the fall in oil prices in the 1980s (see 38.5) led to economic collapse. Boumédienne was overthrown by forces led by one of his former ministers, Kasdi Merbah. His government broke up the costly state farms, allowed greater freedom to industrialists and ended price fixing by government officials.

These reforms led to increased unemployment. In October 1988 the masses rose in revolt because of food shortages, unemployment and inflation. These risings were harshly suppressed. However, Merbah's government was overthrown by a coup inside the ruling party, the National Liberation Front. It was President Bendjedid who had to face:
▶ the growth of Muslim fundamentalism, particularly among the young and unemployed;
▶ demands for more democracy by the Press and a vocal, educated middle class;
▶ the refusal of the army to remain a 'tool' of the Front;
▶ the formation of opposition political parties, particularly among the Berber people;
Early in 1989 Bendjedid's new constitution was approved by a popular referendum. It:
▶ allowed the formation of legitimate political parties;
▶ conceded freedom to critics of the government's policies on human rights;
▶ promised that elections would be held in 1990.
In those elections (June 1990):
▶ voters elected 48 provincial assemblies and 1500 town councils but not a national parliament;
▶ the Islamic Salvation Front, a fundamentalist movement, won an overwhelming majority of seats everywhere: the FLN suffered a humiliating defeat – but remained in control of the national government.

The head of the Islamic Front demanded immediate elections for a national parliament – which had been promised for 1992. The government feared that, in such elections, the Islamic Front would win a majority of seats and create a one-party Islamic state. The army, although no longer tied to the ruling FLN, announced that it would not allow the creation of a fundamentalist Islamic state. Tunisia and Morocco had banned even the formation of Islamic parties and their governments encouraged Algerian opposition to the onward march of Islamic fundamentalism.

Early in 1992, as promised, national elections were held. These followed the pattern of French elections in which many candidates contest each seat in a first round of elections, and only two or three go forward to fight seats in the second round. As the army had feared, Islamic Front candidates won an overwhelming number of votes in the first round which indicated that, in the second round, Front candidates would win most seats and form a huge majority in Parliament. At that point the army stepped in, forced the willing government to cancel the second round of elections and, to date, has maintained an unpopular government in power. It remains to be seen whether fundamentalism can be halted by the power of the gun – in Algeria, Tunisia and Morocco.

45.2 Israel

DOMESTIC POLITICS

1984 After the general election there was an uneasy coalition government: Shamir, right-wing leader of the Likud Party, shared the post of Prime Minister with Peres, leader of the Labour Party. The main difficulty facing this government was the problem of the Palestinians (see below). Likud, led by a former freedom fighter, took a harder line than the Labour Party which wanted better relations with the Arabs in the areas of Palestine which had been occupied following the 1973 War (see 37.12).

The Israeli population as a whole was similarly divided. There were those on the right wing who claimed that these occupied areas were the Biblical regions of Judea and Samaria and so were part of historic Israel: they supported those who built settlements there, demanded that the government support these new Jewish towns and defend them against Arab attack. Indeed, there were right-wing extremists who seemed willing to make war against Arabs in the name of Judea and Samaria. Labour supporters, including many young men in the Israeli army, argued against such expansionism.

1987 In December 1987 Palestinians in the occupied regions rose in what seemed to be a spontaneous uprising (*intifidah*): young children attacked Israeli troops and offices with stones and petrol bombs, Arab workers went on strike and Arab traders kept their businesses closed. The Israeli army was sent to restore order and from this arose the well-publicized scenes of soldiers beating children, firing at mobs and killing young people. British MPs were among those who visited the region and criticized the Israelis.

1988 Following a general election there was an increase in the number of right-wing members in the Knesset (Israeli Parliament), including about twenty representing Orthodox religious groups. They shared Shamir's hardline attitude towards the Arabs. However, some Likud ministers, notably Ariel Sharon, thought that Shamir was not tough enough in his attitude towards the Arabs, the PLO and the Palestinian *intifadah*. It was clear, and remained so through the next four years, that Israeli domestic politics were dominated by the Palestinian problem.

PALESTINIAN PROBLEMS

1948 The UNO had suggested the division of Palestine between Israel and the Arabs, with the creation of an Arab-Palestinian state (see Unit 37 and Fig 37.4(a)). This had been rejected by the Arabs. In the subsequent war, Jordan occupied the land on the West Bank of the Jordan, and, in the following years, claimed to be the spokesman for the Palestinians.

1973 Following the series of Arab-Israeli wars (see Unit 37) Israel occupied more Palestinian territory (Fig 37.4(b)). As mentioned, some Israelis saw this expansionist policy as merely an attempt to regain the biblical lands of Judea and Samaria.

The PLO (see 37.11) had been formed by Arabs who wanted to 'abolish Israel, drive Jews into the sea' and regain Palestine for the Arabs. It was a coalition of parties, most of whom accepted the leadership of Arafat. He approved of the terrorist attacks on Israel, the wars of 1967 and 1973 and, once it had started, the uprising of 1988. He was also

politically active, seeking the support of Arab nations and of the UNO against Israel. His relations with Arab states was always uneasy and uncertain: he quarrelled with Hussein of Jordan, with Sadat of Egypt, with Hussein of Syria, who drove the PLO out of Lebanon (see 37.14), and with other leaders who feared, on the one hand, his brand of extremism and, on the other hand, Israeli retaliation against them if they supported the PLO.

1986–88 Mubarak of Egypt (Sadat's successor) was welcomed back into the Arab fold, in spite of the peace with Israel: only Syria, Libya and Lebanon refused to enter into friendly relations with Egypt. The price which Egypt paid for this *rapprochement* was the recognition of 'the state of Palestine' (November 1988).

The 1987–89 uprising in the occupied regions owed nothing to PLO leadership. Indeed, it seemed as if the people had despaired of the smooth-tongued but ineffective Arafat. Their problem was to find someone who might speak for them at any international conference which might be called to find a solution to their dispute with Israel. Hussein of Jordan gave up his claim to be the Arab spokesman in mid-1988 when he also gave up his claim for a restoration of the West Bank to Jordan.

A PLO 'REVOLUTION'?

In November 1988 the Palestinian National Council, meeting in Damascus, announced that it accepted the UN resolutions 242 and 338 which called for recognition of the state of Israel and of the boundaries of the states as they had been before the 1967 War. The PNC is a coalition of many Palestinian groups, the most publicized of which is the PLO. Arafat of the PLO agreed that his organization would not support terrorism against Israel, would not call for the suppression of that state and would attend a conference aimed at peacemaking in the region.

SHAMIR'S PEACE PLAN 1989

In May 1989 Shamir announced that elections would be held on the West Bank and the Gaza, the areas which Palestinians regard as 'illegally occupied' by the Israelis. Many members of his own party opposed this policy and feared that it would lead to negotiations on a Palestinian state alongside Israel. On the other hand, Arab members of the Israeli Parliament argued that the policy did not go far enough: they wanted just that Palestinian state. Shamir told both groups of critics that he would not agree to giving up any land on the West Bank although he would agree to Palestinian self-rule pending a final settlement which would have to include Jordan. Jewish settlers on the West Bank were alarmed by Shamir's apparent 'softness' to the Palestinians and they clashed with Israeli police and armed forces in a series of riots.

THE USA PEACE PLAN 1991–2

Israel has always been heavily indebted to the USA which gives it more than $2 billion a year to help it to survive. This gives the US government a good deal of influence over the Israeli government. In 1991 it used that influence to force Shamir to agree to the holding of an international conference on the Palestinian issue. The conference opened in Madrid and was attended by statesmen from the USA, the UK, France, most Arab states, Israel and, most controversially, Palestinian representatives. It became clear that there were major differences in outlook between, for example, Syria on the one hand and Israel on the other, and that both hoped that the parts they had played in the Gulf War (see 45.6) entitled them to look for US support for their differing points of view.

After the initial meeting in Madrid the conference moved to Washington where, to date, the differing factions have been unable to come up with any proposals satisfactory to every side. This is hardly surprising in view of the Palestinians' demand for an independent state and Israel's continued need for extra living space for the influx of Jews from the old Soviet Union and Eastern Europe.

45.3 Lebanon

For most of this period, 1987–92, Lebanon continued to be a war-torn country in which:

▶rival Christian factions fought one another (see 37.17);

▶rival Shi'ite Muslim groups fought one another, with Syria supporting a group called Amal, and Iran supporting a group called Hezbollah;

▶Christian groups fought Muslim groups;

▶Syria tried to gain control of the whole country, first by trying to defeat the official Lebanese (mainly Christian) army and then by defeating rival Muslim groups;

▶Iraq, angered by Syrian support for Iran in the Iran–Iraq war (see 45.4) supported anti-Syrian forces;

▶Israel opposed Syrian efforts to dominate Lebanon.

Israel continued to hold part of southern Lebanon as a 'safety zone' to ensure that Arab terrorists would find it difficult to cross into Israel. Israeli forces in this zone were attacked by Arab extremists who also launched air and sea attacks on Israel itself. In retaliation, Israeli forces attacked cities, towns and camps in Lebanon, claiming that they were seeking out terrorists.

For much of 1989 a Christian, General Aoun, head of the largely Christian Lebanese official army, set out to drive Syria from the Lebanon. It was never clear which outside agencies provided him with money and help: the USA, which feared Syria as a main provider of aid to international terrorists? France, which had once controlled Lebanon and opposed Syria's efforts to control the country? Israel, which saw Aoun as a counterweight to Syrian power? Iraq, seeking revenge for its failure in the Iran–Iraq war? Moderate Arabs, such as Saudi Arabia, fearful of the growing power of anti-royalist Syria?

Aoun's efforts led to even more bitter fighting, heavier bombing and shelling, and more destruction, particularly of Beirut, the capital. And no outside agency was able to bring the fighting to an end. The UN and the Pope called in vain for a ceasefire: the USA was unwilling to get involved after its failure in 1984 (see 37.17). In December 1989 the war-weary Lebanese elected a new President. He was a moderate Catholic whose election was welcomed by Syria and who promised to limit his powers as Christian President while increasing the powers of the Muslim-controlled Parliament. Within a few days of being elected he was assassinated – allegedly by Aoun supporters unwilling to see any diminution of Christian influence.

But in 1990 Aoun fled the country, leaving Syria with even greater power than before. In July 1990 Assad of Syria showed that he was anxious to bring the fighting to an end: in particular he indicated that he was willing to talk to Israel about their countries' common problems and differences. He was driven to this 'diplomatic revolution' by:

▶the growing belligerence of Saddam Hussein of Iraq, his rival in the Arab world;

▶the Soviet Union's withdrawal of aid and arms to Syria which had wanted 'parity with Israel'. This limited Syria's chances of being able to withstand an Israeli attack;

▶the effect on his own economy of the years of fighting in Lebanon.

However, Assad continued to demand that Israel hand back the Golan Heights (see 37.12 and Fig 37.4) and attend an international conference aimed at settling the problems of Lebanon and of the Middle East in general.

One fortunate by-product of this new peace-seeking policy was a change in the fortunes of Western hostages held by one or other of the Muslim groups in Lebanon. With Iran seeking better relations with the West and with Syria seeking to make peace, there was pressure on these Muslim groups to hand back the hostages as part of the process of improving relations between the Muslim world and the West. So it was that in 1990 and 1991 Western media

showed the release, after many years of captivity, of men such as Terry Waite.

45.4 The Iran–Iraq War

Until his death in June 1989, Iran was ruled by Khomeini, whose fundamentalist revolution had overthrown the Shah in 1979 (see 32.6). He called on Muslims everywhere to return to the fundamentals of their faith and to reject westernization (see 37.18). Khomeini, a Shia Muslim, was opposed to Sunni Muslims (37.17) and to the rule of what he saw as 'backsliders' such as the royal families of Saudi Arabia, Kuwait and other Gulf States.

Between 1980 and 1988 Iran was at war with Iraq (see 37.18). In August 1988 the UN helped negotiate an end to the fighting and start peace talks which went on for a year. Among the issues discussed at these talks were:

▶Iraq's demand that the Shat al-Arab be cleared of war debris to allow free movement of shipping;

▶Iraq's demand for return of all prisoners of war;

▶Iran's demand that all Iraqi troops be evacuated from Iranian territory.

In August 1990 Saddam Hussein of Iraq accepted Iran's terms for a peace treaty, finally ending a war which had cost 500,000 lives and about £500 billion. Saddam accepted a humiliating peace treaty because:

▶he wanted to concentrate on his new venture against Kuwait (see 45.7);

▶he needed to move half of his army from the Iranian front to the Saudi border to confront US forces arriving there;

▶he hoped that by evacuating occupied Iranian territory he would be able to call on 'Islamic principles' and so gain the support of Iran and the rulers of the Gulf States in his confrontation with the USA: he failed to see that Iran, Syria and the rulers of the Gulf States might see him as a potential enemy rather than a potential ally.

SADDAM HUSSEIN

He had become dictator of Iraq in 1979 and was supported by the Soviet Union which saw him as an ally in its contest for control of the Gulf. This struggle saw the Soviet Union confronting the USA and its main ally, Saudi Arabia.

Hussein was supported by most Western countries which saw Khomeini's Iranian fundamentalism as a major threat to peace in the Gulf and danger to their oil supplies; almost every country loaned him money (by 1989 he had borrowed over $200 billion) and provided him with a variety of arms – Italy provided warships, France gave aircraft and missiles, Germany and Britain provided him with chemical and biological capability, and France sold him a nuclear reactor.

While he governed ruthlessly with the aid of a well-paid army, an efficient secret police and the supine Baath political party, he also carried out wholesale social reforms. These were financed out of the revenue from Iraqi oil sales. He had once talked of 'liberating Palestine' but by 1988 he had abandoned this as a policy, leaving room for his rival, Assad of Syria, to gain influence in that region (see 45.2 and 45.3).

45.5 Oil Politics

Iraq and other Gulf States were dependent on oil as an export (which paid for imports) and as a source for most government revenue (paying for armies and social reform). The fall in oil prices in the 1980s (see 38.5) affected the economies of all oil-producing states, including Iraq. The oil-producing states tried, but failed, to agree on reductions in output – which might have led to increased prices. Indeed, some states increased output in the hope that a larger output, even at lower prices, would maintain their total income.

One cause of the Iran–Iraq war had been Iraq's ambition to gain control of some of Iran's oilfields. The end of that war saw Iraqi and Iranian oil come back on to the world market, so that prices fell even more dramatically: by the end of 1988 oil was selling at less than ten dollars a barrel. OPEC (see 38.4) managed to get states to agree to some cuts in output and with Russia's oil exports falling off, prices rose to $17 a barrel.

However, there was always the threat of a fresh fall in prices, and Iraq asked its OPEC partners to make further cuts in output, claiming that this would push prices above $20 a barrel. At that price, Saddam claimed, he could afford to repay his debts to the West, finance a new programme of rearmament and continue his policy of social reform.

45.6　The Gulf War, 1990–91

Iraq was clearly the strongest military power in the Gulf region and replaced Iran as the West's 'bogeyman'. Saddam had always been seen as an enemy by the royalist states of the Gulf – Saudi Arabia, Kuwait, Bahrein and the rest, although they had supported him financially during his long war with Iran, whose fundamentalism was an immediate danger to these westernized rulers.

In July 1990 Saddam claimed that Kuwait was over-producing oil and so helping to keep prices down below the $20-a-barrel limit. His enmity towards Kuwait was also due to:

▶ long-standing border disputes: did this or that section of an oilfield lie in Iraq or in Kuwait?
▶ Kuwait's refusal to lease him an offshore island which he could develop as an oil terminal;
▶ the speedy re-establishment of Iranian–Kuwaiti relations: Saddam overlooked the massive aid he had received from Kuwait throughout the long war with Iran;
▶ his confidence that, in the event of a crisis, the rulers of Kuwait and other Gulf states would give him whatever he wanted – rather than face his powerful military machine.

On 25 July 1990 Saddam sent a large part of his army to the border with Kuwait, although he said that he had no intention of invading that country:

▶ Mubarak of Egypt, acting as leader of Arab opinion, met Saddam and was assured that there would be no war against 'fellow Arabs';
▶ the US Ambassador left for a vacation, having been told that there was no real crisis.

However, Saddam made it clear that he expected Kuwait to cut its oil production and to concede his claim to parts of an oilfield which Kuwait had developed along the border. No Gulf State came forward to support Kuwait in its dispute with Saddam:

▶ none of them had armed forces to match Iraq's;
▶ they had not evolved any common defence policy, in spite of much talk of 'brotherhood' and 'Arab unity';
▶ many states were as suspicious of the rich Saudis as they were of the armed Iraqis.

Kuwait agreed to pay $1 billion in compensation to Iraq 'for oil taken illegally from the Iraqi section of the common oilfield'. However, this failed to satisfy Saddam. On 2 August 1990 his forces invaded and quickly overran Kuwait: they pushed on to the Kuwaiti-Saudi border and, it was feared, prepared to invade Saudi Arabia and other Gulf states.

The USA gained almost total support at the UN for its demand that Saddam had to withdraw from Kuwait. In the new atmosphere of *glasnost* the Soviet Union sided with the USA so that the UN Security Council was able to pass a resolution calling for Iraq's withdrawal and for the UN to send forces to the Gulf to help ensure the carrying out of that resolution. During the next few months US, UK and other forces arrived in the area: there were naval patrols, air force units and armies from many countries, including forces from Egypt and Syria. Germany's constitution forbade the sending of German troops but, along with Japan, Germany made massive financial contributions to meet the costs borne by the participants.

This Iraq–Kuwait crisis created problems for rulers of the Gulf states:

▶ Should they support the West against Iraq? Extreme Arab

nationalists said 'No', claiming that the West was interested only in its oil supplies and not in the rights and wrongs of the dispute. 'Would the USA have intervened if Kuwait produced cabbages and not oil?'

▶ Should they take account of the possibility that, if Saddam succeeded in Kuwait, he might, like Hitler in the 1930s, be encouraged to adopt an expansionist programme and seek to conquer one Gulf state after another?
▶ Should they allow Western forces to occupy bases in their countries? If so, what would be the reaction of Muslim fundamentalists? One result of attempts to answer this question was that Western forces in Saudi Arabia were not allowed to celebrate Christmas 1990 in public for fear of annoying Muslims.

The build-up of UN (mainly US) forces went on through the rest of 1990 and into 1991. Saddam promised that any attack would be met with massive retaliation: the West was aware of his capability to wage nuclear, chemical and bio-logical warfare. It knew that he had used chemical weapons against his own Kurdish population and feared that he would not hesitate to use such weapons against Western forces in what he promised would be 'the mother of all battles'.

In the event, when the Western forces did invade Kuwait, the war lasted only a few days and casualities were very light. This was because:

▶ the Iraqi airforce had fled to Iran and safety;
▶ Western airforces, mainly US and British, had had months in which to bomb Iraqi bases, roads, bridges and installations;
▶ Western technology was much superior to that of Iraq – as witnessed by TV viewers who saw bombs being dropped down chimneys or onto bridges;

Saddam kept his highly-trained Revolutionary Guards away from any fighting – fearing, perhaps, that he might need them to put down any dissidence at home.

He tried to widen the war by attacking Israel with Scud missiles. Perhaps he hoped to involve Israel in the war and thus deepen Arab suspicion of the Western alliance. In fact his attacks did relatively little harm and Israel, perhaps surprisingly, agreed not to retaliate but to allow Western forces to destroy Saddam's capabilities.

Once Kuwait had been liberated, at little cost to the West but at a high cost in lives for the Iraqis, the fighting stopped. There was no attempt to overthrow Saddam, or to punish him for any war crimes. He had to agree to pay compensation to Kuwait for the damage done to that country and for the destruction of much of its oil industry. Western forces did nothing to help the Kurds who rebelled in northern Iraq or the Muslims who rebelled in the marshes in the south. Saddam's forces were free to put down these rebellions which led to much suffering, particularly for the Kurds caught in the mountains in the winter of 1991.

Trade sanctions had been imposed on Iraq in August 1990 at the time of the invasion of Kuwait. These remain in place in March 1992. However, Iraq has still not complied with UN demands for the destruction of its capability to produce nuclear, chemical and biological weapons. Nor does the UN appear willing to act militarily to force it to do so.

45.7　Libya

Since 1969 Libya had been ruled by Gadaffi, a Muslim extremist. Many Westerners thought that he was responsible for much of what was called 'state terrorism' (see 37.19). Others though that Syria and Iran deserved to be condemned for such activities, but it was politically and militarily more convenient to blame Gadaffi than to blame the Soviet's ally, Syria, or the powerful Iran.

Certainly Gadaffi supported the IRA which he supplied with arms and finance:

▶ in 1987 he welcomed to Tripoli the terrorist leader Abu Nidal, recognized as the most ruthless leader of terrorist groups;
▶ in 1988 Libya was accused of complicity in the destruction

of a PanAm plane which blew up over Lockerbie in Scotland. Subsequent investigation proved that two Libyans were responsible or this crime;

▶ also in 1988 Libyan terrorists were shown to have been responsible for the blowing up of a French plane over Niger with the loss of 411 lives;

▶ later in 1988 German police arrested a dozen Libyans who were found guilty of plotting to blow up an Iberian plane.

In May 1986 US planes had bombed Tripoli (see 37.19) to punish Gadaffi for sponsoring terrorist activities. In 1992 the UN demanded that Libya hand over the two men responsible for the Lockerbie crime: the intention was that they should be tried either in the USA (where Pan Am was registered) or in Scotland (where the plane crashed and where many Scots were killed).

Gadaffi was unwilling to hand over 'his' men to Western courts; he used a variety of moves in the hope that their trial might be held by an Arab League court, or by the International Court of Justice, or by some other non-Western court. The UN, through the Security Council, voted to impose a variety of sanctions on Libya if she did not conform to the UN resolution. These included:

▶ a trade embargo, including a ban on the purchase of Libyan oil by the outside world. This might be difficult to impose because of the long borders which Libya has with Egypt, (which might not want to be seen as submitting to Western pressure) and Algeria, increasingly an anti-Western and Muslim fundamentalist state (see 45.1);

▶ a ban on airlines flying to Libya.

Unit 45 Summary

▶ The growth of fundamentalism in Maghreb.
▶ Moves towards peace in Palestine.
▶ Continued unrest in the Lebanon.
▶ A truce for the Iran–Iraq war, 1990.
▶ The Gulf War, 1990–91 and its consequences.
▶ Western pressure exerted on Libya.

ABM Anti-ballistic missile. A ballistic missile is first powered by some explosive or fuel, then depends only on gravity. ABMs are meant to shoot these down.

abdicate (to) To give up some office or power. Nicholas II (Unit 10), Alfonso XIII (Unit 24), and Edward VIII of Britain gave up their thrones.

amnesty The granting of forgiveness, a pardon, usually to political offenders.

anarchy A country without effective government (the aim of Spanish Anarchists (Unit 24)), or the political and social disorder following from the inability of government to control things.

ANC The African National Congress, a predominantly black organization opposed to the whites-only policies of the South African government (see apartheid).

annexation The taking of territory, often without any right.

anti-clericalism A policy opposed to the strong influence of the clergy or the Church in political and social life.

ANZAC The Australian and New Zealand Army Corps (1914–18). ANZAC Day, 25 April, commemorates the landing of the Corps in Gallipoli in 1915.

ANZUS The Australian, New Zealand and United States Pact signed in 1951.

apartheid The South African system for separating the races.

appeasement Reaching agreement by negotiating with and conciliation of a potential aggressor. In the late 1930s it came to be identified with giving way to Hitler.

arbitration The settlement of disputes through the verdict of someone not involved in the dispute.

armistice An agreement to end fighting so that negotiations for a peace treaty can take place.

autarky The plan for economic self-sufficiency in Germany in the 1930s. Nazi Germany wanted to be economically independent.

authoritarian The opposite of 'liberal'. An authoritarian government imposes strict discipline and represses opposition (see totalitarianism).

autocracy Rule by one person, a dictatorship (see dictatorship).

Bolsheviks Those members of the Russian Social Democratic Party who believed that a Marxist revolution would be brought about only by a small, dedicated organization. They were led by Lenin. The name comes from the Russian word for the majority which Lenin and his followers had after a debate in 1903.

BOSS The Bureau of State Security, the South African force mainly used to crush anti-apartheid opposition.

bourgeoisie A French word used to describe the middle classes, the capitalist owners of industry.

boycott (to) To unite to refuse to deal with someone or some nation; to refuse to handle someone's goods.

Bundesrat The Upper House of the German Parliament set up in 1871. It represented the Princes of the federal state (see p. 170. See also Reichstat).

caste The term applied to the 2000 divisions of Hindu society in India. There are four main divisions: priests, rulers and warriors, traders and farmers, and artisans. Those outside these divisions are called Untouchables (see p. 172). Caste is hereditary and the members of each caste are equal and united in religion. Caste largely determines occupation. It is an exclusive system, with little contact with those outside the caste.

Caudillo The Spanish word for leader; the title taken by Franco.

centre Political parties of the centre are neither extreme socialists (see p. 172) nor extremely conservative (i.e. the right). They have middle-of-the-road policies.

Cheka Lenin's secret police, the name coming from the Russian initials for Extraordinary Commission.

CIA The Central Intelligence Agency (USA).

co-existence A state of international relations in which rivals (such as the USA and USSR) tolerate one another. Neither seeks to bring down the other by force (a 'hot war'), although dislike remains. When the dislike becomes very strong the world may have a period of 'cold war'—see below.

cold war Such a 'war' is fought by various 'peaceful' weapons—such as propaganda (see p. 171), economic sanctions (see p. 172), aid (even military) to opponents of the rival régime. The rivals (since 1945 the USA and USSR) have stopped short of military confrontation although they have supported rivals in various 'local' wars as in Vietnam.

colonialism The policy of obtaining and maintaining colonies; opponents of this policy use the word to argue that the colonial (or occupying) power exploits backward or weak people for its own economic benefit.

collectivization The policy of joining small farms into one large holding. Stalin implemented this policy to destroy the bourgeois (see bourgeoisie) kulaks.

Comecon The Council for Mutual Economic Assistance.

Cominform The Communist Information Bureau.

concordat An agreement, usually between the Church and State.

congress A meeting of delegates. In the USA it is the national legislative body (or Parliament); in India the name was used by Indian politicians campaigning against British colonialism (see above). They were, by using the word, claiming to be the Indian 'Parliament' even though they had no power.

constitution The principles by which a country is governed. In many countries there is a written constitution which expresses these principles.

containment The building of alliances in an effort to frighten an enemy and prevent its expansion.

convoy A number of merchant ships sailing together under the escort of warships.

Cortes The Legislative Assembly (or Parliament) of Spain or Portugal.

coup d'état A violent or illegal change of government; the seizure of power by a non-elected group, or by an individual (see putsch).

covenant An agreement setting out the aims and rules (of the League of Nations).

Czech Legion While they were being evacuated from eastern Russia along the Trans-Siberian Railway in 1918,

Czech prisoners-of-war overpowered their guards and began a private march to Moscow. They were halted by Trotsky's Red Army outside Kazan. The plight of this Legion was the official reason for the various foreign interventions in the Russian Civil War.

Dail The Lower House of the Irish Parliament.

democracy (from demos, the Greek word for 'the people') Rule by the people; a system of government which allows the mass of the people (the electorate) to have some control over their rulers; a system which tolerates minority views.

DMZ A demilitarized zone as in the Rhineland after 1919 (Unit 12) and in Korea after 1953 (Unit 28) and such as was proposed by various people for Central Europe in the 1960s.

depression A fall or reduction in the amount of industrial and trading activity such as followed (a) the First World War, (b) the Wall Street Crash, 1929 and (c) the rise in oil prices after 1973.

desegregation The ending of segregation (see p. 172).

détente The easing of strained relations between rival States. It is a part of the policy of co-existence (see p. 169).

dictatorship Rule by one person who has usually gained power by a coup d'état (see p. 169) and who suppresses democracy (see above) in his or her totalitarian state (see totalitarianism).

diktat The imposition of severe terms by a victor on a defeated nation. Often used of the Treaty of Versailles—by Germans.

distressed areas Those areas of Britain which suffered severe unemployment during the depression (see above) during the inter-war period.

dole The amount of money paid weekly by the State to unemployed workers.

dominion A term used to describe the first self-governing (and therefore independent) parts of the British Empire—Australia, Canada, New Zealand and South Africa. Dominion status was defined in 1926 and in the Statute of Westminster, 1931. Dominions were free from British control but retained a connection with the British Throne.

Duma Originally this described the Russian elected town councils. It was more commonly used in the 19th century by liberals as the title of their proposed Russian Council of State—or Parliament.

EEC The European Economic Community, or Common Market.

EFTA The European Free Trade Association.

emancipation The setting free of people—from slavery (in the USA) or serfdom (in Russia) or from legal disabilities (such as women suffered).

Enosis The proposed political union between Cyprus and Greece.

entente A friendly understanding between people in which they settle their past differences. The Entente Cordiale between Britain and France, 1904, was followed by an Anglo-Russian Entente in 1907.

EOKA The initials of the Greek words meaning Revolutionary Organization for Cypriot Struggle. The organization was founded in 1955 and had a campaign of anti-British sabotage and terrorism in the hope that this would force the British to agree to enosis (see above).

FAO The Food and Agricultural Organization (of the United Nations).

federal This is used to describe the system of government in which several states form a unity (or union) but remain independent in internal affairs. It is also used to describe the policy of supporting a central government as opposed to those who favour government by separate states or provinces. Australia, Canada, West Germany and the USA have federal systems of government.

FLN The initials of the French words for the National Liberation Front (of Algeria).

franchise The right to vote (see suffrage).

Führer The German word for leader, taken by Hitler in 1934.

GDR The German Federal Republic (East Germany).

GPU The Russian initials for the State Political Department, once the name for the Russian secret police, later the OGPU (see p. 171).

guerrilla A fighter engaged in irregular warfare, usually as a member of an organization resisting the government. Guerrilla warfare describes the methods used by resistance movements who use hit-and-run tactics and sabotage. Urban guerrillas refers to groups operating in towns. Guerrilla is a Spanish word and was first used to describe fighters resisting Napoleon's rule in Spain.

humanitarian Someone campaigning for some humane purpose or welfare.

ICBM Intercontinental ballistic missiles (see ABM above).

immigrants People who come to live, as permanent residents, in a foreign country.

imperialism The extension of the power of one country over other (usually backward) countries. Dollar imperialism is a term used by critics to describe the process by which the US government and US firms gain control of the economy of a country. Russian imperialism is used to describe the extension of Russian control of Eastern Europe and, more recently, Afghanistan.

indemnity Usually used to describe a sum of money, a sort of fine, forced out of one country by another after a war (see reparations).

independence The freedom granted to former colonies when the colonial power gives up control. Independence movements are organizations campaigning for independence. They often use guerrilla tactics (see above) when the colonialist power (see p. 169) refuses to accept their demands (see FLN).

infallibility Strictly this means the inability to err (or make a mistake). Papal infallibility is one aspect of the power of a Pope when speaking *ex cathedra* as defined in 1870 by the Vatican Council (see Vatican).

inflation A general increase of prices and a fall in the purchasing value of money. It usually results from an increase in the quantity of currency, as in Germany in 1923. It may also be the result of increased raw material prices, as with oil after 1973.

integration The merging together of peoples of different races into one society; the integration in US schools refers to the attempts to abolish segregated schools (see below) so that black and white children attended the same school.

investment The spending of money on stocks and shares; the spending of money by individuals or governments on various projects. Such spending creates employment, but may lead to inflation (see above).

IRA The Irish Republican Army which used guerrilla tactics (see guerrilla) in its fight for Irish independence (see above) from Britain. Since 1922 it has campaigned for the incorporation of Ulster into a United Ireland.

isolationism The policy of staying out of involvement in the affairs of other countries. It is particularly used to refer to US foreign policy after 1920.

Izvestia One of the two official Soviet newspapers. It means 'news'. See also *Pravda.*

Jesuits Members of a religious order (see p. 171) in the Catholic Church founded by St Ignatius of Loyola in 1534. Often very influential with Catholic rulers and politicians, it was usually the first to be attacked by anti-clericals (see anti-clericalism).

Junkers The exclusive Prussian aristocracy.

KGB The Russian 'secret branch', as the secret police was known after Stalin's death. (See MVD below.)

Lebensraum (living space) Territory which Germans (particularly the Nazis) claimed was necessary for natural development. Such territory was often rich in natural resources.

Mafia Criminal gangs originating in Sicily which were hostile to government and police. Italian immigrants (see immigrants) into the USA organized crime through Mafia families.

Mandates Areas of the German and Turkish colonial empires which were placed under the control of powers named by the League of Nations so that they could be prepared for independence (see independence).

manifesto The publicly stated policy (usually in writing) of an organization, usually of a political party.

MBFR Mutual and Balanced Force Reduction.

mediate (to) To intervene, or form the connecting link, between two rival groups in the hope of bringing them to agreement (see arbitration).

Mig The Russian air design team of Mikoyan and Gurevich.

ministerial responsibility The responsibility of government ministers to parliament, where ministers have to answer for their actions. In many countries this is regarded as an essential part of democracy (see democracy). It does not exist in an autocracy (see autocracy or dictatorship).

MIRV Multiple Independently-targeted Re-entry Vehicle, a ballistic missile.

MVD The initials of the Russian secret police when it changed from being the NKVD and before it became the KGB.

NASA National Aeronautics and Space Administration (USA).

nation The people of a country under one government.

nationalism Patriotic feeling; pride in one's own country. It may take the form of a campaign for independence (see p. 170) in a colonial country. It may lead to a campaign to make one's nation united and strong. It may lead to a desire to make one's country supreme over others.

nationalization The taking over of the ownership of private property, e.g. the nationalization of the coal industry made it the property of the nation instead of the property of private mine owners.

NATO The North Atlantic Treaty Organization.

NEP The New Economic Policy developed by Lenin and ended by Stalin.

NKVD The name of the Russian secret police during its most notorious period under Stalin's direction (see MVD above).

NLF The National Liberation Front, a title used by nationalists fighting a guerrilla war (see guerrilla) in (a) Aden and (b) Vietnam.

OEEC The Organization for European Economic Co-operation.

OGPU The Central State Political Department, the name of the Russian secret police which succeeded the Cheka (see Cheka).

OPEC The Organization of Petroleum Exporting Countries.

pacifism The belief that all war is wrong. Pacifists refuse to take an active part in fighting during a war.

pact An agreement or treaty.

Pan-Slavism A belief that the whole (*pan* = Greek for 'all') Slavonic peoples should work together; they shared a common (orthodox) religion and common enemies (Austria and Turkey).

partisan A word used in the Second World War to describe anti-German guerrillas (see guerrilla), particularly in Yugoslavia, Italy and France.

panzer German armoured troops.

plebiscite A vote of all the people in a given area on a particular issue. In 1935 the people of the Saar voted in a plebiscite to be re-united with Germany.

PLO The Palestine Liberation Organization which engages in guerrilla war (see p. 170) against Israel.

pogrom The organized massacre of a minority group, especially of Jews in Russia (from the Russian word for 'destroy').

police state A state in which a secret police supervises the people's activities.

Politburo The small group of leaders who control Soviet policy-making. It takes charge of the Communist Party of the Soviet Union when its Central Committee is not in session.

Pravda Another official Soviet newspaper. It means 'Truth'. (See *Izvestia*, 'News'). Russians joke that they get plenty of Izvestia but not much Pravda in their newspapers.

proletariat Wage-earners who have no property and depend on their daily labour for their subsistence. Marxists use it to describe the working masses who, they say, are kept down by the bourgeoisie (see bourgeoisie).

propaganda A word used by critics of attempts to spread a certain doctrine or belief; the means of spreading a belief. It comes from the Latin *propagare* (meaning to multiply plants by layering).

prohibition This usually refers to the attempt to ban the manufacture and sale of alcoholic drink in the USA between 1920 and 1933.

protection A system of tariffs to protect home industries against foreign imports. It is the opposite of free trade.

protectorate A country which is controlled and/or developed by a stronger country. Some mandated territories (see Mandates) became known as protectorates.

puppet (state) A country which claims to be independent but which is actually controlled by a greater power (see satellite).

purge (to) To get rid of 'undesirable' people in the army or state; particularly applied to Stalin's policy in the 1930s.

putsch From the Swiss word for 'blow'. A German attempt at a coup d'état; particularly applied to Hitler's attempt to seize power in 1923.

race People of common descent, perhaps of a distinctive ethnic group. People of different races may be found in one nation (see nation) as in the USA and South Africa.

radical From the Latin word for root. Someone who campaigns for major reforms and changes.

reactionary Someone opposed to change who may, even, want to 'turn back the clock' and undo past reforms.

referendum A vote on a single issue (see plebiscite).

Reichstat The Upper House of the German Parliament in the Weimar Republic. It replaced the Bundesrat (see Bundesrat) and represented the states in the Federal state.

Reichstag The Lower (or popularly-elected) House of the German Parliament.

religious order A society of men or women who have bound themselves by vows (of poverty, chastity and obedience) to live together and to serve God in a special way. Many are particularly concerned with education and were enemies of the anti-clericals (see anti-clericalism; see also Jesuits).

reparations Compensation for injury or damages imposed by the victorious country and paid by the conquered.

They were similar to an indemnity (see indemnity) but were a compensation rather than a fine.

republic A state without a monarchy, that has a president as the head of state.

revisionism (a) The demand for change of some treaty such as the Treaty of Versailles. (b) More recently it has been used about communists who seek to 'revise' Marx's teachings. It is most often used by those who think that a violent revolution is essential as an attack on revisionists who think that communism can be achieved by peaceful means. Mao Tse-tung denounced Khrushchev as a revisionist; China is now ruled by such revisionists.

SALT The Strategic Arms Limitation Talks.

SAM Surface-to-Air Missiles.

sanctions Penalties or methods used to put pressure on nations committing what others condemn as illegal actions. Economic sanctions involve restrictions on trade. Military sanctions involve entering into war.

satellite (a) A country, seemingly independent, but in reality controlled by a greater power (see puppet). (b) One of the artificial bodies sent into orbit around the earth or other planet.

SD Social Democrat.

secession A separation or breaking away of one part of a union (of states or races). The Southern States wanted to break away from the Federal United States; Biafra wanted to break away from Nigeria.

segregation A separation, usually imposed, of different groups of people. (See apartheid, desegregation and integration.)

Senate The Upper House of the US Congress.

socialism A political and social theory which argues that the community as a whole should own and control the means of production (see nationalization), distribution and exchange. In its extreme form it is Marxist.

soviet A council or committee elected in a district of Russia. In 1905 and 1917 soviets were formed by revolutionaries. (See USSR.)

SR Social Revolutionary.

suffrage The right to vote (see franchise).

SWAPO The South West African People's Organization which campaigns for the independence (see independence) of the mandated territory which was formerly German South West Africa.

tariffs Taxes on imports. (See protection.)

totalitarianism A system of government which does not allow a rival to the ruling party. Nazi Germany and Soviet Russia are examples of totalitarian régimes.

tribalism Loyalty to the tribe rather than to the nation (see nation), a feature of some independent African states.

TVA The Tennessee Valley Authority (USA).

U-2 The Lockheed spy-plane (USA).

UDI A Unilateral Declaration of Independence by a country claiming independence (see independence) without the permission of the colonial power (e.g. Rhodesia, 1965).

ultimatum A final proposal or statement of terms, the rejection of which by the opposition (party or nation) leads to a break in friendly relations and may lead to war.

USSR The Union of Soviet Socialist Republics. (See soviet, socialist and republic.)

UNICEF The United Nations International Children's Emergency Fund.

UNO The United Nations Organization.

UNRRA United Nations Relief and Rehabilitation Administration.

Untouchables Those who are outside the Indian caste system (see caste). They do the most menial jobs and are the most underprivileged.

V1; V2 From the initial of the German *Vergeltungswaffen*; reprisal weapons. V1 was a flying bomb (or 'doodle bug'); V2 was a supersonic rocket.

VSO Voluntary Service Overseas.

Vatican (a) The Pope's palace and official residence in Rome; (b) Vatican City is an independent state created by the Lateran Treaty, 1929. (c) Vatican Council of the world's Catholic hierarchy held in (i) 1870 (see infallibility) and (ii) 1962–5.

veto The right to reject a law or a proposal. Such a power is possessed by rulers, presidents, some Upper Houses of Parliament and by the permanent members of the Security Council of the UNO (see above). Every member of the League of Nations had such a veto.

Watergate This complex of buildings contained the headquarters of the Democratic Party during the Presidential election in 1971. Republican burglars broke in and the subsequent scandals surrounding this break-in led to the resignation and imprisonment of the Vice-President, Spiro Agnew, and the resignation of the President, Richard Nixon.

WHO The World Health Organization.

welfare state A state with comprehensive social services and social security systems in health and education and against sickness, unemployment and old age.

ZAPU The Zimbabwe African People's Union which led to the guerrilla war (see guerrilla) by African nationalists (see nationalism) trying to overthrow the whites-only government which had declared UDI (see UDI).

Zionist A supporter of the colonization of Palestine by the Jews. The World Zionist Organization was founded in 1897.

47.1 Topics and Examination Questions

In the table below you will find a guide to the questions in the sections which follow, which are relevant to the topics you have studied. Section 47.2 (pp 185–201) contains typical structured questions based on evidence, but calling for no source evaluation. Section 47.3 (pp 201–210) contains structured questions based on evidence, and asking for some source evaluation. Section 47.4 (pp 210–244) contains multi-sourced questions which ask for a good deal of source evaluation and interpretation.

Topic	47.2	47.3	47.4
Germany, 1870–1914		1	1
France, 1870–1914	1		
Russia, 1855–1914	3+4	2	
The Eastern Question, 1870–1914	5		
Africa, 1870–1914	2		
The Far East, 1870–1918			
The USA, 1870–1917			
International relations, 1870–1914	6+7		3
The First World War, 1914–18	8–10		4
Russia, 1914–28	11+12	3+4	5+27
Russia, 1928–41		9	6+7
Peacemaking – Germany and Austria	13+14	5+6	
Peacemaking – Turkey		5	
The League of Nations	15, 18	7+8	8
Germany, 1919–33		10	
The USA, 1917–32	17	11+12	10
China and Japan, 1914–49	20		11
International affairs, 1919–29	16	8	
The USA, 1932–41	19+21		12
Hitler's Germany, 1933–39	19+22		9, 13, 30

Topic	47.2	47.3	47.4
Italy, 1919–39	23		
The British Empire, 1918–39	41		
International relations, 1930–39	24		
Spain, 1919–39	25		
The Second World War from 1939 to 1942	26		14
The Second World War from 1942 to 1945	27–29		
The United Nations Organization	30, 39		15+16
International relations, 1945–53	31	13+14	2+16
Russia, 1945–88	32		28
Eastern Europe, 1945–86			17+18
Western European integration			19+20
The United States of America, 1945–88	33	16	21+28
China, 1949–86	34		22
The Indian sub-continent, 1939–86	35	15	
The Far East, 1945–86			29
Africa, south of the Sahara, 1945–86	36	17	23+24
North Africa and the Middle East, 1945–86	37		25
The Third World and some of its problems	38+39	18	26
The road to détente	40		28

 ## 47.2 Structured Questions Based on Evidence, but Calling for No Source Evaluation

Candidates are not asked to make any evaluation of this evidence: source-evaluation questions can be found in 47.3 and 47.4.

1 The Third Republic

(a) Study the information below and then answer questions **i** to **iv** which follow.

DIFFICULTIES AND CRISES OF THE THIRD REPUBLIC
1 The struggle against clericalism and syndicalism.
2 Political crises: General Boulanger (1889); The Panama Scandal (1892);
The Dreyfus Affair (1894–1906).
3 Isolation in foreign affairs.

i Write a sentence to explain the meaning of the term 'clericalism'. (2)
ii Write a sentence to explain the meaning of the term 'syndicalism'. (2)
iii Write one or two sentences to explain why General Boulanger caused problems for the Third Republic. (3)
iv Write a paragraph to explain the changes in the relations between the church and the state (e.g. in education) during the Third Republic. (5)

ESSAY QUESTIONS

(b)
EITHER
i   Why did the Dreyfus affair cause such great difficulties for the Third Republic?   (15)
OR
ii The basic problem in foreign affairs was to break out of isolation and to find allies. Why was France isolated until the mid-1890s and what were the advantages of the alliances she later formed?   (15)

LEAG, 1990

2   The 'Scramble for Africa', 1880–1914

(a) Study the maps below, which show Africa in 1880 and in 1914, and then answer questions **i** to **v** which follow.

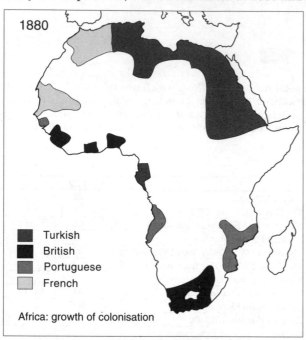

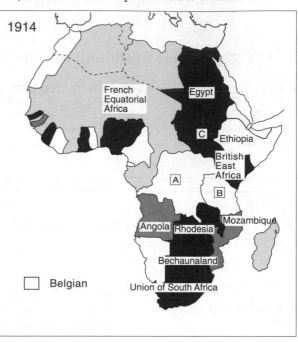

i   Write a sentence to explain the meaning of the term 'imperialism'.   (2)
ii Write a sentence to explain why Africa was known as the 'Dark Continent' in 1880.   (2)
iii Write one or two sentences to explain how Belgium became involved in State A.   (3)
iv Write one or two sentences to explain how Germany became involved in State B.   (3)
v   Write a paragraph to explain why Britain and France came close to war in 1898 over Place C.   (5)

ESSAY QUESTIONS

(b)
EITHER
i   What were the motives for the involvement of European powers in the 'Scramble for Africa'?   (15)
OR
ii How did European powers set about developing and ruling their new African territories and to what extent were there differences in the methods used?   (15)

LEAG, 1990

3   Tsar Alexander's reign in Russia up to 1870

(a) Study the information below and then answer questions **i** to **v** which follow.

'Alexander II was a well-meaning reformer and relatively liberal at first but later became reactionary.'

ALEXANDER'S REFORMS
EMANCIPATION OF THE SERFS
ZEMSTVOS
THE ARMY
LAW AND EDUCATION

i   Write a sentence to explain the meaning of the term 'emancipation'.   (2)
ii Write a sentence to explain the meaning of the term 'serfs'.   (2)
iii Write one or two sentences to describe the situation in Russia in 1855 when Alexander II became Tsar.   (3)
iv Write one or two sentences to explain the purpose of his changes in either the army or in law and education   (3)
v   Write a paragraph to explain how far his introduction of Zemstvos gave any real power to the people of Russia.   (5)

ESSAY QUESTIONS

(b)
EITHER
i   Why did Alexander II decide to emancipate the serfs in 1861 and why were the results of this emancipation far from satisfactory for the peasants?   (15)

OR
ii   The apparent 'new dawn' of reform in Russia proved false. In what ways were the later years of Alexander's reign different from the earlier years (up to 1870) and what events caused this change of heart on the part of Alexander II?

(15)

LEAG, 1990

4   Russia from 1905

(a) Study the passage below, which is about the 1905 revolution, and then answer questions **i** to **v** which follow.

> 'There were only two ways open; the first was to crush the revolution by sheer force. There would then be time to breathe, but, as likely as not, one would have to use force again in a few months and that would mean rivers of blood and in the end we would be back where we started.
>   The other way out would be to give the people their civil rights, to have all the laws confirmed by a State Duma. That of course would mean a constitution.'

Tsar Nicholas II in 1905

i   Write a sentence explaining the meaning of the term 'civil rights' as used in the passage.   (2)
ii   Write one or two sentences to explain why there was a revolution in Russia in 1905.   (3)
iii   Write one or two sentences explaining the part played by the St. Petersburg Soviet in the events of 1905.   (3)
iv   Write a sentence to explain what Tsar Nicholas II mean by a 'State Duma'.   (2)
v   This passage describes two different methods of dealing with the rebellion. Write a paragraph explaining how, during the year 1905, Tsar Nicholas II tried to solve the problems he faced.   (5)

ESSAY QUESTIONS

(b)
EITHER
i   Between 1906 and 1914 a number of attempts were made to solve the domestic problems of Russia. How successful were these attempts?   (15)
OR
ii   In what ways did the First World War create growing problems for the Russian government and people from August 1914 to February 1917?   (15)

LEAG, 1990

5   The Eastern Question

Study the map below and then attempt all the questions which follow.

The Balkans, 1880–1914

(a) In 1878 an international conference on the Eastern Question was held in Berlin. Why did the Great Powers find it necessary to hold this conference? (8)

(b) Why did the Eastern Question become so important again during the years 1908–13? (10)

(c) 'The Eastern Question was the most important cause of war in 1914.' Do you agree or disagree with this opinion? Explain your answer. (12)

SEG,1991

6 International relations, 1870–1914

(a) Study the passage below and then answer questions **i** to **v** which follow.

'By 1871 Germany had replaced France as the leading power in Western Europe. Bismarck knew that France would try to restore its supremacy, but could only do so with strong allies.

In 1872 Bismarck arranged a meeting of the emperors of Austria-Hungary, Germany and Russia and they agreed upon an entente called 'The League of the Three Emperors' (Dreikaiserbund). After this collapsed Bismarck signed an alliance with Austria-Hungary in 1879 (the Dual Alliance).

In 1881 Bismarck signed a treaty with Austria-Hungary and Russia which was renewed in 1884. In June 1887 Bismarck signed the Reinsurance Treaty with Russia.'

i Write a sentence explaining the meaning of the term 'entente'. (2)
ii Write one or two sentences to explain one of Bismarck's main aims in foreign policy during this period. (3)
iii Write one or two sentences explaining why 'the League of the three Emperors' collapsed in 1879. (3)
iv Write a sentence explaining the main purpose of the 'Reinsurance Treaty'. (2)
v Write a paragraph explaining how France tried to gain the 'strong allies' it needed in the years from 1890 to 1904.(5)

ESSAY QUESTIONS

(b)
EITHER
i In what ways did the dismissal of Bismarck in 1890 lead to changes in German foreign policy? (15)
OR
ii Apart from the alliances mentioned in the passage, in what other ways was international tension increased in the years from 1880 to 1908? (15)

LEAG, 1991

7 Causes of the First World War

'No one planned the First World War; it came about by accident.'

Do you agree or disagree with this view? In explaining your answer you might refer to:

the arms race;

the Moroccan crises;

the Balkan crises;

the Alliance system;

the pattern of events from June to August 1914;

any other relevant information. (30)

SEG, 1990

8 The Western Front

(a) Study the passage below and then answer questions **i** to **v** which follow.

'On 1 August 1914 Germany declared war on Russia and two days later on France. No one expected it to be a long war. The Germans thought the first campaigns would be decisive. Germany's task was to deal a knockout blow to France in the west before Russia mobilized her vast armies in the east.

On 4 August the German armies rolled into Belgium. Only the small Belgian army barred their way.'

i Write a sentence explaining one reason why Germany declared war on Russia on 1 August 1914. (2)
ii Write a sentence explaining one reason why Germany declared war on France on 3 August 1914. (2)
iii Write one or two sentences explaining why Germany invaded Belgium in 1914. (3)
iv Write one or two sentences explaining why few people in 1914 expected that the war would be a long one. (3)
v Write a paragraph explaining why the German advance into Belgium and Northern France in 1914 did not go as planned. (5)

ESSAY QUESTIONS

(b)
EITHER
i From October 1914 until March 1918 the war in the West dragged on almost in stalemate. Why was neither side able to win a decisive victory during this period? (15)
OR
ii Between March and November 1918, the Western Allies were able to bring the war to an end. Why did the pattern of the war change so suddenly in its last months? (15)

LEAG,1991

9 The First World War, 1914–18

(a) Study the map of the Somme trench lines, and then answer questions **i** to **v** which follow.

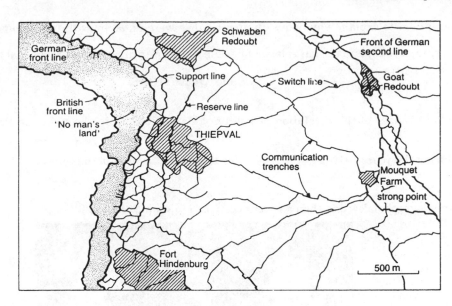

No man's land

i   Write a sentence to explain the term '*no man's land*'. (2)
ii Write a sentence to explain the term '*war of attrition*'. (2)
iii Write one or two sentences to describe the role played by women on the Western Front during the First World War. (3)
iv Write a paragraph to explain why trench warfare developed in the First World War. (4)
v   Write a paragraph to explain how soldiers were affected by trench warfare. (4)

ESSAY QUESTIONS

(b)
EITHER
i   How did the way in which the First World War was fought affect British civilians? (15)
OR
ii 'None of the new techniques of warfare succeeded in bringing the First World War to a speedy end.' Do you agree? Give reasons for your answer. (15)

ULEAC, 1992

10 The First World War, 1914–18

(a) Study this passage from a report by a German submarine captain, and then answer questions **i** to **v** which follow.

'The explosion of the torpedo must have been followed by a second one...The ship stopped immediately and heeled over to starboard...On the bow the name LUSITANIA became visible in golden letters.'

i   Write a sentence to explain why the sinking caused such an outrage. (2)
ii Write a sentence to show the effect of German submarine warfare on British shipping. (2)
iii Write a paragraph to show how Britain tried to fight back against enemy submarines. (4)
iv Write one or two sentences to describe how the war affected supplies of essential goods to the public. (3)
v   Write a paragraph to describe and explain the measures taken to make up for shortages of goods. (4)

ESSAY QUESTIONS

(b)
EITHER
i   The First World War saw the development of many new weapons of warfare. How important were these new weapons (*exclude* submarines) to the outcome of the war? (15)
OR
ii 'When I got back to England in 1917 there were food shortages, but there was little other evidence that we were fighting a war.'
    Do you think that this soldier's first impression of life on the home front was correct? Support your answer with detailed examples. (15)

LEAG, 1990

11 The Russian Revolution and the establishment of the Soviet State, 1917–41

(a) Study this passage from a poster issued by Lenin in October/November 1917, and then answer questions **i** to **v** which follow.

'To the Citizens of Russia! The Provisional Government is overthrown. State power has passed into the hands of the Military Revolutionary Committee...The cause for which the people have fought has triumphed. Long live the Revolution of Workers, Soldiers and Peasants.'

i   Write a sentence explaining why the Provisional Government was so called. (2)
ii Write a sentence explaining the part played by Kerensky in the Provisional Government. (2)
iii Write one or two sentences to explain why the domestic policy of the Provisional Government was so widely unpopular. (3)

iv Write a paragraph to explain why many Russian citizens were unhappy with the foreign policy of the Provisional Government. (4)

v Write a paragraph to explain the part played by Lenin in the overthrow of the Provisional Government. (4)

ESSAY QUESTIONS

(b)

EITHER

i What were the causes of the revolution of February/March 1917 which brought the Provisional Government to power? (15)

OR

ii How far, during the years 1917–24, was Lenin able to achieve the aims of the Bolshevik Revolution? (15)

LEAG, 1990

12 Stalin

(a) Study the photograph below and then answer questions **i** to **v** which follow:

A photograph (possibly faked) of Vladimir Lenin and Joseph Stalin taken in 1922

i Write a sentence describing the work Stalin was doing in the Russian Communist Party in 1922, the date of the photograph. (2)

ii Stalin believed in 'socialism in one country'. Write a sentence to explain the meaning of this phrase. (2)

iii Write one or two sentences explaining why Lenin and other Russian leaders did not at first consider Stalin to be a threat. (3)

iv Write one or two sentences explaining why Stalin made great use of photographs such as this after Lenin's death. (3)

v Write a paragraph describing the ways that Stalin used to gain complete power in the Soviet Union in the years to 1928. (5)

ESSAY QUESTIONS

(b)

EITHER

i Lenin introduced the New Economic Policy in 1921. Stalin changed this policy when he gained complete power. What effects did this change have upon the USSR in the 1930s? (15)

OR

ii In what ways did Stalin deal with opposition to his policies and threats to his position from 1928 to 1941? (15)

LEAG, 1991; WJEC used same source for similar questions

13 Peacemaking, 1918

Towards the end of World War I, President Wilson of the USA suggested that Fourteen Points should be considered when writing the Peace Treaties. Read the extract which lists the Fourteen Points, and then answer the questions which follow.

1   There should be no secret treaties and agreements.
2   The seas should be free in times of peace and war.
3   Customs barriers between countries should be abolished.
4   Armaments to be reduced.
5   The wishes of colonial peoples should be considered when settling colonial claims.
6   German forces to leave Russia.
7   Belgium to have all its territories returned.
8   Alsace-Lorraine to be returned to France.
9   Italy's frontier to be changed to avoid fighting with Austria.
10   Self-determination for the peoples of Austria-Hungary.

11   Serbia, Montenegro and Romania to be independent and Serbia to be given access to the sea.
12   Self-determination for the peoples of the Turkish Empire.
13   Poland to be independent and given access to the sea.
14   The setting up of an organization that would try to keep world peace by guaranteeing the independence of all states.

Adapted from a speech by President Wilson, 8 January 1918

(a) i   There were another two countries mainly involved in the drawing up to the Peace Treaties besides the USA. Name the two countries.   (2)
ii   What was the name of the treaty between Germany and the Allies?   (1)
iii   The term 'self-determination' is used in the above extract (Points 10 and 12). What did it mean?   (1)
(b) In what ways were the terms of the Peace Treaties similar to the Fourteen Points?   (6)
(c) How and why were the terms of the Peace Treaty between Germany and the Allies harsher towards Germany than Wilson's Fourteen Points?   (15)

MEG, 1990

14 Versailles and the League of Nations

Candidates had a map of Europe in the 1920s. They had to answer the questions:

(a) 'The Treaty of Versailles was too harsh on Germany.'
Do you agree or disagree with this statement?
Explain your answer.   (10)

(b) 'The most important weakness of the League of Nations was the fact that the Covenant of the League was part of the Peace Treaties.'
Do you agree or disagree with this statement?
Explain your answer.   (10)

(c) How well during the 1920s did the League of Nations deal with the problems arising from the Peace Treaties?
Explain your answer.   (10)

SEG, 1993

15 The League of Nations

(a) Study this passage which refers to the formation of the League of Nations, and then answer questions **i** to **v** which follow.

The first session of the Assembly ... was a landmark in the history of the world. But from the start the League was incomplete in membership. The United States, Germany, Russia and Austria were amongst those countries not present at the first meeting.

i   Write a sentence to explain what is meant by the term '*Assembly*' as used in this passage.   (2)
ii   Write a sentence to explain why Germany was not present at the first meeting of the League.   (2)
iii   Write one or two sentences to explain why Russia was not present at the first meeting.   (3)
iv   Write a paragraph to show how the Council of the League worked.   (4)
v   Write a paragraph to explain the work of the International Labour Organisation.   (4)

ESSAY QUESTIONS

(b)
EITHER
i   The League became involved in the crisis over Corfu (1923) and Abyssinia (1935). In what ways did the League's handling of these two crises highlight the weakness of the League of Nations?   (15)
OR
ii   'By 1936 the League of Nations had failed completely.' Do you agree? Explain your answer by reference to the period up to 1936.   (15)

ULEAC, 1992

16 International relations, 1919–29

After the First World War many countries were keen to avoid further conflicts. As a result the League of Nations was formed and, during the 1920s, international agreements were signed. Read the following extract and then answer the questions which follow.

'The League should at all times try to keep the peace between nations.'

Adapted from the Covenant of the League of Nations, 1920

(a) i   Name two countries which were permanent members on the Council of the League of Nations in 1920.   (2)
ii   In 1928 many countries signed agreements known as the Kellogg–Briand Pacts. Why were these agreements given this name?   (2)
(b) Were the aims of the League of Nations and Kellogg–Briand Pacts the same? Explain your answer.   (6)
(c) Which one of the following did more to encourage world peace in the 1920s?
1   The League of Nations
2   The Kellogg–Briand Pacts
Explain your answer fully by referring to 1 and 2.   (15)

MEG, 1991

17 Internal developments in the USA, 1919–41

Study the extract below and then attempt *all* parts of the question.

'Business was booming. Factories which had made guns and tanks for the war now made cars and refrigerators. Mass production meant that goods could be made more cheaply, so that more people could afford to buy them.
But there was a dark side to America in the 1920s. Prohibition was one example of this; the Ku Klux Klan was a far worse one. Furthermore, half the families in America scarcely earned enough to live on.'

adapted from The Twentieth Century, 1980, by J Hamer

(a) Sales of consumer goods such as 'cars and refrigerators' increased enormously in the 1920s. Did this happen only because methods of mass production were used? Explain your answer.   (8)
(b) Do you agree that the Ku Klux Klan was 'far worse' than Prohibition? Give reasons for your answer.   (10)
(c) The years of boom and increasing prosperity came to an end during the Depression that followed the Wall Street Crash of 1929. How were people's lives affected by the Depression?   (12)

SEG, 1991

18 The League of Nations

The League of Nations attempted to bring order to international relations in the 1920s. Look at the cartoon which was drawn in 1920 when the League of Nations was formed. Then answer the questions which follow.

READY TO START.

(a) i   The League of Nations set up several different agencies. Name one of these agencies.   (1)
ii   What is meant by the term *'collective security'*? Briefly use your knowledge of the League of Nations to support your answer.   (3)

(b) In what ways were the following events different?
i   The dispute over the Aaland Islands in 1921.
ii   The Corfu Incident in 1923.   (6)

(c) 'The League of Nations was weak in the 1920s only because of these two reasons:
i   The USA was not a member of the League of Nations;
ii   The League of Nations did not have its own army.'
Do you agree or disagree with this statement? Explain your answer carefully.   (15)

MEG, 1992

19 The Depression: Hitler and Roosevelt compared

Below are statements regarding the policies used by Hitler and Roosevelt in dealing with the economic problems of the '30s in their respective countries. If the statement applies to Hitler, put a tick in the column headed 'Hitler'. Do the same with the column headed 'Roosevelt' if it applies to Roosevelt.

	Hitler	Roosevelt
Built up the armed forces		
Developed a programme of public works		
Encouraged trade unions		
Used propaganda to win the support of the people		
Controlled big business		

Using the above information, explain, in more detail, the similarities and differences in the methods by which Hitler and Roosevelt dealt with the economic problems each faced.

WJEC, 1993

20 China, 1934–49

Study the material that follows and then attempt *all* parts of the question.

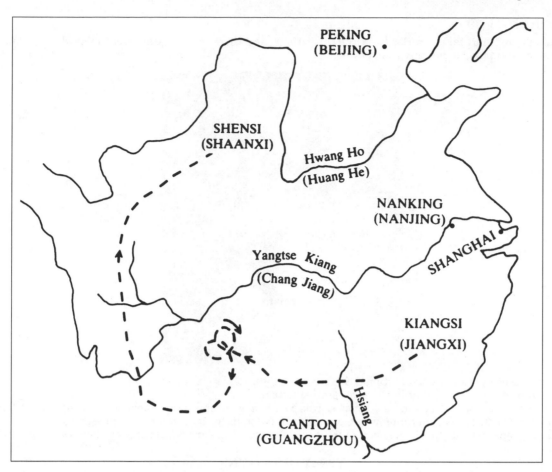

'Since 1935, the Long March has become a legend in China, the epic story of an army of courageous peasants and soldiers who put the interests of their country and political beliefs before their own personal interests.'

D Wilson, *The Long March*, 1971

(a) What were the circumstances that led the Communists into China to carry out the Long March? (8)

(b) Why do Chinese Communists regard the Long March as an 'epic story' and a 'legend'? In your answer you may give examples of incidents and hardships which occurred during the Long March. (10)

(c) Did the Long March bring about a strengthening of the Communists in China? Give reasons for your answer. (12)

SEG, 1991

21 Internal developments in the USA, 1933–41

Study the cartoon below and then attempt *all* parts of the question.

an American cartoon, March 1933

The cartoon shows Franklin D Roosevelt, the new President, putting a dustbin full of Republican policies and slogans outside the White House. Herbert Hoover, the outgoing President, is walking away.

(a) Why did Roosevelt win such an overwhelming victory in the 1932 election for President? (10)

(b) Did the New Deal policies solve the problems facing the USA in the 1930s? (12)

(c) Roosevelt again won convincing victories in the elections for President in 1936 and 1940. In spite of this, there was much opposition to his policies. Was this opposition effective? Explain your answer. (8)

SEG, 1991

22 Germany, 1933–39

(a) Study this photograph taken in Berlin in the early 1930s and then answer questions **i** to **v** which follow: The sign translated reads 'Germans, do not buy from Jews'.

i Write a sentence explaining what National Socialists meant by the word 'Aryan'. (2)
ii Write a sentence explaining what is meant by 'anti-semitism'. (2)
iii Write one or two sentences explaining why there was so much anti-semitism in Germany during the 1930s. (3)
iv Write one or two sentences explaining why German Jews found it difficult to combat anti-semitism. (3)
v Write a paragraph describing the measures that were taken against Jews in Germany during the years 1933-39. (5)

ESSAY QUESTIONS

(b)
EITHER

i 'German dislike of the Treaty of Versailles was mostly responsible for Hitler's rise to power.' Do you agree with this statement? Give reasons for your answer. (15)

OR

ii How successful were the domestic policies of the German government in the years 1933–39? (15)

LEAG, 1991

23 Fascism in Italy, 1919–39

(a) Study this passage, which refers to events in Italy during the early 1920s, and then answer questions **i** to **v** which follow.

> 'The Fascist action squads turned their attention to those suburbs firmly held by communists and socialists. These left-wing parties had encouraged the breakdown of law and order. The swift decisive work of the Fascists put them into flight. Before the action squads came, the authorities were powerless: they could not control the disorders and disturbances...The squads were defenders of civil life, protectors of order and citizenship.'

Adapted from Mussolini, *My Autobiography*, 1936

i Write a sentence explaining what is meant by 'the authorities' referred to in the passage. (2)
ii Write a sentence explaining why the authorities could not control disorders and disturbances. (2)
iii Write one or two sentences explaining why there was a great deal of support for Socialists in Italy after 1919. (3)
iv Write one or two sentences showing how Fascist action squads operated at this time. (3)
v Write a paragraph describing the main beliefs of Italian Fascists in the early 1920s. (5)

ESSAY QUESTIONS

(b)
EITHER

i 'The impact of the First World War was mostly responsible for the rise of Fascism in Italy.'
Do you agree with this statement? Give reasons for your answer. (15)

OR

ii Did the Italians benefit from Mussolini's domestic policies during the years 1922–39? Give reasons for your answer. (15)

LEAG, 1991

24 International Relations 1933–39

During the 1930s, Germany, Italy and Japan all seemed to be threatening international peace. Look at the cartoon, which refers to the attitude of Germany and Italy towards international agreements in the 1930s. Then answer the questions which follow.

(a) i In the 1930s Germany and Italy were ruled by dictators. What does the term 'dictator' mean?   (1)

ii Name the 1935 agreement which aimed to prevent Germany changing the terms of the Versailles Peace Treaty.
     (1)

iii State *two* reasons why the League of Nations failed to control the actions of Germany, Italy and Japan in the 1930s.   (2)

(b) Explain *three* ways in which the foreign policies of Germany, Italy and Japan were similar in the 1930s.   (6)

(c) Which *one* of the following countries caused most harm to international peace in the 1930s?
 1 Germany
 2 Italy
 3 Japan

Explain your answer fully by referring to *1, 2* and *3*.   (15)

MEG, 1991

25 The Spanish Civil War, 1936–39

(a) Study the passage below and then answer questions **i** to **v** which follow:

> 'In 1931 the Spanish king abdicated. From 1931–36 the Spaniards had democratic governments. In 1936 the Popular Front came to power in the election and was at once faced with a military uprising under General Franco and the Falange. A bitter civil war was fought between the Republicans (the government) and the Nationalists (the followers of Franco) which lasted from 1936 to 1939.'

i Write a sentence to explain the term 'Popular Front'.   (2)
ii Write a sentence to explain what the 'Falange' was.   (2)
iii Write one or two sentences to explain why the king had been forced to leave in 1931.   (3)
iv Write one or two sentences to explain the part played by the Condor Legion in the civil war.   (3)
v Write a paragraph to explain the importance of the Spanish Civil War for the future of Europe.   (5)

ESSAY QUESTIONS

(b)
EITHER

i What were the causes of the civil war which broke out in Spain in 1936? What differences in attitude to the war itself were shown by the leading powers in Europe?   (15)

ii Why did the Nationalists win the civil war in Spain?   (15)

LEAG, 1991

26 The Second World War, 1939–45

Study Map A below and then answer **all** parts of the question.

Map A: The Mediterranean

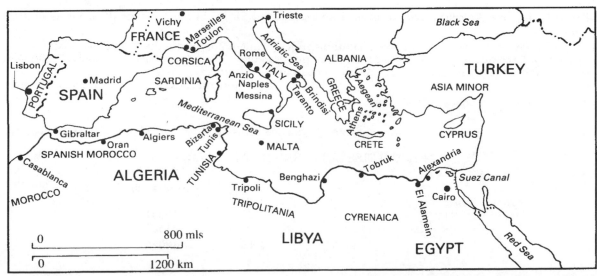

from *The Second World War*, (1989) by M. Gilbert

(a) 'If Britain had lost control of the Mediterranean during the years 1940–43, Britain could easily have lost the war.'
Do you agree or disagree with this statement?
Explain your answer. (8)

(b) 'Air attacks on armies and navies achieved much more than air attacks on civilian targets.'
Do you agree or disagree with this statement?
Explain your answer. (10)

(c) 'Russia's campaigns in Eastern Europe were the main reason for the defeat of Germany.'
Do you agree or disagree with this statement?
Explain your answer. (12)

SEG, 1993

27   The Second World War, 1941–45

Study the following sources carefully. Use the information to help you answer the questions which follow.

SOURCE A:
In March 1941, Hitler sent Rommel to recover the ground lost by the Italians in North Africa.

'Dearest Lu,
   Who knows whether I'll have a chance to sit down and write in peace in the next few days or ever again. Today there's a chance.
   The battle is raging. Perhaps we will still manage to be able to stick it out, in spite of all that's against us – but it may go wrong and that would have very grave consequences for the whole course of the war. For North Africa would then fall to the British in a few days, almost without a fight. We will do all we can to pull it off. But the enemy's superiority is terrific and our resources very small.'

Rommel, letter to his wife, October 1942

Why was Rommel eventually defeated in the Desert War?

SOURCE B:
In June 1941, Hitler launched his attack on Russia, code-named Operation Barbarossa.

Describe briefly the Russian campaign of 1941–2.

SOURCE C:
In July 1943, British and American troops invaded and conquered Sicily. In September, Allied forces landed on the mainland of Italy.

'Those who have not seen the Appenine Mountains in Italy cannot appreciate the formidable obstacle they present to a force advancing from the south. This great stretch of mountains, rising to nearly 7,000 feet, stretches across the peninsula from the Mediterranean to the Adriatic.'

General Alexander, *The Alexander Memoirs*, 1962

Describe briefly the Allied conquest of Italy, 1943–4.

SOURCE D:
On 6 June 1944, Allied troops landed in Normandy and began the invasion which would end with the defeat and death of Hitler.

CASUALTIES SUFFERED BY THE ALLIES

		British	American
From 6 June to 19 July 1944:	killed	6010	10641
	wounded	28690	51387
		34700	**62028**

What problems faced the Allies during the D-Day campaign?

What explanation for the defeat of Nazi Germany is contained in the accounts of the four campaigns you have written about in your answers to the above questions?

WJEC, 1991

28 The USA and the war

Study the extract below and then attempt all parts of the question.

Churchill's delight at the American entry into the war, December 1941

> 'To have the USA at our side was the greatest joy to me. After the horrors of the invasion threat, and after the deadly struggle of the U-boat war, we were at last on the road to victory.
> How long the war would last I did not know. But Hitler's fate was sealed; Mussolini's fate was sealed. As for the Japanese, they would be ground to powder. The British Empire, the Soviet Union and now the USA had twice or even three times the power and strength of the enemy.'
> from Winston Churchill, *The Second World War*, 1949

(a) Why did the USA remain neutral during the early years of the Second World War? (8)
(b) Why did the USA join the war in December 1941? (8)
(c) 'Of all the factors leading to Allied success in the war, the entry of the USA was the most important.'
Do you agree or disagree with this opinion? Explain your answer. (14)

SEG, 1991

29 Germany's alliances with Italy and Japan

(a) 'If, in spite of all our our efforts, we fail to win this war, the Italian alliance will have contributed to our defeat.'
Adolf Hitler

Was the Italian alliance a burden for Germany during the Second World War? Explain your answer. (15)
(b) Did the Japanese bring added strength to the Axis Powers from 1941 onwards? Explain your answer. (15)

SEG, 1991

30 The United Nations

(a) Study this passage, which refers to the formation of the United Nations, and then answer questions **i** to **v** which follow.

> 'When the United Nations' Charter was signed by representatives of 50 allied nations on 26 June 1945, General Smuts said "It provides for a peace with teeth…".'

i Write a sentence to explain the term '*Charter*' as used in the passage. (2)
ii Write a sentence to explain what you think General Smuts meant when he used the phrase '*peace with teeth*'. (2)
iii Write one or two sentences to explain the part played by the Secretary-General in the United Nations. (3)
iv Write one or two sentences to show the work of the General Assembly. (3)
v Write a paragraph to explain the work of the Security Council. (5)

ESSAY QUESTIONS

(b)
EITHER
i Describe the United Nations' involvement in the Korean War of 1950–1953. How has the United Nations tried to maintain peace there since 1953? (15)
OR
ii 'The United Nations is a failure because it has not prevented wars.' Do you agree? Explain your answer by reference to the United Nations' work. (15)

ULEAC, 1992

31 The Cold War

Victory over Nazi Germany in 1945 was followed by a Cold War between the former allies. Some of the causes and consequences of this Cold War are listed below. Identify which, in the list, are *causes* and which are *consequences* of the Cold War by putting a tick in the appropriate column.

	Cause	Consequence
American fear of world communism		
Russia's distrust of American policy in Europe		
NATO and the Warsaw Pact		
The Berlin Airlift		
The arms race		

Using the above factors, explain the causes and consequences of the Cold War during the period 1945–55.

WJEC, 1993

32 The USSR 1953–80

(a) Study the table and then answer questions **i** to **v** which follow.

1976–1980	Target percentage increase in production	Actual percentage increase in production
Heavy Industry	38–42	26
Consumer Goods	30–32	21
Agriculture	14–17	9

A table showing what the Tenth *Five-Year Plan* aimed to achieve, and what was actually achieved.

i Write a sentence explaining the term 'Consumer Goods'. (2)
ii Write a sentence explaining the term 'Five-Year Plan'. (2)
iii In the past, the Soviet Union has often paid more attention to heavy industry than to consumer goods. Write one or two sentences explaining why this has been the case. (3)
iv Write one or two sentences explaining why Five-Year Plans have often failed to meet their targets. (3)
v Write a paragraph explaining why Soviet agriculture remained a problem in the 1970s. (5)

ESSAY QUESTIONS

(b)
EITHER
ii How did Nikita Khrushchev gain power in the mid-1950s?
What were the reasons for his fall from power in 1964? (15)
i Between the mid-1950s and 1980, leaders of the USSR made several attempts to improve East-West relations. How successful were these attempts? (15)

LEAG, 1991

33 The USA

(a) Study the following passage, which refers to civil rights demonstrations in 1963, and then answer questions **i** to **v** which follow:

'In August 1963, a quarter of a million people, black and white, representing a great number of civil rights groups, met at a giant rally in Washington to register their plea for the many rights that were still denied to American blacks. President Kennedy...listened sympathetically.'

i Write a sentence to explain the term 'civil rights'. (2)
ii Write one or two sentences to explain why the early 1960s were so important to the civil rights movement. (2)
iii Write a paragraph to explain why the desegregation of public facilities was so important to the civil rights movement. (4)
iv Write one or two sentences to describe the importance of the war in Vietnam to the civil rights movement. (3)
v Write a paragraph to explain why education was such an important issue to the civil rights movements in the 1960s. (4)

ESSAY QUESTIONS

(b)
EITHER
i What attempts were made by US Presidents, in the period 1947–65, to bring about equality for black people and how successful were they? (15)
OR
ii Assess the significance of Martin Luther King as leader of the civil rights movement in the 1960s. (15)

LEAG, 1990

34 China

Study the photograph below and then attempt all parts of the question.

Members of a commune building a canal in 1958.

Members of a commune building a canal in 1958

(a) This photograph was taken during the Great Leap Forward.
Why did Mao Tse-tung (Mao Zedong) introduce the Great Leap Forward? (6)
(b) This photograph helps to show what happened in China during the Great Leap Forward.
Was China much changed by the Great Leap Forward? Explain your answer. (12)
(c) In 1966 Mao introduced the Cultural Revolution. Was this because the Great Leap Forward had failed? Explain
your answer. (12)

SEG, 1991

35 India

(a) Study this passage, which relates to Indian Independence, and then answer questions **i** to **v** which follow.

> 'In June 1947, Mountbatten took the decision to bring forward independence to 15 August. The parliament
> of each province would have to decide whether to join India or Pakistan, so would the 565 princes.'

i Write a sentence to explain the position held by Mountbatten at this time. (2)
ii Write a sentence to explain what is meant by the reference in the passage to the '*565 princes*'. (2)
iii Write a paragraph to explain why Mountbatten brought forward the date for independence. (4)
iv Write a paragraph to describe the partition of India. (4)
v Write one or two sentences to explain the part played by Gandhi between independence and his death in January
1948. (3)

ESSAY QUESTIONS

(b)
EITHER
i 'The creation of a separate India and Pakistan destroyed everything that Gandhi had worked for.' Do you agree?
Explain your answer. (15)
OR
ii 'World War II was the most important reason for India's independence.' Do you agree? Explain your answer. (15)

ULEAC, 1993

36 Africa, south of the Sahara

Study carefully the sources below, and then answer the question which follows.

> 'I will reform African education so that the Natives will be taught from childhood to realise that equality
> with Europeans is not for them ...'

Dr. Verwoerd, Minister of National Affairs

Signs of segregation

How did the system of apartheid work in South Africa?

WJEC, 1993

37 Arab-Israeli Relations since 1948

(a) Study the following map, which shows the areas occupied by Israel after the Six Days War of 1967 and then answer
questions **i** to **v**.

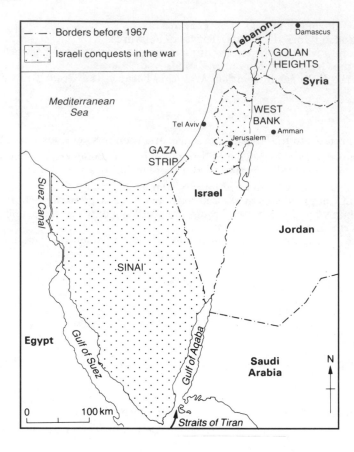

- — - Borders before 1967

Israeli conquests in the war

i The Six Days War has been described as a 'pre-emptive strike' by Israel. Write a sentence to explain in your own words what 'pre-emptive strike' means. (2)

ii Write a sentence to explain what you learn from the map about Israel's position in relation to its Arab neighbours. (2)

iii Write one or two sentences explaining the long-term causes of the Six Days War. (3)

iv Write one or two sentences explaining the short-term causes of the Six Days War. (3)

v Write a paragraph explaining why Israel was so successful in the Six Days War. (5)

ESSAY QUESTIONS

(b)

EITHER

i 'Israel's wars with its neighbours have always followed a similar pattern.'
Referring to at least two of the Arab-Israeli wars of 1956, 1967 or 1973, show whether you agree with this statement.

(15)

OR

ii 'The creation of the state of Israel in 1948 had a dramatic effect on the position of Arabs in the Middle East.'
Show how since 1948, Palestinian Arabs and neighbouring Arab states have been affected by the creation of the state of Israel. (15)

LEAG, 1991

38 Third World problems

Since 1945 the difficulties of the developing world have increased. Read the extract, and then answer the questions which follow.

'The real problem facing us today is the division of the world into rich and poor countries.'

Adapted from a speech by Julius Nyerere, President of Tanzania

(a) i Briefly describe *three* ways by which the developed countries have tried to solve the problem of 'the division of the world into rich and poor countries'. (3)

ii Why are poorer countries often described as 'Third World' countries? (1)

(b) i Why have the difficulties of the developing world increased since 1945? (6)

ii Why does that concern the governments of developed countries? (15)

MEG, 1991

39 The United Nations and the Third World

One of the main challenges of the second half of the twentieth century is the poverty of the developing world and its results. The United Nations has attempted to change the situation through the work of its agencies. On the next page is a list of the problems of the developing world. Indicate, by placing a tick in the appropriate column, whether the UN has largely succeeded in changing the situation or whether the problem still exists.

	Has changed	Continues
Disease		
Starvation		
Illiteracy		
Overpopulation		

Using the above factors, describe the degree of success of the UN agencies in meeting the challenges of the developing world.

WJEC, 1993

40 The road to détente

(a) Study the passage below and then answer questions **i** to **v** which follow.

'Huge sums of money have been spent since 1945 in producing weapons, a large proportion because of the Cold War. In the 1970s people spoke of détente but, by 1980, 450 000 million dollars a year was still being spent. Military leaders said nuclear weapons have been a deterrent. In 1962 an American journalist calculated that, since 1946, 863 international disarmament meetings have been held, involving 1700 hours and 18 million words, but with little success.'

i   Write a sentence to explain the meaning of the term 'détente'. (2)
ii Write a sentence to explain the meaning of the term 'deterrent'. (2)
iii Write one or two sentences to explain which types of weapons were mainly discussed at disarmament meetings. (3)
iv Write one or two sentences to explain how space exploration has made the problem of nuclear warfare even worse. (3)
v   Write a paragraph to explain the importance of the Helsinki Conference (1973–5) in improving international relations. (5)

ESSAY QUESTIONS

(b)
EITHER
i   What progress was made in the field of arms control between 1946 and 1980? (15)
OR
ii Why was it so difficult to achieve disarmament in the period 1946 to 1980? (15)

LEAG, 1990

41 India, 1918–48

(a) Study this passage, which relates to British rule in India, and then answer questions **i** to **v** which follow.

'On 13 April 1919, 10,000 unarmed Indians gathered inside an enclosed square in Amritsar. Some of these people were supporters of Gandhi, others were agitators and many were there for the annual horse fair. Brigadier-General Dyer arrived with British and Indian troops and without warning-shots the troops opened fire on the crowd, killing 379 people.'

i   Write a sentence to explain the term *'caste system'*. (2)
ii Write a sentence to explain the term *'untouchables'*. (2)
iii Write one or two sentences to explain why Brigadier-General Dyer ordered the Amritsar shootings. (3)
iv Write one or two sentences to explain why the Indians fought on the British side during the First World War. (3)
v   Write a paragraph to explain the impact of the Amritsar Massacre on the Indian people. (5)

ESSAY QUESTIONS

(b)
EITHER
i   How did Britain try to change the system it used to govern India between 1919 and 1939? (15)
OR
ii Why did the Indian National Congress and the Muslim League become such rivals between 1919–1940? What consequences did this rivalry have for the coming of independence? (15)

ULEAC, 1993

47.3 Structured Questions Based on Evidence; Some Source Evaluation

1 Germany 1870–14

Study the source below and then attempt all parts of the question.

i   'The State must provide the funds for pensions, not as charity, but in recognition of the workers' right to State help when they are unable to provide for themselves. Why should a worker not receive a pension, just as a soldier or civil servant?'

ii 'Someone who is looking forward to an Old Age Pension is far more contented and easier to control. Money spent in this way is well invested; it is used to prevent revolution, which would cost a great deal more.'

From remarks made by Bismarck at different times during the 1880s

(a) Why did Bismarck quarrel with the Roman Catholic Church? (6)
(b) Why did Bismarck wish to weaken the socialists? (7)
(c) How valuable are Bismarck's comments in the source as evidence about his reasons for introducing Old Age Pensions? (5)
(d) How successful was Bismarck in controlling political opposition in Germany after 1871? (7)

SEG, 1991

2 Russia 1894–1914

Study the source below and then attempt all parts of the question.

(a) Why was there revolution in Russia in 1905? (6)
(b) The photograph shows part of a procession which was later fired on by the troops at the Winter Palace. How useful is this photograph to historians writing about the events of 1905? (5)
(c) 'The revolution of 1905 was a complete failure.' Do you agree or disagree with this opinion? Explain your answer. (7)
(d) During the years 1905–14, did conditions in Russia improve or get worse? Explain your answer. (7)

SEG, 1991

3 Russia, 1894–1917

Study Source A below and then answer all parts of the question.

SOURCE A: Rasputin with the Tsar and Tsarina

a Russian cartoon drawn in about 1913

(a) The purpose of this cartoon was to lower respect for the Russian monarchy.
Do you think it succeeds in doing so?
Explain your answer. (5)

(b) In March 1917 the Tsar fell from power.
Was the influence of Rasputin
   i   the only reason, *or*
   ii the main reason, *or*
   iii just one of many reasons for this?
Explain your answer. (10)

(c) Why were the Bolsheviks able to overthrow the Provisional Government in November 1917?

(10)
SEG, 1993

4   Russia, 1924–53

Study the source below and then attempt *all* parts of the question.

'Stalin was a bloodthirsty tyrant. He deliberately carried out mass murder. He cared nothing for the people of Russia, he cared only for personal power. His policies caused famine, a weakening of Russian agriculture from which it has never recovered, and the decline of Russian industry. He became a friend of Hitler and only fought against him when war was forced on him. He enslaved Eastern Europe in the prison of communism. The Russian people have nothing to thank him for.'

An historian's view, 1989

(a) Why had Stalin emerged as leader of Russia by 1929? (6)
(b) Were Stalin's policies in the 1930s aimed at strengthening Russia, or strengthening Stalin's dictatorship? Explain your answer. (9)
(c) 'Stalin's power and reputation in Russia were strengthened by the war of 1941–45.'
Do you agree or disagree with this opinion? Explain your answer. (5)
(d) 'The source gives a modern historian's judgement of Stalin. It is therefore likely to be accurate.'
Do you agree or disagree with this opinion? Explain your answer. (5)
SEG, 1991

5   The peace treaties following the First World War

Study Source A below and then answer all parts of the question.

SOURCE A

'The German representatives had half-expected that they would be presented with terms. They thought that they would be invited to discuss these terms with the Allies. But the Allies had decided that there would be no discussion. The Treaty of Versailles was to be forced upon Germany.
   On 7 May 1919 the Germans realised this. They were brought before the Allies like prisoners in the dock. At last they learned how harsh the terms of the treaty would be.'

from *The Post-War World*, (1935) by J. Hampden Jackson

(a) Source A was written by a British author.
Does this prove that some British people were against the terms of the Treaty of Versailles from the start?
Explain your answer. (5)

(b) Source A says that the Germans had hoped to have discussions with the Allies, but these did not happen.
Is that why the Germans were so angry about the Treaty of Versailles?
Explain your answer. (8)

(c) Source A says that the Allies took a harsh line with Germany in 1919.
Did the attitude of the Allies towards Germany change in the years 1919–29?
Explain your answer. (6)

(d) In 1919–20 peace treaties were also signed with the other defeated countries – Austria, Hungary, Bulgaria and Turkey.
In the 1920s these other treaties did not lead to as much international argument and discussion as the Treaty of Versailles.
Was this because they were not so harsh?
Explain your answer. (6)
SEG, 1993

6   Attitudes towards the Treaty of Versailles

Study the source below and then attempt *all* parts of the question.

'Germany is going to pay and I have no doubt that we will get everything out of her that you can squeeze out of a lemon, and a bit more. Not only all the gold Germany has got, but all her silver and jewels shall be handed over. All her pictures and libraries should be sold to the Allies and the proceeds used to pay reparations. I would strip Germany as she stripped Belgium.'

from a speech made in 1919 by Sir Eric Geddes, a British politician

(a) Does the source prove that in 1919 the British people wanted to punish Germany as severely as possible after the First World War? Explain your answer. (5)
(b) Many German people felt extremely bitter and angry about the terms of the Treaty of Versailles. Was this only because of the reparations referred to in the extract? Explain your answer. (8)
(c) 'The Treaty of Versailles was not fully carried out between 1919 and January 1933.'
Do you agree or disagree with this opinion? Explain your answer. (6)
(d) Hitler became Chancellor of Germany in January 1933. By the end of 1936 he had broken the Treaty of Versailles in a number of ways. Why did Britain and France fail to prevent the breaking of the Treaty? (6)
SEG, 1991

7   The League of Nations

The following sources give evidence about the search for security through the League of Nations.

Source A is part of the Covenant of the League of Nations, 1919.

SOURCE A

League members undertook the following obligations:

Art 10   to respect and preserve as against external aggression the territorial integrity and existing political independence of all members of the League.

Art 16   Should any member of the League resort to war in disregard of its covenants, it shall be deemed to have committed an act of war against all other members of the League, which hereby undertake immediately to subject it to the severence of all trade or financial relations... .

How did the members of the League of Nations expect to guarantee international security?

Source B is a 1920 cartoon on the American failure to join the League of Nations.

SOURCE B

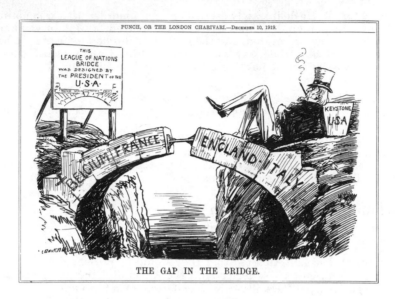

PUNCH, OR THE LONDON CHARIVARI.—December 10, 1919.

THIS LEAGUE OF NATIONS BRIDGE WAS DESIGNED BY THE PRESIDENT of the U·S·A·

THE GAP IN THE BRIDGE.

In Source C, the historian R Henig comments on the American failure to join the League of Nations.

R Henig *The Origins of the Second World War*, published 1985

SOURCE C

'The refusal of the United States Senate to ratify the Paris Peace Treaties, in which the League Covenant constituted the first twenty-six articles, meant the absence of the world's leading economic and political power from the League of Nations. The guarantee treaty of assistance promised to France also fell to the ground, unratified even by Britain whose participation had been made carefully conditional upon American ratification. France was left without the Rhine frontier and without powerful allies. The League was now her only hope of security, apart from alliances hastily concluded with Poland and Czechosolvakia. It must be strengthened and made to work; article 10 at least provided a foundation on which French delegates could build.'

How damaging to European security was the absence of the USA from the League of Nations?

(Note: For this question, you should write a short essay of several paragraphs.)

SCE, Credit Level, 1990

8   The League of Nations

Study Source A below and then answer all parts of the question.

SOURCE A

"THE STRENGTH OF A CHAIN IS THAT OF ITS WEAKEST LINK"

a British cartoon, (18 October 1935) drawn by David Low

The cartoon shows Italy (Mussolini) on the way to Abyssinia.
The main countries of the League of Nations, the Soviet Union (Litvinov), France (Laval) and Britain (Eden), are joined against him.

(a) When the League of Nations was formed in 1919, the Soviet Union and the United States were not members.
Were the reasons for this the same?
Explain your answer.   (6)

(b) When the League was formed, some countries became Permanent Members of the Council.
Why were they given this important position in the League?   (6)

(c) Is Source A useful as evidence about the problems facing the League in the 1930s?
Explain your answer.   (5)

(d) 'The Italian conquest of Abyssinia clearly showed that the League of Nations had no power.'
Do you agree or disagree with this statement?
Explain your answer.   (8)

SEG, 1993

9   Russia, 1924–53

Study Source A below and then answer **all** parts of the question.

SOURCE A: a British lawyer's opinion of Stalin's show trials

> Zinoviev and Kamenev admitted that they plotted to murder Kirov, Stalin and others. People who do not believe their confessions face a very great difficulty. For it follows that Stalin and others, including the judges and prosecutor, would themselves be guilty of a foul plot.
> But it is clear that the Russian judges and prosecutors have helped to make the Russian legal system among the best in the modern world.

from *The Zinoviev Trial*, (1936) by D.N. Pritt

(a) 'Source A is convincing proof that those accused in Stalin's purges must have been guilty.'
Do you agree or disagree with this statement?
Explain your answer.   (5)

(b) 'Stalin was certain to win the struggle for power with Trotsky.'
Do you agree or disagree with this statement?
Explain your answer.   (8)

(c) 'Stalin achieved very little. He was no more than a brutal dictator.'
Do you agree or disagree with this statement?
Explain your answer.   (12)

SEG, 1993

10 Germany, 1918–45

Study the source below and then attempt *all* parts of the question.

Seats held by the Nazi Party in the Reichstag (Parliament), 1920–32			Unemployment, 1929–1932		
1920		0			
1924	May	32			
1924	December	14			
1928		13	1929	September	1.3 millions
1930		107	1931	August	4.0 millions
1932	July	230	1932	February	6.0 millions

from official figures

(a) Hitler made his first attempt to seize power in November 1923. Why did this seem to be a good time to choose for such an attempt? (7)

(b) Why did the Nazis make very little progress between 1923 and 1929? (6)

(c) Between 1929 and 1932, support for the Nazis increased enormously and they became the largest party in the Reichstag. Why did this change come about? (7)

(d) 'These statistics provide solid facts and are therefore of great use to historians in explaining the rise of the Nazis.' Do you agree or disagree with this view? Explain your answer. (5)

SEG, 1991

11 The USA, 1917–32

Study Source A below and then answer all parts of the question

SOURCE A: part of a crowd demonstrating against Prohibition

photograph taken in 1931 in Newark, New Jersey

(a) Why was Prohibition introduced in the USA in 1920? (5)

(b) Does Source A prove that in 1931 the American people wanted Prohibition to end? Explain your answer. (5)

(c) 'Popular demand was not the only reason why Prohibition was abandoned in 1933.' Do you agree or disagree with this statement? Explain your answer. (5)

(d) 'The activities of the Ku Klux Klan showed that racism was very strong in the USA during the 1920s and 1930s.' Do you agree or disagree with this statement? Explain your answer. (5)

(e) 'In the 1920s the USA was a lawless society.' Do you agree or disagree with this statement? Explain your answer. (5)

SEG, 1993

12 The USA, 1919–45

Study the source below and then attempt *all* parts of the question.

photograph taken in New York, October 1920

(a) The American economy grew very quickly during the 1920s.
How far was this growth caused by government policies? (10)

(b) How valuable is this photograph as evidence of the effects of the Wall Street Crash in 1929? (5)

(c) In the years 1929–32 the Republicans were unable to control the financial and economic crisis. Why was this? (10)

SEG, 1991

13 International relations, 1945–65

Study Source A below and then answer all parts of the question

SOURCE A

"AND HOW ARE WE FEELING TO-DAY?"

a British cartoon, (4 February 1945) drawn by B. Partridge

The cartoon shows the world as the patient and Churchill, Roosevelt and Stalin as doctors. The war against Germany had nearly ended.

(a) 'The cartoon was drawn to show that, at the time, Britain, the United States and the Soviet Union were working together.'
Do you agree or disagree with this opinion?
Explain your answer. (5)

(b) Just over a year later, in March 1946, Churchill made an important speech. In this speech, Churchill referred to an Iron Curtain which had cut Europe in two.
Why, by this time, had the Superpowers become more suspicious of each other? (6)

(c) Stalin died in 1953.
Did Stalin's death make any difference to relations between the Superpowers in the 1950s?
Explain your answer. (6)

(d) 'Until the mid-1950s the Superpowers were mainly concerned with Europe.
For the next ten years (1955–65) they were mainly concerned with the world outside Europe.'
Do you agree or disagree with these statements?
Explain your answer.   (8)

SEG, 1993

14 Relations between the Superpowers, 1945–60

Study the source below and then attempt all parts of the question.

> 'American military intervention in Korea in the summer of 1950 made an already tense situation even
> worse. The South Koreans, backed by the United States, started a civil war in June 1950. This turned
> Korea into an area of fierce international fighting. The South Koreans failed, however, to achieve the aims
> of their American masters. Soviet and Chinese assistance to the People's Democratic Republic of Korea
> spoiled the plan to take over North Korea.'

> from Vadim Nekrasov (a Soviet writer), *The Roots of European Security* (1984).

(a) The source says the situation between the Superpowers was already tense when war broke out in Korea. Why was
the situation already so tense by the Summer of 1950?   (8)
(b) The source above is clearly biased against the South Koreans. Does this mean that it has no value for a study of the
outbreak of war in Korea? Explain your answer.   (5)
(c) When the Korean War broke out, the South Koreans received massive support from the United States. Why was the
United States so ready to give this support in 1950?   (4)
(d) The fighting in Korea was ended with a ceasefire in 1953. Did relations between the Superpowers improve during
the rest of the 1950s? Explain your answer.   (8)

SEG, 1991

15 India

Study the source below and then attempt all parts of the question.

In the 1930s, Michael Carritt was a District Officer, a British local official in India. In this extract, written 50 years
later, he remembers his time in India.

> 'It was the effect of a series of shocks to my conscience that produced a change in my attitude to the British
> Raj in India: the beating-up of whole villages organized by police after the murder of a District Officer; the
> daily misery of dealing with the detention camps; the thickening atmosphere of fear and hostility between
> the communities.
>   All the fine and caring work of many hundreds of Indian civil servants for over 150 years was a front
> behind which the Raj encouraged exploitation on an ever bigger scale.'

> adapted from an article by Michael Carritt in *The Guardian*, (September 1985)

(a) The source refers to 'fear and hostility between the communities'. How did this fear and hostility make it more
difficult to achieve independence?   (5)
(b) The source also refers to 'the fine and caring work' of civil servants in British India. Was Britain responsible for 'fine
and caring' work in India? Explain your answer.   (6)
(c) Gandhi was a leading opponent of British rule. Did his opposition have much effect? Give reasons for your answer.
                                                                                                       (8)
(d) Would this source be useful to an historian studying the causes of the Indian revolt against the British in the 1930s
and 1940s? Explain your answer.   (6)

SEG, 1991

16 The USA, 1945–92

Study Source A below and then answer all parts of the question.

SOURCE A: Kennedy and civil rights

> 'Kennedy proposed his civil rights laws to Congress in February 1963. The liberals condemned them as not
> going far enough. Mass black demonstrations soon began in Birmingham, Alabama. These were in support
> of the proposed new civil rights laws. Before the end of the summer there were peaceful black protests in
> over 800 towns and cities, including Washington DC. The police often used dogs and firehoses against
> them. In June the government strengthened the proposed new laws. But white opposition to these
> proposals developed in response to increasing black pressure. Even in 1963 the brutal way in which some
> peaceful demonstrations were broken up made headlines around the world.'

> from *A New History of the Unites States*, (1968) by W. Miller, published by Bantam Doubleday Dell

(a) 'Source A proves that the civil rights proposals had no chance of becoming law in the mid-1960s.'
Do you agree or disagree with this statement?
Explain your answer.   (5)
(b) 'During the years 1945–74 the coloured people of the USA were second-class citizens.'
Do you agree or disagree with this statement?
Explain your answer.   (7)
(c) During the 1960s the Women's Liberation Movement claimed that women were second-class citizens.
Do you agree or disagree that they were?
Explain your answer.   (5)
(d) How far did Presidents Kennedy and Johnson give their support to the aims of the Civil Rights and Women's
Liberation Movements?
Explain your answer.   (8)

SEG, 1993

17 South Africa and Apartheid

Study the source below and then attempt all parts of the question.

This cartoon shows Dr Verwoerd, the South African Prime Minister, in the deck chair. It appeared in the Daily Mirror just after Dr Verwoerd had made a speech in which he said, 'Apartheid is better described as a policy of good neighbours'.

(a) Is this cartoon useful as historical evidence? Explain your answer. (5)

(b) How might Dr Verwoerd have explained his use of the words 'good neighbours' to describe the policy of Apartheid? (4)

(c) Very few, if any, non-white South Africans have agreed that they were treated as 'good neighbours'. They have always been strongly opposed to apartheid. Why is this so? (8)

(d) Has the policy of Apartheid affected South Africa's relations with other countries? Explain your answer. (8)

SEG, 1991

18 Population growth: a Third World problem

Study Source A below and then answer all parts of the question

SOURCE A: the population of Britain and Bangladesh, 1950–2000

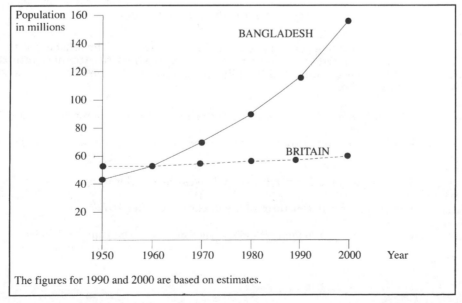

The figures for 1990 and 2000 are based on estimates.

from a computer database, (1989)

(a) 'Source A is based on figures which are readily available.
Therefore it is reliable as evidence.'
Do you agree or disagree with this statement?
Explain your answer.　(5)

(b) Source A shows that the population of Bangladesh increased a great deal between 1950 and 1980.
During this time the population of Britain changed very little.
Why has there been such a difference in the rate of population growth?　(6)

(c) 'For countries with a rapidly growing population, the greatest problem is to find enough food.'
Do you agree or disagree with this statement?
Explain your answer.　(8)

(d) In 1950 there was little international concern about the problems of countries like Bangladesh.
By 1980 there was far more concern.
Why did this change happen?　(6)

SEG, 1993

47.4 Questions Based on a Number of Sources of Various Kinds Requiring Candidates to Evaluate and Interpret the Material

1　Bismarck and Germany, 1870–14

Study sources A, B, C, D and E and then answer questions (a) to (e) which follow.

SOURCE A:

'In the palace of Versailles ... the German Empire was solemnly proclaimed on January 18th ... At a quarter past twelve His Majesty entered the hall ... the King then walked up to where the colours were displayed, and read the document proclaiming the German empire, the grand duke of Baden stepped forth and shouted "Long live his Majesty the Emperor!" '

SOURCE B: (a painting of the time showing Wilhelm I being proclaimed Emperor of Germany).

SOURCE C: (from Bismarck's memoirs).

'It has always been my ideal aim, after we had established our unity, to win the confidence not only of the smaller European states, but also of the Great Powers, and to convince them that German policy would be first and foremost peaceful, now that our nation was united.'

SOURCE D: (from an essay entitled *Our Empire*, published in Germany in 1886).

'... Prussia occupies in reality a position altogether different from that of the other states of the empire. Prussia alone remains a free state and cannot be forced to carry out her imperial duties by an order. Only the emperor can issue such orders and the emperor is the King of Prussia.'

SOURCE E: (a German recalls his schooldays in the 1870s).

'The German victory (of 1871) led to a general adoption of Prussian ideals. The schools felt the first results of this ... When the teacher entered the classroom the boys stood stiffly to attention until the command 'Sit' rang out. Simple words, good nature and friendly encouragement ... were regarded as soft ... Behind the teacher was the Prussian army.'

(a) Study source A.
What can you learn from this source about the way in which Wilhelm I became Emperor of Germany?　(2)
(b) Study sources A and B.
Do these sources provide a full and reliable account of the events surrounding the setting up of the German Empire?
Explain your answer.　(5)
(c) Study source C.
In what ways does this source help you to understand Bismarck's policies for Germany?　(3)
(d) Study sources D and E.
In what ways do these sources present similar pictures of life in Germany after 1871?　(4)
(e) Study all the sources.
How useful are these sources in helping you to understand the significance of the year 1871 in German history?　(6)

LEAG, 1990

2 Superpower Relations, 1945–50

Study Sources A, B, C and D, which are about the Berlin blockade, and then answer questions (**a**) to (**e**) which follow:

SOURCE A: (adapted from a school textbook, 1984)

> 'Stalin closed all access to Berlin. He hoped to force an Allied retreat, but Truman was firm: "We are going to stay!" he said. The Americans thought of using their army and air force, and even the atom bomb, but decided to ferry supplies into West Berlin by air.
>
> The crisis came in January 1949 when the western city was down to one week's supply of coal and three weeks' supply of food. By March though, the Americans and British were flying in 8,000 tons per day and the crisis was over.
>
> Stalin stopped short of violence. He did not order any planes to be shot down. In May 1949 Stalin called off the blockade.'

SOURCE B: (a cartoon from a British magazine, July 1948)

SOURCE C: (written by an inhabitant of Berlin, June 1948)

> 'Then the day came when the airlift started. Father didn't believe it. He rode to Tempelhof airport on his bicycle. He was away a long time. When he came home, he said "They're actually doing it. They're flying food into Berlin. But they won't be able to bring in enough. Think of this huge city with its millions of people!" '

SOURCE D: (a photograph of a U.S. plane being loaded with supplies for Berlin, 1948)

(**a**) Study Source A.

According to this source, what choices of action did the United States consider? (3)

(**b**) Study Sources A and B.

Does the evidence of Source B support the account given in Source A? Give reasons for your answer. (4)

(**c**) Study Source B

'Source B is a British cartoon and so is sure to be biased against Stalin.' With reference to the source, explain whether you agree or disagree with this statement. (4)

(d) Study Sources A, C and D.

Are sources written after the event, like Source A, of more use to someone studying the Berlin airlift, than are Sources C and D? Give reasons for your answer by referring to the sources. (4)

(e) Use your own knowledge to explain why there was a crisis concerning Berlin in 1948–9. (5)

ULEAC, 1992

3 International relations 1870–1914

Look carefully at Sources A to E. Then answer *all* the questions.

SOURCE A:

i (The following extract is from a speech made by Lord Salisbury in 1888.)

'We belong to the community of Europe and we have no right to avoid those duties to look after the interests of the whole community. There is a big difference between trying to get on well with your neighbours and that mood of superior isolation which we proudly like to call 'non-intervention.'

ii A recent book puts forward Lord Salisbury's view about alliances with other countries in Europe.

'Lord Salisbury, the British Prime Minister, believed that no government based on a parliamentary democracy could enter into a permanent alliance with a foreign power. He said this because a later government under a different political party could ignore the promises made by an earlier government.'

SOURCE B: (The following cartoon was printed in a British magazine on Christmas Day, 1901. Britannia and Colonia represent Britain and her Empire. The other three figures represent Germany, France and Russia.)

BRITANNIA: "After all, my dear, we needn't trouble ourselves about the others.
COLONIA: "No; we can always dance together, you and I!"

SOURCE C: (A recent book looks at relations between Britain and Germany at the beginning of this century.)

'Germany produced half as much steel as Britain in 1860, was level by 1900, and was to produce twice as much by 1914. So, although Germany was Britain's biggest customer, she was also regarded as Britain's biggest rival in trade. Therefore, Britain was ready to welcome friendly approaches made by France in 1903.'

SOURCE D: (A recent historian describes Britain's diplomatic position in 1914.)

'There can be no doubt that Britain's diplomatic position in 1914 was dangerously misunderstood. British military and naval officers expected to be drawn into a war between France and Germany; but many politicians and the general public were unaware of the obligations Britain had agreed with France.'

SOURCE E: (Part of a note written during a Cabinet meeting on 30 July 1914 by the Prime Minister, Herbert Asquith, to a close personal friend, Venetia Stanley.)

'We have no obligation to help France or Russia ... We mustn't forget the tie created by our friendship with France ... It is against British interests that France should be destroyed as a great power.'

(a) Read source C.

Give *two* other ways in which Britain considered Germany a 'rival'. (2)

(b) Read source C.

    i   What is the name of the 'agreement' which was made as a result of 'friendly approaches' made by France to Britain in 1903? (1)

    ii   Which other country joined Britain and France in this 'agreement' in 1907? (1)

(c) Read source A **i** and source A **ii**.

What similarities and differences are there in the statements about Salisbury's foreign policy given in these two sources? (6)

(d) Read sources A **i** and E.

Source A i and source E are statements made by British prime ministers. Does this mean they are of equal value to the historian? Explain your answer. (8)

(e) Look at *all* the sources.

'Britain's policy of "Splendid Isolation" only existed in popular imagination, not in practice.' How far do Sources A to E show this to be true? Explain your answer fully. (12)

MEG, 1990

4 The First World War

Look carefully at Sources A to E which refer to the Battle of Passchendaele (3rd Ypres), 31 July to 12 November 1917. Then answer all the questions.

SOURCE A

An entry dated 19 June 1917 from the diary of Field Marshal Haig, Commander-in-Chief of British forces on the Western Front. He had met the War Cabinet in London to discuss a new offensive.

> 'The members of the War Cabinet asked me many questions, all tending to show that each of them was more pessimistic than the other. Lloyd George seemed to believe the decisive moment of the war would be 1918. Until then we ought to do little or nothing except support Italy with guns and gunners. I strongly argued that Germany was nearer to her end than they seemed to think. I stated that Germany was within six months of the total exhaustion of her available manpower if the fighting continues at its present level on the Western Front.'

SOURCE B

An extract from an account of the Battle of Passchendaele published in 1931 and written by General Gough. Gough was a British general during the battle.

> 'The state of the ground was frightful on 17 August. The task of bringing up supplies and ammunition, or moving or firing the guns, which had often sunk up to their axles, was a fearful strain on the officers and men. When it came to an infantry attack across the water-logged shell-holes, movement was so slow and tiring that only the shortest advance could be considered. I informed the Commander-in-Chief that success was not possible, or would be too costly, under such conditions, and advised that the attack should now be abandoned.'

SOURCE C

A photograph taken in the battle area on 1 August 1917

SOURCE D

Two differing views of the battle

(i) *An extract from the diary of an important New Zealand officer whose men fought in the battle. It was written after the battle.*

> 'My opinion is that the generals who direct these battles do not know of the conditions, mud, cold, rain and lack of shelter for the men. The Germans are not so played out as our High Command think. Exhausted men struggling through mud cannot compete against dry men with machine-guns.'

(ii) *A telegram sent from Lloyd George to Field Marshal Haig on 16 October 1917.*

> 'The War Cabinet desires to congratulate you upon the achievements of the British Armies in the great battle which has been raging since 31 July. Starting from positions in which the enemy had every advantage and despite being hampered by most unfavourable weather, you and your men have nevertheless driven the enemy back with skill and courage and have filled the enemy with alarm. I am personally glad to pass this message to you, and to your gallant troops, and to state again my confidence in your leadership.'

SOURCE E

A comment on the Battle of Passchendaele taken from a German history of the war published in the 1920s.

> 'Above everything else the battle had used up German strength. Losses had been so high that they could no longer be replaced and the fighting strength of battalions was further reduced. Our enemies were well-prepared, greater in number and brave. However they had been able to achieve little, partly because of the bad weather conditions which made movement extremely difficult. But water and mud were no less a disadvantage to the defenders. These conditions, more than the bloody fighting, led to a rapid wearing out of the troops.

(a) Look at Source C.

Why was there so much mud in the battle area?   (2)

(b) Read Source D(ii).

State two advantages which German soldiers had in the battle.   (2)

(c) Read Source A.

In what ways may Haig's account of his meeting with the War Cabinet be biased? Explain your answer.   (6)

(d) Read Source D(ii) and Source E.

Which of these two sources gives the more reliable view of the battle? Explain your answer. (8)

(e) Look at all the sources.

In his war memoirs written in the 1930s Lloyd George called Passchendaele 'the senseless campaign'.

Do these sources show his view to be true? Explain your answer fully. (12)

MEG, 1992

5 The Civil War in Russia, 1918–21

Study sources A to G and then attempt *all* parts of the question.

To answer the questions, use *only* the information given in the sources.

In your answers, you should refer to the sources by letter.

(a) Is source A more friendly towards Denikin than source B? Explain your answer. (3)

(b) Study source C. Why do you think Trotsky had so much to say about England? (4)

(c) 'All the written sources (C, D, E and G) are biased to some extent.'

Do you agree or disagree with this opinion? Explain your answer, referring to these four sources. (6)

(d) 'Sources A to G are all equally valuable to historians.'

Do you agree or disagree with this opinion? Explain your answer, referring to each of the sources. (8)

(e) 'Sources A to G show that the Whites had no chance of winning the Civil War.'

Using only sources A to G, explain whether you agree with this opinion. (9)

SEG, 1991

SOURCE A: (General Denikin inspecting his British-trained tank corps in the White Russian army.)

a photograph from the *Illustrated London News*, 1919

SOURCE B: (General Denikin)

a Russian cartoon from the Civil War

SOURCE C: (Trotsky's appeal to the Red Army)

'Red fighters, on all fronts you are meeting with the hostile English. It is from English guns that counter-revolutionary troops fire at you. The prisoners you take have English equipment on them. Women and children are murdered and mutilated by English airmen and English high explosives. English ships shell our coasts.

But even now, at the moment of the most bitter fight against England's puppet, the White general Yudenich, I call upon you: never forget that this is not the only England that exists. Apart from the England of profits, bribery, violence and bloodthirstiness, there exists the England of the labouring classes, full of ideals and international working-class solidarity. It is the England of the Stock Exchange, the vile and honourless England, that fights against us. Toiling England, its people, is with us.'

from Trotsky, *Order 159 to the Red Army and Navy*, 1919

SOURCE D: (a Russian historian praises the Bolsheviks' efforts in the Civil War)

'The working people performed miracles of achievement on the battlefronts for several years. There were desperate shortages of arms, equipment and food. The people had been exhausted to the limit by several years of bloody world war. On every battlefront the Red Army had to fight against an enemy who was better equipped, better trained and superior in numbers.'

from Y Kukushkin, *History of the USSR*, 1981

SOURCE E: (a Russian historian comments on the Bolshevik war effort)

'The Bolsheviks had learned the art of war. At one of the very first sessions of the Council of Defence, a decree was issued: "The Council of Defence approves the plan of forming an army with a total strength of 1,500,000 men and 300,000 horses". It is difficult even to imagine the poverty and ruin facing Lenin and his comrades-in-arms in their task of building a mass army and organizing its supply of weapons, clothing, equipment, and food.'

from an article by *S V Liptsky*, 1968

SOURCE F: (Russia during the Civil War)

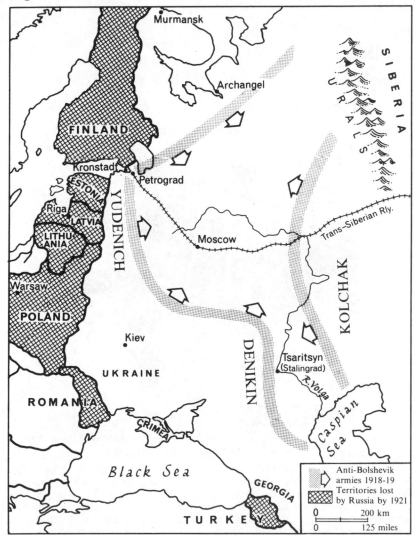

from R D Cornwell, *World History in the Twentieth Century*, 1969

SOURCE G: (a British historian gives his explanation of the Bolshevik success)

'The Bolsheviks had better lines of communication. Trotsky organized and controlled the Red Army with energy and ability. The Whites were divided into too many political groups. Western help for the Whites was half-hearted and was soon withdrawn, but it did give the Bolsheviks the advantage of nationalist support. The peasants had little enthusiasm for either side. They were less opposed to the Bolsheviks, who had at least given them land, while the Whites said they would restore the landlords.'

from R D Cornwell, *World History in the Twentieth Century*, 1969
SEG, 1991

6   Russia, 1917–39

(a) Study the following statements and answer each of the questions which follow by writing the number of the speaker in the box provided.

Speaker 1:   Our aims are simple. We want three things – land, peace and bread.

Speaker 2:   Let us look to the achievements of Stakhanov and follow his example.

Speaker 3:   Now that the Duma has been granted, our hopes have been realized.

Speaker 4:   Father Gapon was our leader. We were dressed in our best clothes and many of our members carried pictures of the Tsar.

Speaker 5:   We gained our land at the time of the Revolution and have no desire to lose everything now.

Speaker 6:   We are proud to be members of the CHEKA and to have helped to defeat the Whites.

Speaker 7:   Our friend, Gregory Rasputin, is our one hope. Russia will not be blessed if we fail to listen to his advice.

Which speaker –

i   is probably a kulak?

ii   must have been in the secret police?

iii   would have suffered from the introduction of collectivization?

iv   supports a parliamentary system of government?

v   best represents the view of Tsarina Alexandra?

vi   would most likely have supported Stalin's Five-Year Plans?

vii   best puts forward the view of Lenin in 1917?

viii was at 'Bloody Sunday' in 1905?

ix   most probably fought in the Civil War?

x   would definitely have been against the Bolshevik Party?   (5)

(b) Study the sources below and then answer the questions which follow.

SOURCE A: (A French cartoon published in the 1930s.)

The banner held by the Russian citizen reads, 'We are really happy'

SOURCE B: (From a history text book by Stalin, used in Russian schools, 1938.)

'In 1937 new factors were discovered regarding the terrible crimes of the Bukharin-Trotsky gang. The trials showed that these dregs of humanity, these enemies of the people, had been plotting against Lenin, the Party and the Soviet State ever since the early days of the Revolution. They worked as spies in the pay of foreign powers working to assist foreign military intervention to prepare the way for the break-up of the USSR. They were wreckers who sought to destroy the gains of the workers and the collective farmers and to restore capitalist slavery to the country. The Soviet court sentenced these traitors and the Soviet people approved of their execution.'

SOURCE C: (Timechart of the 'Purges' 1934–38)

1934 – Kirov, the Leningrad Party Secretary, shot dead. Wholesale purge of Bolshevik party ordered.

1936 – Show Trials. Kamanev and Zinoviev and other Bolshevik leaders executed.

1937 – Leading Army and Navy Commanders tried and executed.

1938 – Bukharin, Rykov, Yagoda and other leading Bolsheviks tried and executed. Those on trial were accused of plots to murder Lenin and Stalin, spying for Germany and Japan, plans to sabotage the Russian economy by attacking factories and railways. All the accused confessed their guilt.

SOURCE D: (From an historian writing in 1989.)

'By 1940 every important member of the Bolshevik Party from Lenin's era, except one, had been eliminated. Old heroes of the 1917 Revolution confessed in open court to a whole series of unbelievable crimes from trying to poison Stalin to plotting Lenin's murder, from spying for Nazi Germany to sabotaging Russian industry.'

i What evidence is there in the cartoon in source A to indicate that it is referring to life in the USSR? (2)

ii Explain the meaning of the cartoon in source A and say why it might be thought to be anti-communist. (5)

iii Compare sources B and C. How far are they in agreement about the purges that took place in the USSR in the 1930s? Give reasons for your answer. (5)

iv What were the 'Show Trials' mentioned in source C and why were they so called? (2)

v Name the Russian leader responsible for the purges and Show Trials mentioned in the sources. (1)

vi Using the information in the sources and your knowledge of the period, explain the reasons why the purges were carried out. (5)

NEA, 1990

7 Stalin's Russia

Study the following sources carefully. Use the information to help you complete the exercises which follow.

(a) Stalin was determined to make Soviet Russia one of the strongest of industrial nations.

	1928	1933	1937
Electricity (100 m. kwts.)	5.1	13.4 (17.0)	36.2 (38.0)
Coal (m. tonnes)	35.4	64.3 (68.0)	128.0 (152.5)
Steel (m. tonnes)	4.0	5.9 (8.3)	17.7 (17.0)
Oil (m. tonnes)	11.7	21.4 (19.0)	28.5 (46.5)

Soviet industrial production, 1928–1937
(Targets are shown in brackets)

What measures did Stalin take to improve industry?

(b) To feed this new industrial nation, Soviet agriculture had to be improved.

A group of peasants carrying a banner with the inscription, 'We demand collectivisation and the liquidisation of the kulaks as a class', 1931

How did Stalin reorganize Soviet Russia's farms?

(c) There was much opposition to the agricultural reorganization ordered by Stalin.

'A middle-aged peasant, his face black and blue and his clothes ripped, was led off by two secret police. His grief-stricken wife stood outside her home. The woman held a flaming sheaf of grain in her hands. She tossed the burning sheaf on the thatched roof of her house which burst into flames. "Infidels! Murderers!" the woman was shrieking. "We worked all our lives for our house. You won't have it."'

Eye-witness account of a scene in one village (1930)

Why was Stalin's agricultural policy unpopular?

(d) In spite of opposition, Stalin was ruthless in forcing through his industrial and agricultural policies.

'In the 1930s Stalin was systematically slaughtering anyone who incurred his displeasure or his suspicion. The dark record, which still awaits full disclosure in the Soviet Union, has been carefully analysed by Western scholars. On a sober estimate, about 700,000 people were executed and 12 million died in the camps, where the average survival was two years.'

R. Cornwell, *The Independent* (7 November 1987)

How did Stalin deal with people who opposed him?

(e) Were Stalin's economic policies good or bad for the Russian people? Explain your answer fully.

WJEC, 1993

8 The League of Nations

Study sources A, B, C and D and then answer the questions which follow.

SOURCE A: (Membership of the League – the Great Powers)

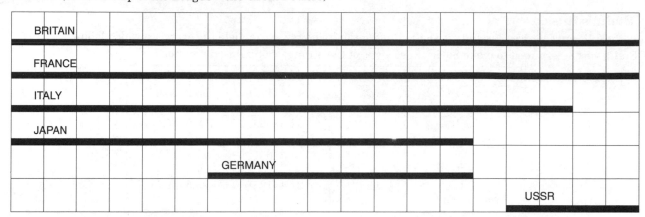

	1919	1920	1921	1922	1923	1924	1925	1926	1927	1928	1929	1930	1931	1932	1933	1934	1935	1936	1937

BRITAIN
FRANCE
ITALY
JAPAN
GERMANY
USSR

SOURCE B: (The Covenant of the League of Nations, 1919 – Article 16.)

'Should any member of the League resort to war in disregard of its covenants, it shall be deemed to have committed an act of war against all members of the League, which immediately undertake to end all trade and financial relations with the covenant-breaking state.

It shall be the duty of the Council, in such cases, to recommend to all governments what effective military, naval or airforces the members of the League shall contribute to the armed force to be used by the League.'

SOURCE C: (A cartoon published in the British magazine Punch in 1936)

MORAL PERSUASION
The Rabbit: "My power and sanctions being practically nil, it remains for me to control him by the hypnotic power of my eye."

SOURCE D: (Benito Mussolini speaking in May 1936)

'We have won a great victory. Italy has her Empire – a Fascist Empire. An Empire of peace, because Italy is a peace-loving nation and she decided upon war only when it was forced upon her.'

(a) One of the Great Powers is not included in source A because it never joined the League of Nations. Name this great power. (1)

(b) Explain the problems caused for the League by its changing membership. (6)

(c) Use the information in source B to explain what League members could do against a country that 'resorted to war in disregard of its covenants.' (4)

(d) Explain the meaning of the cartoon in source C. (7)

(e) 'The criticisms of the League, given in source C, are largely supported by the information provided in Article 16 in source B.' Give reasons why you agree or disagree with this statement. (7)

(f) 'Source D is biased and therefore of little value to an historian studying the League of Nations.' How far do you agree or disagree with this statement? Given reasons for your answer. (5)

NEA, 1991

9 Hitler's Germany, 1933–1939

Study carefully the sources which follow, and then answer the questions which are based upon them.

SOURCE A

A Nazi badge; the words read, 'He who buys from a Jew is a traitor to his people.'

SOURCE B

'Section 4, 1929–33. Germany's Misery and Want.

The period of inflation was noted for the inflation swindlers and Jewish profiteers. What a good time the foreigners (Eastern Jews) had; how they bought German land.

Section 5, 1933. Germany awakes.

What does our Chancellor Hitler want? He wants to lock up the Godless Communists. He wants to drive out the Jews. He wants to give every German work.'

Chapter summaries from a German history textbook for schools (1934)

SOURCE C

'1. Marriages between Jews and citizens of German blood are forbidden.

2. Jews are not permitted to employ female citizens of German blood under forty-five years of age as domestic help.

3. No Jew can be a German citizen. The right to vote on any political question is not extended to him.'

From the Nuremberg Laws (1935)

SOURCE D

'Berlin had (in 1933) 32% Jewish chemists, 48% Jewish doctors, 50% Jewish lawyers, 8.5% Jewish newspaper editors … No people on earth with any pride in itself could put up with such domination of many professions by members of a completely alien race.'

Dr. Gross, Head of the Reich Bureau for Enlightenment on Population Policy and Racial Welfare – quoted in a book published for British readers by the German Embassy in London (1938)

SOURCE E

'(The region of) Oldenburg had the distinction of being the first Nazi state government, even before Hitler came to power in Berlin. It is strange to recall, however, that there was very little active anti-Semitism, at least until 1938. The Jews – small shop-keepers, farmers, cattle-dealers and breeders – were submerged in the local population so far as their residences and occupations were concerned.'

Joe de Haas (now living in England) remembering the Germany of his early days in an article in *The Guardian* (26 June 1985)

(a) Give *one* reason why Source A may be said to suggest that life was difficult for the Jews in Nazi Germany. (1)

(b) Give *one* reason why Source E may be said to suggest that life was still not difficult for Jews in Nazi Germany. (1)

(c) What is the meaning of the phrase underlined in Source B? (1)

(d) How does Source E contradict Source C? (3)

(e) How reliable is Source E as evidence? Give reasons for your answer. (4)

(f) Which *one* of the sources do you regard as being the most biased? Explain your answer. (6)

(g) i What evidence do you find *in the sources provided* which would help in a description of the situation in which German Jews found themselves between 1933 and 1938? (6)

ii What other *types of evidence* would you have wished to examine, and why? (3)

WJEC, 1993

10 The United States of America, 1931–39

Read the following information and sources carefully and then answer the questions that follow.

After the boom times of the 1920s, the USA was affected by the economic problems of the 1930s.

SOURCE A

'We can say with satisfaction of this period of nearly twenty months of continuous economic decline that we have had fewer strikes and lock-outs than in normal times; that we have had no mob violence worth noting; and with only local and unnecessary exceptions there has been no starvation.'

President Herbert Hoover (May 1931)

SOURCE B

'We got more wheat, more corn, more food, more cotton, more money in the banks, more everything in the world than any nation that ever lived ever had, yet we are starving to death. We are the first nation in the history of the world to go to the poorhouse in an automobile.'

The American humorist, Will Rogers (November 1931)

SOURCE C

'I remember it was fun. It was fun going to the soup-line 'cause we all went down the road, and we laughed and we played. The only thing we felt was that we were hungry and we were going to get food. Nobody made us feel ashamed.'

Peggy Terry talking about her childhood in America in the early thirties, quoted in Stud Terkel, *Hard Times* (1970)

SOURCE D

'Oh no, the Depression was not a romantic time. It was a time of terrible suffering. The contradictions were so obvious it didn't take a very bright person to realise something was terribly wrong. Have you ever seen a child with rickets? No proteins. No milk – and the companies pouring milk into the gutters. People with nothing to wear – and they were ploughing up cotton. People with nothing to eat – and they slaughtered pigs.'

Virginia Durr, quoted in Stud Terkel, *Hard Times* (1970)

SOURCE E

Average annual income per head in the USA

1928	$643
1929	$682
1930	$621
1931	$580

Bernard Barker, *The Great Crash* (1979)

SOURCE F

'I never saw one bread line, never in New York. If they were there, they were in Harlem or down in Greenwich Village ... To me, the '30s was a glamorous, glittering moment.'

A high-society photographer from the wealthy district of Manhattan, New York

SOURCE G

Some of the 10,000 poor and unemployed waiting in the streets of New York for a free meal, Christmas 1931

(a) Which of the above sources suggest:
   i   that things were not as bad as all that in the Depression;   (1)
   ii that things were very bad in the Depression;   (1)
   iii that there was plenty of food available, but it was not getting to the people?   (1)
(b) Can a photograph, such as Source G, be always regarded as completely reliable?
Explain your answer.   (4)
(c) Sources C and D are memories of individuals recorded long after the event. How useful is such evidence to the historian?   (4)

(d) i How do Sources A and F support each other? (3)
ii How do Sources C and D contradict each other? (3)
(e) *Having studied all the evidence*, was the American Depression as bad as it is usually described? Explain your answer fully.

WJEC, 1993

11 China, 1914–49

Study sources A, B, C and D which relate to the Long March, and then answer questions **(a)** to **(d)** which follow:

SOURCE A: (adapted from a book about the Long March written in 1971)

'The 'historian' of the Long March, Hsu Meng-chui, said "We lost nearly all our official documents in the Grasslands and in crossing rivers. We also burned many documents that could not be conveniently carried." Much weight had therefore to be put on the memory of the men involved, and that is only too human. General Pen Teh-huai was once explaining how they planned a breakthrough in one of the Encirclement campaigns, when he paused suddenly. He had made a mistake. The battle he was describing was a quite different one, in Szechuan, several hundred miles away. "There were so many battles", he remembered.

Since 1935 there has been a gradual process of 'tidying up' history on the part of the Chinese Communists, whose interest lies in portraying the Long March as a fully successful result of perfect decision-making on the part of the present leadership.'

SOURCE B: (from a description of his experiences in the Long March by Tung Pi-wu. Here he remembers the Great Snow Mountain)

'So we started straight up the mountain, heading for a pass near the summit. Heavy fogs swirled up, there was a high wind and half way up it began to rain. As we climbed higher and higher we were caught in a terrible hailstorm, and the air became so thin we could hardly breathe at all. Speech was completely impossible and the cold so dreadful that our breath froze and our hands and lips turned blue. Men and animals staggered and fell into chasms and disappeared forever.

Those who sat down to rest or relieve themselves froze to death on the spot. Exhausted political workers encouraged men by sign and touch to continue moving, indicating that the pass was just ahead.'

SOURCE C: (from a speech made by [Mao Zedong Mao Tse-tung] in 1935)

'We say that the Long March is the first of its kind ever recorded in history ... For twelve months we were under daily reconnaissance and bombing from the air by scores of planes; we were encircled, pursued, obstructed and intercepted on the ground by a big force of several thousand men; we encountered untold difficulties and great obstacles on the way, but by keeping our two feet going we swept across a distance of more than 20,000 li* ... Well, has there ever been in history a long march like ours? No, never. The Long March also ... proclaims that the Red Army is an army of heroes, and that the imperialists and their jackals, Chiang Kai-shek and the like, are perfect non-entities. The Long March also has sown seeds in many provinces, which will bear fruit and yield a crop in future.'

*20,000 li = 6,000 miles

SOURCE D: (a picture showing an incident from the Long March)

Study sources A, B and C.

(a) i Using the sources and your own knowledge, explain the causes of the Long March. (5)
ii Use the sources and your own knowledge to explain the effects of the Long March on the conflict between the Communists and the Guomindang (Kuomintang). (5)
(b) Study source A.
According to the author of source A, what are the difficulties facing the historian studying the Long March? (3)

(c) Study sources B and C.

To what extent do these sources demonstrate the difficulties referred to in source A? Refer in detail to each source in your answer.   (4)

(d) Do you think that source D is of any value to historians studying the Long March? Explain your answer.   (3)

LEAG, 1990

12 The USA, 1932–34

Study sources A, B, C and D and then answer the questions which follow.

SOURCE A: (A flow chart explaining the New Deal.)

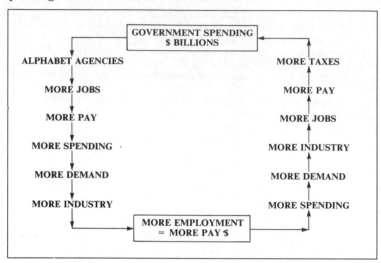

SOURCE B: (A cartoon published during the New Deal.)

SOURCE C: (An American businessman remembers the New Deal.)

'The New Deal hurt us. The President was a rich man's son and he betrayed his own class by wasting billions of dollars of our money on his schemes. He didn't understand that when you give to people you hurt them. We had the soup lines and the depression because people lost confidence in themselves. Welfare kills a man's spirit because it makes him lose the will to fend for himself. If you want a dog to hunt you have to let him go hungry. If you want a man to be successful, he needs to face the setbacks of life. You're free to eat if you can pay for your food and free to starve if you don't pay for it.'

SOURCE D: (A reporter talking about the New Deal in 1936.)

'Everyone is against the New Deal except the voters.'

(a) According to source A, what action needed to be taken by the government to overcome the depression?   (1)

(b) Explain source A and show how the New Deal was meant to end the depression.   (6)

(c) What were the Alphabet Agencies mentioned in source A? Explain how successful they were in dealing with the depression.   (6)

(d) Explain whether the cartoonist in source B is for or against the New Deal. Give reasons for your answer.   (4)

(e) Would the writer of source C have agreed or disagreed with the cartoonist in source B? Give reasons for your answer.   (2)

(f) Explain in your own words the arguments used by the writer of source C against giving welfare to people.   (3)

(g) Explain the statement made in source D.   (3)

NEA, 1991

13 Germany, 1933-39

Study the sources below and answer the questions which follow.

SOURCE A: (A photo-cartoon published in a German Communist newspaper in 1933.)

Goering – the butcher of the Third Reich

SOURCE B: (Martin Niemoller* explains why Germans did not oppose the Nazis.)

'First they came for the Jews. I was silent. I was not a Jew. Then they came for the Communists. I was silent. I was not a Communist. Then they came for the trade unionists. I was not a trade unionist. Then they came for me. There was no one left to speak for me.'

*Arrested by the Gestapo and died in a concentration camp.

SOURCE C: (From the autobiography of Christabel Bielenberg, who lived in Germany 1932–1945.)

'What had Hitler provided which seemed to satisfy so many Germans and persuaded them so easily to give up their freedom and to accept without protest the brutal acts carried out by the state?

There was, in fact, something for everyone. There was plenty of work for the unemployed, an army for the generals, a sort of phoney religion for the simple-minded and a restored pride in their nation for all Germans. There were also the detention camps and carefully broadcast hints at what might happen to anyone who voiced the slightest opposition to the regime.'

SOURCE D: (Germany 1928–1939 – Some statistics)

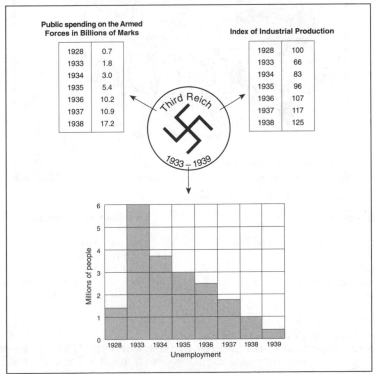

Public spending on the Armed Forces in Billions of Marks	
1928	0.7
1933	1.8
1934	3.0
1935	5.4
1936	10.2
1937	10.9
1938	17.2

Index of Industrial Production	
1928	100
1933	66
1934	83
1935	96
1936	107
1937	117
1938	125

Third Reich 1933 – 1939

(a) To which event is source A referring? (1)
(b) Explain the meaning of source A. Say why it might be thought to be a biased piece of evidence. (7)
(c) Explain why the writer of source B thought himself a failure. (5)
(d) 'The main reason why the German people supported the Nazis was fear.' Would the writer of source C have agreed or disagreed with this statement? Give reasons for your answer. (6)

(e) The writer of source C thought that many Germans liked Nazi policies because they were better off under Hitler's rule. Does the information in source D support this point of view? Give reasons for your answer. (5)

(f) Use the information in the sources, and your knowledge of the period, to explain the success of the Nazis in reducing unemployment. (6)

NEA, 1991

14 Military events of the Second World War, 1939–45

Study sources A and B and then attempt *all* parts of the question.

SOURCE A

'The aim of our attack is to destroy what armies the Russians have left. We must also stop the Russians from building up new armies by breaking their economy. All possible force will be used in the south of Russia. We must smash the enemy on the River Don and at Stalingrad. Then we will control the oilfields in the Caucasus area.'

from a directive issued by Hitler on 5 April 1942

SOURCE B

STALINGRAD ARMY WIPED OUT
16 AXIS GENERALS AMONG THE 46,000 CAPTURED
MARSHALL PAULUS IS A PRISONER

from *The Daily Mail*, 1 February 1943

(a) In source A, Hitler said that a successful attack would lead to control of the oilfields in the Caucasus area. Was control of these oilfields the main reason why Germany had invaded Russia? Explain your answer. (10)

(b) 'In the summer of 1942, Germany intended to attack Russia only in the South.' Does source A support this statement? Explain your answer. (5)

(c) Does source B prove that the German attack on Stalingrad was a failure? Explain your answer. (5)

(d) After the final defeat of Germany in 1945, the Russian victory at Stalingrad was seen as a major turning-point. What is really a major turning-point? Explain your answer. (10)

SEG, 1991

15 The United Nations

Study the sources below and then answer the questions which follow.

SOURCE A: (A cartoon on the United Nations published in 1945)

SOURCE B: (A chart on the main parts of the United Nations)

The General Assembly	The Security Council
Each member-nation represented and has one vote. Debates World Issues Passes resolutions but members are not forced to obey them.	Five permanent members. Each permanent member has the power of the veto. Ten non-permanent members. Aim: to prevent conflict.

SOURCE C: (A Russian historian's view of the United Nations, 1955.)

'Over the years since 1945 the United Nations has reflected the world outside. The Cold War between the Great Powers was being played out in the Security Council, where the USA and its capitalist allies had a built-in majority. Therefore, the veto was used frequently by the USSR. Similarly, in the General Assembly, Western influence was dominant because so many of its members dared not offend the USA. They were dependent on American dollar aid. Certainly, to many Communist countries, the United Nations must have appeared little more than a puppet of the American Government. The non-admission of China served only to prove this fact.'

SOURCE D: (An historian's view of the United Nations in 1989.)

'Since 1945, 34 African and 17 Asian nations have joined the UN and this means that the 'Third World' countries have a majority in the General Assembly. The UN, set up by the Great Powers, has now become the voice of the weaker and poorer nations of the world. The Great Powers no longer dominate and often prefer to act on their own without referring the problem to the UN.'

(a) Explain the cartoon shown in source A. (3)

(b) Which permanent member of the Security Council is not named in the cartoon in source A?(1)

(c) What evidence is there in source B to suggest that the cartoonist may be correct in his view of the UN? Explain your answer. (2)

(d) What was the veto mentioned in sources B and C? (2)

(e) Explain whether or not source C supports the view that the United Nations was 'little more than a puppet of the American Government' in the 1950s. (4)

(f) Explain what the historian in source C means when he writes about 'the non-admission of China' in this period. (4)

(g) How do sources C and D differ in their descriptions of the Untied Nations? Explain your answer. (5)

(h) Using the sources and your knowledge of the period, show how the Great Powers have often acted on their own and ignored the United Nations. (4)

NEA, 1990

16 The United Nations

Study the sources below and then answer the questions which follow.

SOURCE A: (A cartoon published in 1950)

'Come on, your help is needed in Korea.'

SOURCE B: (Statement by the US Secretary of State in 1951)

'The attack on Korea was a challenge to the whole system of collective security and a threat to the independence of all nations.

The decision to meet force with force was essential. The authority and very survival of the United Nations was involved. The operation in Korea has been a success. The Soviet plot for a communist takeover of Korea from the North has been stopped and the attempts by the North Koreans and the Chinese communists to drive out United Nations forces have failed.'

SOURCE C: (From an historian writing in 1953)

'The so-called UN action in Korea is a fraud. It is almost entirely an American Imperialist operation in support of a puppet dictatorship. The Security Council resolution recommending military intervention is illegal because neither the USSR nor the People's Republic of China were present when it was passed. The wanton American aggression into North Korea is clear proof that the real intention of the USA was to destroy communism in the whole area. Only the valiant and heroic actions of the Chinese volunteers have stopped this evil plan.'

SOURCE D: (Two maps of the Korean War)

War in Korea up to October 1950

War in Korea, October 1950–1953

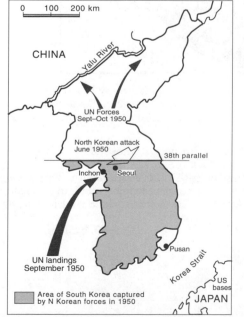

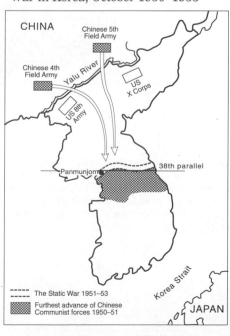

(a) What position did the man shown in the cartoon in source A hold? (1)
(b) Explain the cartoon in source A. (5)
(c) Explain the reasons given in source B for the action of the United States in Korea. (6)
(d) Do the views expressed in the cartoon in source A agree or disagree with the views expressed in source B? Give reasons for your answer. (4)
(e) 'Source C is biased and therefore of little value to an historian writing about the war in Korea.' Give reasons why you agree or disagree with this statement. (8)
(f) Source C says that neither the USSR nor the People's Republic of China was present when the Security Council passed its resolution recommending military intervention in Korea. Explain why these two powers were not present at this time. (2)
(g) Using the information in source D, and your knowledge of the period, say how far you think that the action of the United Nations in Korea was a success. (4)

17 The Berlin Wall

Study the Introduction and Sources A to E and then answer *all* parts of the question.

Introduction

'In 1945, when the Second World War had ended, Germany and Berlin were divided. After this the Superpowers often argued about Berlin. The most serious dispute was the blockade and airlift of 1948–49. Twelve years later, on 13 August 1961, a wall was built to separate West Berlin from the German Democratic Republic (East Germany).'

SOURCE A

'The Western powers use West Berlin as a centre of activities aimed against the German Democratic Republic. There are more centres of spying in West Berlin than anywhere else in the world. These centres smuggle their agents into the German Democratic Republic. Their job is to commit sabotage, to recruit spies and to set up disturbances.

The government's plans will stop all this activity. Effective control will be established around West Berlin including its border with democratic Berlin. Protecting ourselves will contribute to peace.'

from a statement made on 10 August 1961 by the
Government of the German Democratic Republic

SOURCE B

a British cartoon drawn by Ronald Searle in late August 1961
At this time American, Soviet and British representatives
were meeting to discuss nuclear disarmament.

SOURCE C

'East Germany and the Soviet Union thought of West Berlin as an island of Western influence. Most important of all, it was an exit to the West. East Germans took full advantage.

For twelve years, from 1949 to 1961, they escaped at the rate of 20 000 a month. This showed how bad the East German system was. It was also a drain on East Germany's economy and had to be stopped.

In early August 1961 Warsaw Pact leaders met in Moscow, Khrushchev, the Soviet leader, agreed to the East German demand to close the border.'

from *The Coming of the Wall*, (1969) by John Man, a British historian

SOURCE D

a photograph of the Berlin Wall, taken in about 1967

SOURCE E

'When the East Germans built the Berlin Wall in 1961, they claimed that by closing the Berlin border they had saved the peace. It happened at the time of Nikita Khrushchev. A rush of people to the West was threatening to cause the collapse of the East German state. That collapse would have brought the two Superpowers into violent collision.'

from an article by Neil Ascherson in *The Independent*, a British newspaper, (10 November 1989)

To answer the questions, use the information given in the Introduction and Sources. In your answers, you should refer to the Sources by their letters.

(a) The Berlin Wall was built soon after the East German government made the statement in Source A.
Does this statement prove that the East German government had good reasons for building the Wall?
Explain your answer. (6)

(b) 'As Source B was drawn at the time of the Berlin Crisis of 1961, it is very useful as evidence.'
Do you agree or disagree with this statement?
Explain your answer. (5)

(c) In Source C John Man says the Wall was built to stop East Germans escaping to the West.
Does the photograph, Source D, prove that he was right?
Explain your answer. (5)

(d) 'Source E was written 28 years after the Berlin Crisis of 1961.
Therefore it is more reliable than Source C.'
Do you agree or disagree with this statement?
Explain your answer. (6)

(e) In Source A the East German government claimed that the building of the Berlin Wall would 'contribute to peace'.
Does the evidence of the Introduction and Sources B, C, D and E support this East German claim?
Explain your answer. (8)

SEG, 1993

18 Eastern Europe since 1945

Study Sources A, B, C and D, which are about the U.S.S.R.'s relations with Eastern Europe, and then answer questions **(a)** to **(e)** which follow:

SOURCE A: (adapted from N. R. MacMahon, *The Hungarian Revolution*, published in 1969)

'After the death of Stalin some things began to change. Khrushchev began to talk with the Yugoslavs, who had never followed Stalin's methods. Khrushchev blamed Soviet problems on Stalin. The Secret Police (NKVD) were abolished. This relaxation led to riots in Poland where Gomulka, a popular Polish Communist, was brought to power. Then there were a similar rising in Hungary. A government was formed by Imre Nagy which included some non-Communists. Nagy promised free elections in Hungary and even talked of leaving the Warsaw Pact.'

SOURCE B: (a cartoon from a British magazine, 31 October 1956)

SOURCE C: (quoted in D. Pryce-Jones, *The Hungarian Revolution*, published in 1969)

'As I moved deeper into the city (Budapest), every street was smashed. Hardly a stretch of tramcar rails was left intact ... Hundreds of yards of paving stones had been torn up, the streets were littered with burnt-out cars. Even before I reached the Duna Hotel, I counted the remains of at least forty tanks ... at the corner of Stalin Avenue ... two monster Russian T54 tanks lumbered past, dragging bodies behind them, a warning to all Hungarians of what happened to fighters ...'

SOURCE D: (a photograph showing a huge statue of Stalin being pulled down in Budapest, capital of Hungary, 1956)

(a) Study Source A.

According to Source A, how did the death of Stalin change the situation in Eastern Europe? (3)

(b) Study Sources A and B.

In what ways does the information in Source A help you to understand Source B? Explain your answer. (4)

(c) Study Sources C and D.

To what extent does Source D support the evidence of the eye-witness in Source C? (4)

(d) Study Sources B and D.

'Source D is more useful to someone studying the events in Eastern Europe in the 1950s than is Source B.' Do you agree? Give reasons for your answer. (4)

(e) Use your knowledge to explain why Khrushchev ordered Soviet troops and tanks into Hungary in 1956.

ULEAC, 1992

19 Co-operation in Western Europe from 1945

Look carefully at sources A to E. Then answer *all* the questions.

SOURCE A: (Harry Truman, President of the USA from 1945 to 1952, explained in an interview he gave in 1961 why he decided to set up the Marshall Plan in 1947)

> 'I doubt if things in Europe had ever been worse. People were starving and dying of disease. There had been food riots in France and Italy, everywhere. I said, if we don't do it, hundreds of thousands of people will starve to death, and we don't want that on our consciences. If we let Europe go down the drain, we're going to have a bad depression in this country.'

SOURCE B: (In May 1947 General Marshall's assistant spoke about plans for European aid.)

> 'We should remove the impression that the United States' approach to world problems is a defensive reaction to Communist pressure. We would still be interested in the effort to restore sound economic conditions even if there were no Communist menace.'

SOURCE C: (In June 1947 General Marshall, US Secretary of State, announced the Marshall Plan.)

> 'Our policy is directed not against any country or doctrine but against hunger, poverty and chaos. Its purpose is the revival of a working economy in the world so as to allow the political and social conditions in which free institutions can exist.'

SOURCE D: (A recent historian describes the reluctance of the US Congress to approve money for Marshall Aid to Europe.)

> 'Sixteen Western European nations drew up a plan by August 1947 calling for $28 billion of aid over the next four years. Truman reduced the figure to around $17 billion, but Congress still refused to approve the money because the Republican Party wanted Truman to lose the 1948 election. However, at the end of February 1948, Communists took control of Czechoslovakia. In mid March Congress approved the Plan, and in April 1948 the Organization for European Economic Co-operation was set up to put the Marshall Plan into action.'

SOURCE E:

i (In 1980 an American historian gave this view of Marshall Aid.)

> 'The Marshall Plan gave around $16 billion in aid to Western Europe in four years. Its aim was to build up markets for American exports. It also had a political motive. The Communist parties of Italy and France were strong, so the USA used pressure and money to keep Communists out of governments in those countries.'
>
> (Note: one billion = one thousand million)

ii (Countries which received most in Marshall Aid (figures are in millions of dollars).)

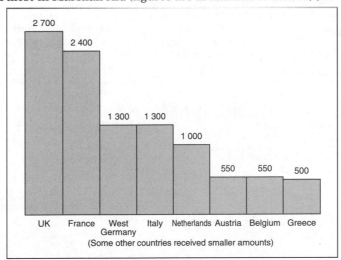

2 700 UK
2 400 France
1 300 West Germany
1 300 Italy
1 000 Netherlands
550 Austria
550 Belgium
500 Greece

(Some other countries received smaller amounts)

(a) Look at source B.
  i   What is the name usually given to the policy announced by the USA in March 1947 which promised political support to countries threatened by Communists? (1)
  ii Name the European country in which a civil war between Communist and anti-Communist forces took place in 1947. (1)

(b) Look at source D.
Why was it Western European rather than Eastern European countries which received economic aid from the USA after 1947? (2)

(c) Look at source E i and source E ii.
How far does the information contained in the chart support the views expressed by the historian in source E i? Explain your answer. (6)

(d) Refer to the sources in answering this question.
Source A is a statement by a former President of the USA. Does this mean it is the most reliable source of evidence on the Marshall Plan out of sources A to E? Explain your answer. (8)

(e) Look at all the sources.
'The Americans' motive behind the Marshall Plan was to look after the welfare of the peoples of Europe.' How far do sources A to E show this to be true? Explain your answer fully. (12)

MEG, 1990

20 Post-War Co-operation in Western Europe

Study the sources below and then answer the questions which follow.

SOURCE A: (A journalist discusses Britain's entry into the EEC, 1970)

'Britain's reluctance to join the EEC in its early years has made entry more difficult, and De Gaulle has already prevented our attempts to join in 1963 and 1967. Certainly the peoples of the Six are better off now then ever before. Between 1960 and 1965 their industrial output rose twice as fast as that of Britain. The vast market of 250 million customers offers enormous scope to industry. An Italian factory owner can sell his goods in France and Germany as well as in Italy, whereas the British businessman cannot do this because we are not members. More and more people are asking the question "Why has Britain not joined?".'

SOURCE B: (A cartoon published in a British newspaper in 1970)

The tide's coming in...and time's running out!

SOURCE C: (An opponent argues against Britain's membership of the EEC.)

'The British people have a long tradition of independence and no desire to lose our identity in some silly European Club. Nobody wants to join with the French, who never can be trusted, and few would welcome the Germans as friends after two World Wars. Historically our true links are not with foreigners on the continent but with our English-speaking friends overseas.'

SOURCE D: (A chart about the Common Agricultural Policy.)

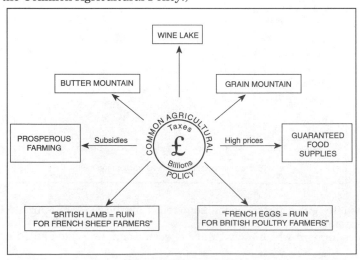

(a) Name the countries which made up 'the Six' mentioned in source A. (3)

(b) Explain the arguments used in source A, for Britain entering the EEC. (5)

(c) Would the cartoonist in source B have agreed with the point of view of the writer of ? source A? Give reasons for your answer. (5)

(d) 'Source C is biased and therefore of little value to an historian studying Britain's application to join the EEC.' Say whether you agree or disagree with this statement. Give reasons for your answer.

(e) 'The writer of source C is against British membership of the EEC.' What policies would the writer of source C prefer for Britain? Explain your answer. (4)

(f) Using source D, and your knowledge of the period, explain the advantages and disadvantages of the Common Agricultural Policy. (8)

NEA, 1991

21 Race Relations in the USA

Look carefully at Sources A to E which refer to Civil Rights issues in the USA. Then answer all the questions.

SOURCE A: (A photograph showing housing for Blacks in Harlem, New York City, in the late 1970s.)

SOURCE B: (Two photographs showing Black protests in the 1950s and 1960s.)

i   Two opponents of segregation sit in the whites only part of a bus in Birmingham, Alabama, 1956.

ii Martin Luther King at the Washington Civil Rights demonstration, August 1963.

SOURCE C: (A British newspaper report about the Central High School, Little Rock, Arkansas, published on 5 September 1987.)

> 'Thirty years to the day after Governor Orval Faubus provoked the Eisenhower Government at Little Rock, black and white students stood together outside the Central High School. "This school's great," said a black youth. "Race ain't nothing to worry about here." A white youngster nearby said, "People have got used to the idea that they've got to go to school together." I could see, however, that black and white students keep to their own 'territory' in the school-yard. Furthermore, I learned that still another plan to stop segregation came into force this week.'

SOURCE D: (Statistics collected at the time and published by the US government.)

Unemployment (shown as a % of working population)

Date	All workers	Black workers
1958	6.8	12.6
1961	6.7	12.4
1964	.5.2	9.6
1967	3.8	7.4
1970	4.9	8.2

Figures for 1974 showing deaths per 100,000 from certain causes.

	Whites	Blacks
Tuberculosis	1.3	4.1
Infancy diseases	11.3	29.0

SOURCE E: (Race relations in the USA in the 1970s and 1980s.)

i A newspaper photograph of a Ku Klux Klan rally in Little Rock, Arkansas, 1979.

ii A US newspaper report published on 16 August 1985.

WHITE HOUSE PLANS CIVIL RIGHTS U TURN

'Rules concerning equal rights in employment which were made by President Lyndon Johnson are to be abolished, making higher black unemployment likely.

(a) Look at source A.

In what ways does the photograph indicate that Harlem was a poor area of New York?   (2)

(b) Look at source B **ii**.

Why did Martin Luther King lead this demonstration to Washington in 1963?   (2)

(c) Read source D.

How would these statistics be useful to an historian of race relations in the USA? Explain your answer.   (6)

(d) Look at sources E **i** and E **ii**.

Which of these sources gives the more reliable account of race relations in the USA? Explain your answer.   (8)

(e) Look at *all* the sources.

'The Civil Rights protests of the 1950s and 1960s achieved nothing for the Blacks of the USA.' Do these sources show this view to be true? Explain your answer fully.   (12)

MEG, 1991

22 China since 1949

Look carefully at Sources A to E which refer to the Cultural Revolution, 1966–69. Then answer all the questions.

SOURCE A

A British journalist, who lived in China at the time, describes the beginning of 'the Great Cultural Revolution of the proletariat' in a book published in 1985.

'In August 1966, Mao showed that he wanted to get rid of leading members of the Party by publishing a poster calling on the young people of the Red Guards to "Bombard the Headquarters". "Some leading comrades have set up a dictatorship. They have silenced opinions that differed from their own." '

From *Mao*, Clare Hollingsworth (1985), published by Jonathan Cape

SOURCE B
Two examples of posters published in China during the Cultural Revolution.

(i) *The Red Guards are shown attacking landlords.*

(ii) *The Red Guards set out their aims.*

> 'We are the Red Guards and we carry out the Revolution. We tear up and smash old paintings, British and American records, precious vases. We put up pictures of the Chairman.
>
> Gentlemen of the capitalist classes, you stink, you are just rotten trash, we hate you, we shall beat you, our bayonets shall taste blood.'

SOURCE C
Lu Hong, a Red Guard, recalls what happened when Mao sent her to work in the countryside.

> 'They put us on a train. There were 2400 other students on that train. After four days of travelling, they let us off at a state farm. I lived, with 60 others, in a large room made of mud, with mud walls and mud floors. We got up at 5 am to work in the fields and were too tired to read at night. Some young people even forgot how to read and write.'

SOURCE D
A photograph, taken during the Cultural Revolution, showing a group of Red Guards listening to an old peasant.

SOURCE E
Lu Hong sums up her opinion of the results of the Cultural Revolution.

'I spent eight years fanning the flames of revolution. It was like losing a big chunk of your life. Now I would like to help the motherland, but what do I have? I never finished my schooling. It's like my friends say, the Chinese people don't live, they just exist.'

(a) Read Source B(ii).
Who was known as 'the Chairman' in China at this time? (1)

(b) Read Source A.
  i Name one of 'the leading members of the Party' who was dismissed during the Cultural Revolution. (1)
  ii Why did Mao appeal especially to young people to carry out the revolution? (2)

(c) Look at Source B(i) and read Source B(ii).
What evidence is there in these sources that the posters are propaganda? Explain your answer. (6)

(d) Read Source C and look at Source D.
Which of these two sources gives the more reliable view of the work of the Red Guards in the Chinese countryside? Explain your answer. (8)

(e) Look at *all* the sources.
'The Cultural Revolution was a complete disaster for China.'

Do these sources show this view to be true? Explain your answer fully. (12)

MEG, 1992

23 Apartheid in South Africa and its opponents

Study sources A, B and C, which refer to the origins of apartheid, and answer questions **(a)** to **(e)** which follow:

SOURCE A: (adapted from a speech by the leader of the Nationalist Party, Dr Malan, during the 1948 election campaign)

'Will the European race in the future be able to maintain its rule, its purity, and its civilization? Or will it float along until it vanishes for ever, without honour, in the black sea of South Africa's non-European population? If the European can save itself, then can it do so without oppression? Can it do so in consideration of the non-European's natural right to a proper living? Can Europeans respect non-Europeans' right to their own development in accordance with their own requirements and capabilities? Will the all-destroying Communist cancer be checked, or will it be allowed to undermine our freedom, our religion, our own South African nationhood and our European existence?'

SOURCE B: (adapted from a letter written in 1952 from Dr Malan to the African National Congress)

'The road to peace and goodwill lies in the acceptance of the fact that separate population groups exist. Each group should have the opportunity of developing its ambitions and abilities in its own area or within its own community. It should be clearly understood that the government is not prepared to grant the Bantu political equality with the European community. It is, however, only too willing to encourage Bantu initiative, Bantu services, and Bantu administration within the Bantu community, and to allow the Bantu people full scope to fulfil their potential.'

SOURCE C: (adapted from a letter written in 1952 from the African National Congress to Dr Malan)

'We refer to the campaign of mass action which the ANC intends to launch. As a defenceless and voteless people, we have explored other channels without success. The African people are left with no alternative but to set out on the campaign referred to. It is our firm intention to conduct this campaign in a peaceful manner. Any disturbances, if they must occur, will not be of our making.'

SOURCE D: (adapted from a speech by P W Botha, Prime Minister of South Africa, 1980)

'We are moving in a changing world, we must adapt otherwise we shall die ... The moment you start oppressing people ... they fight back ... We must acknowledge people's rights and ... give to others in a spirit of justice what we demand for ourselves. A white monopoly of power is impossible in the Africa of today ... A division of power between all racial groups is needed ... Apartheid is a recipe for permanent conflict.'

(a) Study source A. In what ways does this source show the policies of apartheid adopted by Nationalist governments in South Africa? (4)
(b) Study source B. Is source B a reliable source of information about Bantu attitudes towards the policies of the South African government? Explain your answer. (4)
(c) Both sources A and B express strong opinions. In view of this, how useful are they to someone studying South African history? Give reasons for your answer, referring to the sources. (4)
(d) Study source C. How useful if this source as evidence of the part played by Black Africans in the government of South Africa? (3)
(e) Study sources C and D. Do sources C and D indicate that there had been a major change since the 1950s in the racial policies pursued within South Africa by the South African government? Explain your answer. (5)

LEAG, 1991

24 The Achievement of Independence in Africa

Look carefully at sources A to E. Then answer all the questions.

SOURCE A: (Africa in 1960.)

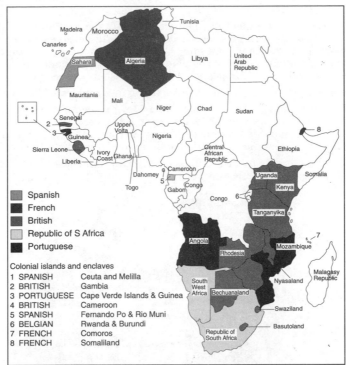

SOURCE B: (Photographs illustrating the conflicts in Algeria and Zimbabwe.)

i A house destroyed by an OAS bomb (OAS = the Secret Army Organization, led by former French army commanders, which was opposed to Algerian independence).

ii White golfers make use of a black armed guard of Ian Smith's army to carry their golf clubs. This photograph was published in 1978.

SOURCE C: (Extract from a report on Algeria, published in 1955, made by a group of French MPs appointed by the French Parliament.)

'The money given by the French government has benefited chiefly the big landowners, mostly Europeans, who have concentrated on growing wine and vegetables for export. These exports compete unnecessarily with the French home market, where there is a glut. On the other hand very little has been done for the small Moslem farmers. At the same time the taxes paid by the big landowners are ridiculously low. There cannot be any peace between Arabs and Europeans so long as these injustices and inequalities continue.'

SOURCE D: (Joshua Nkomo sets out the grievances of Africans living in Zimbabwe. This article was published in 1966.)

'The result of the Land Apportionment Act was that many towns became the homes only of Europeans. Africans were allowed into these areas only as workers for Europeans. After the Second World War all industrial and commercial expansion was confined to these European areas. Our enemy in Zimbabwe is not the white man, but political, economic and social domination of a majority by a very small minority.'

SOURCE E: (A comment on African attitudes to UDI, published in Britain in the 1960s. The person trying to defuse the mine is Harold Wilson, Prime Minister of Great Britain.)

"You're getting nowhere, man—let us try."

(a) Look at source A.
Name a country, independent by 1960, which had previously been a colony of
   i   Britain;
   ii   France? (1)
(b) Look at source B i.
Explain why the OAS was opposed to Algerian independence. (2)
(c) Look at source E.
In what ways can this cartoon be of use to an historian studying African decolonization? (6)
(d) Read sources C and D.
Which of these two sources do you consider to provide the more reliable evidence about white settlers in Africa? Explain your answer. (8)
(e) Look at all the sources.
'Independence was delayed in both Algeria and Zimbabwe because of the determination of white settlers to keep their privileges.' Do these sources show this view to be true? Explain your answer fully. (12)

MEG, 1990

25　The Arab-Israeli conflict, 1945–79

Study sources A and B and then attempt all parts of the question.

SOURCE A:

'After 1967, we Palestinians began to realize that we should organize for ourselves; that would be the only way to return to Palestine. We could not do this openly. It was a crime to announce our Palestinian identity. This was the case, even in those Arab countries which said they supported our cause. We feared that there might be strong action against us if we said in public. 'We want to return home' or 'The Arab countries are causing us misery.'

from comments made by Abu Jihad, quoted in *The Palestinians*, (1979)

SOURCE B:

an Arab cartoon, (31 May 1967) from a newspaper hostile to Israel

(a) In the years 1948-66 the Palestinians were seen as a problem by some of the countries of the Middle East. Why was this? (10)

(b) Abu Jihad, who is quoted in source A, was a leading member of the Palestine Liberation Organization. What he says is, therefore, bound to be biased and of little use to a study of the Palestinian issue. Explain whether or not you agree with this view. (5)

(c) In source A, Abu Jihad criticises some Arab countries for not fully supporting the Palestinians. Source B shows Israel being threatened by a number of Arab countries. Does this prove that Abu Jihad was wrong? Explain your answer. (5)

(d) 'The Palestinian Liberation Organisation was formed in 1969. Since then it has caused more trouble for the Arab countries than for Israel.' Do you agree or disagree with this opinion? Explain your answer. (10)

SEG, 1991

26 Third World Problems

Study Sources A, B, C and D and then answer questions (**a**) to (**e**) which follow:

SOURCE A: (a photograph taken during Live Aid's 'Feed the World' campaign, 1985. The photograph shows Bob Geldof, a rock musician who organised Live Aid, and a Japanese businessman)

SOURCE B: (Richard M. Nixon, former U.S. President, 1983)

'Let us remember the main purpose of American aid is not to help other nations but to help ourselves.'

SOURCE C: (from '*Social Issues: The world*', by Coutts, Coutts and Rae, 1986)

'The British government gives aid to the value of about 0.4 per cent of the United Kingdom's GNP*. About half of this is in the form of loans that must be repaid with interest. Many countries give aid mostly in the form of such loans. Other countries include military equipment as aid.

Aid is given for a variety of reasons by governments. The Brandt Report, produced under the chairmanship of the former West German Chancellor, Willi Brandt, argued that aid should be greatly increased in order to help Third World economies and so increase the demand for produce from the industrialised world.'

*GNP = Gross National Product, a way of measuring a nation's wealth.

SOURCE D: (the main diseases of malnutrition, World Health Organisation, 1989)

Disease/illness	Lack of:	Areas of world affected	Food lacking
Anaemia	Iron	Central, South and North America, Africa, Asia, Australia, Europe	Red meat, liver, cereals/fruit, green vegetables
Kwashiorkor	Protein	Parts of Latin America, Africa, South East Asia	Dairy products, meat and fish, eggs, legumes
Marasmus	Calories	Parts of Central and South America, South East Asia, Africa	Mother's milk, cereals, tubers, fats
Xerophthalmia	Vitamin A	Central America, parts of South America, Africa, Near East, Far East, Asia	Dairy products, vegetables, fruits

(a) Study Source A.

What evidence does this source contain about the importance of the media in raising money for 'Live Aid'? (3)

(b) Study Sources A and B.

Both of these sources deal with aid. In what ways do they show differences of attitude towards this issue? (4)

(c) Study Sources B and C.

How can the information in Source C be used to support Richard Nixon's point of view in Source B? (4)

(d) Study Sources A, B and C.

Which source do you think is the most biased? Explain your answer by referring to the sources. (4)

(e) Study Source D.

Use your own knowledge to explain how aid has been used to try to overcome some of the problems listed in this source.

(5)

ULEAC, 1992

27 Russia, 1917–41

Look carefully at Sources A to E which refer to the New Economic Policy (NEP). Then answer *all* the questions.

SOURCE A

Lenin introduced the NEP at the Tenth Party Congress, March 1921.

'Our large factories have been so ruined that it will take a long time to restore them. We must therefore help to restore small industry. This will mean the revival of private profit and capitalism.

The workers are in no danger as long as they firmly hold power over the most important parts of the economy.

This is a retreat, but only for a new attack.'

SOURCE B

Two views of NEP

(i) *Bukharin, one of Lenin's economic advisors, spoke of the future in 1922.*

'Poor, starving old Russia, Russia of primitive lighting and the meal of a crust of black bread, is going to be covered by a network of electric power stations. The NEP will transform the Russian economy and rebuild a broken nation. The future is endless and beautiful.'

(ii) *Kopelev, a former Soviet Communist Party member, spoke in a British television programme in 1990.*

'We thought at the time that the NEP was a retreat, that maybe it was necessary but it must be ended as quickly as possible. The NEP meant the recovery of capitalism. I was 15 years old and I wrote a poem called 'The NEP' where I said things like how awful it was but at some point it would come to an end because there were still true Bolsheviks alive. We were lads in 1927. We thought that stealing from an NEP man was not a sin; to steal sweets or apples or beer, that was part of the class struggle.'

SOURCE C

A British historian in 1985 noted these comments about the NEP.

'In 1925 the Soviet Commissar for Finance admitted that the pay of miners, metal workers and engine drivers was still lower than it had been before 1914. This in turn meant that workers' housing and food were poor. The factory committee of a cement works in Smolensk reported, for example, in 1929: "Every day there are many complaints about apartments: many workers have families of six or seven people, and live in one room." '

From *A History of the Soviet Union*, G. Hosking, published by HarperCollins Publishers Ltd

SOURCE D

(i) *A Soviet painting of 1927 entitled 'Forward Heavy Industry'.*

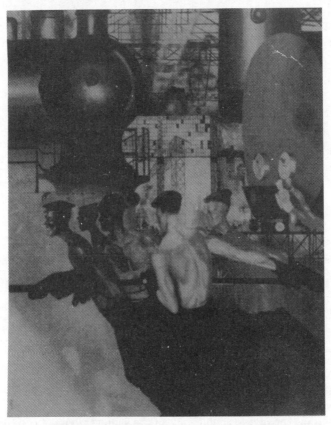

(ii) *A poster advertising the new film 'October', 1927*

SOURCE E
A graph which shows production under the NEP. The lines on the graph show the change in production of four basic commodities compared with 1913. The graph was compiled from statistics taken from Russian sources by a British historian in the 1960s.

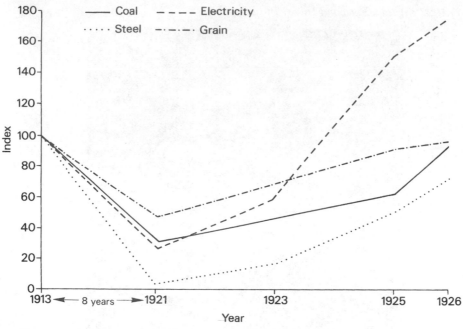

(a) Look at Source E.
Give two reasons why production fell between 1913 and 1921.   (2)

(b) Read Source B(ii).
Why did Kopelev think that stealing from an NEP man was 'part of the class struggle'?   (2)

(c) Read Source B(i).
What evidence is there that Bukharin's statement is propaganda? Explain your answer.   (6)

(d) Look at Sources D(i) and D(ii) and Source E.
Do the illustrations or the graph give the more reliable view of the achievements of the NEP? Explain your answer.   (8)

(e) Look at all the sources.

'NEP was abandoned in 1927 because it was failing.'
Do these sources show this view to be true? Explain your answer fully.   (12)

MEG, 1992

28 The Cuban Crisis, 1962

Study Sources A, B and C, which are about the Cuban Missile Crisis, and then answer questions (**a**) to (**e**) which follow:

SOURCE A: (adapted from a letter sent by Khrushchev (U.S.S.R.) to President Kennedy (U.S.A.), October 1962)

> 'I have learned with great pleasure of your reply to Mr U Thant (the Secretary-General to the United Nations) that you will take steps to avoid contact between our ships. This will avoid any dangerous results.
>
> line 5   You have been worried that we have helped Cuba to strengthen her defences by supplying weapons. Yes, but you are still more powerful than Cuba.
>
> We aim to help Cuba to live in peace and develop the way her people want. All countries want to make themselves safe.
>
> But how are we, the U.S.S.R., to understand your actions? You have surrounded the U.S.S.R. with military bases, you have rockets in Britain, Italy and Turkey which are
> line 10   aimed at us! You say you are worried by rockets in Cuba which is 90 miles from the coast of your country, but Turkey is next to us. Do you have the right to demand security by the removal of our rockets from Cuba and not give us the same right to security?
>
> I make this proposal: we agree to remove our rockets from Cuba if you will make a declaration that you will remove yours from Turkey.'

SOURCE B: (from a history textbook, 1988)

> 'Kennedy replied to the Russian leader's letter with counterproposals of his own: firstly, the Russians would dismantle their nuclear missile bases in Cuba and undertake "to halt the further introduction of such weapons systems to Cuba"; secondly, the Americans on their part would end the quarantine measures then in effect and "give assurances
> line 5   against the invasion of Cuba". For a week the world waited as the Soviet vessels approached Cuba. The two super-powers seemed on the brink of a nuclear war.'

SOURCE C: (a cartoon from a British newspaper, *The Daily Mail*, October 1962)

(a) Study Source A.
According to Source A, in what ways did the U.S.S.R. wish to help Cuba? (3)

(b) Study Sources A and B.
How does Source A help you to understand the part of Source B which says '*and give assurances against the invasion of Cuba*' (lines 4 and 5)? (4)

(c) Study Sources A, B and C.
In what ways is the cartoonist's view of the crisis (Source C) supported by the other two sources? (4)

(d) Which of Sources A, B and C do you think is the most biased? Give reasons for your answer by referring to the sources. (4)

(e) Use your own knowledge to explain the consequences of the 1962 missile crisis for relations between the U.S.A. and the U.S.S.R. in the 1960s. (5)

ULEAC, 1993

29 The Vietnam War

Study Sources A, B, C and D, which are about the Vietnam War, and then answer questions (**a**) to (**e**) which follow:

SOURCE A: (from an account of the Vietnam War, written by an Austrian newspaper reporter, 1970)

'The Vietcong are not only afraid of rockets and napalm bombs and aircraft cannon shells. It is above all the American rifles which have inflicted heavy losses on them. The newest American rifles fire bullets with the effect of shells. Without even hitting the enemy it is enough if one of these shells strikes the ground two yards away from him, and the result at this distance is terrible. I have seen Vietcong snipers open fire on American troops who answered with 25 rounds per rifle in a few seconds; the trees were stripped of their leaves and the snipers swept away.'

SOURCE B: (from '*Death in the Rice Fields*', written by a West German journalist, 1976)

'How on earth could a victory like this ever have happened? How could this divided country, robbed of its richest provinces, survive thirty years of war and not only survive but win? How did North Vietnam, this poor, under-fed dwarf, manage to take on the spectacular might of the American army and beat it? Every time you walked through the streets of Saigon these questions would come to you again and again.'

SOURCE C: (a photograph of U.S. troops in Vietnam, 1969)

SOURCE D: (from a statement by Vo Nguyen Giap, Commander-in-Chief of the North Vietnamese army, 1967)

'When they sent troops into the south, the United States imperialists wanted to use their great military superiority, concentrate their forces and attack and wipe out the Liberation Armed Forces (Vietcong). Yet, although they have more than one million troops they have not been able to do this. Although they wanted to concentrate their forces they have had to scatter them in many theatres of war, and give them many tasks.

In sending U.S. troops to South Vietnam, the U.S. imperialists have met a people's war. This people's war has successfully developed the people's strength, has succeeded in gathering all the people to fight their attackers in all ways and with all kinds of weapons – from primitive to modern, and has created a very great strength.'

(a) Study Source A
According to this source, what were the Vietcong afraid of, and why? (3)

(b) Study Sources B and D.
The author of Source B seems surprised that the U.S. lost the war. How can the information in Source D be used to explain this defeat? (4)

(c) Study Sources C and D.
Which of these sources do you think is the more valuable evidence about the Vietnam War? Explain your answer. (4)

(d) Study Sources A, B, C and D.
'All accounts of the war are biased'. With reference to these sources, explain whether you agree or disagree with this statement. (4)

(e) Use your own knowledge to explain how the war affected the lives of the citizens of both North and South Vietnam.
(5)
ULEAC, 1992

30 Germany, 1919–39

Look carefully at Sources A to E which refer to the rise to power of the Nazi Party. Then answer *all* the questions.

SOURCE A
Table showing seats won by some parties in elections to the Reichstag.

Parties	1928	1930	July 1932	Nov 1932
NSDAP (Nazi)	12	107	230	196
Nationalists	73	41	37	51
Catholic Party	62	68	75	70
SPD (Social Democrats)	153	143	133	121
KPD (Communists)	54	77	89	100
Others	121	129	22	26

SOURCE B
Otto Strasser, a Nazi supporter, describes Hitler's powers as an orator.

'Adolf Hitler enters the hall. For a minute he feels his way, senses the atmosphere. Suddenly he bursts forth. His words appeal to the hopes of his listeners. If he tries to put a reasoned argument, quoting ideas from books he has only imperfectly understood, his speech becomes mediocre. But let him step out boldly, speaking as the spirit moves him, and he is transformed into one of the greatest speakers of the century.'

SOURCE C
A cartoon published in 1932

SOURCE D
Two views of the SA

(i) *A photograph taken of a parade in the 1930s.*

(ii) *An English writer, who worked in Berlin from 1930 to 1933, describes an incident in that city in a novel, published in 1939.*

'Walking along the pavement ahead of me were three SA men. All at once they came face to face with a youth of 17 or 18. I heard one of the Nazis shout, "That's him!" and immediately all three flung themselves on the young man and began kicking him and stabbing him with the sharp metal points of their banners. His left eye was half poked out and blood poured from the wound. A group of policemen standing nearby took no notice of the whole affair.'

Courtesy of the Estate of Christopher Isherwood, *Goodbye to Berlin*, published by Hogarth Press

SOURCE E
Nazi election posters.

(i) *The caption reads: 'We want Work and Bread! Vote Hitler.'*

(ii) *The banner reads: 'Loyalty, Honour and Order'. The woman's headband reads: 'Germany'.*

(a) Study Source A.
    i   Which party's support remained most steady through these four elections?   (1)
    ii Which party gained seats in each of the elections of 1930 and 1932?   (1)

(b) Look at Source E(i).
Why would the Nazis use the slogan 'We want Work and Bread' in elections at this time?   (2)

(c) Look at Source C.
What evidence is there in this cartoon that it is propaganda?   (6)

(d) Look at Source D(i) and Source D(ii).
Which of these two sources gives the more reliable view of the SA? Explain your answer.   (8)

(e) Look at *all* the sources.
'The Nazis achieved power in the 1930s because Hitler was able to win over the hearts and minds of the German people.'
Do these sources show this view to be true? Explain your answer fully.
   (12)

MEG, 1993

INDEX